# STREET ATLAS
# Hertfordshire

First published in 1986 by

Philip's, a division of
Octopus Publishing Group Ltd
2-4 Heron Quays, London E14 4JP

Third colour edition 2004
First impression 2004

ISBN-10    0-540-08495-6 (hardback)
ISBN-13    978-0-540-08495-1 (hardback)

ISBN-10    0-540-08496-4 (spiral)
ISBN-13    978-0-540-08496-8 (spiral)

© Philip's 2004

**Ordnance Survey**®

This product includes mapping data licensed
from Ordnance Survey® with the permission of
the Controller of Her Majesty's Stationery Office.
© Crown copyright 2004. All rights reserved.
Licence number 100011710.

Printed and bound in Spain
by Cayfosa-Quebecor

## Contents

III   **Key to map symbols**

IV   **Key to map pages**

VI   **Route planning**

VIII   **Administrative and Postcode boundaries**

1   **Street maps** at 3½ inches to 1 mile

177   **Index** of towns and villages

179   **Index** of streets, hospitals, industrial estates, railway
stations, schools, shopping centres, universities
and places of interest

## Digital Data

The exceptionally high-quality mapping found in this atlas is available as digital data in TIFF format,
which is easily convertible to other bitmapped (raster) image formats.

The index is also available in digital form as a standard database table. It contains all the details
found in the printed index together with the National Grid reference for the map square in which
each entry is named.

For further information and to discuss your requirements, please contact Philip's on
020 7644 6932 or james.mann@philips-maps.co.uk

| | | | |
|---|---|---|---|
| | **Motorway** with junction number | | **Ambulance station** |
| | **Primary route** – dual/single carriageway | | **Coastguard station** |
| | **A road** – dual/single carriageway | | **Fire station** |
| | **B road** – dual/single carriageway | | **Police station** |
| | **Minor road** – dual/single carriageway | | **Accident and Emergency entrance to hospital** |
| | **Other minor road** – dual/single carriageway | H | **Hospital** |
| | **Road under construction** | + | **Place of worship** |
| | **Tunnel, covered road** | i | **Information Centre** (open all year) |
| | **Rural track, private road or narrow road in urban area** | P | **Parking** |
| | **Gate or obstruction to traffic** (restrictions may not apply at all times or to all vehicles) | P&R | **Park and Ride** |
| | **Path, bridleway, byway open to all traffic, road used as a public path** | PO | **Post Office** |
| | **Pedestrianised area** | | **Camping site** |
| DY7 | **Postcode boundaries** | | **Caravan site** |
| | **County and unitary authority boundaries** | | **Golf course** |
| | **Railway, tunnel, railway under construction** | | **Picnic site** |
| | **Tramway, tramway under construction** | Prim Sch | **Important buildings, schools, colleges, universities and hospitals** |
| | **Miniature railway** | | **Built up area** |
| Walsall | **Railway station** | | **Woods** |
| | **Private railway station** | River Medway | **Water name** |
| | **London Underground station** | | **River, weir, stream** |
| | **Tram stop, tram stop under construction** | | **Canal, lock, tunnel** |
| | **Bus, coach station** | | **Water** |
| | | | **Tidal water** |

| | | | | | |
|---|---|---|---|---|---|
| Acad | **Academy** | Inst | **Institute** | Recn Gd | **Recreation Ground** |
| Allot Gdns | **Allotments** | Ct | **Law Court** | | |
| Cemy | **Cemetery** | L Ctr | **Leisure Centre** | Resr | **Reservoir** |
| C Ctr | **Civic Centre** | LC | **Level Crossing** | Ret Pk | **Retail Park** |
| CH | **Club House** | Liby | **Library** | Sch | **School** |
| Coll | **College** | Mkt | **Market** | Sh Ctr | **Shopping Centre** |
| Crem | **Crematorium** | Meml | **Memorial** | TH | **Town Hall/House** |
| Ent | **Enterprise** | Mon | **Monument** | Trad Est | **Trading Estate** |
| Ex H | **Exhibition Hall** | Mus | **Museum** | Univ | **University** |
| Ind Est | **Industrial Estate** | Obsy | **Observatory** | W Twr | **Water Tower** |
| IRB Sta | **Inshore Rescue Boat Station** | Pal | **Royal Palace** | Wks | **Works** |
| | **Boat Station** | PH | **Public House** | YH | **Youth Hostel** |

*Church* **Non-Roman antiquity**

ROMAN FORT **Roman antiquity**

87
58 **Adjoining page indicators**

■ The small numbers around the edges of the maps identify the 1 kilometre National Grid lines

■ The dark grey border on the inside edge of some pages indicates that the mapping does not continue onto the adjacent page

**The scale of the maps on the pages numbered in blue is 5.52 cm to 1 km • 3½ inches to 1 mile • 1: 18103**

| 0 | ¼ | ½ | ¾ | 1 mile |
|---|---|---|---|---|
| 0 | 250 m  500 m | 750 m  1 kilometre | | |

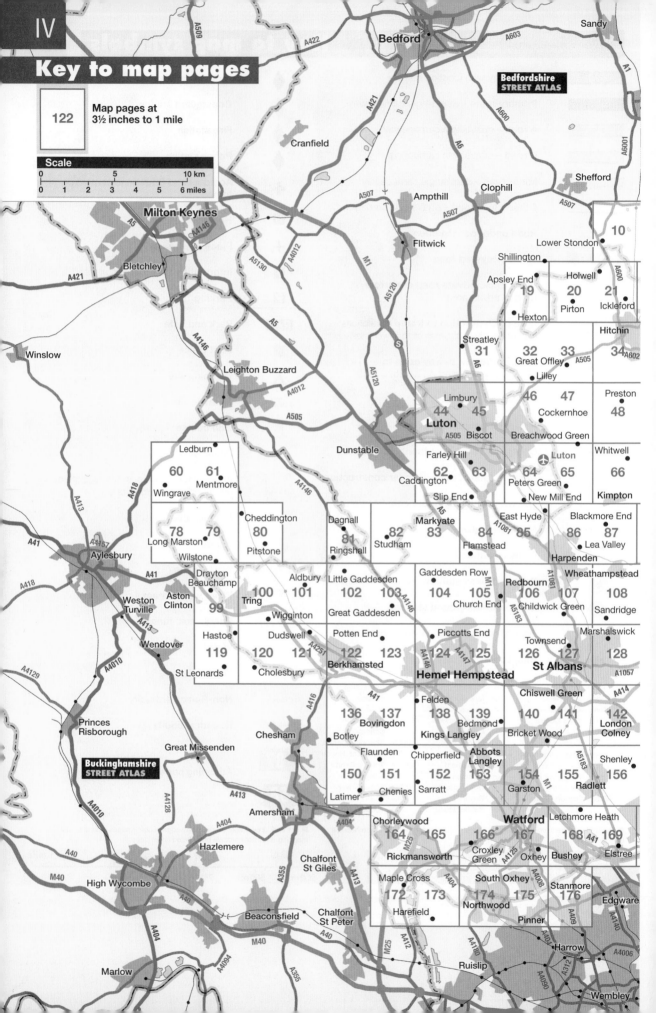

IV

# Key to map pages

122 Map pages at 3½ inches to 1 mile

**Scale**

0 — 5 — 10 km

0 1 2 3 4 5 6 miles

**Bedford**

**Bedfordshire STREET ATLAS**

Sandy

Cranfield

Shefford

Clophill

Ampthill

Milton Keynes

Flitwick

Lower Stondon

10

Bletchley

Shillington

Apsley End

Holwell

19 20 21

Hexton Pirton Ickleford

Streatley

Hitchin

31 32 33 34

Great Offley Lilley

Winslow

Leighton Buzzard

Limbury

46 47 Preston

44 45 Cockernhoe 48

Luton Biscot Breachwood Green

Dunstable

Farley Hill

Whitwell

Luton

62 63 64 65 66

Caddington Peters Green

Slip End New Mill End Kimpton

Ledburn

60 61

Mentmore

Wingrave

Dagnall Markyate East Hyde Blackmore End

82 83 84 85 86 87

Cheddington 81 Studham Flamstead Lea Valley

78 79 80

Long Marston Ringshall Harpenden

Pitstone

Wilstone

Gaddesden Row Wheathampstead

Aylesbury

Drayton Beauchamp Aldbury Little Gaddesden Redbourn

99 100 101 102 103 104 105 106 107 108

Aston Clinton Tring Church End Childwick Green Sandridge

Weston Turville Wigginton Great Gaddesden

Marshalswick

Hastoe Dudswell Potten End Piccotts End Townsend

Wendover 119 120 121 122 123 124 125 126 127 128

St Leonards Berkhamsted

Cholesbury Hemel Hempstead St Albans

Felden Chiswell Green

Princes Risborough

136 137 138 139 140 141 142

Bovingdon Bedmond London Colney

Buckinghamshire STREET ATLAS

Botley Kings Langley Bricket Wood

Great Missenden

Chesham

Flaunden Chipperfield Abbots Langley Shenley

150 151 152 153 154 155 156

Latimer Chenies Sarratt Garston Radlett

Amersham

Chorleywood Watford Letchmore Heath

Hazlemere

164 165 166 167 168 169

Rickmansworth Croxley Green Oxhey Bushey Elstree

High Wycombe

Chalfont St Giles

Maple Cross South Oxhey Stanmore

172 173 174 175 176

Harefield Northwood Pinner Edgware

Beaconsfield Chalfont St Peter

Harrow

Marlow

Ruislip

Wembley

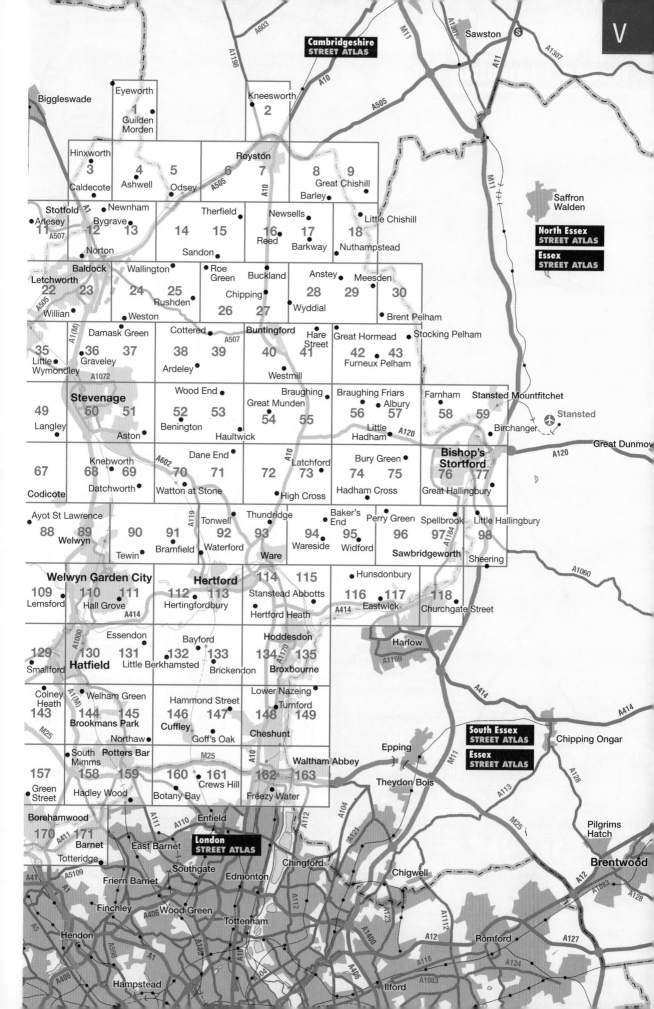

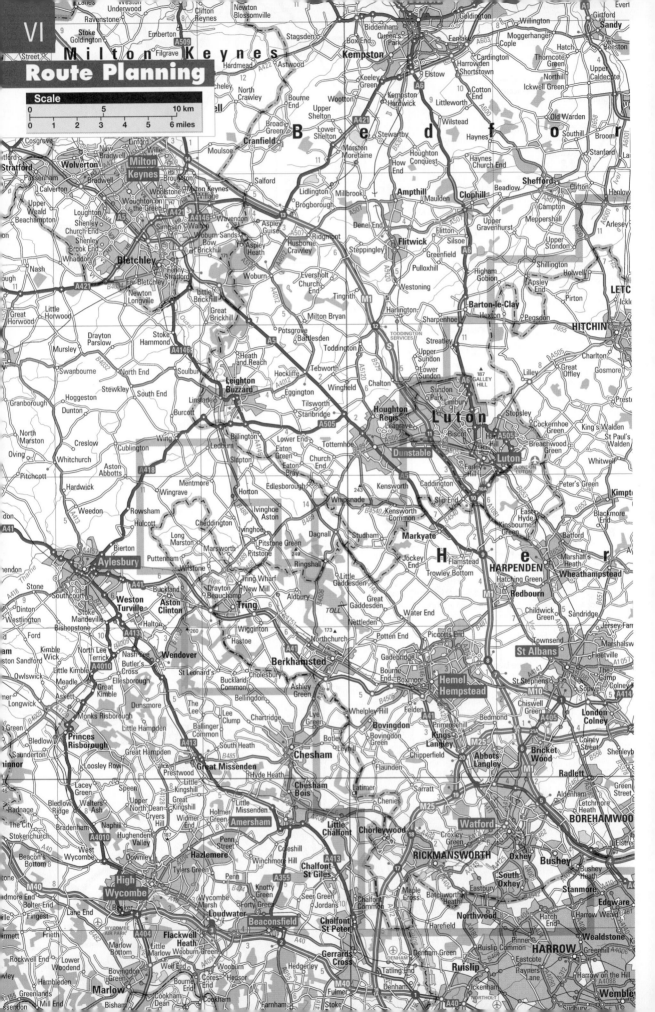

Scale
0        5        10 km
0   1   2   3   4   5   6 miles

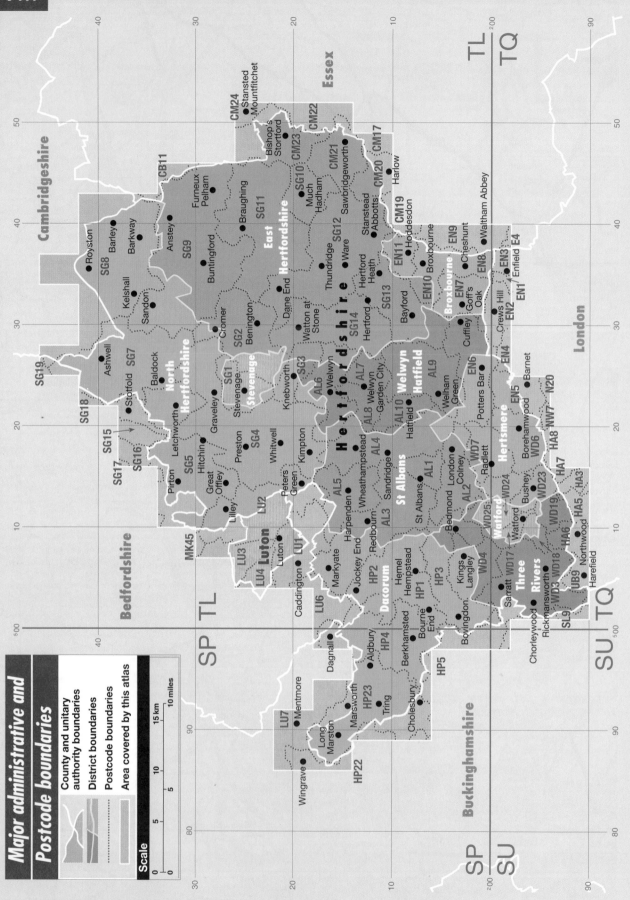

## Major administrative and Postcode boundaries

County and unitary authority boundaries
District boundaries
Postcode boundaries
Area covered by this atlas

**Scale**

0    5    10    15 km

0    5    10 miles

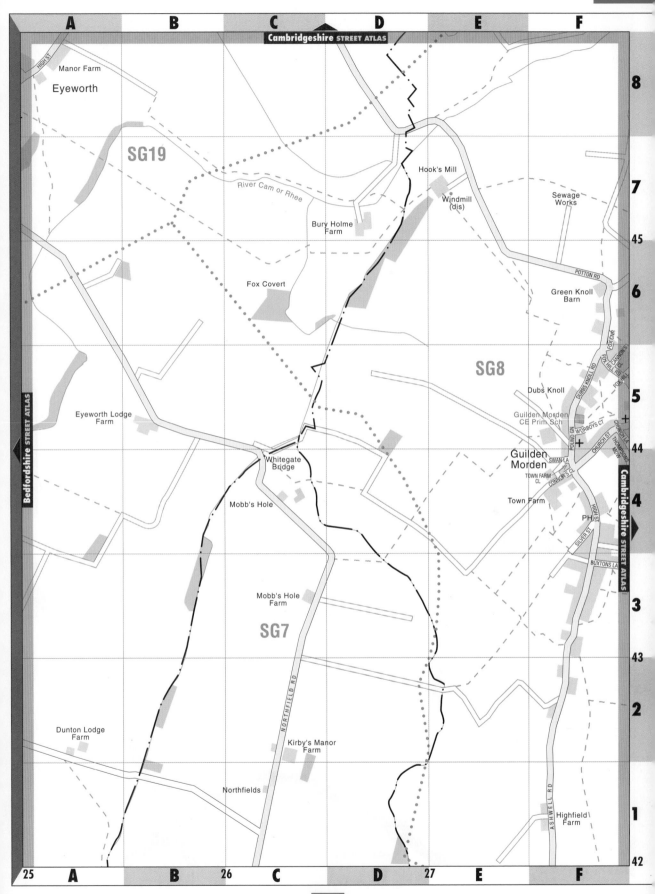

Cambridgeshire STREET ATLAS

A B C D E F

8

Manor Farm
Eyeworth

SG19

River Cam or Rhee

Hook's Mill

Windmill
(dis)

7

Sewage
Works

45

Bury Holme
Farm

POTTON RD

Fox Covert

6

Green Knoll
Barn

SG8

Dubs Knoll

5

Guilden Morden
CE Prim Sch

Eyeworth Lodge
Farm

Guilden
Morden

44

Whitegate
Bridge

SWAN LA

TOWN FARM
CL

CONNOR'S CL

Mobb's Hole

Town Farm

PH

HIGH ST

4

SILVER ST

BUXTONS LA

Mobb's Hole
Farm

3

43

NORTHFIELD RD

SG7

2

Dunton Lodge
Farm

Kirby's Manor
Farm

ASHWELL RD

Highfield
Farm

Northfields

1

42

25 A B 26 C D 27 E F

Bedfordshire STREET ATLAS

Cambridgeshire STREET ATLAS

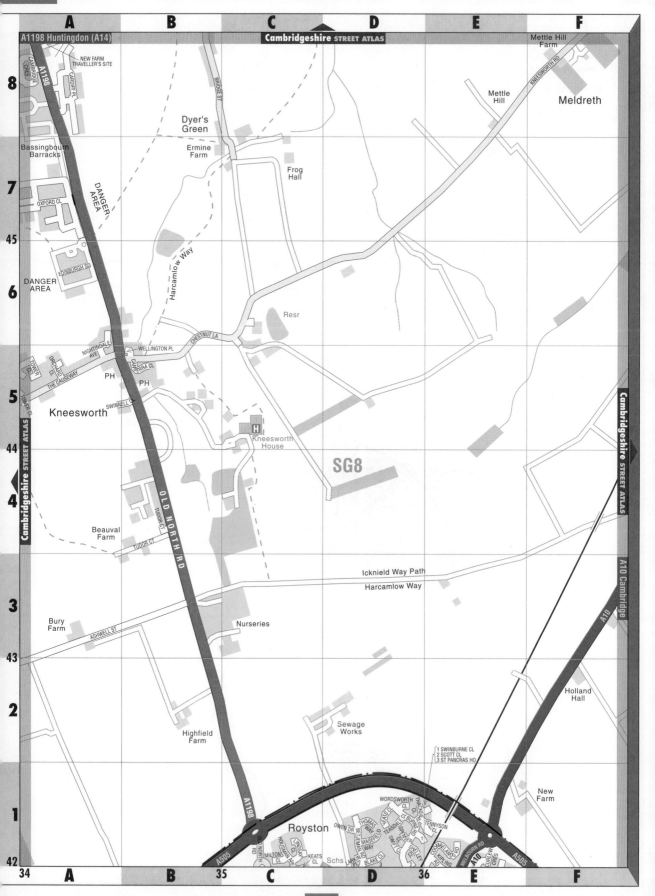

**A1198** Huntingdon (A14)

Mettle Hill Farm

NEW FARM TRAVELLER'S SITE

CARDIFF PL

CAMBRIDGE CRES

Dyer's Green

Mettle Hill

Mettle Hill

Meldreth

KNEESWORTH RD

Bassingbourn Barracks

Ermine Farm

OXFORD CL

DANGER AREA

Frog Hall

EDINBURGH SQ

DANGER AREA

Harcamlow Way

CHESTNUT LA

Resr

NIGHTINGALE AVE

WELLINGTON PL

ORCHARD CL

THE CAUSEWAY

TOWER CL

TOWER RD

PH

CANBERRA CL

PH

SWINNELL CL

Kneesworth

SG8

H

Kneesworth House

OLD NORTH RD

TUDOR CT

Beauval Farm

TUDOR CT

Icknield Way Path

Harcamlow Way

Bury Farm

ASHWELL ST

Nurseries

A10 Cambridge

A10

Holland Hall

Highfield Farm

Sewage Works

1 SWINBURNE CL
2 SCOTT CL
3 ST PANCRAS HO

New Farm

WORDSWORTH CL

THACKERAY CL

TENNYSON CL

KEATS CL

OWEN DR

THOMAS WAY

BETJEMAN

MASEFIELD WAY

TEASDALE CL

BURNS RD

SPENCER RD

SKELTON

SWIFTS

SPENCER

A1198

Royston

MILTON AVE

HOLMAN CL

LINDSAY AVE

KEATS CL

LARKIN

BLAKE CL

Schs

CHAUCER RD

MELBOURN RD

KIPLING

A10

CURLEW CRES

A505

A505

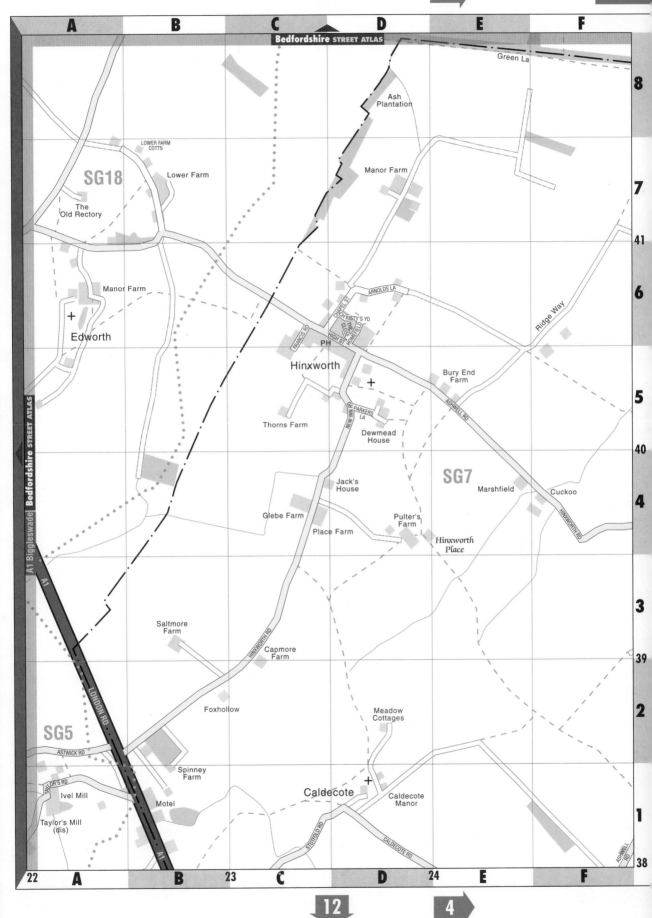

Bedfordshire STREET ATLAS

**A** **B** **C** **D** **E** **F**

8

Green La

Ash Plantation

LOWER FARM COTTS

**SG18**

Lower Farm

Manor Farm

7

The Old Rectory

41

Manor Farm

ARNOLDS LA

6

CHAPEL ST

CHRISTY'S YD

THE CLOSE

Ridge Way

Edworth

FRANCIS RD

HIGH ST

MANFIELD

PH

Hinxworth

Bury End Farm

5

ASHWELL RD

Thorns Farm

PARKERS LA

Dewmead House

40

**SG7**

Jack's House

Marshfield

Cuckoo

4

Glebe Farm

Place Farm

Pulter's Farm

HINXWORTH RD

Hinxworth Place

3

Saltmore Farm

HINXWORTH RD

Capmore Farm

39

Foxhollow

Meadow Cottages

2

**SG5**

ASTWICK RD

Spinney Farm

LONDON RD

Caldecote

Caldecote Manor

TAYLOR'S RD

Ivel Mill

Motel

1

Taylor's Mill (dis)

STOTFOLD RD

CALDECOTE RD

ASHWELL RD

A1

38

**A** **B** **C** **D** **E** **F**

22 23 24

A1 Biggleswade Bedfordshire STREET ATLAS

A B C D E F

8

7

41

6

5

40

4

3

39

2

1

38

25 A B 26 C D 27 E F

Green La
Barrowsford Bridge
Ridge Way
NORTHFIELD RD
ASHWELL RD
SG8
Cold Harbour
Sewage Works
COMMON LA
River Rhee
Bluegates Farm
Ashwell End
Bluegates Dairy
Elbrook House
SG7
Baldwin's Corner
Cemy
GREEN LA
Ashwell Bury
FORDHAM CL
MILL ST
SPRINGHEAD
LUCAS LA
Love's Farm
LOVE LA
Ashridge Farm
Icknield Way Path
ROLLYS LA
ALMS LA
Hotel
Quarry Hills Farm
Ashwell Village Mus
GARDINERS LA
SWAN ST
HODWELL
HIGH ST
PO
Whittington Farm
WOLVERLEY HO 1
THE OLD GRANARY 2
THE DOVECOTE 3
BACON'S YD
SILVER ST
WOODFORDE CL
STATION RD
HINXWORTH RD
COLBROOK CL
JOHN SALE CT
WEST END
WILSOVER END
BACK ST
PH
THE RICKYARDS
SILVER ST CT
ANGEL'S MEADOW
KINGSLAND WAY
ASHWELL ST
DIXIES CL
BOAT LA
Ashwell Prim Sch
CLAYBUSH RD
Ashwell
PARTRIDGE HILL
Newnham Hill
NEWNHAM WAY
Arbury Banks
Claybush Hill
Icknield Way Path
ASHWELL RD
Ash Hill

Steeple
Morden

Wyndmere
Farm

ASHWELL RD

PLOUGH CL

WESTBROOK CL

Gatley
End

Icknield Way Path

Upper
Gatley End

High
Farm

Ashwell St

SG8

Morden
Grange
Farm

STATION RD

Chalk
Pit

Shire Balk

Morden
Grange
Plantation

New
Part

Caravan
Site

Next
Odsey

Cheyneys
Lodge

Chain Walk

A505

STATION RD

Redlands
Farm

SG7

Ashwell
Fields

PH

Ashwell &
Morden

Highley
Hill

Odsey

A505

Gallows
Hill

Heath
Barn

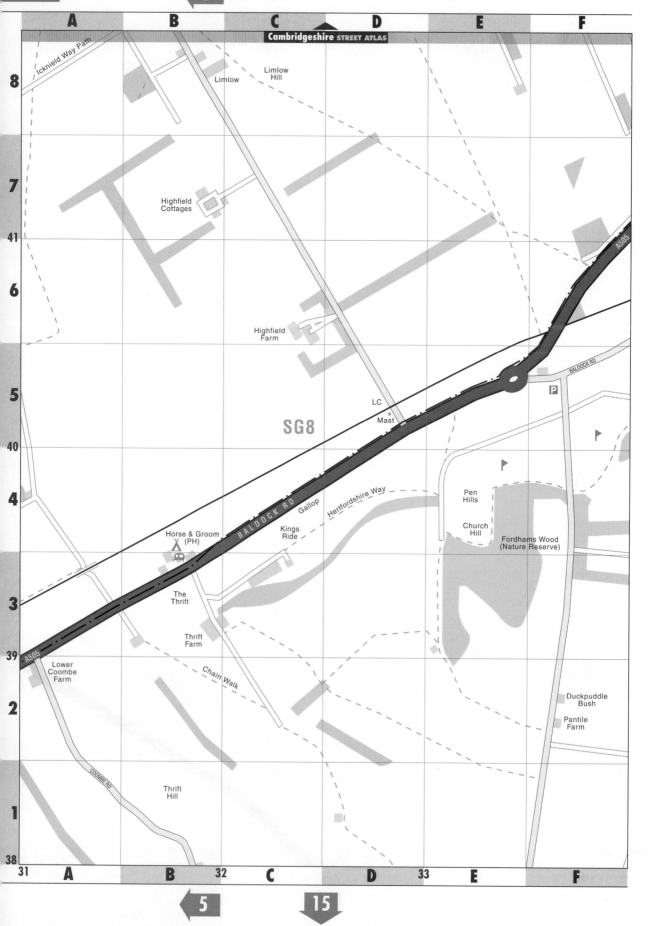

A  B  C  D  E  F

**Cambridgeshire** STREET ATLAS

8

Icknield Way Path

Limlow

Limlow Hill

7

Highfield Cottages

41

6

Highfield Farm

5

LC

Mast

SG8

40

Baldock Rd

A505

4

Gallop

Hertfordshire Way

Baldock Rd

Kings Ride

Pen Hills

Church Hill

Fordhams Wood (Nature Reserve)

Horse & Groom (PH)

3

The Thrift

Thrift Farm

39

A505

Lower Coombe Farm

Chain Walk

Duckpuddle Bush

2

Pantile Farm

Coombe Rd

Thrift Hill

1

38

31  A  B  32  C  D  33  E  F

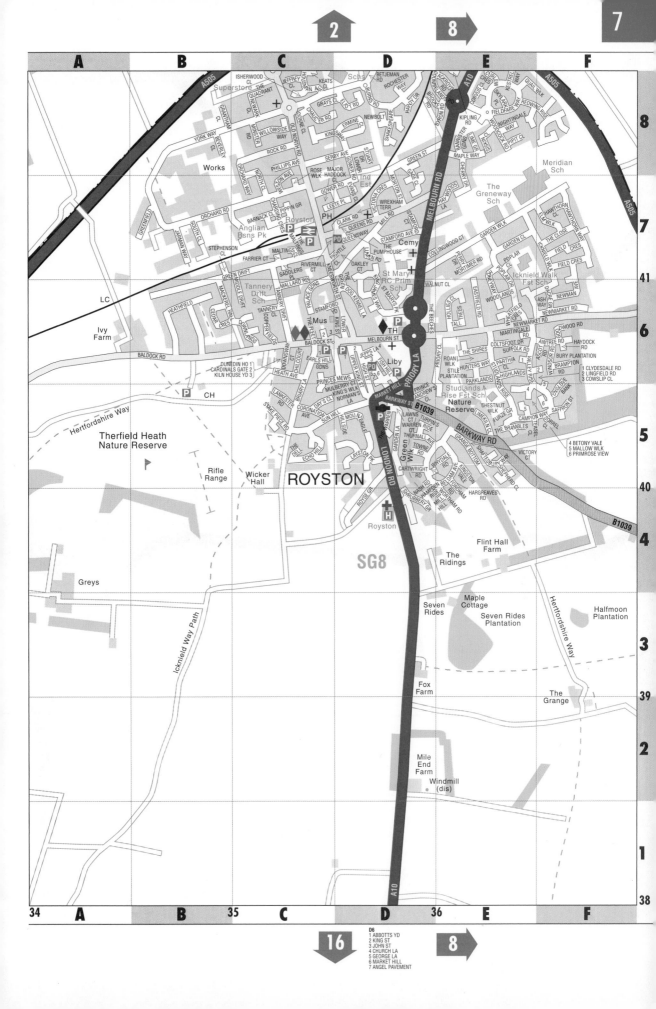

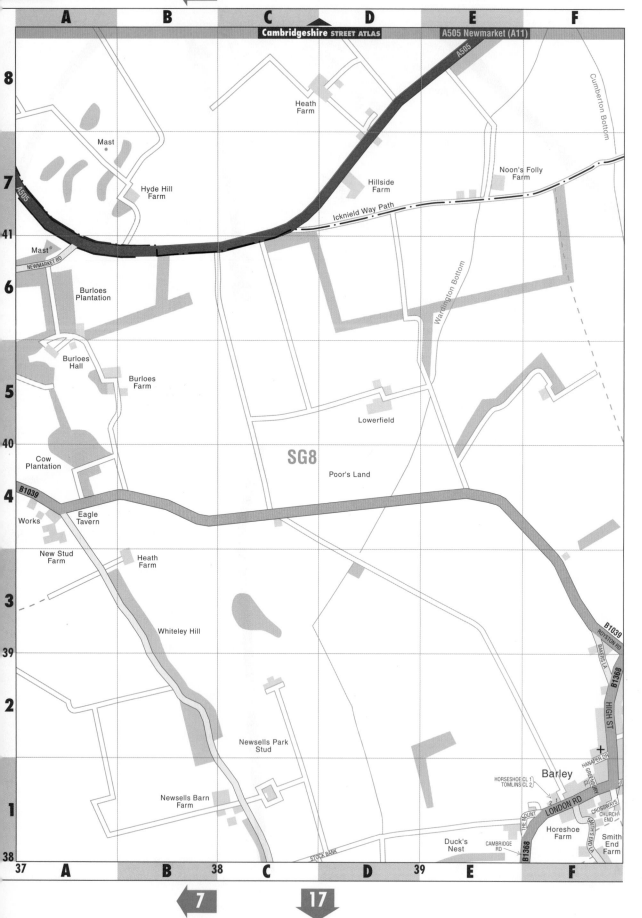

A B C D E F

A505 Newmarket (A11)

A505

8

Heath Farm

Cumberton Bottom

Mast

Hyde Hill Farm

7

A505

Hillside Farm

Noon's Folly Farm

41

Mast

Icknield Way Path

NEWMARKET RD

6

Burloes Plantation

Wardington Bottom

Burloes Hall

Burloes Farm

5

Lowerfield

40

Cow Plantation

SG8

Poor's Land

4

B1039

Eagle Tavern

Works

New Stud Farm

Heath Farm

B1039

ROYSTON RD

BAKERS LA

B1368

3

Whiteley Hill

39

HIGH ST

2

Newsells Park Stud

HANAPER DR

GREENBURY CL

Barley

HORSESHOE CL 1
TOMLINS CL 2

1

Newsells Barn Farm

LONDON RD

THE MOUNT

CROSSWAYS

CHURCH END

SMITH'S END LA

Horeshoe Farm

Smith End Farm

38

Duck's Nest

CAMBRIDGE RD

B1368

STOCK BANK

37 A B 38 C D 39 E F

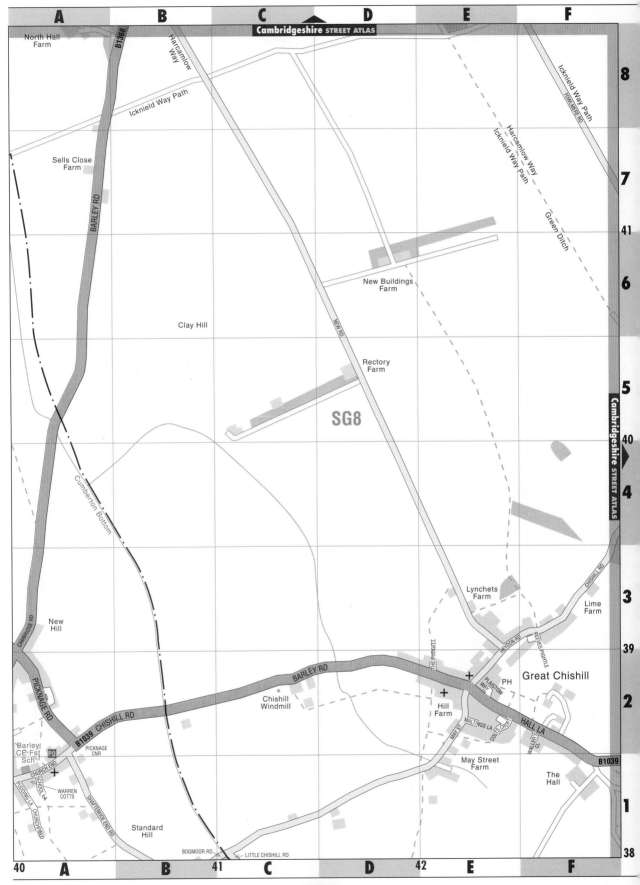

Cambridgeshire STREET ATLAS

North Hall Farm

B1368

Harcamlow Way

Icknield Way Path

Sells Close Farm

BARLEY RD

Clay Hill

Icknield Way Path

Fowlmere Rd

Harcamlow Way

Icknield Way Path

Green Ditch

New Buildings Farm

NEW RD

Rectory Farm

SG8

Cambridgeshire STREET ATLAS

Cumberton Bottom

New Hill

CAMBRIDGE RD

Lynchets Farm

CHISHILL RD

Lime Farm

HEYDON RD

REEVES PIGHTLE

THE PIDGETT

Great Chishill

PH

PLAISTOW WAY

PICKNAGE RD

BARLEY RD

Chishill Windmill

Hill Farm

MALTINGS LA

COTS CROFT

HALL LA

WALLERS CL

B1039 CHISHILL RD

Barley CE Fst Sch

PO

PICKNAGE CNR

MAY ST

May Street Farm

B1039

The Hall

CHURCH END

SCHOOL LA

WARREN COTTS

SHAFTENHOE END RD

PUDDING LA

CHURCHFIELD

Standard Hill

BOGMOOR RD

LITTLE CHISHILL RD

18

8
7
41
6
5
40
4
3
39
2
1
38

40  A  B  41  C  D  42  E  F

A507 Flitwick

A6001 Biggleswade

A507

SG17

8

Henlow

THE GARDENS

ARLESEY RD PARK FARM CL

PH

Arlesey Bridge

7

Henlow Airfield

Old Manor Farm

Cityfield Farm

37

Westfield Farm

Middlefield Farm

MIDDLEFIELD LA

Middle Water

6

HITCHIN RD

Sewage Works

SG16

River Hiz

5

Camp

Playing Field

Derwent Lower Sch

Laurels Grove

SG15

SPRECKLEY CL

WHITWORTH JONES AVE

DAWSON CL

OWEN JONES

MORRIS CL

WEEDON RD

TEDDER AVE

36

WHITTLE CL

FRANKS CL

OLDFIELD FARM RD

Susans Grove

MILL LA

KAREN HO

OLYMPUS RD

NENE RD

DERWENT RD

AVON CHASE

Oldfield Farm

STRAW PLAIT WAY

P

P

Greyhound Stadium

A6001

PO

BURNET AVE

AVON RD

THE CRESCENT

OLDFIELD FARM RD

4

STATION RD

ALLOWAY RD

PH

WILLOW TREES CVN SITE

Henlow Ind Est

BORTON AVE

Peckworth Ind Est

Lower Stondon

Playing Field

Lindas Grove

Works

THREE STAR CVN PK

ASTRAL CL

JUBILEE CL

SIGNAL CL

FLIGHT PATH

CHESTNUT AVE

NORTHERN AVE

THE OVAL

3

Cherry Tree Nurseries

APPLECROFT

ORCHARD WAY

MIDLAND WAY

BEDFORD RD

CHERRY TREES

WESTERN AVE

CENTRAL AVE

EASTERN AVE

PEAR TREE CL

PLUM TREE RD

SOUTHERN AVE

35

Old Ramerick

Holwellbury Farm

Holwell Bury House

2

Holwellbury

LC

1

Ramerick Nursery

Ramerick Bottom

A600

SG5

34

Bedfordshire STREET ATLAS

A600 Bedford

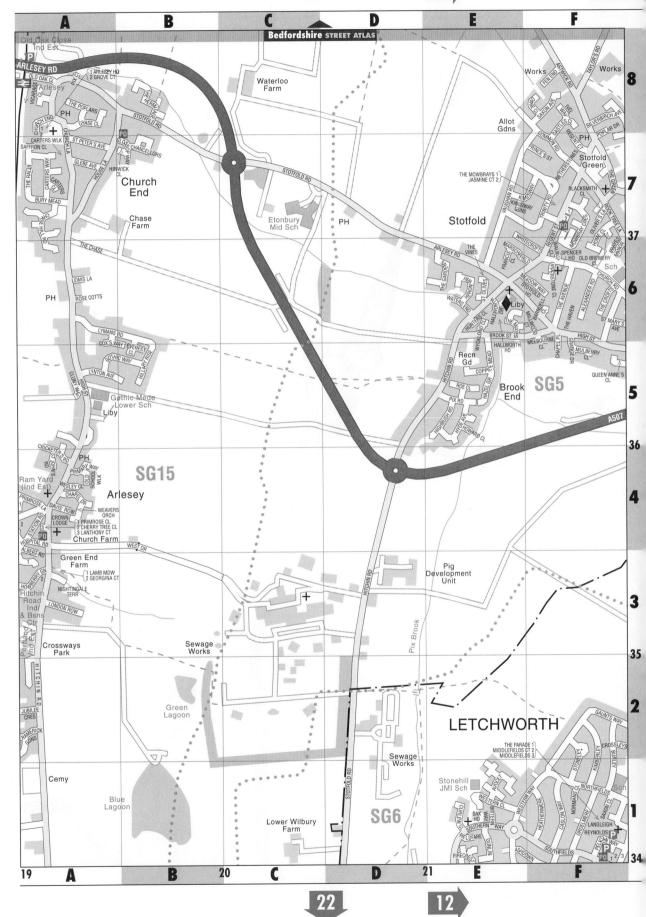

**Bedfordshire** STREET ATLAS

Old Oak Close
Ind Est

ARLESEY RD

Old Oak Cl

1 ARLESEY HO
2 GROVE CT

Arlesey

PH

THE POPLARS

CHASE CL

STOTFOLD RD

ST PETER'S AVE

GLEBE AVE

HINWICK CL

CHANCELLORS

PO

Church
End

Chase
Farm

THE CHASE

Waterloo
Farm

STOTFOLD RD

Etonbury
Mid Sch

PH

Works

Works

Allot
Gdns

COMMON RD

SAXON AVE

PRINCE'S ST

WETHERSTONES RD

THE MOWBRAYS 1
JASMINE CT 2

Stotfold
Green

PH

POPLAR DR

SILVERBIRCH AVE

8

Stotfold

BLACKSMITH
CL

37

7

ARLESEY RD

THE
VINES

WHITECROFTS

MARSCHEFIELD

SPENCER
HO

Old Brewery

Sch

6

LEWIS LA

ROSE COTTS

PH

LYMANS RD

COX'S WAY

EVEREST
CL

GOTHIC WAY

HILLARY RISE

LYNTON AVE

CLUNI WAY

HIGH ST

WATERS END

THE GARDENS

HERON WAY

BROOK ST

HALLWORTH
HO

Recn
Gd

COPPER

ROE CL

PIX RD

HITCHIN RD

HIGHBUSH RD

HYDE AVE

HOWARD CL

Liby

Brook
End

SG5

MELBOURNE
CL

CHAPEL RD

HIGH ST

MULBERRY
CL

QUEEN ANNE'S
CL

ST MARY'S
AVE

5

36

A507

Gothic Mede
Lower Sch

Liby

CRICKETER'S
RD

ST JOHN'S RD

PH

PRIMLY WAY

OLD
SCHOOL
WLK

HIGH ST

SG15

Ram Yard
(Ind Est)

WESLEY CL

CHAPEL LA

DAVIS' ROW

Arlesey

WEAVERS
ORCH

CROWN
LODGE

1 PRIMROSE CL
2 CHERRY TREE CL
3 LANTHONY CT

Church Farm

WEST DR

4

PRIMROSE LA

STATION RD

PO

ALBERT RD

HOWBERRY GN

LONDON ROW

Green End
Farm

1 LAMB MDW
2 GEORGINA CT

NIGHTINGALE
TERR

Hitchin
Road
Ind/
& Bsns
Ctr

Portland
Ind Est

Crossways
Park

Sewage
Works

Green
Lagoon

HITCHIN RD

Pig
Development
Unit

Pix Brook

3

35

JUBILEE
CRES

TAMERICK
GDNS

Cemy

Blue
Lagoon

STOTFOLD RD

Sewage
Works

SG6

Lower Wilbury
Farm

LETCHWORTH

GAUNTS WAY

THE PARADE 1
MIDDLEFIELDS CT 2
MIDDLEFIELDS 3

Stonehill
JMI Sch

WESTERN CL

WESTERN WAY

SOUTHERN WAY

STONELEY

KIMBERLY

NORTHFIELDS

NORMANS CL

HEATHERMERE

SOUTHFIELDS

CROSSLEY'S

BURLEY

SAXON CL

DRIPELMERE

LANGLEIGH

REYNOLDS

PELHAM WAY

PO

CRIPLEY

BITTERN WAY

DUNLIN

FELDFARE

FIRECREST

ASHDOWN

2

1

34

**A** **B** **C** **D** **E** **F**

8

White House

Nursery

Newnham Hall

CALDECOTE RD

Cat Ditch

Newnham

Radwell Grange Spinney

SILVERBIRCH AVE

THE GREEN

Manor Farm

ASHWELL RD

PO

7

MALTHOUSE LA

P

Ford Bridge

SG5

Radwell Grange

37

Cemy

MILL LA

St Mary's Lower Sch

ROOK TREE CL

Grange Cottages

Hullockpit Hill

NEWNHAM RD

6

ROOK TREE LA

CHEQUERS CL

MILL CL

PH

ST MARY'S AVE

Baldock Services

SG7

Hullockpit Plantation

A1 (M)

VICTORIA DR

Works

A1

5

A507

QUEEN ANNE'S LA

New Bridge

BALDOCK RD

THE COPSE

GROVELAND WAY

LITTLEBURY CL

A507

10

A507

36

Boundary Farm

Mill House

Radwell

COUNCIL COTTS

RADWELL LA

THE PEBBLES

4

Capra

Garden Cottages

Bury Farm

Radwell House

Landing Strip

Poultry Farm

River Ivel

Icknield Way Path

3

Countryside Walk

NORTON MILL LA

The Nook

GREAT NORTH RD

35

NORTON RD

NORTON BURY LA

P

Norton Mill (disused)

2

Grange Playing Field

SG6

Norton Bury

Blackhorse Farm

BALDOCK

1 BRAMLEY CL
2 LAUREL MEWS
3 RABAN CT
4 PRYORS CT
5 GROSVENOR RD W
6 MAGDALENE CT
7 PEARL CT

GRANGE JUN SCH

GAUNTS WAY

SPARHAWKE

WHITHICKS

MAYCROFT

Nursery

Payne's Farm

PH

CHURCH LA

St Nicholas CE Prim Sch

Equitation Ctr

NORTH RD

Laymore Farm

SALISBURY RD

BYGRAVE RD

FARRIERS CL 1
FOOTBALL CL 2
MEETING HOUSE LA 3
EAGLE CT 4
LAVENDER CT 5
ALDRIDGE CT 6
BUTLERS YD 7
BREWERY COTTS 8
BREWERY LA 9

Works

1

GRANGE CT

NORTHFIELDS

EASTERN WAY

DANESCROFT

PAYNES CL

FARM CL

CASHIO LA

CROFT LA

THE MEWS

THE MALTINGS

THE RICKYARD

Allet Gdns

Norton

GREEN LA

TALBOT RD

CADE CL

PO

A1 (M)

LARKINS CL

A507

Baldock

ICKNIELD WAY

STATION RD

ROYSTON RD

A505

CALIFORNIA

SALE DR

GROSVENOR RD

Hartsfield JMI Sch

34

LINDENCROFT

Playing Field

THE SYCAMORES

CHURCH ST

ORCHARD RD

WHITEHORSE ST

A505

PO

BLOFIELD

34

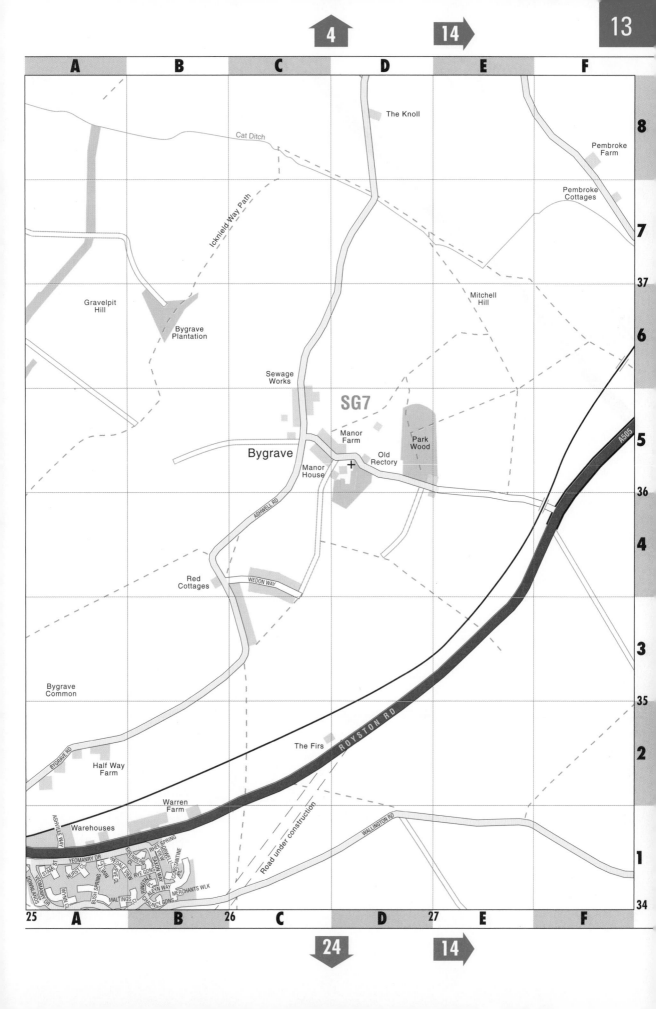

A B C D E F

8

The Knoll

Cat Ditch

Pembroke
Farm

Pembroke
Cottages

7

37

Ickneld Way Path

Gravelpit
Hill

Bygrave
Plantation

Mitchell
Hill

6

Sewage
Works

SG7

A505

Manor
Farm

Park
Wood

5

Bygrave

Old
Rectory

Manor
House

36

ASHWELL RD

4

Red
Cottages

WEDON WAY

3

Bygrave
Common

35

ROYSTON RD

The Firs

2

BYGRAVE RD

Half Way
Farm

Warren
Farm

Warehouses

Road under construction

WALLINGTON RD

1

ASHVILLE WAY

YEOMANRY DR

STANK ST

HURST CL

WYNN CL

DOWNLANDS

YEOMANRY DR

BUSH SPRING

RHEE SPRING

EISENBERG CL

IKEDALE TREN

IKEDALE CL

RUNSTALE

RHEE SPRING

RYE GDNS

ORWELL PL

SAXON WAY

CONSTANTINE PL

ALEYN WAY

CHAUNCY GDNS

MALTINGS

MERCHANTS WLK

34

25 A 26 B C 27 D E F

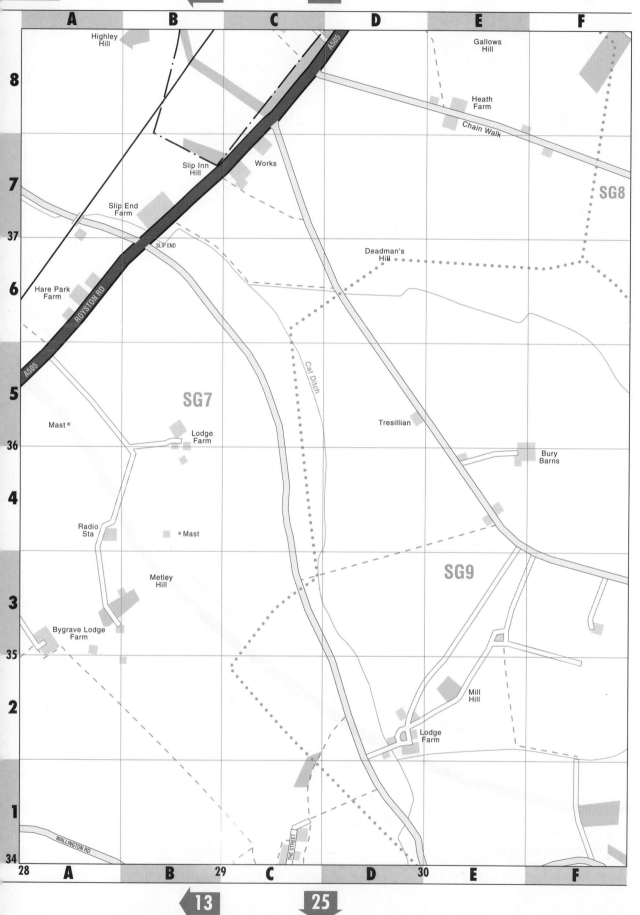

A  B  C  D  E  F

8

Icknield Way Path

Hatchpen

7

37

Hertfordshire Way

6

MEADOW WAY

Washingditch
Green

HAYWOOD LA

River Rib

Mardlebury

THE JOINT

BRICKYARD LA

Mast

JACKSON'S LA

Reed
End

WILLOW CL

HOBBS HAYES

CROW LA

Reed
Fst Sch

Wisbridge
Farm

SG8

BLACKSMITH'S LA

5

Holborn
Farm

Mast

Reed

ROOKS NEST LA

CHURCH LA

The Cabinet
(PH)

HIGH ST

36

Southview

DRIFTWAY

Dane
End

Queenbury

4

Rooksnest
Farm

DANE END

Mast

CHURCH CL

+

Reed
Hall

Gannock
Grove

Kelshall La

Gannock
Green

3

Icknield
Way Path

Chapel
Green

Reed
Wood

35

River Rib

Sewage
Works

Hilly
Wood

Southfield
Grove

2

Brandish
Wood

SG9

Slate Hall
Farm

1

34

A10

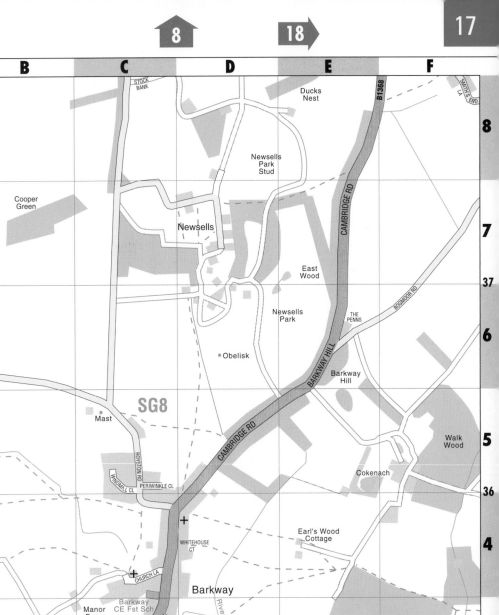

A    B    C    D    E    F

8

7

37

6

36

5

4

3

35

2

1

34

SMITH'S LA

B1368

Ducks
Nest

Newsells
Park
Stud

Newsells

Cooper
Green

East
Wood

Newsells
Park

CAMBRIDGE RD

BOGMOOR RD

THE
PENNS

Obelisk

BARKWAY HILL

Barkway
Hill

THE JOINT

Mast

SG8

Mast

Walk
Wood

Sallow
Wood

Cokenach

Periwinkle
Hill

ROYSTON RD

WINDMILL CL

PERIWINKLE CL

Bush
Wood

Rokey
Wood

WHITEHOUSE
CT

Earl's Wood
Cottage

CHURCH LA

Barkway

Manor
Farm

Barkway
CE Fst Sch

BURRS LA

River Quin

Earl's
Wood

Ashgrove

ASH MILL

TOWNSEND CL

HIGH ST

Rushing
Wells

Hertfordshire Way

Strawberry
Grove

GAS LA

Sewage
Works

Howlet's
Farm

PH

NUTHAMPSTEAD RD

CH

LONDON RD

B1368

Barkway
Equestrian Ctr

SG9

SG9

37    A    B    38    C    D    39    E    F

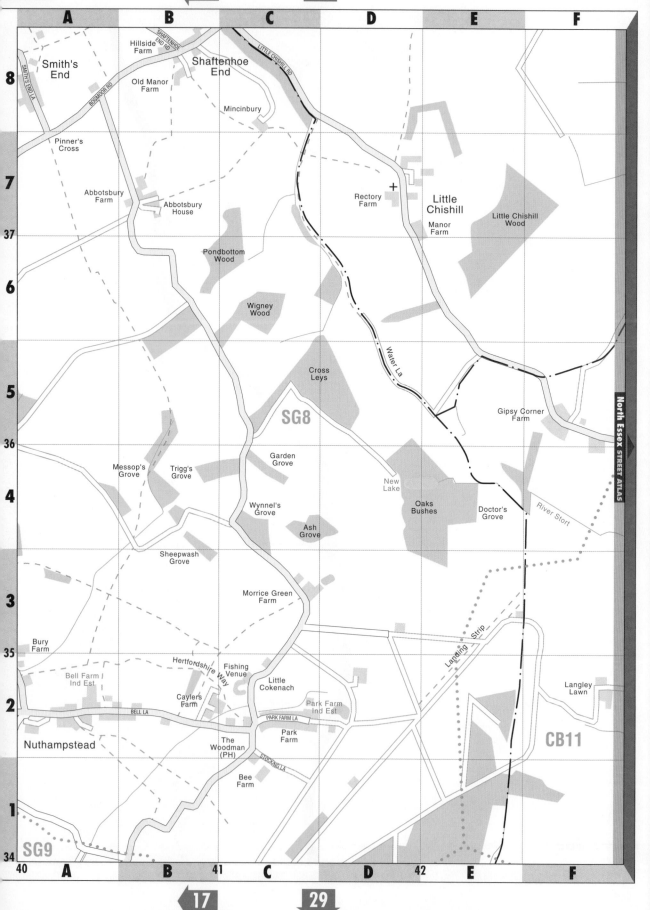

## 9

A B C D E F

**8**

Smith's End

Hillside Farm

Shaftenhoe End

Old Manor Farm

LITTLE CHISHILL RD

Mincinbury

**7**

Pinner's Cross

Abbotsbury Farm

Abbotsbury House

Rectory Farm

Little Chishill

Manor Farm

Little Chishill Wood

**37**

Pondbottom Wood

**6**

Wigney Wood

Water La

**5**

Cross Leys

SG8

Gipsy Corner Farm

**36**

Messop's Grove

Trigg's Grove

Garden Grove

New Lake

**4**

Wynnel's Grove

Oaks Bushes

Doctor's Grove

River Stort

Ash Grove

Sheepwash Grove

**3**

Morrice Green Farm

Landing Strip

**35**

Bury Farm

Hertfordshire Way

Fishing Venue

Bell Farm Ind Est

Langley Lawn

**2**

Caylers Farm

Little Cokenach

Park Farm Ind Est

CB11

BELL LA

PARK FARM LA

Nuthampstead

The Woodman (PH)

Park Farm

STOCKING LA

Bee Farm

**1**

SG9

**34**

40 A B 41 C D 42 E F

North Essex STREET ATLAS

A   B   C   D   E   F

Bedfordshire STREET ATLAS

Ion Bridge Farm

Archers Farm

Hanscombe End Farm

MK45

Hanscombe End

HANSCOMBE END RD

Parsonage Farm

CHURCH ST
THE OLD SCHOOL
SCAGGS CL
PH
Shillington
HIGH RD

8

Chalkybush Farm

Apsley End

7

Manor Cottage

Higham Cottages

Green Farm

Pirton Grange Farm

33

Manor Farm

Pirton Grange

Pirton Hall

Manor Farm Bsns Pk

PH

APSLEY END RD

Wesley Spinney

Higham Gobion

Apsleybury Wood

SHILLINGTON RD

6

Lowerpiece Spinnies

Ravendale Farm

Apsley Bury Farm

Shillington Manor

5

32

Hexton Common

Common La

Kettledean Farm

4

John Bunyan Trail

SG5

3

The Mill

MILL LA

31

Sewage Works

Manor Farm

Pegsdon Common Farm

The Curl Paper

Green End Farm

2

PH
PO
Hexton

Pegsdon Belt

Church Wood

DAIRY COTTS

Hexton Manor

The Rookery

Bury Farm

Pegsdon

Hexton JMI Sch

PEGSDON WAY
LONG ROW
PH

B655
BARTON RD

HITCHIN RD

1

The Butts

Bonfirehill Knoll

B655

30

10   A   B   11   C   D   12   E   F

Bedfordshire STREET ATLAS

Bedfordshire STREET ATLAS

SG16

SG5

**Burge End**

**Pirton**

Rosehill Farm

New Wrights Farm

Burge End Farm

Hammonds Farm

West Lane Farm

Rectory Farm

SHILLINGTON RD

BURGE END LA

WEST LA

FRANKLIN CL

LITTLE LA

DANSCL

BUNYAN CL

CROMWELL WAY

ROYAL OAK LA

COLEMANS CL

HIGH ST

PO

Pirton Sch

ST MARY'S CL

DOCKLANDS

CRAB TREE LA

HAMBRIDGE WAY

Ickenield Way Path

PRIORS HILL

POLLARDS WAY

DANEFIELD RD

Wr Twr

Hill Farm

THREE CLOSES

GREAT GREEN END

NO BURY END

Toot Hill

WALNUT TREE RD

Hill Farm

MALTINGS ORCH

WALNUT TREE RD

Walnut Tree Farm

Knocking Knoll

Ickenield Way Path

Wood La

Ickenield Way Path

HITCHIN RD

Highdown Farm

Lower Plantation

Tingley Wood

High Down House

Highdown Plantation

Hanginghill Plantation

Punch's Cross

Tingley Field Platation

B655

Shrub Wood

B655

| A | B | C | D | E | F |
|---|---|---|---|---|---|

**8**

White Hill
Fairfield Kennels

Standalone Farm

SG15

SG6

PH STOTFOLD RD

HITCHIN RD

**7**

Wilbury Farm

ARLESEY NEW RD

ARLESEY RD

COOPERS FIELD 1
HAMMERDELL 2
WYSELLS CT 3

DAVID EVANS CT
FURLAY CL
BEECH HILL
LONGFIELD CT
WARREN CL
CHASTEN HILL
HIBBERTS CT

Pix Brook
Norton Common

WHEAT HILL
HAWTHORN HILL
HAYMOOR
LONGMEAD

STATION PAR 1
THE GALLERY 2
THE ARCADE 3
THE WYND 4
CENTRAL APP 5
COMMERCE WAY 6

**33**

Fox Covert

Wilburyhill Farm

Cvn Pk

WILBURY HILLS RD
WILBURY CL
ROMANY RD
MULLWAY
HALL MEAD

ELDEFIELD

BEDFORD RD

Wilbury Jun Sch

CORNER CL
NEVELLS RD

NEVELLS CL
CROSS ST
THE QUADRANT

**6**

PH

Wilbury Hill

Cemy

MONKS CL
ABBOTTS RD

Icknield Inf Sch

ROMAN CRES
REDHOODS WAY E
COWSLIP HILL

TA Ctr Letchworth

Superstore

BENNETT CT
STATION RD
LEYS AVE
PAW LANE

Icknield Way Path

SG5

Cadwell Farm

Allot Gdns
Fearnhill Sch

CAMPFIELD WAY
MARTIN WAY
HIGHOVER RD

Icknield Inf Sch
SUMMERS LODGE
SAFFRON HILL
ICKNIELD WAY

THE MEADS
STATION WAY

Coll
Liby
TH
Letchworth Mus & Art Gall

EASTCHEAP
ROWLAND WAY
ARENA PAR
GERNON RD
PIXMORE WAY

**5**

LETCHWORTH

BURNELL RISE
BURNELL
CAMPERS RD
CHILTERN VIEW
HILLBROW

CAMPERS AVE
WEST VIEW
HIGH AVE

BROADWATER DALE
BROADWATER AVE
THE DALE

Sch

St Francis' Coll

WEST VIEW
SOUBERIE AVE
LYTTON
PADDOCK CL
MEADOW WAY

**32**

ROBERT SAUNDERS CT
UNWIN CL
OAK TREE CL
PARKER CL

St Thomas More RC Prim Sch

The Highfield Sch

SOLLERSHOTT W
HIGHFIELD

SOLLERSHOTT
SOLLERSHOTT HALL

SOUTH VIEW
BALDOCK RD
A505
CLOISTERS RD
CLOISTER LAWNS

**4**

STOTFOLD RD

North Area Pupil Referral Unit
Briar Patch

BRIAR PATCH LA

BROADWAY CT

PO

BARRINGTON RD

St Christopher Sch

**3**

The Hitchin Bsns Ctr
Theobald Bsns Ctr
KNOWL PIECE
HILL GATE

Cam Sln
Cam Ctr
HUNTING GATE

SG4

Playing Field
HITCHIN RD

PASTURE RD
THE GLADE

MANOR CL
MANOR WAY
LETCHWORTH LA
AUBREYS RD
EARLSMEAD

CH

**31**

WALLACE WAY
WILBURY WAY

HIGH DANE

COLLISON CL
ROUNDWOOD CT

Nursery

PASTURE RD
GARTH RD

ALINGTON LA
ST MARY'S RD
BROADCROFT

**2**

HITCHIN
Highover Farm

CADWELL LA
HILLFIELD AVE
GIRDLE RD
CADWELL

STURGEON'S WAY
ARMOUR RISE
GROVE ANGS AVE
GAINSFORD CRES

COLLISON CL

CAMBRIDGE RD

Garden Ctr
Lodge
Keysheath

Hotel

Fiveways House

**1**

MILLSTREAM
GROVE HO
REDOUBT CL
GROVE RD

Walsworth Common
Walsworth

River Purwell

WOOLGROVE RD
EAST CL
ORCHARD CL
ST STAINS CL

Highover JMI Sch

GREEN LA
P PO

QUEENSWOOD DR
GRANVILLE RD
HAMPDEN RD
KINGSWOOD AVE

The Orchard

Longwood

WILLIAN RD

WILSHERE CRES

**30**

SG5
MIDLAND COTTS

A505

| A | B | C | D | E | F |
|---|---|---|---|---|---|

23
13

A B C D E F

8

Nursery
Home
Land
YEOMANRY
DR
WEAVERS
WAY
MERCIA RD
J. OMANRY RD
WESTEL CL
BARLY RISE

Clothall Common

7

Cambrai
Farm
LIMEKILN
SOUTH RD
WALNU'T
LAYTON GDNS
WALLINGTON RD

Sch

BYRD WLK
PENFOLD RD
PRYOR RD

The Homestead

33

Icknield Way Path

Warren La

Cockpit

Quickswood

6

Nature Trail

Baldock By-Pass under construction

CLOTHALL RD

Welbury
Farm

Windmill Hill

Bird Hill

Icknield Way Path

SG7

Weston Hills

5

Newfield Hill

Clothall
Bury

32

Ashanger Hill

Clothall

4

Hertfordshire Way

Green
Grove

Bush Wood

HICKMAN'S HILL

ASHANGER LA

The Barley Mow
(PH)

A507

3

HATCH LA

SG4

31

Green End

2

Mill
Farm

Weston Windmill
(dis)

Old
Farm

PH

Darnall's Hall
Farm

Weston

Weston
Prim Sch

Weston
Bury

1

THE SNIPE
FRIARS RD
HITCHIN RD
POST
OFFICE
ROW
FORE ST
MILL LA
MILL
GROUND
COTTS
MAIDEN ST
MOUNT'S
MEADOW
SCHOOL LA
CHURCH LA

Oakley's
Farm

30

Town
Farm
DAMASK GREEN RD
PO
Manor
House
Works
Recn
Gd
Church
End

25 A B 26 C D 27 E F

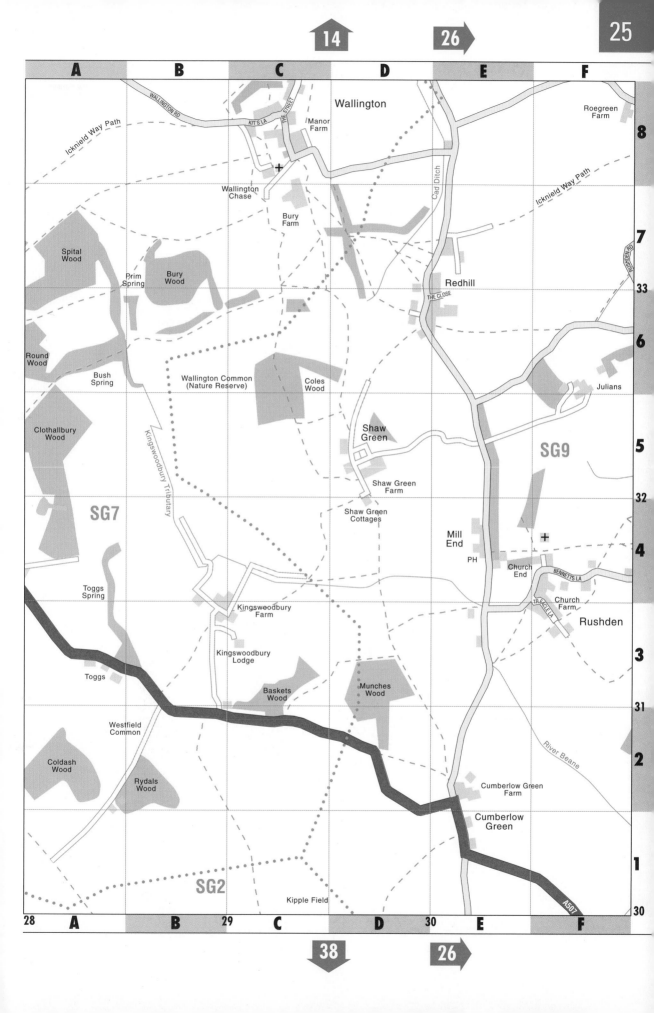

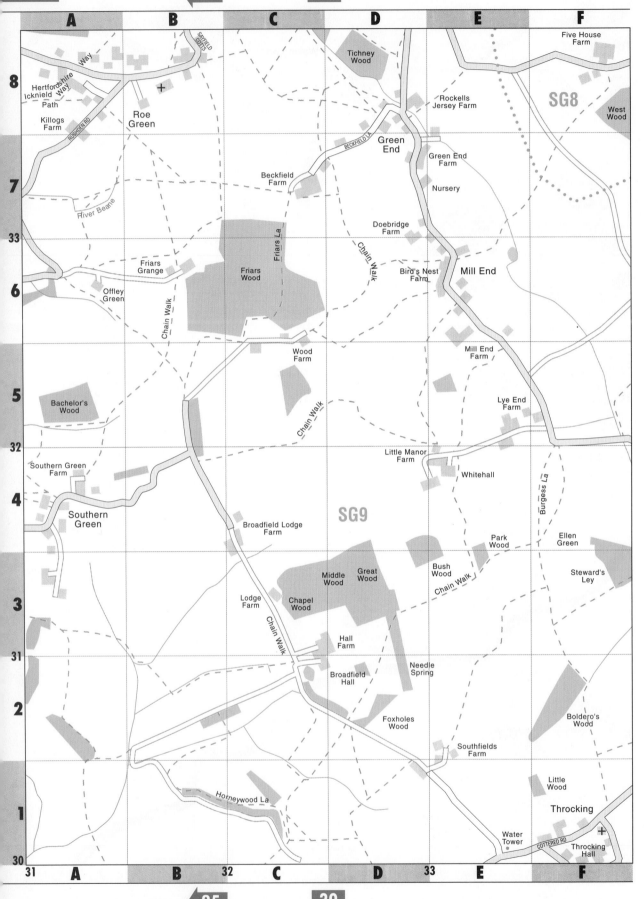

A B C D E F

8

Five House
Farm

Hertfordshire
Way
Icknield Way
Path

SG8

West
Wood

Killogs
Farm

Roe
Green

Tichney
Wood

Rockells
Jersey Farm

Green
End

BECKFIELD LA

7

Beckfield
Farm

Green End
Farm

Nursery

River Beane

33

Doebridge
Farm

Friars
Grange

Friars
Wood

Chain Walk

Bird's Nest
Farm

Mill End

6

Offley
Green

Chain Walk

Wood
Farm

Mill End
Farm

5

Bachelor's
Wood

Chain Walk

Lye End
Farm

32

Little Manor
Farm

Burgess La

Southern Green
Farm

Whitehall

4

Southern
Green

Broadfield Lodge
Farm

SG9

Park
Wood

Ellen
Green

Middle
Wood

Great
Wood

Bush
Wood

Chain Walk

Steward's
Ley

3

Lodge
Farm

Chapel
Wood

Chain Walk

Hall
Farm

31

Broadfield
Hall

Needle
Spring

2

Foxholes
Wood

Boldero's
Wood

Southfields
Farm

Little
Wood

1

Horneywood La

Throcking

Water
Tower

COTTERED RD

Throcking
Hall

30

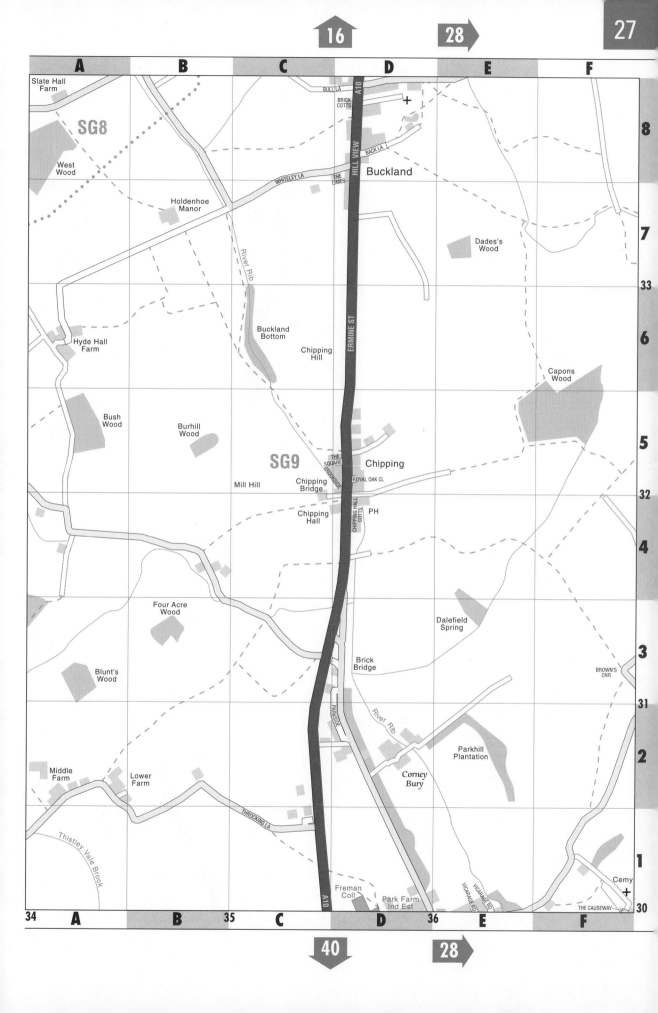

A B C D E F

SG8

8

B1368 LONDON RD

North End Farm

Biggin Bridge

7

Biggin Manor

Northey Wood

River Quin

33

BIGGIN HILL

CAVE GATE

6

Cave Bridge

Stapleton Bridge

Lincoln Hill

5

Forty Acre Plantation

Cavehall Plantation

32

Cherry Orchard Plantation

SG9

New Barns

Wyddial Hall

+

4

Peartree Field Wood

Bushleys Grove

Fox Hill

CHERRY ORCHARD LA

ROSE COTTS

SOUTHSIDE Wyddial

Beauchamps

River Quin

Home Farm

Flint Cottages

3

MOLES LA

Silkmead Farm

31

Moles Farm

Beauchamp's Wood

2

Beauchamp's Plantation

Bradbury Farm

Works

1

B1368

30

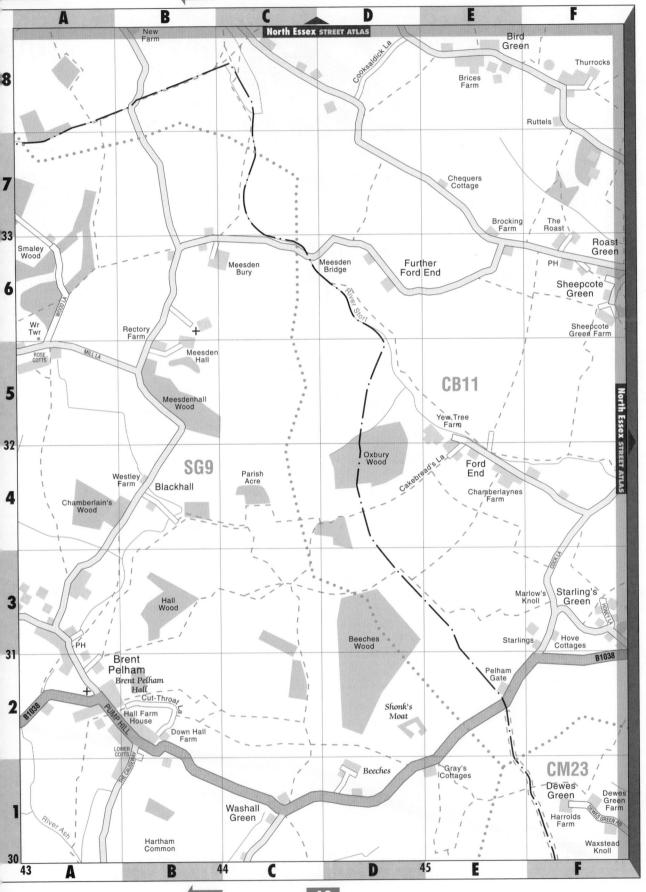

A B C D E F

8

7

33

6

32

5

4

3

31

2

1

30

43 A B 44 C D 45 E F

New Farm

Cooksaldick La

Bird Green

Thurrocks

Brices Farm

Ruttels

Chequers Cottage

Smaley Wood

Meesden Bury

Meesden Bridge

Further Ford End

Brocking Farm

The Roast

Roast Green

PH

Sheepcote Green

WOOD LA

Wr Twr

Rectory Farm

Meesden Hall

River Short

Sheepcote Green Farm

ROSE COTTS

MILL LA

Meesdenhall Wood

CB11

SG9

Yew Tree Farm

Cakebread's La

Ford End

Westley Farm

Blackhall

Parish Acre

Oxbury Wood

Chamberlaynes Farm

Chamberlain's Wood

DUCK LA

Hall Wood

Marlow's Knoll

Starling's Green

HONEY LA

PH

Beeches Wood

Starlings

Hove Cottages

B1038

Brent Pelham

Pelham Gate

Brent Pelham Hall

Cut-Throat La

Shonk's Moat

B1038

PUMP HILL

Hall Farm House

Down Hall Farm

CM23

LOWER COTTS

Beeches

Gray's Cottages

Dewes Green

Dewes Green Farm

THE CAUSEWAY

Washall Green

DEWES GREEN RD

Harrolds Farm

River Ash

Hartham Common

Waxstead Knoll

North Essex STREET ATLAS

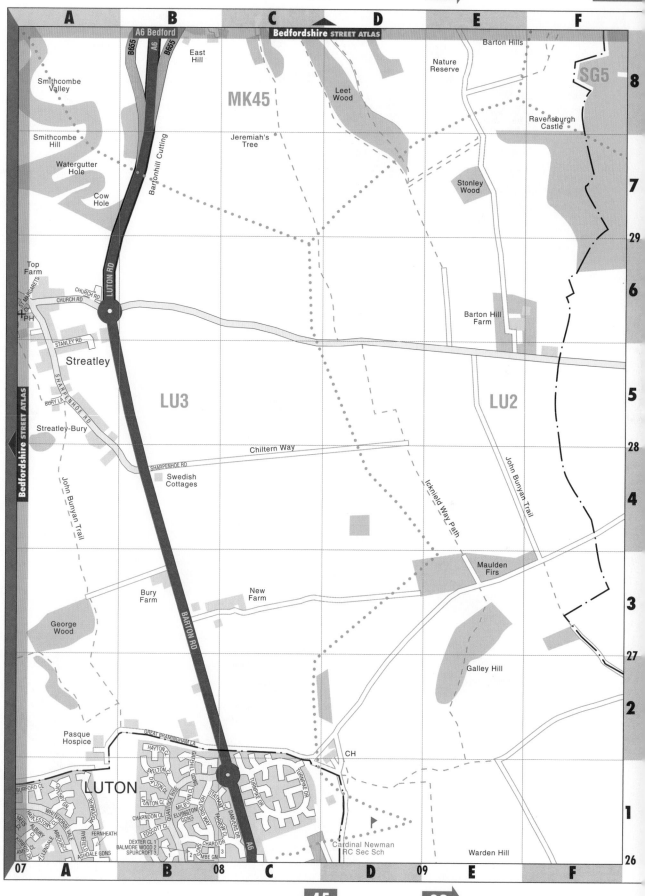

Bedfordshire STREET ATLAS

A6 Bedford

East Hill

Smithcombe Valley

MK45

Leet Wood

Nature Reserve

Barton Hills

SG5

Ravensburgh Castle

Smithcombe Hill

Jeremiah's Tree

Watergutter Hole

Cow Hole

Bartonhill Cutting

Stonley Wood

Top Farm

LUTON RD

CHURCH RD

CHURCH RD

ST MARGARETS CL

PH

STANLEY RD

Streatley

Barton Hill Farm

LU3

LU2

BURY LA

SHARPENHOE RD

Streatley-Bury

Chiltern Way

John Bunyan Trail

SHARPENHOE RD

Swedish Cottages

Icknield Way Path

John Bunyan Trail

Maulden Firs

Bury Farm

New Farm

George Wood

BARTON RD

Galley Hill

Pasque Hospice

GREAT BRAMINGHAM LA

CH

HAYTON CL

SKELTON CL

GAYHILL GDNS

TO LYTON CL

HOT FORD WAY

STATION

MILTON

TURNPIKE DR

TURNPIKE DR

LUTON

BURFORD CL

OTTERS GN

WHITEHORSE VALE

FERNHEATH

CHARNDON CL

ELVINGTON GDNS

LINTON CL

EDGCOTT CL

DANTERS DR

FAIRWAY CL

CHARD DR

DEXTER CL 1
BALMORE WOOD 2
SPURCROFT 3

SHAMBE GN

Cardinal Newman RC Sec Sch

Warden Hill

Bedfordshire STREET ATLAS

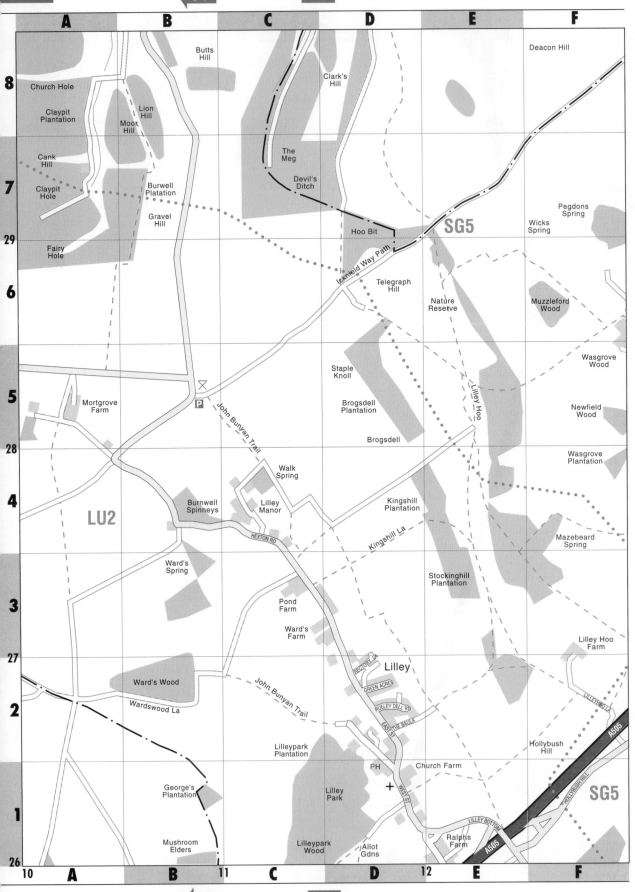

A  B  C  D  E  F

8  Church Hole

Butts Hill

Clark's Hill

Deacon Hill

Claypit Plantation

Lion Hill

Moor Hill

The Meg

7  Cank Hill

Burwell Platation

Devil's Ditch

SG5

Pegdons Spring

Wicks Spring

29  Claypit Hole

Gravel Hill

Hoo Bit

Fairy Hole

Icknield Way Path

Telegraph Hill

Nature Reserve

Muzzleford Wood

6

Wasgrove Wood

Staple Knoll

Lilley Hoo

Newfield Wood

5  Mortgrove Farm

P

John Bunyan Trail

Brogsdell Plantation

Brogsdell

28

Wasgrove Plantation

Walk Spring

Kingshill Plantation

4  Burnwell Spinneys

Lilley Manor

Mazebeard Spring

**LU2**

HEXTON RD

Kingshill La

Ward's Spring

Stockinghill Plantation

3  Pond Farm

Ward's Farm

27

Lilley Hoo Farm

Ward's Wood

John Bunyan Trail

Lilley

LILLEYHOO LA

2  Wardswood La

RECTORY LA

GREEN ACRES

RUELEY DELL RD

A505

Lilleypark Plantation

EAST ST  THE BAULK

Hollybush Hill

PH

Church Farm

George's Plantation

Lilley Park

WEST ST

HOLLYBUSH HILL

SG5

1

Lilley Bottom

Ralphs Farm

A505

Mushroom Elders

Lilleypark Wood

Allot Gdns

26

10  A  B  11  C  D  12  E  F

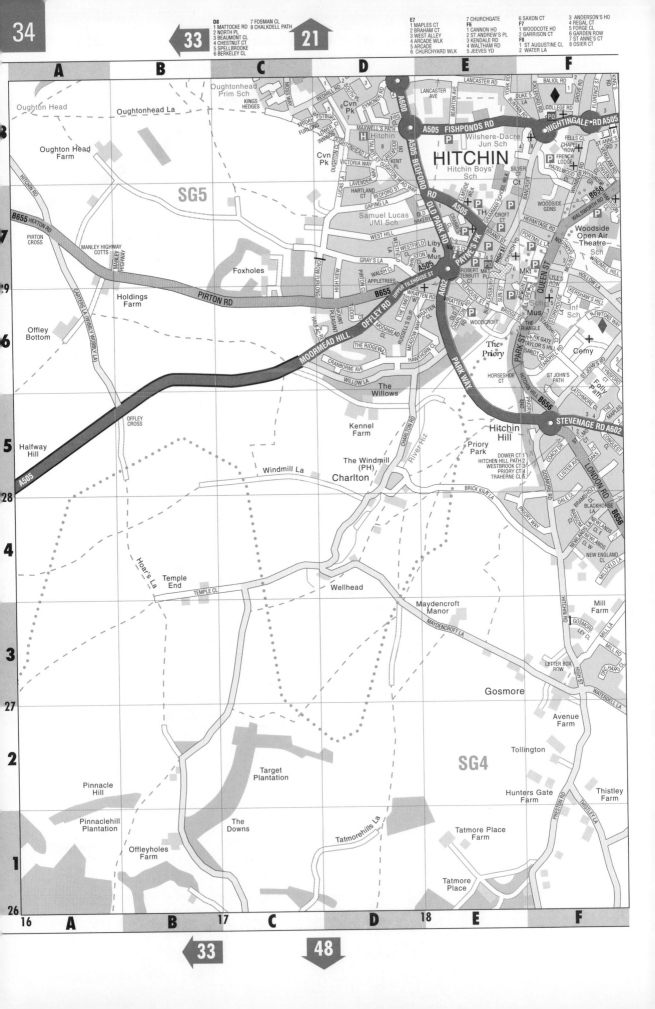

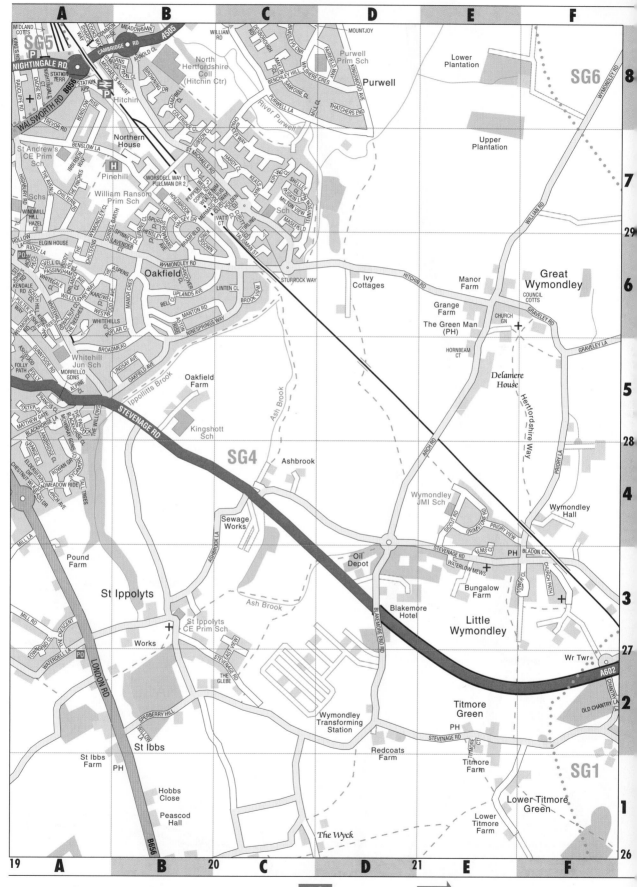

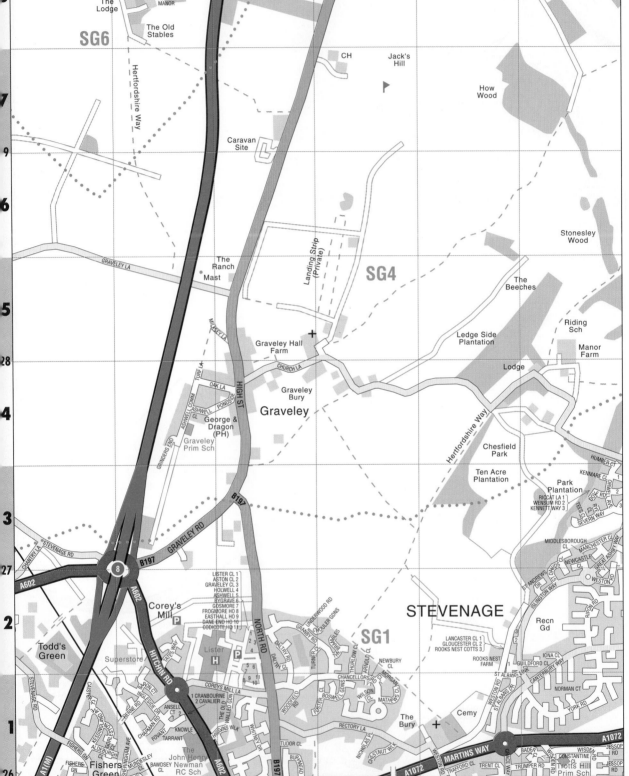

WYMONDLEY RD

The Lodge

ROXLEY MANOR

The Old Stables

SG6

Hertfordshire Way

B197

Jack's Hill Farm

CH

Jack's Hill

How Wood

Caravan Site

Stonesley Wood

GRAVELEY LA

The Ranch

Mast

Landing Strip (Private)

SG4

The Beeches

Riding Sch

MILKSEY LA

Graveley Hall Farm

Ledge Side Plantation

Manor Farm

Lodge

TURF LA

CHURCH LA

OAK LA

PONDSIDE

ASHWELL

Graveley Bury

Graveley

Hertfordshire Way

Chesfield Park

ASHWELL COMM

GRINDERS END

George & Dragon (PH)

Graveley Prim Sch

Ten Acre Plantation

Park Plantation

HUMBER CT

KENMARE CL

DOVE RD

ORWELL RD

RICCAT LA 1
WENSUM RD 2
KENNETT WAY 3

TEES

PIFFS

SEVERN WAY

B197

MIDDLESBOROUGH CL

MANCHESTER CT

GREAT ASHBY WAY

GRAVELEY RD

STEVENAGE RD

CHANTRY LA

B197

A602

NEWCASTLE

ST ANDREWS DR

DOWDS

ISLINGTON WAY

WESTON

8

LISTER CL 1
ASTON CL 2
GRAVELEY CL 3
HOLWELL 4
ASHWELL 5
BYGRAVE 6
GOSMORE 7
FROGMORE HO 8
EASTHALL HO 9
DANE END HO 10
CODICOTE HO 11

STEVENAGE

Recn Gd

Corey's Mill

P

Todd's Green

Superstore

YATES WAY

HITCHIN RD

NORTH RD

Lister

H

P

LINDERWOOD RD

GRANBY RD

CAZIER GDNS

DC TRY RD

DALTRY

TURNER

RD

GRANBY

THURLOW CL

ARNOLD CL

NEWBURY CL

MORGAN CL

SG1

LANCASTER CL 1
GLOUCESTER CL 2
ROOKS NEST COTTS 3

ROOKS NEST FARM

ST ALBANS LINK

ST ALBANS RD

GUILDFORD CL

IONA CL

WESTON RD

CANTERBURY WAY

NORMAN CT

STEVENAGE RD

CAISTER

INGLESIDE

BERIE RD

CHAPMAN RD

ANSELL CT

FOVANT

KNOWLE

TARRANT

COREYS MILL LA

1 CRANBOURNE
2 CAVALIER

THE OLD WALLED GDN

TARGANS WLK

WHITNEY RD

DALTRY RD

WOODFIELD

PEXTER CL

BOSWELL

CHANCELLORS RD

WILSON

MATHEWS

The Bury

Cemy

YORK RD

RITSON RD

A602

FISHERS GN

Fishers Green

SHERINGHAM AVE

MUNDESLEY

BAWDSEY CL

NEWMAN RC Sch

The John Henry Newman RC Sch

TUDOR CL

BURTMEAD

RECTORY LA

NICHOLAS PL

CHESTNUT WLK

MARTINS WAY

TRAFFORD CL

TRENT CL

A1072

GRACE WAY

BADER

TRUMPER RD

CONSTANTINE

WISDEN RD

JESSOP RD

JESSOP RD

Trotts Hill Prim Sch

A1(M)

A602

A1072

A B C D E F

8 Barnacks Hill Wood

Kipple Field

Dolls Field

A507

Weston Tributary

7 Lolleywood La

Harveyshill Farm

Luffenhall

Swamstey Common

SG9

29 Luffenhall Common

Church Farm

Newell La

6 Whitehall Farm

Manor Farm

Newell Common

Cromer Windmill

B1037

Hare Street

SG4

Walnut Tree Farm

Cromer

Cromerfield Common

Bancroft Farm

BLIND LA

5 Hick's Grove Cottages

Hick's Grove

Cromerhill Common

Cromer Farm

The Ainage (Pearson's Charity)

28 Howell's Wood

SG2

Brookfield Comomon

4 Sloggar's Wood

Cornhill Common

Bury Grange

Markham's Wood

Ardeley Brook

River Beane

Ardeley

3 Churchend Common

Ardeley Bury

THE GLEBE

Ardeley St Lawrence CE Prim Sch

SCHOOL LA

27 White Hill

The Bungalow

The Old Rectory

THE CRESCENT

2 Dovehouse La

Manor Farm

GLEBE

BEECROFT LA

CHURCH END

Squitmore Spring

KITCHENERS LA

Bridgefoot Farm

BOCKINGS

FROGHALL LA

BROCKWELL SHOTT

HIGH ST

WINTERS LA

Nursery

TOTTS LA

1 Walkern

ALBRIES

CHERRY TREE RISE

B1037

PO

The Yew Tree (PH)

Chancey Hall

Walkern Bury Farm

26 MOORS LEY

28 A B 29 C D 30 E F

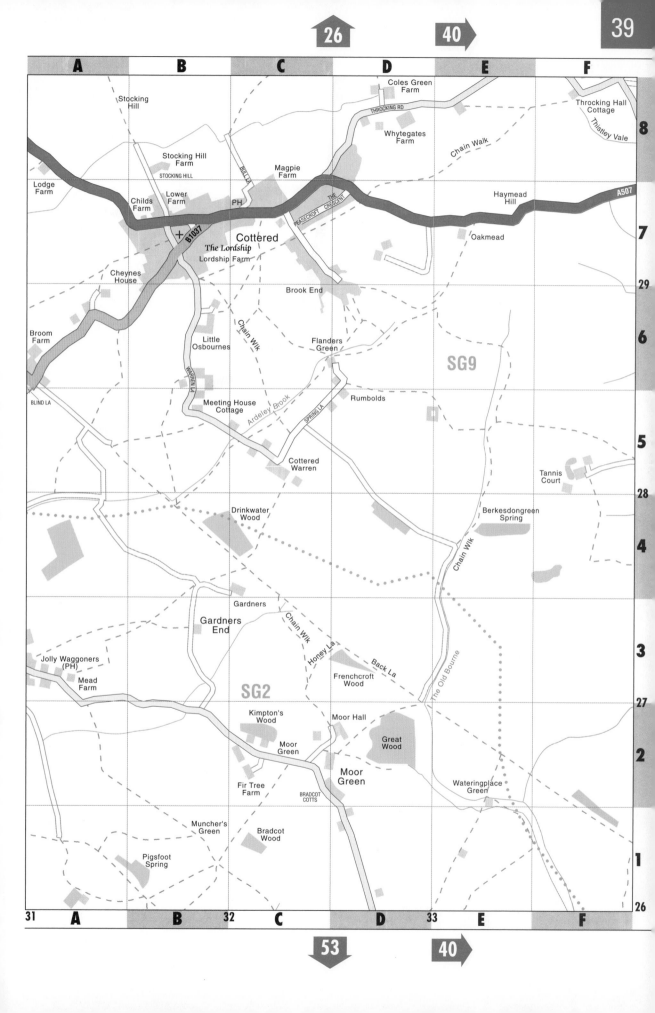

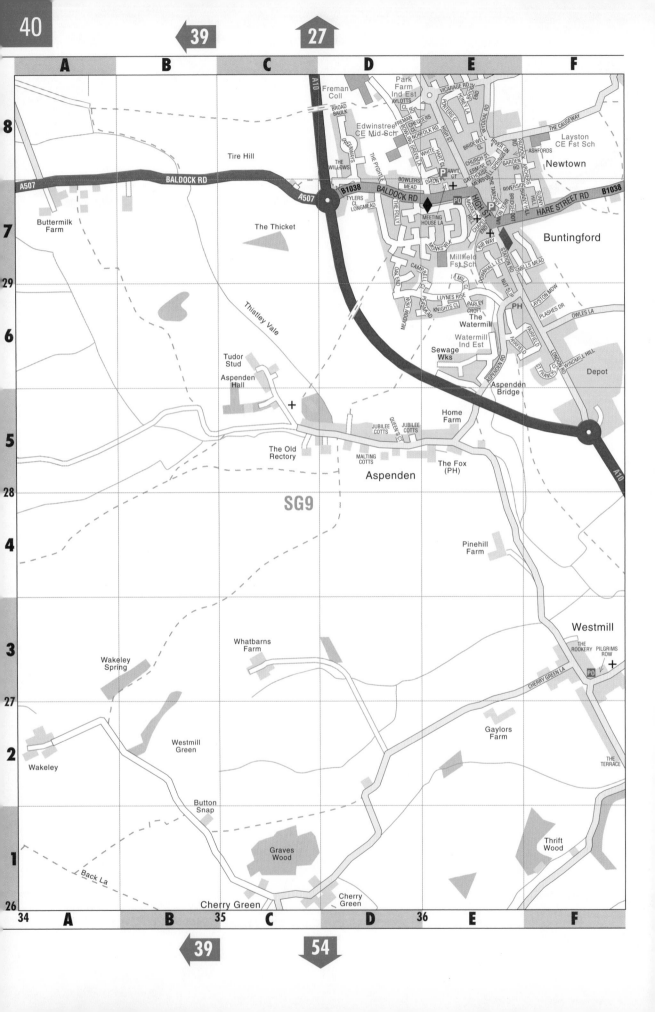

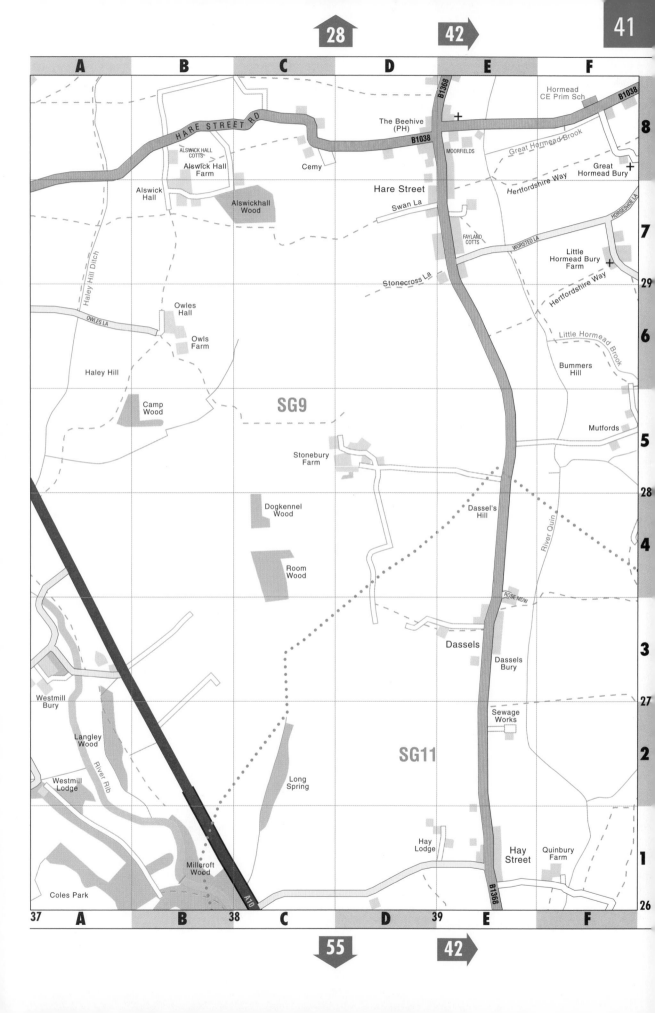

A B C D E F

8

7

29

6

5

28

4

3

27

2

1

26

HARE STREET RD

ALSWICK HALL COTTS

Alswick Hall Farm

Alswick Hall

Alswickhall Wood

Cemy

The Beehive (PH)

B1038

B1038

MOORFIELDS

Hormead CE Prim Sch

B1038

Great Hormead Brook

Great Hormead Bury

Hertfordshire Way

Hare Street

Swan La

FAYLAND COTTS

Worsted La

HORSESHOE LA

Little Hormead Bury Farm

Stonecross La

Hertfordshire Way

Haley Hill Ditch

OWLES LA

Owles Hall

Owls Farm

Little Hormead Brook

Bummers Hill

Haley Hill

Camp Wood

SG9

Mutfords

Stonebury Farm

Dogkennel Wood

Dassel's Hill

River Quin

Room Wood

Dassels

Dassels Bury

ROSE MDW

Westmill Bury

Langley Wood

River Rib

Westmill Lodge

Long Spring

SG11

Sewage Works

A10

Millcroft Wood

Hay Lodge

Hay Street

Quinbury Farm

B1368

Coles Park

41
29

**A** **B** **C** **D** **E** **F**

B1038

Three Tuns (PH)

HORSESHOE HILL

Great Hormead

St Patrick's Wood

**8**

JUBILEE COTTS

WILLOW CL

Church End Cottage

HORSESHOE LA

Sparksfield

**7**

The Thrift

Great Hormead Park

PARK VIEW

Glebe House

**29**

Little Hormead Brook

SG9

Balons Farm

Little Hormead

Bulls Farm

**6**

Fair Lady Wood

The Willows

Lady Wood

Mutfords

**5**

Mutton Hall

Duck Street Cottage

Hertfordshire Way

**28**

HALL BARNS

THE STREET

**4**

Shirley

Bradley Spring

High Wood

Hoare's La

**3**

Bozengreen Farm

Rotten Row

Hertfordshire Way

Patient End Farm

Patient End

**27**

Bozen Green

**2**

SG11

THE CAUSEWAY

Hole Farm Cott

**1**

Hole Farm

**26**

41
56

Hall Wood

Stocking Farm

Stocking Pelham Hall

CM23

The Cock (PH)

Stocking Pelham

White Hart

Violets Spring

Whitebarns

MEAD VIEW

CRABB'S LA

Sports Ground

Crabb's Green

Crabb's Green Farm

Silla Farm

GINNS RD

The Willows

El Sub Sta

Whitebarns Cottages

Willows Farm

SG9

Furneux Pelham

River Ash

VIOLETS LA

Brewery

THE WASH

GINNS RD

Lower Farm

East End

Green's Farm

WHITEBARNS LA

The Street

PO

Furneux Pelham CE Sch

The Brewery Tap (PH)

LAKE VILLAS

Old Mill House

Eastend Farm

The Star (PH)

THE OLD COMMON

Barleycroft End

Recn Gd

BROOKSIDE

Clay Chimneys

The Brook

Pheasant Hall

THE CAUSEWAY

Sewage Works

Hixham Cottages

Hixham Hall

Kings Cottage

SG11

Kings

CM23

Oaken Spring

Heath Farm

North Essex STREET ATLAS

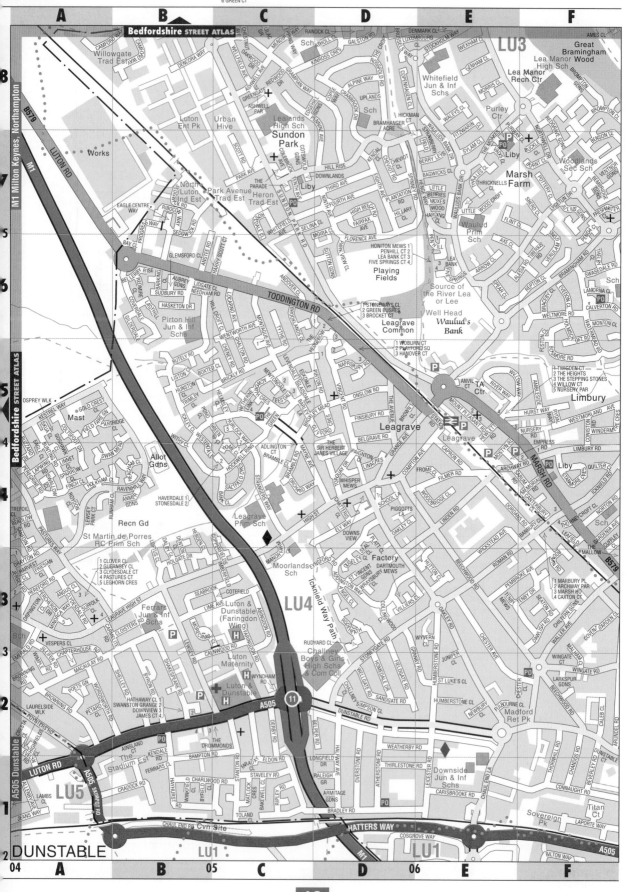

C5
1 CHAWORTH GN
2 ACWORTH CT
3 MOSSDALE CT
4 WOLFSBURG CT
5 THORNTONDALE
6 GREEN CT
7 WHARFDALE

**Bedfordshire** STREET ATLAS

LU3

LU4

LU5

DUNSTABLE

LU1

LU1

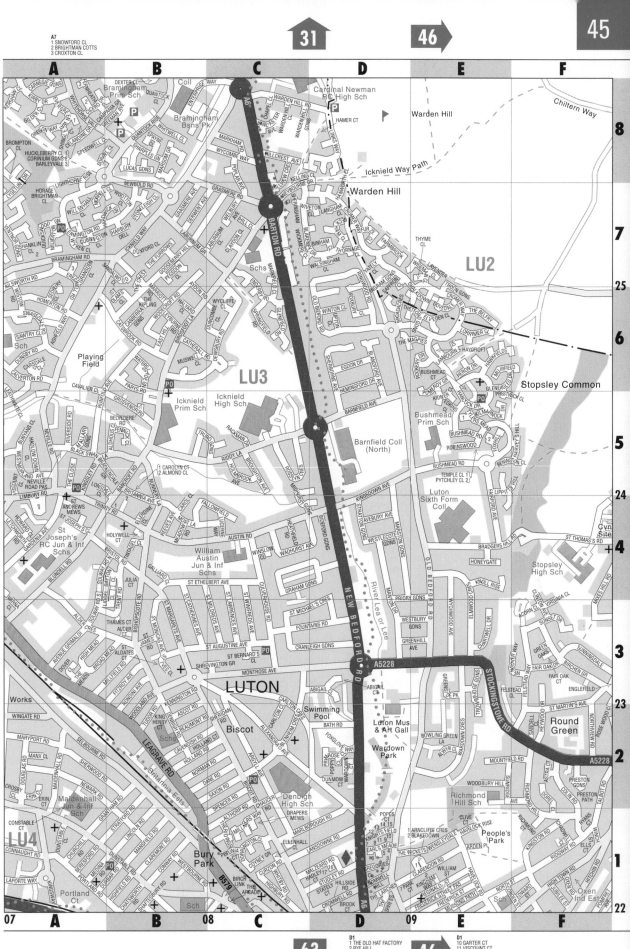

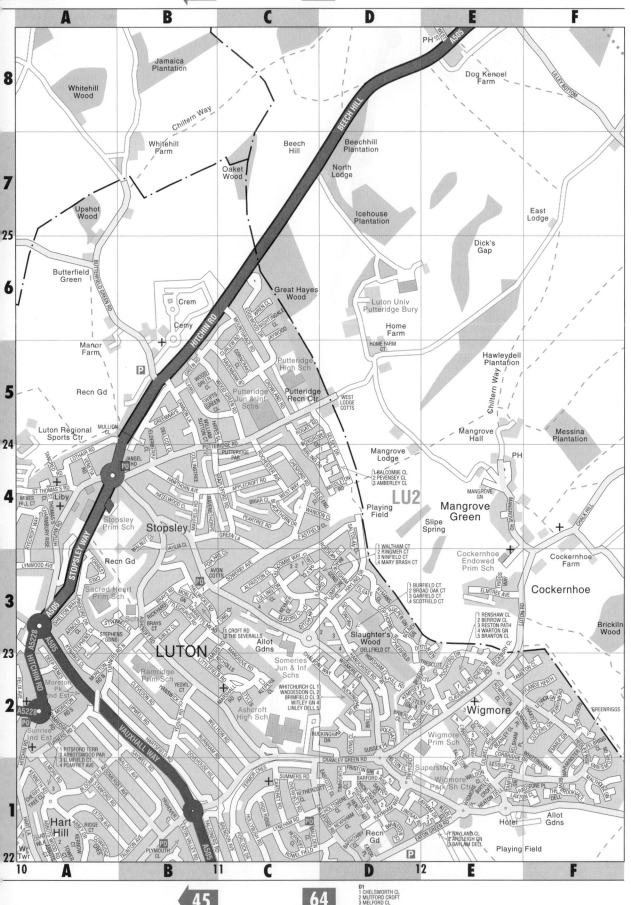

D1
1 CHELSWORTH CL
2 MUTFORD CROFT
3 MELFORD CL
4 PINFORD DELL
5 ALDERTON CL

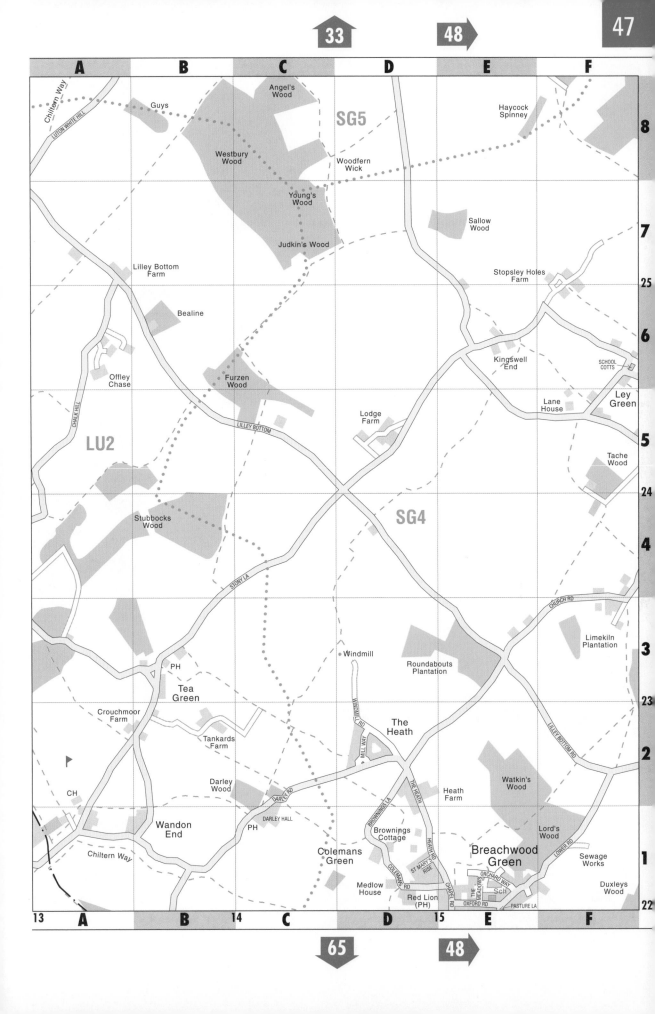

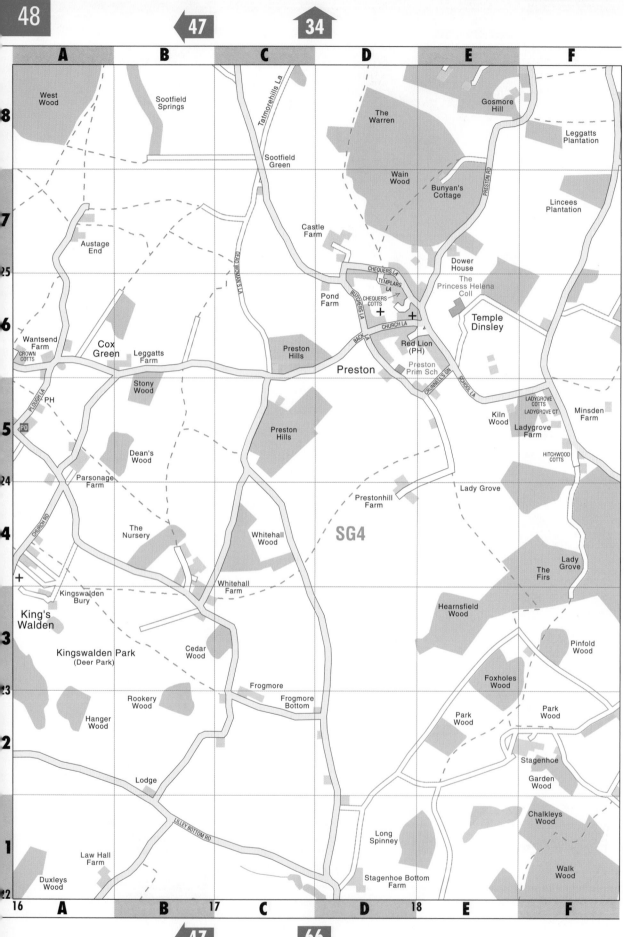

A  B  C  D  E  F

**8**

West Wood

Sootfield Springs

Talmorehills La

The Warren

Gosmore Hill

Leggatts Plantation

Wain Wood

Bunyan's Cottage

Lincees Plantation

**7**

Austage End

Castle Farm

DEAD WOMAN'S LA

PRESTON RD

**25**

CHEQUERS LA

TEMPLARS LA

Dower House

The Princess Helena Coll

Pond Farm

BUTCHERS LA

CHEQUERS COTTS

+  +

Temple Dinsley

**6**

Wantsend Farm

CROWN COTTS

Cox Green

Leggatts Farm

Preston Hills

CHURCH LA

Red Lion (PH)

BACK LA

Preston Prim Sch

Preston

GRUNNELL'S GN

SCHOOL LA

LADYGROVE COTTS

LADYGROVE CT

Minsden Farm

PLOUGH LA

PH

Stony Wood

Kiln Wood

Ladygrove Farm

**5**

PO

Preston Hills

HITCHWOOD COTTS

Dean's Wood

**24**

Parsonage Farm

CHURCH RD

Prestonhill Farm

Lady Grove

The Nursery

Whitehall Wood

**SG4**

**4**

Whitehall Farm

The Firs

Lady Grove

Kingswalden Bury

Hearnsfield Wood

King's Walden

+

Pinfold Wood

**3**

Kingswalden Park (Deer Park)

Cedar Wood

Foxholes Wood

Frogmore

Park Wood

Park Wood

**23**

Rookery Wood

Frogmore Bottom

Hanger Wood

Stagenhoe

**2**

Garden Wood

Lodge

LILLEY BOTTOM RD

Chalkleys Wood

**1**

Law Hall Farm

Long Spinney

Walk Wood

Duxleys Wood

Stagenhoe Bottom Farm

**22**

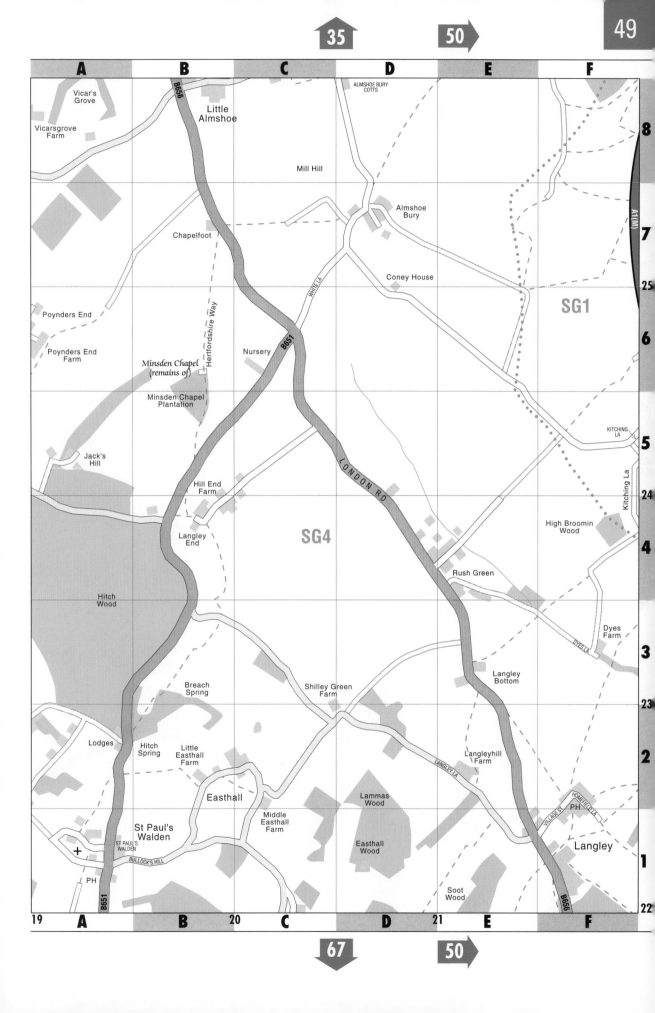

A  B  C  D  E  F

8

Vicar's
Grove

Vicarsgrove
Farm

Little
Almshoe

B656

ALMSHOE BURY
COTTS

Mill Hill

Almshoe
Bury

7

25

Chapelfoot

Coney House

SG1

Poynders End

Hertfordshire Way

Nursery

WHITE LA

B651

LONDON RD

6

Poynders End
Farm

Minsden Chapel
(remains of)

Minsden Chapel
Plantation

KITCHING
LA

5

Jack's
Hill

Hill End
Farm

High Broomin
Wood

Kitching La

24

Langley
End

SG4

Rush Green

4

Hitch
Wood

Dyes
Farm

DYES LA

3

Breach
Spring

Shilley Green
Farm

Langley
Bottom

23

Lodges

Hitch
Spring

Little
Easthall
Farm

Langleyhill
Farm

LANGLEY LA

2

Easthall

Middle
Easthall
Farm

Lammas
Wood

HOMEFIELD LA

PH

VILLAGE ST

St Paul's
Walden

ST PAUL'S
WALDEN

BULLOCK'S HILL

Easthall
Wood

Langley

1

+

PH

B651

Soot
Wood

B656

22

B8
1 BAWDSEY CL
2 SHERINGHAM AVE
3 BOURNEMOUTH RD
49

C7
1 MIDDLE ROW
2 BAKER ST
36

E6
1 JOWITT HO
2 BATES HO
3 CHAUNCY HO
4 BERTRAM HO
5 EDWARDS HO
6 BLOOMFIELD HO

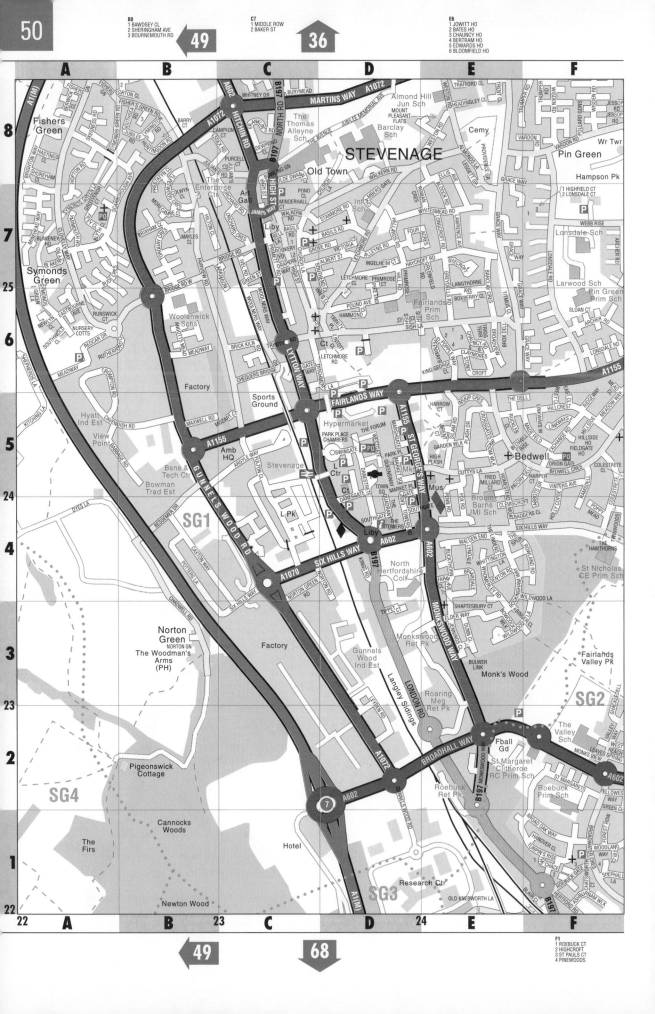

F1
1 ROEBUCK CT
2 HIGHCROFT
3 ST PAULS CT
4 PINEWOODS

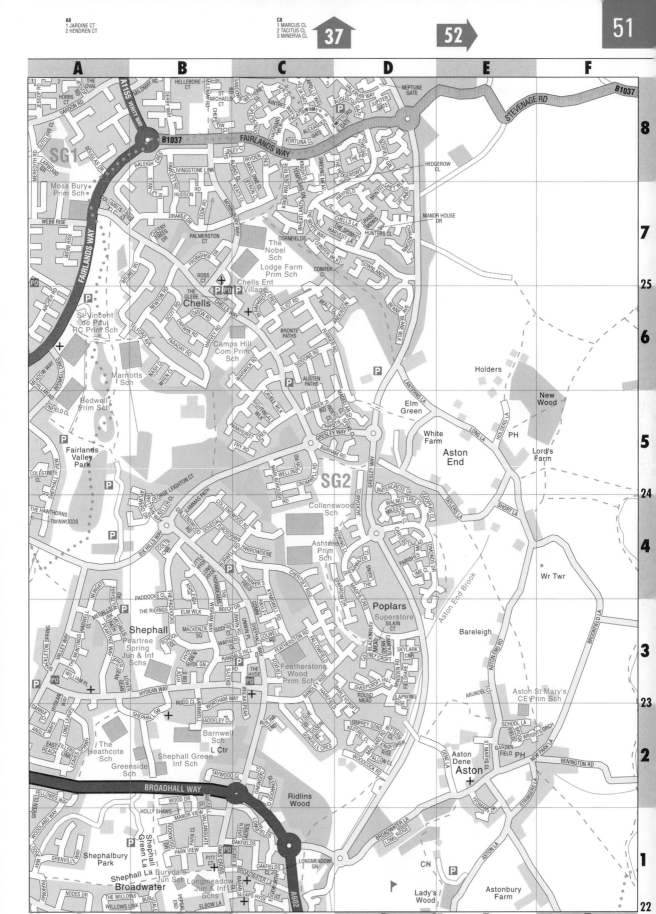

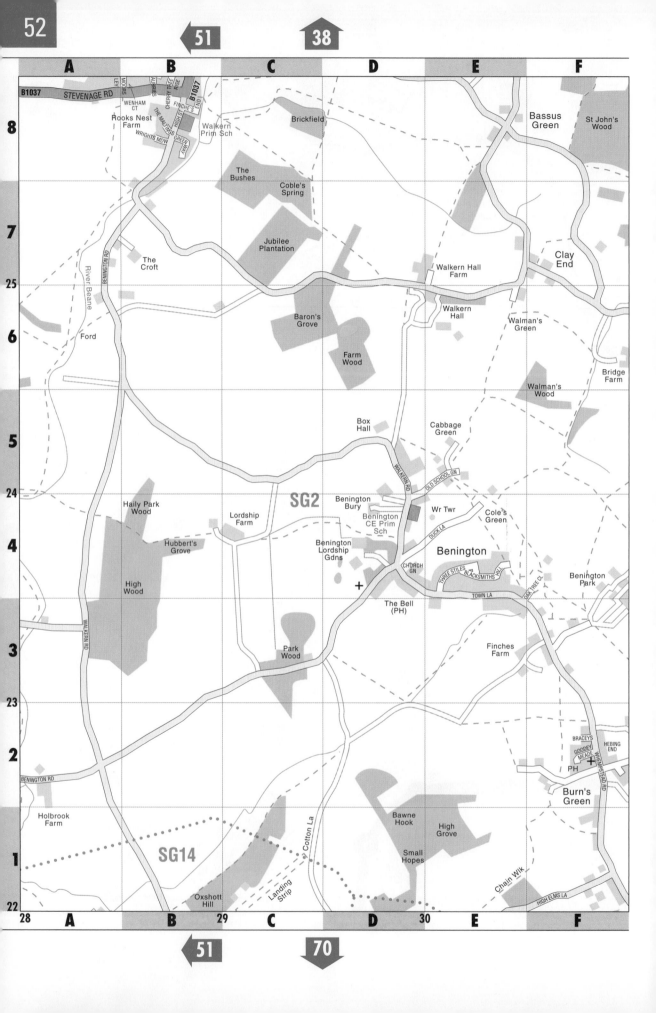

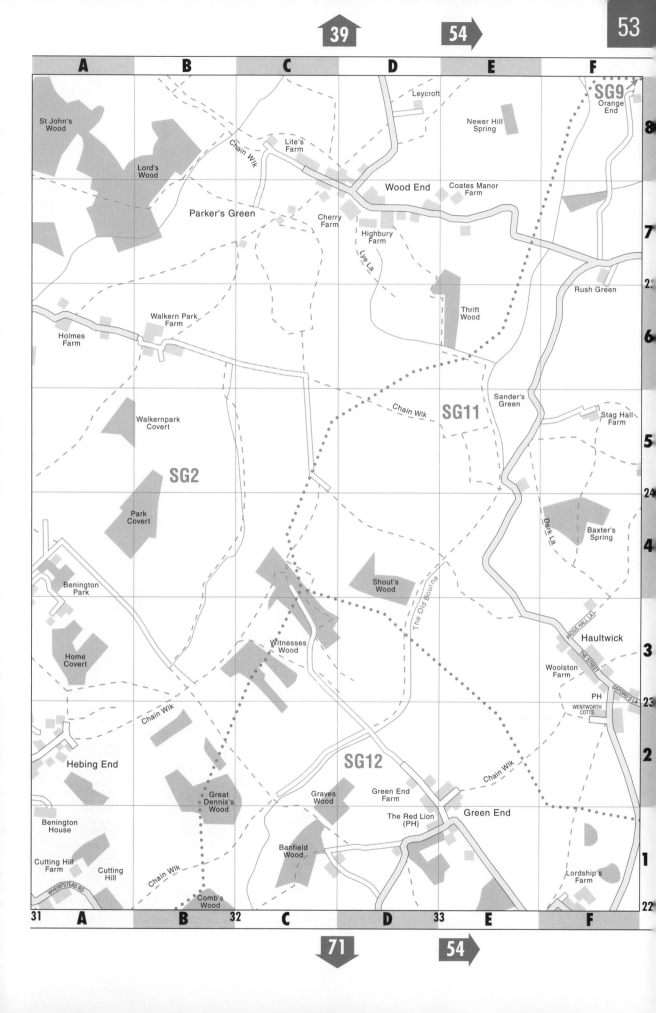

A B C D E F

8
7
2.
6
2.
5
24
4
22
3
23
2
1
22

St John's
Wood

Lord's
Wood

Chain Wlk

Lite's
Farm

Parker's Green

Leycroft

Newer Hill
Spring

SG9
Orange
End

Wood End

Cherry
Farm

Highbury
Farm

Lye La

Coates Manor
Farm

Rush Green

Holmes
Farm

Walkern Park
Farm

Thrift
Wood

Walkernpark
Covert

SG2

Chain Wlk

SG11

Sander's
Green

Stag Hall
Farm

Park
Covert

Shout's
Wood

The Old Bourne

Dark La

Baxter's
Spring

Benington
Park

Witnesses
Wood

FROGS HALL LA

Haultwick

Home
Covert

Chain Wlk

Woolston
Farm

THE STREET

PH

GIFFORD'S LA

WENTWORTH
COTTS

23

Hebing End

SG12

Chain Wlk

Green End
Farm

Chain Wlk

Great
Dennis's
Wood

Graves
Wood

Green End

Benington
House

The Red Lion
(PH)

Cutting Hill
Farm

Cutting
Hill

Banfield
Wood

Lordship's
Farm

WHEMPSTEAD RD

Chain Wlk

Comb's
Wood

A B
C D
E F

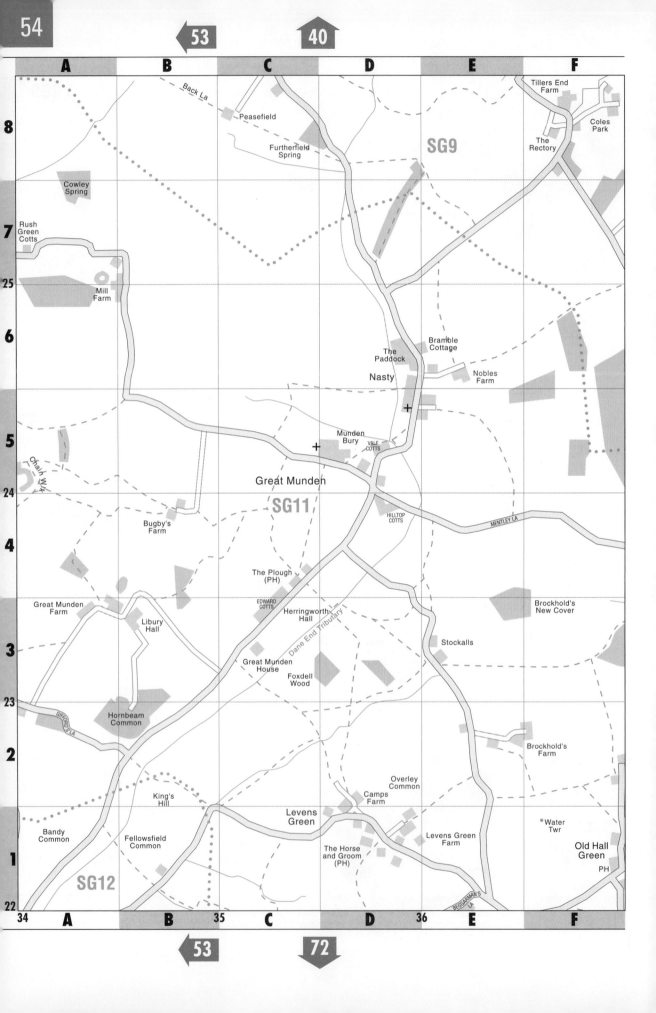

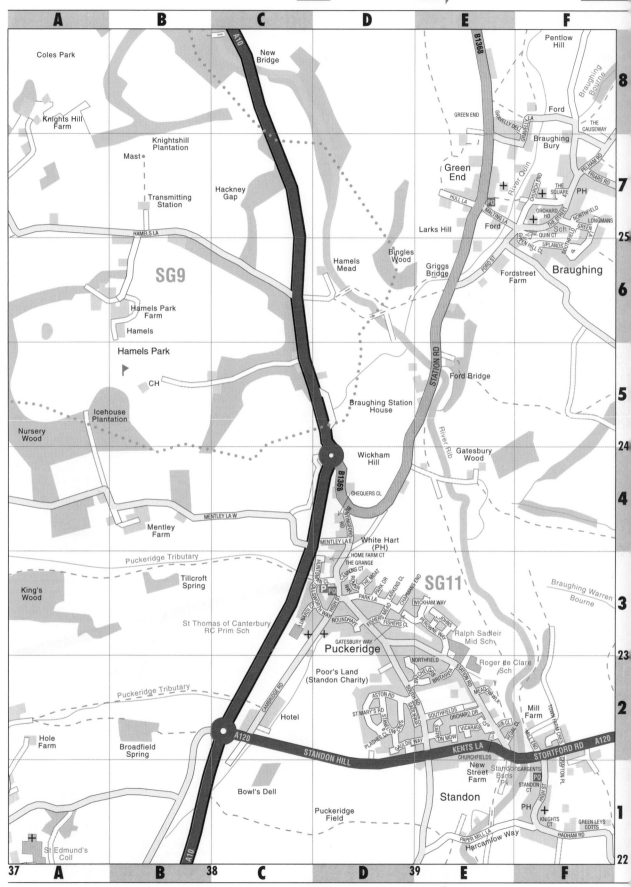

55
42

| | A | B | C | D | E | F |

Braughing Bourne

THE CAUSEWAY

**8**

Hole Spring

Charleston House

Albury Hall Farm

**7**

FRIARS RD

Allot Gdns

Harcamlow Way

Windcott

Cockhamstead

Albury Hall Cottages

Flowerlands

**25**

**6**

Fryers House

Nursery

Ferricks Wood

PARSONAGE LA

Braughing Friars

Albury Wr Twr

**5**

Sacombe Wood

Oldfield Cottages

Upp Hall

Ideal Farm

**24**

Braughing Warren Bourne

Piggotts Farm

Harcamlow Way

The Warren

**SG11**

Albury End

**4**

Ash Plantation

New Wood

Darney Wood

Keepers Cottage

**3**

HORSE CROSS

STANDON RD

Tilekiln Farm

Pockendon Field

A120

**23**

Ten Acre Wood

Poor's Land (Standon Charity)

BROKEN GREEN COTTS

**2**

A120

Frogs Hall House

Broken Green

Twiney Wood

Foxearth Wood

Standon Friars

Wellpond Green

Queer Wood

**1**

PH

Westland Green

Lodge Farm

Highfield Farm

**22**

| 40 | A | B | 41 | C | D | 42 | E | F |

55
74

**A** **B** **C** **D** **E** **F**

8

Gravesend

Catherine Wheel (PH)

Patmore Heath (Nature Reserve)

Harcamlow Way

Bogs Cottage

Patmore Hall

Hertfordshire Way

Bogs Wood

7

BARNCROFT

Itch La

High Hall

Mansfield Cottages

CM23

25

Clapgate

SIX COTTS

MILL LA

Ypres

THE BOURNE

Albury CE Prim Sch

6

Parsonage Farm

PARSONAGE LA

The Close

Sewage Works

Salmon Mead Spring

The Common

Albury

Ninno Wood

Upwick Wood

Green Farm

Upwick Green

5

Albury Lodge

River Ash

SG11

Hoy's Farm

Upwick Hall

Walnuttree Green

24

Albury Lodge House

4

Folly Gorse

Hertfordshire Way

Alburyend Wood

3

23

HIGHFIELD

WATTS PL

ALBURY RD

STANDON RD

Little Hadham

Church End Farm

STABLE COTTS

Church End

CAPEL CT

Haddam Hall

2

LLOYD-TAYLOR CL

THE SMITHY

Little Hadham Prim Sch

STORTFORD RD

BAUD CL

HADDAM HALL

The Causeway

Little Hadham Place

Halfway House

Stone House Farm

CM23

1

RIDGEWAY

PO

RED BRICK COTTS

MILLFIELD LA

HADHAM RD

Green Street Farm

A120

22

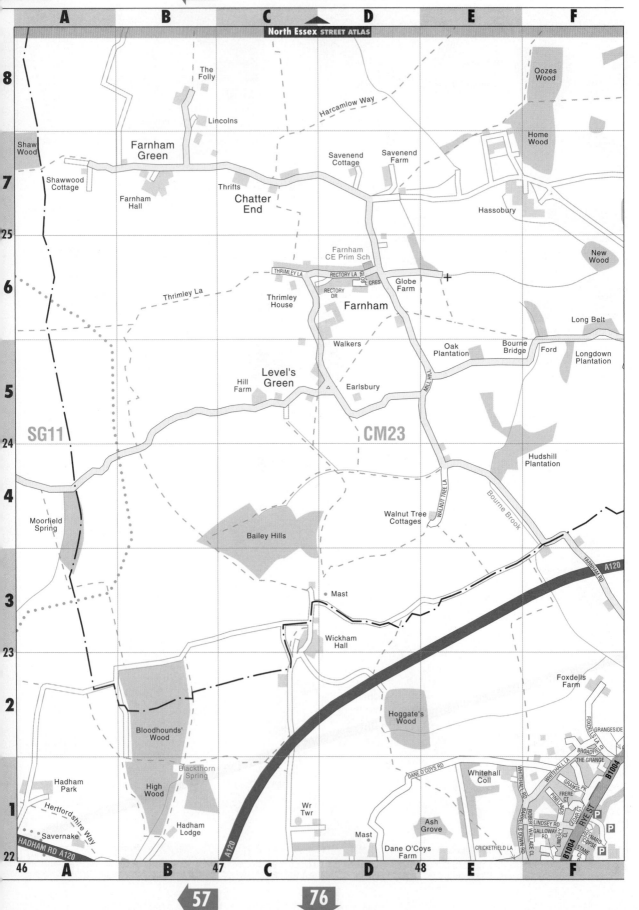

A B C D E F

8

Oozes Wood

The Folly

Lincolns

Harcamlow Way

Home Wood

Shaw Wood

Farnham Green

Savenend Cottage

Savenend Farm

7

Shawwood Cottage

Thrifts

Chatter End

Hassobury

Farnham Hall

25

New Wood

Farnham CE Prim Sch

6

Thrimley La

THRIMLEY LA

RECTORY LA

GLOBE CRES

Globe Farm

Thrimley La

Thrimley House

RECTORY DR

Farnham

Long Belt

Walkers

Oak Plantation

Bourne Bridge

Ford

Longdown Plantation

5

Level's Green

Hill Farm

Earlsbury

MILL HILL

SG11

24

CM23

Hudshill Plantation

4

Moorfield Spring

Bailey Hills

Walnut Tree Cottages

WALNUT TREE LA

Bourne Brook

A120

FARNHAM RD

3

Mast

Wickham Hall

23

Foxdells Farm

GRANGESIDE

2

Bloodhounds' Wood

Hoggate's Wood

FOXDELLS LA CL

BROADFIELD

THE GRANGE

B1004

Blackthorn Spring

DANE O'COYS RD

Whitehall Coll

WHITEHALL LA

GRANGE PK

FRERE CT

PINE END

LINDSEY RD

CEDAR CT

RYE ST

Hadham Park

High Wood

WHITEHALL RD

ROBERT WALLACE RD

BARRELLS DOWN RD

HEYNARD COPSE

1

Hertfordshire Way

Wr Twr

Ash Grove

GALLOWAY RD

STANE

B1004

P

Savernake

Hadham Lodge

Mast

Dane O'Coys Farm

CRICKETFIELD LA

P

P

22

HADHAM RD A120

A120

46 A 47 B C 48 D E F

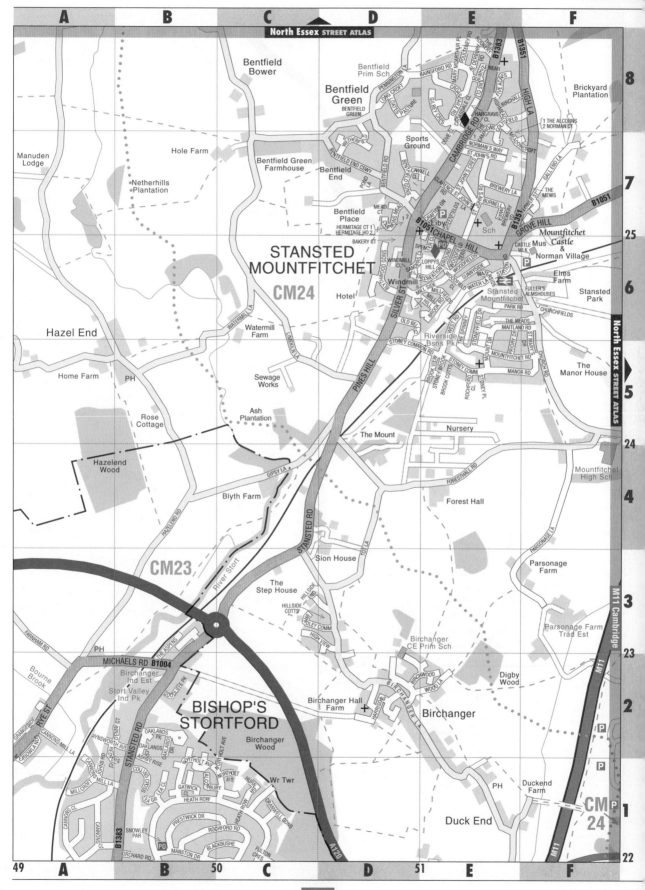

Manuden
Lodge

Bentfield
Bower

Bentfield
Prim Sch

Brickyard
Plantation

Bentfield
Green

BENTFIELD
GREEN

1 THE ALCORNS
2 NORMAN CT

Hole Farm

Netherhills
Plantation

Bentfield Green
Farmhouse

Bentfield
End

THE
MEWS

B1051

Bentfield
Place

HERMITAGE CT 1
HERMITAGE HO 2

BAKERY CT

Mountfitchet
Castle
&
Norman Village

Castle Mus

25

STANSTED
MOUNTFITCHET

CM24

Stansted
Mountfitchet

Elms
Farm

Stansted
Park

Hotel

Windmill

Fuller's
Almshouses

6

Hazel End

Watermill
Farm

Riverside
Bsns Pk

The
Manor House

Home Farm

PH

5

Rose
Cottage

Sewage
Works

24

Ash
Plantation

The Mount

Nursery

Hazelend
Wood

GIPSY LA

Mountfitchet
High Sch

Blyth Farm

Forest Hall

4

CM23

River Stort

Sion House

Parsonage
Farm

The
Step House

HILLSIDE
COTTS

Birchanger
CE Prim Sch

Parsonage Farm
Trad Est

3

23

MICHAELS RD B1004

Birchanger
Ind Est

Digby
Wood

PH

Stort Valley
Ind Pk

Bourne
Brook

Birchanger
Wood

Birchanger Hall
Farm

Birchanger

2

BISHOP'S
STORTFORD

GATWICK
CL

Wr Twr

PH

Duckend
Farm

CM
24

SNOWLEY
PAR

Duck End

1

49        50        51        22

North Essex STREET ATLAS

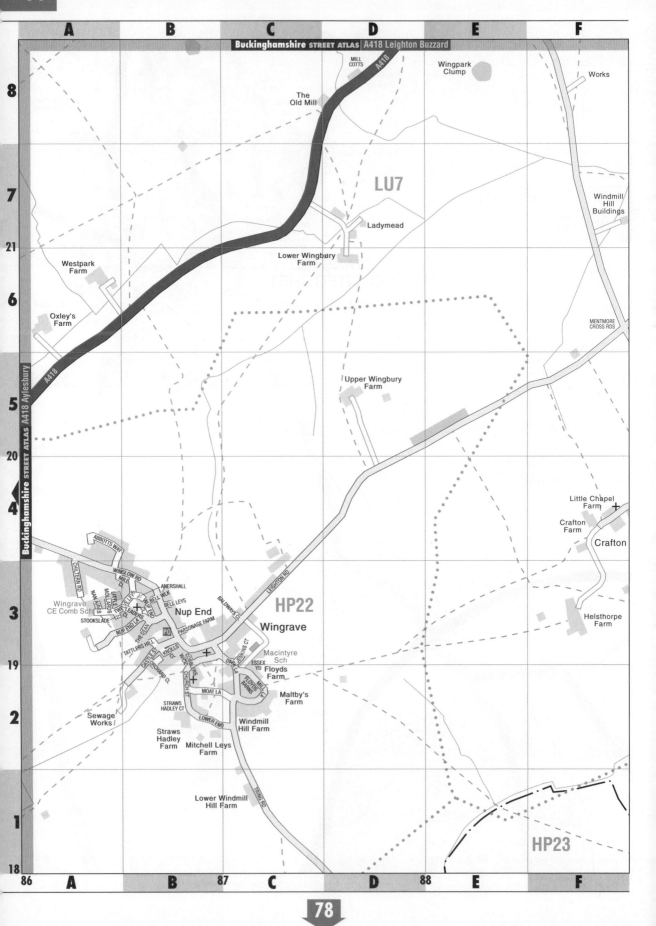

A　B　C　D　E　F

8

7

21

6

5

20

4

3

19

2

1

18

86　87　88

LU7

Mill Cotts

A418

The Old Mill

Wingpark Clump

Works

Windmill Hill Buildings

Ladymead

Lower Wingbury Farm

Westpark Farm

Oxley's Farm

MENTMORE CROSS RDS

Upper Wingbury Farm

Little Chapel Farm

Crafton Farm

Crafton

LEIGHTON RD

HP22

Helsthorpe Farm

ABBOTTS WAY

WINSLOW RD

CHILTERN RD

MILL CL

NAN AIRES

LITTLE MOLLARDS

THE BEAN

TWELVE LEYS

NUP END

BELL WLK

ANERSHALL

BELL LEYS

BALDWAYS CL

Wingrave CE Comb Sch

STOOKSLADE

NUP END LA

Nup End

PARSONAGE FARM

Wingrave

PO

TATTLERS HILL

CASTLE ST

KNOLLS CL

ORCHARD CL

COBBLERS WICK

CHURCH ST

MOAT LA

DOVE LA

JENKINS CT

ESSEX YD

Macintyre Sch

Floyds Farm

FLOYDS BARNS

MILL LA

Maltby's Farm

Sewage Works

STRAWS HADLEY CT

LOWER END

Windmill Hill Farm

Straws Hadley Farm

Mitchell Leys Farm

FRING RD

Lower Windmill Hill Farm

HP23

Ledburn

Manor Farm

MANOR FARM LA

LEYBOURNE CL

Ledburn Farm

Windmill Hill

WELL LA

Whaddon Farm Cottages

Rowden Farm

B488

Bedfordshire STREET ATLAS

LU7

The Belt

Cricket Ground

Mentmore Stud

Wing Lodge

HOWELL HILL CL

Mentmore

PH

Home Farm

Crafton Stud Farm

Mentmore

Big Wood

ROSEBERY MEWS

Mansom

New Spinney

Mentmore Park

Crafton Stud

Crafton Lodge

Model Farm

CH

The Belt

HP23

STATION RD

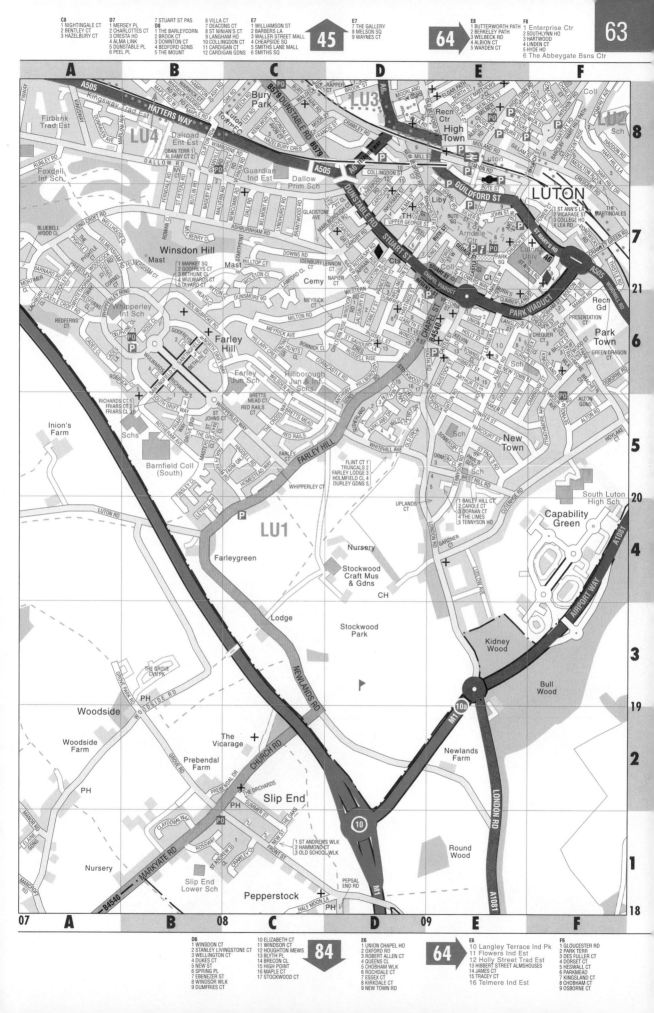

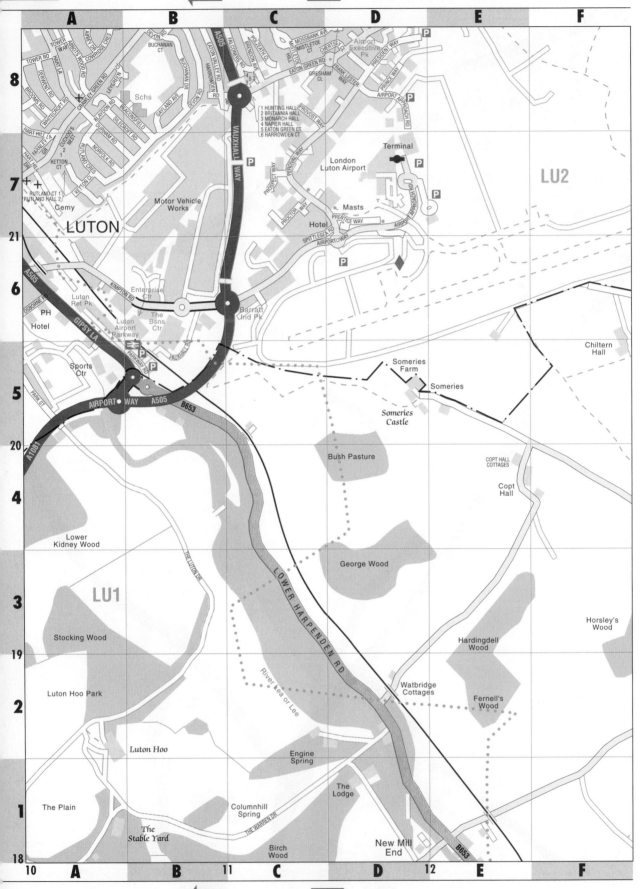

A  B  C  D  E  F

8

7

21

6

5

20

4

3

19

2

1

18

LU2

LU1

Luton

Chiltern Hall

Somereis Farm

Somereis

Someries Castle

Copt Hall Cottages

Copt Hall

Horsley's Wood

Hardingdell Wood

Fernell's Wood

Watbridge Cottages

George Wood

Bush Pasture

Lower Harpenden Rd

River Lea or Lee

Stocking Wood

Lower Kidney Wood

Luton Hoo Park

Luton Hoo

The Plain

The Stable Yard

Columnhill Spring

Birch Wood

Engine Spring

The Lodge

New Mill End

Terminal

London Luton Airport

Hotel

Masts

Motor Vehicle Works

Sports Ctr

Enterprise Ctr

Luton Ret Pk

Luton Airport Parkway

The Bsns Ctr

Barratt Ind Pk

Airport Executive Pk

PH

Hotel

Gemy

Schs

1 HUNTING HALL
2 BRITANNIA HALL
3 MONARCH HALL
4 NAPIER HALL
5 EATON GREEN CT
6 HARROWDEN CT

AIRPORT WAY  A505  B653

GIPSY LA

VAUXHALL WAY

A505

A1061

PARK ST

OSBORNE RD

KIMPTON RD

FAUXHALL RD

THE LUTON DR

THE WARREN DR

B653

A505

EATON VALLEY RD

FALCONERS RD

HARROWDEN RD

BUCHANAN DR

BUCHANAN CT

DEVON RD

GAYLAND AVE

BEACONSFIELD

SILECROFT RD

DURHAM RD

BLAXTON RD

NORFOLK RD

RUTLAND CRES

LEYGREEN RD

CRAWLEY GREEN RD

COWRIDGE CRES

ABBOTS WOOD RD

ABBEY DR

TOWER WAY

TOWER RD

HART LA

HART HILL DR

HART HILL A

FARLEY A GR

BROOMS RD

WHITECROFT RD

DERWENT RD

CROOKS 'S WEST

KETTON CT

RUTLAND HALL 1

RUTLAND CT 1
RUTLAND HALL 2

RUTLAND CT 2

KETTON CL

BRENDON AVE

POLLOEATH CL

MOSSBANK AVE

MISTLETOE HILL

MISTLETOE CT

CHERTSEY CT

EATON GREEN RD

GRESHAM CL

FRANK LESTER WAY

PROVOST WAY

PERCIVAL WAY

PROSPECT WAY

PROCTOR WAY

PRENTICE WAY

SPITTLESEA RD

AIRPORTWAY

PRESIDENT WAY

PRINCE WAY

AIRPORT APPROACH RD

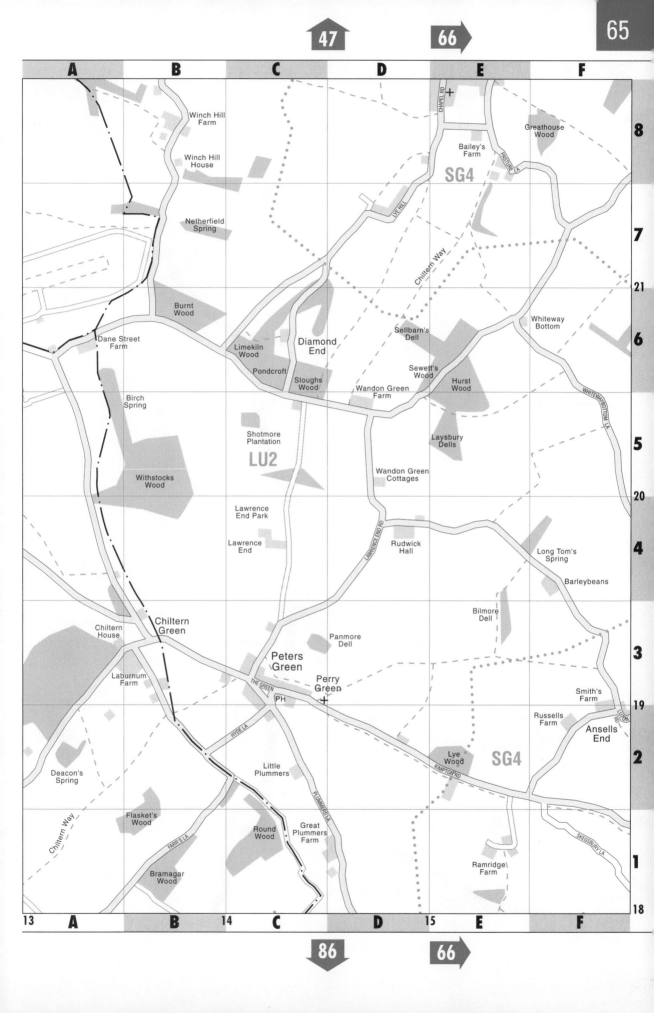

A B C D E F

8

Winch Hill
Farm

Winch Hill
House

Netherfield
Spring

7

Chapel Rd

Bailey's
Farm

Greathouse
Wood

Pasture La

SG4

21

Burnt
Wood

Dane Street
Farm

Lye Hill

Chiltern Way

Whiteway
Bottom

6

Limekiln
Wood

Diamond
End

Sellbarn's
Dell

Pondcroft

Sloughs
Wood

Sewett's
Wood

Wandon Green
Farm

Hurst
Wood

Whiteway Bottom La

Birch
Spring

Shotmore
Plantation

LU2

Laysbury
Dells

5

Withstocks
Wood

20

Lawrence
End Park

Wandon Green
Cottages

Lawrence End Rd

Long Tom's
Spring

4

Lawrence
End

Rudwick
Hall

Barleybeans

Chiltern
House

Chiltern
Green

Panmore
Dell

Bilmore
Dell

3

Laburnum
Farm

Peters
Green

Perry
Green

Smith's
Farm

Lea La

19

The Green

PH

Russells
Farm

Ansells
End

SG4

Deacon's
Spring

Hyde La

Lye
Wood

Kimpton Rd

2

Chiltern Way

Flasket's
Wood

Little
Plummers

Farr's La

Round
Wood

Plummers La

Great
Plummers
Farm

Skegsbury La

Ramridge
Farm

1

Bramagar
Wood

18

13 A 14 B C 14 C D 15 E F

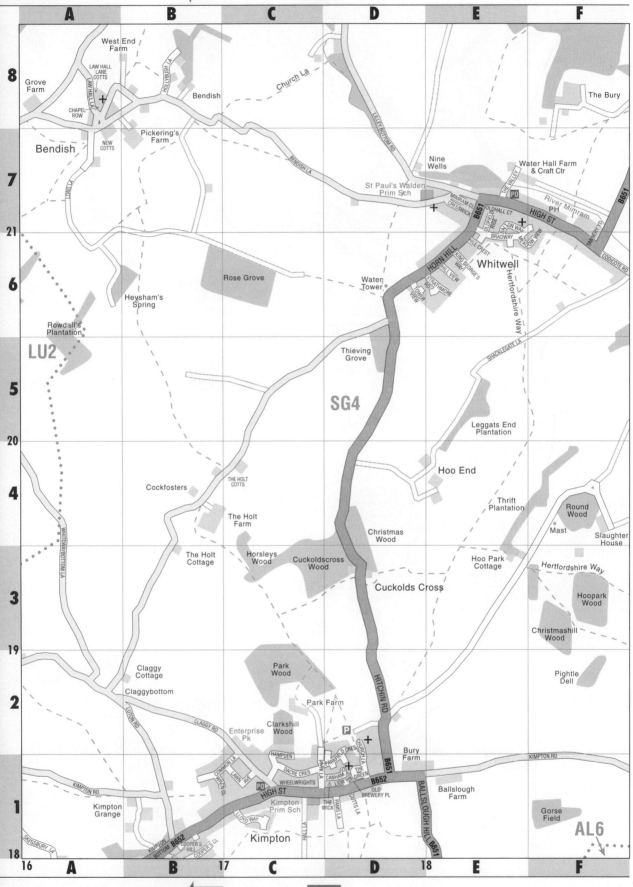

A    B    C    D    E    F

8    Grove Farm    West End Farm    LAW HALL LANE COTTS    Bendish    Church La    The Bury

Bendish    CHAPEL ROW    NEW COTTS    Pickering's Farm    HOLLYBUSH LA    Nine Wells    Water Hall Farm & Craft Ctr

7    LUTON LA    BENDISH LA    LILLEY BOTTOM RD    St Paul's Walden Prim Sch    River Mimram    PH    HIGH ST    B651    PO

21    Rose Grove    Heysham's Spring    Water Tower    Whitwell    HORN HILL    MIMRAM CL    CRESSWICK    OLDHALL CT    OLDFIELD RISE    HILL CREST    KING GEORGE'S WAY    HILL VIEW    LION WAY    MEADOW VIEW    BRADWAY    TANNERY YD    CODICOTE RD

6    Rowdall's Plantation    Thieving Grove    STRATHMORE RD    TOWER VIEW    Hertfordshire Way

LU2    SG4    Shacklegate La

5

20    Leggats End Plantation    Hoo End

4    Cockfosters    THE HOLT COTTS    The Holt Farm    Thrift Plantation    Round Wood    Mast    Slaughter House

The Holt Cottage    Horsleys Wood    Cuckoldscross Wood    Christmas Wood    Hoo Park Cottage    Hertfordshire Way    Hoopark Wood

3    WHITEWAYBOTTOM LA    Cuckolds Cross    Christmashill Wood

19    Claggy Cottage    Park Wood    Pightle Dell

2    Claggybottom    LUTON RD    CLAGGY RD    Enterprise Pk    Clarkshill Wood    Park Farm    HITCHIN RD    Bury Farm    KIMPTON RD

COMMON LA    WEST CL    HAMPDEN    LAWN AVE    DACRE CRES    PARK LA    PARKFIELD CRES    CHURCH LA    CANHAM    LION YD    THE GREEN    B651    Ballslough Farm

1    KIMPTON RD    WHEELWRIGHTS    PO    HIGH ST    Kimpton Prim Sch    THE WICK    OLD BREWERY PL    PAMS LA    CUTTS LA    B652    BALLSLOUGH HILL    B651    Gorse Field    AL6

Kimpton Grange    SKEGSBURY LA    KIMPTON BOTTOM    B652    COOPER'S HILL    COOPER'S CL    LLOYD WAY    Kimpton    HALL LA

18    16    A    B    17    C    D    18    E    F

A B C D E F

8
7
21
6
SG14
5
20
4
SG3
3
19
2
1
18

STEVENAGE

SG2

Crem

Knebworth

Mast

Sundown

Pinker
Wood

Badger
CL

Swangley's
Farm

Baines's
Spring

Knebworth
Prim Sch

Bragbury

The Chequers
(PH)

Bragbury
End

PH

Caravan
Pk

Hook's
Cross

The
Wood

Hale's
Wood

Skegg's
Wood

Hazel
Farm

Staples
Farm

Aston
Bury

Aston Bury
Manor

Astonbury
Wood

Stevenage Brook

Bury Farm
Pound Farm
All Saints
CE Prim Sch

Bury
Wood

Raffin Green
Farm

Raffin
Green

Painter's
Green

Datchworth

Woolmer
Green

Mardleybury

Cave
Wood

Mardleybury
Farm

Hay
Wains

St Michael's
Woolmer Green
CE Prim Sch

PH

AL6

Datchworth
Green

Hooper's
Hall

The Inn
on the Green
(PH)

Hawkins Hall
Farm

Pennyfather
CL

Nash
CL

Beechcroft

Watton Rd

Back La

LONDON RD

STEVENAGE RD

B197 MARDLEY HILL

THE DRIVE

HEATH RD

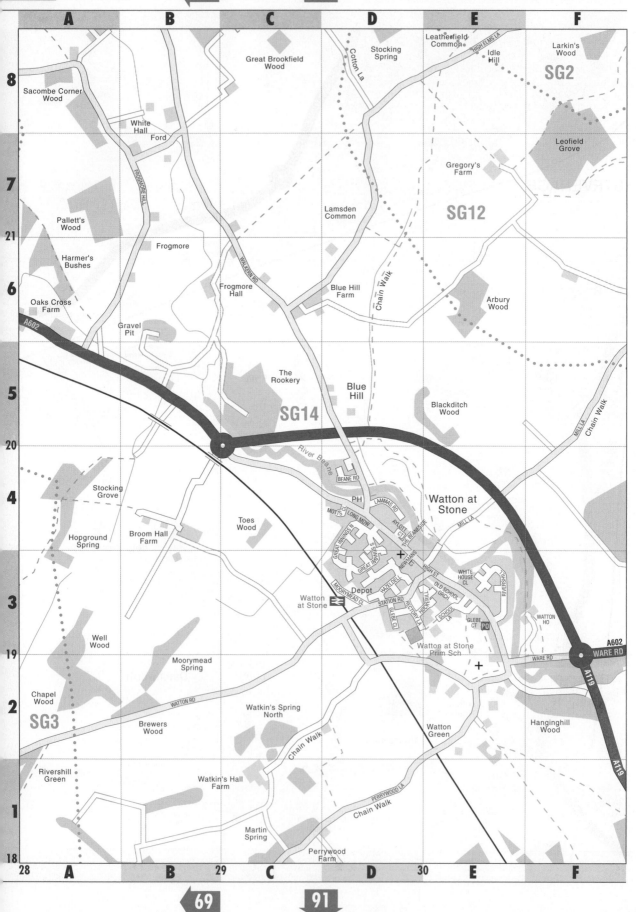

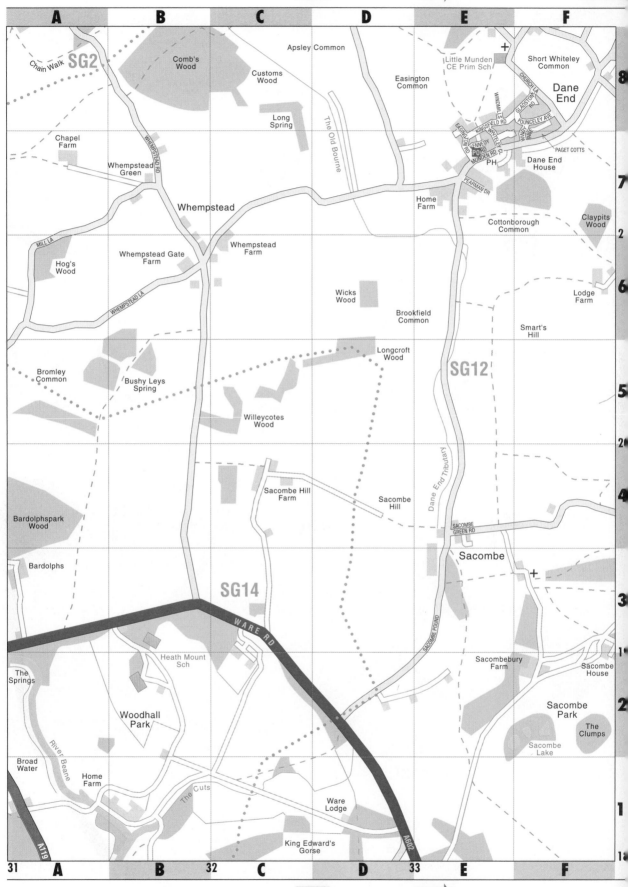

71 54

A  B  C  D  E  F

8
High Trees Farm
Hatchett Farm
Fullar's Common
Moorfield Common
Hatchett Poultry Farm
Beggarman's Wood
BEGGARMAN'S LA
Hill Farm
Trenchern Hills

7
Whitehill Farm
Langton's La
Shelly's Wood
Roughground Wood

21
CH
Cock's Wood
Rigery Farm
6
Potter's Green
Potter's Hall Farm
Labdens Farm

5
ROWNEY LA
Rowney Priory
Black Grove
Standon Green End Farm
Willowtree Farm
Rowney Wood
LOWGATE LA
Knoll Farm

20
SG12
Standon Green End
SG11

4
LOWGATE LA
Sacombe Green
Mott's Wood
Banwick Tributary

Church Wood
Dilly Wood
The Bourne
Salmonsley Wood
DANE END RD
A10

3
Low Wood
Home Wood

19
Home Farm
MARSHALL'S LA
Sutes
CAMBRIDGE COTTS
Pullar Memorial Prim Sch

2
Gages Wood
Marshall's Farm PH
High Cross
Marshall's
Furzeground Wood
NORTH DR
POPLAR LA
PASSFIELD COTTS

1
Hazelwood Farm
Rennesley Garden Wood
Mark's Wood
SG12
Highcross Hill
Gravelpit Wood
A10

48
34  A  B  35  C  D  36  E  F

71 93

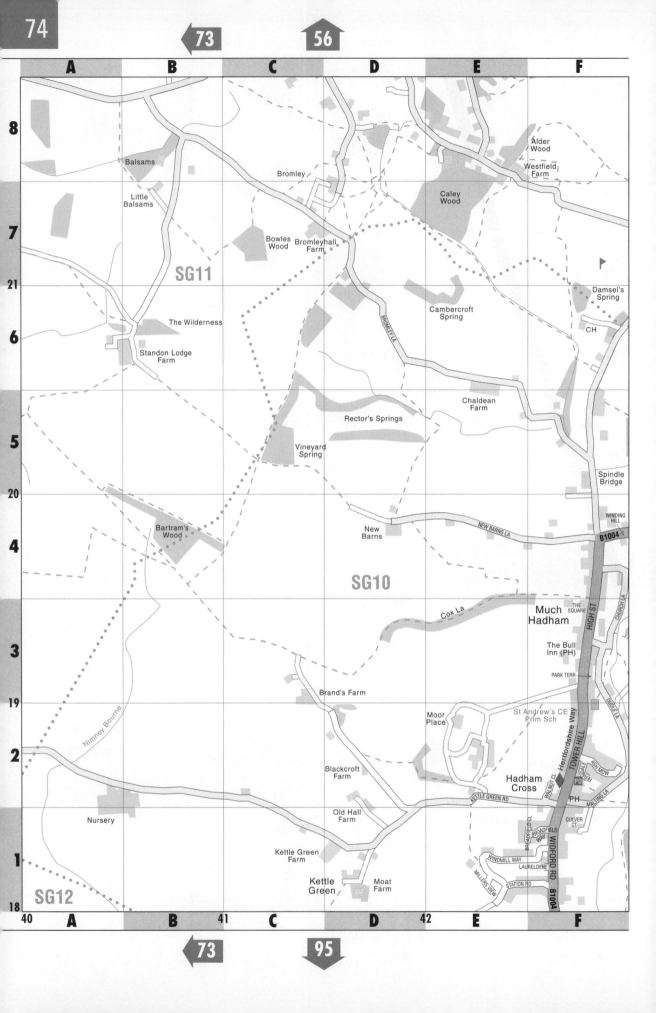

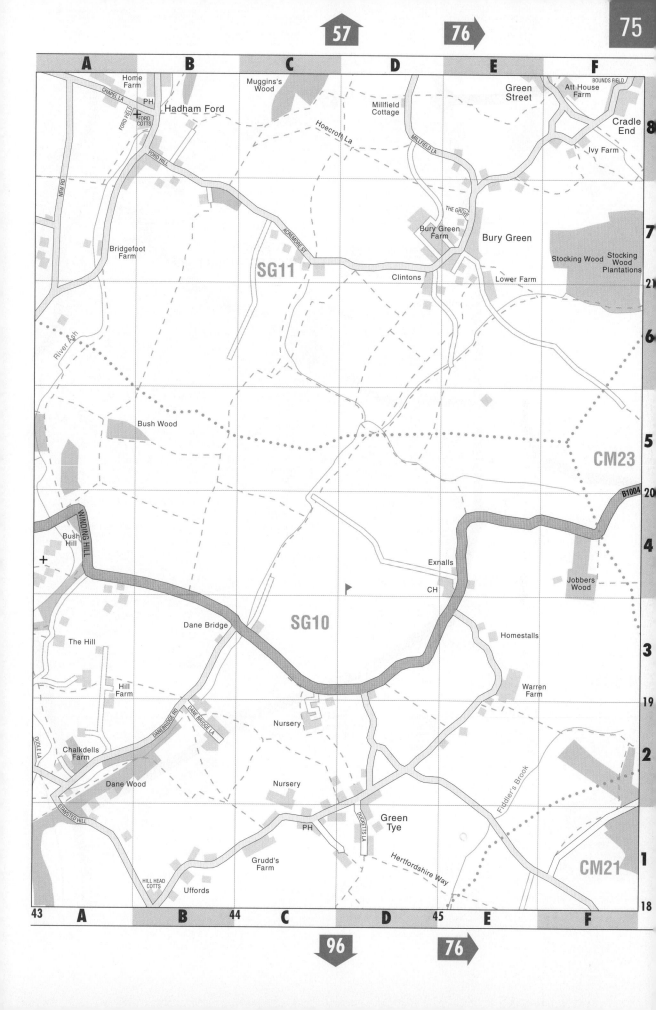

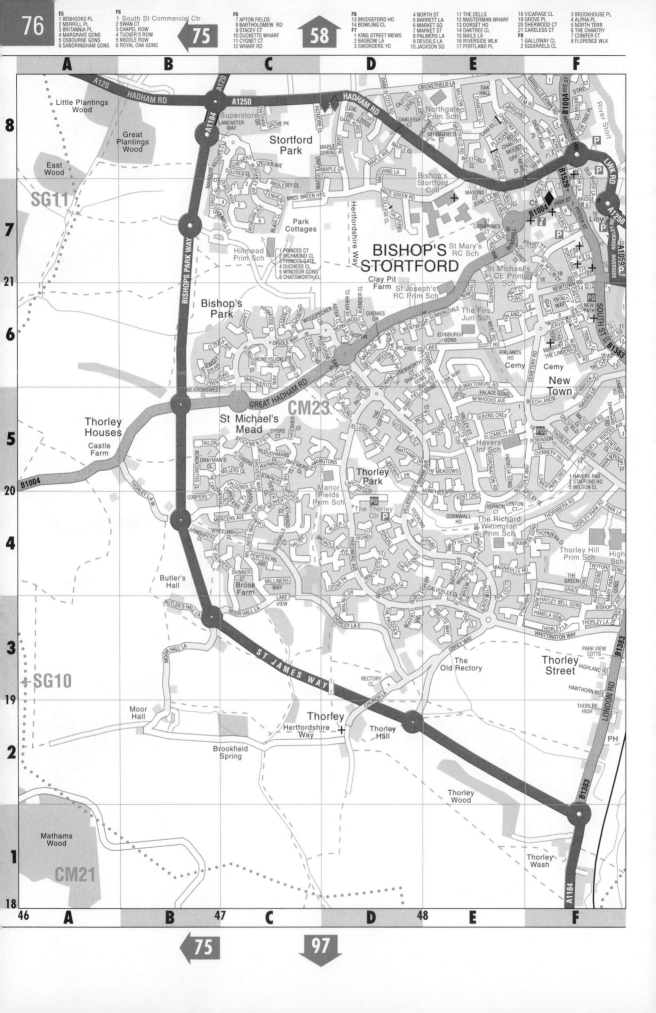

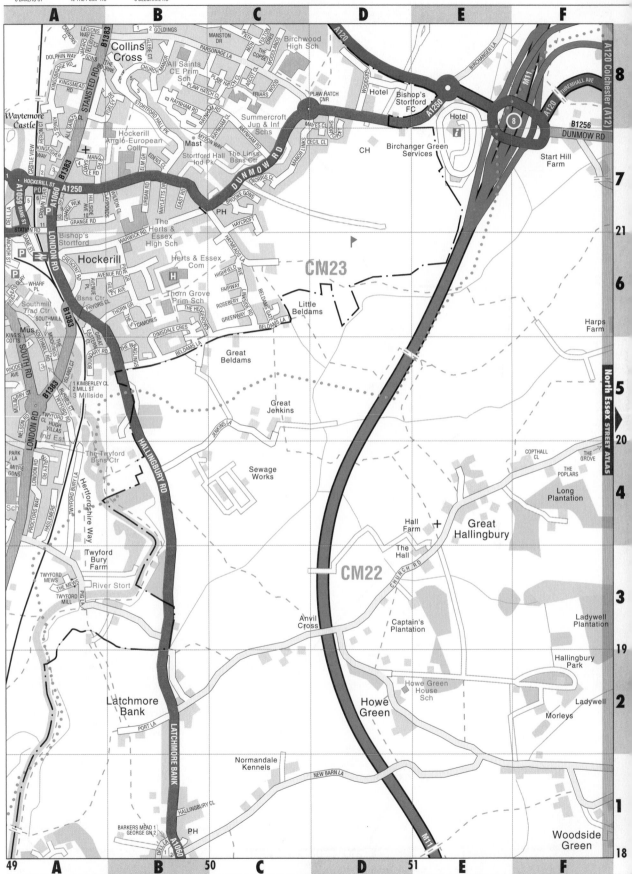

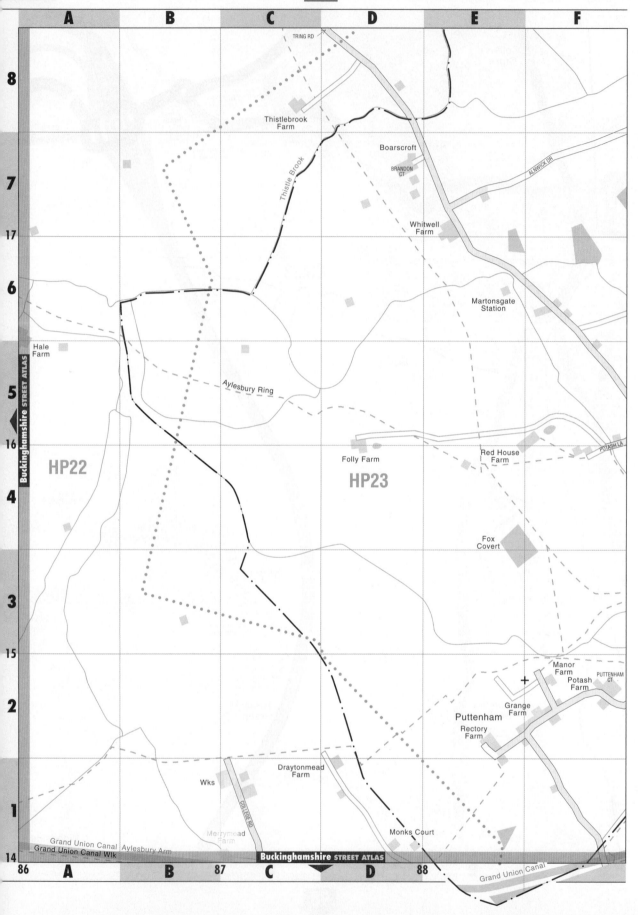

8

7

17

6

5

16

4

3

15

2

1

14

TRING RD

Thistlebrook
Farm

Thistle Brook

Boarscroft

BRANDON
CT

Whitwell
Farm

ALNWICK DR

Martonsgate
Station

Hale
Farm

Aylesbury Ring

HP22

HP23

Folly Farm

Red House
Farm

POTASH LA

Fox
Covert

Manor
Farm

Potash
Farm

PUTTENHAM
CT

Grange
Farm

Puttenham

Rectory
Farm

Draytonmead
Farm

Wks

COLLEGE RD

Monks Court

Merrymead
Farm

Grand Union Canal Aylesbury Arm
Grand Union Canal Wlk

Grand Union Canal

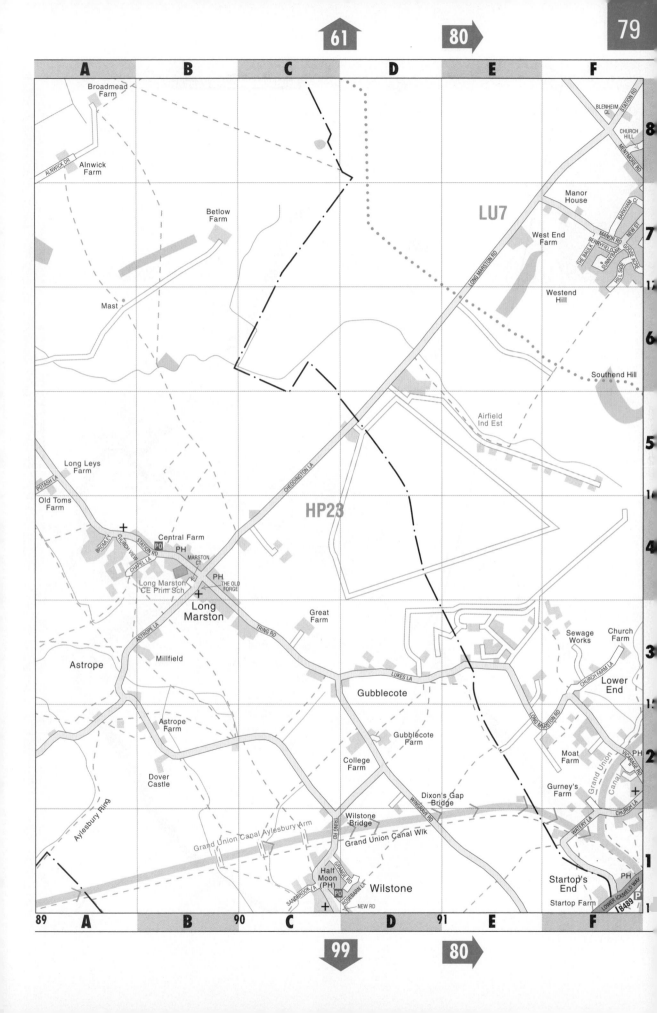

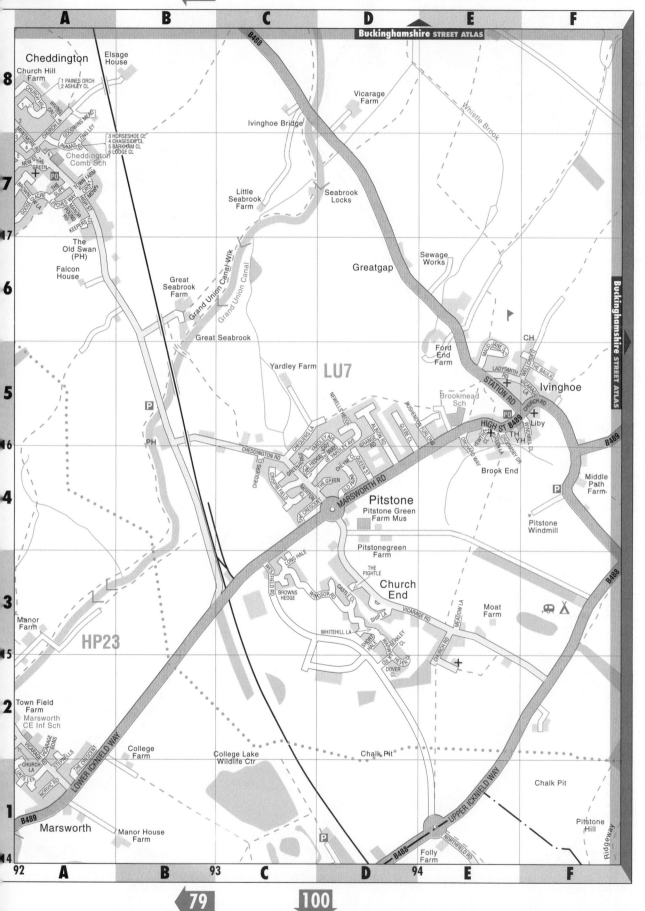

Cheddington

Church Hill Farm
1 PAINES ORCH
2 ASHLEY CL

Elsage House

Ivinghoe Bridge

Vicarage Farm

Whistle Brook

3 HORSESHOE CL
4 CHASESIDE CL
5 BARKHAM CL
6 LODGE CL

Cheddington Comb Sch

Little Seabrook Farm

Seabrook Locks

Buckinghamshire STREET ATLAS

The Old Swan (PH)

Falcon House

Great Seabrook Farm

Greatgap

Sewage Works

CH

Great Seabrook

Yardley Farm

LU7

Ford End Farm

MAUD JANE'S
LADYSMITH RD
STATION RD
VICARAGE LA
WELLCROFT
THE BAULK

Ivinghoe

PO

Liby

Brookmead Sch

Grand Union Canal Wlk
Grand Union Canal

HIGH ST  B489
TH
YH
WINDMILL CL
CHURCH RD
GROOMSBY DR

B489

PH

CHEDDINGTON RD
CHEQUERS CL
CHRISPIN FIELD
CHEQUERS LA
GREENACRES
THE HENGE
YARDLEY AVE
SGT WAY
LONG YARDLEY AVE
CHEYNE LA
QUEEN'S WAY
GRANGE RD
GLEBE CL
ALBION RD
NEWELLS HEDGE
RUSHENDON FURLONG
PEWTER LA
GREEN LA
ORCHARD WAY

Brook End

Middle Path Farm

MOSSOM
THE GREEN
OLD PARK
FIELD CRESCENT

MARSWORTH RD

Pitstone

Pitstone Green Farm Mus

Pitstone Windmill

HP23

Manor Farm

Pitstonegreen Farm

THE PIGHTLE

Church End

Moat Farm

Long Hale

WESTFIELD RD
WINDSOR RD
CASTLE CL
SHIP LA
VICARAGE RD
MEADOW LA
CHURCH RD

BROWNS HEDGE

WHITEHILL LA

SHORT HALE
WARWICK RD
BERKLEY CL
HELEN CL
DOVER CL

Town Field Farm

Marsworth CE Inf Sch

College Farm

College Lake Wildlife Ctr

Chalk Pit

Chalk Pit

Pitstone Hill

VICARAGE RD
VICARAGE GDNS
STEPNELLS
THE CRESCENT
LOWER ICKNIELD WAY
CHURCH LA
LUCKS LEA
NORVIC RD

Marsworth

Manor House Farm

UPPER ICKNIELD WAY
NORTHFIELD RD

Ridgeway

B489

B489

Folly Farm

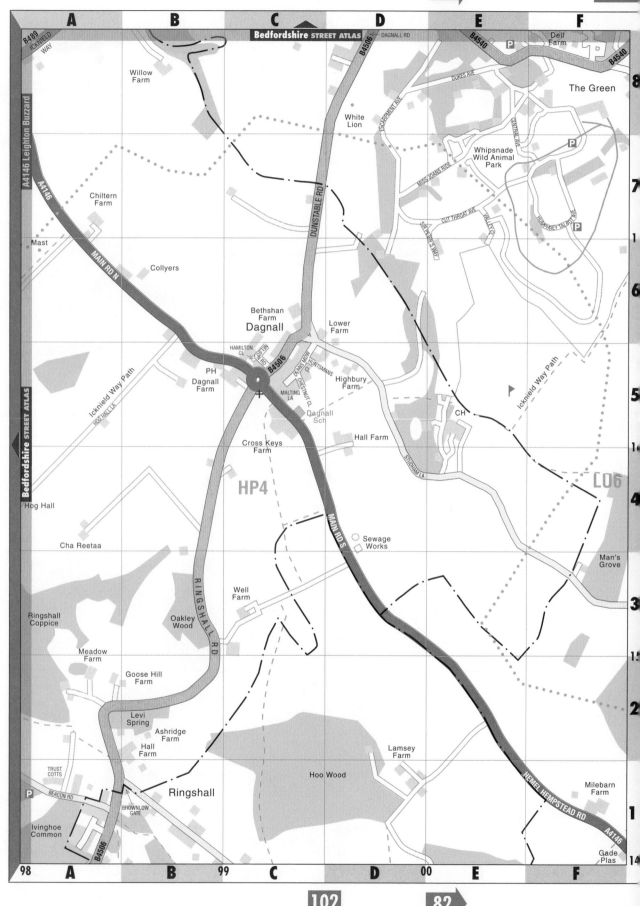

Bedfordshire STREET ATLAS

Dagnall Rd

The Green

Willow Farm

White Lion

Whipsnade Wild Animal Park

Dell Farm

Chiltern Farm

Dukes Ave

Escarpment Ave

Miss Joans Ride

Central Ave

Mast

Collyers

Cut Throat Ave

Valley Ct

Humphrey Talbot

Sub Peter's Way

Bethshan Farm

Dagnall

Lower Farm

Hamilton Cl

PH Dagnall Farm

Nelson Cl

Deans Row

Huntsmans Cl

Chestnut Cl

Malting La

Highbury Farm

Icknield Way Path

Dagnall Sch

Icknield Way Path

CH

Hall Farm

Cross Keys Farm

Studham La

LU6

HP4

Hog Hall

Cha Reetaa

Sewage Works

Man's Grove

Ringshall Coppice

Well Farm

Oakley Wood

Ringshall Rd

Meadow Farm

Goose Hill Farm

Levi Spring

Ashridge Farm

Hall Farm

Lamsey Farm

Hoo Wood

Hemel Hempstead Rd

Milebarn Farm

Trust Cotts

Beacon Rd

Ivinghoe Common

Brownlow Gate

Ringshall

Gade Plas

A4146 Leighton Buzzard

B489 Icknield Way

A4146

Main Rd N

B4506

Dunstable Rd

B4506

B4540

Main Rd S

A4146

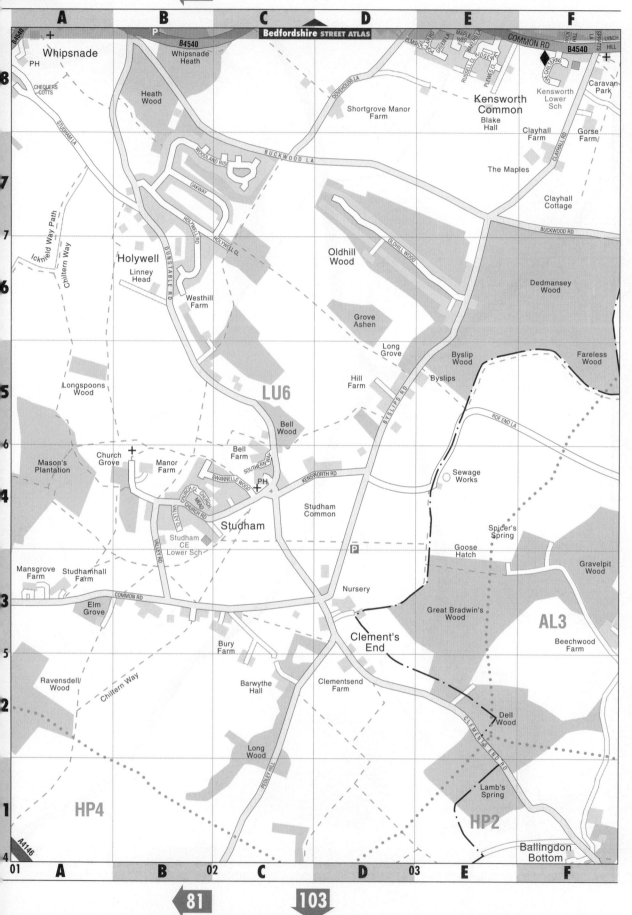

**Bedfordshire STREET ATLAS**

A B C D E F

COMMON RD

B4540

Whipsnade
PH

P
B4540
Whipsnade
Heath

Heath
Wood

DOVEHOUSE LA

Shortgrove Manor
Farm

ELMSIDE CL
SALT RD
GREEN LA
MAPLE WAY
RUSSELL CL
HODGEW
PLEWS CL
WALERS CL
WICK HILL
SPROTS
LYNCH HILL

THE CHILTERNS

Kensworth
Common

Blake
Hall

Kensworth
Lower
Sch

Caravan
Park

Clayhall
Farm

CLAYHALL RD

Gorse
Farm

WOODLAND RISE

BUCKWOOD LA

The Maples

Clayhall
Cottage

OAKWAY

BUCKWOOD RD

HOLYWELL RD
HOLYWELL CL

Holywell

Linney
Head

DUNSTABLE RD

Westhill
Farm

Oldhill
Wood

OLDHILL WOOD

Dedmansey
Wood

Ickheld Way Path

Chiltern Way

CHEQUERS
COTTS
PH

STUDHAM LA

Grove
Ashen

Long
Grove

Byslip
Wood

Fareless
Wood

Longspoons
Wood

Hill
Farm

Byslips

LU6

BYSLIPS RD

Bell
Wood

Mason's
Plantation

Church
Grove

Manor
Farm

Bell
Farm

SOUTHERN WAY
SWANNELLS WOOD
PH

KENSWORTH RD

ROE END LA

Sewage
Works

CHURCH CL
CHURCH MEAD
CHURCH RD
VALLEY CL
VALLEY RD

Studham

Studham
CE
Lower Sch

Studham
Common

Spicer's
Spring

Goose
Hatch

Gravelpit
Wood

Mansgrove
Farm

Studhamhall
Farm

COMMON RD

Elm
Grove

P

Nursery

Great Bradwin's
Wood

AL3

Beechwood
Farm

Ravensdell
Wood

Chiltern Way

Bury
Farm

Barwythe
Hall

Clement's
End

Clementsend
Farm

Dell
Wood

CLEMENTS END RD

Long
Wood

PEDLEY HILL

Lamb's
Spring

HP4

HP2

A4146

Ballingdon
Bottom

01 A 02 B C 03 D E F

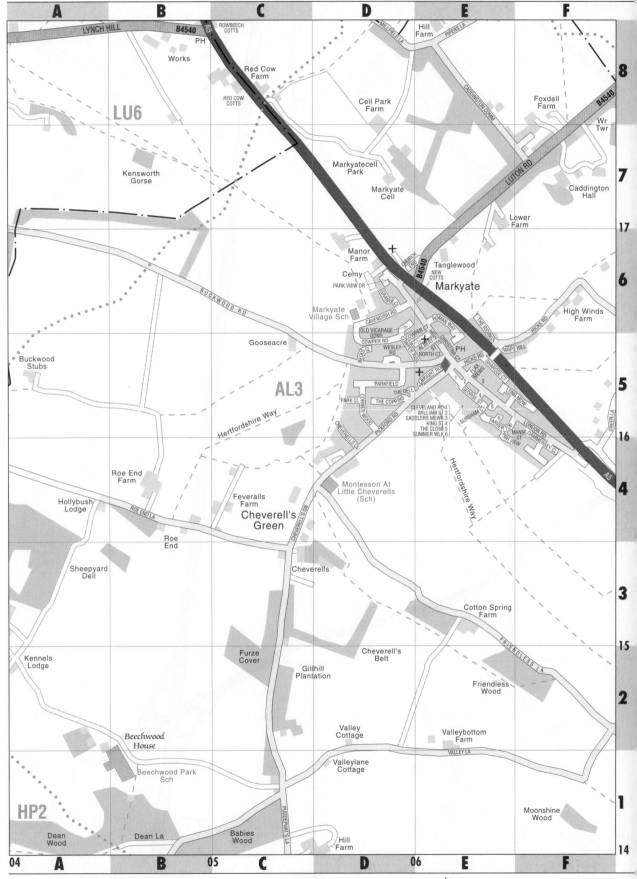

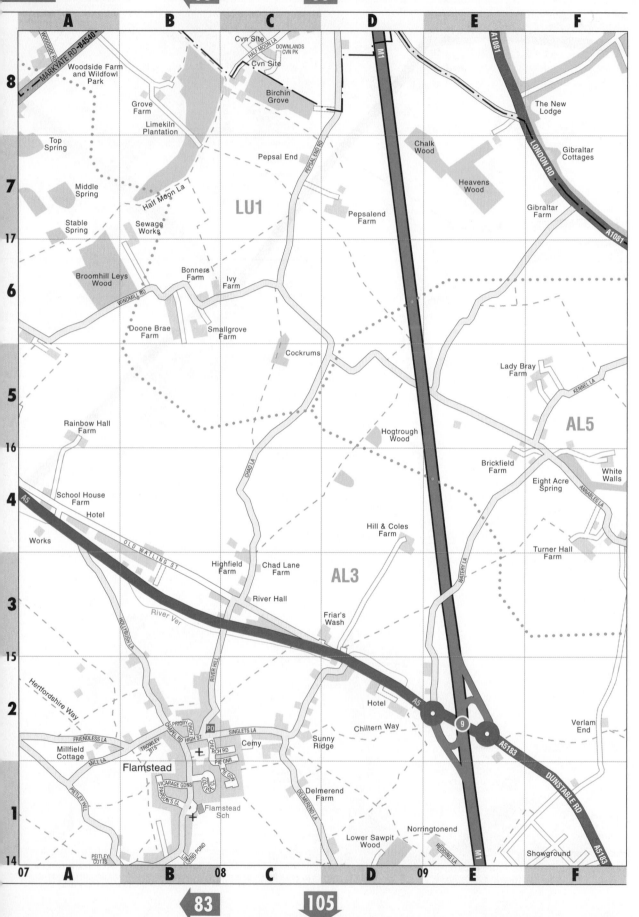

A1
1 THE COPPICE
2 THE BOURNE APARTMENTS
3 THE BOURNE

**8** | **7** | **17** | **6** | **5** | **16** | **4** | **3** | **15** | **2** | **1** | **14**

A | B | C | D | E | F

Chiltern Way
Garden Wood
The Hyde
Home Wood
Hyde Home Farm
Little Cutts Farm
Hill Farm
East Hyde Park
Bishey Wood
Tallents Farm
SG4
B652

LU2
B653
LOWER HARPENDEN RD
Ladies Spring
Dane Farm
Dane Spring
KIMPTON BOTTOM
Animal Welfare Centre

Hyde Mill Farm
Broadlands
Wall Wood
BOWER HEATH LA
Bower Heath
KINGS HEATH PK
Bower Heath Farm
HOLLY LA
Holly Farm
Old Raisins Farm
THE SLYPE

River Lea or Lee
Lea Valley Wlk
B652
COMMON LA
SAUCEY WOOD LA
Turners Hall Farm

AL5
Cold Hartbour
Westfield Wood
The Lea Prim Sch
Cemy
Harpenden (private)
H
SAUNCEY WOOD
Sauncey Wood
Mackerye End
Mackerye End
Mackerye End Farm

1 RIVERBANKS CL
2 BARLEY RISE
3 ST MARTINS CL

Sauncey Wood Prim Sch

ST JAMES'S CT 1
CLARENDON CT 2
Riverside Est
Allied Bsns Ctr
LOWER LUTON RD
Batford
LEACROFT

Manland Prim Sch
Sir John Lawes Sch
B652
SALISBURY RD

St George's Sch
HARPENDEN
Harpenden Memorial Gdns
Ford
Lea Valley

A1081 LUTON RD
H
Harpenden
Sewage Works
AL4
Lea Valley Wlk
B653

Rothamsted Sch
Liby
Crabtree Inf Sch
1 DALEWOOD
2 FAIRFIELD CL
3 ENGLEHURST
Piggottshill Wood

James Marshall Commercial Ctr
Harpenden
High Beeches Prim Sch
CH

13 | A | B | 14 | C | D | 15 | E | F

A2
1 LYDEKKER MEWS
2 GERARD CT
3 CORNELIA CL
4 HARDENWICK CT
5 SOUTHGATE CT
6 BERKELEY CT
7 FERNDALE
8 ANVIL HO

B1
1 CARLTON CT
2 CARLTON BANK
3 THE MEWS
4 CROFT CT
5 DEVONSHIRE RD
6 KINLOCH CT
7 VICTORIA RD
8 HARDING PAR
9 COLERIDGE CT

B1
10 BEAUMONT CT
11 COPPER BEECHES
12 MILTON CT
13 THE CEDARS
14 YARDLEY CT
15 KEATS HO
16 SHELLEY CT
17 AVON CT
18 FURZEDOWN CT

19 CHILTERN CT
20 HADDON CT

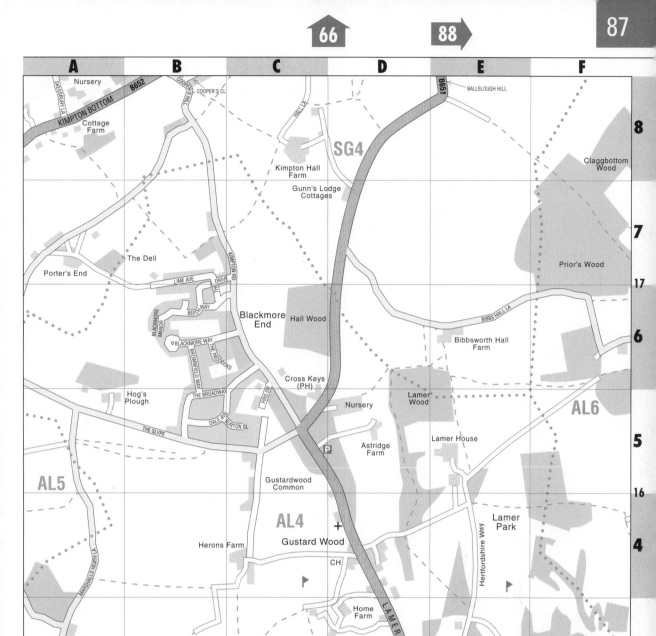

Nursery
B652
COOPER'S HILL
COOPER'S CL
KIMPTON BOTTOM
SKEGSBURY LA
Cottage Farm
B651
BALLSLOUGH HILL
SG4
Claggbottom Wood
Kimpton Hall Farm
HALL LA
Gunn's Lodge Cottages
The Dell
Porter's End
KIMPTON RD
LIME AVE
Prior's Wood
DRIVE
THE
BEECH WAY
BLACKMORE MANOR
BLACKMORE WAY
THE PADDOCKS
BROWNFIELD WAY
Blackmore End
Hall Wood
BIBBS HALL LA
Bibbsworth Hall Farm
Hog's Plough
THE BROADWAY
FIRS DR
Cross Keys (PH)
Nursery
Lamer Wood
AL6
THE SLYPE
DALE AVE
BURTON CL
Lamer House
AL5
P
Astridge Farm
Gustardwood Common
AL4
MARSHALLS HEATH LA
Herons Farm
Gustard Wood
CH
Lamer Park
HERTFORDSHIRE WAY
CH
Home Farm
LAMER LA
Cromwell Piggeries
Delaport House
Marshalls Heath
Dairy Cottage
CODICOTE RD
P
MARSHALLS WAY
The Folly
FOLLY FIELDS
PH
ROSE LA
D1
4 ABBOT JOHN MEWS
5 OLD WADDLING LA
6 PIKES LEAP
7 PALMERSTON DR
8 LATCHFORD MEWS
CHERRY TREE LA
LEASEY DELL DR
Cherry Trees
PH
LOWER LUTON RD
GARDEN
CODICOTE RD
WADDLING LA
CORY-WRIGHT WAY
SHEEPCOTE LA
Leasey Bridge
LEASEY BRIDGE LA
KINGFISHER CL
STATION RD
MOUNT RD
DAWES LA
Lea Valley Wlk
Leasey Bridge Farm
Lea Valley Wlk
River Lea or Lee
ASH GR
P.O
B651
HIGH ST
EAST LA
MEADS LA
Sewage Works
1 OLD RECTORY GDNS
2 EAST MOUNT
3 BROCKET VIEW
CANONS FIELD
B653

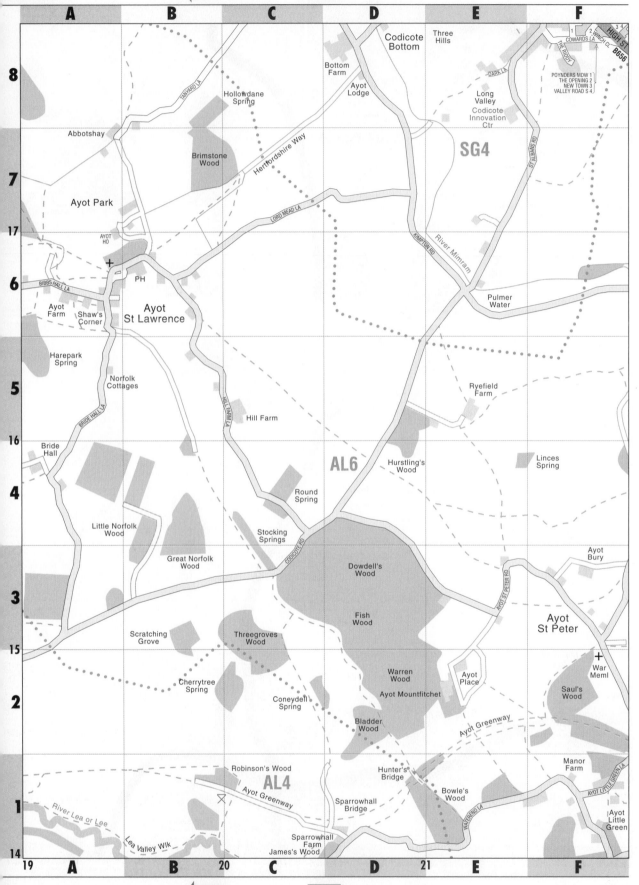

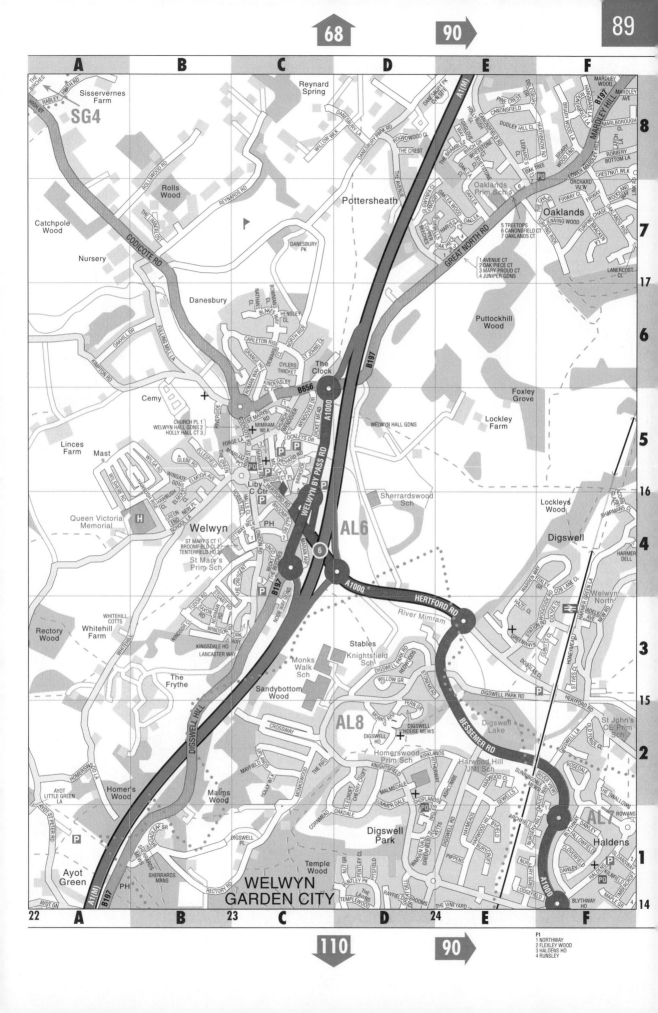

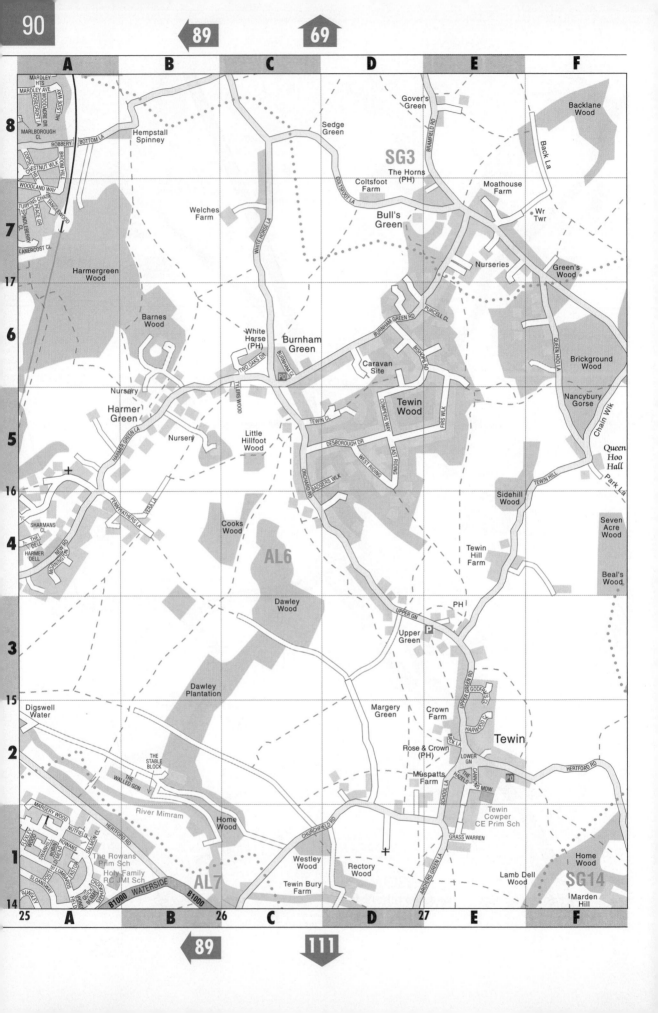

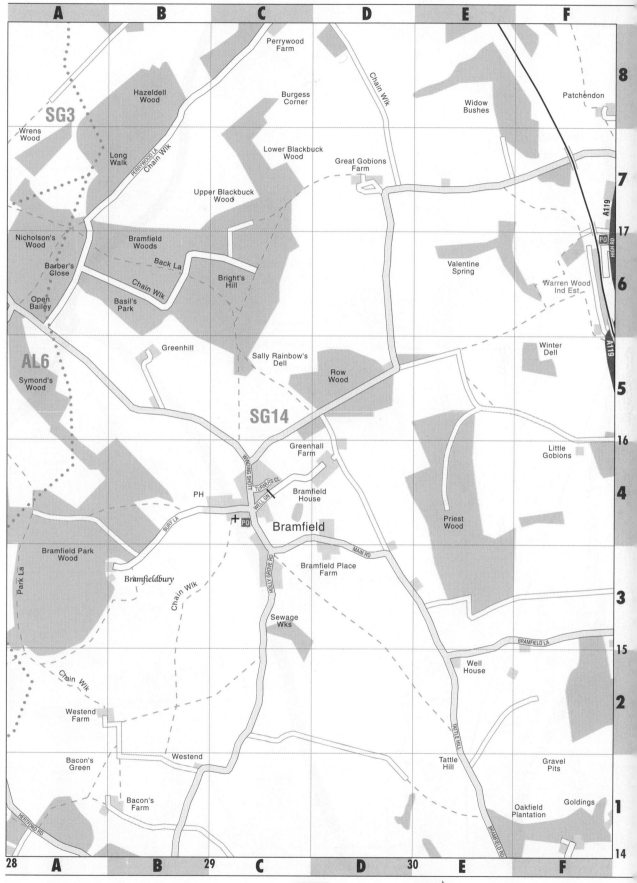

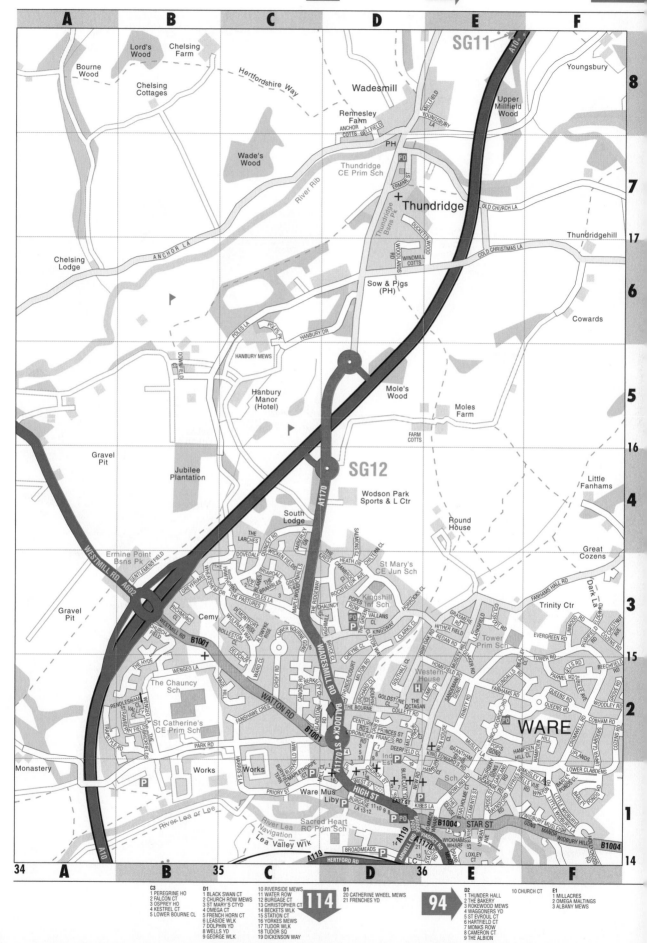

**C3**
1 PEREGRINE HO
2 FALCON CT
3 OSPREY HO
4 KESTREL CT
5 LOWER BOURNE CL

**D1**
1 BLACK SWAN CT
2 CHURCH ROW MEWS
3 ST MARY'S CTYD
4 OMEGA CT
5 FRENCH HORN CT
6 LEASIDE WLK
7 DOLPHIN YD
8 WELLS YD
9 GEORGE WLK
10 RIVERSIDE MEWS
11 WATER ROW
12 BURGAGE CT
13 CHRISTOPHER CT
14 BECKETS WLK
15 STATION CT
16 YORKES MEWS
17 TUDOR WLK
18 TUDOR SQ
19 DICKENSON WAY

**D1**
20 CATHERINE WHEEL MEWS
21 FRENCHES YD

**D2**
1 THUNDER HALL
2 THE BAKERY
3 ROKEWOOD MEWS
4 WAGGONERS YD
5 ST EVROUL CT
6 HARTFIELD CT
7 MONKS ROW
8 CAMERON CT
9 THE ALBION
10 CHURCH CT

**E1**
1 MILLACRES
2 OMEGA MALTINGS
3 ALBANY MEWS

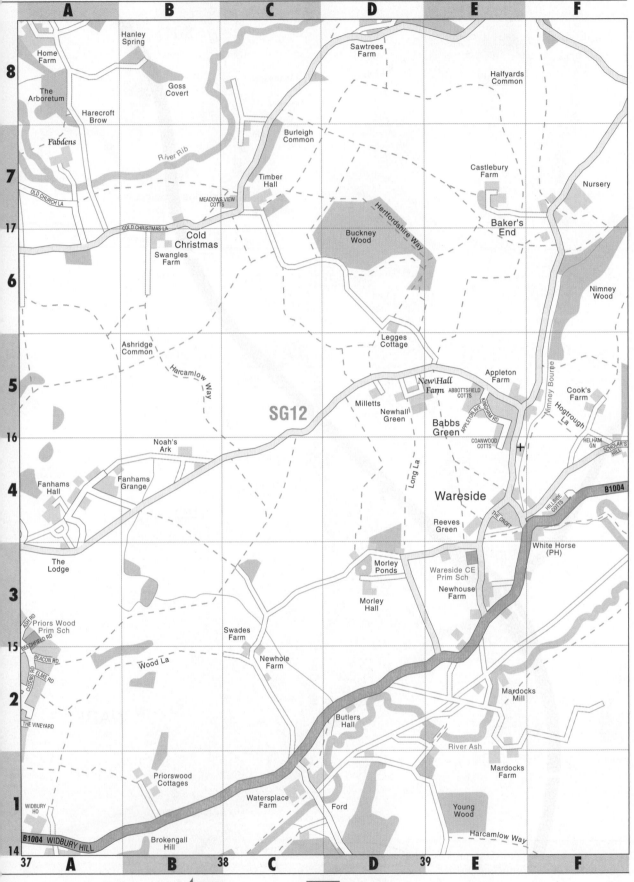

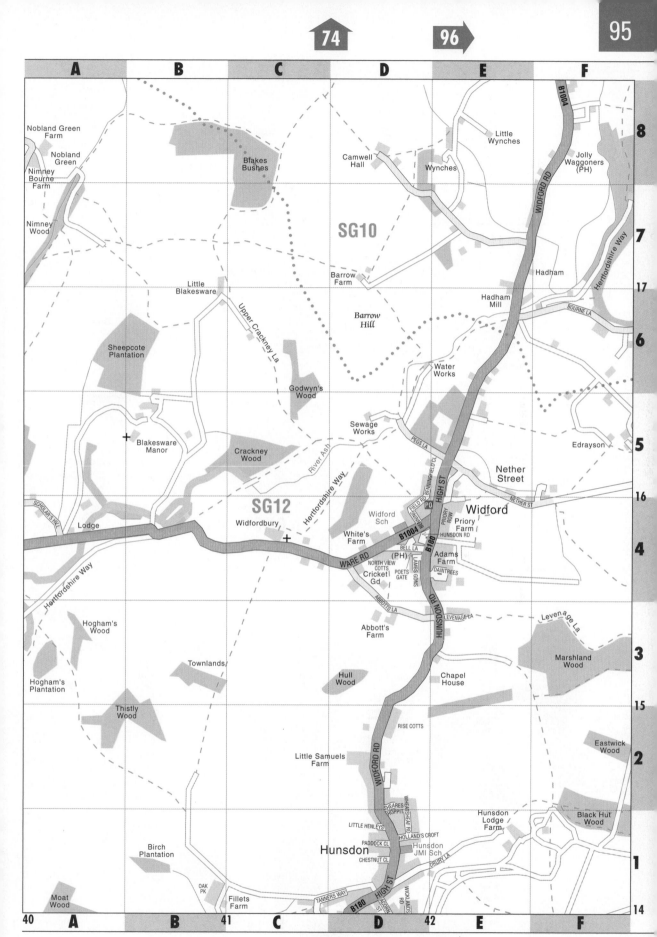

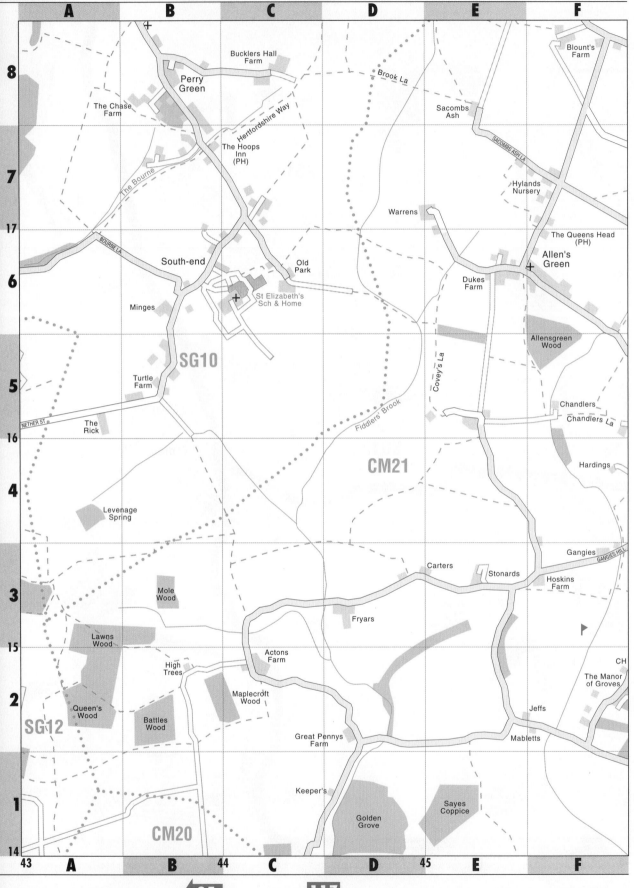

A B C D E F

8

7

17

6

5

16

4

3

15

2

1

14

Blount's Farm

Bucklers Hall Farm

Perry Green

Brook La

The Chase Farm

Sacombs Ash

Hertfordshire Way

The Hoops Inn (PH)

Hylands Nursery

The Bourne

Warrens

The Queens Head (PH)

Allen's Green

BOURNE LA

South-end

Old Park

Dukes Farm

Minges

St Elizabeth's Sch & Home

Allensgreen Wood

SG10

Covey's La

Chandlers

Turtle Farm

Chandlers La

NETHER ST

The Rick

CM21

Hardings

Levenage Spring

Gangies

GANGIES HILL

Carters

Stonards

Hoskins Farm

Mole Wood

Fryars

Lawns Wood

CH

The Manor of Groves

High Trees

Actons Farm

Maplecroft Wood

SG12

Queen's Wood

Jeffs

Battles Wood

Great Pennys Farm

Mabletts

Keeper's

Sayes Coppice

Golden Grove

CM20

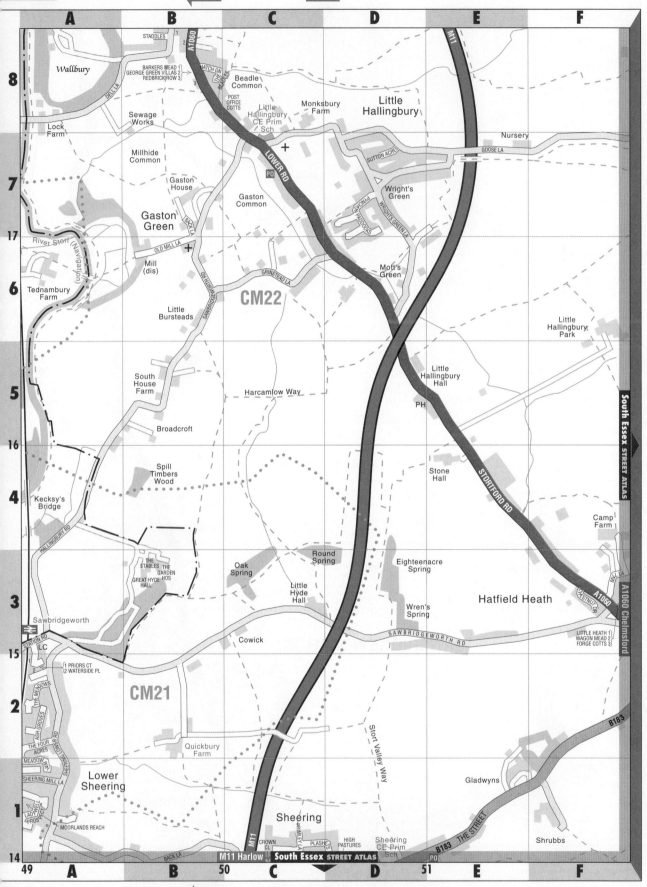

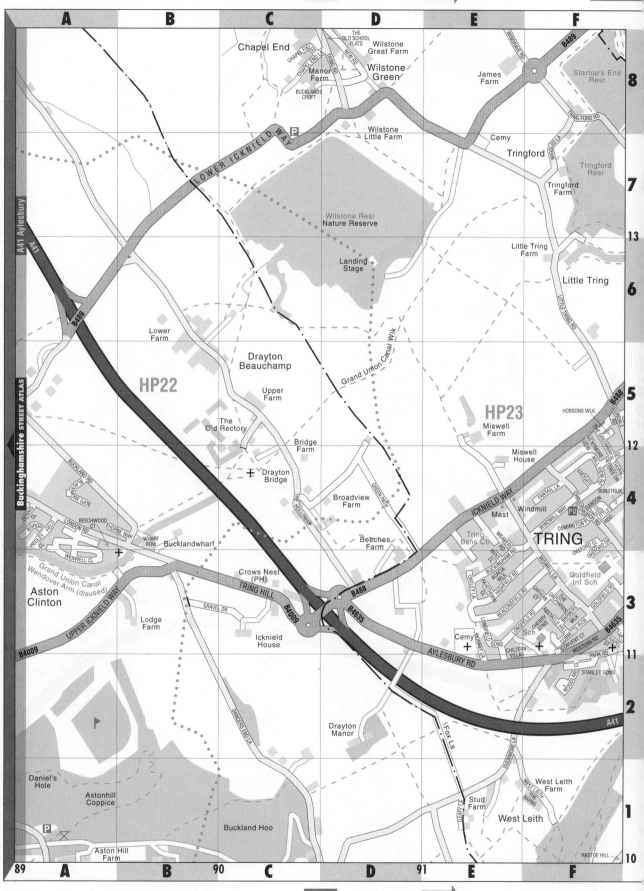

Chapel End

THE OLD SCHOOL FLATS

Wilstone Great Farm

Wilstone Green

James Farm

Startop's End Resr

8

Manor Farm

BUCKLANDS CROFT

Wilstone Little Farm

Cemy

Tringford

WINGRAVE RD

B489

TRING FORD RD

WIGGLES LA

Tringford Resr

LOWER ICKNIELD WAY

P

Tringford Farm

7

13

Wilstone Resr
Nature Reserve

Landing Stage

Little Tring Farm

Little Tring

6

LITTLE TRING RD

Lower Farm

Drayton Beauchamp

Grand Union Canal Wlk

HP22

Upper Farm

HP23

Miswell Farm

HOBSONS WLK

B488

5

The Old Rectory

Bridge Farm

Miswell House

12

GREEN PATH

Broadview Farm

ICKNIELD WAY

Windmill

PO

TRING

4

Mast

Tring Bsns Ctr

Beeches Farm

Crows Nest (PH)

TRING HILL

B488

AYLESBURY RD

Goldfield Inf Sch

3

Aston Clinton

Grand Union Canal Wendover Arm (disused)

UPPER ICKNIELD WAY

GRAVEL DR

Icknield House

B4009

B4635

Cemy

CHILTERN VILLAS

PARK RD

STANLEY GDNS

11

B4009

Lodge Farm

DANGERS END LA

A41

2

Drayton Manor

FOX LA

Daniel's Hole

Astonhill Coppice

Stud Farm

West Leith Farm

THE BARNS

1

P

Buckland Hoo

LEADY LA

DUCKMORE LA

WEST LEITH

West Leith

Aston Hill Farm

HASTOE HILL

10

A B C D E F

8

Marsworth Resr
Nature Reserve
College Lake Wildlife Ctr
UPPER ICKNIELD WAY
B488
Folly Bridge
Northfield Grange

Works
Grand Junction Arms (PH)
Bulbourne
MYRTLE COTTS
Bulbourne Farm
Park Hill Farm

NORTHFIELD RD

7

TRING FORD RD
Gamnel Farm
BULBOURNE RD
Grand Union Canal
Grand Union Canal Wlk

Sewage Works
BULBOURNE CT
GAMNEL MEWS
Mill

13

BUSHE WHARF
LONGRIDGE
Tring Wharf
MARSHCROFT LA

6

New Mill
ELIZABETH DR
SUTTON CL
PHEASANT MDW
B486
CHAPEL MDW
ALBANY TERR
Marshcroft Cottages

ICKNIELD WAY
NEW RD
FIELDS END
WINGRAVE RD
MCDONOUGH RD
ALDBURY GDNS
NEW MILL TERR
NETHERBY CL
HOLLYFIELD CL
RIDGE VIEW

Clarke's Spring

5

B488
EGGLETON DR
GRENADINE WAY
GWYNNE
SILK MILL WAY
GROVE RD
HOLLYFIELD
BEACON
THE GROVE
KATO
FLAX TREE WLK
ROSEBERY WAY
Grove Road Prim Sch
DANVERS CROFT
CHILTERN WAY
BULGRAVE CRES
GROVE PK
CLARKE'S SPRING

NATHANIEL WLK
DRUMMOND RIDGE
EMMA ROTHSCHILD
Dundale Prim Sch
BEECH WLK
GRANGE RD
HP23

12

MANOR BETTY'S LA
EIGHT ACRES
KINGSLEY RD
CARRINGTON PL
HARCOURT RD
WHYTINGHAM RD
STATION RD
Court Theatre
Pendley Farm
BEGGARS LA

4

BUNSTRUX
DUNDALE
MEADOW
ST PETERS HILL
FAVERSHAM CL
Tring Sch
MORTIMER HILL
EVANS GDNS
WEST RD
NURSERY GDNS
TREEHANGER
SYCAMORE DR
THE BEECHES
HAZELY
HAWKWELL
DAMASK CL
Cow Lane Farm
Pendley Manor (Hotel)
Chestnut Wood

PARSONAGE CL
DEANS FURLONG
PLATTERS
BEECH GR
THE MEADS
MORTIMER RISE
Upper Dunsley
Sports Ctr
Lodge Bushes

3

CHRISTCHURCH
FRIARS WLK
DEANS
Pond CL
CHURCH YD
B486
DUNSLEY PL
Dunsley Farm
Pendley Beeches

REGAL
WESTERN RD
WEST CROFT
B4635
HIGH ST
Liby
PO
HARROW RD
OAKLAWN
MANSION DR
LONDON RD
TRING
1 GOLDFIELD RD
2 CHRISTCHURCH HO
3 DOLPHIN SQ
4 CLEMENT PL
5 GRACES MALTINGS
6 CROWN ROSE CT
7 THE TERRACE
8 MUSEUM CT
9 LOUISA COTTS
10 WEST PAS

11

KING ST
HENRY ST
CHARLES ST
ALBERT ST
ACKMANS
RODWELL
SURREY PL
Mus
PARK
Wellbrook Mews
Parsonage
Jun Sch
The Arts Educational Sch
CARPENTERS YD
A4251
B4635
Ridgeway

THE FURLONG
PARK RD
CASTLE ROW
Woodlands Farm
ODDY HILL
FOX RD
Langton Wood
THE TWIST
A4251

2

A41
HASTOE LA
HASTOE HILL
Tring Park Nature Reserve
Park Farm
HEMP LA

1

MARTIN HILL
Bull's Wood
HIGHFIELD RD
MARY CROSSFIELD RD
FOX CL
POLLYWICK RD
GRIMSDYKE RD
COMMON FIELD WAY
BELLMERS
WICK RD
Sch
VICARAGE RD
THE FIRS
Wigginton
THE HOLLIES
FIELDWAY
THE BIT
FIELD END CL 1
VALPY CL
2
CHESHAM RD
1 RED COTTAGE
2 VALPY CL
Hill Green Farm

10

92 A B 93 C D 94 E F

Buckinghamshire STREET ATLAS

| | A | B | C | D | E | F |

**8**

B4506

ALDERTON DR

Chiltern Way

RINGSHALL DR

GATESHEDE CL

PO

BRIDGEWATER CT

Bridgewater Arms (PH)

BELL CT

CHURCH RD

Church Farm

Badger Wood

+

Little Gaddesden CE Prim Sch

Little Gaddesden

Hudnall Common Plantation

**7**

Pitstone Park Copse

B4506

Hudnall Common

HUDNALL LA

POND LA

Hudnall

**13**

Ashridge

CH

Hudnall Farm

**6**

Old Park Lodge

Ashridge Park

Golden Valley

CHAPEL CL

THE LYE

Robin Hood Farm

Little Brownlow Farm

LITTLE GADDESDEN HO

Prince's Riding

The Rookery

Lady Grove

Home Farm

**5**

Thunderdell Wood

Hertfordshire Way

Ashridge College Gdns

Ashridge Management Coll

Cromer Wood

CROMER CL

ASHRIDGE COTTS

**12**

HP4

Harding's Rookery

CROMER CL

NETTLEDEN RD

**4**

Woodyard Cottage

Berkhamstead Common

Toll

Pulridge Wood

**3**

Little Coldharbour Farm

Coldharbour Spring

Coldharbour Farm

Golden Valley Farm

**11**

Furzefield Wood

Nettleden Lodge

**2**

Hertfordshire Way

Ashridge

Webb's Copse

Bluebell Spring

HP1

**1**

Brickkiln Cottage

Frithsden Beeches

Frithsden Gardens

**10**

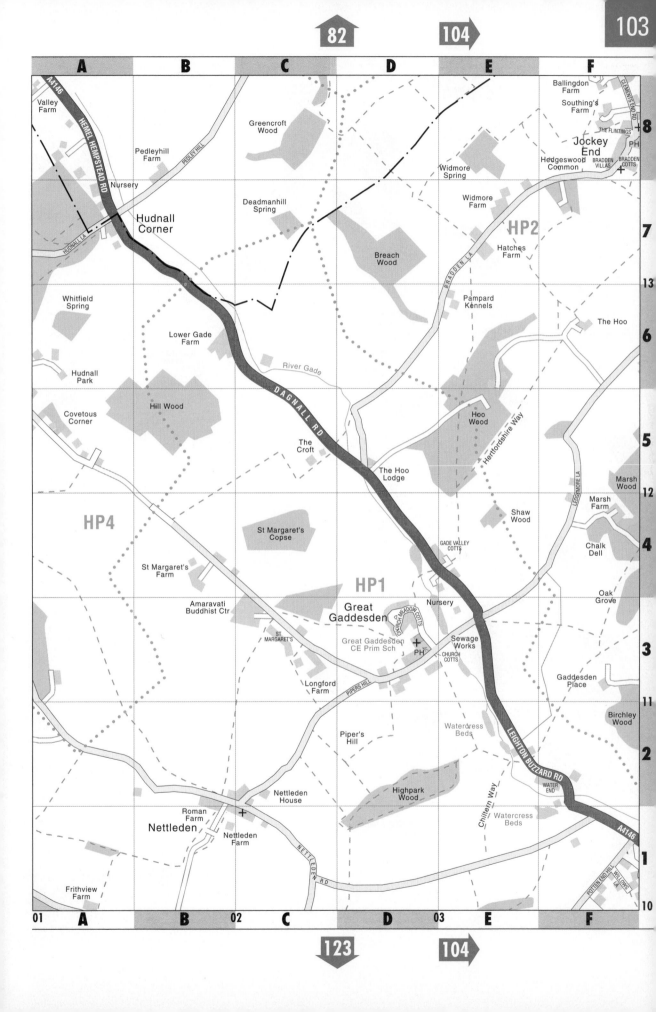

103
83

A B C D E F

Dean La
Babies Wood
Little Woodend Cottages

8
WEST DENE
SOUTH DENE
Newland's Wood
Prior's Spring
Yewtree Spring
Scratch Wood
AL3
WOOD END LA

Hertfordshire Way
Six Tunnels Farm
Whitehouse Farm
Chiltern Way
Abel's Grove
Wood End Farm
PUDDEPHAT'S LA

7

Water Twr
Puddephats' Farm

13

Ledgemore La
Gaddesden Row JMI Sch
Gaddesden Row
Teakettle Wood
Upper Wood Farm
Green La

Hoo Cotts
The Lane House
GADDESDEN ROW

6

Ledgemore Farm
New Gorse
Golden Parsonage
Round Spring Wood
Greenlane Wood

Long Wood

5
CHEQUERS END
Ye Olde Chequers (PH)
Elmtree Farm

12
Marsh Wood
Stags End

Home Farm
London Wood
Threecraft Wood
HP2
Hawbush Farm
Corner Farm
THE GRANARY
GADDESDEN LA

4

Stable Wood
Big Wood

3

Crown & Sceptre (PH)
Thomas's Wood
CUPID GREEN LA

Birchley Wood

11
Briden's Camp
Millhill Farm
Millhill Gorse
Eastbrookhay Farm

Hogstrough Dell
Chalkpit Dell

2

Lovetts End Farm

Varney's Wood

1
Red Lion (PH)
HP1
DODDS LA
Little Lovetts End Farm
ESSEX MEAD 1
ST AGNELLS LA 2
THE DEE 3
OLD MAPLE 4
SQUIRES RIDE

Wood Farm

LEIGHTON BUZZARD RD
A4146
WOOTTON DR

10

04 A 05 B C 05 D 06 E F

103
124

107
87

A  B  C  D  E  F

8

WHEATHAMPSTEAD RD
PIPERS LA
CH
Down Green House
Lea Valley Wlk
BURY GN 1
BURY MEAD 2
ASH GR 1
OLD RECTORY GDNS 2
BREWHOUSE HILL
CHURCH ST
ST HELEN'S CL
GRANARY CL
ST THOMAS'S CL
HIGH ST
B651
TOWN FARM CL
BROCKET VIEW
NECTON RD
Marford Farm
The Nelson (PH)
CORY-WRIGHT WAY
B653

Sch
Liby
FOUR LIMES
WALNUT CT
GARRARD WAY
OFFAS WAY
SAXON RD
CAESARS RD
CONQUERORS HILL
NURSERIES RD
TUDOR RD
BATTLEVIEW
MARFORD RD

AL5

Pipers

7

Amwell
HARPENDEN RD
AMWELL LA
HILLTOP VIEW
HIGH ASH RD
LATTIMORE RD
BARTON RD
WICK AVE
MALTINGS DR
BUTTERFIELD RD
Wheathampstead
HEWITT CL
PEN CL
WRIGHT CL
HOUSDEN CL
SMALLWOOD CL
LAMB CT
Sch
Belgic Oppidum

Little Piggotts Wood
The Elephant & Castle (PH)
DOWN GREEN LA
VALE CT
BEECH CRES
HALL DYKE RD
DAVYS CL
DYKE LA
Beech Hyde Farm
BEECH HYDE LA

13

Stocking Wood

BULL LA

6

West Farm
Glen Nurseries
PH
Nomansland
Wicked Lady (PH)
Pearman's Spring
PH

P
FERRERS LA

5

P
Nomansland Common
AL4
Nomansland Farm
Coleman Green LA
Darblay
DARBLAY CL
Coleman Green
TOWER HILL LA

12

Round Wood

4

Hillend Farm
Hammond's Farm Cottages
Hammond's Farm

3

HAMMONDS LA

11

Langley Wood
AL3
Hertfordshire Way
Harlowdell Spring

2

SANDRIDGEBURY LA
POUND CL
SPENCER PL
HIGH ST
LANGLEY GR
SHOTFIELD RD
Sandridge Sch
FAIRSHOT CT

Sandridgebury
Sandridgebury Farm
The Green Man (PH)
CHURCH END
ST LEONARD'S CR
LYNDON MEAD
GILES CL
NISON CL
ST LEONARDS CRES
Cemy
HOUSE LA
JERSEY LA
Harefield
WOODCOCK HILL
Harlowdell Spring
Fairfolds

HOPKINS CRES
GIBBONS CL
NORTHSIDE
Mast
Fairfold's Farm

1

ST ALBANS RD
B651
HIGHFIELD RD
Sandridge
REYNOLDS CRES

10

16  A  B  17  C  D  18  E  F

107
128

109
89

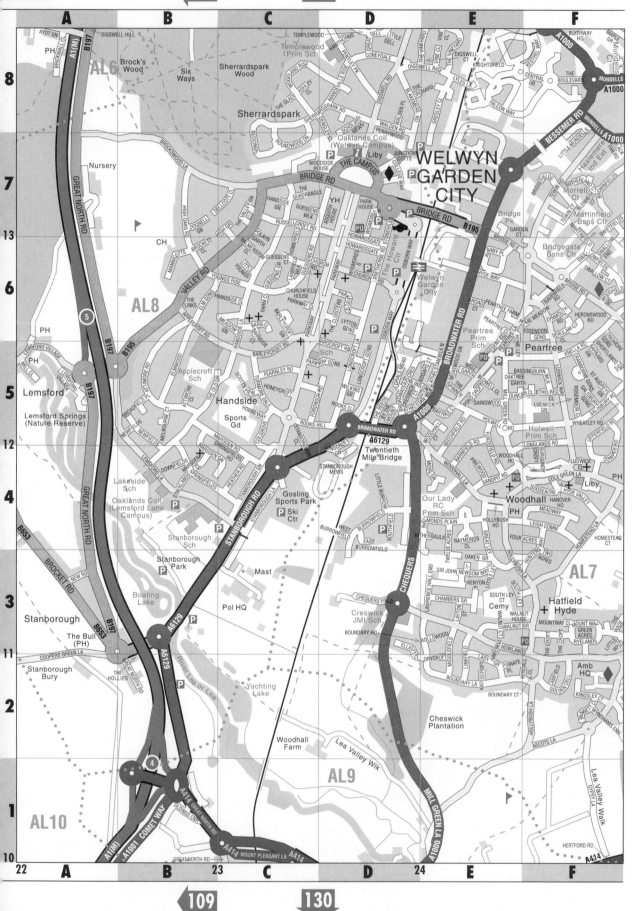

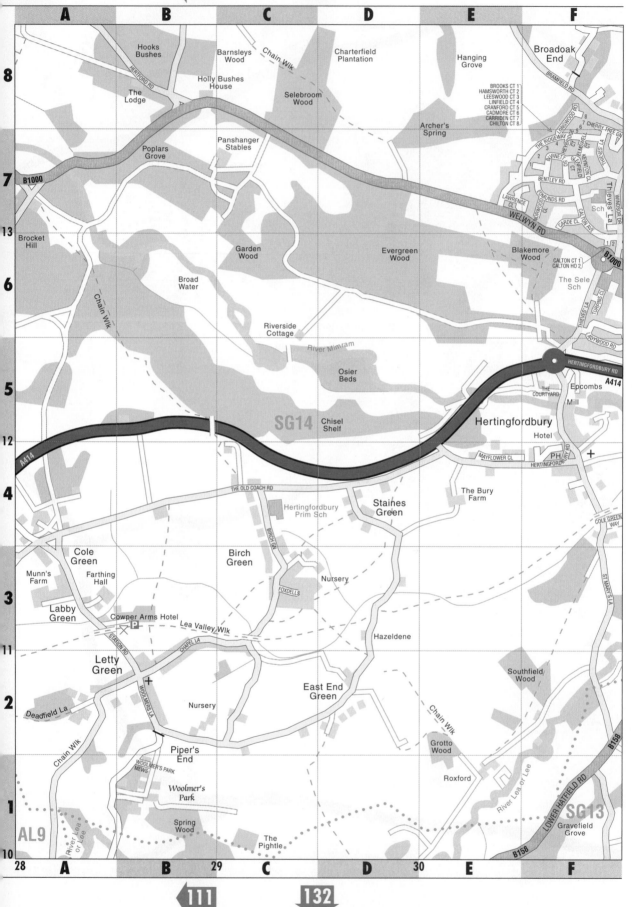

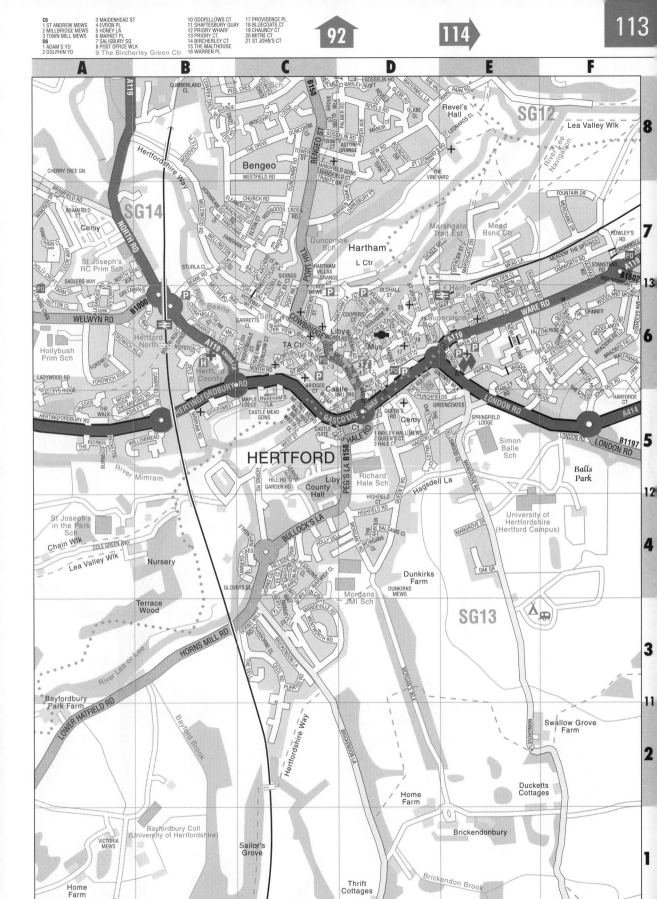

**C6**
1 ST ANDREW MEWS
2 MILLBRIDGE MEWS
3 TOWN MILL MEWS
**D6**
1 ADAM'S YD
2 DOLPHIN YD

3 MAIDENHEAD ST
4 EVRON PL
5 HONEY LA
6 MARKET PL
7 SALISBURY SQ
8 POST OFFICE WLK
9 The Bircherley Green Ctr

10 ODDFELLOWS CT
11 SHAFTESBURY QUAY
12 PRIORY WHARF
13 PRIORY CT
14 BIRCHERLEY CT
15 THE MALTHOUSE
16 WARREN PL

17 PROVIDENCE PL
18 BLUECOATS CT
19 CHAUNCY CT
20 MITRE CT
21 ST JOHN'S CT

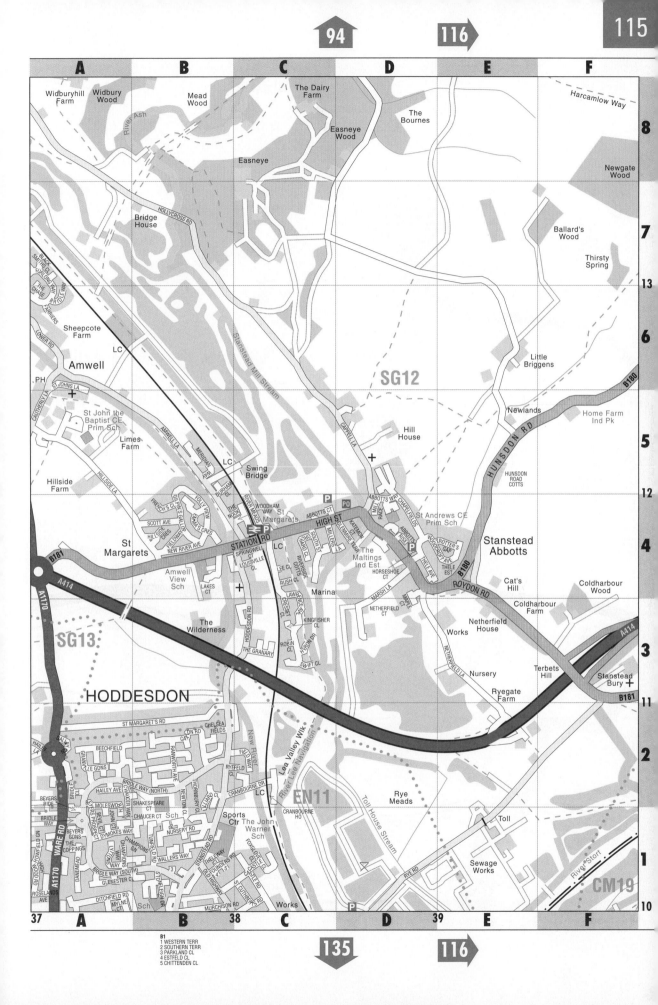

B1
1 WESTERN TERR
2 SOUTHERN TERR
3 PARKLAND CL
4 ESTFELD CL
5 CHITTENDEN CL

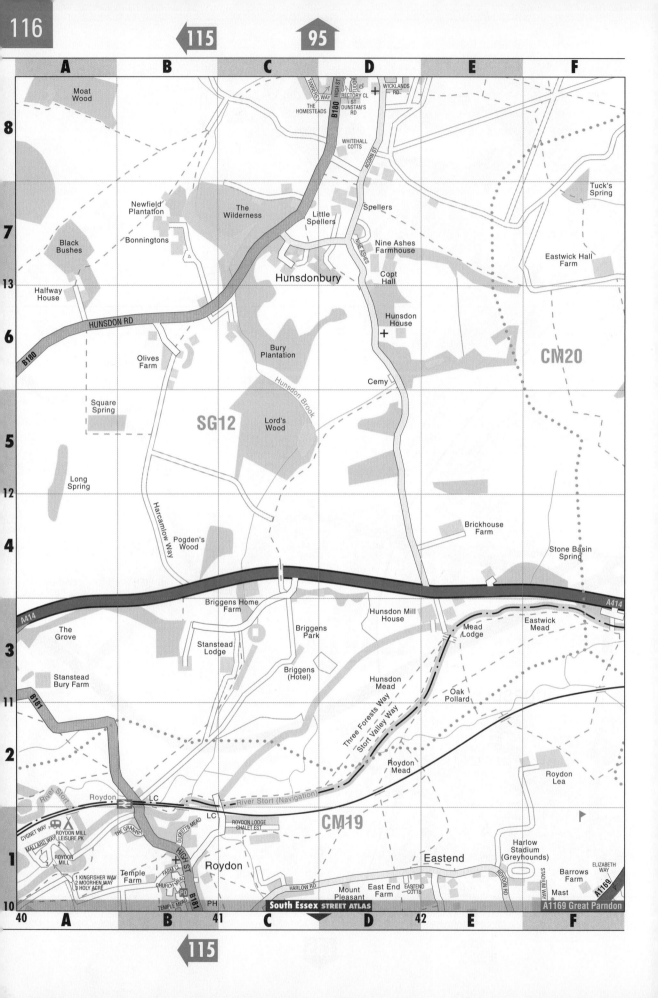

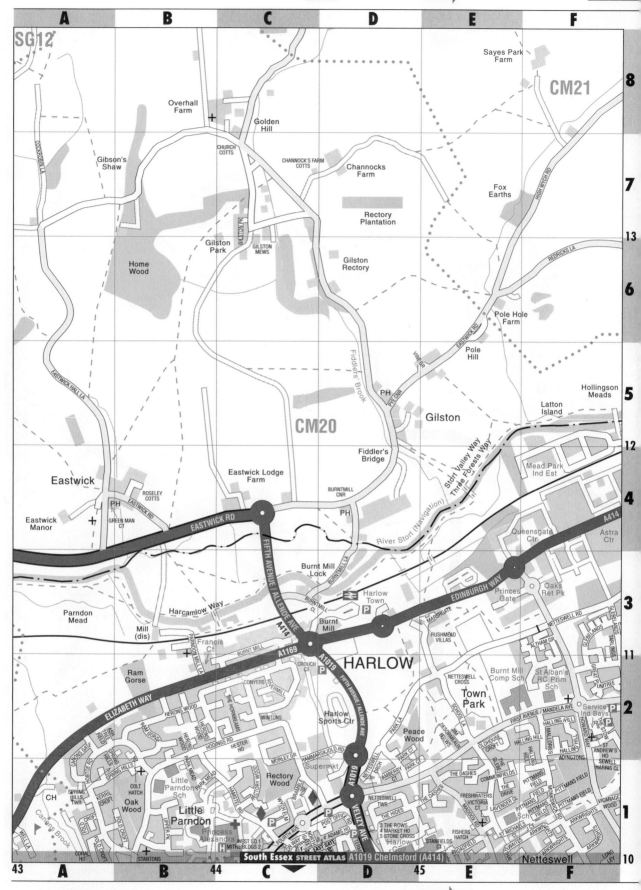

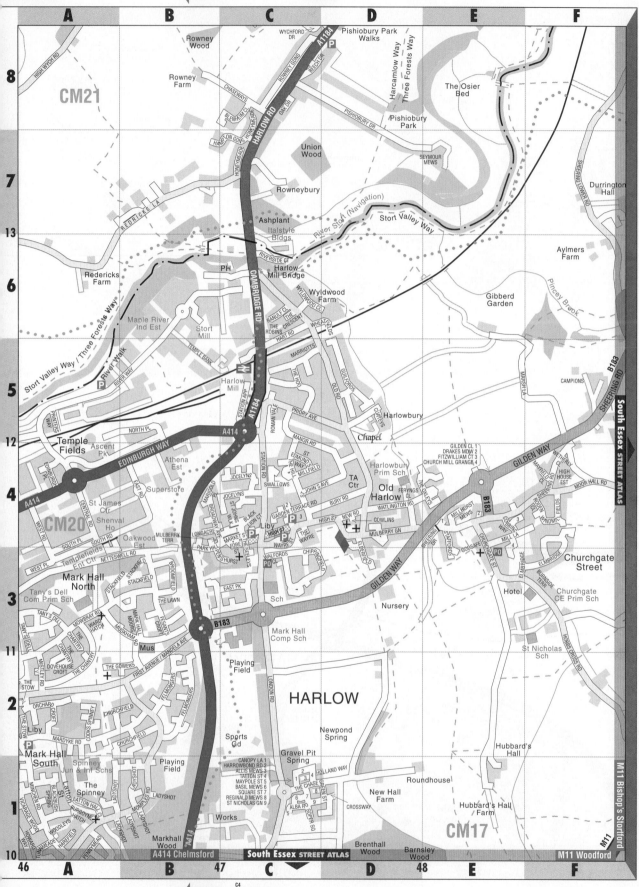

C4
1 DELLFIELD CT
2 CHERRY BLOSSOM CL
3 ROSEMARY CL

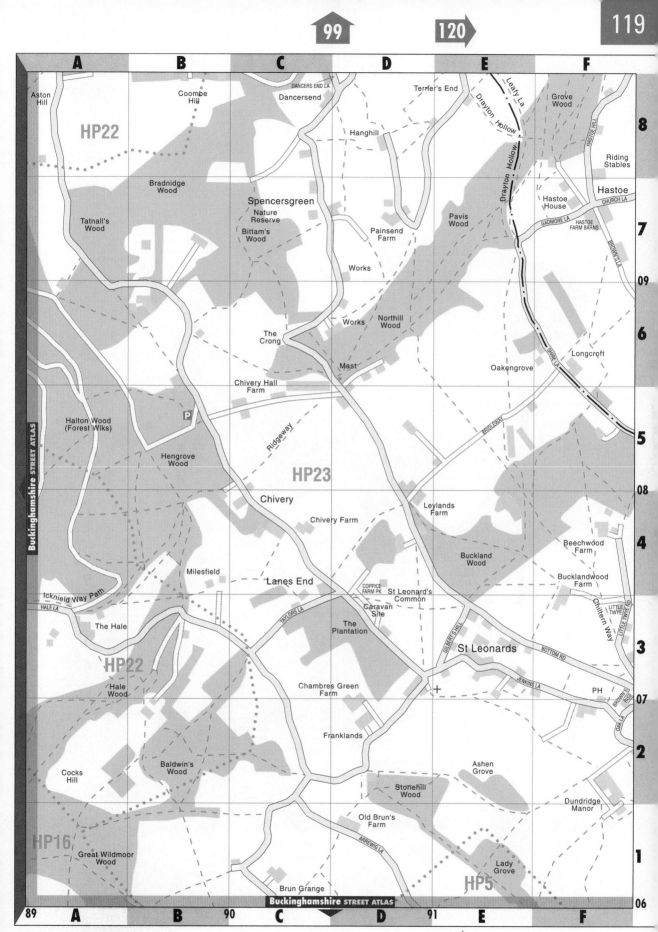

Aston Hill

HP22

Coombe Hill

DANCERS END LA

Dancersend

Terrier's End

Leafy La

Drayton Hollow

Grove Wood

8

Bradnidge Wood

Hanghill

Drayton Hollow

Riding Stables

Hastoe

Tatnall's Wood

Spencersgreen

Nature Reserve

Painsend Farm

Pavis Wood

Hastoe House

CHURCH LA

7

Bittam's Wood

GADMORE LA

HASTOE FARM BARNS

BROWN'S LA

Works

09

Works

Northill Wood

SHIRE LA

Longcroft

6

The Crong

Works

Mast

Oakengrove

Chivery Hall Farm

P

Ridgeway

BRIDLEWAY

5

Halton Wood (Forest Wlks)

Hengrove Wood

HP23

08

Chivery

Leylands Farm

Chivery Farm

Beechwood Farm

4

Milesfield

Lanes End

Buckland Wood

Bucklandwood Farm

Icknield Way Path

HALE LA

COPPICE FARM PK

St Leonard's Common

LITTLE TWYE RD

Chiltern Way

LITTLE TWYE

The Hale

Caravan Site

GILBERT'S HILL

St Leonards

BOTTOM RD

PH

3

HP22

TAYLORS LA

The Plantation

JENKINS LA

BROWN'S RISE

OAK LA

07

Hale Wood

Chambres Green Farm

+

Franklands

Cocks Hill

Baldwin's Wood

Ashen Grove

2

Stonehill Wood

Dundridge Manor

HP16

Old Brun's Farm

ARREWIG LA

1

Great Wildmoor Wood

Lady Grove

HP5

Brun Grange

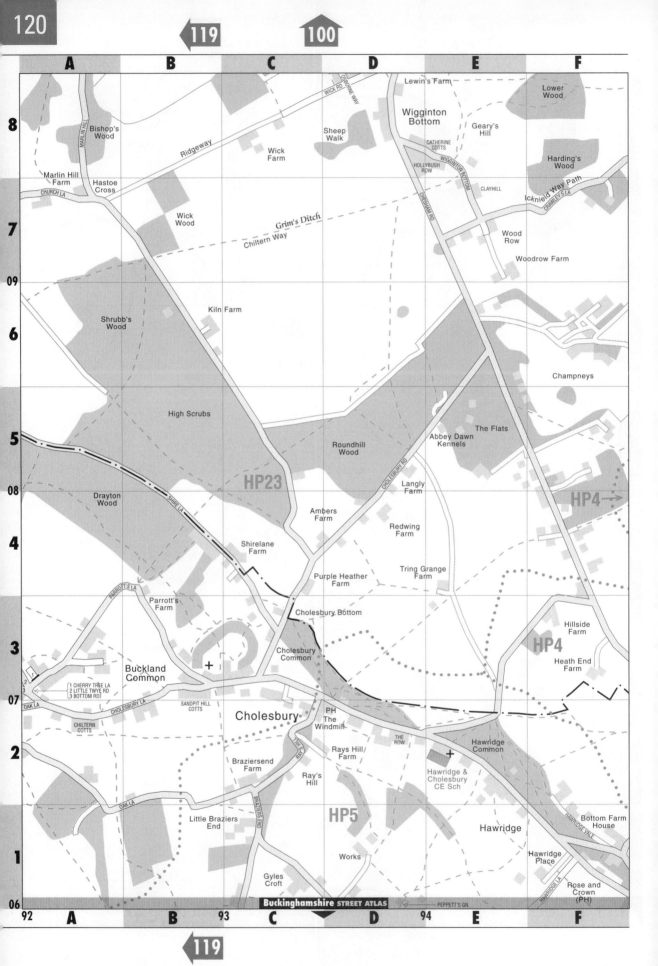

A B C D E F

8

7

09

6

5

08

4

3

07

2

1

06

92 A B 93 C D 94 E F

Marlin Hill Farm
Bishop's Wood
CHURCH LA
MARLIN HILL
Hastoe Cross
Ridgeway
WICK RD
OSBORNE WAY
Lewin's Farm
Wigginton Bottom
Lower Wood
Geary's Hill
CATHERINE COTTS
Harding's Wood
HOLLYBUSH RDW
WIGGINTON BOTTOM
Clayhill
CHESHAM RD
Icknield Way Path
CRAWLEY'S LA
Wick Farm
Sheep Walk
Wick Wood
Grim's Ditch
Chiltern Way
Wood Row
Woodrow Farm
Kiln Farm
Shrubb's Wood
Champneys
High Scrubs
Roundhill Wood
Abbey Dawn Kennels
The Flats
HP23
Drayton Wood
SHIRE LA
Ambers Farm
Langly Farm
Redwing Farm
HP4
Shirelane Farm
Purple Heather Farm
Tring Grange Farm
Parrott's Farm
PARROTT'S LA
Cholesbury Bottom
Cholesbury Common
Hillside Farm
HP4
Heath End Farm
Buckland Common
1 CHERRY TREE LA
2 LITTLE TWYE RD
3 BOTTOM RD
OAK LA
CHOLESBURY LA
SANDPIT HILL COTTS
Cholesbury
PH The Windmill
THE ROW
Hawridge Common
CHILTERN COTTS
TRIL LANE
Braziersend Farm
Rays Hill Farm
Hawridge & Cholesbury CE Sch
OAK LA
Ray's Hill
BRAZIERS END
Little Braziers End
HP5
Hawridge
HAWRIDGE VALE
Bottom Farm House
Works
Hawridge Place
HAWRIDGE LA
Gyles Croft
Rose and Crown (PH)

PEPPETT'S GN

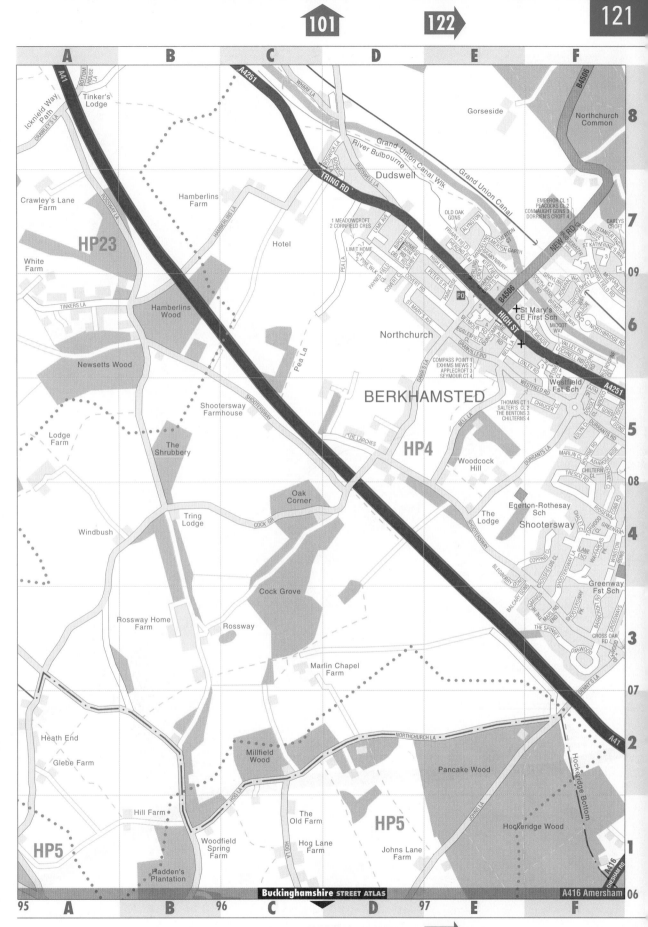

A B C D E F

8

7

09

6

5

08

4

3

07

2

1

06

Icknield Way Path
A41
Bottom House La
Tinker's Lodge
Crawley's Lane Farm
HP23
White Farm
TINKERS LA
CRAWLEY'S LA
ROSSWAY LA
Hamberlins Farm
Hamberlins Wood
HAMBERLINS LA
Newsetts Wood
Lodge Farm
Windbush
The Shrubbery
Shootersway Farmhouse
SHOOTERSWAY
Tring Lodge
Rossway Home Farm
Rossway
COCK GR
Cock Grove
Oak Corner
Heath End
Glebe Farm
Hill Farm
HP5
Hadden's Plantation
Woodfield Spring Farm
HOG LA
Millfield Wood
The Old Farm
HOG LA
Hog Lane Farm
Marlin Chapel Farm
NORTHCHURCH LA
HP5
Johns Lane Farm
JOHNS LA
Pancake Wood
Hockeridge Wood
Hockeridge Bottom
A41
A416
CHESHAM RD
A416 Amersham

A4251
WHARF LA
Grand Union Canal Wlk
River Bulbourne
Dudswell
TRING RD
Grand Union Canal
Hotel
Gorseside
Northchurch Common
B4506
EMPEROR CL 1
PEACOCKS CL 2
CONNAUGHT GDNS 3
DORRIEN'S CROFT 4
NEW RD
CAREYS CROFT
STANIER RD
CREW CURVE
ST KATHERINE'S WAY
LYME AVE
Old Oak Gdns
ALYNGTON
FRIARS FIELD
HERONS ELM
1 MEADOWCROFT
2 CORNFIELD CRES
LIMIT HOME PK
PINE WLK
PAYNES FIELD
COVERT RD
COVERT RD
PARK RISE
ST MARY'S AVE
PETER'S PL
P.O
HIGH ST
B4506
St Mary's CE First Sch
SOUTH BANK
GRAYLING RD
ADMIRAL WAY
BRISTONE DR
NORTHBRIDGE RD
SPRINGFIELD RD
MORTAIN DR
Northchurch
DARR'S LA
EGGLESHELD
GRANVILLE RD
BELL LA
MICDOT WAY
THE HEADS
VALLEY RD
LOCHNELL RD
BOURNE
LOXLEY RD
COMPASS POINT 1
EXHIMS MEWS 2
APPLECROFT 3
SEYMOUR CT 4
BERKHAMSTED
WESTFIELD RD
Westfield Fst Sch
A4251
THOMAS CT 2
SALTER'S CL 2
THE BENTONS 3
CHILTERNS 4
CHAUCER
DORSET CL
GONVILLE RD
DURRANT'S RD
HP4
THE LARCHES
Woodcock Hill
BELL LA
DURRANT'S LA
MARLIN CL
ASHLYNS RD
CHILTERN CL
TRESCO RD
EDLYN CL
KITSBURY RD
RAVENS CL
The Lodge
SHOOTERSWAY
Egerton-Rothesay Sch
Shootersway
RIDGEWAY
COBB RD
CHALET CL
TORWOOD
GREENWAY
WINSTON
Greenway Fst Sch
BLEGBERRY GDNS
CROSSFIELDS CL
SHOOTERSWAY LA
LANE END
WATERSIDE PK
SMITHS
MARLINS
THE SPINEY
OAKWOOD
CROSS OAK RD
SHOOTERSWAY
CROSSWAYS
BARCROFT
DENNY'S LA

Buckinghamshire STREET ATLAS

95 96 97

A B C D E F

8 Northchurch Farm
Berkhamsted Common
Hertfordshire Way

7 Well Farm
CAREYS CROFT

09 1 ST KATHERINE'S WAY
2 MORTAIN DR
3 MONTGOMERIE CL
4 BECKETS SQ
CH
WHYBROW GDNS
FARMERY CT
PRIESTLAND GDNS
BRITWELL DR
LADY COOPER CT
THE MANSION
RAVENS CT

Bridgewater Mid Sch
Castle Hill Farm
CASTLE HILL CT

6 **BERKHAMSTED**
NORTHBRIDGE RD
A4251
River Park Ind Est
CASTLE HILL AVE
BROWNLOW RD
HEADLANDS DR
BENSTONE HILL
Gutteridge Farm
THE COMMON
BRACKENHILL
LANRICK COPSE

5 GOSSOM'S END
SP Ct
VICTORY RD
Berkhamsted Castle
HP4
Berkhamsted Castle
GRAVEL PATH
GILPIN'S RIDE
MEADOW
HUNTERS PK

08 Nightingale Lodge
PARK VIEW
Berkhamsted Sch
Berkhamsted Castle
WHITEHILL
MILL FIELD
IVY HOUSE LA
GRANTHAM MEWS
ELLESMERE RD
THE CEDARS

4 St Thomas More RC Prim Sch
Liby
C Ctr
Victoria CE Fst Sch
FROST HO
Cemy
WATERSIDE
GEORGE ST
OLD MILL GDNS
CANAL FIELDS
BANK MILL
Grand Union Canal Wlk

3 Greenway Fst Sch
KINGS RD
Berkhamsted Collegiate Sch
Cemy
Swing Gate Fst Sch
CURTIS WAY
HILLSIDE GDNS
CEDAR RD
HALL PK
LONDON RD
River Bulbourne
Bankmill Bridge
BLUE BEGGARS LA
A4251

07 SHOOTERSWAY
OLD MEADOW
Ashlyns Sch
Coram Cl
BRIAR WAY
UPPER HALL PK
HALL PARK HILL
FIELDWAY
GARDEN FIELD LA

2 National Film Archive
Kingshill
Cemy
KINGSHILL WAY
A416
Ashlyn's Hall
The Thomas Coram CE Mid Sch
SWING GATE LA
Long Green
A41

1 A416 CHESHAM RD
Haresfoot Sch
Sandpit Green
Bottom Farm
HP1
A41

06
98 A 99 B C 00 D E F

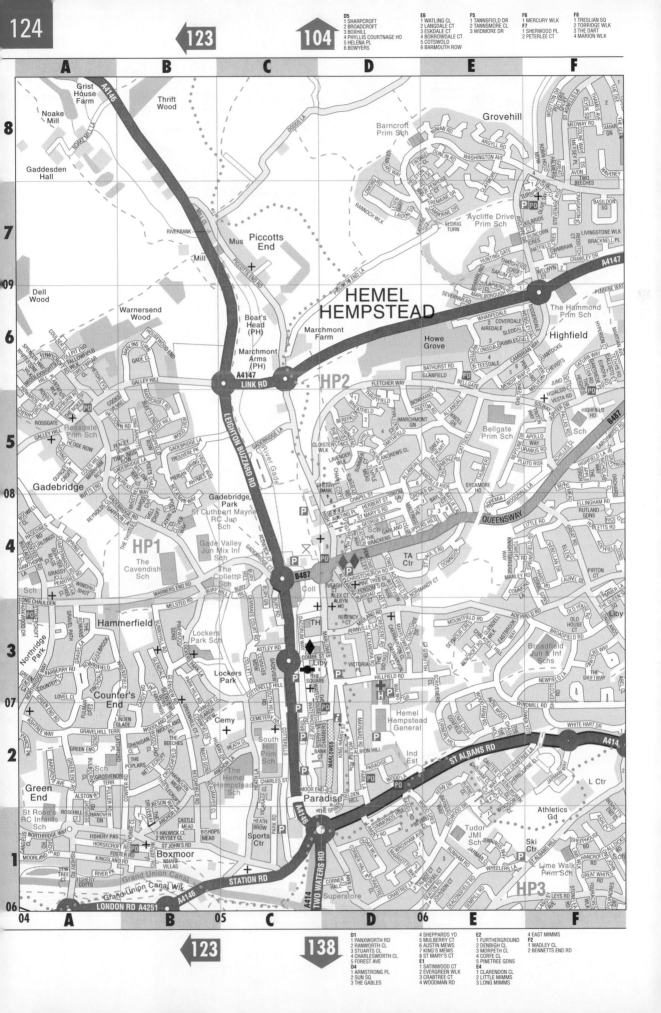

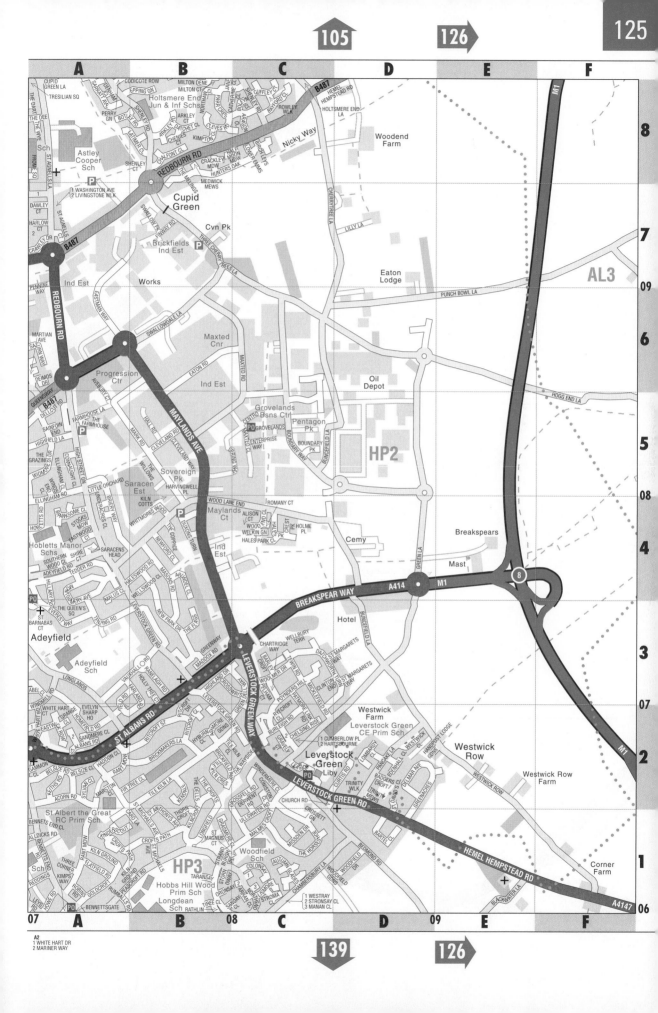

A  B  C  D  E  F

8

7

09

6

5

08

4

**HP2**

3

07

2

1

**HP3**

A4147

06

10  A  B  11  C  D  12  E  F

WILL FARM LA

Hill Farm

New Jerome Cottage

PUNCH BOWL LA

Baker's Farm

Southend Farm

Hogg End

Beech Hyde

HOGG END LA

Old Jeromes

Butlers Farm

Kettlewell's Farm

Kentish Wood

Windmillhill Wood

The Vistas

Bruce's Plantation

Old Gorhambury House (remains of)

Brickkiln Wood

Temple Cottage

Temple Wood

Stud Cottages

BECHTREE LA

Square Wood

Westwick Hall

Hill End Farm

AL3

Gorhambury

Shepherds Cottages

Cypress Wood

Lord Bacon's Mount

Prae Wood

Maynes Farm

A5183

REDBOURN RD

Shafford Farm

Whitehedge Spring

SHAFFORD COTTS

Bow Bridge

River Ver

A5183

Hertfordshire Way

Prae Wood House

Praewood Farm

A4147

M1

M10

⑦

M1

HEMEL HEMPSTEAD RD

AL2

REDMOND LA

LINDUM PL
APPLETINE CT
BEVUM CT
MAINE GYNE
GAMMAN CT
GATE
CAVIAN CT
HADRIAN CT

POTTERSROUGH LA

OKNIC CT

AKEMAN CL 1
MEAUTYS 2

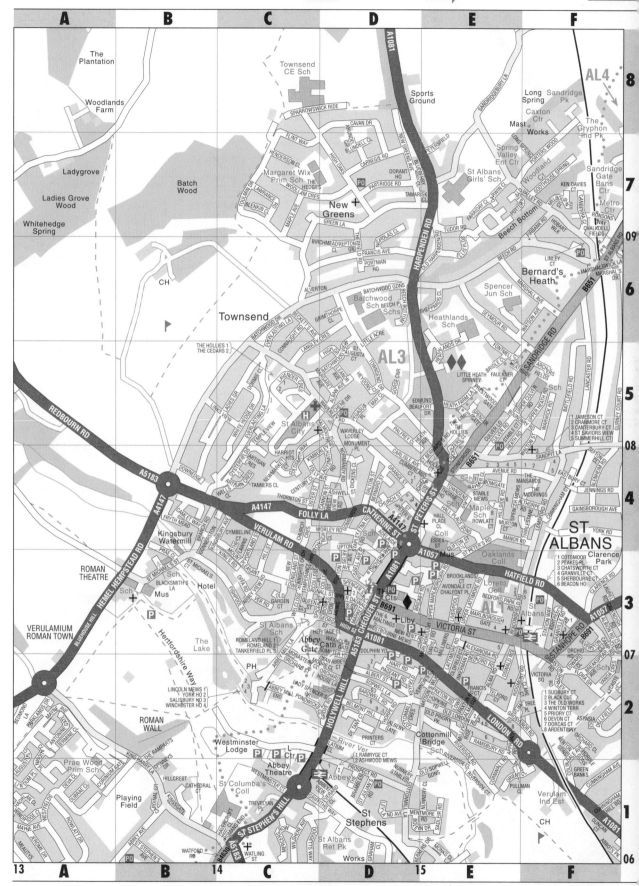

ST ALBANS

AL4

AL1

AL3

129
110

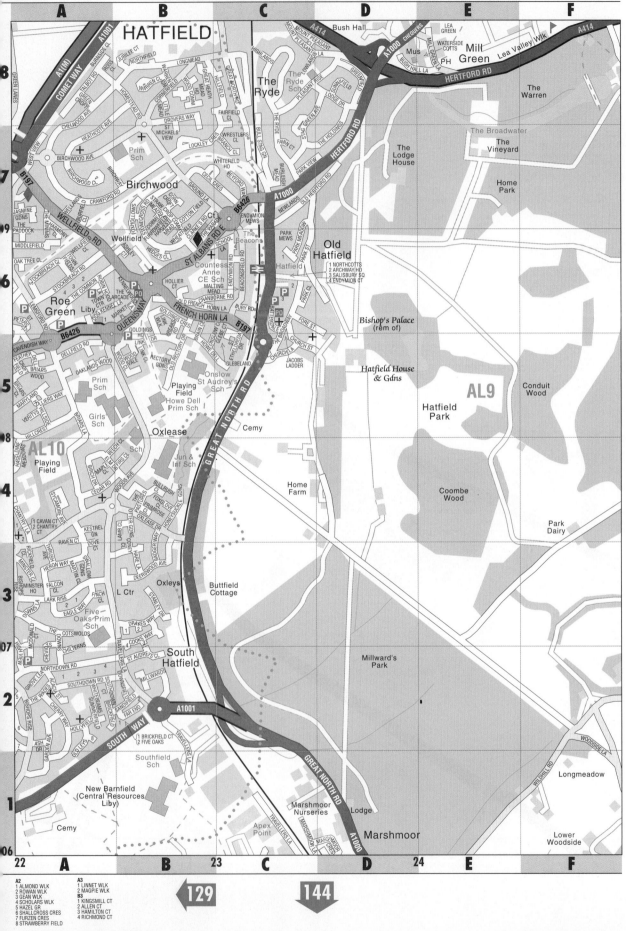

129
144

**A2**
1 ALMOND WLK
2 ROWAN WLK
3 GEAN WLK
4 SCHOLARS WLK
5 HAZEL GR
6 SHALLCROSS CRES
7 FURZEN CRES
8 STRAWBERRY FIELD

**A3**
1 LINNET WLK
2 MAGPIE WLK
**B3**
1 KINGSMILL CT
2 ALLEN CT
3 HAMILTON CT
4 RICHMOND CT

Lodge

Hillend Farm

Hillend Cottages

The Furze Field

Pollard Wood

Brickkiln Wood

Wellington Wood

The Roughs

Green St

Woodside

Woodside Place Farm

Brewhouse Farm

WILDHILL RD

Woodside Green

GRUBBS LA

WOODSIDE LA

WESTFIELD

Pope's Pondholes

Pope's Farm

ROSE LA

WEST END LA

Lower Westend Farm

West End

The Candlestick (PH)

Edwards Wood

AL9

Hertfordshire Way

Harefield Wood

Bath Wood

Home Wood

Camfield Place

The Woodman (PH)

Wildhill

KENTISH LA

B158

Larkinshill Grove

Ox Wood

Hanbury Cotts

THE TERRACE

CHURCH COTTS

CHURCH ST

CALTON ST

RECTORY

FORGE COTTS

GLEBE CL

GLEBE COTTS

GLEBE HO.

SCHOOL LA

SCHOOL CL

EAST VIEW

Essendon CE Prim Sch

Rose & Crown (PH)

Essendon

Parsonage

ESSENDON HILL

HIGH RD

Essendonbury Farm

Holwell Manor

HOLWELL LA B1455

B1455

Holwell Bridge

B158

LOW RD

MILLGREEN COTTS

THE BUNGALOWS

Essendon Place

Essendon Place Farm

Bedwell Park

CH

Belvedere Farm

Duncan's Wood

Panther's Wood

CUMCUM HILL

Hoppett's Wood

HORNBEAM LA

Warrenwood Park

BERKHAMSTED LA

Bedwell Lodge Farm

CUCUMBER LA

Whitbury Wood

Nine Acre Wood

8
7
09
6
5
08
4
3
07
2
1
06

25    26    27
A    B    C    D    E    F

A B C D E F

8

7

09

6

5

08

4

3

07

2

1

06

28 A B 29 C D 30 E F

B158

Water Hall Farm

Spring Wood

Sandpit Danes

Broadgreen Wood

BROAD GREEN WOOD

BROAD GN

River Lea or Lee

LOWER HATFIELD RD

B158

Howe Green

BEDWELL AVE

Kennel Hall Farm

Longacre Wood

Bunkers Hill

WATERHALL COTTS

Pollard Wood

Stocking La

Bayford Hall Farm

Bayford Hall

BAYFORD LA

WELL RDN

Ashfield Farm

Chain Wlk

Culver Wood

Culverwood House

Culverwood Farm

Great Stockings

Chain Wlk

STOCKINGS LA

Bayford

WILLOW CNR

CH

Furze Field

Breach La

ROBINS NEST HILL

Manor House

SG13

Twr

Chain Wlk

Bayford Wood

Caravan Pk

Bayford CE Prim Sch

Bayford Grange

Bayford House

AL9

Danes Farm

ORCHARD CL

CHURCH RD

CHURCH CL

GODDARDS CL

Five Horse Shoes (PH)

Little Berkhamsted

The Gage

BUCKS ALLEY

ASHENDENE RD

Berkhamsted Lane Plantation

LITTLE BERKHAMSTED LA

Chain Wlk

Bush Farm

Buck's Alley Wood

Bucks Farm

Bell's Wood

The Wilderness

WHITE STUBBS LA

Chain Wlk

The Beehive (PH)

Epping Green

Woodcock Lodge

HENDERSON PL

Mast

Wr Twr

Epping Green Farm

Ashendene Farm

Ashen Grove

Calves Grove

CUCUMBER LA

Woodcock Lodge Farm

Birch Wood

Chain Wlk

TYLERS CSWY

Tylers Causeway

Chain Wlk

133 114

A B C D E F

8

Mast

Elbowlane Farm

The Woodman (PH)

Woollensbrook

HERTFORD RD

Cutthroat La

A10

HIGH MORRICE... AVE
ROSELANDS AVE
BRISCOE COLLEGE CT
BRISCOE RD
APPLEFORD'S CL
WEST HILL RD
B1197

7

SG13

Box Wood

Dalmonds

Dalmond's Wood

Wr Twr

Goose Green

The Huntsman (PH)

Lanthorn's Wood

Bramble La

Woollers Brook

Westfield Com Prim Sch

HILL SIDE
FENLAND CL
SAFFRON CL
WESTFIELD RD
NORRIS RISE
WATERSCROFT RD
A10

09

MANGROVE LA

ELBOW LA

EN11

High Leigh Farm

BOX LA

High Leigh

KENNEDY AVE
BURNSIDE
LANGTON HOUSE
WHITEHANDS CL
A10

6

Highfield Farm

LORD ST

ROSEHILL
ROSEHILL CL
FOXTON RD
BEECH HO
Beech Wlk
BEECH HO

5

Highfield Wood

Red Hills

Hoddesdonpark Wood

Hoddesdon Lodge

Spital Brook

Recn Gd

08

Danemead Wood

COCK LA

Sheredes Sch

Sheredes Prim Sch

THE AVENUE

WARNERS AVE
SHEREDES DR
BENFORD RD
ANTHONY CL
LONG GROVE
CRABTREE WLK
PARKWOOD CL
THE SPINNEY
ST DAVID'S DR

4

P

Nursery Grove

Chestnut Grove

GLENWOOD
THE ROWANS
BUTTON CL
STRATFIELD DR
PARK LA
ST AUGUSTINES DR
GARDEN CT
SPRINGFIELDS
A1170

3

Great Grove

BROXBOURNEBURY MEWS

Broxbournebury Mansion
CH

Icehouse Grove

ALAMEIN CL
SWORD CL
GOLD CL
SHERIDEN WLK
CHINDIT CL
CARNABY RD
OXFORD CL
NORRIS GR
MANDEVILLE CL
BASSINGBOURNE CL
THE PRECINCT
BOURNE CL
ST AUGUSTINES RD
HIGH RD
PO
RAVENSCROFT
GROSVENOR RD
B194
STATION RD
P

Broxbourne

07

PEMBRIDGE LA

Edgewood Farm

EN10

PULHAM AVE
HICKMAN CL
ALLARD WAY
BORRELL WE
COPTHORNE
CHRISTIE
SAWLEY CRES
ELPPIN CT
RICHMOND RD
CHURCH VIEW
MILL LA

Lower White Stubbs

WOOD HOUSE LA

Baas Hill

BAAS HILL

GRAHAM AVE
RAMSAY CL
ROYCE
GRENVILLE AVE
TRAFALGAR AVE

Sports Gd

2

WHITE STUBBS LA

Cold Hall

SPRING WLK

BAAS HILL

BAAS HILL CL
BADGERS CROFT
HIGHFIELD CL
TUDOR RISE
BEVERLY
BELL LA
BAAS LA
BOLEYN CT
WILLOUGHBY RD
HIPKINS CL

Cozens Grove

The Broxbourne Sch

Broxbourne CE Prim Sch

THE LAWNS
THE REDHOUSE
HIGH ROAD
BROXBOURNE
New River
ASHCROFT CT
WINFORD DR
WINFORD CL

White Stubbs Farm

Carneles Green

CHURCH LA

Baas Manor Farm

COZENS LA W
BRIARLEY CL
CHILWORTH GATE
LICHFIELD
WAR BUCKLERS
CALDECOT WAY
SILVERFIELD
BUSHBY AVE
Ley Park Prim Sch

1

WEST END RD

Tudor Farm

Manor House

Bury Farm

WENTWORTH COTTS

A1170

06

133 148

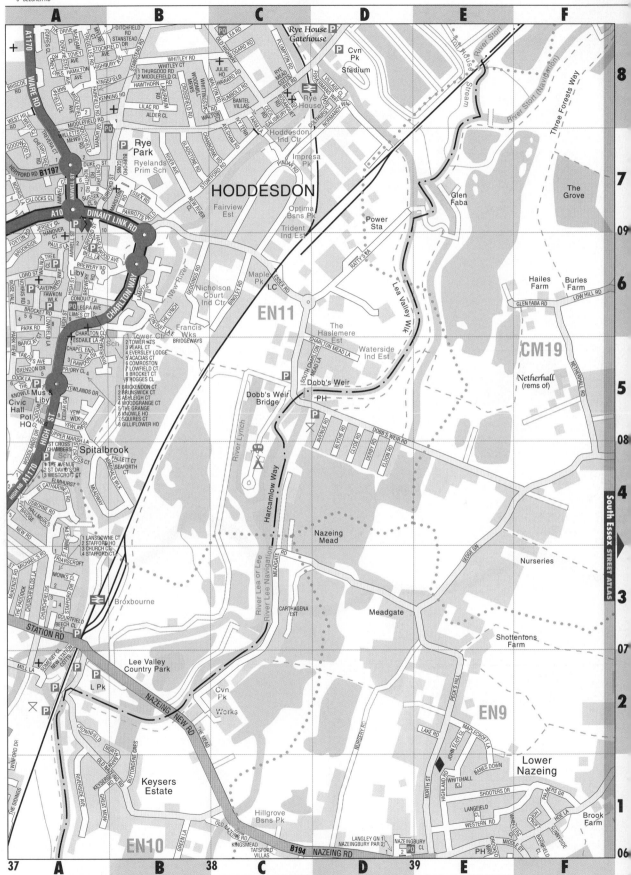

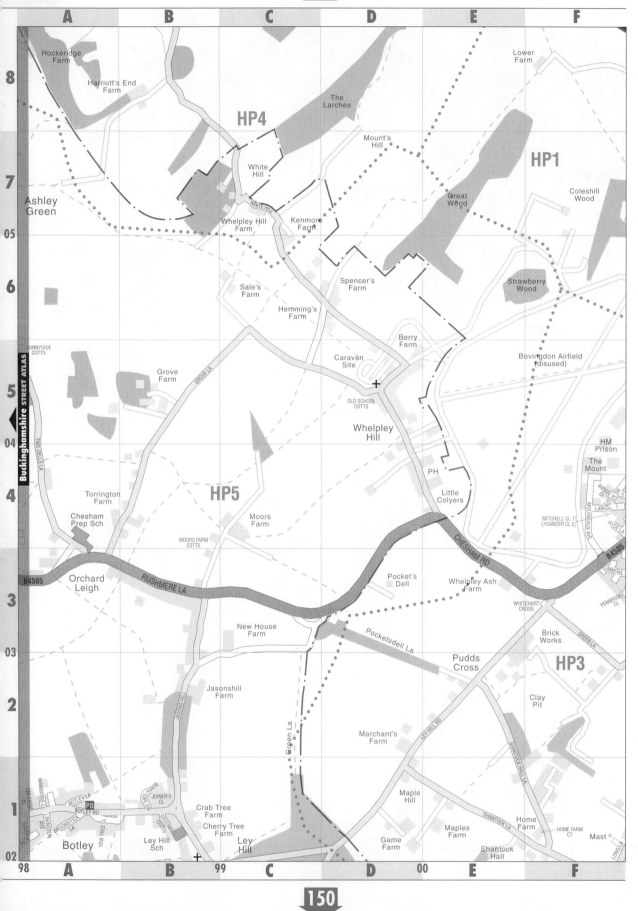

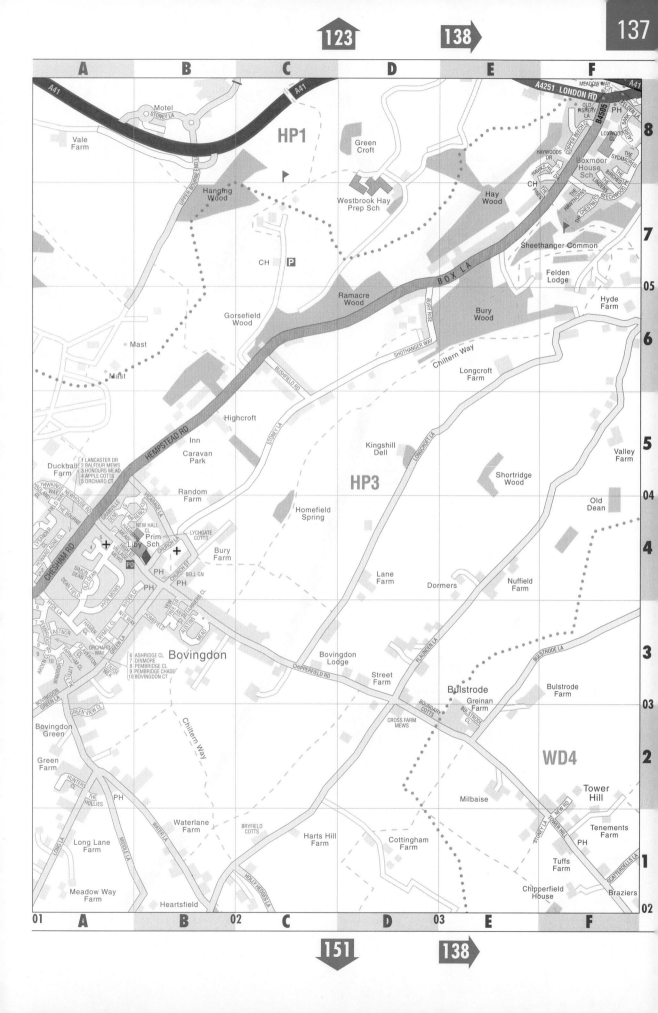

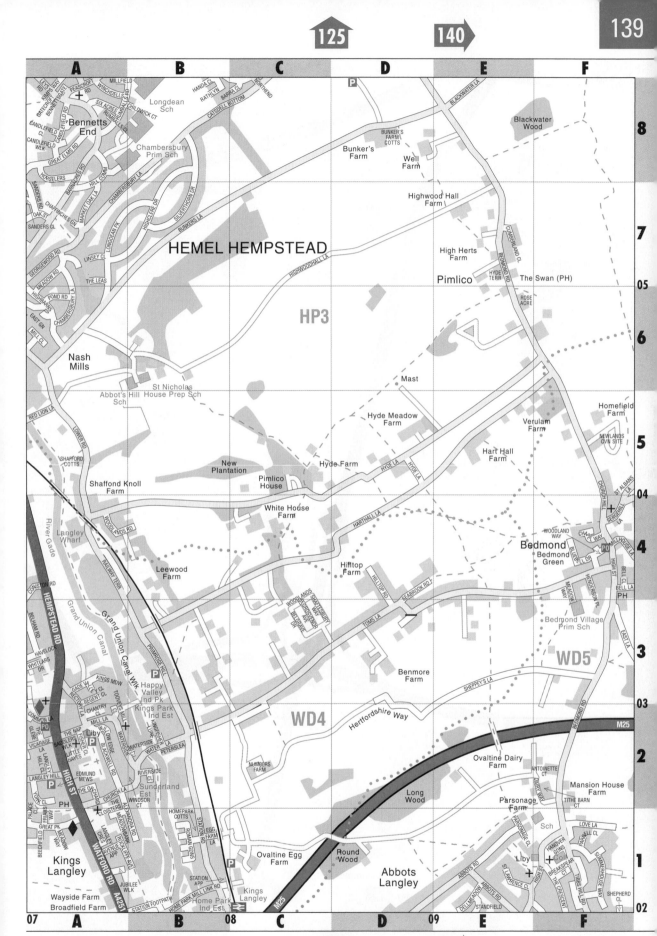

A B C D E F

8
7
05
6
5
04
4
3
03
2
1
02

07 A B 08 C D 09 E F

**HEMEL HEMPSTEAD**

HP3

WD4

WD5

Bennetts End

Longdean Sch

Chambersbury Prim Sch

Bunker's Farm

Bunker's Farm Cotts

Well Farm

Blackwater Wood

Highwood Hall Farm

High Herts Farm

Pimlico

The Swan (PH)

Rose Acre

Nash Mills

St Nicholas

Abbot's Hill House Prep Sch

Mast

Hyde Meadow Farm

Verulam Farm

Homefield Farm

Newlands Cvn Site

Hart Hall Farm

Shaffond Knoll Farm

New Plantation

Hyde Farm

St Albans

Pimlico House

White House Farm

Woodland Way

Bedmond

Bedmond Green

Leewood Farm

Hilltop Farm

Harthall La

PH

Langley Wharf

River Gade

Grand Union Canal

Grand Union Canal Wlk

Hempstead Rd

Benmore Farm

Bedmond Village Prim Sch

Happy Valley Ind Pk

Kings Park Ind Est

Liby

Hertfordshire Way

Ovaltine Dairy Farm

M25

Antoinette Ct

Mansion House Farm

Tithe Barn

Sunderland Est

Numbers Farm

Long Wood

Parsonage Farm

Sch

Liby

Coll

Kings Langley

Homepark Cotts

Ovaltine Egg Farm

Round Wood

Abbots Langley

Wayside Farm
Broadfield Farm

Kings Langley Ind Est

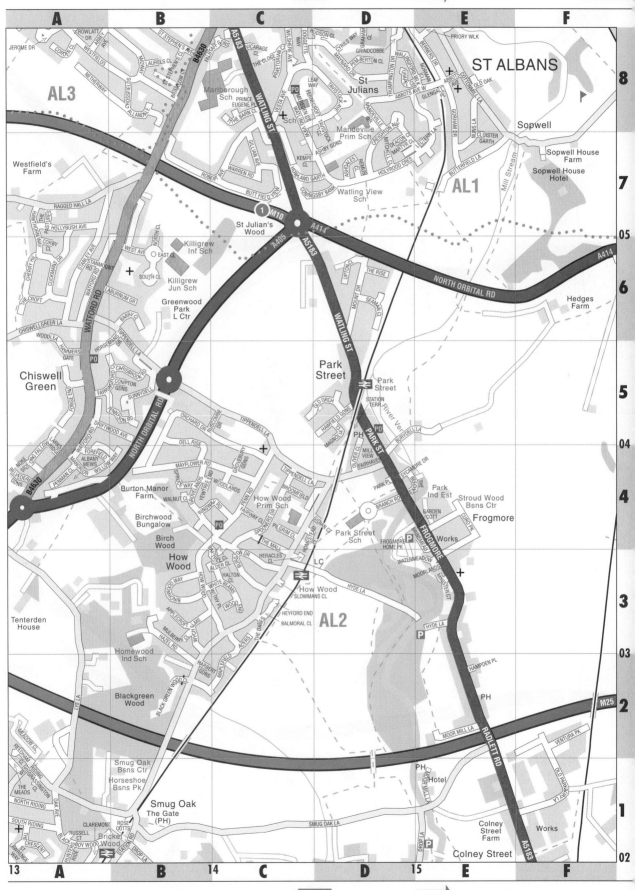

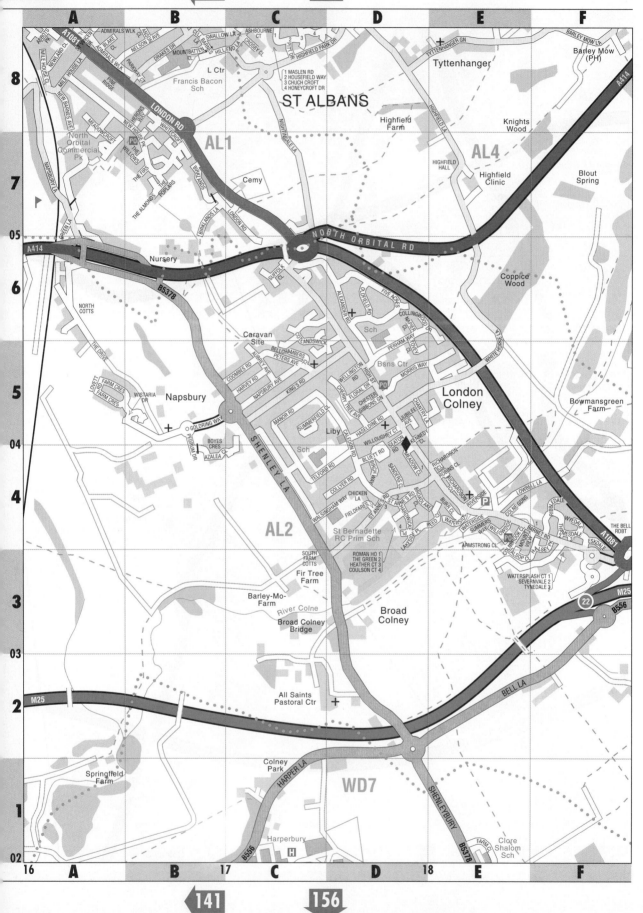

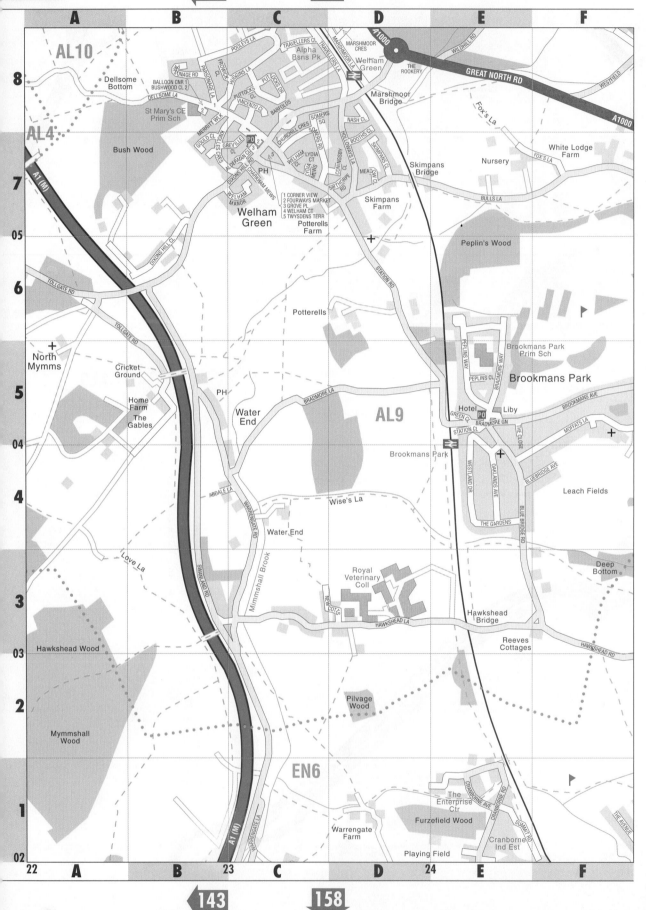

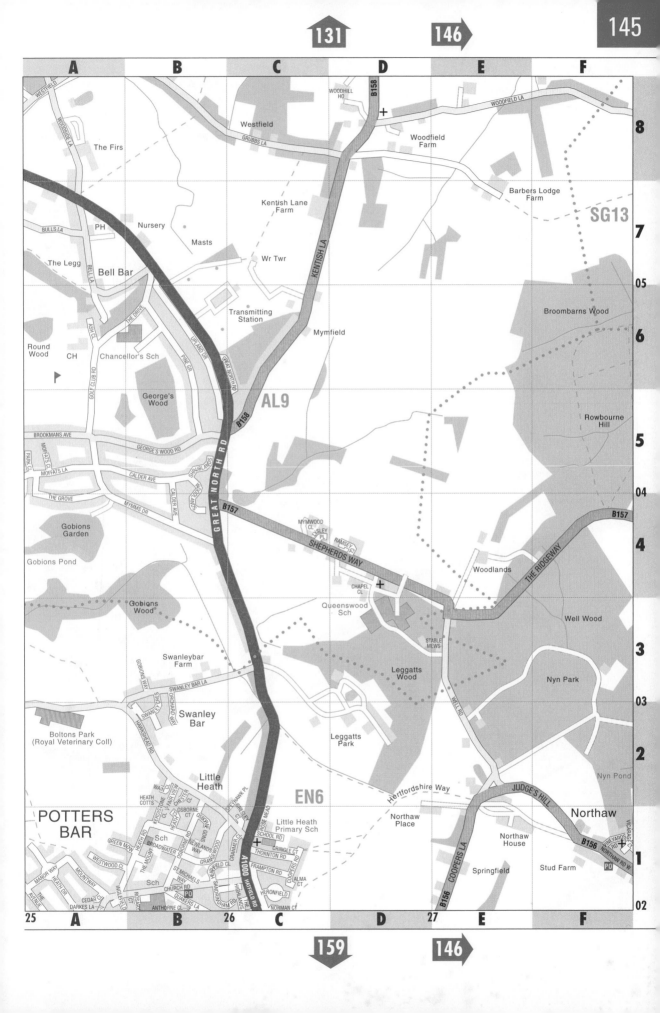

145
132

A B C D E F

8

Birchwood Cottages
CUCUMBER LA
WOODFIELD LA
TYLERS CSWY
Coldharbour Farm

Ponsfall Farm

The Warren
HOME FARM COTTS
Home Farm
Chain Wlk

Hertfordshire Way

NEWGATE ST
Ponsbourne House

7

Hell Wood

SG13

New Park Farm
NEW PARK RD
Home Farm

CH
Ponsbourne Park

Ponsbourne St Mary's CE Prim Sch
PO
PH
Newgate Street

05

Coldharbour Plantation

NEWGATE STREET VILLAGE

Tolmers Park Farm

Newgate Street Bridge

DARNICLE HILL

6

Chain Wlk

TOLMERS MEWS

EN 7

Nature Trail

Justice Hill

Great Wood Country Park
Grimes Brook

Grimes Bottom

Postern Gate

Postern Bridge

CARBONE HILL

Tolmers

5

County School Camp

Visitor Ctr
P
The Cottage

TOLMERS RD

Home Wood

04

B157

THE RIDGEWAY

Carbone Bottom
Bradgate

FARM CL

BROXSIDE CRES

HOMEWOOD AVENUE

Cuffley Brook

4

HOMEWOOD LA

EN6

Warwick Ave
WARWICK CL

HANYARDS END
HIGHFIELD
HILL RISE
HILL PRIDGE
HIGH BRIDGE
ROBINS WAY
ORCHARD CL
TOLMERS
HILL LEYS
THRUSH LA
STARLING LA

Nyn Manor Farm

BRADGATE CL

HANYARDS LA
ROWBOURNE PL
SPRINGS
LEEFE WAY
LAND AVE
TOLMERS RD
FOX'S LA

Cuffley

3

Thornton's Farm

SUTHERLAND WAY
THE DRIVEWAY

EAST RIDGEWAY
KINGSMEAD
MANN LA
OAK LA

03

High Willows

CROXFIELD CRES
BACONS DR
LAUREL CT
Cuffley
PLOUGH HILL
B151
Liby
P
B156

VINEYARDS HILL

Cuffley Hills Farm

STATION RD
SOPERS RD
P

2

Vineyard Bridge

Hertfordshire Way

Hemps Hill

KING JAMES AVE
CHURCH CL
LAMBS CL
THEOBALD'S CL

B156
CUFFLEY HILL

The Vineyard

KINGSWELL RIDE
KINGSWAY
SOUTH DR
GREENFIELDS

NORTHAW RD E

THE MEADWAY

Chain Wlk

Northaw CE Prim Sch

Chain Wlk

1

Northaw
CHURCH LA

Waterworks Cottages

Cuffley Sch

VICARAGE CL
PARK RD
B156
NORTHAW RD W
HOOK LA

Wells Farm
B156

02

28 A B 29 C D 30 E F

E5
1 SOUTHVIEW CL
2 THE POPLARS
3 HAZEL CL
4 WHITEBEAM CL
5 NUTWOOD GDNS
6 FRIERN CL
7 CONY CL

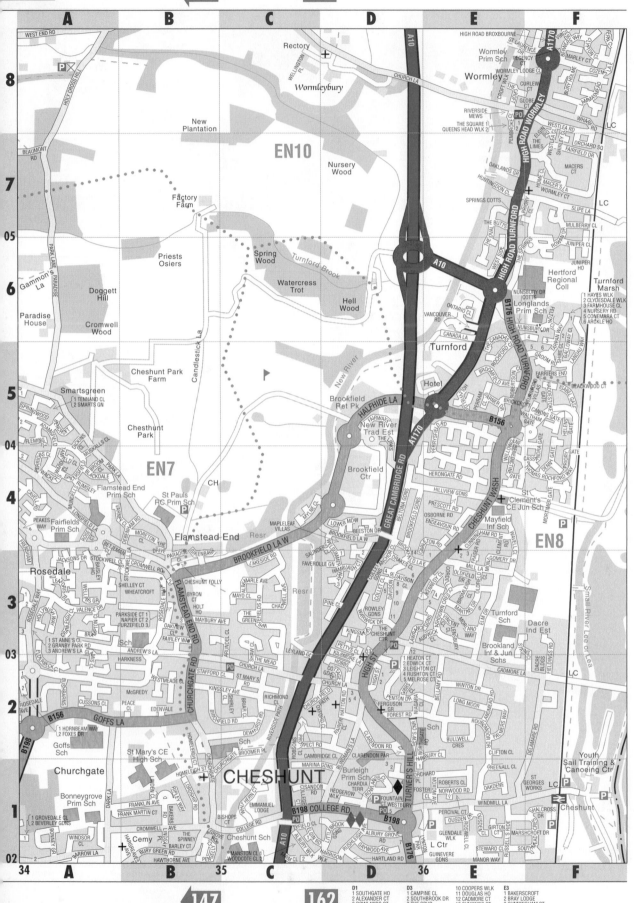

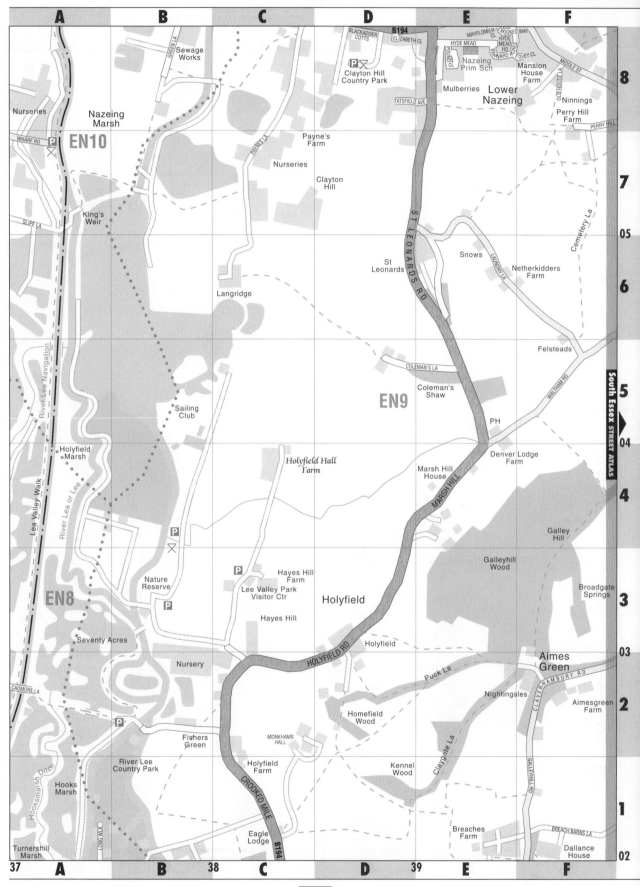

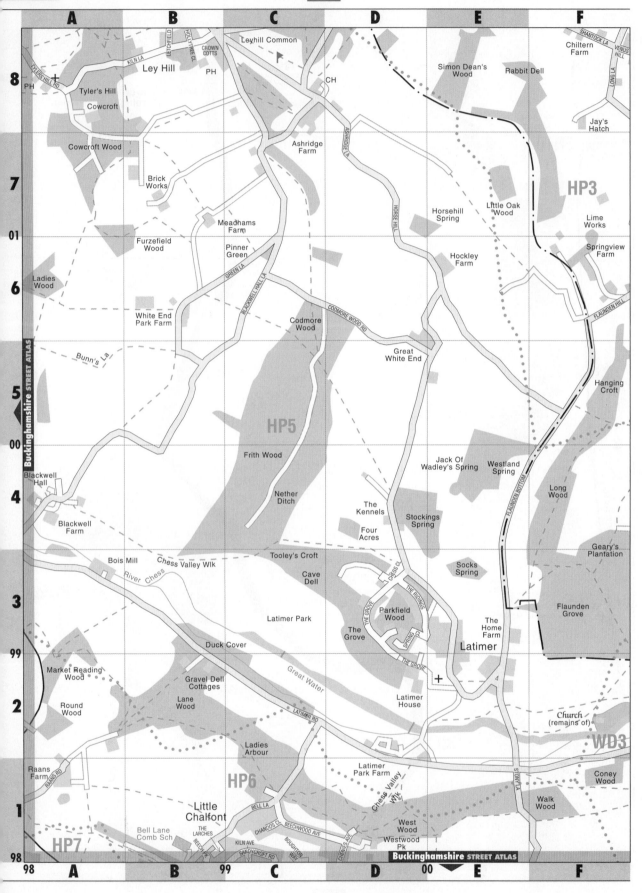

A B C D E F

**8**

PH
Tyler's Hill
Cowcroft
Cowcroft Wood

Ley Hill
PH

Leyhill Common
CH

Simon Dean's Wood
Rabbit Dell

Chiltern Farm
VENUS HILL

SHANTOCK LA
LONG LA
Jay's Hatch

KILN LA
LETCHFIELD
HOLLYTREE CL
CROWN COTTS

**7**

Brick Works

Ashridge Farm

ASHRIDGE LA

Horsehill Spring

Little Oak Wood

HP3

Lime Works

**01**

Furzefield Wood

Meadhams Farm

Pinner Green

Hockley Farm

Springview Farm

**6**

Ladies Wood

White End Park Farm

GREEN LA

BLACKWELL HALL LA

Codmore Wood

CODMORE WOOD RD

HORSE HILL

Great White End

FLAUNDEN HILL

Hanging Croft

**5**

Bunn's La

HP5

Jack Of Wadley's Spring

Westland Spring

FLAUNDEN BOTTOM

Long Wood

**00**

Frith Wood

**4**

Blackwell Hall

Blackwell Farm

Nether Ditch

The Kennels

Four Acres

Stockings Spring

Geary's Plantation

**3**

Bois Mill

Chess Valley Wlk

River Chess

Tooley's Croft

Cave Dell

Latimer Park

THE GROVE

THE RIDINGS

CHESS CL

Parkfield Wood

The Grove

SPRING CL

Socks Spring

The Home Farm

Latimer

Flaunden Grove

**99**

Market Reading Wood

Duck Cover

Great Water

THE GROVE

Latimer House

Church (remains of)

**2**

Round Wood

Gravel Dell Cottages

Lane Wood

LATIMER RD

WD3

**1**

Raans Farm

RAANS RD

Ladies Arbour

HP6

Little Chalfont

BELL LA

Chess Valley Wlk

Latimer Park Farm

STORY LA

Walk Wood

Coney Wood

**98**

HP7

Bell Lane Comb Sch

THE LARCHES

BEECH PK

CHANDOS CL

BEECHWOOD AVE

KILN AVE

SANDYCROFT RD

BOUGHTON WAY

CHENIES AVE

West Wood

Westwood Pk

Buckinghamshire STREET ATLAS

98 A 99 B C 99 C D 00 E F

Buckinghamshire STREET ATLAS

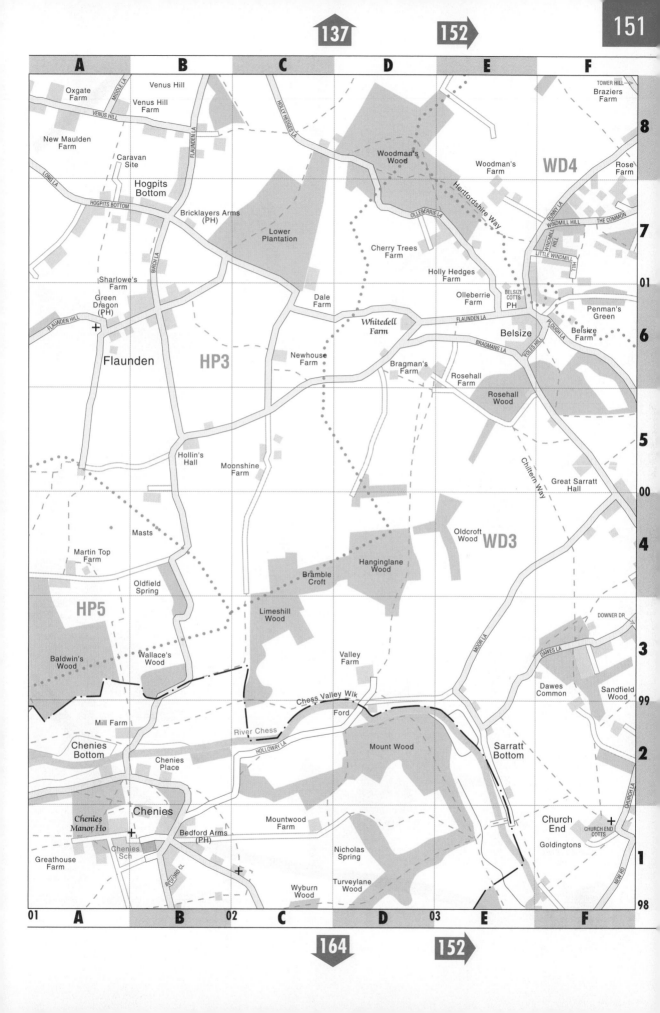

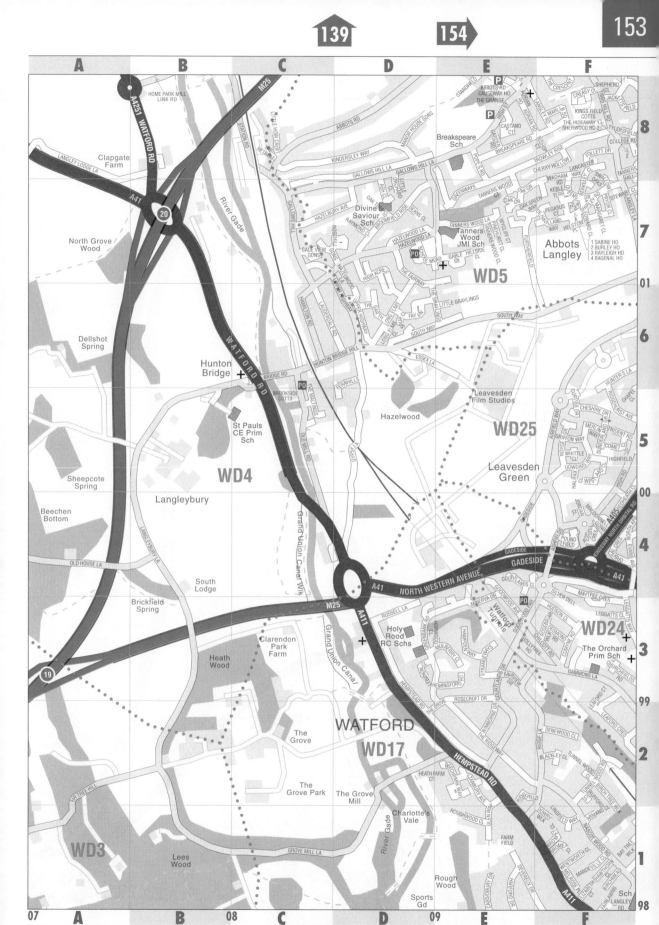

153 140

A B C D E F

**8**

NIGHTINGALE CL
REDWING WLK
LINNET RD
HIGH ELMS
ORIOLE CT
PEACOCK WLK
LEAVESDEN CT
LAPWING WAY

Parmiter's Sch

HIGH ELMS LA
COOPERS MEWS

WD5

COLLEGE RD
MEADOWSIDE
ORCHARD AVE

St Andrews Montessori Prep Sch

Crem

Brookdell Farm

AL2

THE KESTRELS
MORAN CL
ST LAWRENCE WAY
HALIFAX CL
FERNDENE
ASH COPSE
MOUNT PLEASANT LA

**7**

SHACKLETON SPRING
CARDIFF RD
MAGNOLIA AVE
BLENHEIM CL
HURRICANE CT

Woodside

BOUNDARY WAY

Francis Combe Sch & Com Coll

St Michael's RC High Sch

Garston Manor Sch

NORTH ORBITAL RD

TUDOR MANOR GDNS

BUCKNALLS CL
BUCKNALLS LA
AVALON
CRANFIELD DR
LAMONIED DR

Building Research Sta

**01**

Alban Wood Inf Sch

THE BROW
ABBOTSBURY CT

BRIDGER CL

1 GLEBE CT
2 CEDAR CT
3 DEAN CT
4 THE GABLES

Mutchetts Wood

**6**

HAMMER PAR
SHERWOOD CT

GANDERS ASH

Alban Wood Jun Sch

L Ctr

Woodside Playing Fields

**WATFORD**

LYCH GATE

Coates Way JMI Sch

COATES DELL
MUTCHETTS CL
CHICHESTER WAY

Coldharbour Plantation

AL2

The Old Fox (PH)
Munden Spring

**5**

Leavesden Green Sch

LYMINGTON CT
FOXLANDS CL
BADGERS CL

**KINGSWAY NORTH ORBITAL RD**

NORTH APP
HILLINGDON RD
KINGSWOOD RD

**Kingswood**

Kingsway Schs

PERIVALE GDNS
MOSS RD
SHEEPCOT DR
MEDWAY
ROTHER CL

PARK LODGE

BOVIN GDNS

GADDESDEN CRES

PEREGRINE CL
KESTREL CL
OSPREY CL

RAVENSCROFT

**00**

ROSS CLOSE
HARRIS RD
GOODRICH CL

BRIAR RD

BRAMBLE CL
SYCAMORE CL
CYPRESS WLK
ALDER WLK
CEDAR WOOD

Stanborough Prim Sch

ST ALBANS RD

GARDNER

SIXTH AVE

Garston

TIBBLES CL
WHITWELL RD
THE GOSSAMERS

**4**

SUMMERFIELD RD
CLARKE WAY
GREEN EDGE
RUSHTON AVE

**Garston**

Stanborough Sec Sch

FERN WAY
ELDERBERRY WAY
HAZEL GR

AVON CL
ROCHESTER DR
BEKEN CT
FIRST AVE

COLLISMERE CL

THIRD AVE
FOURTH AVE

THE PELHAMS
FAIRFOLDS

Meriden

**A41**

LEGGATTS RISE

North Watford Cemy

WEST DR
EAST DR
PURBROCK AVE

HOLLAND GDNS
SPRING GDNS

EDWARD AVE

COW LA

Superstore

Works

HARVEST
MANG GN

PINETREE HO
TEAL HO

The Turnstiles

BUTTERWICK

**3**

West Herts Coll Leggatts Campus

Cherry Tree Prim Sch

CHURCHFIELDS RD
FOXHILL

BERRY AVE

LEGGATTS WOOD AVE
CHERRY TREE RD
POMEROY CRES
OAKDENE RD

**NORTH WESTERN AVE**

Superstore

Liby

Meriden Sch

ABBEY VIEW
COLDHARBOUR RD
BEATTREE CT

MAPLE
YORK WAY

MERIDEN AVE
KELSHALL

**99**

WOODSIDE
ACORN
CHESTNUT WLK
BEECH RD

HAZEL TREE RD
BEECHWOOD RISE

RUSHEY MILL LA

Works

SWANLEY CT

Parkgate Inf Sch

Oldhams Trad Est

GREYCAINE RD

BROOKSIDE
COLNE MEAD

Wenta Bsns Ctr

MERIDEN WAY
WILLARD WAY
WIGEON WAY
WIDMORE AVE
EASTLEA AVE
WESTLEA AVE

River Colne

Otterspool

**2**

LEAFORD CRES
BRANSCOMBE DR
BEECHFIELD Sch
Recn Gnd

COWPER RD
HABERDASHERS

North Watford

ST ALBANS RD

NISTON RD
BUCKINGHAM RD
WINDSOR RD

Paramount Ind Est
Mowat Ind Est

LC

GREYCAINE RD
TUDOR AVE
TUDOR DR

**COLNE WAY**

OLEANDER GDNS

**WD24**

WD23

M1
(5)

**1**

WD17

JUNIPER GR
BROOM CL

Shakespeare Ind Est
Coll

JUBILEE RD
DIAMOND RD

GAMMONS LA
COLLEGE YD
RIDGE LA

JUDGE ST

CROMER RD
YARMOUTH

OSBORNE

SOUTHFIELD AVE
NORFOLK AVE
MUNDELLA GR

Watford North

BUSHEY MILL LA

WESTFIELD AVE
KNUTSFORD AVE

Knutsford Sch

RADLETT RD

BERRY GROVE LA

**OTTERSPOOL WAY**

A41

**98**

CECIL ST
REGENT ST
VICTORIA RD
MILTON RD
GARFIELD

BRUCE GR
SALISBURY

FEDERAL WAY
DEVON RD

BALMORAL RD

**A4008 STEPHENSON WAY**

10 A B 11 C D 12 E F

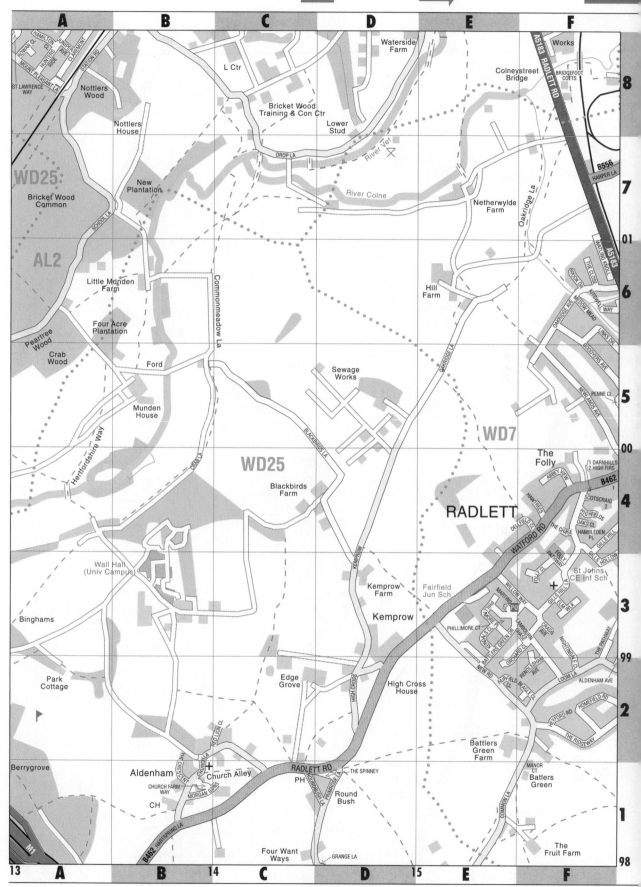

**A B C D E F**

**8**

B556
HARPER LA
Radlett Lodge Sch
Houndswood Farm
Harperbury
Nine Acres
Margaret Cotts
RIDGEWAY
HEATH WAY
LINE WAY
THE COMMON
MEADOW WAY
COLNEY LANE

B5378
HUGO GRYN WAY
SHENLEYBURY VILLAS
Clore Shalom Sch
Dell Grove
Shenleybury
SHENLEYBURY COTTS
Shenleybury House
BROADLEY GDNS

**7**

B556
Houndswood House
Wild Farm
Harper Lodge Farm
Harper House

QUEENS WAY
BOSWELL CL
NORTH AVE
DE HAVILLAND
TRENT CL
HEADINGLEY CL
EDGBA
LORDS
NEL
DR
HALLIDAY
PORTERS
HOWE
KING
CHARLES
RAPHAEL CL
COX CL
POULTNEY CL
WYNN CL
MYERS
BLACK LION HILL
HERTFORDSHIRE WAY
Combe Wood

**01**

KITSWELL WAY
THE HEATH
MADDESFIELD
RUSTON CL
CLOSE DR
COCKLE
PIPPIN CL
WICKS
PHILARIN CL
GRACE AVE
HAWKLINGS
WAYSIDE
EMMITT
WOOD GDNS
CHARWOOD
OVERTON WAY
JUNIPER CL
MULBERRY CL
WHITEBEAM
HAZEL CT
THE LAWNS
RECTORY LA
POND LA
CAGE POND RD
PH
LONDON RD B5378
KING EDWARD

**6**

A5183
LINKS DR
DOVERS AVE
PENNE CL
EVERETT CT
WOODLANDS
THE GROVE
PARK AVE
THE WARREN
THE AVENUE
LONGRIDGE
BEECH AVE
LODGE END
PARK WALK
THE DRIVE
THE WOODS
Sand Plantation
Cricket Gd
P
RADLETT LA
MONARCH WALK
Shenley Prim Sch

**5**

REGENTS CL
HAWTHORNE
MORNINGTON RD
ALDENHAM GR
LLAMORNA CL
THE SYCAMORES
WALTERS
SHENLEY HILL
CH
RADLETT
WD7
Auriol Lodge

**00**

MALTHOUSE PL
NEWLANDS PARK RD
Radlett
NIGHTINGALE CT
REGENCY HO
STATION RD
BEAUMONT GATE
HILLSIDE CL
BROADLANDS
FAGGOTS CL
SHENLEY RD
The Gorse
Auriol Farm
WOODHALL LA

**4**

WATFORD RD
B462
ALDENHAM RD
PRIMROSE
THE CROSSPATH
SLADE
PRIMROSE CL
CANONS CL
WILLIAMS WAY
BRIDGE CT
CRAIG MOUNT
NEWBERRIES AVE
Newberries Prim Sch
Wood Hall Farm
WOODHALL LA

**99**

GILLS HILL
GILLS HOLLOW
HIGH FIRS
THE LISSOM
WOODFIELD RD
LETCHMORE RD
WATLING MANS
Liby
1 CONINGSBY CT
2 SCRUBBITTS CT
3 SHERLAND CT
OAKBANK
ATHLONE CL
CHRISTCHURCH CRES
CHURCH CL
ALDENHAM AVE
Buckfield
Radlett Inf Sch
COBDEN HILL
LOOM LA
Mile Ash
THEOBALD ST
Wood Hall
Lyndhurst
Hertfordshire Way

**3**

HOMEFIELD RD
THE RIDGEWAY
MAYTREES
THE ROSE WLK
Wellhouse Dell
Rifle Range
Cobdenhill Dell
Kendal Wood
Tykes Water
Hertfordshire Way
WD6

**2**

Moses Dell
Kendal Hall Farm
FULTON CT 1
GARETH CT 2
DELMER CT 3
EMERALD CT 4
BURGESS CT 5
CARMEN CT 6
ALMA CT 7
BERWICK RD
FENWICK PATH
Parkside Com Prim Sch

**1**

Little Kendals Farm
Hertfordshire Way
A5183
Radlett Prep Sch
Organ Hall Farm
STAINER RD
TUXFORD CL
FELTON CL
ROSSINGTON AVE
HAGGERSTON RD
STRETTON PATH
MORPETH AVE
ALLERTON RD
BUCKTON RD
BEDFORD CL
REDFORD CL
FORDWICH RISE
NORTHGATE
RADCLIFFE RD

**98**

**16 A B 17 C D 18 E F**

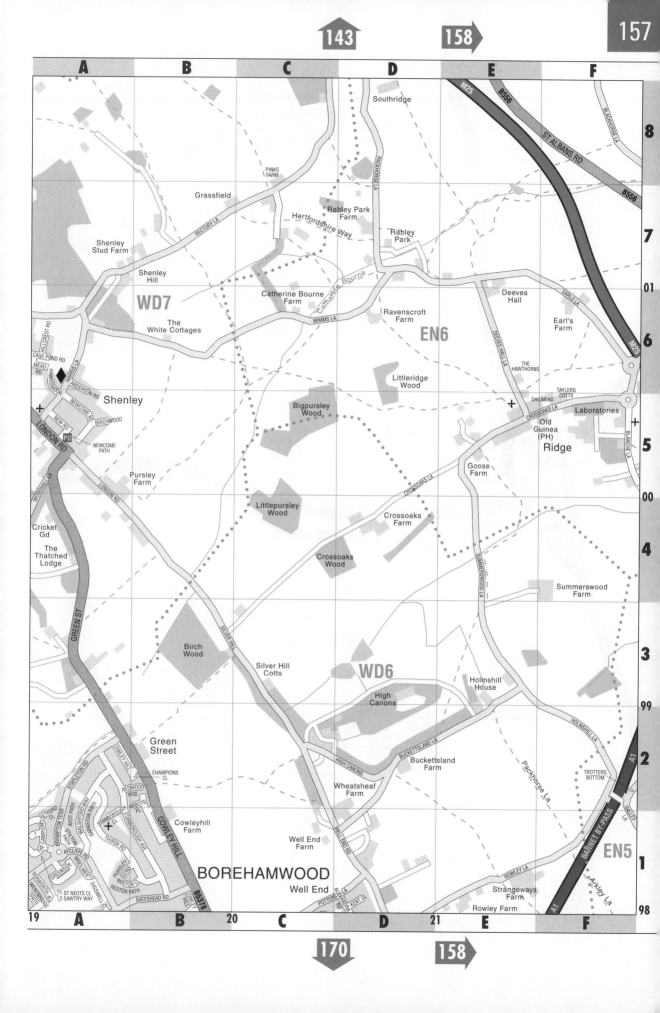

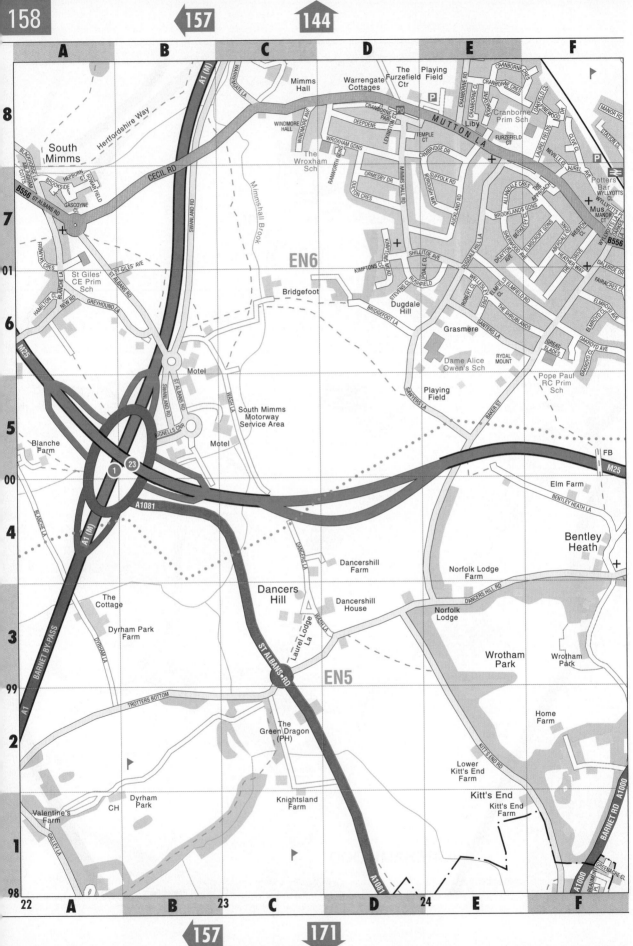

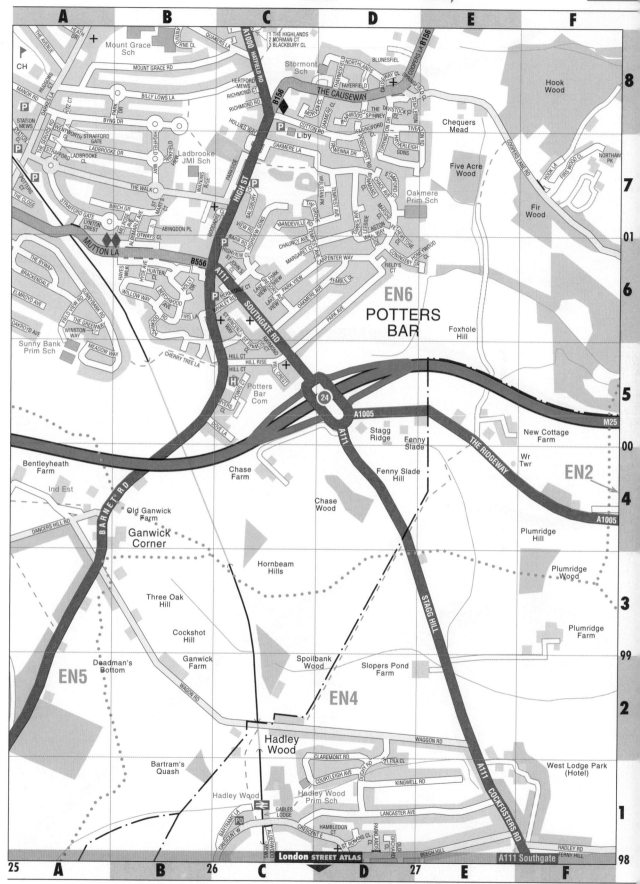

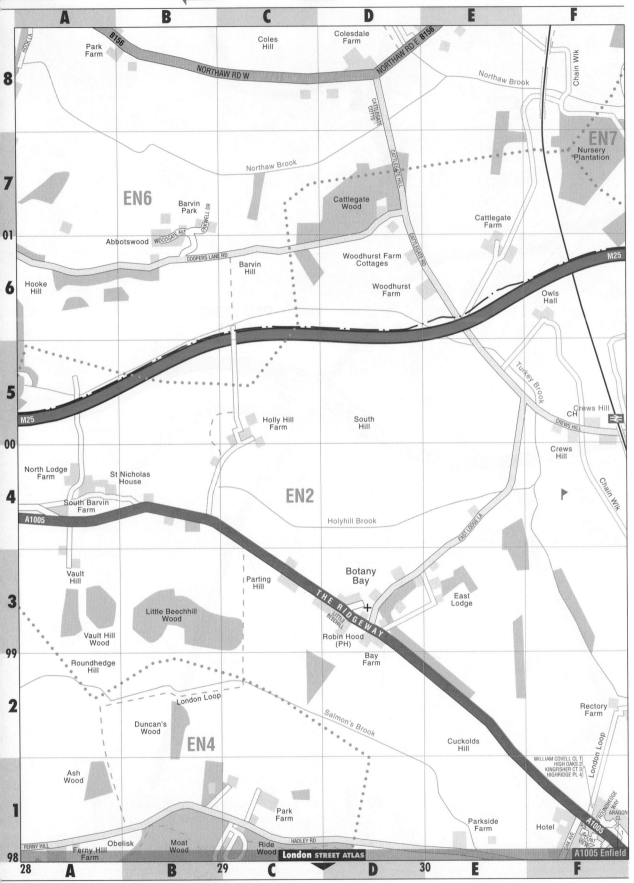

**A** **B** **C** **D** **E** **F**

Woodgreen Farm

Burnt Farm

Chain Wlk

Theobalds

BARROW LA

Broadfield Farm

B198

LIEUTENANT ELLIS WAY

**8**

Burnt Farm Cottage

Cattlins

Dysons Osiers

OLDPARK RIDE

Home Wood

Chain Wlk

Hanging Plantation

**7**

BURNT FARM RIDE

**EN7**

**01**

Tilekiln Osiers

Home Plantation

Spring Farm

Theobalds Manor

**6**

The Paddocks

Chain Wlk

Gunsite Stud

Crews Hill Piggeries

Glasgow Stud

South Osiers

Cemy

**5**

Nurseries

Sloemans Farm

Whitewebbs Farm

M25

**00**

CATTLEGATE RD

SANDER'S CNR

Crews Hill

WHITEWEBBS RD

WHITEWEBBS LA

**4**

BEECH AVE
ROSEWOOD DR
ASH RIDE
GOLF RIDE
CYPRESS AVE
WROXHAM GDNS

Whitewebbs Mus of Transport

Nurseries

Whitewebbs Wood

P

King & Tinker (PH)

Water Garden Ctr

Chain Wlk

Whitewebbs Park

White Webbs

New River (Old Course)

Turkey Brook

**3**

Nurseries

THEOBALDS PARK RD

FLASH LA

**EN2**

Cuffley Brook

London Loop

King's Oak Plain

Chain Wlk

ROSSENDALE CL

St John's CE Prim Sch

STRAYFIELD RD

Brayside Farm

CH

**99**

London Loop

The Red House

Queenswood Farm

Clay Hill

Turkey Brook

PH

Forty Hall Farm

P

Forty Hall

THE CLOCK HO

**2**

TUDOR CRES 1
YORK TERR 2
RIPLEY RD 3
WETHERBY RD 4

Hilly Fields Park

Clay Hill

PARK NOOK GDNS

ELM GDNS

**ENFIELD**

Allot Gdns

CARTERHATCH LA 1
BRIDGENHALL RD 2
LAYARD RD 3
CHINNERY CL 4
DOWLAND HO 5

KENILWORTH CRES

The Kings Oak Private

Cemy

COOK'S HOLE RD

PHIPPS HATCH LA

ACACIA RD 1
LAVENDER RD 2
VIOLET AVE 3

BRAMLEY HOUSE CT
ST JOHN'S TERR
STRATTON AVE

WOODBINE GR

1 WADDESTON CT
2 KENSINGTON CT
3 HOWARD CT

BURNHAM CL

Worcesters Primary Sch

PH

ST GEORGE'S RD

GOAT LA

**1**

Chase Farm

H
P
H
THE RIDGEWAY

SPRING COURT RD

RENDLESHAM RD

CEDAR RD
LAVENDER GDNS

LIME TREE WLK

BLOSSOM

GLOUCESTER RD
BRIGADIER AVE
BRODIE RD
BRIGADIER HILL

GLENVILLE AVE
MERTON
HAWTHORN GR
STERLING

WOODLANDS

ST LUKE'S
MORLEY HILL
BIRKBECK RD
MYRTLE GR

KYMTON DR

CONWAY GDNS
HENRY

PORTLAND GR
RIDLER RD
BAKER ST

Lavender Prim Sch

Enfield Cty Lwr Sch

FORTY HILL

RUSSELL RD

GARNAULT RD

**EN1**

**98**

**31** **A** **B** **32** **C** **D** **33** **E** **F** **98**

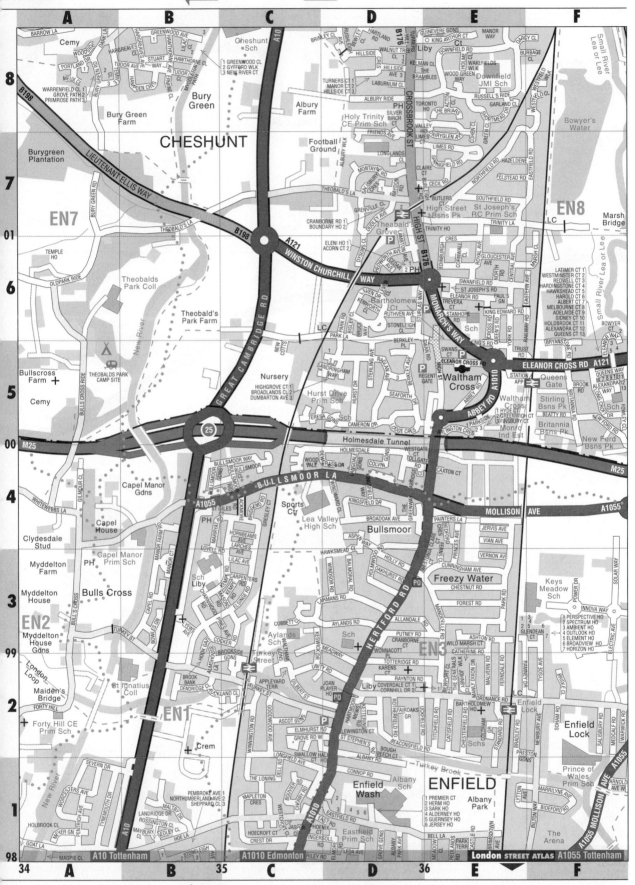

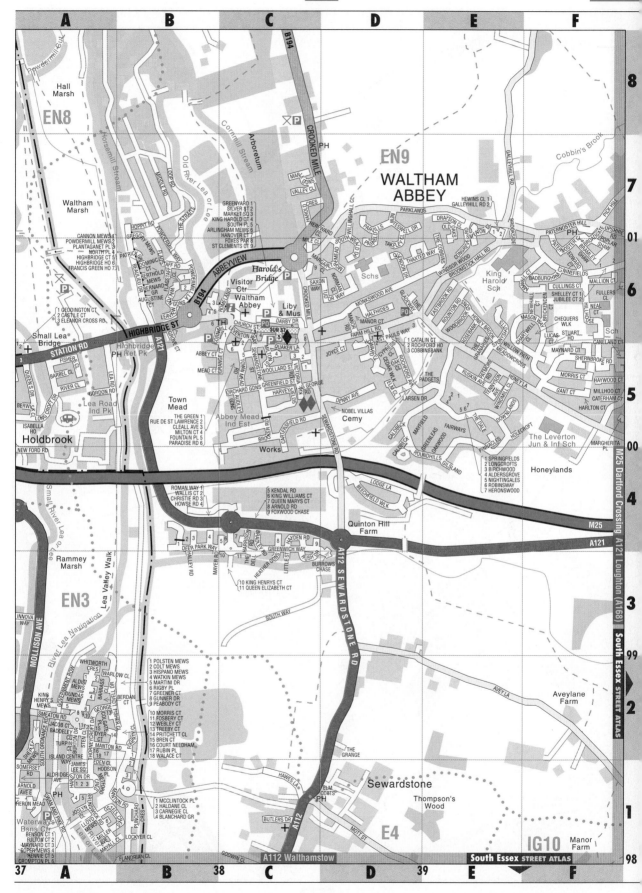

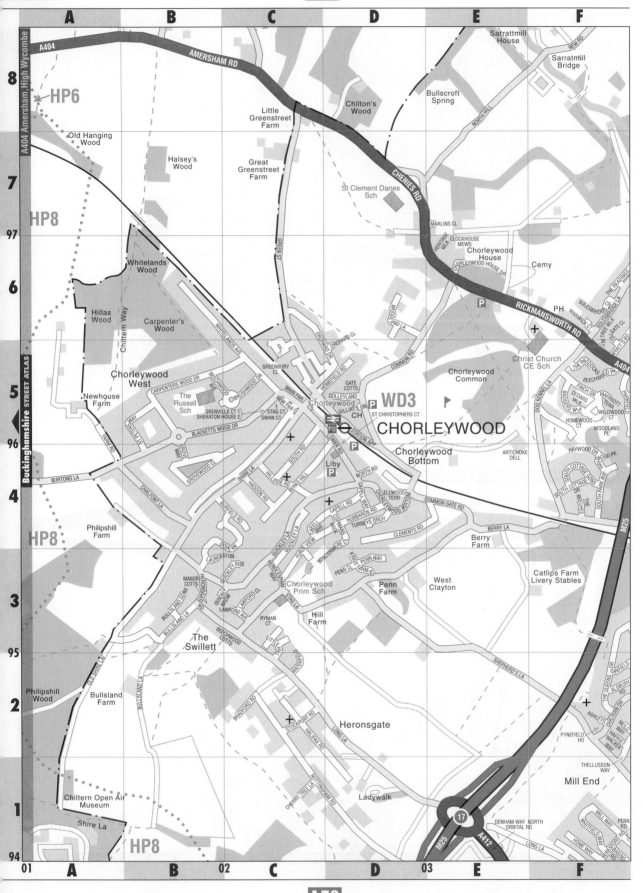

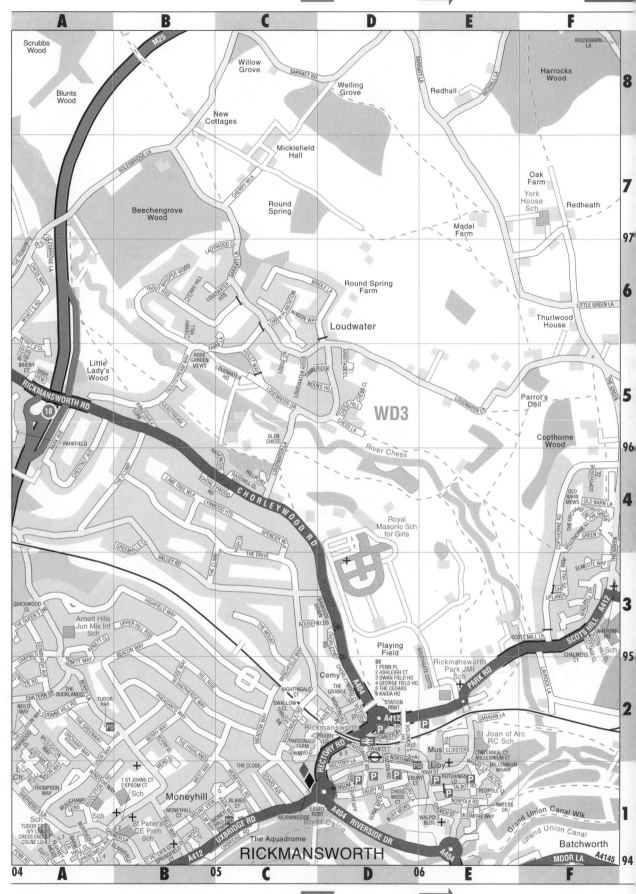

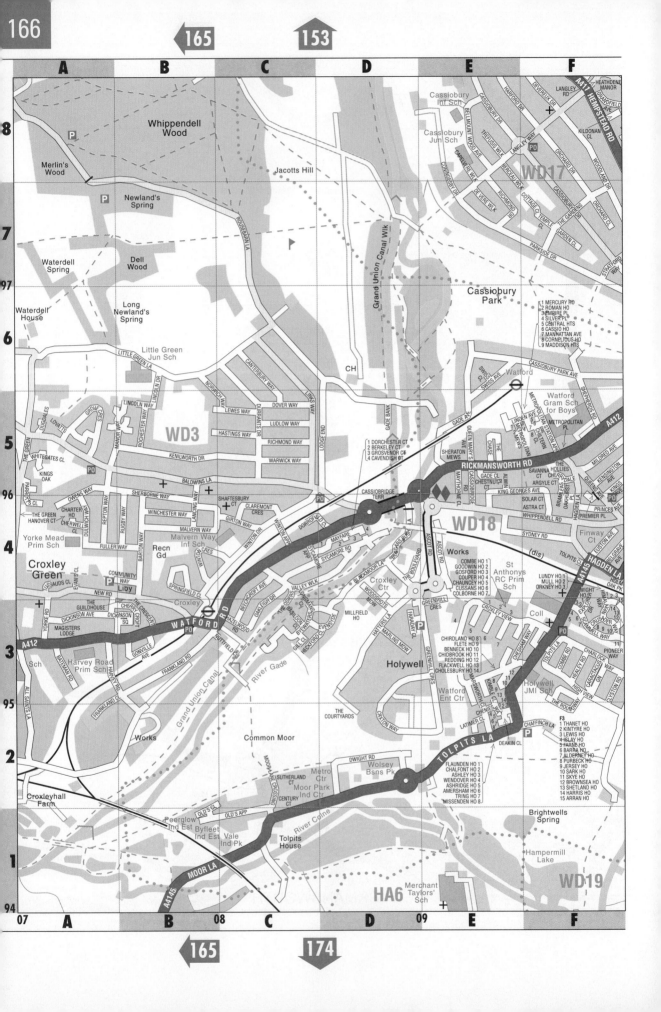

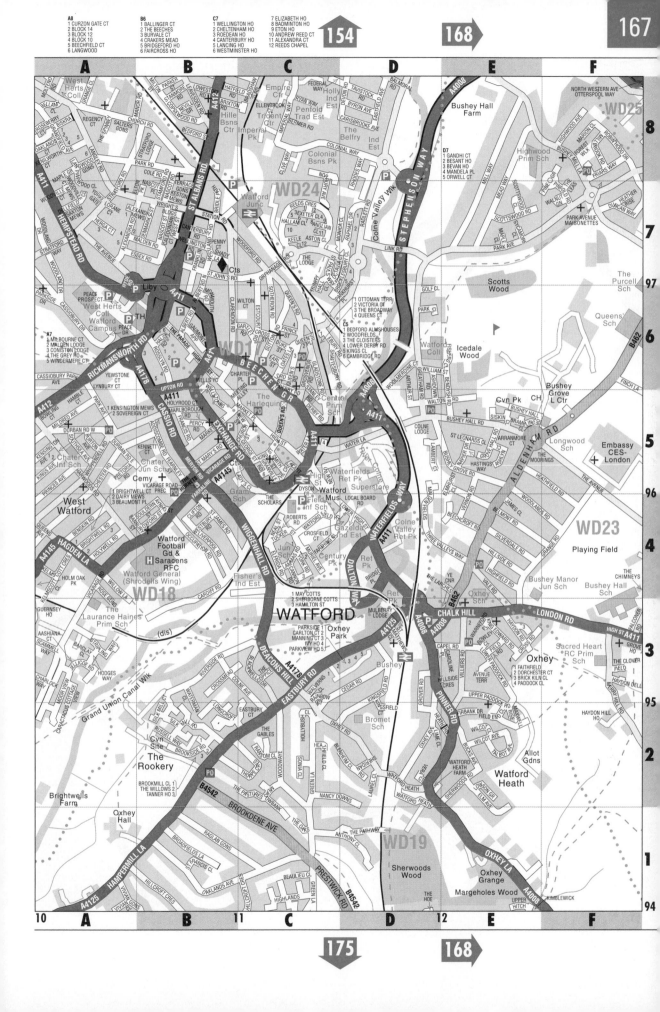

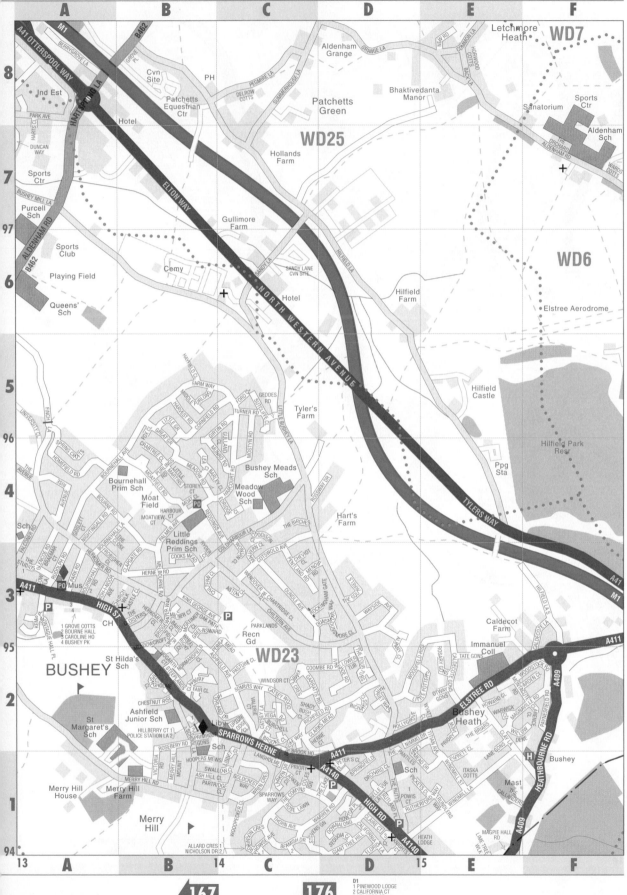

167
155

A    B    C    D    E    F

8

7

97

6

5

96

4

3

95

2

1

94

167
176

D1
1 PINEWOOD LODGE
2 CALIFORNIA CT
3 UPLANDS CT

13    A    B    14    C    D    15    E    F

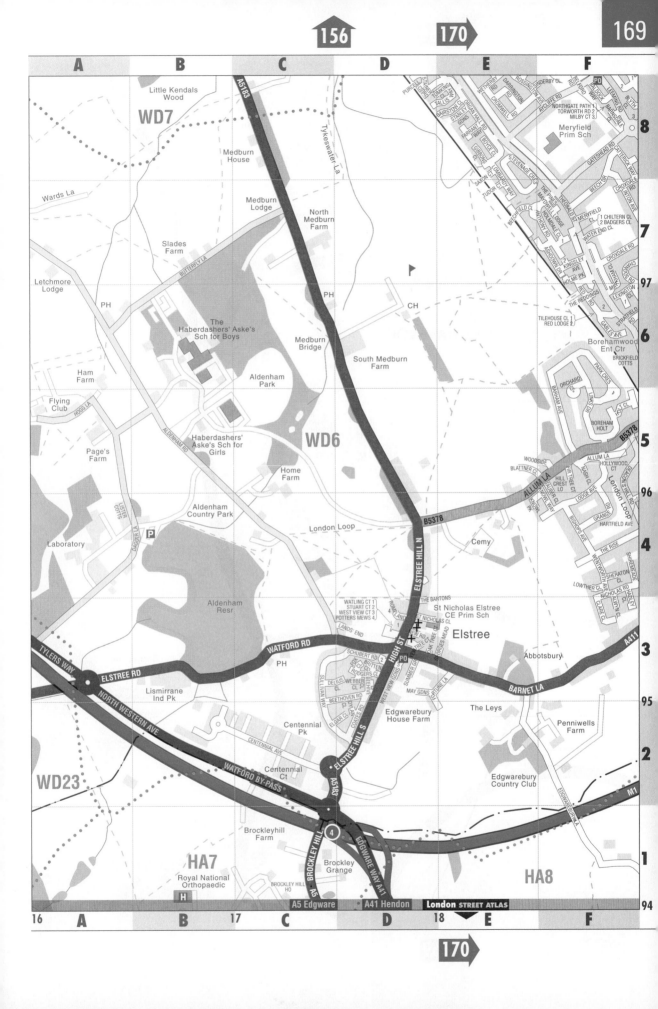

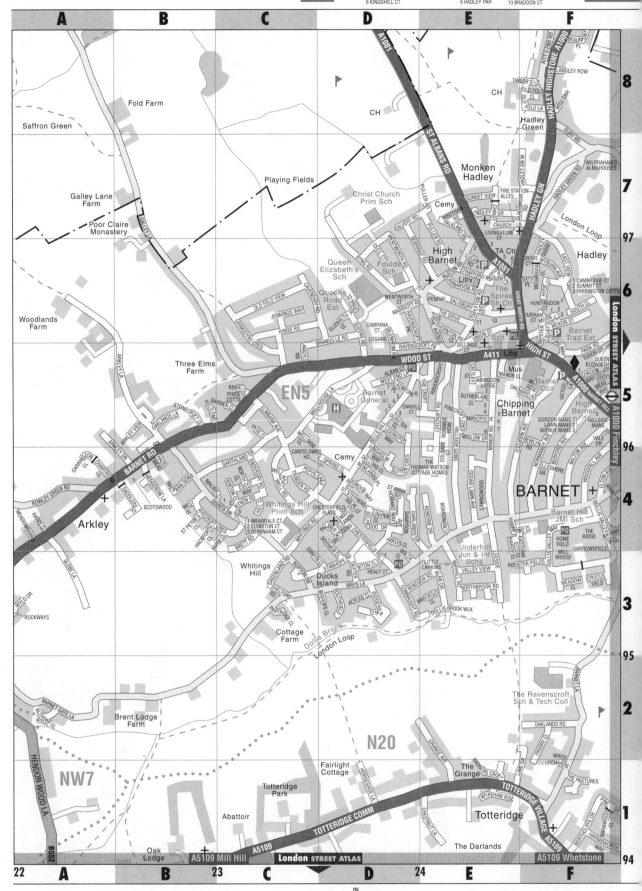

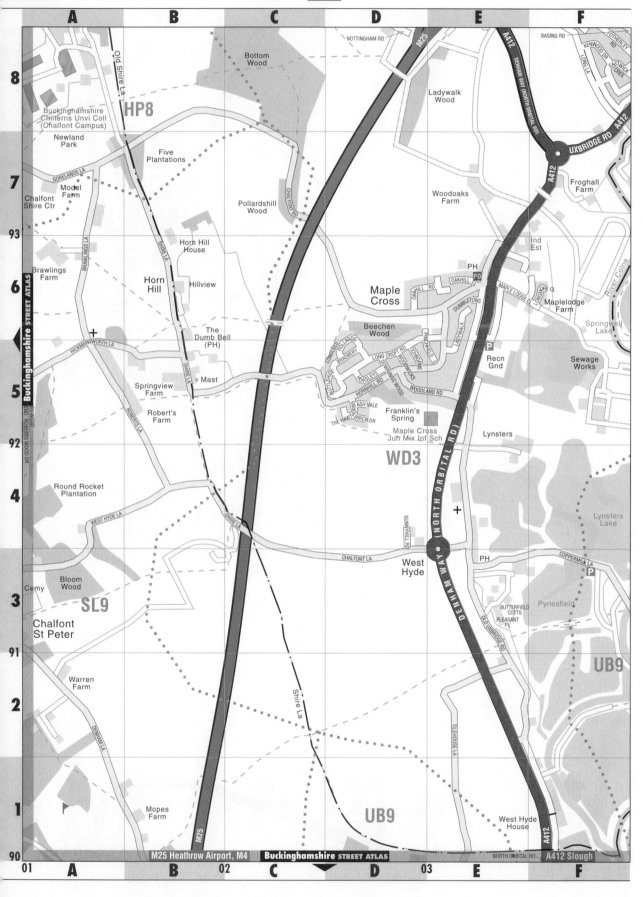

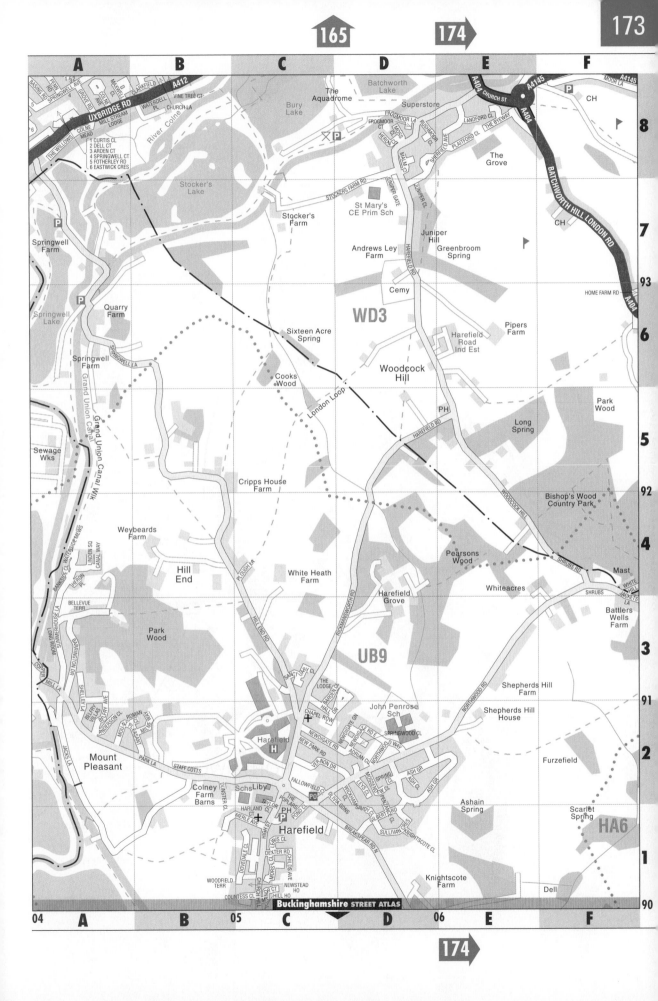

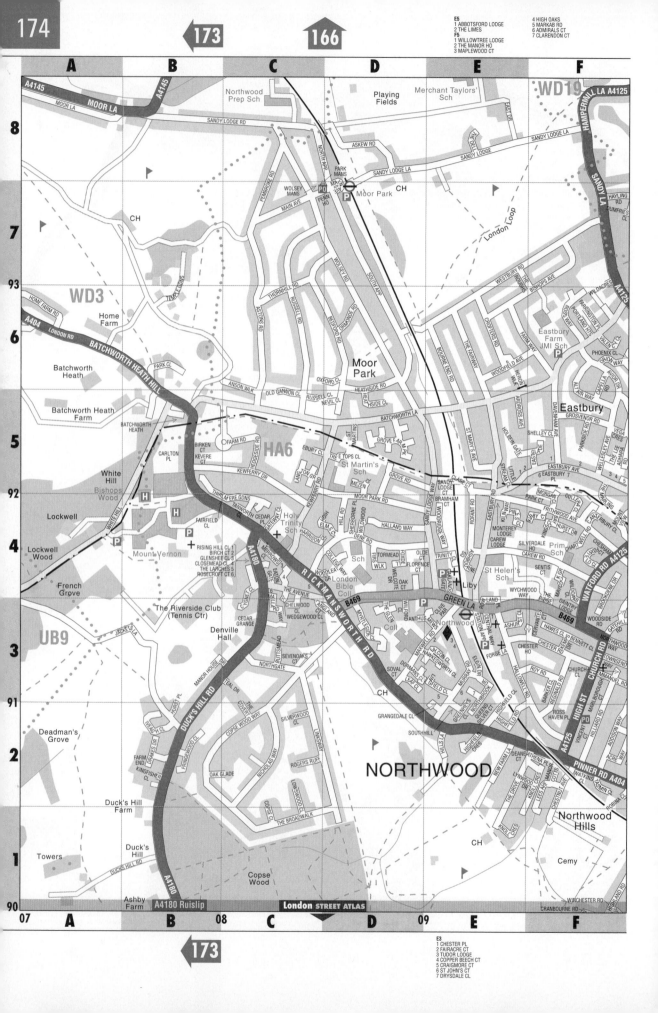

BUSHEY

WD23

WD19

Hartsbourne Ctry Club

Hartsbourne Prim Sch

Harrow Weald Common

Mutton Wood

Levels Wood

Grimsdyke Hotel

Weald Wood

The Kiln

HA7

Heriot's Wood

Deer Park

STANMORE

Bentley Priory

Priory House

Lower Priory Farm

Valley View Farm

Burnt Oak Farm

Oxheylane Farm

Stony Wood

Copse Farm

Hillside

Harrow Coll Harrow Weald Campus

Harrow Weald Cemy

Bentley Wood High Sch

HA5

HA3

The Bannister Sports Ctr

UXBRIDGE RD (HARROW WEALD)

UXBRIDGE RD (STANMORE)

Hatch End

Superstore

Hatch End High Sch

UXBRIDGE RD (HATCH END)

Harrow Weald

Shaftesbury High Sch

St Teresa's RC Fst & Mid Sch

Cedars Fst & Mid Schs

St Barnabas Sch

High View Superstore

Azure Appartments

Weald Fst & Mid Schs

Playing Field

Headstone Lane

Pinner Park Farm

HA2

Sports Gd

Harrow

Coll

HARROW

Belmont Fst & Mid Schs

Whitefriars Trad Est

Pinner Park Sch

A404 Harrow

A409 Harrow

## Church Rd 6 Beckenham BR2..........53 C6

| Place name | Location number | Locality, town or village | Postcode district | Page and grid square |
|---|---|---|---|---|
| May be abbreviated on the map | Present when a number indicates the place's position in a crowded area of mapping | Shown when more than one place has the same name | District for the indexed place | Page number and grid reference for the standard mapping |

**Public and commercial buildings** are highlighted in magenta   **Places of interest** are highlighted in blue with a star★

## Abbreviations used in the index

| | | | | | | | | | |
|---|---|---|---|---|---|---|---|---|---|
| Acad | Academy | Comm | Common | Gd | Ground | L | Leisure | Prom | Prom |
| App | Approach | Cott | Cottage | Gdn | Garden | La | Lane | Rd | Road |
| Arc | Arcade | Cres | Crescent | Gn | Green | Liby | Library | Recn | Recreation |
| Ave | Avenue | Cswy | Causeway | Gr | Grove | Mdw | Meadow | Ret | Retail |
| Bglw | Bungalow | Ct | Court | H | Hall | Meml | Memorial | Sh | Shopping |
| Bldg | Building | Ctr | Centre | Ho | House | Mkt | Market | Sq | Square |
| Bsns, Bus | Business | Ctry | Country | Hospl | Hospital | Mus | Museum | St | Street |
| Bvd | Boulevard | Cty | County | HQ | Headquarters | Orch | Orchard | Sta | Station |
| Cath | Cathedral | Dr | Drive | Hts | Heights | Pal | Palace | Terr | Terrace |
| Cir | Circus | Dro | Drove | Ind | Industrial | Par | Parade | TH | Town Hall |
| Cl | Close | Ed | Education | Inst | Institute | Pas | Passage | Univ | University |
| Cnr | Corner | Emb | Embankment | Int | International | Pk | Park | Wk, Wlk | Walk |
| Coll | College | Est | Estate | Intc | Interchange | Pl | Place | Wr | Water |
| Com | Community | Ex | Exhibition | Junc | Junction | Prec | Precinct | Yd | Yard |

## Index of localities, towns and villages

**A**

Abbots Langley .......153 F7
Adeyfield ...........125 A3
Aimes Green .........149 F2
Albury ...............57 A6
Albury End ...........56 F4
Aldbury .............101 C5
Aldenham ............155 B3
Aley Green ...........62 E1
Allen's Green .........96 F6
Amwell .............115 A6
Ansells End ..........65 F2
Anstey ..............29 B6
Apsley End ...........19 E7
Ardeley .............38 F3
Arkley ..............171 A4
Arlesey .............11 A4
Ashley Green ........136 A7
Ashwell ..............4 D3
Ashwell End ..........4 A5
Aspenden ............40 D5
Aston ...............51 E2
Aston Clinton ........99 A3
Aston End ...........51 E5
Astrope .............79 A3
Ayot Green ...........89 A1
Ayot St Lawrence .....88 B6
Ayot St Peter ........88 F3
Ayres End ...........107 E5

**B**

Babbs Green ..........94 E5
Baker's End ..........94 E7
Baldock .............23 E8
Ballingdon Bottom ....82 F1
Barkway .............17 D4

Barley ...............8 F1
Barleycroft End ......43 B4
Barnet .............171 F4
Barnet Gate ........170 F3
Barwick .............73 C3
Bassus Green .........52 F8
Batchworth .........165 F1
Batford .............86 D3
Bayford ............132 F6
Bedmond ............139 F4
Bedwell .............50 E5
Bell Bar ...........145 A7
Belsize .............151 E6
Bendish .............66 A7
Bengeo .............113 C8
Benington ...........52 E4
Bennetts End .......139 A8
Bentfield Green ......59 D8
Bentley Heath .......158 F4
Berkhamsted ........122 C6
Bernard's Heath .....127 F6
Birchanger ..........59 E2
Birch Green ........112 C3
Birchwood ..........130 B7
Biscot ..............45 C2
Bishop's Park ........76 B6
Bishop's Stortford ....76 D7
Blackmore End .......87 C6
Blue Hill ............70 D5
Borehamwood .......170 B6
Botany Bay .........160 D3
Botley .............136 A1
Bourne End .........123 E2
Bovingdon ..........137 B3
Boxmoor ...........124 B1
Bragbury End ........69 D6
Bramfield ...........91 C4
Braughing ...........55 F6
Braughing Friars .....56 C5
Breachwood Green ....47 E1
Brent Pelham ........30 A2

Brickendon .........133 C4
Bricket Wood .......140 F1
Broad Colney .......142 D3
Broadgreen Wood ...132 F8
Broadoak End .......112 F8
Broadwater ..........51 A1
Broken Green ........56 C2
Brookmans Park .....144 F5
Broxbourne ........134 F3
Buckland ............27 D8
Buckland Common ...120 B3
Bulbourne ..........100 C8
Bulls Cross ........162 A3
Bull's Green .........90 D7
Bullsmoor ..........162 D4
Bullstrode .........137 E3
Buntingford .........40 F7
Burge End ...........20 D5
Burnham Green .......90 C6
Burns Green .........52 F2
Bury Green
  Bishop's Stortford ...75 E7
Bury Green Cheshunt ...162 B8
Bury Park ...........45 B1
Bushey .............168 A2
Bushey Heath .......168 E3
Bygrave .............13 C5

**C**

Caddington ..........62 D3
Cadwell .............21 F5
Caldecote ............3 C1
Capability Green .....63 F4
Chalfont St Peter ...172 A3
Chandler's Cross ...152 F1
Chapel End ..........99 C8
Chapmore End ........92 D5
Charlton ............34 D5

Chatter End ..........58 C7
Chaulden ...........123 E2
Chaul End ...........62 C7
Cheapside ...........29 B7
Cheddington ........80 A8
Chells ..............51 B6
Chenies ............151 B1
Cherry Green ........40 C1
Cheshunt ...........148 C1
Cheverell's Green ....83 C4
Childwick Green .....107 C2
Chiltern Green .......65 B3
Chipperfield .......152 B8
Chipping ............27 D5
Chipping Barnet ....171 F5
Chiswellgreen ......141 A5
Cholesbury .........120 C2
Chorleywood .......164 E5
Chorleywood West ..164 B5
Church End Arlesey ....11 B7
Church End Little Hadham .57 D2
Church End Pitstone ...80 D3
Church End Redbourn ..105 F4
Church End Sarratt ..151 F1
Churchgate .........148 A1
Churchgate Street ...118 F3
Clapgate ............57 C6
Clay End ............52 F7
Clement's End ........82 D3
Clothall ............24 E4
Cockernhoe ..........46 F3
Codicote ............67 E1
Codicote Bottom .....88 D8
Cold Christmas ......94 B6
Cole Green .........112 A3
Colliers End .........73 A6
Collins Cross ........77 B8
Colney Heath .......143 D8
Colney Street ......141 E1
Commonwood .......152 B5
Corey's Mill .........36 B2

Cottered ............39 C7
Counter's End ......124 A3
Cow Roast ..........101 B1
Cradle End ..........75 F8
Crafton .............60 F4
Crews Hill .........161 B4
Cromer .............38 D5
Croxley Green ......166 A4
Cuckolds Cross ......66 D3
Cuffley ............146 E3
Cumberlow Green .....25 E1
Cupid Green ........125 B7

**D**

Dagnall .............81 C6
Damask Green ........37 B8
Dancers Hill .......158 C3
Dane End ............71 F8
Datchworth ..........69 E2
Datchworth Green ....69 C1
Deacons Hill .......170 A3
Dewes Green .........30 F1
Digswell ............89 F4
Digswell Park .......89 D1
Drayton Beauchamp ...99 C5
Duck End ............59 E1
Dudswell ...........121 D7
Dunstable ...........44 A1
Dyer's Green .........2 B8

**E**

Eastbury ...........174 F5
Eastend ............116 E1
East End ............43 E4
East End Green .....112 D2

Easthall . . . . . . . . . . . .49 B2
East Hyde . . . . . . . . . . .85 F8
Eastwick . . . . . . . . . . .117 A4
Edgware . . . . . . . . . . .170 E1
Edworth . . . . . . . . . . . . .3 A6
Ellenbrook . . . . . . . . . .129 C5
Elstree . . . . . . . . . . . .169 E3
Enfield . . . . . . . . . . . .162 E1
Enfield Lock . . . . . . . . .162 F2
Enfield Wash . . . . . . . . .162 D1
Epping Green . . . . . . . . .132 D2
Essendon . . . . . . . . . . .131 F6
Eyeworth . . . . . . . . . . . . .1 A8

**F**
Farley Hill . . . . . . . . . . .63 B6
Farnham . . . . . . . . . . . .58 D6
Farnham Green . . . . . . . .58 B7
Felden . . . . . . . . . . . . .138 A8
Fields End . . . . . . . . . . .123 D4
Fishers Green . . . . . . . . .50 A4
Flamstead . . . . . . . . . . .84 B1
Flamstead End . . . . . . . .148 B4
Flaunden . . . . . . . . . . .151 A6
Fleetville . . . . . . . . . . .128 B4
Ford End . . . . . . . . . . . .30 E4
Freezy Water . . . . . . . . .162 E3
Frithsden . . . . . . . . . . .123 B8
Frogmore . . . . . . . . . . .141 E4
Frogmore End . . . . . . . .138 E7
Furneux Pelham . . . . . . .43 A5
Further Ford End . . . . . . .30 D6

**G**
Gaddesden Row . . . . . .104 C6
Gadebridge . . . . . . . . . .124 A5
Ganwick Corner . . . . . . .159 B4
Garston . . . . . . . . . . . .154 C4
Gaston Green . . . . . . . . .98 B7
Gilston . . . . . . . . . . . .117 E5
Goff's Oak . . . . . . . . . .147 C3
Gorhambury . . . . . . . . .126 C4
Graveley . . . . . . . . . . . .36 C4
Gravesend . . . . . . . . . . .57 B8
Great Amwell . . . . . . . .114 F5
Great Ashby . . . . . . . . . .37 D3
Great Chishill . . . . . . . . . .9 F2
Great Gaddesden . . . . . .103 D3
Great Hallingbury . . . . . .77 E4
Great Hormead . . . . . . . .42 A8
Great Munden . . . . . . . .54 C5
Great Offley . . . . . . . . . .33 D2
Great Wymondley . . . . . .35 F6
Green End Braughing . . . .55 E7
Green End Buntingford . . .26 D7
Green End Dane End . . . .53 E1
Green End
  Hemel Hempstead . . . . . .124 A2
Green Street
  Bishop's Stortford . . . . . . .75 E8
Green Street
  Borehamwood . . . . . . . .157 B2
Green Tye . . . . . . . . . . .75 D1
Grovehill . . . . . . . . . . .124 E8
Gubblecote . . . . . . . . . .79 D3
Guilden Morden . . . . . . . .1 F4
Gustard Wood . . . . . . . .87 D4

**H**
Hadham Cross . . . . . . . .74 E2
Hadham Ford . . . . . . . . .75 B8
Hadley . . . . . . . . . . . . .171 F6
Hadley Wood . . . . . . . . .159 C2
Haldens . . . . . . . . . . . . .89 F1
Hall Grove . . . . . . . . . .111 B4
Hammerfield . . . . . . . . .124 A3
Hammond Street . . . . . . .147 D5
Handside . . . . . . . . . . .110 C5
Hanscombe End . . . . . . . .19 C8
Harefield . . . . . . . . . . .173 C1
Hare Street Buntingford . . .41 D7
Hare Street Cottered . . . . .38 F6
Harlow . . . . . . . . . . . . .117 D2
Harmer Green . . . . . . . . .90 B5
Harpenden . . . . . . . . . . .86 B2
Harpenden Common . . .107 B7
Harrow . . . . . . . . . . . . .176 A1
Harrow Weald . . . . . . . .176 D2
Hart Hill . . . . . . . . . . . .46 A1
Hastoe . . . . . . . . . . . . .119 F7
Hatch End . . . . . . . . . . .175 E3
Hatching Green . . . . . . .107 A6
Hatfield . . . . . . . . . . . .130 B8
Hatfield Garden Village . .129 E8
Hatfield Heath . . . . . . . .98 E3
Hatfield Hyde . . . . . . . .110 F3
Haultwick . . . . . . . . . . .53 F3
Hawridge . . . . . . . . . . .120 E1
Hay Green . . . . . . . . . . .15 F6

Hazel End . . . . . . . . . . .59 A6
Hebing End . . . . . . . . . .53 A2
Hemel Hempstead . . . . .124 D6
Henlow . . . . . . . . . . . . .10 D8
Heronsgate . . . . . . . . . .164 D2
Hertford . . . . . . . . . . . .113 C5
Hertford Heath . . . . . . . .114 B3
Hertingfordbury . . . . . . .112 E5
Hexton . . . . . . . . . . . . .19 B2
Higham Gobion . . . . . . . .19 A6
High Barnet . . . . . . . . . .171 E6
High Cross . . . . . . . . . . .72 F2
Highfield . . . . . . . . . . .124 F6
High Town . . . . . . . . . . .63 E8
High Wych . . . . . . . . . . .97 B1
Hill End . . . . . . . . . . . .173 B4
Hinxworth . . . . . . . . . . . .3 C5
Hitchen Hill . . . . . . . . . .34 E5
Hitchin . . . . . . . . . . . . .34 E8
Hockerill . . . . . . . . . . . .77 A6
Hoddesdon . . . . . . . . . .135 C7
Hogpits Bottom . . . . . . .151 B7
Holdbrook . . . . . . . . . . .163 A5
Holwell . . . . . . . . . . . . .21 B7
Holwellbury . . . . . . . . . .10 B1
Holyfield . . . . . . . . . . .149 D3
Holywell Watford . . . . . .166 D3
Holywell Whipsnade . . . . .82 B6
Hoo End . . . . . . . . . . . .66 E4
Hook's Cross . . . . . . . . .69 F6
Horn Hill . . . . . . . . . . .172 B6
Howe Green . . . . . . . . . .77 D2
How Wood . . . . . . . . . .141 B3
Hudnall . . . . . . . . . . . .102 F7
Hudnall Corner . . . . . . .103 B7
Hunsdon . . . . . . . . . . . .95 D1
Hunsdonbury . . . . . . . . .116 D7
Hunton Bridge . . . . . . . .153 C6

**I**
Ickleford . . . . . . . . . . . .21 E4
Ivinghoe . . . . . . . . . . . .80 F5

**J**
Jockey End . . . . . . . . . .103 F8

**K**
Kelshall . . . . . . . . . . . . .15 D5
Kemprow . . . . . . . . . . .155 D3
Kensworth Common . . . .82 E8
Kensworth Lynch . . . . . . .62 A1
Kettle Green . . . . . . . . .74 C1
Keysers Estate . . . . . . . .135 B1
Kimpton . . . . . . . . . . . .66 C1
Kings Langley . . . . . . . .139 A1
King's Walden . . . . . . . . .48 A3
Kinsbourne Green . . . . . .85 C5
Kitt's End . . . . . . . . . . .158 E1
Knebworth . . . . . . . . . . .69 A5
Kneesworth . . . . . . . . . . .2 A5

**L**
Lanes End . . . . . . . . . . .119 C4
Langley . . . . . . . . . . . . .49 F1
Langleybury . . . . . . . . .153 B4
Latchford . . . . . . . . . . . .73 F5
Latchmore Bank . . . . . . .77 B2
Latimer . . . . . . . . . . . .150 E3
Leagrave . . . . . . . . . . . .44 D5
Lea Valley . . . . . . . . . . .86 F2
Leavesden Green . . . . . .153 E5
Ledburn . . . . . . . . . . . . .61 C8
Lemsford . . . . . . . . . . .110 A5
Letchmore Heath . . . . . .168 B8
Letchworth . . . . . . . . . . .22 C5
Letty Green . . . . . . . . . .112 B2
Level's End . . . . . . . . . . .58 C5
Levens Green . . . . . . . . .54 C1
Leverstock Green . . . . . .125 C2
Ley Green . . . . . . . . . . .47 F5
Ley Hill . . . . . . . . . . . . .150 B8
Lilley . . . . . . . . . . . . . . .32 D2
Limbury . . . . . . . . . . . . .44 F5
Little Berkhamsted . . . . .132 C4
Little Chalfont . . . . . . . .150 B1
Little Chishill . . . . . . . . .18 E7
Little Gaddesden . . . . . .102 D7
Little Hadham . . . . . . . . .57 C2
Little Hallingbury . . . . . .98 D8
Little Heath
  Hemel Hempstead . . . . . .123 B5
Little Heath Potters Bar . .145 B2
Little Hormead . . . . . . . .42 A4
Little Parndon . . . . . . . .117 B1
Little Tring . . . . . . . . . . .99 F6
Little Wymondley . . . . . .35 E3

London Colney . . . . . . . .142 E5
Long Marston . . . . . . . . .79 B3
Loudwater . . . . . . . . . . .165 D6
Lower End . . . . . . . . . . .79 F3
Lower Green Ickleford . . .21 E5
Lower Green Meesden . . .29 E6
Lower Nazeing . . . . . . . .149 E8
Lower Sheering . . . . . . . .98 A1
Lower Stondon . . . . . . . .10 A3
Lower Titmore Green . . . .35 F1
Luffenhall . . . . . . . . . . .38 C7
Luton . . . . . . . . . . . . . .45 C3

**M**
Mackerye End . . . . . . . . .86 F4
Mangrove Green . . . . . . .46 E4
Maple Cross . . . . . . . . . .172 D6
Mardleybury . . . . . . . . . .69 C2
Mark Hall North . . . . . . .118 A3
Mark Hall South . . . . . . .118 A1
Markyate . . . . . . . . . . . .83 E6
Marshalls Heath . . . . . . .87 A2
Marshalswick . . . . . . . . .128 B6
Marsh Farm . . . . . . . . . .44 E7
Marsworth . . . . . . . . . . .80 A1
Meesden . . . . . . . . . . . .29 E6
Meldreth . . . . . . . . . . . . .2 F8
Mentmore . . . . . . . . . . .61 D4
Meriden . . . . . . . . . . . .154 E3
Merry Hill . . . . . . . . . . .168 B1
Micklefield Green . . . . . .152 B1
Mill End Buntingford . . . .26 E6
Mill End Rickmansworth . .164 F1
Mill Green . . . . . . . . . . .130 E8
Moneyhill . . . . . . . . . . .165 B1
Monken Hadley . . . . . . .171 E6
Moor Green . . . . . . . . . .39 D2
Moor Park . . . . . . . . . . .174 D6
Mount Pleasant . . . . . . .173 A2
Much Hadham . . . . . . . . .74 F3

**N**
Napsbury . . . . . . . . . . .142 B5
Nash Mills . . . . . . . . . . .139 A6
Nasty . . . . . . . . . . . . . .54 D6
Nazeing Marsh . . . . . . . .149 A8
Nether Street . . . . . . . . .95 E5
Nettleden . . . . . . . . . . .103 B1
Newgate Street . . . . . . .146 F7
New Greens . . . . . . . . . .127 D7
New Ground . . . . . . . . .101 A7
New Mill . . . . . . . . . . . .100 A6
Newmill End . . . . . . . . . .64 D1
Newnham . . . . . . . . . . .12 E8
Newsells . . . . . . . . . . . .17 D7
Newtown . . . . . . . . . . . .40 F8
New Town
  Bishop's Stortford . . . . . . .76 F6
New Town Luton . . . . . . .63 E5
Northaw . . . . . . . . . . . .146 A1
North End . . . . . . . . . . .15 D6
North Mymms . . . . . . . .144 A5
North Watford . . . . . . . .154 B8
Northwood . . . . . . . . . .174 E2
Northwood Hills . . . . . . .174 F1
Norton . . . . . . . . . . . . .12 C1
Norton Green . . . . . . . . .50 B3
Nup End . . . . . . . . . . . .60 B3
Nuthampstead . . . . . . . .18 A2

**O**
Oakfield . . . . . . . . . . . . .35 B6
Oaklands . . . . . . . . . . . .89 F7
Odsey . . . . . . . . . . . . . . .5 C1
Old Hall Green . . . . . . . .54 F1
Old Harlow . . . . . . . . . .118 D4
Old Hatfield . . . . . . . . . .130 D6
Old Knebworth . . . . . . . .68 C5
Old Town . . . . . . . . . . . .50 C8
Orchard Leigh . . . . . . . .136 A3
Oxhey . . . . . . . . . . . . .167 E3
Oxlease . . . . . . . . . . . .130 B5

**P**
Painter's Green . . . . . . . .69 D2
Panshanger . . . . . . . . . .111 B7
Park Street . . . . . . . . . .141 D5
Patchetts Green . . . . . . .168 D8
Peartree . . . . . . . . . . . .110 F5
Pegsdon . . . . . . . . . . . .19 D1
Pepperstock . . . . . . . . . .63 C1
Perry Green . . . . . . . . . .96 B8
Peters Green . . . . . . . . . .65 C3
Piccotts End . . . . . . . . . .124 C7
Pimlico . . . . . . . . . . . . .139 E7

Pin Green . . . . . . . . . . . .50 F8
Pinner . . . . . . . . . . . . . .175 E1
Pinner Green . . . . . . . . .175 C1
Pirton . . . . . . . . . . . . . .20 D1
Pitstone . . . . . . . . . . . . .80 D4
Poplars . . . . . . . . . . . . .51 D3
Potten End . . . . . . . . . . .123 C7
Potters Bar . . . . . . . . . . .159 D6
Potters Crouch . . . . . . . .140 D7
Pottersheath . . . . . . . . . .89 D7
Pouchen End . . . . . . . . .123 D2
Presdales . . . . . . . . . . .114 E7
Preston . . . . . . . . . . . . .48 D6
Puckeridge . . . . . . . . . . .55 D3
Pudds Cross . . . . . . . . . .136 E2
Purwell . . . . . . . . . . . . .35 D8
Puttenham . . . . . . . . . . .78 E2

**R**
Rableyheath . . . . . . . . . .68 D3
Radlett . . . . . . . . . . . . .156 C5
Radwell . . . . . . . . . . . . .12 C4
Redbourn . . . . . . . . . . .106 B6
Reed . . . . . . . . . . . . . . .16 B5
Reed End . . . . . . . . . . . .16 B5
Rickmansworth . . . . . . . .165 C1
Ridge . . . . . . . . . . . . . .157 F5
Ringshall . . . . . . . . . . . .81 B1
Roast Green . . . . . . . . . .30 F6
Roe Green Hatfield . . . . .130 A6
Roe Green Sandon . . . . . .26 B8
Roestock . . . . . . . . . . . .143 E8
Rosedale . . . . . . . . . . . .148 A3
Round Green . . . . . . . . . .45 F2
Rowley Green . . . . . . . . .170 F5
Roydon . . . . . . . . . . . . .116 C1
Royston . . . . . . . . . . . . . .7 C5
Rucklers Lane . . . . . . . . .138 C5
Rushden . . . . . . . . . . . .25 F3
Rusling End . . . . . . . . . .67 D7
Rye Park . . . . . . . . . . . .135 B7

**S**
Sacombe . . . . . . . . . . . .71 E3
Sacombe Green . . . . . . . .72 A4
St Albans . . . . . . . . . . .127 F4
St Ibbs . . . . . . . . . . . . .35 B2
St Ippolyts . . . . . . . . . . .35 B3
St Julians . . . . . . . . . . .141 D8
St Leonards . . . . . . . . . .119 E3
St Margarets . . . . . . . . .115 B4
St Michael's Mead . . . . . .76 C5
St Nicholas . . . . . . . . . . .37 A2
St Paul's Walden . . . . . . .49 B1
St Stephens . . . . . . . . . .127 C1
Sandon . . . . . . . . . . . . .15 B1
Sandridge . . . . . . . . . . .108 C1
Sarratt . . . . . . . . . . . . .152 A4
Sarrett Bottom . . . . . . . .151 E2
Sawbridgeworth . . . . . . .97 C3
Sewardstone . . . . . . . . .163 D1
Shaftenhoe End . . . . . . . .18 B8
Shaw Green . . . . . . . . . .25 D5
Sheepcote Green . . . . . . .30 F6
Sheering . . . . . . . . . . . .98 C1
Shenley . . . . . . . . . . . .157 A5
Shenleybury . . . . . . . . . .156 E8
Shephall . . . . . . . . . . . .51 B3
Sherrardspark . . . . . . . .110 C8
Shillington . . . . . . . . . . .19 F8
Shootersway . . . . . . . . .121 F4
Sleapshyde . . . . . . . . . .129 C2
Slip End . . . . . . . . . . . . .63 C2
Smallford . . . . . . . . . . .129 B4
Smith's End . . . . . . . . . .18 A8
Smug Oak . . . . . . . . . . .141 B1
Snailswell . . . . . . . . . . . .21 E6
Sopwell . . . . . . . . . . . .141 F8
South-end . . . . . . . . . . .96 B6
Southern Green . . . . . . . .26 A4
South Hatfield . . . . . . . .130 B2
South Mimms . . . . . . . .158 A8
South Oxhey . . . . . . . . .175 B7
Spellbrook . . . . . . . . . . .97 E8
Spencerswood . . . . . . . .119 C7
Spitalbrook . . . . . . . . . .135 A4
Staines Green . . . . . . . .112 D4
Stanborough . . . . . . . . .110 A3
Standon . . . . . . . . . . . . .55 E1
Standon Green End . . . . .72 E4
Stanmore . . . . . . . . . . .176 F5
Stanstead Abbotts . . . . .115 E4
Stansted Mountfitchet . .59 C6
Stapleford . . . . . . . . . . .92 A7
Starling's Green . . . . . . . .30 F3
Startop's End . . . . . . . . .79 F1
Steeple Morden . . . . . . . .5 B8
Stevenage . . . . . . . . . . .50 D8
Stocking Pelham . . . . . . .43 E7
Stopsley . . . . . . . . . . . .46 B4
Stotfold . . . . . . . . . . . . .11 E7

Streatley . . . . . . . . . . . .31 A5
Studham . . . . . . . . . . . .82 C4
Sundon Park . . . . . . . . .44 E7
Swanley Bar . . . . . . . . . .145 B2
Symonds Green . . . . . . .50 A7

**T**
Temple Fields . . . . . . . . .118 A4
Tewin . . . . . . . . . . . . . .90 E2
Tewin Wood . . . . . . . . . .90 D5
The Camp . . . . . . . . . . .128 B2
The Green . . . . . . . . . . .81 F8
Therfield . . . . . . . . . . . .15 F7
The Rookery . . . . . . . . .167 B2
The Ryde . . . . . . . . . . . .130 C8
The Swillett . . . . . . . . . .164 B3
Thorley . . . . . . . . . . . . .76 C3
Thorley Park . . . . . . . . . .76 D5
Thorley Street . . . . . . . . .76 F3
Throcking . . . . . . . . . . .26 F1
Thundridge . . . . . . . . . .93 E7
Titmore Green . . . . . . . .35 E2
Todd's Green . . . . . . . . .36 A2
Tonwell . . . . . . . . . . . . .92 F7
Totteridge . . . . . . . . . . .171 E1
Tower Hill . . . . . . . . . . .137 F2
Town Park . . . . . . . . . . .117 E2
Townsend . . . . . . . . . . .127 C6
Trims Green . . . . . . . . . .97 C7
Tring . . . . . . . . . . . . . .100 B3
Tringford . . . . . . . . . . . .99 F7
Tring Wharf . . . . . . . . . .100 B6
Trowley Bottom . . . . . . .105 B8
Turnford . . . . . . . . . . . .148 E5
Two Waters . . . . . . . . . .138 C6
Tylers Causeway . . . . . . .132 D1
Tyttenhanger . . . . . . . . .142 E8

**U**
Upper Dunsley . . . . . . . .100 C4

**W**
Wadesmill . . . . . . . . . . .93 D8
Walkern . . . . . . . . . . . . .38 A1
Wallington . . . . . . . . . . .25 D8
Walsworth . . . . . . . . . . .22 A1
Waltham Abbey . . . . . . .163 D7
Waltham Cross . . . . . . . .162 E5
Warden Hill . . . . . . . . . .45 D7
Ware . . . . . . . . . . . . . .93 F2
Wareside . . . . . . . . . . . .94 E4
Warners End . . . . . . . . .123 F4
Warren's Green . . . . . . . .37 D6
Washall Green . . . . . . . . .30 C1
Waterdale . . . . . . . . . . .140 C1
Waterford . . . . . . . . . . .92 A2
Watford . . . . . . . . . . . .167 C3
Watford Heath . . . . . . . .167 E2
Watton at Stone . . . . . . .70 D4
Welham Green . . . . . . . .144 C7
Well End . . . . . . . . . . . .157 C1
Wellpond Green . . . . . . .56 D1
Welwyn . . . . . . . . . . . . .89 B4
Welwyn Garden City . . . .110 E2
West End . . . . . . . . . . . .131 C5
Westland Green . . . . . . .56 E1
West Leith . . . . . . . . . . .99 F1
Westmill Buntingford . . . .40 F3
Westmill Hitchin . . . . . . .21 C1
Weston . . . . . . . . . . . . .24 C1
West Watford . . . . . . . . .167 A4
Westwick Row . . . . . . . .125 E2
Wheathampstead . . . . . .108 C7
Whelpley Hill . . . . . . . . .136 D5
Whempstead . . . . . . . . .71 B7
Whippendell Bottom . . . .138 C5
Whipsnade . . . . . . . . . . .82 A8
Whitwell . . . . . . . . . . . .66 E6
Widford . . . . . . . . . . . . .95 E4
Wigginton . . . . . . . . . . .100 D1
Wigginton Bottom . . . . .120 D8
Wigmore . . . . . . . . . . . .46 E2
Wildhill . . . . . . . . . . . . .131 D2
Willian . . . . . . . . . . . . .23 B2
Wilstone . . . . . . . . . . . .79 D1
Wilstone Green . . . . . . . .99 D8
Wingrave . . . . . . . . . . . .60 C3
Winsdon Hill . . . . . . . . . .63 B7
Woodcock Hill . . . . . . . .173 D6
Wood End . . . . . . . . . . .53 D7
Woodhall . . . . . . . . . . .110 E4
Woodside Luton . . . . . . .63 A2
Woodside Watford . . . . .154 B7
Woodside . . . . . . . . . . .131 A2
Woodside Green . . . . . . .77 F1
Woolmer Green . . . . . . . .69 B2
Wormley . . . . . . . . . . . .148 E8
Wormley West End . . . . .147 F8
Wyddial . . . . . . . . . . . . .28 A3

Aashiana Ct WD18 ......167 A3
Abbey Ave AL3 .........127 B1
Abbey CE Prim Sch The
  AL1 .................127 D2
Abbey Ct St Albans AL1 ..127 D2
  Waltham Abbey EN9 ....163 B5
Abbey Dr
  Abbots Langley WD5 ....154 A7
  Luton LU2 .............46 A1
Abbey Mead Ind Est
  EN9 .................163 C5
Abbey Mill End AL3 ....127 C2
Abbey Mill La AL3 ....127 C2
Abbey Rd EN8 .........162 E6
Abbey Sta AL1 .........127 D1
Abbey Theatre AL1 ....127 C1
Abbey View Radlett WD7 .155 F4
  St Albans AL1 .........127 D1
  Watford WD25 .........154 D3
Abbey View Rd AL3 ....127 C3
Abbeygate Bsns Ctr The [6]
  LU2 .................63 F8
Abbeyview EN9 ........163 C6
Abbis Orch SG5 .........21 E5
Abbot John Mews [4]
  AL4 .................87 D1
Abbots Ave AL1 .......141 E8
Abbots Ave W AL1 .....141 D8
Abbots Cl SG3 .........69 D1
Abbots Ct LU2 .........46 A1
Abbots Gr SG1 .........50 F5
Abbots Langley Sch
  WD5 ................139 D1
Abbots Pk AL1 ........128 A1
Abbots Pl WD6 ........157 B2
Abbots Rd WD5 .......139 E1
Abbots Rise WD4 ......138 F5
Abbots View WD4 .....138 F4
Abbots Wood Rd LU2 ...64 A8
Abbotsbury Ct WD25 ...154 B7
Abbotsford Lodge [1]
  HA6 ................174 F5
Abbotswood Par LU2 ...46 A1
Abbotts Ct SG12 ......115 C4
Abbotts La SG12 ........95 D3
Abbotts Rd SG6 ........22 D6
Abbotts Rise SG12 ....115 D4
Abbotts Way
  Bishop's Stortford CM23 ..76 E3
  Stansted Abbotts SG12 ..115 D4
  Wingrave HP22 .........60 A4
Abbotts Yd [1] SG8 ......7 D6
Abbottsfield Cotts SG12 .94 E5
Abdale La AL9 .........144 C4
Abel Cl HP2 ...........125 A3
Abel Smith Sch SG13 ...113 D6
Aberdale Gdns EN6 ....158 F7
Aberdeen Rd HA3 .....176 F1
Aberford Rd WD6 .....170 A7
Abigail Cl LU3 .........45 D3
Abigail Ct LU3 .........45 D3
Abingdon Lodge EN5 ..171 E5
Abingdon Pl EN6 ......159 B7
Abingdon Rd LU4 ......44 C3
Abinger Cl SG1 .........50 E3
Aboyne Lodge Jun Mix Inf
  Sch AL3 .............127 D4
Abraham Cl WD19 .....175 B6
Abridge Cl EN8 ........162 D4
Abstacle Hill HP23 ......99 F3
Acacia Cl
  Hammond Street EN7 ..147 A4
  Stanmore HA7 ........176 E4
Acacia Gr HP2 .........122 B3
Acacia Rd EN2 ........161 D1
Acacia Rd AL10 .......130 A2
Acacia Wlk
  Harpenden AL5 .......107 D6
  Tring HP23 ............99 E3
Acacias Ct EN11 ......135 A6
Academy Ho [4] WD6 ..170 A5
Achilles Cl HP2 .......124 F5
Ackroyd Rd SG8 .........7 B3
Acme Rd WD24 .......154 B1
Acorn Cl LU2 ...........45 F3
Acorn Ct EN8 .........162 D6
Acorn Glade AL6 .......89 F4
Acorn La EN6 .........146 E2
Acorn Pl WD24 .......154 A2
Acorn Rd HP3 .........125 A2
Acorns The AL4 .......128 D3
Acre Piece SG4 .........35 A6
Acre Way HA6 ........174 F2
Acre Wood HP2 .......124 E2
Acremore St SG11 ......75 C7
Acrewood Way AL4 ....128 F3
Acton Cl EN8 .........162 E6
Acworth Cres LU4 ......44 C5
Acworth Ct [2] LU4 .....44 C5
Adam's Yd [1] SG14 ...113 D6
Adams Ho CM20 ......117 D1
Adams Way HP23 .....100 B6
Adamsfield EN7 .......148 A5
Adderley Rd
  Bishop's Stortford CM23 ..76 F7
  Harrow HA3 ..........176 F2
Addington Way LU4 ....44 D3
Addiscombe Rd WD18 .167 B5
Addison Cl HA6 .......175 D4
Addison Way HA6 .....174 F2
Adelaide Cl EN1 ......161 F1
Adelaide Ct EN8 ......162 F5
Adelaide St Luton LU1 ...63 D7
  St Albans AL3 ........127 D4

Adele Ave AL6 .........89 F3
Adeyfield Gdns HP2 ...124 F4
Adeyfield Rd HP2 .....124 F3
Adeyfield Sch HP2 ....125 A3
Adhara Rd HA6 .......175 A5
Adingtons CM20 ......117 F2
Adlington Ct LU4 .......44 C4
Admiral St SG13 ......114 A6
Admiral Way HP4 .....121 F6
Admirals Cl AL4 ......143 E8
Admirals Ct [6] HA6 ..174 F5
Admirals Wlk
  Hoddesdon EN11 .....135 B4
  St Albans AL1 ........142 A8
Adrian Cl Barnet EN5 .171 D3
  Harefield UB9 ........173 D2
Adrian Ho WD5 .......153 B4
Adrian Rd WD5 .......153 B8
Adstone Rd LU1 .......62 F3
Ailsworth Rd LU3 ......45 A7
Ainsdale Rd WD19 ....175 C7
Ainsland Ct LU4 ........44 B2
Aintree Rd SG8 .........7 F6
Aintree Way SG1 .......51 C8
Airedale HP2 .........124 E6
Airfield Ind Est HP23 ...79 E5
Airfield Way WD25 ....153 F5
Airport Approach Rd
  Luton LU2 .............64 D7
Airport Executive Pk LU2 64 D8
Airport Way LU1,LU2 ...64 A5
Aitken Rd EN5 ........171 C4
Akeman Cl AL3 .......126 F1
Akeman St HP23 .....100 A3
Akrill Ho AL5 ..........86 A3
Alamein Cl EN10 .....134 E3
Alan Dr EN5 ..........171 E3
Alandale Dr HA5 .....175 B2
Alba Rd CM17 ........118 C1
Alban Ave AL3 ........127 D5
Alban Cres WD6 .....170 B8
Alban Ct Barnet EN5 ..171 C3
  St Albans AL1 ........128 C3
Alban Ho WD6 .......170 B8
Alban Pk Ind Est AL4 .128 F3
Alban Rd SG6 .........23 C3
Alban Wood Inf Sch
  WD25 ...............154 B7
Alban Wood Jun Sch
  WD25 ...............154 B6
Albanian Ct AL1 ......128 A3
Albans View WD25 ....154 B6
Albany Cl WD23 ......168 E3
Albany Ct Harpenden AL5 107 C8
  Luton LU1 .............63 B8
Albany Mews
  Chiswell Green AL2 ...141 A4
  [3] Ware SG12 ........93 E1
Albany Park Ave EN3 ..162 D1
Albany Pl AL7 ........110 E6
Albany Rd EN3 .......162 D1
Albany Sch EN3 ......162 D1
Albany Terr HP23 ....100 B6
Albatross Ct SG13 ....114 B7
Albemarle Ave
  Cheshunt EN8 .......148 C3
  Potters Bar EN6 .....159 B7
Albeny Gate AL1 .....127 D2
Albert Rd Arlesey SG15 ..11 A4
  Luton LU1 .............63 F8
Albert Rd N WD17 ....167 B6
Albert Rd S WD17 ....167 B6
Albert St Markyate AL3 ..83 E5
  St Albans AL1 ........127 D2
  Stevenage SG1 ........50 A7
  Tring HP23 ...........100 A3
Albion Cl SG13 .......113 E7
Albion Ct [4] LU2 ......63 E8
Albion Hill HP2 ......124 D2
Albion Rd Luton LU2 ...63 E8
  Pitstone LU7 ..........80 D5
  St Albans AL1 ........127 F3
Albion The [9] SG12 ...93 D2
Albury CE Prim Sch
  SG11 ................57 A6
Albury Cl LU3 .........31 A1
Albury Dr Pinner HA5 .175 D3
  Pinner HA5 ..........175 E3
Albury Grove Rd EN8 .148 D1
Albury Ride SG11 .....57 C2
Albury Ride EN8 .....162 D8
Albury Wlk EN8 ......148 C1
Albyn Ho HP2 ........124 D3
Alconbury
  Bishop's Stortford CM23 ..59 B1
  Welwyn Garden City AL7 .111 E6
Alcorns The CM24 .....59 E7
Aldbury CE Prim Sch
  HP23 ................101 C6
Aldbury Cl St Albans AL4 128 C8
  Watford WD25 .......154 C3
Aldbury Gdns HP23 ...100 B6
Aldbury Rd AL7 .......111 B6
Aldbury Rd WD3 .....164 F2
Aldeburgh Cl SG1 ......36 A1
Alden Mead [6] HA5 ..176 A3
Aldenham Ave WD7 ..156 A3
Aldenham Ctry Pk★
  WD6 ................169 B4
Aldenham Gr WD7 ...156 B5
Aldenham Rd
  Bushey WD23 ........168 A6
  Elstree WD6,WD25 ...169 B5
  Radlett WD7 .........156 A4
  Watford WD23 .......167 E5
Aldenham Sch WD6 ..168 F7

Alder Cl Baldock SG7 ...23 F7
  Bishop's Stortford CM23 ..76 F4
  Chiswell Green AL2 ...141 C3
  Hoddesdon EN11 .....135 B8
Alder Cres LU3 .........45 A3
Alder Cl LU3 ...........45 B3
Alder Wlk WD25 .....154 B4
Alderbury Rd CM24 ...59 E8
Alderley Ct HP4 ......122 C3
Alderman Cl AL9 .....144 C7
Alderney Ho Enfield EN3 162 D1
  [7] Watford WD18 ...166 F3
Alders Ct AL7 .........111 A6
Alders End La AL5 .....85 F2
Alders Wlk CM21 ......97 E2
Aldersgrove EN9 .....163 E5
Alderton Cl [5] LU2 ....46 D1
Alderton Dr HP4 ......122 B4
Alderwood Ho [6] WD19 175 C7
Alderwood Mews EN4 .159 C1
Aldhous Cl LU3 ........45 B5
Aldis Mews EN3 .....163 A2
Aldock AL7 ...........111 A3
Aldock Rd SG1 .........50 E7
Aldridge Ave AL3 ....163 A1
Aldridge Ct SG7 .......12 E1
Aldwick AL1 .........128 B1
Aldwick Ct AL1 ......128 B1
Aldwick Rd AL5 ......107 E8
Aldwickbury Cres AL5 ..86 D1
Aldwickbury Sch AL5 ..107 E8
Aldwyck Cl HP1 ......124 C4
Aldwyke Rise SG12 ....93 C3
Aldykes AL10 ........129 F5
Alesia Rd LU3 .........44 F6
Alex Ct HP2 ..........124 D4
Alexander Ct [2] EN8 ..148 D1
Alexander Gate SG1 ...51 C8
Alexander Rd
  Hertford SG14 .......113 A6
  London Colney AL2 ...142 D6
  Stotfold SG5 ..........11 F6
Alexandra Ave LU3 ....45 C2
Alexandra Ct
  Cheshunt EN8 .......162 F5
  [11] Watford WD24 ..167 C7
Alexandra Mews WD17 .167 A7
Alexandra Rd
  Borehamwood WD6 ..170 D8
  Chipperfield WD4 ....138 A1
  Hemel Hempstead HP2 .124 D4
  Hitchin SG5 ...........21 F1
  Sarratt WD3 .........152 A3
  St Albans AL1 ........127 E3
  Watford WD17 .......167 A7
  Kings Langley WD4 ..139 B1
Alexandra Way EN8 ..162 F5
Aleyn Way SG7 ........13 B1
Alfriston Cl LU2 .......46 A3
Algar Cl HA7 .........176 F5
Alington La SG6 ........22 F3
Alison Ct HP2 ........125 C4
All Saints CE Prim Sch
  Bishop's Stortford CM23 ..77 B8
  Datchworth SG3 ......69 D3
All Saints Cl CM23 ....77 A8
All Saints Cres WD25 ..154 D6
All Saints La WD3 ....166 A3
All Saints Mews HA3 .176 E4
Allandale
  Hemel Hempstead HP2 .124 D5
  St Albans AL3 ........141 B8
Allandale Cres EN6 ...158 E7
Allandale Rd EN3 ....162 D3
Allard Cl EN7 .........147 E4
Allard Cres WD23 ....168 C1
Allard Way AL10 .....134 E2
Alldicks Rd HP3 ......124 F1
Allen Cl Shenley WD7 .156 E7
  Wheathampstead AL4 .108 D7
Allen Ct [2] AL10 .....130 B3
Allenby Ave LU5 .......44 A1
Allendale LU3 .........31 A1
Allerton Cl WD6 .....156 F1
Allerton Rd WD6 .....156 F1
Alleyns Rd SG1 ........50 D7
Allied Bsns Ctr AL5 ...86 C3
Allis Mews CM17 .....118 C1
Allison SG6 ...........23 C5
Allton Rd SG16 ........10 A4
Allum La WD6 .......169 E5
Allwood Rd EN7 .....147 F4
Alma Ct
  Borehamwood WD6 ..156 F1
  Potters Bar EN6 .....145 C1
Alma Cut AL1 ........127 E2
Alma Link [4] LU1 .....63 D7
Alma Rd
  Berkhamsted HP4 ....121 E6
  St Albans AL1 ........127 E2
Alma Row HA3 .......176 D2
Alma St LU1 ...........63 D7
Almond Cl LU3 ........45 B4
Almond Hill Jun Sch SG1 50 E8
Almond Way
  Borehamwood WD6 ..170 B5
  Harrow HA2 ..........176 D1
Almond Wlk [1] AL10 .130 A2
Almonds La SG1 .......50 E8
Almonds The AL1 ....142 B7
Alms La SG7 ...........49 D8
Almshoe Bury Cotts SG4 49 D8
Almshouse La EN1 ...162 B2
Almshouses SG5 .......68 B5
Alnwick Dr HP23 ......78 F7
Alpha Bsns Pk AL9 ...144 C8
Alpha Pl [4] CM23 .....76 F8
Alpine Cl SG4 .........35 A5

Alpine Way LU3 .......44 D8
Alpine Wlk HA7 ......176 E8
Alsford Wharf [1] HP4 .122 C4
Alsop Cl AL2 .........142 E3
Alston Ct [2] EN5 ....171 E6
Alston Rd Barnet EN5 .171 E6
  Hemel Hempstead HP1 .124 A2
Alswick Hall Cotts SG9 .41 B8
Altair Way HA6 ......174 F5
Altham Gdns WD19 ..175 D6
Altham Gr CM20 .....117 F3
Altham Rd HA5 ......175 D5
Althorp Cl EN5 .......171 A2
Althorp Rd LU3 ........45 C1
Althorpe Rd AL1 .....127 F4
Alton Ave HA7 .......176 E3
Alton Gdns LU1 ........63 C5
Alton Rd LU1 ..........63 C5
Altwood AL5 ..........86 D1
Alva Way WD19 ......175 D8
Alverton AL3 .........127 C6
Alwin Pl WD18 .......166 E5
Alwyn Cl
  Borehamwood WD6 ..169 D3
  Luton LU2 .............45 E2
Alyngton HP4 ........121 E7
Alzey Gdns AL5 ......107 D8
Amberdene [3] HA7 ..176 F4
Amberley Cl
  Harpenden AL5 .......86 B2
  Luton LU2 .............46 D4
Amberley Gn AL5 .....93 C4
Amberley Rd CM20 ..117 D1
Ambient Ho EN3 .....162 F3
Ambleside Harpenden AL5 86 D2
  Luton LU3 .............44 F5
Ambrose La AL5 .......85 F4
Amenbury Ct AL5 .....86 A1
Amenbury La AL5 .....86 A1
Amersham Ho WD18 .166 E2
Amersham Rd WD3 ..164 B8
Ames Cl Luton LU3 ....31 A1
  Luton LU3 .............44 F4
Amor Way SG6 ........23 B6
Amwell Cl WD25 .....154 E4
Amwell Comm AL7 ..111 C5
Amwell Ct
  Hoddesdon EN11 .....135 A7
  Waltham Abbey EN9 .163 E6
Amwell End SG12 ......93 D1
Amwell Hill SG12 ....114 F6
Amwell La
  Stanstead Abbotts SG12 ..115 B5
  Wheathampstead AL4 ..108 B7
Amwell Pl SG13 ......114 C4
Amwell St EN11 .....135 A7
Amwell View Sch SG12 .115 B4
Anchor Cl EN8 .......148 D3
Anchor Cotts SG12 ....93 D7
Anchor La
  Hemel Hempstead HP1 .124 B1
  Hemel Hempstead HP1 .124 C2
  Tonwell SG12 .........93 B6
Anchor Rd SG7 ........23 F7
Anchor St SG12 ........77 A6
Ancient Almhos [4] EN8 148 D1
Anderson Rd
  Shenley WD7 ........157 A6
  Stevenage SG2 ........51 D6
Anderson's Ho [3] AL5 .34 F8
Anderson's La SG9 ....29 A1
Andover Cl LU4 .......44 C4
Andrew Cl WD7 ......156 F6
Andrew Reed Ct [10]
  WD24 ...............167 C3
Andrew's La
  Cheshunt EN7 .......148 B3
  Goff's Oak EN7 ......147 B3
Andrews Cl HP2 .....124 D5
Andrews Lane Prim Sch
  EN7 .................148 B3
Andrewsfield AL7 ....111 C6
Anelle Rise HP3 ......138 C7
Anershall HP22 ........60 B3
Angel Cl LU4 ..........44 D3
Angel Cotts SG5 .......33 D2
Angel Pavement [7] SG8 ..7 D6
Angell's Mdw SG7 ......4 D4
Angle Ways SG2 .......51 B1
Anglefield Rd HP4 ...122 A4
Anglesey Cl CM23 .....76 C2
Anglesey Rd WD19 ..175 C5
Anglian Bsns Pk SG8 ...7 D7
Anglian Cl WD24 ....167 C2
Angotts Mead SG1 ....50 B6
Angus Cl LU4 ..........44 A3
Anmer Gdns LU4 ......44 A4
Annables La AL5 .......85 A4
Annette Cl HA3 ......176 E1
Anns Cl HP23 .........99 E3
Ansell Ct SG1 .........36 B1
Anselm Rd HA5 ......175 F3
Anson Cl Bovingdon HP3 .136 F4
  Sandridge AL4 .......108 A3
  St Albans AL1 ........128 B1
Anson Wlk HA6 ......174 C6
Anstee Rd LU4 ........44 B6
Anstey Fst Sch SG9 ...29 A6
Anthony Cl WD19 ....167 D1
Anthony Gdns LU1 ....63 D6
Anthony Rd WD6 .....169 D5
Anthorne Ct EN6 ....159 B8
Anthus Mews HA6 ...174 E3
Antoinette Ct WD5 ..139 F2
Antoneys Cl HA5 ....175 D1
Antonine Gate AL3 ..127 A4

Anvil Cl HP3 .........137 B3
Anvil Ct Buntingford SG9 .40 E8
  Luton LU3 .............44 E5
Anvil Ho [8] AL5 .......86 A5
Apex Point AL9 ......130 C1
Aplins Cl AL5 .........86 A2
Apollo Ave HA6 ......175 A5
Apollo Way
  Hemel Hempstead HP2 .124 F5
  Stevenage SG2 ........51 C8
Apple Cotts HP3 .....137 A4
Apple Orch The HP2 .124 F5
Appleby St EN7 ......147 E5
Applecroft
  Berkhamsted HP4 ...121 E6
  Chiswell Green AL2 ..141 B3
  Lower Stondon SG16 ...10 B3
Applecroft Rd Luton LU2 .46 C4
  Welwyn Garden City AL8 .110 B6
Applecroft Sch AL8 ..110 B5
Appleford's Cl EN11 .134 D4
Appleton Ave SG12 ...94 E5
Appleton Fields CM23 .76 E4
Appletree Gr AL3 ....106 B6
Appletree Wlk WD25 .154 B4
Appletrees SG5 .......34 D6
Applewood Cl AL5 .....85 E3
Appleyard Terr EN3 ..162 C2
Approach Rd AL1 ....127 E2
Approach The EN6 ...158 F7
Appspond La AL2 ....140 C8
April Pl CM21 .........97 F3
Apsley Cl CM23 ......76 F4
Apsley End Rd SG5 ...19 E6
Apsley Grange HP3 ..138 E4
Apsley Sta End HP3 ..138 D7
Apsley Manor Farm Barns
  HP3 .................138 D5
Apsley Mills Ret Pk
  HP3 .................138 E7
Apsley Sta HP3 ......138 E6
Apton Cl CM23 .......76 F4
Apton Fields [7] CM23 .76 F6
Apton Rd CM23 .......76 F7
Aquarius Way HA6 ...175 A6
Aragon Cl Enfield EN2 .160 F1
  Hemel Hempstead HP2 .125 C8
Aran Cl AL5 ..........107 D6
Arbour Cl LU3 .........31 A1
Arbour The SG13 ....113 D4
Arbroath Gn WD19 ..175 D7
Arcade [5] SG5 ........34 E7
Arcade The Hatfield AL10 130 B6
  Letchworth SG6 .......22 F6
  Luton LU1 .............45 C1
Arcade Wlk [4] SG5 ...34 E7
Arcadian Ct AL5 .......86 A2
Arch Rd SG4 ..........35 E4
Archer Cl WD4 .......138 F2
Archer Rd SG1 ........51 A6
Archers SG9 ..........40 F8
Archers Ct Hertford SG14 113 C7
  Redbourn AL3 .......106 B5
Archers Fields AL1 ..127 F5
Archers Green La AL6 .111 E8
Archers Ride AL7 ....111 B4
Archers Way SG6 .....22 B6
Arches Hall Cotts SG11 .73 E5
Archfield AL7 .........89 E1
Archway Ho AL9 ....130 C6
Archway Par LU3 ....44 F4
Archway Rd LU3 .....44 F4
Arckle Ho EN10 .....148 F5
Ardeley St Lawrence CE Prim
  Sch SG2 ..............38 F3
Arden Cl Bovingdon HP3 .137 A3
  Bushey WD23 .......168 F2
Arden Ct WD3 .......173 A8
Arden Gr AL5 .........86 B1
Arden Pl LU2 ..........45 E1
Arden Press Way SG6 .23 B6
Ardens Way AL4 .....128 D6
Ardentinny AL1 ......127 E2
Ardleigh Gn LU2 ......46 E1
Ardross Ave HA6 ....174 E5
Arena Par SG2 ........22 F6
Arena The EN3 ......162 F1
Argent Way EN7 ....147 D5
Argyle Ct WD18 .....166 F5
Argyle Rd EN5 .......171 C5
Argyle Way SG1 ......50 C5
Argyll Ave LU3 .......45 C2
Argyll Rd HP2 .......124 D8
Arkley Ct HP2 .......125 B8
Arkley Dr EN5 .......171 B5
Arkley La EN5 .......171 B5
Arkley Pk Cvn Pk EN5 .170 D3
Arkley Rd HP2 .......125 B8
Arkley View EN5 .....171 B5
Arkwrights CM20 ...117 F1
Arlesey Ho SG15 ......11 A8
Arlesey New Rd SG15,SG6 22 B7
Arlesey Rd Henlow SG16 .10 D8
  Henlow SG16 .........10 E8
  Ickleford SG5 .........21 F5
  Stotfold SG5 ..........11 E6
Arlesey Sta SG15 ......11 A8
Arlingham Cotts EN6 .158 A7
Arlingham Mews EN9 .163 C6
Arlington Cres EN8 ..162 E5
Armand Cl WD17 ....153 F1
Armitage Cl WD3 ....165 D5
Armitage Gdns LU4 ...44 D1
Armour Rise SG4 .....22 E4
Armourers Cl CM23 ..76 B4

**Armstrong Cl**
Borehamwood WD6 .......170 C6
London Colney AL2 .......142 E4
**Armstrong Gdns** WD7 ..156 E7
**Armstrong Pl** ∎ HP1 ..124 D4
**Arncliffe Cres** LU2 .......45 E1
**Arndale Ctr** LU1 .......63 E7
**Arnett Cl** WD3 .......165 A3
**Arnett Hills Jun Mix Inf Sch**
WD3 .......165 A3
**Arnett Way** WD3 .......165 A2
**Arnold Ave E** EN3 .......163 A1
**Arnold Ave W** EN3 .......162 F1
**Arnold Cl** Hitchin SG4 ..35 B8
Luton LU2 .......46 A3
Stevenage SG1 .......36 D2
**Arnold Rd** EN9 .......163 C4
**Arnolds La** SG7 .......3 D6
**Arran Cl** HP3 .......125 C1
**Arran Ct** LU1 .......63 D7
**Arran Ho** ∎ WD18 .......166 F3
**Arranmore Ct** WD23 .....167 E5
**Arretine Cl** AL3 .......126 F1
**Arrewig La** HP5,HP23 ...119 D1
**Arrow Cl** LU3 .......44 E6
**Art School Yd** ∎ AL1 ..127 D3
**Arthur Gibbens Ct** SG1 ..37 A1
**Arthur Rd** AL3 .......128 B3
**Arthur St** Luton LU1 .....63 E6
Watford WD23 .......167 E5
**Artichoke Dell** WD3 .....164 E4
**Artillery Pl** HA3 .......176 E1
**Artisan Cres** AL3 .......127 C4
**Arts Educational Sch The**
HP23 .......100 B3
**Arundel Cl** Aston SG2 .....51 E2
Cheshunt EN8 .......148 C3
Hemel Hempstead HP2 ..125 B4
**Arundel Dr** WD6 .......170 C5
**Arundel Gr** AL3 .......127 D7
**Arundel Ho** WD6 .......170 C5
**Arundel Rd** LU4 .......44 F2
**Arundell Rd** WD5 .......154 A7
**Arwood Mews** SG7 .......23 F7
**Ascent Pk** CM20 .......118 A4
**Ascot Cl**
Bishop's Stortford CM23 ..77 C8
Borehamwood WD6 .......170 A4
**Ascot Cres** SG1 .......37 B1
**Ascot Gdns** SG1 .......162 C2
**Ascot Ind Est** SG6 .......23 B2
**Ascot Rd** Luton LU3 .......45 B2
Royston SG8 .......7 F6
Watford WD18 .......166 E4
**Ascot Terr** SG12 .......114 F7
**Ascots La** AL7 .......110 F2
**Ash Cl**
Abbots Langley WD5 .....153 D7
Brookmans Park AL9 .....145 A6
Harefield UB9 .......173 C1
Harrow HA7 .......176 F4
Watford WD25 .......154 B4
**Ash Copse** AL2 .......154 F8
**Ash Dr** Hatfield AL10 .....130 A2
Hitchin SG4 .......35 A4
**Ash Gr** Harefield UB9 ....173 D2
Hemel Hempstead HP3 ..138 F7
Wheathampstead AL4 .....87 C1
**Ash Groves** CM21 .......98 A2
**Ash Hill Cl** WD23 .......168 B1
**Ash Mdw** SG10 .......74 F2
**Ash Mill** SG8 .......17 C3
**Ash Rd** Luton LU4 .......63 B8
Tring HP23 .......99 F4
Ware SG12 .......94 A3
**Ash Ride** EN2 .......161 A4
**Ash Tree Field** CM20 ....117 A2
**Ash Tree Rd** WD24 .......154 B3
**Ash Vale** WD3 .......172 D5
**Ash Way** SG8 .......7 F6
**Ashanger La** SG7 .......24 D4
**Ashbourne Cl** SG6 .......23 B3
**Ashbourne Ct** AL4 .......142 C8
**Ashbourne Rd** EN10 .....134 F2
**Ashbourne Sq** HA6 .....174 E4
**Ashbrook La** SG4 .......35 C3
**Ashburnam Wlk** SG2 .....50 F1
**Ashburnham Cl** WD19 ...175 A7
**Ashburnham Dr** WD19 ...175 A7
**Ashburnham Rd** LU1 .....63 C7
**Ashbury Cl** AL10 .......129 E5
**Ashby Ct** HP2 .......105 B1
**Ashby Gdns** AL1 .......141 D7
**Ashby Rd**
Berkhamsted HP4 .......121 D7
Watford WD24 .......154 A1
**Ashby Rise** CM23 .......59 B1
**Ashcombe** AL8 .......89 E2
**Ashcroft** HA5 .......176 A4
**Ashcroft Cl** AL5 .......107 E8
**Ashcroft Ct** EN10 .......134 F1
**Ashcroft High Sch** LU2 ...46 C2
**Ashcroft Rd** LU2 .......46 B3
**Ashdale** CM23 .......76 D4
**Ashdale Gdns** LU3 .......31 A1
**Ashdale Gr** HA7 .......176 F4
**Ashdales** AL1 .......141 D7
**Ashdown** SG6 .......11 F1
**Ashdown Cres** EN8 .......148 E3
**Ashdown Dr** WD6 .......169 F7
**Ashdown Rd**
Stevenage SG2 .......69 B8
Watford WD17 .......167 D6
**Ashendene Rd** SG13 .....132 F4
**Ashfield Ave** WD23 ......168 C2

**Ashfield Jun Sch** WD23 ..168 B2
**Ashfield Way** LU3 .......45 A6
**Ashfields** WD24,WD25 ...153 F4
**Ashford Gn** WD19 .......175 D5
**Ashfords** SG9 .......40 E8
**Ashleigh** SG2 .......51 B4
**Ashleigh Ct**
Hoddesdon EN11 .......135 A5
∎ Rickmansworth WD3 ..165 D2
**Ashleigh Cvn Pk** SG11 ....73 C3
**Ashley Cl** Cheddington LU7 80 A8
Hemel Hempstead HP3 ..124 F1
Pinner HA5 .......175 B1
Welwyn Garden City AL8 .110 C8
**Ashley Ct** AL10 .......130 B6
**Ashley Dr** WD6 .......170 D4
**Ashley Gdns** AL5 .......85 D3
**Ashley Ho** WD18 .......166 F3
**Ashley Rd** Hertford SG14 .113 B5
St Albans AL1 .......128 C2
**Ashleys** WD3 .......164 F2
**Ashlyn Cl** WD23 .......167 E5
**Ashlyns Ct** HP4 .......122 B3
**Ashlyns Rd** HP4 .......122 B3
**Ashlyns Sch** HP4 .......122 C2
**Ashmore Gdns** HP3 .....125 B2
**Ashmore Cl** HP3 .......137 C3
**Ashridge College Gdns**★
HP4 .......102 D5
**Ashridge Cotts** HP4 .....102 E5
**Ashridge Dr**
Bricket Wood AL2 .......140 F1
South Oxhey WD19 .......175 C5
**Ashridge Estate Visitor Ctr**★
HP4 .......101 E6
**Ashridge Ho** WD18 .....166 E2
**Ashridge La** HP5 .......150 D7
**Ashridge Management Coll**
HP4 .......102 C5
**Ashridge Rise** HP4 .......121 F5
**Ashton Rd** Enfield EN3 ...162 E3
Luton LU1 .......63 E5
**Ashton's La** SG7 .......23 F6
**Ashtree Ct** AL1 .......127 F3
**Ashtree Prim Sch** SG2 ....51 C4
**Ashtree Way** HP1 .......124 A2
**Ashurst Cl** HA6 .......174 E3
**Ashville Way** SG7 .......13 A1
**Ashwell** SG1 .......36 C2
**Ashwell & Morden Sta**
SG7 .......5 D2
**Ashwell Ave** LU3 .......44 C8
**Ashwell Cl** SG4 .......36 B4
**Ashwell Comm** SG4 .......36 B4
**Ashwell Par** LU3 .......44 C8
**Ashwell Pk** AL5 .......86 D1
**Ashwell Prim Sch** SG7 .....4 D4
**Ashwell Rd** Bygrave SG7 ..13 C4
Guilden Morden SG8 .......1 F1
Hinxworth SG7 .......3 E5
Newnham SG7 .......12 F8
**Ashwell St** Ashwell SG7 .....4 D4
Kneesworth SG8 .......2 A3
St Albans AL3 .......127 D4
**Ashwell Village Mus**★
SG7 .......4 D4
**Ashwood Ho** ∎ HA5 ......176 A3
**Ashwood Mews** AL1 .....127 D1
**Ashwood Pl** SG4 .......35 A5
**Ashwood Rd** EN6 .......159 B6
**Askew Rd** HA6 .......174 D8
**Aspasia Cl** AL1 .......127 F2
**Aspen Cl**
Bricket Wood AL2 .......140 E1
Stevenage SG2 .......69 B7
**Aspen Park Dr** WD25 ....154 B4
**Aspen Way** Enfield EN3 ...162 D4
Welwyn Garden City AL7 .111 C5
**Aspenden Rd** SG9 .......40 E6
**Aspens The**
Bishop's Stortford CM23 ...59 B2
Hitchin SG4 .......35 A6
**Aspfield Row** HP1 .......124 B5
**Asquith Cl** SG2 .......69 C7
**Asquith Ho** AL8 .......110 D7
**Ass House La** HA3 .......176 B6
**Astall Cl** HA3 .......176 E2
**Aster Cl** CM23 .......76 D6
**Asters The** EN7 .......147 D3
**Astley Cooper Sch** HP2 ..125 A8
**Astley Gn** LU2 .......46 C2
**Astley Rd** HP1 .......124 C3
**Aston Bury** SG2 .......69 F8
**Aston Cl** Bushey WD23 ...168 C3
Stevenage SG2 .......36 C2
Watford WD24 .......167 C7
**Aston End Rd** SG2 .......51 E3
**Aston Grange** SG14 .....113 D8
**Aston La** SG2 .......69 E8
**Aston Rd** SG11 .......55 D2
**Aston Rise** SG4 .......35 B6
**Aston St Mary's CE Prim Sch**
SG2 .......51 E2
**Aston View** HP2 .......105 A1
**Aston Way** EN6 .......159 D7
**Astonia Ho** SG7 .......23 F7
**Astons Rd** HA6 .......174 C6
**Astra Ct** Luton LU2 .......45 F2
Watford WD18 .......166 F4
**Astra Ctr** CM20 .......117 F4
**Astral Cl** SG1 .......10 B3
**Astrope La** HP23 .......79 B3
**Astwick Ave** AL10 .......129 F8
**Astwick Manor** AL10 .....129 C8
**Astwick Rd** Stotfold SG5 ..11 F8
Stotfold SG5 .......3 A2
**Athelstan Rd** HP3 .......138 F8
**Athelstan Wlk N** AL7 .....110 E5

**Athelstan Wlk S** AL7 ....110 D5
**Athelstone Rd** HA3 .......176 D1
**Athena Est** CM20 .......118 B4
**Athena Pl** HA6 .......174 F2
**Atherstone Rd** LU4 .......44 D1
**Atherton End** CM21 .......97 E3
**Athlone Cl** WD7 .......156 B3
**Athol Cl** HA5 .......175 B2
**Athol Gdns** HA5 .......175 B2
**Atholl Cl** LU3 .......44 D8
**Atria Rd** HA6 .......175 A5
**Attenborough Cl** WD19 ..175 E7
**Attimore Cl** AL8 .......110 B5
**Attimore Rd** AL8 .......110 B5
**Aubretia Ho** AL7 .......111 B4
**Aubrey Ave** AL2 .......142 C5
**Aubrey Gdns** LU4 .......44 B6
**Aubrey La** AL3 .......105 C2
**Aubreys** SG6 .......23 A2
**Aubreys Rd** HP1 .......123 E3
**Aubries** SG2 .......38 B1
**Auckland Cl** EN1 .......162 B2
**Auckland Rd** EN6 .......158 F7
**Auden Dr** WD6 .......170 A4
**Audley Cl** WD6 .......170 A6
**Audley Ct** HA5 .......175 C1
**Audley Gdns** EN3 .......163 C5
**Audrey Gdns** CM23 .......76 E5
**Audwick Cl** EN8 .......148 E3
**Augustine Ct** EN9 .......163 B6
**Augustine Rd** HA3 .......176 C2
**Augustus Cl** AL3 .......127 A1
**Augustus Gate** SG2 .......51 D8
**Augustus Smith Ho** ∎
HP4 .......122 D4
**Austen Paths** SG2 .......51 C6
**Austin Mews** ∎ HP1 .....124 D4
**Austin Rd** LU3 .......45 C4
**Austins Mead** HP3 .......137 B3
**Austins Pl** HP2 .......124 D4
**Autumn Glades** HP3 .....125 C1
**Autumn Gr** AL7 .......111 B4
**Avalon Cl** WD25 .......154 E7
**Avebury Ave** LU2 .......45 D4
**Avebury Ct** HP2 .......125 A5
**Avenue App** WD4 .......139 A1
**Avenue Ct** AL6 .......89 E7
**Avenue Grimaldi** LU3 .....45 A3
**Avenue Mans** EN5 .......171 C5
**Avenue One** SG6 .......23 C6
**Avenue Pl** CM23 .......77 A6
**Avenue Rd**
Bishop's Stortford CM23 ...77 D5
Hoddesdon EN11 .......135 D5
Pinner HA5 .......175 E1
St Albans AL1 .......128 A5
**Avenue Rise** WD23 .......168 A4
**Avenue St Nicholas** AL5 ..86 A1
**Avenue Terr** WD19 .......167 E3
**Avenue The** Barnet EN5 ..171 C5
Bushey WD23 .......167 F5
Harrow HA3 .......176 F2
Hemel Hempstead HP1 ..123 A4
Hertford SG14 .......113 B8
Hitchin SG4 .......35 B7
Luton LU4 .......44 D5
Northwood HA6 .......174 C4
Oaklands AL6 .......89 D7
Pinner HA5 .......175 F4
Potters Bar EN6 .......145 A1
Radlett WD7 .......156 B5
Stevenage SG1 .......50 D8
Stotfold SG5 .......11 F6
Watford WD17 .......167 A4
**Avey La** EN9 .......163 E2
**Avia Cl** HP3 .......138 D7
**Avior Dr** HA6 .......174 F6
**Avocet Cl** SG6 .......11 E1
**Avon Chase** SG16 .......10 C4
**Avon Cl** WD25 .......154 C5
**Avon Cotts** LU2 .......46 B3
**Avon Ct** ∎ Harpenden AL5 .86 B1
Luton LU3 .......63 C8
**Avon Dr** SG1 .......37 A3
**Avon Mews** HA5 .......175 F2
**Avon Rd** SG16 .......10 B4
**Avon Sq** HP2 .......124 F8
**Avondale Cl** AL1 .......127 E3
**Avondale Rd** LU1 .......63 C8
**Axe Cl** LU3 .......44 E6
**Aycliffe Dr** HP2 .......124 E7
**Aycliffe Drive Prim Sch**
HP2 .......124 E7
**Aycliffe Rd** WD6 .......156 F1
**Aydon Rd** LU3 .......45 B6
**Aylands Rd** EN3 .......162 D3
**Aylands Sch** EN3 .......162 D3
**Aylesbury Rd** HP23 .......99 E3
**Aylott Ct** SG14 .......70 E4
**Aylotts Cl** SG9 .......40 D8
**Aylsham Rd** EN11 .......135 C8
**Aylward Dr** SG2 .......51 B4
**Aynho St** WD18 .......167 B4
**Aynsworth Ave** CM23 .....59 B2
**Ayot Gn** Ayot St Peter AL6 .89 A1
Hatfield AL6 .......109 F8
**Ayot Ho** AL6 .......88 A6
**Ayot Little Green La** AL6 ..88 F1
**Ayot Mt** WD6 .......157 A1
**Ayot St Peter Rd** AL6 .....88 E3
**Ayr Cl** SG1 .......51 C8
**Ayres End La** AL3,AL5 ....107 E5
**Aysgarth Cl** AL5 .......107 B8
**Aysgarth Rd** AL3 .......106 A6
**Azalea Cl** AL2 .......142 B4

**Azure Appartments**
HA3 .......176 E2

**B**

**Baas Hill** EN10 .......134 D2
**Baas Hill Cl** EN10 .......134 E2
**Baas La** EN10 .......134 E3
**Babbage Rd** SG1 .......50 B5
**Back La** Buckland SG9 .....27 C8
Little Hallingbury CM22 ...98 B3
Preston SG4 .......48 D6
Radlett WD25 .......168 E8
Sheering CM22 .......98 B1
Tewin AL6 .......90 E2
**Back St** Ashwell SG7 .......4 C3
Luton LU2 .......63 D8
**Back The** HP4 .......123 B7
**Bacon's Yd** SG7 .......4 D4
**Bacons Dr** EN6 .......146 E2
**Badburgham Ct** EN9 .....163 F6
**Baddeley Cl**
Holdbrook EN3 .......163 A2
Stevenage SG2 .......51 B2
**Bader Cl** Stevenage SG1 ...36 F1
Welwyn Garden City AL7 .111 C6
**Badger Cl** SG3 .......69 A6
**Badger Way** AL10 .......130 B3
**Badgers** CM23 .......76 E5
**Badgers Cl**
Borehamwood WD6 .......169 F7
Hertford SG13 .......114 B6
Stevenage SG1 .......50 E4
**Badgers Croft**
Barnet HP2 .......171 E1
Hemel Hempstead HP2 ..125 D2
Hoddesdon EN10 .......134 E2
Radlett WD25 .......154 A5
**Badgers Wlk**
Chorleywood WD3 .......164 F5
Tewin AL6 .......90 C5
**Badingham Dr** AL5 .......85 E1
**Badminton Cl**
∎ Borehamwood WD6 ...170 A7
Stevenage SG2 .......69 B7
**Badminton Ho** ∎ WD24 167 C2
**Badminton Pl** EN10 .......134 E3
**Bagenal Ho** WD5 .......153 F7
**Bagwicks Cl** LU3 .......44 E7
**Bailey Hill Ct** LU1 .......63 E5
**Bailey St** LU1 .......63 F6
**Baines La** SG3 .......69 C4
**Baird Cl** WD23 .......168 B3
**Bairstow Cl** WD6 .......169 E8
**Baisley Ho** EN7 .......148 A3
**Baker Cl** WD6 .......170 B7
**Baker St** Enfield EN1 .....161 E1
Hertford SG13 .......113 E6
Luton LU1 .......63 E5
Potters Bar EN6 .......158 E5
∎ Stevenage SG1 .......50 C7
**Baker's La** SG4 .......67 F1
**Bakers Ct** ∎ CM23 .......77 A7
**Bakers Gr** AL7 .......111 C7
**Bakers La** Barley SG8 .......8 F7
Kensworth Common LU6 ..82 E8
**Bakers Rd** EN7 .......148 B1
**Bakers Wlk** CM21 .......97 E2
**Bakerscroft** ∎ EN8 .......148 E3
**Bakery Ct** CM24 .......59 D6
**Bakery The** ∎ SG2 .......93 D2
**Bakewell Cl** LU4 .......44 C1
**Balcary Gdns** HP4 .......121 F4
**Balcombe Cl** LU2 .......46 D4
**Balcon Way** WD6 .......170 C8
**Baldock La** SG6 .......23 D4
**Baldock Rd** Aspenden SG9 40 B8
Letchworth SG6 .......23 B5
Royston SG8 .......6 C4
Stotfold SG5 .......12 A5
**Baldock St** Royston SG8 .....7 C6
Ware SG12 .......93 D2
**Baldock Sta** SG7 .......12 F1
**Baldock Way** WD6 .......169 F8
**Baldways Cl** HP22 .......60 C3
**Baldwins** AL7 .......111 C6
**Baldwins La** WD3 .......166 B5
**Balfour Ct** AL5 .......86 C3
**Balfour Mews** HP3 .......137 A4
**Balfour St** SG14 .......113 C7
**Baliol Rd** SG5 .......34 F8
**Ballater Cl** WD19 .......175 C6
**Ballinger Ct**
Berkhamsted HP4 .......122 B3
∎ Watford WD18 .......167 B6
**Balloon Cnr** AL9 .......144 B8
**Ballslough Hill** SG4 .......66 D1
**Balmoral Cl**
Chiswell Green AL2 .......141 C3
Stevenage SG2 .......69 C7
**Balmoral Dr** WD6 .......170 D5
**Balmoral Ho** WD6 .......170 C5
**Balmoral Rd**
Abbots Langley WD5 .....154 A7
Enfield EN3 .......162 D3
Hitchin SG5 .......21 E1
Watford WD24 .......154 C1
**Balmore Wood** LU3 .......31 B1
**Balsams Cl** SG13 .......113 D4
**Bampton Rd** LU4 .......44 B2
**Bamville Wood** AL5 .......107 C5
**Banbury Cl** LU4 .......44 F4
**Banbury St** WD18 .......167 B4
**Bancroft** SG5 .......34 F7
**Bancroft Gdns** HA3 .......176 C2
**Bancroft Rd** Harrow HA3 176 C1

**Bancroft Rd** continued
Luton LU3 .......45 B5
**Bandley Rise** SG2 .......51 C3
**Banes Down** EN9 .......135 E1
**Bank Cl** LU4 .......44 C4
**Bank Ct** HP1 .......124 C2
**Bank Mill** HP4 .......122 E4
**Bank Mill La** HP4 .......122 E3
**Banks Rd** WD6 .......170 C7
**Bankside Cl** UB9 .......173 A4
**Bankside Down** WD3 .....165 D3
**Bannister Gdns** SG8 .......7 E3
**Bantel Villas** EN11 .......135 C8
**Barbel Ct** EN8 .......163 A5
**Barberry Rd** HP1 .......124 A3
**Barbers La** ∎ LU1 .......63 E7
**Barbers Wlk** HP23 .......99 F3
**Barchester Rd** HA3 .......176 D1
**Barclay Cl**
Hertford Heath SG13 .....114 B4
Watford WD18 .......167 A3
**Barclay Cres** SG1 .......50 E7
**Barclay Ct**
Hoddesdon EN11 .......135 A5
Luton LU1 .......63 F8
**Barclay Sch** SG1 .......50 D8
**Barden Cl** UB9 .......173 C3
**Bards Cnr** HP1 .......124 B4
**Bardwell Ct** ∎ AL1 .......127 D2
**Bardwell Rd** AL1 .......127 D2
**Barfolds** AL9 .......144 C8
**Barford Rise** LU2 .......46 D1
**Barge Ho** HP3 .......138 E7
**Bargrove Ave** HP1 .......124 A2
**Barham Ave** WD6 .......169 F5
**Barham Rd** SG2 .......51 C5
**Barker Cl** HA6 .......174 F3
**Barkers Mead**
Bishop's Stortford CM22 ...77 B1
Little Hallingbury CM22 ...98 B8
**Barkham Cl** LU7 .......79 F7
**Barking Cl** LU4 .......44 B6
**Barkston Path** WD6 .....157 A1
**Barkway CE Fst Sch** SG8 ..17 C4
**Barkway Hill** SG8 .......17 E6
**Barkway Rd** SG8 .......7 E5
**Barkway St** SG8 .......7 D5
**Barley Brow** WD25 .......154 C8
**Barley CE Fst Sch** SG8 .....9 A1
**Barley Cl** WD23 .......168 B4
**Barley Croft**
Hemel Hempstead HP2 ..125 C3
Hertford SG14 .......113 D8
Stapleford SG14 .......92 A3
**Barley Ct** EN7 .......148 B1
**Barley Hills** CM23 .......76 C4
**Barley La** LU4 .......44 C5
**Barley Mow La** AL4 .......142 F8
**Barley Ponds Cl** SG12 ....93 F1
**Barley Ponds Rd** SG12 ....93 F1
**Barley Rd** Barley SG8 .......9 A7
Great Chishill SG8 .......9 C2
**Barley Rise** Baldock SG7 ..24 B8
Harpenden AL5 .......86 C4
**Barleycorn The** ∎ LU3 ....63 D8
**Barleycroft**
Buntingford SG9 .......40 E6
Stevenage SG2 .......51 D3
Tonwell SG12 .......92 F7
**Barleycroft Gn** AL8 .......110 C6
**Barleycroft Rd** AL8 .......110 C5
**Barleyvale** LU3 .......45 A8
**Barlings Rd** AL5 .......107 B5
**Barmor Cl** HA2 .......176 B1
**Barmouth Row** ∎ HP2 ...124 E6
**Barn Cl**
Hemel Hempstead HP3 ..138 F8
Radlett WD7 .......156 A4
Welwyn Garden City AL8 .110 C6
**Barn Ct** CM21 .......97 E3
**Barn Lea** WD3 .......165 A1
**Barnack Ct** SG8 .......7 C7
**Barnacres Rd** HP3 .......139 A8
**Barnard Acres** EN9 .......149 E8
**Barnard Gn** AL7 .......110 F5
**Barnard Rd** Luton LU1 ....63 A7
Sawbridgeworth CM21 ....97 E4
**Barnard Way** HP3 .......124 E1
**Barncroft** SG11 .......57 C7
**Barncroft Prim Sch**
HP2 .......124 D8
**Barncroft Rd** HP4 .......121 F3
**Barncroft Way** AL1 .......128 A2
**Barndell Cl** SG5 .......11 F6
**Barndicott** AL7 .......111 C6
**Barndicott Ho** AL7 .......111 C6
**Barnes La** WD4 .......138 D3
**Barnes Rise** WD4 .......138 F4
**Barnet By-Pass**
Borehamwood WD6 .......170 C6
Dancers Hill EN5 .......158 A3
Barnet Coll EN5 .......171 F5
**Barnet Gate La** EN5 .......170 F3
**Barnet General Hospl**
EN5 .......171 D5
**Barnet Hill** EN5 .......171 F5
**Barnet Hill Jun Mix Inf Sch**
EN5 .......171 F5
**Barnet La**
Borehamwood WD6 .......170 B3
Totteridge EN5,N20 .......171 F2
Barnet Mus★ EN5 .......171 E5
**Barnet Rd** Barnet EN5 ....170 E3
Ganwick Corner EN6,EN5 .159 A4
London Colney AL2 .......142 E4
**Barnet Stall Market**
EN5 .......171 E6
**Barnet Trad Est** EN5 .....171 F6

**Barnet Way (Barnet By-Pass)**
NW7 . . . . . . . . . . . .170 D2
**Barnfield** HP3 . . . . . . . .138 F8
**Barnfield Ave** LU2 . . . . .45 D5
**Barnfield Cl**
Hoddesdon EN11 . . . . . .135 A8
Lower Nazeing EN9 . . . . .135 F1
**Barnfield Coll** LU3 . . . . .45 B8
**Barnfield Coll (North)**
Luton LU2 . . . . . . . . . . .63 F8
Luton,Stopsley Common
LU2 . . . . . . . . . . . . . .45 D5
**Barnfield Coll (South)**
LU1 . . . . . . . . . . . . . . .63 B5
**Barnfield Ct** AL5 . . . . .107 C8
**Barnfield Rd**
Harpenden AL5 . . . . . . .107 C8
St Albans AL4 . . . . . . . .128 C5
Welwyn Garden City AL7 .110 E4
**Barnhurst Path** WD19 . .175 C5
**Barns Dene** AL5 . . . . . .85 E2
**Barns The** HP23 . . . . . . .99 F1
**Barnsdale Cl** WD6 . . . . .169 F8
**Barnside Ct** AL8 . . . . . .110 C6
**Barnston Cl** LU2 . . . . . . .46 D1
**Barnsway** WD4 . . . . . . .138 E3
**Barnview Lo** HA3 . . . . . .176 E2
**Barnwell** SG2 . . . . . . . . .51 B2
**Barnwell Sch** SG2 . . . . . .51 B2
**Barnwood Cl** N20 . . . . .171 F1
**Baron Ct** SG1 . . . . . . . . .36 B1
**Barons Ct** 7 LU2 . . . . . .45 D1
**Barons The** CM23 . . . . . .76 D5
**Baronsmere Ct** 7 EN5 .171 E5
**Barr Rd** EN6 . . . . . . . . .159 C6
**Barra Cl** HP3 . . . . . . . . .139 C8
**Barra Ho** 6 WD18 . . . . .166 F3
**Barrass Cl** EN3 . . . . . . .163 A2
**Barratt Ind Pk** LU2 . . . . .64 C6
**Barratt Way** HA3 . . . . . .176 D1
**Barrells Down Rd** CM23 . .58 E1
**Barrett La** 5 CM23 . . . . .76 F7
**Barrington Dr** UB9 . . . . .173 A3
**Barrington Mews** AL7 . . .111 B5
**Barrington Rd** SG6 . . . . . .22 F4
**Barrons Row** AL5 . . . . .107 D7
**Barrow** EN7 . . . . . . . . . .147 F1
**Barrow Point Ave** HA5 . .175 E1
**Barrow Point La** HA5 . . .175 E1
**Barrowby Cl** LU2 . . . . . . .46 D1
**Barrowdene Cl** HA5 . . . .175 E1
**Barry Cl** AL2 . . . . . . . . .141 B6
**Barry Ct** SG1 . . . . . . . . .50 B8
**Bartel Cl** HP3 . . . . . . . .125 D1
**Bartholomew Court Sh**
Pavilion EN8 . . . . . . . .162 E6
**Bartholomew Ho** EN3 . .162 E2
**Bartholomew Rd** 8
CM23 . . . . . . . . . . . . .76 F6
**Bartletts Cotts** 4 EN5 .171 E6
**Bartletts Mead** SG14 . . . .92 D1
**Barton Cl** AL5 . . . . . . . . .86 C3
**Barton Rd** Hexton SG5 . . .19 A1
Luton LU3 . . . . . . . . . . .45 C7
Wheathampstead AL4 . . .108 C8
**Barton Way**
Borehamwood WD6 . . . .170 A7
Croxley Green WD3 . . . .166 B4
**Bartons The** WD6 . . . . .169 D3
**Bartrams La** EN4 . . . . . .159 C1
**Bartrop Ct** EN7 . . . . . . .147 D3
**Bartrum Villas** 4 HP4 . .122 D4
**Barwick La** SG11 . . . . . . .73 C3
**Basbow La** 2 CM23 . . . . .76 F7
**Basil Mews** CM17 . . . . . .118 C4
**Basildon Cl** WD18 . . . . .166 C3
**Basildon Sq** HP2 . . . . . .124 F7
**Basils Rd** SG1 . . . . . . . . .50 D7
**Baslow Cl** HA3 . . . . . . . .176 D2
**Bassett Cl** AL3 . . . . . . . .106 B5
**Bassil Rd** HP2 . . . . . . . .124 D2
**Bassingbourne Cl** EN10 .134 F3
**Bassingburn Wlk** AL7 . . .110 F5
**Bassus Gn** SG2 . . . . . . . .52 F8
**Batchelors** SG11 . . . . . . .55 E2
**Batchwood Dr** AL3 . . . . .127 C6
**Batchwood Gdns** AL3 . . .127 D6
**Batchwood Sch** AL3 . . . .127 D6
**Batchwood View** AL3 . . .127 D5
**Batchworth Heath** WD3 174 B5
**Batchworth Heath Hill**
WD3 . . . . . . . . . . . . .174 A6
**Batchworth Hill London Rd**
WD3 . . . . . . . . . . . . .173 F7
**Batchworth La** HA6 . . . .174 D5
**Bateman Rd** WD3 . . . . . .166 A3
**Bates Ho** 2 SG1 . . . . . . .50 E6
**Batford Cl** AL7 . . . . . . . .111 B5
**Batford Rd** AL5 . . . . . . . .86 D3
**Bath Pl** EN5 . . . . . . . . .171 F6
**Bath Rd** LU3 . . . . . . . . . .45 D2
**Bathurst Rd** HP2 . . . . . .124 E6
**Batterdale** AL9 . . . . . . . .130 C6
**Battlefield Rd** AL1 . . . . .127 F5
**Battlers Green Dr** WD7 . .155 E3
**Battleview** AL4 . . . . . . . .108 E8
**Baud Cl** SG11 . . . . . . . . .57 E2
**Baulk The**
Cheddington LU7 . . . . . . .79 F7
Lilley LU2 . . . . . . . . . . . .32 D2
Pitstone LU7 . . . . . . . . . .80 F5
**Bay Cl** LU4 . . . . . . . . . . .44 B6
**Bay Ct** HP4 . . . . . . . . . .122 B4
**Bay Tree Cl**
Chiswell Green AL2 . . . . .141 C3
Hammond Street EN7 . . . .147 F4
**Bay Tree Wlk** WD17 . . . .154 A1

**Bayford CE Prim Sch**
SG13 . . . . . . . . . . . . .132 F5
**Bayford Cl**
Hemel Hempstead HP2 . .125 C8
Hertford SG13 . . . . . . . .113 C4
**Bayford Gn** SG13 . . . . . .133 A6
**Bayford La** SG13 . . . . . .132 F7
**Bayford Sta** SG13 . . . . . .133 B5
**Bayfordbury Coll (Univ of
Hertfordshire)** SG13 . . .113 B1
**Bayhurst Dr** HA6 . . . . . .174 F4
**Baylam Dell** LU2 . . . . . . .46 E1
**Bayley Hall Mews** SG14 113 D5
**Baylie Ct** HP2 . . . . . . . .124 E4
**Baylie La** HP2 . . . . . . . .124 E4
**Bayworth** SG6 . . . . . . . . .23 B5
**Beacon Ct** SG13 . . . . . . .114 C3
**Beacon Rd** Al1 . . . . . . . .127 F3
**Beacon Rd** Ringshall HP4 . .81 A1
Ware SG12 . . . . . . . . . . .94 A2
**Beacon Way**
Rickmansworth WD3 . . . .165 B3
Tring HP23 . . . . . . . . . .100 C5
**Beacons The**
Hatfield AL10 . . . . . . . .130 C6
Stevenage SG1 . . . . . . . . .37 B3
**Beaconsfield** LU2 . . . . . . .64 B8
**Beaconsfield Rd**
Enfield EN3 . . . . . . . . .162 D2
Hatfield AL10 . . . . . . . .130 C6
St Albans AL1 . . . . . . . .127 E3
Tring HP23 . . . . . . . . . . .99 E3
**Beadles The** CM22 . . . . . .98 B8
**Beadlow Rd** LU4 . . . . . . .44 A4
**Beagle Cl** WD7 . . . . . . .155 F2
**Beale Cl** SG2 . . . . . . . . . .51 C6
**Beamish Dr** WD23 . . . . .168 C1
**Beane Ave** SG2 . . . . . . . .51 D6
**Beane Rd** Hertford SG14 .113 B7
Watton at S SG14 . . . . . . .70 D1
**Beane Wlk** SG2 . . . . . . . .51 D6
**Beaneside The** SG14 . . . . .70 D4
**Beanfield Rd** CM21 . . . . . .97 A4
**Beanley Cl** LU2 . . . . . . . .46 E2
**Bear La** SG7 . . . . . . . . . . .4 D4
**Bearton Ave** SG5 . . . . . . .34 E8
**Bearton Ct** SG5 . . . . . . . .21 E1
**Bearton Gn** SG5 . . . . . . .21 D1
**Bearton Rd** SG5 . . . . . . .21 E1
**Beatty Rd** EN8 . . . . . . . .162 F5
**Beauchamp Gdns** WD3 . .165 A1
**Beauchamps** AL7 . . . . . .111 B5
**Beaulieu** 7 WD19 . . . . . .167 C1
**Beaulieu Dr** EN9 . . . . . .163 B6
**Beaumayes Cl** HP1 . . . . .124 B2
**Beaumont Ave** AL1 . . . . .128 B4
**Beaumont Ct** 3 SG5 . . . . .34 E8
**Beaumont Ct** 10 AL5 . . . . .86 B1
**Beaumont Gate** WD7 . . .156 A4
**Beaumont Hall La** AL3 . .106 C2
**Beaumont Pl** Barnet EN5 171 F8
Watford WD18 . . . . . . .167 A4
**Beaumont Rd**
Hammond Street EN7 . . .147 F7
Luton LU3 . . . . . . . . . . .45 B2
**Beaumont Sch** AL4 . . . . .128 C4
**Beaumont View** EN7 . . . .147 D5
**Beazley Cl** SG13 . . . . . . . .93 E2
**Beckbury Cl** LU2 . . . . . . .46 E2
**Becket Gdns** AL6 . . . . . . .89 C4
**Beckets Sq** HP4 . . . . . . .122 A6
**Beckett's Ave** AL3 . . . . .127 C6
**Becketts** SG14 . . . . . . . .113 A5
**Beckfield La** SG9 . . . . . . .26 D7
**Beckham Cl** LU2 . . . . . . .45 D7
**Beckham Cl** AL3 . . . . . . . .83 D5
**Bede Cl** HA5 . . . . . . . . . .175 D2
**Bede Ct** HP4 . . . . . . . . . .102 C8
**Bedford Almshouses** 1
WD18 . . . . . . . . . . . .167 C5
**Bedford Ave** EN5 . . . . . .171 F4
**Bedford Cl** WD3 . . . . . . .151 B1
**Bedford Cres** EN3 . . . . . .162 E4
**Bedford Gdns** 4 LU2 . . . .63 D8
**Bedford Park Rd** AL1 . . .127 E3
**Bedford Rd** Hitchin SG5 . . .34 D7
Ickleford SG5 . . . . . . . . .21 D5
Letchworth SG6 . . . . . . . .22 D7
Lower Stondon SG16 . . . . .10 B3
Moor Park HA6 . . . . . . .174 D6
St Albans AL1 . . . . . . . .127 E2
**Bedford St**
Berkhamsted HP4 . . . . . .122 D4
Hitchin SG5 . . . . . . . . . .34 D7
Watford WD24 . . . . . . .167 B8
**Bedmond La**
Bricket Wood AL3,WD5 . .140 B6
St Albans AL3 . . . . . . . .126 F1
**Bedmond Rd**
Abbots Langley WD5 . . . .139 F2
Hemel Hempstead HP3 . .125 D1
Pimlico HP3 . . . . . . . . .139 E7
**Bedmond Village Prim Sch**
WD5 . . . . . . . . . . . . .139 F3
**Bedwell Ave** AL9,SG13 . .132 A2
**Bedwell Cl** AL7 . . . . . . . .110 F5
**Bedwell Cres** SG1 . . . . . .50 F5
**Bedwell Prim Sch** SG1 . . .51 A5
**Bedwell Rise** SG1 . . . . . . .50 F5
**Beech Ave**
Crews Hill EN2 . . . . . . . .161 A4
Radlett WD7 . . . . . . . . .156 A5
**Beech Bottom** AL3 . . . . .127 D6
**Beech Cl** Harpenden AL5 .107 C5

**Beech Cl** *continued*
Hatfield AL10 . . . . . . . .130 A4
**Beech Cres** AL4 . . . . . . .108 D7
**Beech Ct** Harpenden AL5 . .85 F3
Hoddesdon EN10 . . . . . .135 A3
**Beech Dr**
Berkhamsted HP4 . . . . . .122 C3
Borehamwood WD6 . . . .169 F7
Sawbridgeworth CM21 . . .118 C8
Stevenage SG2 . . . . . . . . .51 B3
**Beech Farm Dr** AL4 . . . .128 F7
**Beech Gr** HP23 . . . . . . . .100 C4
**Beech Hill**
Hadley Wood EN4 . . . . . .159 E1
Letchworth SG6 . . . . . . . .22 D7
Luton LU2 . . . . . . . . . . .46 D8
**Beech Hill Com Prim Sch**
LU4 . . . . . . . . . . . . . . .45 B1
**Beech Hill Ct** HP4 . . . . . .122 D4
**Beech Ho** EN11 . . . . . . .134 F6
**Beech Hyde La** AL4 . . . . .108 F6
**Beech Hyde Prim Sch**
AL4 . . . . . . . . . . . . . .108 D7
**Beech Mews** SG12 . . . . .114 D7
**Beech Pk** HP6 . . . . . . . .150 B1
**Beech Pl** AL3 . . . . . . . . .127 D6
**Beech Rd** Luton LU1 . . . . .63 C8
St Albans AL3 . . . . . . . .127 E6
Watford WD24 . . . . . . .154 B3
**Beech Ridge** Baldock SG7 . .23 B5
Harpenden AL5 . . . . . . . .85 B5
**Beech Way** AL4 . . . . . . . .87 B6
**Beech Wlk** HP23 . . . . . . .100 C4
**Beechcroft**
Berkhamsted HP4 . . . . . .122 C3
Datchworth SG3 . . . . . . .69 D1
**Beechcroft Ave** WD3 . . .166 C4
**Beechcroft Rd** WD23 . . .167 E4
**Beechen Gr** WD17 . . . . .167 C6
**Beeches The**
Chorleywood WD3 . . . . .164 F4
Hemel Hempstead HP1 . .124 B2
Hitchin SG4 . . . . . . . . . .35 A6
Park Street AL2 . . . . . . .141 D4
Royston SG8 . . . . . . . . . . .7 D6
Tring HP23 . . . . . . . . . .100 C4
**2** Watford WD18 . . . . .167 B6
Welwyn AL6 . . . . . . . . . .89 C4
**Beechfield**
Hoddesdon EN11 . . . . . .115 A2
Kings Langley WD4 . . . . .138 F1
Sawbridgeworth CM21 . . .97 F2
**Beechfield Cl**
Borehamwood WD6 . . . .169 E7
Redbourn AL3 . . . . . . . .106 B5
**Beechfield Ct** 5 WD17 .167 A8
**Beechfield Rd**
Hemel Hempstead HP1 . .124 B2
Ware SG12 . . . . . . . . . . .93 F2
**Beechfield Sch** WD24 . . .154 B4
**Beechfield Wlk** EN9 . . . .163 D4
**Beeching Cl** AL5 . . . . . . .86 B4
**Beechlands** CM23 . . . . . .76 B5
**Beecholm Mews** 5 EN8 148 E3
**Beechpark Way** HP1 . . . .153 D6
**Beechtree La** AL3 . . . . . .126 B2
**Beechwood Ave**
Chorleywood WD3 . . . . .164 B5
Little Chalfont HP6 . . . . .150 C1
Potters Bar EN6 . . . . . . .159 B6
St Albans AL1 . . . . . . . .128 A1
**Beechwood Cl**
Baldock SG7 . . . . . . . . . .23 F5
Hammond Street EN7 . . .147 E5
Hertford SG13 . . . . . . . .113 F6
Hitchin SG5 . . . . . . . . . .21 D2
**Beechwood Cotts** WD3 .164 C3
**Beechwood Ct** HP22 . . . . .99 A4
**Beechwood Dr** HP23 . . . .101 D5
**Beechwood Park Sch**
AL3 . . . . . . . . . . . . . . .83 B1
**Beechwood Pk**
Chorleywood WD3 . . . . .164 F5
Hemel Hempstead HP3 . .137 F7
**Beechwood Rd** LU4 . . . . .44 B3
**Beechwood Rise** WD24 . .154 B2
**Beecroft La** SG2 . . . . . . . .38 C2
**Beehive Cl** WD6 . . . . . . .169 D3
**Beehive Gn** AL7 . . . . . . .111 A4
**Beehive La** AL7 . . . . . . . .111 A3
**Beehive Rd** EN7 . . . . . . .147 B3
**Beesonend Cotts** AL5 . . .107 B4
**Beesonend La** AL3,AL5 . .106 C4
**Beeston Cl** WD19 . . . . . .175 D6
**Beeston Dr** EN8 . . . . . . .148 E4
**Beetham Ct** SG12 . . . . . . .92 E4
**Beethoven Rd** WD6 . . . . .169 D3
**Beeton Cl** HA5 . . . . . . . .176 A3
**Beggarman's La** SG11 . . . .72 D8
**Beggars Bush La** WD18,
WD3 . . . . . . . . . . . . .166 D4
**Beggars La** HP23 . . . . . . .101 A3
**Beken Ct** WD25 . . . . . . .154 C4
**Belcher Rd** EN11 . . . . . . .135 A2
**Beldam Ave** SG8 . . . . . . . .7 E5
**Beldams Gate** CM23 . . . . .77 B5
**Beldams La** CM23 . . . . . .77 B5
**Belfairs** WD19 . . . . . . . .175 D5
**Belford Rd** WD6 . . . . . . .156 F1
**Belfry Ave** UB9 . . . . . . . .173 A2
**Belfry The** Luton LU2 . . . .45 E6
Watford WD24 . . . . . . .167 D8
**Belfry** UB9 . . . . . . . . . . .173 A2
**Belgrave Ave** WD18 . . . .166 F4
**Belgrave Cl** AL4 . . . . . . .128 C7
**Belgrave Dr** WD4 . . . . . .139 C3
**Belgrave Ho** 6 CM23 . . . .77 B8

**Belgrave Mews** SG2 . . . .69 A8
**Belgrave Rd** LU4 . . . . . . .44 D5
**Belgravia Cl** EN5 . . . . . .171 F6
**Belham Rd** WD4 . . . . . . .139 A3
**Bell Acre** SG6 . . . . . . . . .23 B4
**Bell Acre Gdns** SG6 . . . . .23 B4
**Bell Cl** Bedmond WD5 . . .139 F4
Hitchin SG4 . . . . . . . . . .35 B6
Knebworth SG3 . . . . . . . .69 A5
**Bell Gn** HP3 . . . . . . . . . .137 B4
**Bell La**
Abbots Langley WD5 . . . .140 A4
Berkhamsted HP4 . . . . . .121 E5
Brookmans Park AL9 . . . .145 A7
Enfield EN3 . . . . . . . . . .162 E1
Hertford SG13 . . . . . . . .113 D6
Hoddesdon EN11 . . . . . .135 A6
Hoddesdon, Broxbourne
EN11 . . . . . . . . . . . . .134 E2
Little Chalfont HP6 . . . . .150 C1
Nuthampstead SG8 . . . . . .18 B2
Shenley AL2 . . . . . . . . .142 E2
Stevenage SG1 . . . . . . . .50 C7
Widford SG12 . . . . . . . . .95 D4
**Bell Lane Comb Sch**
HP6 . . . . . . . . . . . . . .150 B1
**Bell Leys** HP22 . . . . . . . . .60 B3
**Bell Mead** HP22 . . . . . . . .97 E2
**Bell Rdbt The** AL2 . . . . . .142 F4
**Bell Row** SG7 . . . . . . . . .23 E7
**Bell St** CM21 . . . . . . . . . .97 E2
**Bell View** AL4 . . . . . . . . .128 D3
**Bell Wlk** HP22 . . . . . . . . .60 B3
**Bellamy Cl** Knebworth SG3 68 E5
Watford WD17 . . . . . . . .167 A8
**Bellamy Rd** EN8 . . . . . . .148 E2
**Bellchambers Cl** AL2 . . .142 C5
**Belle Vue La** WD23 . . . . .168 D1
**Belle Vue Rd** SG12 . . . . .93 F1
**Bellerby Rise** LU4 . . . . . . .44 B6
**Bellevue Terr** UB9 . . . . . .173 A2
**Bellfield Ave** HA3 . . . . . .176 D4
**Bellgate** HP2 . . . . . . . . .124 E6
**Bellgate Prim Sch** HP2 . .124 E5
**Bellingdon** WD19 . . . . . .175 E7
**Bellis Ho** AL7 . . . . . . . . .111 B4
**Bellmount Wood Ave**
WD17 . . . . . . . . . . . .166 E8
**Bells Hill** Barnet EN5 . . . .171 D5
Bishop's Stortford CM23 . .76 E3
**Belmers Rd** HP23 . . . . . .100 D1
**Belmont Ct** 7 AL1 . . . . .127 D2
**Belmont Fst Sch** HA3 . . .176 E1
**Belmont Hill** AL1 . . . . . . .127 D2
**Belmont Lodge** HA3 . . . .176 D3
**Belmont Mid Sch** HA3 . .176 F1
**Belmont Rd**
Hemel Hempstead HP3 . .138 E8
Luton LU1 . . . . . . . . . . .63 C7
Watford WD23 . . . . . . .167 E4
**Belmor** WD6 . . . . . . . . . .170 A3
**Belper Rd** LU4 . . . . . . . . .44 D2
**Belsham Pl** LU2 . . . . . . . .46 E2
**Belsize Cotts** WD3 . . . . .151 E6
**Belsize Rd** Harrow HA3 . .176 D3
Hemel Hempstead HP3 . .125 A2
**Belswains La** HP3 . . . . . .138 E8
**Belswains Prim Sch**
HP3 . . . . . . . . . . . . . .138 F7
**Belton Rd** HP4 . . . . . . . .122 A5
**Beltona Gdns** EN8 . . . . .148 D4
**Belvedere Gdns** AL2 . . . .141 B4
**Belvedere Rd** LU3 . . . . . . .45 B5
**Bembridge Gdns** LU3 . . . .44 F4
**Ben Austins** AL3 . . . . . . .106 A4
**Benbow Cl** AL1 . . . . . . . .128 B1
**Benchley Hill** SG4 . . . . . . .35 C8
**Benchleys Rd** HP1 . . . . . .123 F2
**Bencroft** EN7 . . . . . . . . .148 A5
**Bencroft Rd** HP2 . . . . . . .124 E3
**Bencroft Wood** EN10 . .133 D2
**Bendish La** SG2 . . . . . . . .66 C7
**Bendysh Rd** WD23 . . . . .167 E5
**Benedict Ct** HA5 . . . . . . .175 D4
**Benedictine Gate** EN8 . .148 E4
**Benford Rd** EN11 . . . . . .134 F4
**Bengarth Dr** HA3 . . . . . .176 D1
**Bengeo Ho** SG14 . . . . . . .92 C1
**Bengeo Mdws** SG14 . . . . .92 C1
**Bengeo Mews** SG14 . . . . .92 C1
**Bengeo Prim Sch** SG14 . .92 C1
**Bengeo St** SG14 . . . . . . .113 C8
**Benhooks Ave** CM23 . . . . .76 B5
**Benhooks Pl** 1 CM23 . . . . .76 E5
**Benington CE Prim Sch**
SG2 . . . . . . . . . . . . . .52 D4
**Benington Cl** LU2 . . . . . . .45 D1
**Benington Lordship Gdns**★
SG2 . . . . . . . . . . . . . . .52 E6
**Benington Rd** Aston SG2 . .51 F4
Benington SG2 . . . . . . . .52 A7
**Benneck Ho** WD18 . . . . .166 E3
**Bennett Cl**
Northwood HA6 . . . . . . .174 F3
Welwyn Garden City AL7 .110 F7
**Bennett Ct** Letchworth SG6 122 F6
Letchworth SG6 . . . . . . . .23 A5
**Bennetts Cl** AL4 . . . . . . .143 D8
**Bennetts End Cl** HP3 . . .124 E1
**Bennetts End Rd** HP3 . . .125 A1
**Bennetts La** SG9 . . . . . . .25 C4
**Bennettsgate** HP3 . . . . . .139 A8

**Benningfield** SG12 . . . . . .95 D5
**Benningfield Gdns** HP4 .122 E6
**Benningfield Rd** SG12 . . . .95 D4
**Benningfield Rd** WD18 . .167 A4
**Benslow La** SG4 . . . . . . . .35 A7
**Benslow Rise** SG4 . . . . . . .35 A8
**Benskin Rd** WD18 . . . . . .167 A4
**Benson Cl** EN3 . . . . . . . .163 A1
**Benstede** SG2 . . . . . . . . . .69 C8
**Bentfield Bower** CM24 . . .59 C8
**Bentfield End Cswy**
CM24 . . . . . . . . . . . . .59 D7
**Bentfield Gdns** CM24 . . . .59 D7
**Bentfield Gn** CM24 . . . . . .59 D8
**Bentfield Prim Sch** CM24 59 D8
**Bentfield Rd** CM24 . . . . . .59 D7
**Bentick Way** SG4 . . . . . . .67 F2
**Bentley Cl** CM23 . . . . . . .76 F5
**Bentley Ct** 2 LU1 . . . . . . .63 C8
**Bentley Heath La** EN5 . .158 F4
**Bentley Lodge** WD23 . . .176 B3
**Bentley Rd** SG14 . . . . . . .112 F7
**Bentley Wood High Sch**
HA7 . . . . . . . . . . . . . .176 F5
**Benton Rd** WD19 . . . . . .175 D5
**Bentons The** HP4 . . . . . .121 F6
**Bentsley Cl** AL4 . . . . . . .128 C7
**Berceau Wlk** WD17 . . . . .166 E8
**Berdan Ct** EN3 . . . . . . . .163 A2
**Berefeld** HP2 . . . . . . . . .124 D5
**Beresford Rd** Luton LU4 . .45 A1
Rickmansworth WD3 . . . .164 F1
St Albans AL1 . . . . . . . .128 C2
**Bericot Way** AL7 . . . . . . .111 D6
**Berkeley** SG6 . . . . . . . . . .23 A4
**Berkeley Cl**
Abbots Langley WD5 . . . .153 F8
Borehamwood WD6 . . . .170 A4
**6** Hitchin SG5 . . . . . . . .34 D8
Potters Bar EN6 . . . . . . .158 F7
Stevenage SG2 . . . . . . . .69 A8
Ware SG12 . . . . . . . . . . .93 C2
**Berkeley Ct**
Croxley Green WD3 . . . . .166 D4
**6** Harpenden AL5 . . . . .86 A2
**Berkeley Mews** AL1 . . . .128 B2
**Berkeley Path** 2 LU2 . . . .63 E8
**Berkeley Rd** LU2 . . . . . . .105 C1
**Berkhamsted Castle**★
HP4 . . . . . . . . . . . . . .122 C6
**Berkhamsted Collegiate Sch**
Berkhamsted HP4 . . . . . .122 B4
Berkhamsted HP4 . . . . . .122 C4
**Berkhamsted Rd** HP1 . . .123 D7
**Berkhamsted Sta** HP4 . .122 C5
**Berkley Ave** EN8 . . . . . . .162 D5
**Berkley Cl** Pitstone LU7 . . .80 D3
St Albans AL4 . . . . . . . .128 C7
**Berkley Ct** 2 HP4 . . . . . .122 C4
**Berkley Rd** EN8 . . . . . . . .162 D5
**Berks Hill** WD3 . . . . . . . .164 C4
**Bermer Rd** WD24 . . . . . .167 C8
**Bernard Gr** EN9 . . . . . . .163 B6
**Bernard St** AL3 . . . . . . . .127 D4
**Bernard's Heath Inf Sch**
AL1 . . . . . . . . . . . . . .127 F5
**Berners Dr** AL1 . . . . . . . .141 E8
**Berners Way** EN10 . . . . .148 B5
**Bernhardt Cres** SG2 . . . . .51 C6
**Berries The** AL4 . . . . . . .128 A7
**Berrow Cl** LU2 . . . . . . . . .46 E2
**Berry Ave** WD24 . . . . . . .154 B3
**Berry Cl** WD3 . . . . . . . . .165 B2
**Berry Grove La** WD24,
WD25 . . . . . . . . . . . .154 E1
**Berry La** WD3 . . . . . . . . .165 A2
**Berry Leys** LU3 . . . . . . . . .44 E2
**Berry Way** WD3 . . . . . . .165 B2
**Berryfield** LU7 . . . . . . . . .79 F7
**Berrygrove La** WD25 . . . .168 A3
**Berrymead** HP2 . . . . . . . .124 F5
**Berthold Mews** EN9 . . . .163 B6
**Bertram Ho** 4 SG1 . . . . . .50 E6
**Berwick Cl** Harrow HA7 . .176 F4
Holdbrook EN8 . . . . . . .163 A5
Stevenage SG1 . . . . . . . .50 A8
**Berwick Rd** WD6 . . . . . . .156 F1
**Besant Ho** 2 WD24 . . . . .167 D2
**Besford Cl** LU2 . . . . . . . . .46 E2
**Bessemer Cl** SG5 . . . . . . .21 E2
**Bessemer Dr** SG1 . . . . . . .50 B4
**Bessemer Rd** AL7,AL8 . . .89 C2
**Bethune Cl** LU1 . . . . . . . .63 B6
**Bethune Cl** LU1 . . . . . . . .63 B6
**Betjeman Cl**
Cheshunt EN7 . . . . . . . .148 A3
Harpenden AL5 . . . . . . . .86 C1
**Betjeman Rd** SG8 . . . . . . .2 D1
**Betjeman Way** HP1 . . . . .124 B4
**Betony Vale** SG8 . . . . . . . .7 E5
**Bettespol Mdws** AL3 . . .106 A6
**Betty's La** HP23 . . . . . . .100 A4
**Bevan Cl** HP3 . . . . . . . . .124 C1
**Bevan Ho** 3 WD24 . . . . .167 D2
**Beverley Cl** EN10 . . . . . . .7 B5
**Beverley Gdns**
Cheshunt EN7 . . . . . . . .148 A1
St Albans AL4 . . . . . . . .128 D7
Welwyn Garden City AL7 .111 C6
**Beverley Rd** Luton LU4 . . .44 F1
Stevenage SG2 . . . . . . . .37 B2
**Beverly Cl** EN10 . . . . . . .134 C2
**Bevil Ct** EN11 . . . . . . . . .115 A1
**Bewdley Cl** AL5 . . . . . . . .107 D6
**Bewley Cl** EN8 . . . . . . . .162 D8

Bexhill Rd LU2 .........46 D2
Beyers Gdns EN11 ....115 A1
Beyers Prospect EN11 .115 A1
Beyers Ride EN11 ......115 A1
Bibbs Hall La SG4,AL6 .87 E6
Biddenham Turn WD25 .154 C4
Bideford Gdns LU3 .....45 D4
Bideford Rd EN3 .......162 F1
Bidwell Cl SG6 .........23 B5
Biggin Hill SG9 ........28 D7
Biggin La SG5 ..........34 F7
Biggs Grove Rd EN7 ...147 E4
Bignells Cnr EN6 ......158 B5
Billet La HP4 ..........122 A6
Billy Lows La EN6 .....159 B8
Bilton Rd SG4 ..........21 F2
Bilton Way Enfield EN3 .162 F1
  Luton LU1 ............44 F1
Bingen Rd SG5 .........21 C1
Bingham Cl HP1 .......123 F5
Bingham's Park Childrens
  Farm★ HP1 ...........123 E8
Bingley Rd EN11 ......135 C6
Binham Cl LU2 .........45 D7
Binyon Cres HA7 ......176 F5
Birch Copse AL2 ......140 E1
Birch Ct HA6 ..........174 C4
Birch Dr Hatfield AL10 .130 A4
  Maple Cross WD3 .....172 D5
Birch Gn
  Hemel Hempstead HP1 .123 F5
  Hertingfordbury SG14 .112 C4
Birch Gr Oaklands AL6 .89 E8
  Potters Bar EN6 ......159 B7
Birch La HP3 ..........151 B7
Birch Leys HP2 ........125 C8
Birch Link LU4 .........45 C1
Birch Pk HA3 ..........176 C3
Birch Rd
  Berkhamsted HP4 .....121 D7
  Woolmer Green SG3 ...69 B1
Birch Tree Gr HP5 .....136 B1
Birch Tree Wlk WD17 ..153 F2
Birch Way
  Harpenden AL5 .......107 C8
  London Colney AL2 ...142 D4
Birch Wlk WD6 ........170 A8
Birchall La AL5 ........111 E4
Birchall Wood AL7 ....111 E4
Birchalls CM24 .........59 E8
Birchanger CE Prim Sch
  CM23 .................59 D2
Birchanger Ind Est CM23 59 B2
Birchanger La CM23 ....59 D2
Birchen Gr LU2 ........45 F3
Bircherley Ct 14 SG14 .113 D6
Bircherley Green Ctr The 9
  SG14 ................113 D6
Bircherley St SG14 ....113 D6
Birches The
  Bushey WD23 .........168 C4
  Codicote SG4 .........89 A8
  Hemel Hempstead HP3 .137 F8
  Letchworth SG6 .......22 E8
Birchfield Rd EN8 .....148 C2
Birchmead WD17 ......153 F1
Birchmead Cl AL3 .....127 D6
Birchway AL10 ........130 B7
Birchwood
  Birchanger CM23 .....59 D2
  Shenley WD7 .........156 A5
  Waltham Abbey EN9 ...163 E5
Birchwood Cl AL10 ....130 A7
Birchwood Avenue Prim Sch
  AL10 .................130 B3
Birchwood Cl AL10 ....130 A7
Birchwood High Sch
  CM23 .................77 C8
Birchwood Way AL2 ...141 B3
Birdcroft Rd AL8 ......110 D5
Birdie Way SG13 ......114 B7
Birds Cl AL7 ...........111 B4
Birds Hill SG6 .........23 A6
Birdsfoot La LU3 .......45 B6
Birkbeck Rd EN2 ......161 D1
Birken Ct HA6 .........174 B5
Birklands AL1 .........142 B7
Birklands La AL1 ......142 B7
Birling Dr LU2 .........46 C4
Birnbeck Ct 1 EN5 ....171 D5
Birstal Gn WD19 ......175 D6
Birtley Croft LU2 ......46 E1
Biscot Rd LU3 .........45 C2
Bishop Ct WD5 ........153 F8
Bishop Ken Rd HA3 ...176 F2
Bishop Sq AL10 .......129 E5
Bishop Wood CE Jun Sch
  HP23 .................100 A3
Bishop's Ave CM23 ....76 F3
Bishop's Cl AL1 .......127 A7
Bishop's Garth AL4 ...128 A7
Bishop's Hatfield Girls' Sch
  AL10 .................130 A5
Bishop's Palace (rem of)★
  AL9 ..................130 D6
Bishop's Stortford Bsns Ctr
  CM23 .................77 A6
Bishop's Stortford Coll
  CM23 .................76 E7
Bishop's Stortford High Sch
  The CM23 ............76 F4
Bishop's Stortford Sta
  CM23 .................77 A6

Bishop's Wood Ctry Pk★
  WD3 .................173 F4
Bishops Ave
  Borehamwood WD6 ...169 A4
  Moor Park HA6 .......174 F7
Bishops Cl Barnet EN5 .171 D3
  Hatfield AL10 .........129 F5
Bishops Field HP22 .....99 A4
Bishops Mead HP1 ....124 B1
Bishops Park Way CM23 .76 B7
Bishops Rd AL6 ........90 C6
Bishops Rise AL10 .....129 F2
Bishops Wood Hospl
  HA6 .................174 B4
Bishopscote Rd LU3 ...45 B3
Biskra WD17 ..........167 A8
Bisley Cl EN8 .........162 D6
Bit The HP23 .........100 D1
Bittern Cl
  Hammond Street EN7 .147 C6
  Hemel Hempstead HP3 .138 F6
  Stevenage SG2 .......51 D2
Bittern Way SG6 ......11 E1
Black Boy Wood AL2 ..141 A1
Black Cut AL1 .........127 C2
Black Fan Rd
  Welwyn Garden City AL7 .110 F7
  Welwyn Garden City AL7 .111 B6
Black Green Wood Cl
  AL2 .................141 B2
Black Lion Ct CM17 ...118 C4
Black Lion Hill WD7 ...156 F7
Black Smiths Cl SG12 ..115 A7
Black Swan Ct 1 SG12 .93 D1
Black Swan La LU4 ....45 A5
Blackadder Cotts EN9 .149 D8
Blackberry Mead SG2 .51 D3
Blackbirds La WD25 ...155 C5
Blackbury Cl EN6 .....159 C8
Blackbush Spring CM20 118 A4
Blackbushe CM23 .....59 C1
Blackdale EN7 ........148 A4
Blackdown Cl SG1 ....37 B3
Blacketts Wood Dr
  WD3 ................164 B5
Blackford Rd WD19 ...175 D5
Blackhorse La SG4 ...35 A5
Blackhorse La Hitchin SG4 35 A5
  Redbourn AL3 ........106 A6
  Ridge EN6 ...........157 F8
Blackhorse Rd SG6 ...23 C8
Blackley Cl WD17 .....153 F2
Blackmoor La WD18 ...166 D4
Blackmore SG6 .......23 B3
Blackmore Gate HP22 .99 A4
Blackmore Manor AL4 .87 B6
Blackmore Way AL4 ...87 B6
Blacksmith Cl SG5 ....11 F7
Blacksmith's La
  Reed SG8 ...........16 D5
  St Albans AL3 ........127 A4
Blacksmiths Cl CM23 .76 B5
Blacksmiths Hill SG2 ..52 E4
Blacksmiths Way CM21 .97 B1
Blackthorn Cl
  St Albans AL4 ........128 C6
  Watford WD25 ........154 B7
Blackthorn Dr LU2 ....46 C4
Blackthorn Rd AL7 ....111 A5
Blackthorne Ct AL10 ..129 F2
Blackwater La HP3 ....125 E1
Blackwell Cl HA3 .....176 D3
Blackwell Dr WD19 ....167 C3
Blackwell Hall La HP5 .150 C6
Blackwell Rd WD4 ....139 A2
Blackwood Ct EN7 ....148 F5
Bladon Cl SG4 ........35 F3
Blaine Cl HP23 .......100 A6
Blair Cl
  Bishop's Stortford CM23 .76 C7
  Hemel Hempstead HP2 .105 B1
  Stevenage SG2 .......50 F1
Blairhead Dr WD19 ...175 B7
Blake Cl Royston SG8 ..2 D1
  St Albans AL1 ........142 A8
Blakedown LU2 .......45 E1
Blakemere Rd AL8 ....110 D8
Blakemore End Rd SG4 .35 D3
Blakeney Dr LU2 ......45 C2
Blakeney Ho SG1 .....50 A7
Blakeney Rd SG1 .....50 A7
Blakes Ct
  Rickmansworth WD3 ..165 C1
  Sawbridgeworth CM21 .97 E2
Blakes Way AL6 .......89 C6
Blanchard Gr EN3 ....163 B1
Blanche La EN6 .......157 F5
Blandford Ave LU2 ....45 D6
Blandford Rd AL1 .....128 A3
Blanes The SG12 ......93 C3
Blattner Cl WD6 ......169 E5
Blaxland Terr 9 EN8 ..148 D3
Blaydon Rd LU2 ......64 A8
Blegberry Gdns HP4 ..121 E4
Blenheim Cl
  Cheddington LU7 .....79 F8
  Sawbridgeworth CM21 .118 C8
  Watford WD19 ........167 D2
Blenheim Cres LU3 ...45 C2
Blenheim Ct
  Bishop's Stortford CM23 .76 C7
  Welwyn Garden City AL7 .110 F7
  St Albans AL1 ........127 A4
Blenheim Way SG2 ...69 D7
Blenheim Rd WD5 ....154 A7

Blenkin Cl AL3 .......127 C7
Blind La SG2,SG9 .....38 F5
Blindman's La EN8 ....148 D2
Block 10 4 WD17 .....167 A8
Block 12 3 WD17 .....167 A8
Block 14 2 WD17 .....167 A8
Bloomfield Ave LU2 ...46 A1
Bloomfield Ho 6 SG1 .50 E6
Bloomfield Rd
  Hammond Street EN7 .147 C6
  Harpenden AL5 .......85 F3
Blossom La EN2 ......161 C1
Blue Bridge Rd AL9 ...144 E4
Bluebell Cl
  Hemel Hempstead HP1 .123 E2
  Hertford SG13 ........114 A6
Bluebell Dr
  Bedmond WD5 ........139 F4
  Goff's Oak EN7 .......147 D3
Bluebell Way AL10 ....109 F1
Bluebell Wood Cl LU1 .63 A7
Bluebells AL6 .........89 D7
Blueberry Cl AL3 .....127 D7
Bluebird Way AL2 ....140 E1
Bluebridge Ave AL9 ..144 F4
Bluecoat Yd SG12 ....93 D1
Bluecoats Ave SG12 ..113 D6
Bluecoats Ct 18 SG14 .113 D6
Bluehouse Hill AL3 ...127 A3
Bluett Rd AL2 ........142 D4
Blundell Cl AL3 .......127 C7
Blundell Rd LU3 ......45 A4
Blunesfield EN6 ......159 D8
Blunts La AL2 ........140 D5
Blyth Cl
  Borehamwood WD6 ...170 A8
  Stevenage SG2 .......50 A7
Blyth Pl 13 LU1 ......63 D6
Blythe Rd EN11 ......135 D5
Blythway AL7 .........89 F1
Blythway Ho AL7 .....89 F1
Blythwood Gdns CM24 .59 D6
Blythwood Rd HA5 ...175 D2
Boardman Cl EN5 ....171 E4
Bockings SG1 ........38 C1
Bodmin Rd LU4 ......44 F3
Bodwell Cl HP1 ......124 A4
Bogmoor Rd SG8 .....18 A8
Bognor Gdns WD19 ...175 C5
Bohemia HP2 ........124 E4
Boissy Cl AL4 ........128 E2
Boleyn Cl HP2 ........125 C8
Boleyn Ct EN10 ......134 E2
Boleyn Dr AL1 ........127 D1
Boling Brook AL4 .....128 A7
Bolingbroke Rd LU1 ..63 B6
Bolney Gn LU2 ........46 D3
Bolton Rd EN11 ......63 F7
Boltons Park (Royal
  Veterinary Coll) EN6 .145 A2
Bond Ct AL5 ..........85 F2
Bondor Bsns Ctr SG7 ..23 F7
Boniface Gdns HA3 ...176 B3
Boniface Wlk HA3 ....176 B3
Bonks Hill CM21 ......97 D1
Bonney Gr EN7 .......148 A1
Bonneygrove Prim Sch
  EN7 .................148 A1
Bonnick Cl LU1 .......63 C6
Booths Cl AL9 ........144 D7
Boreham Holt WD6 ...169 F5
Borehamwood Ent Ctr
  WD6 .................169 F6
Borehamwood Ind Pk
  WD6 .................170 D7
Bornedene EN6 .......158 E8
Borodale AL5 .........86 A1
Borough Way EN6 ....158 E7
Borrell Cl EN10 ......134 F3
Borrowdale Ct 4 HP2 .124 E6
Borton Ave SG6 ......10 B4
Bosanquet Rd EN11 ..135 C8
Boscombe Cl SG6 ....23 B6
Bosmore Rd LU3 .....44 F5
Boswell Cl WD7 ......156 E7
Boswell Dr SG5 ......21 E4
Boswell Gdns SG1 ...36 D1
Boswick La HP4 ......121 D8
Botley La HP5 ........136 A1
Botley Rd Botley HP5 .136 A1
  Hemel Hempstead HP2 .125 B8
Bottom House La HP23 .101 A1
Bottom La WD3,WD4 .152 C4
Bottom Rd HP23 .....119 F3
Bough Beech Ct EN3 .162 D2
Boughton Way HP6 ..150 C1
Boulevard Ctr The WD6 170 A6
Boulevard The
  Watford WD18 .......166 D4
  Welwyn Garden City AL7 .110 F8
Boulton Rd SG1 ......37 C2
Bounce The HP2 .....124 D5
Boundary Cl EN5 .....171 E8
Boundary Cotts HP3 ..137 D2
Boundary Ct AL7 .....110 F2
Boundary Dr SG14 ...113 D8
Boundary Ho
  Cheshunt EN8 ........162 D7
  Welwyn Garden City AL7 .110 D3
Boundary La AL7 .....110 E2
Boundary Pk HP2 ....125 C5
Boundary Rd
  Bishop's Stortford CM23 .77 A5
  St Albans AL1 ........127 E5
Boundary Way
  Hemel Hempstead HP2 .125 C5
  Watford WD25 ........154 C4
Bounds Field SG11 ...75 F8

Bourne Apartments The 2
  AL5 ..................85 F2
Bourne Cl
  Hoddesdon EN10 .....134 F3
  Ware SG12 ...........93 D2
Bourne End Cotts HP1 .123 C1
Bourne End Rd HA6 ..174 E6
Bourne Hall WD23 ....168 A3
Bourne Honour SG12 .92 E7
Bourne La SG10 ......96 A6
Bourne Rd
  Berkhamsted HP4 ....121 F5
  Bushey WD23 ........168 A4
Bourne The
  Bishop's Stortford CM23 .77 A8
  Bovingdon HP3 .......137 A4
  Clapgate SG11 .......57 C6
  3 Harpenden AL5 ....85 F2
  Ware SG12 ...........93 D2
Bournehall Ave WD23 .168 A4
Bournehall La WD23 ..168 A4
Bournehall Prim Sch
  WD23 ...............168 B4
Bournehall Rd WD23 .168 B4
Bournemouth Rd 3 SG1 .50 B8
Bouvier Rd EN3 .......162 C1
Bovingdon Cres WD25 .154 D5
Bovingdon Ct HP3 ....137 A3
Bovingdon Prim Sch
  HP3 .................137 B4
Bowbrookvale LU2 ....46 F1
Bowcock Wlk SG1 ....50 E3
Bower Heath La AL5 ..86 C6
Bower's Par AL5 ......86 A1
Bowers Way AL5 .....86 A1
Bowershott SG6 ......23 A4
Bowes Lyon Mews AL3 .127 D3
Bowgate AL1 .........127 E4
Bowlers Mead SG9 ...40 D7
Bowles Gn EN1 .......162 B3
Bowling Cl
  14 Bishop's Stortford CM23 76 F6
  Harpenden AL5 .......107 C7
Bowling Ct WD18 .....167 A5
Bowling Gn SG1 ......50 C8
Bowling Green La
  Buntingford SG9 .....40 D8
  Luton LU2 ...........45 E2
Bowling Rd SG12 .....93 E1
Bowman Trad Est SG1 .50 B5
Bowmans Ave SG4 ...35 B6
Bowmans Cl
  Potters Bar EN6 ......159 D7
  Welwyn AL6 ..........89 C6
Bowmans Ct HP2 .....124 E5
Bowmans Gn WD25 ..154 E3
Bowmansgreen Prim Sch
  AL2 .................142 C4
Bowring Gn WD19 ...175 C5
Bowyer Ct EN8 .......162 F6
Bowyer's Cl SG5 .....21 D1
Bowyers 6 HP2 ......124 D5
Box La
  Hemel Hempstead HP3 .137 E7
  Hoddesdon EN11 .....134 E6
Boxberry Cl SG1 .....50 E6
Boxfield AL7 .........111 B3
Boxfield Gn SG2 .....51 D8
Boxgrove Cl LU2 .....46 C5
Boxhill 3 HP2 ........124 D5
Boxmoor House Sch
  HP3 .................137 F8
Boxmoor Prim Sch HP1 124 A2
Boxted Cl LU4 ........44 C5
Boxtree La HA3 ......176 D3
Boxtree Rd HA3 ......176 D3
Boxwell Rd HP4 ......122 B4
Boyce Cl WD6 ........169 E8
Boyd Cl 1 CM23 .....77 B8
Boyes Cres AL2 ......142 B5
Boyle Cl LU2 .........63 E8
Brace Cl EN7 ........147 B6
Braceby Cl LU3 ......44 F6
Braces SG2 ..........52 F2
Brache Cl AL3 .......106 A5
Brache Ct LU1 .......63 E4
Bracken Cl WD6 .....170 B8
Bracken La AL6 ......89 C7
Brackendale EN6 ....159 A6
Brackendale Gr
  Harpenden AL5 ......85 D3
  Luton LU3 ...........45 B5
Brackendene AL2 ....140 F1
Brackenhill HP4 .....122 F5
Brackens The HP2 ...124 D4
Bracklesham Gdns LU2 .46 D3
Bracknell Pl HP2 .....124 F7
Bradbery WD3 .......172 D5
Bradbury Cl WD6 ....170 B8
Bradcot Cotts SG2 ...39 C2
Bradden Cotts HP2 ..103 F8
Bradden La HP1,HP2 .103 E7
Bradden Villas HP2 ..103 F8
Braddon Ct 13 EN5 ..171 E6
Bradford Rd WD3 ....164 C2
Bradgate EN6 ........146 D4
Bradgate Cl EN6 .....146 D3
Bradgers Hill Rd LU2 .45 E4
Bradley Comm CM23 .59 C3
Bradley Rd Enfield EN3 .162 E2
  Luton LU4 ...........44 D1
  Waltham Abbey EN9 ..163 C4
Bradleys Cnr SG4 ....35 C8
Bradman Way SG1 ...37 A1
Bradmore Gn AL9 ....144 E5
Bradmore La AL9 ....144 D5
Bradmore Way AL9 ..144 E5

Bradshaw Rd WD24 ..154 C1
Bradshaws AL10 .....129 F1
Bradway SG4 .........66 E6
Braemar Cl SG2 ......69 B7
Braemar Ct WD23 ....168 A3
Braemar Turn HP2 ...105 B1
Braeside Cl HA5 .....176 A3
Bragbury Cl SG2 .....69 D7
Bragbury La SG2,SG3 .69 D5
Bragmans La WD3 ...151 E6
Braham Ct 2 SG5 ....34 E7
Brain Cl AL10 ........130 B6
Braithwaite Ct 16 LU3 .45 D1
Brakynbery HP4 .....121 E7
Bramble Cl Harpenden AL5 85 F3
  Luton LU4 ...........44 C4
  Watford WD25 .......154 A5
Bramble Rd
  Hatfield AL10 ........129 D5
  Luton LU4 ...........44 C4
Bramble Rise CM20 ..117 C1
Brambles The
  Bishop's Stortford CM23 .76 C6
  Cheshunt EN8 ........162 D8
  Oaklands AL6 ........89 E8
  Royston SG8 .........7 E5
  St Albans AL1 ........127 D1
  Stevenage SG1 .......36 D2
  Ware SG12 ...........93 C3
Brambling Cl WD23 ...167 E5
Brambling Rise HP2 ..124 E6
Bramfield Hitchin SG4 ..35 B6
  Watford WD25 .......154 E5
Bramfield Ct SG14 ...113 A7
Bramfield La AL5 .....91 F3
Bramfield Pl HP2 ....105 A1
Bramfield Rd
  Datchworth SG3 .....90 E8
  Hertford SG14 .......112 F8
Bramham Ct HA6 ....174 E4
Bramhanger Acre LU3 .44 D7
Bramingham Bsns Pk
  LU3 .................45 B8
Bramingham Prim Sch
  LU3 .................45 B8
Bramingham Rd LU3 .44 F6
Bramleas WD18 ......166 F5
Bramley Cl SG7 ......12 F1
Bramley Cr WD25 ....154 B8
Bramley Gdns WD19 .175 C5
Bramley House Ct EN2 .161 D2
Bramley Shaw EN9 ..163 F6
Bramley Way AL4 ....128 C2
Brampton Cl
  Cheshunt EN7 ........148 A3
  Harpenden AL5 .......86 D1
Brampton Park Rd SG5 .21 E1
Brampton Rd Royston SG8 .7 F6
  South Oxhey WD19 ...175 A4
  St Albans AL1 ........128 A4
Brampton Terr WD6 ..157 A1
Bramshaw Gdns WD19 .175 D5
Bramshot Way WD19 .175 A8
Bramshott Cl SG4 ....34 F5
Branch Cl AL10 ......130 C7
Branch Rd
  Park Street AL2 ......141 D4
  St Albans AL2 ........127 B4
Brand St SG5 ........34 E7
Brandles Rd SG7 ....23 E7
Brandles Sch SG7 ...23 E7
Brandon Cl EN7 .....147 F5
Brandon Ct HP23 ....78 D7
Brandon Mobile Home Pk
  AL4 .................128 D2
Branksome Cl HP2 ...125 A4
Branscombe Ho WD24 .154 A2
Branton Cl LU2 ......46 E2
Brantwood Rd LU1 ...63 C7
Brawlings La SL9 ....172 A6
Bray Cl WD6 .........170 C8
Bray Dr SG1 .........37 A3
Bray Lodge 2 EN8 ...148 E3
Brayes Manor SG5 ...11 F6
Brays Ct LU2 .........46 B3
Brays Rd LU2 ........46 B3
Braziers End HP5 ....120 C1
Braziers Field SG13 ..113 F6
Braziers Quay CM23 .77 A6
Breach Barns La EN9 .149 F1
Breachwood Green Jun Mix
  Inf Sch SG4 .........47 E1
Bread & Cheese La EN7 147 D6
Breadcroft La AL5 ...86 B1
Breakmead AL7 ......111 B4
Breaks Rd AL10 .....130 B6
Breaks The HP2 .....124 D4
Breakspear Ave AL1 .127 F2
Breakspear Ct WD5 ..139 F1
Breakspear Coll WD5 .139 F1
Breakspear Rd N UB9 .173 D1
Breakspear Way HP2 .125 C4
Breakspeare Cl WD24 .154 B1
Breakspeare Rd WD5 .153 E8
Breakspeare Sch WD5 .153 E8
Brecken Cl AL4 ......128 A7
Brecon Cl 14 LU1 ....63 D6
Breeze Terr 5 EN8 ...148 D3
Bren Ct EN3 .........163 A2
Brendon Ave LU2 ....46 C1
Brent Cl SG1 .........50 E5
Brent Pl EN5 .........171 E4
Brett Rd EN5 ........171 C4
Bretts Mead LU1 .....63 C5
Bretts Mead Ct LU1 ..63 C5
Brewers Cl CM23 ....76 C5
Brewery Cotts SG7 ...12 E1

Brewery La Baldock SG7 . .23 E8
Stansted Mountfitchet
CM24 . . . . . . . . . . . . . . .59 E7
Brewery Rd EN11 . . . . . .135 A6
Brewery Yd CM24 . . . . . . .59 F7
Brewhouse Hill AL4 . . . .108 C8
Brewhouse La SG14 . . . .113 C6
Briants Cl HA5 . . . . . . . . .175 F1
Briar Cl Cheshunt EN8 . . .148 C2
Luton LU2 . . . . . . . . . . . . . .46 C4
Potten End HP4 . . . . . . . .123 A7
Briar Patch La SG6 . . . . .22 D3
Briar Rd St Albans AL4 . .128 D6
Watford WD25 . . . . . . . . .154 B4
Briar Way HP4 . . . . . . . .122 D3
Briarcliff HP1 . . . . . . . . .123 E4
Briardale Stevenage SG1 . .50 E4
Ware SG12 . . . . . . . . . . . .93 C3
Briarley Cl EN10 . . . . . . .134 F1
Briars Cl AL10 . . . . . . . . .130 A5
Briars La AL10 . . . . . . . . .130 A5
Briars The Bushey WD23 .168 E2
Cheshunt EN8 . . . . . . . . . .162 E8
Hertford SG13 . . . . . . . . .114 A6
Sarratt WD3 . . . . . . . . . . .152 A3
Briars Wood AL10 . . . . .130 A5
Briarswood EN7 . . . . . . .147 E3
Briarwood Dr HA6 . . . . .175 A1
Briary La SG8 . . . . . . . . . . . .7 C5
Briary Wood End AL6 . . . .89 F8
Briary Wood La AL6 . . . . .89 F8
Brick Cotts SG9 . . . . . . . .27 D8
Brick Kiln Cl WD19 . . . . .167 E3
Brick Kiln La SG4 . . . . . . .34 E5
Brick Kiln Rd SG1 . . . . . . .50 C6
Brick Knoll Pk AL1 . . . . .128 C2
Brickcroft EN10 . . . . . . . .148 E5
Brickenden Ct EN9 . . . . .163 F6
Brickendon Ct EN11 . . . .135 A5
Brickendon La SG13 . . . .133 D6
Bricket Rd AL1 . . . . . . . .127 D3
Bricket Wood Sta AL2 . .141 A1
Brickfield AL10 . . . . . . . .130 A2
Brickfield Ave HP3 . . . . .125 B2
Brickfield Cotts WD6 . . .169 F6
Brickfield Ct AL10 . . . . . .130 B2
Brickfield La EN5 . . . . . .170 F3
Brickfields Ind Est HP2 .125 B7
Brickfields The SG12 . . . .93 B2
Brickly Rd LU4 . . . . . . . . . .44 C5
Brickmakers La HP3 . . .125 B2
Brickwall Cl AL6 . . . . . . .110 A8
Brickyard La SG8 . . . . . . .16 E5
Bride Hall La AL6 . . . . . . .88 A5
Bridewell Cl SG9 . . . . . . . .40 E8
Bridge Ct
1 Berkhamsted HP4 . . . .122 D4
Harpenden AL5 . . . . . . . . .85 F3
Radlett WD7 . . . . . . . . . .156 B4
Bridge End SG9 . . . . . . . . .40 E8
Bridge Foot SG12 . . . . . . .93 D1
Bridge Pk AL7 . . . . . . . . .110 E7
Bridge Pl WD17 . . . . . . .167 D4
Bridge Rd
Abbots Langley WD4 . . . . .153 C6
Letchworth SG6 . . . . . . . . . .22 F6
Stevenage SG1 . . . . . . . . . .50 C7
Welwyn Garden City AL8 . .110 C7
Woolmer Green SG3 . . . . . .69 A2
Bridge Rd E AL7 . . . . . . .110 F6
Bridge Rd W SG1 . . . . . . .50 B7
Bridge St
Berkhamsted HP4 . . . . . . .122 D4
Bishop's Stortford CM23 . . .76 F7
Hemel Hempstead HP1 . . .124 C2
Hitchin SG5 . . . . . . . . . . . . .34 E6
Kneesworth SG8 . . . . . . . . . .2 B8
Luton LU1 . . . . . . . . . . . . . .63 E8
Bridgefields AL7 . . . . . . .110 F7
Bridgefoot SG9 . . . . . . . . .40 E7
Bridgefoot Cotts AL2 . . .155 F8
Bridgefoot La EN6 . . . . .158 D6
Bridgeford Ho
13 Bishop's Stortford CM23 76 F6
5 Watford WD18 . . . . . . .167 B6
Bridgegate Bsns Ctr
AL7 . . . . . . . . . . . . . . . . .110 F7
Bridgend Rd EN1 . . . . . .162 C4
Bridgenhall Rd EN1 . . . .161 F1
Bridger Cl WD25 . . . . . . .154 E6
Bridges Ct SG14 . . . . . . .113 C6
Bridges Rd HA7 . . . . . . . .176 F5
Bridgewater Ct HP4 . . . .102 C8
Bridgewater Hill HP4 . . .121 F7
Bridgewater Mid Sch
HP4 . . . . . . . . . . . . . . . . .122 A6
Bridgewater Monument
The* HP4 . . . . . . . . . . . . .101 E7
Bridgewater Rd HP4 . . .122 B5
Bridgewater Way WD23 168 B3
Bridgeways EN11 . . . . . .135 B5
Bridle Cl Enfield EN3 . . . .162 F2
Hoddesdon EN11 . . . . . . . .115 A2
St Albans AL3 . . . . . . . . . .127 E5
Bridle La WD3 . . . . . . . . .165 D6
Bridle Path WD17 . . . . . .167 B7
Bridle Way
Berkhamsted HP4 . . . . . . .122 A6
Great Amwell SG12 . . . . .115 A6
Hoddesdon EN11 . . . . . . . .115 A1
Bridle Way (N) EN11 . . . .115 B2
Bridle Way (S) EN11 . . . .115 A1
Bridleway HP23 . . . . . . . .119 E5
Bridlington Rd WD19 . . .175 D7
Brierley Cl LU2 . . . . . . . . .46 D2
Briery Ct WD3 . . . . . . . . .165 A5
Briery Field WD3 . . . . . .165 A5
Briery Way HP2 . . . . . . . .125 A4
Brigadier Ave EN2 . . . . . .161 C1
Brigadier Hill EN2 . . . . . .161 C1
Brightman Cotts 2 LU3 . .45 A7
Brighton Rd WD24 . . . . . .154 A1
Brighton Way SG1 . . . . . . .50 A8
Brightview Cl AL2 . . . . . .140 E2
Brightwell Ct WD18 . . . .167 A4
Brightwell Rd WD18 . . .167 A4
Brill Cl LU2 . . . . . . . . . . . . .46 D2
Brimfield Cl LU2 . . . . . . . .46 D2
Brimsdown Ave EN3 . . . .162 E1
Brimstone Way HP4 . . . .121 F6
Brindley Way HP3 . . . . . .138 F6
Brinklow Ct AL3 . . . . . . .141 B8
Brinley Cl EN8 . . . . . . . . .162 D8
Brinsley Rd HA3 . . . . . . .176 D1
Brinsmead AL2 . . . . . . . .141 E4
Briscoe Cl EN11 . . . . . . . .134 F8
Briscoe Rd EN11 . . . . . . .134 F8
Bristol Ho 16 WD6 . . . . . .170 A7
Bristol Rd LU3 . . . . . . . . . .45 B4
Britannia SG11 . . . . . . . . .55 E2
Britannia Ave LU3 . . . . . . .45 B4
Britannia Bsns Pk EN8 .162 F5
Britannia Ests LU3,LU4 . . .45 B2
Britannia Hall LU2 . . . . . .64 C8
Britannia Pl 3 CM23 . . . .76 E5
Britannia Rd EN8 . . . . . .162 F5
Brittain Way SG2 . . . . . . . .51 B4
Britten Cl WD6 . . . . . . . .169 D3
Britton Ave AL3 . . . . . . . .127 D3
Britwell Dr HP4 . . . . . . . .122 E6
Brixham Cl SG1 . . . . . . . . .50 B7
Brixton Rd WD24 . . . . . . .167 B8
Broad Acre AL2 . . . . . . . .140 E1
Broad Acres AL10 . . . . . .129 F8
Broad Baulk SG9 . . . . . . . .40 D8
Broad Ct AL7 . . . . . . . . . .110 E6
Broad Gn SG13 . . . . . . . .132 F8
Broad Green Wood
SG13 . . . . . . . . . . . . . . . .133 A8
Broad Mead LU3 . . . . . . . .45 A3
Broad Oak Ct LU2 . . . . . . .46 D3
Broad Oak Way SG2 . . . . .50 F1
Broad St HP2 . . . . . . . . . .124 D4
Broad Wlk CM20 . . . . . . .117 D1
Broadacres LU2 . . . . . . . . .45 D6
Broadcroft
2 Hemel Hempstead HP2 124 D5
Letchworth SG6 . . . . . . . . . .22 F2
Broadfield
Bishop's Stortford CM23 . . .58 F2
Harlow CM20 . . . . . . . . . .117 E1
Broadfield Cl SG10 . . . . . .74 E1
Broadfield Ct WD23 . . . .176 E8
Broadfield Inf Sch HP2 .124 F3
Broadfield Jun Sch HP2 124 F3
Broadfield Pl AL8 . . . . . .110 B5
Broadfield Rd
Hemel Hempstead HP2 . . .124 F3
Woolmer Green SG3 . . . . . .69 B1
Broadfield Way SG10 . . . .74 F1
Broadfields
Goff's Oak EN7 . . . . . . . . .147 B2
Harpenden AL5 . . . . . . . . . .85 F2
Harrow HA2 . . . . . . . . . . . .176 B1
High Wych CM21 . . . . . . . . .97 B1
Broadfields La WD19 . . .167 B1
Broadfields Prim Sch
CM20 . . . . . . . . . . . . . . . .117 E1
Broadgate EN9 . . . . . . . .163 F7
Broadgreen Rd EN7 . . . .147 D5
Broadhall Way SG2 . . . . . .51 B2
Broadlake Cl AL2 . . . . . .142 D4
Broadlands WD7 . . . . . . .156 B4
Broadlands Cl EN8 . . . . .162 D5
Broadlawns Ct HA3 . . . .176 F2
Broadleaf Ave CM23 . . . .76 D4
Broadleaf Gr AL8 . . . . . . . .89 B1
Broadley Gdns WD7 . . . .156 E7
Broadmead SG4 . . . . . . . .35 B5
Broadmead Cl HA5 . . . . .175 E3
Broadmead Ind Sch LU1 .63 E5
Broadmeadow Ride SG4 .35 A4
Broadmeads SG12 . . . . . .93 D1
Broadoak Ave EN3 . . . . .162 D4
Broadstone Rd AL5 . . . .107 D7
Broadview SG1 . . . . . . . . .50 E6
Broadview Ho EN3 . . . . .162 F3
Broadwalk The HA6 . . . .174 C1
Broadwater
Berkhamsted HP4 . . . . . . .122 C5
Potters Bar EN6 . . . . . . . .145 B1
Broadwater Ave SG6 . . . .22 E5
Broadwater Cres
Stevenage SG2 . . . . . . . . . .69 C8
Welwyn Garden City AL7 .110 D5
Broadwater Dale SG6 . . .22 E5
Broadwater La SG2 . . . . .51 D1
Broadwater Rd AL7 . . . .110 E6
Broadway SG6 . . . . . . . . .22 F5
Broadway Ave CM17 . . . .118 B4
Broadway Ct SG6 . . . . . . .22 E3
Broadway The
Harrow HA3 . . . . . . . . . . .176 F1
Hatfield AL9 . . . . . . . . . . .130 C6
Kimpton AL4 . . . . . . . . . . . .87 B5
Pinner HA5 . . . . . . . . . . . .175 F3
Watford WD17 . . . . . . . . .167 C6
Brocket Cnr AL8 . . . . . . .109 F4
Brocket Ct
Hoddesdon EN11 . . . . . . .135 A6
Luton LU4 . . . . . . . . . . . . .44 D5
Brocket Rd Hatfield AL8 .110 A3
Hoddesdon EN11 . . . . . . . .135 A6
Brocket View AL4 . . . . . .108 D8
Brockett Cl AL8 . . . . . . .110 B6
Brockhurst Cl HA7 . . . . .176 F4
Brocklesbury Cl WD24 .167 D7
Brockley Hill HA7 . . . . . .169 C1
Brockley Hill Ho HA7 . . .169 C1
Brockswood La AL8 . . . .110 B7
Brockswood Prim Sch
HP2 . . . . . . . . . . . . . . . . .105 C1
Brockwell Shott SG2 . . . .38 B1
Brodewater Rd WD6 . . .170 B7
Brodie Rd EN2 . . . . . . . .161 C1
Broken Green Cotts
SG11 . . . . . . . . . . . . . . . . .56 C2
Bromborough Gn WD19 175 C5
Bromet Cl WD17 . . . . . . .153 F1
Bromet Sch WD19 . . . . .167 D2
Bromleigh Cl EN8 . . . . . .148 E3
Bromley HP23 . . . . . . . . . .79 A4
Bromley La SG10,SG11 . . .74 D6
Brompton Cl LU3 . . . . . . .44 F8
Brompton Gdns LU3 . . . . .44 F8
Bronte Cres HP2 . . . . . . .105 B1
Bronte Paths SG2 . . . . . . .51 C6
Brook Bank EN1 . . . . . . .162 B2
Brook Cl WD6 . . . . . . . . .170 B7
Brook Cotts CM24 . . . . . . .59 E5
Brook Ct LU3 . . . . . . . . . . .45 D1
Brook Dr Radlett WD7 . . .155 F6
Stevenage SG2 . . . . . . . . . .69 B8
Brook End CM21 . . . . . . . .97 D2
Brook Field SG2 . . . . . . . .51 E2
Brook Ho WD23 . . . . . . .168 C1
Brook La
Berkhamsted HP4 . . . . . . .122 B5
Sawbridgeworth CM21 . . . .97 D2
Brook Rd
Borehamwood WD6 . . . . .170 A7
Cheshunt EN8 . . . . . . . . . .162 F5
Sawbridgeworth CM21 . . . .97 E1
Stansted Mountfitchet
CM24 . . . . . . . . . . . . . . . . .59 E6
Brook St Luton LU3 . . . . . .63 D8
Stotfold SG5 . . . . . . . . . . . .11 E6
Tring HP23 . . . . . . . . . . . .100 B4
Brook View Hitchin SG4 . . .35 C6
Stansted Mountfitchet
CM24 . . . . . . . . . . . . . . . . .59 E5
Brookbridge La SG3 . . . . .69 D2
Brookdene Ave WD19 . .167 C1
Brookdene Dr HA6 . . . . .174 F4
Brooke Cl WD23 . . . . . . .168 C2
Brooke End AL3 . . . . . . .106 A4
Brooke Gdns CM23 . . . . . .77 C7
Brooke Rd SG8 . . . . . . . . . .7 D8
Brooke Way WD23 . . . . .168 C2
Brooker Rd EN9 . . . . . . .163 C5
Brookfield Cl HP23 . . . .100 B4
Brookfield Ct 14 EN8 . . .148 D3
Brookfield Ctr EN8 . . . . .148 D4
Brookfield Gdns EN8 . . .148 D4
Brookfield La SG2 . . . . . . .51 F3
Brookfield La E EN8 . . . .148 D3
Brookfield La W EN8 . . .148 C4
Brookfield Ret Pk EN8 .148 D5
Brookfields CM21 . . . . . .97 D2
Brookhill SG2 . . . . . . . . . .51 A8
Brookhouse Pl 3 CM23 . .76 F8
Brookland Inf Sch EN8 .148 E3
Brookland Jun Sch EN8 148 E3
Brooklands Cl LU4 . . . . . .44 C6
Brooklands Ct AL1 . . . . .127 E3
Brooklands Gdns EN6 . .158 E7
Brookmans Ave AL9 . . . .144 F5
Brookmans Park Prim Sch
AL9 . . . . . . . . . . . . . . . . .144 E5
Brookmans Park Sta
AL9 . . . . . . . . . . . . . . . . .144 E5
Brookmead Sch LU7 . . . . .80 E5
Brookmill Cl WD19 . . . . .167 B2
Brooks Ct SG14 . . . . . . . .112 F7
Brooksfield AL7 . . . . . . .111 B7
Brookshill HA3 . . . . . . . .176 D5
Brookshill Ave HA3 . . . .176 E5
Brookshill Dr HA3 . . . . .176 D5
Brookside Buckland SG9 . .27 D5
Furneux Pelham SG9 . . . . . .43 B4
Hatfield AL10 . . . . . . . . . .129 D5
Hertford SG13 . . . . . . . . .113 E5
Hoddesdon EN11 . . . . . . .135 A6
Letchworth SG6 . . . . . . . . . .22 F5
South Mimms EN6 . . . . . . .158 A7
Waltham Abbey EN9 . . . . .163 E7
Watford WD24 . . . . . . . . .154 D3
Brookside Cl EN5 . . . . . .171 E3
Brookside Cotts WD4 . .153 C5
Brookside Cres EN6 . . . .146 E4
Brookside Gdns EN1 . . .162 C2
Brookside Rd WD19 . . . .167 B2
Broom Barns Jun Mix Inf Sch
SG1 . . . . . . . . . . . . . . . . . .50 E5
Broom Cl
Hammond Street EN7 . . . .148 A4
Hatfield AL10 . . . . . . . . . .129 F2
Broom Cnr AL5 . . . . . . . .107 C8
Broom Gr Knebworth SG3 .68 F5
Watford WD17 . . . . . . . . .154 A1
Broom Hill
Hemel Hempstead HP1 . . .123 E2
Welwyn AL6 . . . . . . . . . . . .90 A8
Broom Wlk SG1 . . . . . . . .50 E5
Broomer Pl EN8 . . . . . . .148 C2
Broomfield
Chiswell Green AL2 . . . . .141 C4
Harlow CM20 . . . . . . . . . .118 B3
Broomfield Ave EN10 . . .148 E5
Broomfield Cl AL6 . . . . . .89 C4
Broomfield Ct 2 AL10 . .130 A6
Broomfield Rd AL6 . . . . . .89 C4
Broomfield Rise WD5 . .153 D7
Broomhills AL7 . . . . . . . .111 B7
Broomleys AL4 . . . . . . . .128 D6
Brooms Cl AL8 . . . . . . . . . .89 D1
Brooms Rd LU2 . . . . . . . . .64 A8
Broomstick Hall Rd
EN9 . . . . . . . . . . . . . . . . .163 E6
Broomstick La HP5 . . . .136 A1
Broughinge Rd WD6 . . . .170 B7
Broughton Ave LU3 . . . . .45 C5
Broughton Hill SG6 . . . . .23 B6
Broughton Way WD3 . . .165 A2
Brow The WD25 . . . . . . .154 B6
Brown's Cl LU4 . . . . . . . . .44 D5
Brown's Cnr SG9 . . . . . . . .27 F3
Brown's La HP23 . . . . . . .119 F7
Brown's Rise HP23 . . . . .119 F3
Brownfield Way AL4 . . . . .87 B6
Brownfields AL7 . . . . . . .110 F7
Brownfields Ct AL7 . . . . .111 A7
Browning Dr SG4 . . . . . . .35 B8
Browning Rd Enfield EN2 161 D1
Harpenden AL5 . . . . . . . . . .86 C2
Luton LU4 . . . . . . . . . . . . . .44 A2
Brownings La SG4 . . . . . .47 D1
Brownlow Gate HP4 . . . . .81 B1
Brownlow La LU7 . . . . . . .80 A7
Brownlow Rd
Berkhamsted HP4 . . . . . . .122 C5
Borehamwood WD6 . . . . .170 A5
Browns Hedge LU7 . . . . . .80 C3
Browns Spring HP4 . . . .123 C7
Brownsea Ho 12 WD18 . .166 F3
Brox Dell SG1 . . . . . . . . . .50 E6
Broxbourne CE Prim Sch
EN10 . . . . . . . . . . . . . . . .134 F2
Broxbourne Sch The
EN10 . . . . . . . . . . . . . . . .134 E1
Broxbourne Sta EN10 . .135 A3
Broxbournebury Mews
EN10 . . . . . . . . . . . . . . . .134 C3
Broxley Mead LU4 . . . . . .44 D5
Bruce Gr WD24 . . . . . . . .154 C1
Bruce Rd 9 Barnet EN5 . .171 E6
Harrow HA3 . . . . . . . . . . .176 E1
Bruce Way EN8 . . . . . . . .162 D6
Brunel Rd SG2 . . . . . . . . .51 B7
Brunswick Ct EN11 . . . .135 A5
Brunswick Rd EN3 . . . . .163 A1
Brunswick St LU2 . . . . . . .63 F8
Brushrise WD24 . . . . . . .154 A3
Brushwood Dr WD3 . . . .164 C5
Brussels Way LU3 . . . . . .44 D8
Bryan Rd CM23 . . . . . . . . .76 F8
Bryanstone Rd EN8 . . . .162 F5
Bryant Cl EN5 . . . . . . . . .171 F4
Bryant Ct AL5 . . . . . . . . . .86 A3
Bryce Cl SG12 . . . . . . . . . .93 D3
Bryfield Cotts HP3 . . . . .137 C1
Bsns Ctr E SG6 . . . . . . . . .23 C6
Bsns Ctr The LU2 . . . . . . .64 B6
Bsns Ctr W SG6 . . . . . . . . .23 C6
Buchanan Ct
Borehamwood WD6 . . . . .170 C7
Luton LU2 . . . . . . . . . . . . . .64 B8
Buchanan Dr LU2 . . . . . . .64 B8
Buckettsland La WD6 . . .157 D2
Buckingham Dr LU2 . . . . .46 D2
Buckingham Rd
Borehamwood WD6 . . . . .170 D5
Tring HP23 . . . . . . . . . . . . .99 E3
Watford WD24 . . . . . . . . .154 C2
Buckinghamshire Chilterns
Unvi Coll (Chalfont Campus)
HP8 . . . . . . . . . . . . . . . . .172 A8
Buckland Rd HP22 . . . . . .99 A4
Buckland Rise HA5 . . . .175 D2
Bucklands Croft HP23 . . . .99 C8
Bucklands The WD3 . . . .165 A2
Buckle Cl LU3 . . . . . . . . . .44 F7
Bucklers Cl EN10 . . . . . .134 F1
Bucklersbury SG5 . . . . . . .34 E6
Bucknalls Cl WD25 . . . . .154 E7
Bucknalls Dr AL2 . . . . . .154 F8
Bucknalls La WD25 . . . . .154 E7
Bucks Alley SG13 . . . . . .132 D4
Bucks Ave WD19 . . . . . . .167 E2
Bucks Hill WD4 . . . . . . . .152 C5
Buckthorn Ave SG1 . . . . .50 E4
Buckton Rd WD6 . . . . . . .156 F1
Buckwood La LU6 . . . . . .82 C7
Buckwood Rd AL3 . . . . . .83 C6
Buddcroft AL7 . . . . . . . .111 B7
Bude Cres SG1 . . . . . . . . .50 A7
Bulbourne Cl
Berkhamsted HP4 . . . . . . .121 F6
Hemel Hempstead HP1 . . .124 A2
Bulbourne Ct HP23 . . . . .100 A7
Bulbourne Rd HP23 . . . .100 B7
Bull La Buckland SG9 . . . .27 C8
Cottered SG9 . . . . . . . . . . .39 C8
Wheathampstead AL4 . . . .108 A6
Bull Plain SG14 . . . . . . .113 D6
Bull Rd AL5 . . . . . . . . . . .107 B8
Bull Stag Gn AL9 . . . . . .130 C7
Bull's Cross EN2 . . . . . . .162 A3
Bullace Cl HP1 . . . . . . . .124 A4
Bullbeggars La HP4 . . . .123 A4
Bullen's Green La AL4 . .143 E8
Bullfields CM21 . . . . . . . . .97 E3
Bullhead Rd WD6 . . . . . .170 C6
Bullock's Hill SG4 . . . . . .49 B1
Bullock's La SG13 . . . . .113 C4
Bullrush Cl AL10 . . . . . . .130 B4
Bulls Cross Ride EN7 . . .162 A5
Bulls La AL9 . . . . . . . . . .144 E7
Bullsland Gdns WD3 . . .164 B3
Bullsland La WD3 . . . . . .164 B2
Bullsmoor Cl EN8 . . . . . .162 C4
Bullsmoor Gdns EN8 . . .162 B4
Bullsmoor La EN1,EN3 . .162 C4
Bullsmoor Ride EN8 . . . .162 C4
Bullsmoor Way EN8 . . . .162 C4
Bullwell Cres EN8 . . . . . .148 E2
Bulstrode Cl WD4 . . . . . .137 E2
Bulstrode La
Chipperfield WD4 . . . . . . .137 F3
Hemel Hempstead HP3 . . .138 A5
Bulwer Link SG1 . . . . . . . .50 E3
Buncefield La HP2 . . . . .125 C5
Bungalows The
Essendon AL9 . . . . . . . . . .131 F7
Harpenden AL5 . . . . . . . . . .86 C3
Bunker's Farm Cotts
HP3 . . . . . . . . . . . . . . . . .139 D8
Bunkers La HP3 . . . . . . .139 B7
Bunnsfield AL7 . . . . . . . .111 C7
Bunstrux HP23 . . . . . . . .100 A4
Bunting Rd LU4 . . . . . . . . .44 A4
Buntingford Rd SG11 . . . .55 D4
Bunyan Cl Pirton SG5 . . . .20 D4
Tring HP23 . . . . . . . . . . . .100 B5
Bunyan Rd SG5 . . . . . . . . .34 F8
Bunyans Cl LU3 . . . . . . . .45 A5
BUPA Bushey Hospl
WD23 . . . . . . . . . . . . . . . .168 F1
Burbage Cl EN8 . . . . . . . .162 F8
Burchell Ct WD23 . . . . . .168 C2
Burfield Cl AL10 . . . . . . .130 A7
Burfield Ct LU2 . . . . . . . . .46 D3
Burfield Rd WD3 . . . . . . .164 C4
Burford Cl LU3 . . . . . . . . . .31 A1
Burford Gdns EN11 . . . . .135 B7
Burford Mews 9 EN11 . . .135 A7
Burford Pl 10 EN11 . . . . .135 A7
Burford St EN11 . . . . . . .135 A7
Burford Way SG5 . . . . . . . .21 D2
Burgage Ct 12 SG12 . . . . .93 D1
Burgage La SG12 . . . . . . . .93 D1
Burge End La SG5 . . . . . . .20 C5
Burgess Cl EN7 . . . . . . . .147 C6
Burgess Ct WD6 . . . . . . .156 F1
Burghley Ave
Bishop's Stortford CM23 . . .76 C7
Borehamwood WD6 . . . . .170 C4
Burghley Cl SG2 . . . . . . . .69 B8
Burgoyne Hatch CM20 . .118 A1
Burgundy Croft AL7 . . . .110 F4
Burhill Gr HA5 . . . . . . . .175 E1
Burleigh Mead AL9 . . . .130 C7
Burleigh Prim Sch EN8 .148 D1
Burleigh Rd
Cheshunt EN8 . . . . . . . . . .162 E7
Hemel Hempstead HP2 . . .125 C2
Hertford SG13 . . . . . . . . .114 A7
St Albans AL1 . . . . . . . . . .128 B3
Burleigh Way EN6 . . . . .146 E1
Burley SG6 . . . . . . . . . . . .11 F2
Burley Ho WD5 . . . . . . . .153 F7
Burley Rd CM23 . . . . . . . .77 A4
Burn's Gn SG2 . . . . . . . . . .52 F2
Burnell Rise SG6 . . . . . . .22 D5
Burnell Wlk SG6 . . . . . . . .22 E5
Burnells Way CM24 . . . . .59 E7
Burnet Cl HP3 . . . . . . . . .124 E2
Burnett Ave SG16 . . . . . . .10 B4
Burnett Sq SG14 . . . . . . .112 F7
Burnham Cl
Datchworth AL6 . . . . . . . . .90 C6
Enfield EN1 . . . . . . . . . . . .161 E1
Burnham Green Rd AL6,
SG3 . . . . . . . . . . . . . . . . . .90 D6
Burnham Rd Luton LU2 . . .46 B2
St Albans AL1 . . . . . . . . . .128 B3
Burnley Cl WD19 . . . . . . .175 C5
Burns Cl Hitchin SG4 . . . .35 B8
Stevenage SG2 . . . . . . . . . .51 C8
Burns Dr HP2 . . . . . . . . .105 B1
Burns Rd SG8 . . . . . . . . . . .7 D8
Burnsall Pl AL5 . . . . . . . .107 C6
Burnside Hertford SG14 .113 A5
Hoddesdon EN11 . . . . . . .134 F6
Sawbridgeworth CM21 . . . .97 D2
St Albans AL1 . . . . . . . . . .128 B1
Burnside Cl AL10 . . . . . .130 A8
Burnside Terr CM17 . . . .118 F3
Burnt Cl LU3 . . . . . . . . . . .44 F7
Burnt Mill CM20 . . . . . . .117 C3
Burnt Mill Comp Sch
CM20 . . . . . . . . . . . . . . . .117 F2
Burntfarm Ride EN2,EN7 161 B7
Burntmill Cl CM20 . . . . .117 C3
Burntmill Cnr CM20 . . . .117 D4
Burntmill La CM20 . . . . .117 D3
Burr Cl AL2 . . . . . . . . . . .142 E4
Burr St LU2 . . . . . . . . . . . .63 E8
Burr's Pl LU1 . . . . . . . . . .63 E6
Burrowfield AL7 . . . . . . .110 D4
Burrows Chase EN9 . . . .163 D3
Burrs La SG8 . . . . . . . . . . .17 C3
Bursland SG6 . . . . . . . . . . .22 D6
Burston Dr AL2 . . . . . . . .141 C3
Burton Ave WD18 . . . . . .167 A5
Burton Cl AL4 . . . . . . . . . .87 C5
Burton Dr EN3 . . . . . . . .163 A2
Burton Grange EN7 . . . .147 E4
Burton La EN7 . . . . . . . . .147 E3
Burtons La WD3 . . . . . . .164 A4
Burtons Mill CM21 . . . . . .97 F3
Burvale Ct 3 WD18 . . . .167 B6
Burwell Rd SG2 . . . . . . . . .51 B4
Bury Cotts AL3 . . . . . . . .105 E5
Bury End SG5 . . . . . . . . . .20 D4
Bury Field SG9 . . . . . . . . .29 B7

**Bury Gn**
Hemel Hempstead HP1 ...124 C4
Wheathampstead AL4 ...108 C8
**Bury Green Rd**
Cheshunt EN7 .........162 A7
Cheshunt EN7 .........162 A8
**Bury Hill** HP1 ........124 C4
**Bury Hill CI** HP1 ......124 C4
**Bury Holme** EN10 ......148 F8
**Bury La** Bramfield SG14 ..91 B4
Codicote SG4 ..........67 F2
Datchworth SG3 .......69 D3
Rickmansworth WD3 ...165 D1
Streatley LU3 ..........31 A5
**Bury Mdws** WD3 ......165 D1
**Bury Mead** SG15 ......11 A4
**Bury Mead Rd** SG5 ....21 F1
**Bury Park Rd** LU1 .....63 C8
**Bury Plantation** SG8 ...7 F6
**Bury Rd** Harlow CM17 ..118 D4
Hatfield AL10 .........130 C6
Hemel Hempstead HP1 ..124 C3
**Bury Rise** HP3 ........137 D6
**Bury The** SG4 ........67 F2
**Burycroft** AL8 ........89 E1
**Burydale** SG2 ........69 B8
**Burydale Jun Sch** SG2 ..51 B1
**Burydell La** AL2 ......141 D1
**Buryfield Terr** SG12 ...93 C1
**Buryfield Way** SG12 ...93 C1
**Burymead** SG1 ........36 C1
**Burywick** AL5 ........107 B5
**Bush Hall La** AL9 ......130 D8
**Bush Spring** SG7 ......13 A1
**Bushbarns** EN7 ........148 A2
**Bushby Ave** EN10 .....134 F1
**Bushell Gn** WD23 .....176 D8
**Bushey CI** AL7 ........111 B5
**Bushey Gn** AL7 ........111 B5
**Bushey Grove Rd** WD23 167 E5
**Bushey Hall Dr** WD23 ..167 E5
**Bushey Hall Rd** WD23 ..167 E5
**Bushey Hall Sch** WD23 .167 F4
**Bushey Heath Prim Sch**
WD23 ...............168 D1
**Bushey Ley** AL7 .......111 B5
**Bushey Manor Jun Sch**
WD23 ...............167 E4
**Bushey Meads Sch**
WD23 ...............168 C4
**Bushey Mill Cres** WD24 154 C3
**Bushey Mill La**
Watford WD23 .........167 E8
Watford,North Watford
WD24 ...............154 D1
**Bushey Mus★** WD23 ...168 A3
**Bushey Pk** WD23 ......168 A3
**Bushey Sta** WD19 .....167 D3
**Bushfield Rd** HP3 .....137 D6
**Bushmead Ct** LU2 .....45 E6
**Bushmead Prim Sch** LU2 45 E5
**Bushmead Rd** LU2 ....45 E5
**Bushwood CI** AL9 .....144 B8
**Butchers La** SG4 ......48 D6
**Bute Sq** LU1 ..........63 E7
**Bute St** LU1 ..........63 E7
**Butely Rd** LU4 ........44 B5
**Butler's Hall La** CM23 ..76 B3
**Butlers Ct** EN8 ........162 E2
**Butlers Dr** E4 ........163 C1
**Butlers Yd** SG7 .......12 C1
**Butlin Rd** LU1 ........63 B7
**Butt Field View** AL1 ...141 C2
**Buttercup CI** AL10 ....109 F1
**Butterfield Cotts** WD3 .172 E3
**Butterfield Ct** SG7 ....23 E8
**Butterfield Green Rd**
LU2 ................46 A6
**Butterfield La** AL1 ....141 E7
**Butterfield Rd** AL4 ....108 C7
**Butterfly La** WD6 .....169 B7
**Buttermere CI** AL1 ....128 B2
**Buttersweet Rise** CM21 .97 E1
**Butterwick** WD25 .....154 E3
**Butterworth Path** 1 LU2 63 E8
**Buttlehide** WD3 .......172 D5
**Butts End** HP1 ........124 A5
**Butts The** EN10 .......148 E7
**Buttsmead** HA6 ......174 C3
**Buxton CI** AL4 ........128 C4
**Buxton Path** WD19 ....175 C7
**Buxton Rd** LU1 .......63 D7
**Buxtons La** SG1 .......1 F3
**Buzzard Rd** LU4 ......44 A4
**By The Mount** AL7 ....110 D5
**By The Wood** WD19 ...175 E8
**By-Wood End** SL9 ....172 A5
**Byde St** SG14 ........113 C7
**Bye Way The** HA3 ....176 F2
**Byers CI** EN5 .........159 C5
**Byeway The** WD3 .....173 E8
**Byfield** AL8 ..........89 E1
**Byfield CI** LU4 .......44 B1
**Byfleet Ind Est** WD18 ..166 B1
**Byford Ho** 5 EN5 .....171 D5
**Bygrave** SG1 .........36 C2
**Bygrave Rd** SG7 ......12 F1
**Bylands CI** CM23 .....76 D6
**Bylands Ho** AL3 ......106 A7
**Byng Dr** EN6 .........159 A8
**Byng Rd** EN5 ........171 D6
**Byrd Wlk** SG7 ........23 F7

**Byron Ave**
Borehamwood WD6 ...170 A4
Watford WD24 .........167 D8
**Byron CI**
Hammond Street EN7 ..147 F4
Hitchin SG4 ...........35 B8
Stevenage SG2 .......51 C7
**Byron Ct** EN8 ........148 B3
**Byron PI** HP2 ........105 B1
**Byron Rd** Harpenden AL5 .86 A2
Harrow HA3 ..........176 F1
Luton LU4 ...........44 B2
Royston SG8 .........7 E8
**Byslips Rd** LU6 ......82 D5
**Byway The** EN6 ......159 A6
**Byways** HP4 .........122 E5

## C

**Cabot CI** SG2 ........51 A7
**Caddington Comm** AL3 .83 E8
**Caddis CI** HA7 .......176 F3
**Cade CI** SG6 .........12 C1
**Cades CI** LU1 ........63 A6
**Cades La** LU1 ........63 A6
**Cadia Ct** LU1 ........62 E4
**Cadmore Ct**
12 Cheshunt EN8 ......148 D3
Hertford AL1 .........112 F7
**Cadmore La** EN8 ......148 E2
**Cadwell CI** SG4 ......22 A2
**Cadwell La** SG4 ......22 A2
**Caernarvon CI**
Hemel Hempstead HP2 .124 D3
Stevenage SG2 .......69 B7
**Caernarvon Ct** HP2 ...124 D3
**Caesars Rd** AL4 ......108 E8
**Cage Pond Rd** WD7 ...156 F6
**Cairn Way** HA7 ......176 F4
**Cairns CI** AL4 ........128 D2
**Caishowe Rd** WD6 ....170 B8
**Caister CI**
Hemel Hempstead HP2 .124 E2
Stevenage SG1 .......36 A1
**Calais Ct** EN7 ........147 D5
**Calbury CI** AL1 ......128 B2
**Caldbeck** EN9 ........163 D5
**Caldecot Ave** EN7 ....147 E4
**Caldecote Gdns** WD23 .168 E2
**Caldecote La** WD23 ..168 F3
**Caldecote Rd** SG7 ....12 E8
**Calder Ave** WD23 ....145 B5
**Calder Way** SG1 .....37 A3
**Caldwell Rd** WD19 ...175 D6
**Caledon Rd** AL2 ......142 D5
**Caledonian Ct** WD17 ..167 B7
**California** SG12 ......12 F1
**California Ct** 2 WD23 .168 D1
**California La** WD23 ...168 D1
**Callaghan Ct** HP4 ....122 D4
**Callanders The** WD23 .168 E1
**Callisto Ct** HP2 ......124 F6
**Callowland PI** WD24 ..154 B1
**Calnwood Rd** LU4 ....44 C3
**Calton Ave** SG14 .....112 F6
**Calton Ct** SG14 ......112 F6
**Calton Ho** SG14 .....112 F6
**Calverley CI** CM23 ...76 E4
**Calvert Rd** EN5 ......171 D7
**Calverton Rd** LU3 ....45 A6
**Cam Ctr** SG4 .........22 A3
**Cam Sq** SG4 .........22 A3
**Camberley PI** AL5 ....107 D6
**Camborne Dr** HP2 ....124 E7
**Cambrian Way** HP2 ...124 F6
**Cambridge CI** EN8 ....148 E2
**Cambridge Cotts** SG11 .72 E2
**Cambridge Cres** SG8 ..2 A8
**Cambridge Ct** EN5 ...171 F6
**Cambridge Dr** EN6 ...158 E4
**Cambridge Rd**
Barkway SG8 .........17 D5
Barley SG8 ..........9 A3
Harlow CM20 ........118 C6
Hitchin SG4 ..........22 C2
Sawbridgeworth CM21 .97 E4
St Albans AL1 ........128 B2
Standon SG11 ........55 C2
Stansted Mountfitchet
CM24 ...............59 E8
6 Watford WD18 .....167 C5
**Cambridge St** LU1 ....63 A6
**Cambridge Terr** 16 HP4 122 D4
**Cameron Ct** 8 SG12 ..93 D2
**Cameron Dr** EN8 .....162 D5
**Camfield** AL7 ........110 F2
**Camford Way** LU3 ....44 A8
**Camlet Way** AL3 .....127 B4
**Camp Prim Sch** AL1 ..128 B2
**Camp Rd** AL1 ........128 B2
**Camp View Rd** AL1 ...128 B2
**Campana Ct** EN5 .....171 D6
**Campania Gr** LU3 ....45 A8
**Campbell CI**
Buntingford SG9 ......40 E7
Hitchin SG4 ..........35 B8
**Campers Ave** SG6 ....22 E5
**Campers Rd** SG6 .....22 E5
**Campers Wlk** SG6 ....22 E5
**Campfield Rd**
Hertford SG14 .......113 B5
St Albans AL1 ........128 A3
**Campfield Way** SG12 ..22 D5
**Campine CI** 1 EN8 ...148 D3
**Campion CI** WD25 ....154 A6

**Campion Ct** SG1 ......50 C8
**Campion Rd**
Hatfield AL10 ........129 F8
Hemel Hempstead HP1 .123 E2
**Campion Way** SG8 ....7 E5
**Campions** CM17 ......118 F5
**Campions Ct** HP4 ....122 B3
**Campions The**
Borehamwood WD6 ...157 A1
Stansted Mountfitchet
CM24 ...............59 E8
**Campkin Mead** SG2 ...51 D3
**Camps Hill Com Prim Sch**
SG2 ................51 C6
**Campus Five** SG6 ....23 C7
**Campus The** AL8 .....110 D7
**Canada La** EN10 .....148 E6
**Canadas The** EN10 ...148 E6
**Canal Ct** HP4 ........122 E4
**Canal Way** LU9 ......173 A4
**Canalside** HP4 .......121 F6
**Canberra CI**
Kneesworth SG8 .....2 B5
St Albans AL3 ........127 F7
**Canberra Gdns** LU3 ..45 B6
**Candlefield CI** HP3 ...139 A8
**Candlefield Rd** HP3 ..139 A8
**Candlefield Wlk** HP3 ..139 A8
**Caneland Ct** EN9 ....163 F5
**Canfield** CM23 ......76 E8
**Cangelis CI** HP1 ......124 A1
**Canham Ct** SG4 ......66 D1
**Cannix CI** SG2 .......51 A2
**Cannon Ho** 1 SG4 ...34 F6
**Cannon La** LU2 ......46 B5
**Cannon Mews** EN9 ...163 B6
**Cannon Rd** WD18 ....167 C4
**Cannon St** AL3 ......127 D4
**Cannon's CI** SG8 .....1 F5
**Cannons Ct** CM23 ....59 A1
**Cannons Ct** SG11 ....55 D3
**Cannons Mdw** AL6 ...90 E2
**Cannons Mead** CM24 .59 D7
**Cannons Mill La** CM23 .59 A1
**Canons CI** WD7 ......156 B4
**Canons Field** AL6 ....87 D1
**Canons Gate**
Cheshunt EN8 ........148 F5
Harlow CM20 ........117 A2
**Canons Rd** SG12 .....93 C2
**Canonsfield** AL6 .....89 E8
**Canonsfield Ct** AL6 ..89 E8
**Canonsfield Rd** AL6 ..89 E8
**Canopus Way** HA6 ...175 A6
**Canopy La** CM17 .....118 C1
**Cantelowes Ho** EN5 ..171 D4
**Canterbury CI** Luton LU3 .44 F4
Northwood HA6 ......174 F4
**Canterbury Ct** AL1 ...127 F4
**Canterbury Ho**
10 Borehamwood WD6 ..170 A7
4 Watford WD24 .....167 C7
**Canterbury Rd**
Borehamwood WD6 ...170 A7
Watford WD17 .......167 B7
**Canterbury Way**
Croxley Green WD3 ..166 C6
Stevenage SG1 .......36 F2
**Cape Rd** AL1 ........128 B3
**Capel Ct** SG11 .......57 E2
**Capel Ho** WD19 ......175 D6
**Capel Manor Gdns★**
EN1,EN7 .............162 B4
**Capel Manor Prim Sch**
EN1 ................162 B4
**Capel Rd** Enfield EN1 ..162 B3
Watford WD19 .......167 E3
**Capell Ave** WD3 .....164 C4
**Capell Rd** WD3 ......164 D4
**Capell Way** WD3 ....164 D4
**Capella Rd** HA6 .....174 F6
**Capelvere Wlk** WD17 .166 E8
**Caponfield** AL7 ......111 B4
**Capron Rd** LU4 ......44 A4
**Captains Wlk** HP4 ...122 D3
**Caractacus Cottage View**
WD18 ...............167 A3
**Caractacus Gn** WD18 .166 F3
**Caravan La** WD3 ....165 D4
**Carbone Hill** EN6,SG13 .146 D5
**Carde CI** SG14 .......112 F7
**Cardiff CI** SG2 .......69 B7
**Cardiff Gr** LU1 ......63 D7
**Cardiff PI** SG8 .......2 A8
**Cardiff Rd** Luton LU1 ..63 D7
Watford WD18 .......167 B4
**Cardiff Way** WD5 ....154 A7
**Cardigan Ct** 11 LU1 ..63 D8
**Cardigan Gdns** 12 LU1 .63 D8
**Cardigan St** LU1 .....63 D7
**Cardinal Ave** WD6 ...170 B5
**Cardinal CI** EN7 .....147 F5
**Cardinal Ct**
Borehamwood WD6 ...170 B6
3 Luton LU2 .........45 D1
**Cardinal Gr** AL3 .....127 B4
**Cardinal Newman RC Sec Sch**
LU2 ................31 C1
**Cardinals Gate** SG8 ..7 C6
**Cardy Rd** HP1 .......124 B3
**Careless Ct** 21 CM23 ..76 F7
**Carew Lodge** HA6 ...174 F4
**Carew Rd** HA6 ......174 F4
**Carew Way** WD19 ...175 F7
**Careys Croft** HP4 ....122 A7
**Carisbrook Rd** AL2 ..141 B5
**Carisbrooke Ave** WD24 .167 D8

**Carisbrooke Rd**
Harpenden AL5 ......86 C2
Luton LU4 ...........44 E1
**Carleton Rd** EN8 .....148 E4
**Carleton Rise** AL6 ...89 C6
**Carlisle Ave** AL3 .....127 D4
**Carlisle Ho** 15 WD6 ..170 A1
**Carlton CI**
Borehamwood WD6 ...170 D5
Luton LU3 ...........45 C2
**Carlton Cres** LU3 ....45 C2
**Carlton Ct**
1 Harpenden AL5 .....86 B1
Watford WD19 .......167 C3
**Carlton PI** HA6 ......174 B5
**Carlton Rd** AL5 ......86 B2
**Carman Ct** HP23 .....99 F3
**Carmelite CI** HA3 ....176 C2
**Carmelite Rd**
Harrow HA3 .........176 C1
Luton LU4 ...........44 A3
**Carmelite Way** HA3 ..176 C1
**Carmelite Wlk** HA3 ..176 C1
**Carmen Ct** WD6 .....156 F1
**Carnaby Rd** EN10 ....134 E3
**Carnarvon Rd** EN5 ..171 E6
**Carnegie CI** EN3 .....163 B1
**Carnegie Gdns** LU3 ..45 A8
**Carnegie Rd** AL3 ....127 D7
**Caro La** HP3 ........125 B1
**Carol CI** LU3 ........45 B4
**Caroline Ho** WD23 ...168 A3
**Caroline PI** WD19 ...167 E3
**Carolyn Ct** LU3 .....45 B4
**Caroon Dr** WD3 .....152 B3
**Carpenders Ave** WD19 175 E8
**Carpenters CI** AL5 ...85 D4
**Carpenders Park Sta**
WD19 ...............175 D7
**Carpenter Way** EN6 ..159 D6
**Carpenters Rd** EN1 ..162 C3
**Carpenters The** 2 ....76 B5
**Carpenters Wood Dr**
WD3 ...............164 B5
**Carriden Ct** SG14 ...112 F8
**Carrigans** CM23 .....76 E8
**Carrington Ave** WD6 .170 C4
**Carrington CI**
Arkley EN5 ..........171 A4
Borehamwood WD6 ...170 C4
**Carrington PI** HP23 ..100 C5
**Carrington Sq** HA3 ..176 C3
**Carsdale CI** LU3 .....45 A6
**Cart Path** WD25 .....154 C6
**Cart Tk The** HP3 ....138 F6
**Carteret Rd** LU2 .....46 C1
**Carterhatch La** EN1 ..161 F1
**Carters CI** Arlesey SG15 .11 A7
Aston SG2 ..........51 D4
**Carters La (Wibbly Wobbly**
**La)** SG5 ............34 A6
**Carters Leys** CM23 ...76 B3
**Carters Way** SG15 ...11 A7
**Carters Wlk** SG15 ...11 A7
**Cartersfield Rd** EN9 ..163 C5
**Carthagena Est** EN9 ..135 C3
**Cartwright Rd** Royston SG8 7 C5
Stevenage SG1 .......37 C2
**Carve Ley** AL7 ......111 B5
**Carvers Croft** SG3 ...69 B2
**Cary Wlk** WD7 ......156 B5
**Cashio La** SG6 ......23 A8
**Caslon Way** SG6 ....11 F1
**Cassandra Gate** EN8 .148 F4
**Cassio Ho** WD18 ....166 F5
**Cassio Rd** WD18 ....167 B5
**Cassiobridge Rd** WD18 166 C5
**Cassiobridge Terr** WD18 166 D4
**Cassiobury Dr** WD17 .166 F7
**Cassiobury Inf Sch**
WD17 ...............166 E8
**Cassiobury Jun Sch**
WD17 ...............166 E8
**Cassiobury Park Ave**
WD18 ...............166 F6
**Castano Ct** WD5 .....153 E8
**Castellane CI** 1 HA7 ..176 F4
**Castile Ct** EN8 ......163 A5
**Castile Gdns** WD4 ...138 F2
**Castings Ho** AL1 .....23 A7
**Castle CI** Bushey WD23 168 B3
Hoddesdon EN11 ....115 C1
Pitstone LU7 .........80 D3
**Castle Cotts** SG9 ....29 B7
**Castle Croft** AL1 ....63 A6
**Castle Ct** SG5 .......21 D1
**Castle Gate** SG4 ....113 C5
**Castle Gate Way** HP4 122 C6
**Castle Hill** HP4 .....122 C6
**Castle Hill Ave** HP4 ..122 C5
**Castle Hill CI** HP4 ...122 C5
**Castle Hill Ct** HP4 ...122 C5
**Castle Mead** HP1 ....124 B1
**Castle Mead Gdns** SG14 113 C6
**Castle Mews** 3 HP4 ..122 C4
**Castle Rise** AL4 .....86 C2
**Castle Row** HP23 ....100 A3
**Castle St**
Berkhamsted HP4 ...122 C4
Bishop's Stortford CM23 .76 F6
Hertford SG14 .......113 D5
Luton,High Town LU1 ..63 E7

**Castle St** continued
Luton,New Town LU1 ..63 E6
Wingrave HP22 ......60 B3
**Castle View** CM23 ....77 A7
**Castle Wlk** CM24 ....59 E6
**Castleford CI** WD6 ...156 F1
**Castles CI** SG5 ......11 F8
**Catalin Ct** EN9 ......163 D6
**Caterham Ct** EN9 ....163 F5
**Catesby Gn** LU3 .....31 A1
**Catham CI** AL1 ......128 B1
**Cathedral & Abbey Church of**
**St Alban★** AL3 ......127 D3
**Cathedral Ct** AL3 ....127 B1
**Catherall Rd** LU3 ...45 B6
**Catherine CI** HP2 ....125 B8
**Catherine Cotts** HP23 .120 E8
**Catherine Ho** WD19 ..175 B7
**Catherine Rd** EN3 ...162 E3
**Catherine St** AL3 ....127 D4
**Catherine Wheel Mews** 20
SG12 ...............93 D1
**Catisfield Rd** EN3 ...162 E2
**Catkin CI** HP1 .......124 B4
**Catlin St** HP3 .......138 B8
**Catsbrook Rd** LU3 ...45 B6
**Catsdell Bottom** HP3 .139 B8
**Catsey La** WD23 ....168 C2
**Catsey Wood** WD23 ..168 C2
**Catterick Way** WD6 ..169 F8
**Cattlegate Cotts** EN6 .160 D8
**Cattlegate Hill** EN6 ..160 D7
**Cattlegate Rd**
Crews Hill EN2 ......161 A3
Northaw EN6 ........160 D6
**Cattley CI** EN5 ......171 E5
**Cattlins CI** EN7 ......147 F2
**Cattsdell** HP2 .......124 E5
**Causeway CI** EN6 ....159 D8
**Causeway Ho** WD5 ..153 E8
**Causeway The**
1 Bishop's Stortford CM23 .77 A7
Braughing SG9,SG11 .42 D1
Brent Pelham SG9 ...30 B1
Buntingford SG9 ....40 F8
Furneux Pelham SG9 .43 A3
Kneesworth SG8 ....2 A5
Potters Bar EN6 ....159 D8
Therfield SG8 .......15 F7
**Cautherly La** SG12 ...115 A5
**Cavalier CI** ..........36 B1
**Cavalier CI** LU3 .....45 A5
**Cavalier Ct** 7 HP4 ...122 C4
**Cavan Ct** AL10 ......130 A4
**Cavan Dr** AL3 .......127 D8
**Cavan Rd** AL3 .......106 A6
**Cave Gate** SG9 ......28 D6
**Cavell Rd** EN7 ......148 A4
**Cavell Wlk** SG2 .....51 C5
**Cavendish Cres** WD6 .170 A5
**Cavendish Ct**
Croxley Green WD3 ..166 D4
Hemel Hempstead HP3 .138 E6
**Cavendish Rd**
Barnet EN5 ..........171 C6
Luton LU3 ...........45 B2
Markyate AL3 .......83 D6
St Albans AL1 .......127 F3
Stevenage SG1 .....50 B5
**Cavendish Sch The** HP1 124 B4
**Cavendish Way** AL10 .129 F5
**Cawkell Ct** CM24 ....59 D7
**Caxton Ctr** AL3 .....127 F8
**Caxton Hill** SG13 ....113 F6
**Caxton Rd** EN11 ....115 B2
**Caxton Way**
Stevenage SG1 .....50 B4
Watford WD18 ......166 D2
**Cecil CI** CM23 ......77 D7
**Cecil Cres** AL10 .....130 B7
**Cecil Ct** EN5 ........171 D6
**Cecil Rd** Brickendon SG13 113 C3
Cheshunt EN8 .......162 E7
Hoddesdon EN11 ....135 C8
South Mimms EN6 ..158 B7
St Albans AL1 .......127 F3
**Cecil St** WD24 ......154 B1
**Cedar Ave** Cheshunt EN8 162 D6
Ickleford SG5 .......21 E4
**Cedar CI** Hertford SG14 113 B6
Potters Bar EN6 ....145 A1
Sawbridgeworth CM21 .97 E1
Ware SG12 ..........114 D8
**Cedar Cres** SG8 .....7 B6
**Cedar Ct**
Bishop's Stortford CM23 58 F1
St Albans AL4 .......128 D3
Watford WD25 ......154 D6
**Cedar Dr** HA5 .......176 A4
**Cedar Gn** EN11 .....135 A5
**Cedar Grange** HA6 ..174 C3
**Cedar Lawn Ave** EN5 .171 E4
**Cedar Lodge** 8 EN8 .148 D3
**Cedar Park Rd** EN2 ..161 C1
**Cedar Pk** CM23 .....76 D4
**Cedar PI** HA6 .......174 C4
**Cedar Rd**
Berkhamsted HP4 ...122 E3
Enfield EN2 .........161 C1
Hatfield AL10 .......130 A4
Watford WD19 ......167 D3
**Cedar Way** HP4 .....122 D3
**Cedar Wlk**
Hemel Hempstead HP3 .124 D1
Waltham Abbey EN9 .163 D5
Welwyn Garden City AL7 .111 B5

Cedar Wood Dr WD25 ..154 B4
Cedars Ave WD3 ........165 C1
Cedars Cl WD6 .........170 B5
Cedars Fst Sch HA3 ....176 C2
Cedars Mid Sch HA3 ...176 C2
Cedars The
　Berkhamsted HP4 .......122 E4
　13 Harpenden AL5 ......86 B1
　5 Rickmansworth WD3 ..165 D2
　St Albans AL3 ..........127 C5
　Stevenage SG2 ..........69 B8
Cedars Wlk WD3 .......164 F5
Cedarwood Dr AL4 .....128 D3
Celandine Dr LU7 .......45 A8
Cell Barnes Cl AL1 .....128 B1
Cell Barnes La AL1 .....128 B1
Cemetery Hill HP1 .....124 C2
Cemetery Rd CM23 .....76 F6
Cemmaes Court Rd
　HP1 ..................124 C3
Cemmaes Mdw HP1 ....124 C3
Centennial Ave WD6 ...169 C2
Centennial Ct
　Rickmansworth WD3 ...165 E2
　Stanmore WD6 .........169 C2
Centennial Pk WD6 ....169 C2
Central App SG6 ........22 F6
Central Ave
　Cheshunt EN8 .........162 E6
　Lower Stondon SG16 ....10 B3
　Whipsnade LU6 .........81 E8
Central Dr St Albans AL4 .128 C4
　Welwyn Garden City AL7 .110 F8
Central Hts WD18 .....166 F5
Central Prim Sch WD18 167 C5
Central Rd CM20 ......118 A4
Central Way HA6 ......174 E3
Centro HP2 ...........125 C5
Century Cl AL3 ........127 C4
Century Ct WD18 ......166 C2
Century Pk WD17 .....167 C4
Century Rd
　Hoddesdon EN11 ......135 A7
　Ware SG12 .............93 C2
Cervantes Ct HA6 .....174 F3
Chace Ave EN6 .......159 D7
Chace The SG2 .........50 F1
Chad La AL3 ...........84 C4
Chadwell SG12 .......114 C4
Chadwell Ave EN8 ....148 C3
Chadwell Cl LU2 ........45 F1
Chadwell Rd SG1 ......50 B3
Chadwell Rise SG12 ..114 C8
Chaffinch La WD18 ...166 F2
Chaffinches Gn HP3 ..139 A7
Chagny Cl SG6 .........22 E6
Chalet Cl HP4 ........121 F4
Chalfont Cl HP2 ......125 B8
Chalfont Ho WD18 ...166 E2
Chalfont La
　Chorleywood WD3 ....164 B4
　Maple Cross WD3 .....172 D3
Chalfont Pl AL1 .......127 C3
Chalfont Rd WD3,SL9,
　HP8 .................172 C7
Chalfont Shire Ctr★
　HP8 .................172 A7
Chalfont Way LU2 ......46 D2
Chalfont Wlk 2 HA5 ..175 C1
Chalgrove AL7 ........111 D7
Chalk Dale AL7 .......111 B7
Chalk Field SG6 .......23 C3
Chalk Hill Great Offley LU2 47 A5
　Watford WD19 ........167 E3
Chalk Hills SG7 ........23 F5
Chalkdell Fields AL4 ..128 A7
Chalkdell Hill HP2 ....124 E3
Chalkdell Path 8 SG5 .34 D8
Chalkdown Luton LU2 ..45 E6
　Stevenage SG2 ........51 D7
Chalks Ave CM21 ......97 D3
Challney Boys High Sch &
　Com Coll LU4 .........44 D2
Challney Cl LU4 ........44 D2
Challney Girls High Sch
　LU4 ..................44 D2
Chalmers Ct WD3 ....165 F3
Chalton Rd LU4 ........44 C5
Chamberlaines AL5 ....85 A5
Chambers Gate SG1 ...50 D7
Chambers Gr AL7 ....110 E3
Chambers La SG5 ......21 E4
Chambers' St SG14 ...113 C6
Chambersbury La HP3 .139 A7
Chambersbury Prim Sch
　HP3 .................139 B8
Champions Cl WD6 ...157 B2
Champions Gn EN11 ..115 A1
Champions Way EN11 .115 A1
Champneys 3 WD19 ..175 E8
Chancellor's Sch AL9 .145 A6
Chancellors SG15 ......11 B7
Chancellors Rd SG1 ...36 D1
Chancery Cl AL4 .....128 D8
Chandler's La WD3 ...152 E2
Chandlers Cl CM23 ....76 C4
Chandlers Rd AL4 ....128 C6
Chandlers Way SG14 .113 A6
Chandos Cl HP6 ......150 C1
Chandos Rd
　Borehamwood WD6 ...170 A7
　Luton LU4 .............44 F1
Channock's Farm Cotts
　CM20 ................117 C7
Chantry Cl
　Bishop's Stortford CM23 ..76 E8
　Edgware NW7 .........170 F2
　Enfield EN2 ...........161 C1

Chantry Cl continued
　Kings Langley WD4 ....139 A2
Chantry Ct AL10 ......130 A4
Chantry La Hatfield AL10 .129 F4
　Hatfield AL10 .........130 A4
　Little Wymondley SG4 ..35 F2
　London Colney AL2 ....142 D5
Chantry Mount CM23 ..76 E8
Chantry Pl HA3 .......176 B2
Chantry Rd
　Bishop's Stortford CM23 ..76 E8
　Harrow HA3 ..........176 B2
Chantry The
　6 Bishop's Stortford CM23 76 F8
　Harlow CM20 .........118 A4
Chaomans SG6 .........22 F3
Chapel Cl
　Brookmans Park AL9 ..145 D4
　Little Gaddesden HP4 .102 D6
　Luton LU2 .............45 C8
　St Albans AL1 ........141 D8
Chapel Cotts HP2 ....124 D4
Chapel Croft WD4 ....152 A8
Chapel Crofts HP4 ...121 E6
Chapel Dr SG15 ........11 A4
Chapel End
　Buntingford SG9 .......40 E7
　Hoddesdon EN11 .....135 A5
Chapel End La HP23 ...99 C8
Chapel Fields HP23 ....99 C8
Chapel Hill CM24 ......59 C6
Chapel La
　Letty Green SG14 ....112 A3
　Little Hadham SG11 ...75 A8
　Long Marston HP23 ...79 B4
Chapel Pl SG5 .........11 F6
Chapel Rd
　Breachwood Green SG4 .65 D8
　Flamstead AL3 .........84 B2
Chapel Row
　3 Bishop's Stortford CM23 76 F6
　Harefield UB9 ........173 C2
　Hitchin SG5 ...........34 F8
　Whitwell SG4 .........66 A8
Chapel St
　Berkhamsted HP4 ....122 C4
　Hemel Hempstead HP2 .124 D4
　Hinxworth SG7 .........3 D6
　Luton,High Town LU1 ..63 E7
　Luton,New Town LU1 ..63 E6
　Tring HP23 ............99 F3
Chapel Viaduct LU1 ...63 E7
Chapel Way WD5 .....139 F4
Chapelfields SG12 ....115 D4
Chapman Rd SG1 ......36 B1
Chapmans End SG11 ...55 D3
Chappel Mdw HP23 ..100 B6
Chappell Ct SG12 ......92 E7
Chapterhouse Rd LU4 .44 A3
Chard Dr LU3 ..........31 B1
Chardia Terr EN8 ....148 D1
Charding Cres SG8 .....7 C7
Chardins Cl HP1 ......123 F4
Charkham Mews AL9 .144 C7
Charles St
　Berkhamsted HP4 ....122 B4
　Hemel Hempstead HP1 .124 C2
　Luton LU2 .............63 D7
　Tring HP23 ...........100 A3
Charlesworth Cl 4 HP3 124 D1
Charlock Way LU4 ....166 F3
Charlotte Cl AL4 .....128 E3
Charlottes Ct 2 LU1 ..63 D7
Charlton Cl EN11 .....135 A6
Charlton Mead La EN11 135 D5
Charlton Rd SG5 .......34 D5
Charlton Way EN11 ..135 B6
Charlwood Cl HA3 ...176 E4
Charlwood Rd LU4 .....44 B1
Charmbury Rise LU2 ..46 A4
Charmouth Ct AL1 ...128 A6
Charmouth Rd AL1 ..128 A5
Charndon Cl LU3 ......31 B1
Charnwood Rd EN1 ..162 B3
Charter Ho WD3 .....166 A4
Charter Pl WD17 ....167 C6
Chartley Ave HA7 ....176 F4
Chartridge WD19 ....175 D8
Chartridge Cl Arkley EN5 171 A4
　Bushey WD23 ........168 C3
Chartridge Way HP2 ..125 C3
Chartwell Ct EN9 ....163 E6
Chartwell Ct 8 EN5 ..171 E5
Chartwell Dr LU2 .....45 E3
Chartwell Rd HA6 ....174 F4
Charwood Cl WD7 ....156 E6
Chasden Rd HP1 .....123 F5
Chase Cl SG15 .........11 A8
Chase Farm Hospl EN2 .161 A1
Chase Hill Rd SG15 ....11 A7
Chase St LU1 ..........63 E6
Chase The Arlesey SG15 ..11 A6
　Bishop's Stortford CM23 .76 E6
　Goff's Oak EN7 ......147 B3
　Great Amwell SG12 ..115 A6
　Harlow CM17 ........118 C4
　Hemel Hempstead HP2 .124 C2
　Hertford SG13 .......113 F6
　Oaklands AL6 .........89 F7
　Radlett WD7 ........155 F4
　Watford WD18 ......166 E5
Chaseside LU7 .........80 A7
Chaseways CM21 ....118 C8
Chasten Hill SG6 ......22 D7
Chater Inf Sch WD18 .167 A5
Chater Jun Sch WD18 167 B5
Chatsworth Cl
　Bishop's Stortford CM23 .76 C7

Chatsworth Cl continued
　Borehamwood WD6 ...170 A6
Chatsworth Ct
　St Albans AL1 ........127 F3
　Stevenage SG2 .......50 F1
Chatsworth Mews
　WD24 ................154 A1
Chatsworth Rd LU4 ...45 B1
Chatter End CM23 ....58 C7
Chatteris Cl LU4 ......44 D4
Chatton Cl LU2 ........46 E2
Chaucer Cl HP4 ......121 F5
Chaucer Ct EN11 ....115 A1
Chaucer Ho 3 EN5 ..171 D5
Chaucer Rd Luton LU3 .45 C2
　Royston SG8 ...........7 C8
Chaucer Way Hitchin SG4 .35 C7
　Hoddesdon EN11 .....115 A2
Chaucer Wlk HP2 ....105 B1
Chaul End La LU4 .....44 E1
Chaul End Rd
　Caddington LU1 .......62 D6
　Luton LU4 .............44 B1
Chaulden House Gdns
　HP1 .................123 F1
Chaulden Jun & Inf Schs
　HP1 .................123 F2
Chaulden La HP1 ....123 E1
Chaulden Terr HP1 ..123 F2
Chauncey Ho WD18 .166 E3
Chauncy Ave EN6 ...159 C6
Chauncy Cl SG12 ......93 D3
Chauncy Ct 19 SG14 .113 D6
Chauncy Gdns SG7 ...13 B1
Chauncy Ho 3 SG1 ...50 E6
Chauncy Rd SG1 ......50 E6
Chauncy Sch The SG12 .93 D3
Chaworth Gn 1 LU4 ..44 D8
Cheapside LU1 .........63 E7
Cheapside Sq 4 LU1 ..63 E7
Chedburgh AL7 ......111 D7
Cheddington Comb Sch
　LU7 ...................80 A7
Cheddington La HP23 .79 C5
Cheddington Rd LU7 ..80 C4
Cheffins Rd EN11 ....114 F1
Chells La SG2 ..........51 D7
Chells Way SG2 .......51 B6
Chelmsford Rd SG4 ..113 B5
Chelsea Fields EN11 .115 D4
Chelsing Rise HP2 ....125 C2
Chelsworth Cl 1 LU2 .46 D1
Cheltenham Ct AL1 ..128 A2
Cheltenham Ho 2
　WD24 ................167 C7
Chelveston AL7 ......111 D7
Chelwood Ave AL10 .130 A8
Chelwood Cl HA6 ....174 C3
Chenduit Way HA7 ..176 F5
Chene Dr AL3 ........127 D5
Cheney Rd LU4 ........44 C5
Chenies Ave HP6 ....150 D1
Chenies Ct HP2 ......125 B8
Chenies Gn CM23 .....76 D6
Chenies Manor Ho★
　WD3 ................151 A1
Chenies Rd WD3 ....164 D7
Chenies Sch WD3 ...151 B1
Chenies Way WD18 ..166 E2
Chennells AL10 ......129 F4
Chennells Cl SG4 ......22 B2
Chennies The AL5 ...107 C2
Chepstow AL5 .........85 F2
Chepstow Cl SG1 ......51 B8
Chequer Ct LU1 .......63 F6
Chequer La AL3 .....106 B4
Chequer St Luton LU1 ..63 F6
　St Albans AL1 .......127 D3
Chequers
　Bishop's Stortford CM23 .76 C8
　Hatfield AL9 .........130 D8
　Welwyn Garden City AL7 .110 D3
Chequers Bridge Rd SG1 50 C6
Chequers Cl
　Buntingford SG9 .......40 D8
　Pitstone LU7 ...........80 C4
　Standon SG11 .........55 D4
　Stotfold SG5 ...........12 A6
Chequers Cotts
　Preston SG4 ...........48 D6
　Whipsnade LU6 .......82 A8
Chequers End HP2 ...104 D5
Chequers Field AL7 ..110 D3
Chequers La
　Abbots Langley WD2 .140 C1
　Pitstone LU7 ...........80 C5
　Preston SG4 ...........48 D7
Chequers Wlk EN9 ..163 F6
Cheriton Cl AL4 .....128 C4
Cherry Bank HP2 ....124 D5
Cherry Blossom Cl 2
　CM17 ................118 C4
Cherry Cl SG3 .........68 F4
Cherry Croft
　Croxley Green WD3 ..166 B3
　Welwyn Garden City AL8 .89 D2
Cherry Croft Gdns 4
　HA5 .................175 F3
Cherry Ct HA5 .......175 D2
Cherry Dr SG8 ..........7 E7
Cherry Gdns
　Bishop's Stortford CM23 .77 A8
　Sawbridgeworth CM21 .97 E4
　Tring HP23 ............99 F3
Cherry Green La SG9 ..40 F3

Cherry Hill
　Chiswell Green AL2 ..141 A6
　Harrow HA3 ..........176 E4
　Rickmansworth WD3 ..165 B6
Cherry Hills WD19 ...175 E5
Cherry Hollow WD5 ..153 F8
Cherry Orch HP1 ....124 A5
Cherry Orchard La SG9 .28 A3
Cherry Rd EN3 ......162 C1
Cherry Tree Ave AL2 .142 D5
Cherry Tree Cl
　Arlesey SG15 ..........11 A4
　Luton LU2 .............46 A1
Cherry Tree Gn SG14 .112 F7
Cherry Tree La
　Cholesbury HP23 ....120 A3
　Chorleywood WD3 ...164 C1
　Potters Bar EN6 .....159 B5
　Wheathampstead AL4 .87 A2
Cherry Tree Prim Sch
　WD24 ................154 A3
Cherry Tree Rd
　Hoddesdon EN11 ....135 A7
　Watford WD24 .......154 A7
Cherry Tree Rise SG2 .38 B1
Cherry Trees SG16 ....10 B3
Cherry Trees Dr SG2 .51 B7
Cherry Way AL10 ....130 A2
Cherry Wlk WD3 ....165 C7
Cherrydale WD18 ...166 F5
Cherrytree La HP2 ..125 C3
Chertsey Cl LU2 ......64 D8
Chertsey Rise SG2 ...51 C4
Cherwell Cl WD3 ....166 A3
Cherwell Dr SG1 ......37 A3
Chesfield Cl CM23 ...76 F5
Chesford Rd LU2 ......46 C4
Chesham Cl HA6 .....174 F4
Chesham Prep Sch HP5 136 A4
Chesham Rd
　Berkhamsted HP4 ....122 C3
　Bovingdon HP3,HP3 ..136 E3
　Wigginton HP23 .....120 E7
Chesham Way WD18 .166 F3
Cheshire Dr WD25 ...153 F5
Cheshunt Centre The
　EN8 .................148 D3
Cheshunt Folly EN8 ..148 B3
Cheshunt Sch EN8 ..148 C1
Cheshunt Sta EN8 ...148 F1
Cheshunt Wash EN8 .148 E4
Cheslyn Cl LU2 ........46 E2
Chess Cl Latimer HP5 .150 D3
　Rickmansworth WD3 ..165 D5
Chess Hill WD3 ......165 D5
Chess La WD3 .......165 D5
Chess Vale Rise WD3 .165 F3
Chess Way WD3 .....165 A6
Chesswood Ct WD3 .165 D1
Chesswood Way HA5 .175 C1
Chester Ave LU4 ......44 E3
Chester Cl Luton LU4 ..44 F2
　Potters Bar EN6 .....145 B2
Chester Gibbons Gn
　AL2 .................142 D5
Chester Ho HA4 ....174 F3
Chester Pl 1 HA6 ...174 E3
Chester Rd
　Borehamwood WD6 ..170 D6
　Northwood HA6 .....174 F3
　Stevenage SG1 ........37 A1
　Watford WD18 ......167 A5
Chesterfield Flats EN5 171 D4
Chesterfield Inf & Jun Schs
　EN3 .................162 C4
Chesterfield Rd
　Barnet EN5 ..........171 D4
　Enfield EN3 ..........162 C4
Chesterton Ave AL5 ..86 D1
Chestnut Ave
　Lower Stondon SG16 ..10 C3
　Luton LU4 ............44 C8
　Northwood HA6 .....174 F2
　Rickmansworth WD3 ..165 A4
　Ware SG12 ............93 F3
Chestnut Cl
　Bishop's Stortford CM23 .76 E6
　Dagnall HP4 ...........81 C5
　Hunsdon SG12 ........95 D1
　Potten End HP4 .....123 B6
Chestnut Ct
　4 Hitchin SG5 ........34 D8
　Watford WD18 ......166 E5
Chestnut Dr
　Berkhamsted HP4 ....122 D4
　Harrow HA3 ..........176 F4
　Hatfield Heath CM22 .98 F3
　St Albans AL4 .......128 C5
Chestnut La
　Kneesworth SG8 .......2 B6
　Totteridge N20 ......171 E1
Chestnut Rd EN3 ....162 E3
Chestnut Rise WD23 .168 B2
Chestnut Wlk Hitchin SG4 .35 A4
　Royston SG8 ...........7 E5
　Stevenage SG1 ........36 D1
　Watford WD24 .......154 A2
Chestnuts The
　Codicote SG4 .........67 F2
　Hemel Hempstead HP3 .137 F7
　Hertford SG13 ......113 D5
Cheverell's Gn AL3 ...83 C4
Cheverells Cl AL3 .....83 D1
Cheviot Cl Bushey WD23 .168 C3
　Luton LU3 .............44 D7
Cheviot Rd LU3 ........44 D7
Cheviots Hatfield AL10 .130 A3
　Hemel Hempstead HP2 .124 F6

Cheyne Cl Pitstone LU7 .80 D4
　Ware SG12 .............93 D3
Cheynes Inf Sch LU3 ..44 D8
Chicheley Gdns HA3 ..176 C3
Chicheley Rd HA3 ...176 C3
Chichester Way WD25 .154 E6
Chicken La AL2 ......142 D4
Chidbrook Ho WD18 .166 F1
Chigwell Hurst Ct HA5 .175 D1
Chilcott Rd WD24 ...153 D2
Chilcourt 5 ..............7 C6
Childs Ave UB9 .......173 C1
Childwick Ct HP3 ....139 B8
Childwick Gn AL3 ...107 C2
Chilham Cl HP2 ......124 E2
Chiltern Ave WD23 ..168 C3
Chiltern Cl
　Borehamwood WD6 ..169 F7
　Bushey WD23 ........168 B3
　Goff's Oak EN7 ......147 B4
　Ware SG12 .............93 D3
　Watford WD18 ......166 F5
Chiltern Cnr HP4 ....122 A5
Chiltern Cotts HP23 .120 A2
Chiltern Ct
　19 Harpenden AL5 ....86 B1
　St Albans AL4 .......128 C8
Chiltern Dr WD3 ....165 A2
Chiltern Gdns LU4 ....44 F3
Chiltern Open Air Mus★
　HP8 .................164 A1
Chiltern Park Ave HP4 .122 A6
Chiltern Rd Baldock SG7 .23 F6
　Hitchin SG4 ...........35 A7
　St Albans AL4 .......128 C7
　Wingrave HP22 .......60 A3
Chiltern Rise LU1 .....63 D6
Chiltern View SG6 ....22 D5
Chiltern Villas HP23 ..99 E3
Chiltern Way HP23 ..100 C5
Chilterns
　Berkhamsted HP4 ...121 F6
　Hatfield AL10 .......130 A2
　Hemel Hempstead HP2 .124 E2
Chilterns The Hitchin SG4 .35 A6
　Kensworth Common LU6 .82 C8
　Stevenage SG1 ........37 B3
Chilton Ct SG14 .....112 F8
Chilton Gn AL7 ......111 C6
Chilvers Bank SG7 ....23 F7
Chilwell Gdns WD19 .175 C6
Chilworth Gate EN10 .134 F1
Chime Sq AL3 ........127 C4
Chimneys The WD23 .167 F4
Chindit Cl EN10 .....134 F1
Chinneck Ho 10 HP4 .122 C4
Chinnery Cl EN1 .....161 F1
Chinnery Hill CM23 ..76 F5
Chipperfield Rd
　Bovingdon HP3 ......137 C3
　Hemel Hempstead HP3 .138 C2
　Kings Langley WD4 ..138 D2
Chipping Cl 8 EN5 ...171 E6
Chipping Hall Cotts SG9 .27 C4
Chippingfield CM17 ..118 C3
Chirdland Ho WD18 .166 E3
Chishill Rd Barley SG8 ..9 A2
　Great Chishill SG8 ......9 F3
Chishill Windmill★ SG8 .9 C2
Chiswell Ct WD24 ....154 C1
Chiswell Green La AL2 .140 E6
Chittenden Cl 5 EN9 .115 B1
Chivenor Pl AL4 .....128 C1
Chobham Ct 8 LU1 ..63 E6
Chobham St LU1 ......63 F6
Chobham Wlk 5 LU1 .63 E6
Cholesbury 1 WD19 .175 E8
Cholesbury Ho WD18 .166 E1
Cholesbury La HP23 .120 B2
Cholesbury Rd HP23 .120 D5
Chorleywood Bottom
　WD3 ................164 D4
Chorleywood Cl WD3 .165 D2
Chorleywood House Dr
　WD3 ................164 E6
Chorleywood Prim Sch
　WD3 ................164 F5
Chorleywood Rd WD3 .165 C4
Chorleywood Sta WD3 .164 D5
Chouler Gdns SG1 ....36 C2
Chowns The AL5 ....107 A5
Christ Church CE Prim Sch
　SG12 .................93 E1
Christ Church CE Sch
　WD3 ................164 F5
Christ Church La EN5 .171 E7
Christ Church Prim Sch
　EN5 .................171 D7
Christchurch Cl AL3 ..127 D4
Christchurch Cres WD7 156 A3
Christchurch Ho HP2 .100 A3
Christchurch Pl SG14 .113 C6
Christchurch Rd
　Hemel Hempstead HP2 .124 D4
　Tring HP23 ............99 F4
Christie Cl EN10 .....134 F3
Christie Rd Stevenage SG2 51 D5
　Waltham Abbey EN9 .163 B4
Christina Ct AL3 ......83 E5
Christopher Ct
　Hemel Hempstead HP3 .138 D8
　18 Ware SG12 .........93 D1
Christopher Pl 3 AL3 .127 D3
Christy's Yd SG7 .......3 D6

**Church Cl** Codicote SG4 . .**67** F2
Cuffley EN6 . . . . . . . . .**146** E4
Little Berkhamsted SG13 .**132** C4
Northwood HA6 . . . . . . .**174** F3
Radlett WD7 . . . . . . . . .**156** A4
Reed SG8 . . . . . . . . . . . .**16** E4
Studham LU6 . . . . . . . . .**82** B4
**Church Cotts**
Essendon AL9 . . . . . . . .**131** E6
Gilston CM20 . . . . . . . .**117** C7
Great Gaddesden HP1 . .**103** D3
**Church Cres**
Sawbridgeworth CM21 . . . .**97** F2
St Albans AL3 . . . . . . . .**127** C4
**Church Ct**
Hoddesdon EN10 . . . . . .**135** A3
**10** Ware SG12 . . . . . . . . .**93** D2
**Church End** Arlesey SG15 . .**11** A8
Barley SG8 . . . . . . . . . . . .**9** A1
Braughing SG11 . . . . . . .**55** F7
Markyate AL3 . . . . . . . . .**83** D6
Redbourn AL3 . . . . . . . .**106** A4
Sandridge AL4 . . . . . . . .**108** C2
Walkern SG2 . . . . . . . . . .**38** C2
**Church End Cotts** WD3 .**151** F1
**Church Farm La** HP23 . . .**79** F3
**Church Farm Way**
WD25 . . . . . . . . . . . . . .**155** B1
**Church Field** SG12 . . . . .**93** B3
**Church Field Path** EN8 .**148** C2
**Church Gates 4** HP4 . . .**122** C4
**Church Gn** Benington SG2 .**52** D4
Great Wymondley SG4 . . .**35** E6
Harpenden AL5 . . . . . . . .**86** A1
**Church Green Row** AL5 .**86** A1
**Church Hill**
Bedmond WD5 . . . . . . .**139** F4
Cheddington LU7 . . . . . . .**80** A8
Harefield UB9 . . . . . . . .**173** C1
Hertford Heath SG13 . . .**114** C4
**Church La** Arlesey SG15 . .**11** A7
Ashwell SG7 . . . . . . . . . . .**4** C4
Barkway SG8 . . . . . . . . .**17** C4
Berkhamsted HP4 . . . . . .**122** C4
Bishop's Stortford CM23 . .**76** D3
Bovingdon HP3 . . . . . . .**137** B4
Cheddington LU7 . . . . . . .**80** A8
Cheshunt EN8 . . . . . . . .**148** C2
Colney Heath AL4 . . . . .**143** B8
Dane End SG12 . . . . . . . .**71** F8
Graveley SG4 . . . . . . . . .**36** C4
Guilden Morden SG8 . . . . .**1** F5
Harrow HA2 . . . . . . . . .**176** F2
Hatfield AL9 . . . . . . . . .**130** C5
Hoddesdon EN10 . . . . . .**134** C1
Kimpton SG4 . . . . . . . . .**66** D1
Kings Langley WD4 . . . .**139** A2
Letchworth SG6 . . . . . . .**12** C1
Marsworth HP23 . . . . . . .**79** F1
Much Hadham SG10 . . . . .**74** F3
Northaw EN6 . . . . . . . . .**146** A1
Preston SG4 . . . . . . . . . .**48** D6
Radlett WD25 . . . . . . . .**155** B1
Reed SG8 . . . . . . . . . . . .**16** E5
Rickmansworth WD3 . . . .**165** B1
**4** Royston SG8 . . . . . . . . .**7** D6
Sarratt WD3 . . . . . . . . .**152** A2
Stapleford SG14 . . . . . . .**92** A6
Stevenage SG1 . . . . . . . .**50** C7
Therfield SG8 . . . . . . . . .**15** F7
Tring HP23 . . . . . . . . . .**120** A7
Weston SG4 . . . . . . . . . .**24** D1
**Church Manor** CM23 . . . .**77** B8
**Church Mead**
Roydon CM19 . . . . . . . .**116** B1
Studham LU6 . . . . . . . . .**82** B4
**Church Meadow Cotts**
HP1 . . . . . . . . . . . . . . .**103** D3
**Church Mill Grange**
CM17 . . . . . . . . . . . . . .**118** E4
**Church Path**
Great Amwell SG12 . . . . .**114** F6
Little Wymondley SG4 . . . .**35** F3
**Church Pl** AL6 . . . . . . . . .**89** C5
**Church Rd** Flamstead AL3 . .**84** B2
Great Hallingbury CM22 . . .**77** D3
Hemel Hempstead HP3 . . .**125** C2
Hertford SG14 . . . . . . . .**113** C7
King's Walden SG4 . . . . .**47** F3
Little Berkhamsted SG13 .**132** C4
Little Gaddesden HP4 . . .**102** D8
Northwood HA6 . . . . . . .**174** F3
Pitstone, Church End LU7 . .**80** F5
Pitstone, Ivinghoe LU7 . . . .**80** F5
Potten End HP4 . . . . . . .**123** B6
Potters Bar EN6 . . . . . . .**145** B1
Slip End LU1 . . . . . . . . . .**63** C2
Stansted Mountfitchet CM24 **59** F5
Stotfold SG5 . . . . . . . . . .**11** F6
Streatley LU3 . . . . . . . . .**31** A6
Studham LU6 . . . . . . . . .**82** B4
Watford WD17 . . . . . . . .**167** B8
Welwyn Garden City AL8 .**110** D6
**Church Row Mews 2**
SG12 . . . . . . . . . . . . . . .**93** D1
**Church St** Baldock SG7 . .**12** E1
Bishop's Stortford CM23 . .**76** F7
Bovingdon HP3 . . . . . . .**137** B4
Buntingford SG9 . . . . . . .**40** E8
Essendon AL9 . . . . . . . .**131** E6
Guilden Morden SG8 . . . . .**1** F5
Hatfield AL9 . . . . . . . . .**130** C5
Hemel Hempstead HP2 . .**124** D5
Hertford SG14 . . . . . . . .**113** D6
Luton LU2 . . . . . . . . . . .**63** E7

**Church St** continued
Luton,High Town LU2 . . . . . .**63** F8
Rickmansworth WD3 . . . .**165** E1
Sawbridgeworth CM21 . . . .**97** E2
Shillington SG5 . . . . . . . . .**19** E8
St Albans AL3 . . . . . . . . .**127** D4
Waltham Abbey EN9 . . . .**163** C6
Ware SG12 . . . . . . . . . . .**93** D1
Watford WD18 . . . . . . . .**167** C5
Welwyn AL6 . . . . . . . . . .**89** C5
Wheathampstead AL4 . . .**108** D8
Wingrave HP22 . . . . . . . .**60** B2
**Church Street Ind Est**
SG12 . . . . . . . . . . . . . . .**93** D1
**Church View**
Hoddesdon EN10 . . . . . .**134** F3
Long Marston HP23 . . . . .**79** A4
**Church Wlk**
Bushey WD23 . . . . . . . .**168** A3
Sawbridgeworth CM21 . . . .**97** F2
**Church Yd** Hitchin SG5 . .**34** E7
Tring HP23 . . . . . . . . . .**100** A3
**Churchfield** Barley SG8 . . .**9** A1
Harlow CM20 . . . . . . . .**118** B2
Harpenden AL5 . . . . . . . .**107** C8
**Churchfield Ho** AL8 . . . .**110** C6
**Churchfield Rd** AL6 . . . . .**90** C1
**Churchfields**
Hertford SG13 . . . . . . . .**113** D5
Hoddesdon EN10 . . . . . .**135** A3
Standon SG11 . . . . . . . . .**55** E2
Stansted Mountfitchet CM24 **59** F6
**Churchfields La** EN10 . . .**135** A4
**Churchfields Rd** WD24 . .**153** F3
**Churchgate**
Cheshunt EN8 . . . . . . . .**148** B1
**7** Hitchin SG5 . . . . . . . .**34** E7
**Churchgate CE Prim Sch**
CM17 . . . . . . . . . . . . . .**118** F3
**Churchgate Rd** EN8 . . . .**148** B2
**Churchgate St** CM17 . . .**118** E4
**Churchill Cres** SG4 . . . .**144** C8
**Churchill Rd** Luton LU4 . . .**45** A1
St Albans AL1 . . . . . . . .**128** A4
**Churchyard Wlk 6** SG5 . .**34** E7
**Cicero Dr** LU3 . . . . . . . .**45** A8
**Cillocks Cl** EN11 . . . . . .**135** A7
**Claggy Rd** SG4 . . . . . . . .**66** B2
**Claire Ct** Bushey WD23 . .**168** D1
Cheshunt EN8 . . . . . . . .**162** D7
**5** Pinner HA5 . . . . . . . . .**175** F3
**Clamp Hill** HA7 . . . . . . .**176** E5
**Clapgate Rd** WD23 . . . .**168** B3
**Clare Cl** WD6 . . . . . . . . .**169** F3
**Clare Cres** SG7 . . . . . . . .**23** E6
**Clare Ct** Enfield EN3 . . . .**162** E4
Northwood HA6 . . . . . . .**174** E5
St Albans AL1 . . . . . . . .**127** F2
**Claremont**
Bricket Wood AL2 . . . . . .**155** A8
Goff's Oak EN7 . . . . . . .**147** D2
**Claremont Cres** WD3 . .**166** C4
**Claremont Rd**
Hadley Wood EN4 . . . . . .**159** D2
Harrow HA3 . . . . . . . . .**176** E1
Luton LU4 . . . . . . . . . . .**45** B1
**Clarence Cl** WD23 . . . . .**168** F2
**Clarence Rd**
Berkhamsted HP4 . . . . . .**122** C4
Harpenden AL5 . . . . . . . .**86** A3
St Albans AL1 . . . . . . . .**128** A4
Stansted Mountfitchet
CM24 . . . . . . . . . . . . . .**59** E7
**Clarendon Cl 1** HP2 . . .**124** E4
**Clarendon Ct**
Harpenden AL5 . . . . . . . .**86** B3
**7** Northwood HA6 . . . . .**174** F5
**Clarendon Mews** WD6 . .**170** A6
**Clarendon Par** EN8 . . . .**148** D2
**Clarendon Rd**
Borehamwood WD6 . . . .**170** A6
Cheshunt EN8 . . . . . . . .**148** C2
Harpenden AL5 . . . . . . . .**86** B3
Luton LU2 . . . . . . . . . . .**45** E1
Watford WD17 . . . . . . . .**167** B6
**Clarion Cl** SG5 . . . . . . . .**33** C2
**Clarion Ho** SG5 . . . . . . . .**33** C2
**Clark Rd** SG4 . . . . . . . . . .**7** D7
**Clarke Way** WD25 . . . . .**154** A4
**Clarke's Rd** AL10 . . . . . .**130** B7
**Clarke's Spring** HP23 . .**100** F5
**Clarkfield** WD3 . . . . . . .**165** B1
**Clarklands Ind Est** ★
CM21 . . . . . . . . . . . . . . .**97** E5
**Clarks Cl** SG12 . . . . . . . .**93** D3
**Clarks Mead** WD23 . . . .**168** D2
**Claudian Pl** AL3 . . . . . . .**127** A1
**Claverhambury Rd** EN9 .**149** F2
**Claverley Gn** LU2 . . . . . . .**46** E2
**Claverton Cl** HP3 . . . . . .**137** A3
**Clay End** SG2 . . . . . . . . .**52** F7
**Clay Hill** EN2 . . . . . . . .**161** D2
**Clay La** WD23 . . . . . . . .**168** B2
**Claybury** WD23 . . . . . . .**168** B2
**Claybush Rd** SG7 . . . . . . . .**4** D3
**Claycroft** AL7 . . . . . . . .**111** B7
**Claydon Cl** LU3 . . . . . . . .**45** C7
**Claydown Way** LU1 . . . . .**63** B1
**Claygate Ave** AL5 . . . . . .**85** E2
**Clayhall Rd** LU6 . . . . . . . .**82** F7
**Clayhill** HP23 . . . . . . . .**120** E7
**Claymore** HP2 . . . . . . . .**124** E7
**Claymore Dr** SG5 . . . . . .**21** F5
**Claymores** SG1 . . . . . . . .**50** E6
**Clayponds** CM23 . . . . . . .**77** B7
**Clayton Hill Cntry Pk** ★
EN9 . . . . . . . . . . . . . . .**149** D8
**Clayton Par 7** EN8 . . . .**148** D1

**Cleall Ave** EN9 . . . . . . .**163** C5
**Cleave The** AL5 . . . . . . . .**86** D1
**Clement Pl** HP23 . . . . . .**100** A3
**Clement Rd** EN8 . . . . . .**148** E4
**Clements End Rd** LU6,
HP2 . . . . . . . . . . . . . . . .**82** E2
**Clements Rd** WD3 . . . . .**164** D4
**Clements St** SG12 . . . . . .**93** E1
**Clementsbury** SG13 . . . .**133** C8
**Clevedon Rd** LU2 . . . . . . .**46** B2
**Cleveland Cres** WD6 . . .**170** A4
**Cleveland Rd**
Hemel Hempstead HP2 . .**125** B5
Markyate AL3 . . . . . . . . .**83** E5
**Cleveland Way**
Hemel Hempstead HP2 . .**125** B5
Stevenage SG1 . . . . . . . .**37** C3
**Cleves Rd** HP2 . . . . . . . .**125** B8
**Cleviscroft** SG1 . . . . . . . .**50** E4
**Clewer Cres** HA3 . . . . . .**176** C1
**Clifford Cres** SG4 . . . . . .**44** D5
**Clifford Ct 10** CM23 . . . .**77** A7
**Clifton Cl** EN8 . . . . . . . .**148** E2
**Clifton Rd** Luton LU1 . . . .**63** B8
Watford WD17 . . . . . . . .**167** B4
**Clifton St** AL1 . . . . . . . .**127** E4
**Clifton Way**
Borehamwood WD6 . . . .**170** A8
Ware SG12 . . . . . . . . . . .**93** D3
**Climb The** WD3 . . . . . . .**165** B3
**Clinton Ave** LU2 . . . . . . .**45** F3
**Clinton End** HP2 . . . . . .**125** C3
**Clitheroe Gdns** WD19 . .**175** D7
**Clive Cl** EN6 . . . . . . . . . .**158** F8
**Clive Ct** LU2 . . . . . . . . . .**45** E1
**Clive Par** HA6 . . . . . . . .**174** E3
**Clive Way** WD24 . . . . . .**167** C8
**Clock Ho The** EN2 . . . . .**161** F2
**Clockhouse Mews** WD3 .**164** E6
**Cloister Garth**
Berkhamsted HP4 . . . . . .**122** C4
St Albans AL1 . . . . . . . .**141** E7
**Cloister Lawns** SG6 . . . . .**22** F4
**Cloister Wlk** HP2 . . . . . .**124** D5
**Cloisters Rd**
Letchworth SG6 . . . . . . . .**23** A4
Luton LU4 . . . . . . . . . . .**44** B3
**Cloisters The**
Bushey WD23 . . . . . . . .**168** B3
Kings Langley WD4 . . . .**139** A2
Rickmansworth WD3 . . . .**165** E2
**3** Watford WD18 . . . . . .**167** C5
Welwyn Garden City AL8 .**110** D6
**Clonard Way** HA5 . . . . .**176** A4
**Clore Shalom Sch**
London Colney WD7 . . . .**142** E1
Shenleybury WD7 . . . . . .**156** E8
**Close The** Baldock SG7 . . .**23** E7
Brookmans Park AL9 . . . .**144** E5
Bushey WD23 . . . . . . . .**168** A4
Codicote SG4 . . . . . . . . .**67** F1
Harpenden AL5 . . . . . . . .**85** D4
Harrow HA2 . . . . . . . . .**176** C1
Hinxworth SG7 . . . . . . . . .**3** D6
Luton LU3 . . . . . . . . . . .**45** A5
Markyate AL3 . . . . . . . . .**83** E5
Potters Bar EN6 . . . . . . .**159** A7
Radlett WD7 . . . . . . . . .**155** F6
Rickmansworth WD3 . . . .**165** B1
Royston SG8 . . . . . . . . . . .**7** F7
St Albans AL1 . . . . . . . .**141** C8
Wallington SG9 . . . . . . . .**25** E6
Ware SG12 . . . . . . . . . . .**93** E1
**Closemead Cl** HA6 . . . . .**174** C4
**Clothall Rd** Baldock SG7 . .**23** F8
**Clothall The** SG7 . . . . . . .**24** C6
**Clovelly Way** SG1 . . . . . .**50** A7
**Clover Ave** CM23 . . . . . .**76** B6
**Clover Cl** LU4 . . . . . . . . .**44** A3
**Clover Field The** WD23 . .**167** F3
**Clover Way** Hatfield AL10 .**129** E8
Hemel Hempstead HP1 . . .**124** B4
**Cloverfield** AL7 . . . . . . . .**89** F1
**Cloverland** AL10 . . . . . . .**129** F2
**Clump The** WD3 . . . . . . .**165** B4
**Cluny Way** SG15 . . . . . . .**11** A5
**Clusterbolts** SG14 . . . . . .**92** A7
**Clutterbucks** WD3 . . . . .**152** A3
**Clyde Rd** EN11 . . . . . . . .**135** D5
**Clyde Sq** HP2 . . . . . . . .**124** F8
**Clyde Terr** SG12 . . . . . .**114** A6
**Clydesdale Cl** WD6 . . . .**170** A4
**Clydesdale Ct** LU4 . . . . . .**44** A3
**Clydesdale Path** WD6 . . .**170** A4
**Clydesdale Rd** Luton LU4 . .**44** A3
Royston SG8 . . . . . . . . . . .**7** E6
**Clydesdale Wlk** EN10 . . .**148** F6
**Clyfton Cl** EN10 . . . . . . .**148** F6
**Clyston Rd** WD18 . . . . . .**166** F3
**Coach Dr** SG4 . . . . . . . . .**34** F5
**Coach House Cloisters**
SG7 . . . . . . . . . . . . . . . .**23** E7
**Coach Mews** AL1 . . . . . .**128** B3
**Coachman's La** SG7 . . . . .**23** D8
**Coanwood Cotts** SG12 . . .**94** E4
**Coates Dell** WD25 . . . . .**154** E6
**Coates Rd** WD6 . . . . . . .**169** D2
**Coates Way** WD25 . . . . .**154** E6
**Coates Way Jun Mix Inf Sch**
WD25 . . . . . . . . . . . . . .**154** E6
**Cob Lane Cl** AL6 . . . . . . .**89** C4
**Cobb Cl** WD6 . . . . . . . . .**170** C4
**Cobb Gn** WD25 . . . . . . .**154** B7
**Cobb Rd** HP4 . . . . . . . . .**121** F4
**Cobbett Cl** EN3 . . . . . . .**162** C3
**Cobbetts Ride** HP23 . . . . .**99** F3
**Cobbins The** EN9 . . . . . .**163** E6
**Cobbins Way** CM17 . . . .**118** E4

**Cobbinsbank** EN9 . . . . .**163** D6
**Cobblers Wick** HP22 . . . .**60** B3
**Cobden Hill** WD7 . . . . . .**156** A2
**Cobden St** LU2 . . . . . . . .**45** F1
**Cobham Rd** SG12 . . . . . .**93** F2
**Cobmead** AL10 . . . . . . . .**130** B7
**Cock Gr** HP23 . . . . . . . .**121** C4
**Cock La** Brent Pelham CB11 **30** F3
Hoddesdon EN11 . . . . . .**134** D4
**Cockbush Ave** SG13 . . . .**114** B3
**Cockernhoe Endowed Prim
Sch** LU2 . . . . . . . . . . . .**46** E3
**Cockfosters Rd** EN4 . . . .**159** E1
**Cockle Way** WD7 . . . . . .**156** E6
**Cockrobin La** CM20 . . . .**117** A7
**Codicote CE Prim Sch**
SG4 . . . . . . . . . . . . . . . .**67** C1
**Codicote Dr** WD25 . . . . .**154** D5
**Codicote Ho** SG1 . . . . . . .**36** C1
**Codicote Hts** SG4 . . . . . .**68** B1
**Codicote Innovation Ctr**
SG4 . . . . . . . . . . . . . . . .**88** E8
**Codicote Rd**
Ayot St Lawrence AL4,AL6,
SG4 . . . . . . . . . . . . . . . .**88** C3
Welwyn AL6 . . . . . . . . . .**89** B7
Wheathampstead AL4 . . . .**87** D1
Whitwell SG4 . . . . . . . . .**66** F6
**Codicote Row** HP2 . . . . .**105** B1
**Codmore Wood Rd** HP5 .**150** D6
**Cohen Cl** EN8 . . . . . . . .**162** E8
**Colborne Ho** WD18 . . . .**166** E3
**Colburn Ave** HA5 . . . . . .**175** E4
**Colchester Rd** HA6 . . . .**175** A1
**Cold Christmas La** SG12 . .**93** E6
**Coldham Gr** EN3 . . . . . .**162** E2
**Coldharbour La**
Bushey WD23 . . . . . . . .**168** C4
Harpenden AL5 . . . . . . . .**86** C4
**Cole Green La** AL7 . . . . .**111** B4
**Cole Green Way** SG14 . .**113** A4
**Cole Rd** WD17 . . . . . . . .**167** B8
**Colebrook Ave** LU3 . . . . .**44** C7
**Coleman Green La**
Sandridge AL4 . . . . . . . .**108** A4
Wheathampstead AL4 . . .**109** A7
**Coleman's La** EN9 . . . . .**149** E5
**Colemans Cl** SG5 . . . . . . .**20** C3
**Colemans Rd** SG4 . . . . . .**47** D1
**Coleridge Cl**
Hammond Street EN7 . . .**147** F4
Hitchin SG4 . . . . . . . . . .**35** B8
**Coleridge Cres** HP2 . . . .**105** B1
**Coleridge Ct 9** AL5 . . . . .**86** B1
**Coleridge Way** WD6 . . . .**170** A5
**Coles Gn** WD23 . . . . . . .**168** C1
**Coles Hill** HP1 . . . . . . . .**124** A5
**Colesdale** EN6 . . . . . . . .**146** E1
**Colestrete** SG1 . . . . . . . .**50** E6
**Colestrete Cl** SG1 . . . . . .**51** A5
**Coleswood Rd** AL5 . . . . .**107** C7
**Colgate Ct** EN5 . . . . . . .**171** E4
**Colgate Pl** EN3 . . . . . . .**163** A2
**Colgrove** AL8 . . . . . . . . .**110** C5
**Colin Rd** LU2 . . . . . . . . .**45** F2
**Colindale Ave** AL1 . . . . .**127** F1
**College Ave** HA3 . . . . . .**176** E2
**College Cl**
Bishop's Stortford CM23 . .**76** D7
Flamstead AL3 . . . . . . . .**84** B1
Harrow HA3 . . . . . . . . .**176** E3
Ware SG12 . . . . . . . . . .**114** D8
**College Ct** Cheshunt EN8 .**148** C1
Hoddesdon EN11 . . . . . .**134** F8
**College Hill Rd** HA3 . . . .**176** E3
**College Ho** LU1 . . . . . . . .**63** F7
**College La** LU2 . . . . . . . .**45** E1
**College Lake Wildlife Ctr** ★
HP23 . . . . . . . . . . . . . .**100** C8
**College Pl** AL3 . . . . . . . .**127** D3
**College Rd**
Abbots Langley WD5 . . . .**154** A8
Aston Clinton HP22 . . . . .**78** C1
Cheshunt EN8 . . . . . . . .**148** D1
Harrow HA3 . . . . . . . . .**176** E1
Hertford Heath SG13 . . .**114** D2
Hitchin SG5 . . . . . . . . . .**34** F8
Hoddesdon EN11 . . . . . .**134** F8
St Albans AL1 . . . . . . . .**128** B2
**College St** AL3 . . . . . . . .**127** D3
**College Way**
Northwood HA6 . . . . . . .**174** D4
Welwyn Garden City AL8 .**110** D7
**College Yd** WD24 . . . . . .**154** B1
**Collens Rd** AL5 . . . . . . .**107** B5
**Collenswood Rd** SG2 . . . .**51** B4
**Collenswood Sch** SG2 . . .**51** C4
**Collet Cl** EN8 . . . . . . . . .**148** D3
**Collet Gdns** EN8 . . . . . .**148** D3
**Collett Rd**
Hemel Hempstead HP1 . . .**124** C3
Ware SG12 . . . . . . . . . . .**93** D2
**Collett Sch The** HP1 . . . .**124** B4
**Colleyland** WD3 . . . . . . .**164** D5
**Collingdon Ct 10** LU1 . . . .**63** D8
**Collingdon St** LU1 . . . . . .**63** D8
**Collings Wells Cl** LU1 . . . .**62** E4
**Collingtree** LU2 . . . . . . . .**46** B4
**Collingwood Cl** LU4 . . . . .**44** D3
**Collingwood Ct** SG8 . . . . . .**7** D7
**Collingwood Dr** AL2 . . . .**142** D6
**Collins Cross** CM23 . . . . .**59** B1
**Collison Cl** SG4 . . . . . . . .**22** C4
**Collyer Rd** AL2 . . . . . . . .**142** D4
**Colmer Pl** HA3 . . . . . . . .**176** C1
**Colnbrook Cl** AL2 . . . . . .**142** E4

**Colnbrook Sch** WD19 . .**175** C7
**Colne Ave**
Rickmansworth WD3 . . . .**173** A8
Watford WD19 . . . . . . . .**167** C3
**Colne Gdns** AL2 . . . . . . .**142** E4
**Colne Lo** WD3 . . . . . . . .**165** A1
**Colne Lodge** WD3 . . . . .**167** C5
**Colne Mead** WD3 . . . . . .**173** A8
**Colne Valley Ret Pk**
WD17 . . . . . . . . . . . . . .**167** D4
**Colne Way**
Hemel Hempstead HP2 . .**124** F8
Watford WD24,WD25 . . .**154** E2
**Colne Way Ct** WD24 . . . .**154** D3
**Colney Heath Jun & Inf Sch**
AL4 . . . . . . . . . . . . . . .**129** C1
**Colney Heath La** AL4 . . .**128** C3
**Colonial Bsns Pk** WD24 .**167** C8
**Colonial Way** WD24 . . . .**167** C8
**Colonnade The 7** EN8 . .**148** D3
**Colonsay** HP3 . . . . . . . .**125** C1
**Colston Cres** EN7 . . . . . .**147** B4
**Colt Hatch** CM20 . . . . . .**117** B1
**Colt Mews** EN3 . . . . . . .**163** A2
**Colthurst Gdns** EN11 . . .**135** D8
**Colts Cnr** SG2 . . . . . . . . .**51** B4
**Colts Croft** SG8 . . . . . . . . .**9** E2
**Colts The** CM23 . . . . . . .**76** E4
**Coltsfield** CM24 . . . . . . . .**59** E8
**Coltsfoot** AL7 . . . . . . . .**111** B4
**Coltsfoot Dr** SG8 . . . . . . . .**7** E6
**Coltsfoot Gn** LU4 . . . . . .**44** A5
**Coltsfoot La** SG3 . . . . . . .**90** D7
**Coltsfoot Rd** SG12 . . . . . .**93** E3
**Coltsfoot The** HP1 . . . . .**123** E2
**Columbus Cl** SG2 . . . . . .**51** A7
**Columbus Gdns** HA6 . . .**175** A2
**Colvin Gdns** EN8 . . . . . .**162** D4
**Colwell Rd** SG2 . . . . . . . .**51** C3
**Colwell Rise** LU2 . . . . . . .**46** E2
**Colwyn Cl** SG1 . . . . . . . .**50** B7
**Colyer Cl** AL6 . . . . . . . . .**89** F3
**Combe Ho** WD18 . . . . . .**166** E3
**Combe Rd** WD18 . . . . . .**166** F3
**Combe St** HP1 . . . . . . . .**124** C3
**Combewood** WD25 . . . . .**154** C7
**Comet Cl** WD25 . . . . . . .**153** F5
**Comet Rd** AL10 . . . . . . .**129** F6
**Comet Way** AL10 . . . . . .**129** E5
**Commerce Way** SG6 . . . . .**22** F4
**Common Field** HP23 . . . .**100** D1
**Common Gate Rd** WD3 . .**164** E4
**Common Gdns** HP4 . . . . .**123** B6
**Common La** Ashwell SG7 . . .**4** B6
Harpenden AL5 . . . . . . . .**86** C3
Kimpton SG4 . . . . . . . . .**66** B1
Kings Langley WD4 . . . .**138** F3
Radlett WD7,WD25 . . . . .**155** E1
**Common Rd**
Chorleywood WD3 . . . . .**164** D5
Kensworth Common LU6 . .**82** F8
Stanmore HA7 . . . . . . . .**176** D7
Stotfold SG5 . . . . . . . . . .**11** F7
Studham LU6 . . . . . . . . .**82** B3
**Common Rise** SG4 . . . . . .**22** A1
**Common The**
Chipperfield WD4 . . . . . .**152** B8
Harpenden AL5 . . . . . . . .**85** C4
Hatfield AL10 . . . . . . . .**130** A6
London Colney WD7 . . . .**156** B8
Potten End HP4 . . . . . . .**123** A6
Stanmore HA7 . . . . . . . .**176** F8
**Common View** SG6 . . . . . .**23** B8
**Common View Sq** SG6 . . . .**23** A8
**Common Wharf** SG12 . . . .**93** E1
**Commonfields** CM20 . . . .**117** E1
**Commons La** HP2 . . . . . .**124** E4
**Commons The** AL7 . . . . .**111** B3
**Commonswood Sch**
AL7 . . . . . . . . . . . . . . .**111** B3
**Community Way** WD3 . . .**166** B4
**Compass Point** HP4 . . . .**121** E6
**Compton Ave** LU4 . . . . . .**44** D4
**Compton Gdns** AL2 . . . .**141** B5
**Compton Pl** WD19 . . . . .**175** E6
**Comroston** EN11 . . . . . .**135** A6
**Comyne Rd** WD24 . . . . .**153** F2
**Comyns The** WD23 . . . . .**168** C1
**Concorde Dr** HP2 . . . . . .**124** D3
**Concorde St** LU2 . . . . . . .**63** F8
**Conduit La**
Great Hormead SG9 . . . . .**29** B1
Hoddesdon EN11 . . . . . .**135** A6
**Conduit La E** EN11 . . . . .**135** B6
**Conemara Ct** EN10 . . . . .**148** F5
**Coney Cl** AL10 . . . . . . . .**130** B3
**Coneydale** AL8 . . . . . . . .**110** D8
**Congreve Rd** EN9 . . . . . .**163** E6
**Conifer Cl**
Goff's Oak EN7 . . . . . . .**147** F2
Stevenage SG2 . . . . . . . .**51** D7
**Conifer Ct 7** CM23 . . . . .**76** F8
**Conifer Wlk** SG2 . . . . . . .**51** C7
**Conifers The** WD25 . . . .**154** C4
**Coningesby Dr** WD17 . . .**166** E7
**Coningsby Bank** AL1 . . . .**141** D7
**Coningsby Cl** AL9 . . . . . .**144** D7
**Coningsby Ct** WD7 . . . . .**156** A3
**Coniston Cl** HP3 . . . . . . .**125** C2
**Coniston Lodge 3**
WD17 . . . . . . . . . . . . . .**167** A7
**Coniston Rd**
Kings Langley WD4 . . . .**138** F3
Luton LU3 . . . . . . . . . . .**44** F5

Connaught Cl HP2 .....125 A5
Connaught Gdns HP4 ..121 F7
Connaught Rd
Barnet EN5 .........171 D3
Harpenden AL5 .........86 B2
Harrow HA3 .........176 F2
Luton LU4 .........44 F1
St Albans AL3 .........127 C6
Connemara Cl WD6 ....170 D3
Connop Rd EN3 .......162 D1
Connor's Cl SG8 ........1 F4
Conquerors Hill AL4 ...108 E8
Conquest Cl SG4 .......34 F5
Constable Ct LU4 ......45 A1
Constantine Cl SG1 .....36 F1
Constantine Pl SG7 .....13 B1
Convent Cl SG5 .........34 F8
Convent Ct HP23 .......99 F3
Conway Gdns EN2 .....161 E1
Conway Ho WD6 .....170 C5
Conway Rd LU4 .........45 B1
Cony Cl 7 EN7 .......147 E5
Conyers CM20 .........117 C2
Cook Rd SG2 ...........51 B7
Cook's Hole Rd EN2 ...161 C1
Cooks Mead WD23 .....168 B3
Cooks Spinney CM20 ...118 A2
Cooks Vennel HP1 ......124 B5
Cooks Way Hatfield AL10 130 B3
Hitchin SG4 .............22 A1
Coombe Gdns HP4 .....121 F5
Coombe Hill Rd WD3 ..165 A2
Coombe Rd
Bushey WD23 .........168 D2
Kelshall SG8 .............6 A1
Coombelands Rd SG8 ....2 E1
Coombes Rd AL2 .......142 C5
Cooper Way 10 HP4 ....122 D4
Cooper's Cl SG4 ........66 B1
Cooper's Ct SG12 ......114 E8
Cooper's Hill SG4 .......87 B8
Coopers Cl Aston SG2 ....51 D4
Bishop's Stortford CM23 ...76 B4
Coopers Cres WD6 .....170 C8
Coopers Ct SG14 .......113 D6
Coopers Field SG6 ......22 D7
Coopers Gate AL4 .....129 B1
Coopers Green La AL4,
AL10 .................109 D1
Coopers La EN6 .......145 E1
Coopers Lane Rd EN6 ..160 B6
Coopers Mdw AL3 .....106 A6
Coopers Mews
Harpenden AL5 .........107 A8
Watford WD25 .........154 C8
Coopers Rd EN6 .......145 C1
Coopers Wlk 10 EN8 ...148 D3
Cooters End La AL5 .....85 F5
Copenhagen Cl LU3 .....44 D8
Copmans Wick WD3 ...164 D4
Coppens The SG5 .......12 A5
Copper Beech Cl HP3 ..137 F8
Copper Beech Ct 4
HA6 .................174 E3
Copper Beeches
11 Harpenden AL5 .......86 B1
Oaklands AL6 ...........89 D7
Copper Ct CM21 .........97 E2
Copperfields Luton LU4 ..44 C3
Royston SG8 .............7 C6
Welwyn Garden City AL7 ..111 C5
Coppermill La WD3,UB9 .172 F3
Copperwood SG13 .....113 F6
Coppice Cl Harrow HA7 .176 F4
Hatfield AL10 .........129 F1
Coppice Farm Pk HP23 .119 D4
Coppice Mead SG5 ......11 E5
Coppice The
Bishop's Stortford CM23 ...76 D5
1 Harpenden AL5 .......85 F2
Hemel Hempstead HP2 ...125 B4
Watford WD19 .........167 C3
Wigginton HP23 .......100 C1
Coppings The EN11 .....115 A1
Coppins Cl HP4 ........121 F4
Coppins The
Harrow HA3 ...........176 E4
Markyate AL3 ...........83 D5
Copse Cl HA6 .........174 C1
Copse Hill AL6 ..........90 A8
Copse The
Bishop's Stortford CM23 ...77 C8
Hemel Hempstead HP1 ...123 E5
Hertford SG13 .........114 A6
Copse Way LU3 .........44 D8
Copse Wood Way HA6 .174 C2
Copsewood Rd WD24 ..167 B8
Copt Hall Cotts LU2 .....64 E4
Copthall Cl CM22 .......77 F4
Copthorne LU2 .........46 D3
Copthorne Ave EN10 ...134 F3
Copthorne Cl WD3 .....165 F4
Copthorne Rd WD3 ....165 F4
Coral Gdns HP2 ........124 F3
Coral Ho CM20 .........117 A1
Corals Mead AL7 ......110 D5
Coram Cl HP4 .........122 C3
Corbridge Dr LU2 .......46 E1
Corby Cl AL2 ..........141 A6
Cordell Cl EN8 .........148 E3
Corder Cl AL3 .........141 A8
Coreys Mill La SG1 .....36 C1
Corfe Cl
Borehamwood WD6 .....170 D6
4 Hemel Hempstead HP2 124 E2
Corinium Gate AL3 .....127 A1
Corinium Gdns LU3 .....45 A8
Corncastle Rd LU1 ......63 D6
Corncrake Cl LU2 .......46 C5
Corncroft AL10 ........130 B7
Cornel Cl LU1 ..........63 A7
Cornel Ct LU1 ..........63 A7
Cornelia Ct 3 AL5 ......86 A2
Cornelious Ho WD18 ...166 F5
Corner Cl SG6 ..........22 E6
Corner Hall HP3 .......124 D1
Corner Hall Ave HP3 ...124 D1
Corner View AL9 ......144 C7
Corner Wood AL3 .......83 D5
Cornerfield AL10 .......130 B8
Corners AL7 ...........111 A7
Cornfield Cres HP4 ....121 D7
Cornfield Rd WD23 .....168 B5
Cornfields
Hemel Hempstead HP1 ...124 B2
Stevenage SG2 ..........51 C7
Cornflower Way AL10 ..129 E8
Cornhill Dr EN3 .......162 E2
Cornmead AL8 ..........89 C1
Cornmill EN9 ..........163 C6
Cornwall Cl EN8 .......162 E6
Cornwall Ct 6 HA6 ....175 F3
Cornwall Ho CM23 ......76 E4
Cornwall Rd
Harpenden AL5 ..........86 B2
Pinner HA5 ...........175 F3
St Albans AL1 .........127 E1
Coronation Ave SG8 ......7 C5
Coronation Rd
Bishop's Stortford CM23 ...76 E5
Ware SG12 .............93 D2
Coronet Ho 2 HA7 .....176 F4
Corringham Ct AL1 ....127 F4
Corton Cl SG1 ..........50 B8
Corvus Cl SG8 ...........7 E8
Cory-Wright Way AL4 ...87 E1
Cosgrove Way LU1 ......44 D1
Cosne Mews AL5 ......107 C7
Costins Wlk 12 HP4 ...122 D4
Cotefield LU4 ..........44 C3
Cotesmore Rd HP1 .....123 E2
Cotlandswick AL2 ......142 C5
Cotney Croft SG2 .......51 D3
Cotsmoor AL1 .........127 F3
Cotswold HP2 .........124 E6
Cotswold Ave WD23 ....168 C3
Cotswold Bsns Pk LU1 ..62 D2
Cotswold Cl AL4 .......128 C8
Cotswold Gdns LU3 .....44 C7
Cotswolds AL10 .......130 A3
Cottage Cl
Croxley Green WD3 .....165 F3
Watford WD17 .........166 F7
Cottage Gdns EN8 .....148 D2
Cotter Ho SG1 ..........37 A3
Cottered Rd SG9 ........26 F1
Cotterells HP1 .........124 C2
Cotterells Hill HP1 .....124 C3
Cotton Dr SG13 ........114 B7
Cotton Field AL10 .....130 B7
Cotton Rd EN6 ........159 C8
Cottonmill Cres AL1 ...127 D2
Cottonmill La AL1 .....127 D1
Coulser Cl HP1 ........124 A6
Coulson Ct
London Colney AL2 .....142 D4
Luton LU1 ..............62 F8
Coulter Cl EN6 ........146 D4
Council Cotts
Great Wymondley SG4 .....35 F6
Letchworth SG6 ..........23 B2
Radwell SG7 ...........12 C4
Counters Cl HP1 .......124 A3
Countess Anne CE Prim Sch
AL9 ..................130 C6
Countess Cl UB9 .......173 C1
Countess Ct 4 LU2 .....45 D1
Couper Ho WD18 .....166 E3
Coursers Farm Cotts
AL4 ..................143 C6
Coursers Rd AL2,AL4 ...143 C6
Court Cl CM23 ..........76 E5
Court Needham EN3 ...163 A2
Courtaulds WD4 .......138 B1
Courtenay Ave HA3 ...176 C2
Courtenay Gdns HA3 ...176 C1
Courtfield Cl EN10 .....135 A3
Courtfields AL5 .........86 D1
Courtlands Cl WD24 ...153 E4
Courtlands Dr WD17 ...153 E3
Courtleigh Ave EN4 ....159 D1
Courtway The WD19 ....175 E8
Courtyard Mews SG12 ...92 E4
Courtyard The
Hemel Hempstead HP3 ...138 D5
Hertingfordbury SG14 .....112 F5
St Albans AL4 .........128 F3
Courtyards The WD18 ..166 D2
Covent Garden Cl LU4 ...44 F3
Coventry Cl SG1 ........37 B1
Coverdale
Hemel Hempstead HP2 ...124 E6
Luton LU4 ..............44 B6
Coverdale Ct EN3 ......162 E2
Covert Cl HP4 .........121 D6
Covert Rd HP4 ........121 D6
Covert The HA6 .......174 C2
Cow La Bushey WD23 ...168 A3
Tring HP23 ...........100 D4
Watford WD25 .........154 C3
Cowards La SG4 .........88 F8
Cowbridge SG14 ......113 C6
Cowdray Cl LU2 ........46 C3
Cowles EN7 ...........147 F4
Cowley Hill WD6 ......157 B1
Cowley Hill Sch WD6 ...170 A8
Cowlins CM17 .........118 D4
Cowper Cres SG14 ......92 B1
Cowper Ct Markyate AL3 ..83 D5
Watford WD24 .........154 A2
Cowper Rd
Berkhamsted HP4 .......122 B4
Harpenden AL5 ..........86 C1
Hemel Hempstead HP1 ...124 B2
Markyate AL3 ...........83 D5
Welwyn Garden City AL7 ..110 F4
Cowper Rise AL3 ........83 D5
Cowper St LU1 ..........63 E5
Cowpers Way AL6 .......90 D5
Cowridge Cres LU2 .....64 A8
Cowslip Cl SG8 ..........7 F5
Cowslip Hill SG6 ........22 E7
Cowslips AL7 ..........111 C5
Cox Cl WD7 ...........156 F7
Cox's Way SG15 .........11 A6
Coxfield Cl HP2 ........124 E2
Coyney Gn LU3 .........45 C1
Cozens La E EN10 .....134 F1
Cozens La W EN10 .....134 F1
Cozens Rd SG12 ........94 A2
Crab La WD25 .........155 B4
Crab Tree La SG5 .......20 D4
Crab Tree Rd SG3 .......68 F4
Crabb's La SG9 .........43 F6
Crabbes Cl SG5 .........34 E7
Crabtree Cl
Bushey WD23 .........168 B4
Hemel Hempstead HP3 ...124 D1
Crabtree Ct 3 HP3 ....124 E1
Crabtree Dell SG6 .......23 B3
Crabtree Inf Sch AL5 ....86 C1
Crabtree La
Harpenden AL5 ..........86 C1
Hemel Hempstead HP3 ...124 D1
Crabtree Wlk EN10 ....134 E4
Crackley Mdw HP2 .....125 B8
Cradock Rd LU4 .........44 B1
Crafton Gn CM24 .......59 E7
Cragg Ave WD7 ........155 F3
Cragside SG2 ...........69 C7
Craig Mount WD7 ......156 B4
Craigavon Rd HP2 .....124 F7
Craiglands AL4 ........128 D7
Craigmore Ct 5 HA6 ...174 E3
Craigs Wlk 4 EN8 .....148 D3
Craigweil Ave WD7 ....156 B4
Crakers Mead 4 WD18 .167 B6
Cranborne Ave
Hitchin SG5 .............34 D6
Potters Bar EN6 ........144 E1
Cranborne Cl
Brickendon SG13 .......113 C3
Potters Bar EN6 ........158 E8
Cranborne Cres EN6 ...158 E8
Cranborne Ct EN3 .....162 D3
Cranborne Gdns AL7 ...110 F5
Cranborne Ind Est EN6 .144 E1
Cranborne Par EN6 ....158 D8
Cranborne Prim Sch
EN6 ..................158 F8
Cranborne Rd
Cheshunt EN8 ..........162 D7
Hatfield AL10 ..........130 B6
Hoddesdon EN11 .......135 C7
Potters Bar EN6 ........144 E1
Cranbourne SG1 ........36 B1
Cranbourne Dr
Harpenden AL5 .........107 D6
Hoddesdon EN11 .......115 C2
Cranbourne Ho EN11 ...115 C2
Cranbourne Prim Sch The
EN11 .................115 B2
Cranbourne Rd HA6 ....174 F1
Cranbrook Cl SG12 .....93 D3
Cranbrook Dr Luton LU3 ..44 D8
St Albans AL4 .........128 E3
Crane Mead SG12 ......114 E8
Crane Mead Bsns Pk
SG12 .................114 E8
Cranefield Dr WD25 ...154 E6
Cranes Way WD6 ......170 C4
Cranfield Cres EN6 .....146 E2
Cranford Ct
Harpenden AL5 ..........86 C1
Hertford SG14 .........112 F7
Cranleigh Cl EN7 .......148 A3
Cranleigh Gdns LU3 .....45 D3
Cranmer Cl EN6 .......145 C1
Cranmore Ct AL1 .......127 F4
Cranwell Cl AL4 .......128 C1
Cranwell Gdns CM23 ....59 C1
Cravells Ct AL5 ........107 C7
Cravells Rd AL5 ........107 C7
Crawford Rd AL10 .....130 A7
Crawley Cl LU1 .........63 C1
Crawley Dr HP2 .......124 F7
Crawley Green Inf Sch
LU2 ...................64 B8
Crawley Green Rd
Luton, Hart Hill LU2 ......64 A8
Luton, Wigmore LU2 ......46 D1
Crawley Rd LU1 .........63 D8
Crawley's La HP23 .....120 F7
Creamery Ct SG6 .......23 C3
Creasy Cl WD5 .........153 F8
Crecy Gdns AL3 .......106 A6
Creighton Ave AL1 .....141 D8
Crescent E EN4 ........159 C1
Crescent Rd
Bishop's Stortford CM23 ...77 A6
Hemel Hempstead HP2 ...124 D3
Luton LU2 ..............63 F8
Crescent Rise LU2 ......63 F8
Crescent The
Abbots Langley WD5 .....139 F1
Ardeley SG2 ............38 F2
Bricket Wood AL2 .......141 A1
Caddington LU1 .........62 E3
Cottered SG9 ...........39 D7
Croxley Green WD3 .....166 B3
Harlow CM17 ..........118 C6
Hitchin SG5 .............21 D1
Letchworth SG6 .........23 A5
Lower Stondon SG16 .....10 C4
Marsworth HP23 .........80 A1
Pitstone LU7 ............80 C4
Radlett WD25 ..........155 B1
St Ippolyts SG4 ..........35 A3
Watford WD18 .........167 C5
Welwyn AL6 .............89 C4
Crescent W EN4 .......159 C1
Cress End WD3 .......165 A1
Cresset Cl SG12 ........115 C3
Cresswick SG4 ..........66 E7
Crest Dr EN3 ..........162 C1
Crest Pk HP2 ..........125 C4
Crest The
Goff's Oak EN7 .........147 B4
Luton LU3 ..............45 B7
Oaklands AL6 ...........89 D8
Sawbridgeworth CM21 ....97 D2
Ware SG12 .............93 D3
Cresta Cl LU5 ..........44 A2
Cresta Ho 3 LU1 .......63 D7
Creswick Ct AL7 .......110 D5
Creswick Jun Mix Inf Sch
AL7 ..................110 D3
Crew Curve HP4 .......121 F7
Crews Hill EN2 ........160 F5
Crews Hill Sta EN2 .....160 F5
Crib St SG12 ...........93 D2
Cricketer's Rd SG15 .....11 A4
Cricketers Cl AL3 ......127 E4
Cricketfield La CM23 ....76 E8
Cringle Ct EN6 ........145 C1
Crispin Field LU7 .......80 C4
Croasdaile Rd CM24 .....59 E8
Croasdale Cl CM24 ......59 E8
Crocus Field EN5 ......171 F3
Croft Cl WD4 ..........138 A1
Croft Ct
Borehamwood WD6 .....170 D6
4 Harpenden AL5 .......86 B1
Hitchin SG5 .............34 E7
Croft End Rd WD4 .....138 A1
Croft Field
Chipperfield WD4 .......138 A1
Hatfield AL10 ..........130 A5
Croft La
Chipperfield WD4 .......138 A1
Letchworth SG6 ..........12 B1
Croft Mdw WD4 .......138 A1
Croft Mdws LU7 .........80 A7
Croft Rd Luton LU2 ......46 B3
Ware SG12 .............93 C2
Croft The Barnet EN5 ....171 E5
Chiswell Green AL2 .....141 A6
Hoddesdon EN10 .......148 E8
Luton LU3 ..............44 D8
Wareside SG12 ..........94 E4
Welwyn Garden City AL7 ..110 F3
Croft Wlk EN10 ........148 E8
Crofters CM21 ..........97 E3
Crofters End CM21 ......97 E3
Crofters Rd HA6 .......174 E6
Crofts Path HP3 .......125 B1
Crofts The
Hemel Hempstead HP3 ...125 B2
Stotfold SG5 ............11 F6
Croftwell AL5 ..........107 F8
Cromer Cl HP4 ........102 E5
Cromer Rd WD24 ......154 C1
Cromer Way
Luton, Stopsley Common
LU2 ...................45 E6
Luton, Warden Hill LU2 ....45 D7
Cromer Windmill★ SG2 .38 E6
Crompton Pl EN3 ......163 A1
Crompton Rd SG1 .......50 A6
Cromwell Ave EN7 .....148 B1
Cromwell Cl
Bishop's Stortford CM23 ...76 B7
St Albans AL4 .........128 D8
Cromwell Gn SG6 .......23 B8
Cromwell Hill LU2 ......45 D1
Cromwell Rd
Borehamwood WD6 .....169 E8
Cheshunt EN7 ..........148 B3
Hertford SG13 .........114 A7
Letchworth SG6 .........23 B8
Luton LU3 ..............45 D1
Stevenage SG2 ..........51 C5
Ware SG12 .............93 F2
Cromwell Way SG5 .....20 D4
Crooked Mile
Waltham Abbey EN9 .....163 C6
Waltham Abbey EN9 .....163 C7
Crooked Way EN9 .....135 E1
Crookhams AL7 .........90 A1
Crop Comm AL10 ......130 B7
Crosby Cl Luton LU4 .....45 A2
St Albans AL4 .........142 C8
Crosfield Ct WD17 .....167 D4
Cross Farm Mews HP3 .137 D2
Cross La Harpenden AL5 .107 C5
Hertford SG14 .........113 B6
Cross Oak Rd HP4 .....122 A4
Cross Rd Cheshunt EN8 ..162 E6
Hertford SG14 .........113 C7
Watford WD19 .........167 E3
Cross St Letchworth SG6 ..22 F7
Cross St *continued*
Luton LU2 ..............63 E8
2 St Albans AL3 .......127 D3
Ware SG12 .............93 E1
Watford WD17 .........167 C6
Cross Way AL5 ..........86 C3
Cross Way The
Harrow HA3 ...........176 E1
Luton LU1 ..............63 C5
Crossbrook AL10 ......129 E4
Crossbrook St EN8 ....162 D8
Crossett Gn HP3 .......125 C1
Crossfell Rd HP3 .......125 C2
Crossfield Rd EN11 .....135 B8
Crossfields AL3 ........141 B8
Crossfields Cl HP4 .....121 F4
Crossgates SG1 .........50 E5
Crosslands LU1 .........62 E3
Crossleys SG6 ...........11 F2
Crossmead WD19 ......167 B3
Crossoaks La EN6 ......157 F5
Crosspath The WD7 ....156 A4
Crosspaths AL5 .........85 C4
Crossway Harlow CM17 ..118 D1
Pinner HA5 ...........175 B1
Welwyn Garden City AL8 ..89 C2
Crossways Barley SG8 .....8 F1
Berkhamsted HP4 .......121 F3
Hemel Hempstead HP3 ...125 B3
Crouch Ct CM20 .......117 C3
Crouch Hall Gdns AL3 ..106 A6
Crouch Hall La AL3 ....106 A6
Crouch La EN7 ........147 C4
Crouchfield
Hemel Hempstead HP1 ...124 B2
Hertford SG14 ..........92 C1
Crouchfield La SG12 ....92 E4
Crow Furlong SG5 ......34 D7
Crow La SG8 ............16 F5
Crowborough Path
WD19 .................175 D6
Crowland Rd LU2 .......46 C5
Crown Cl CM22 .........98 C1
Crown Cotts Botley HP5 .150 B8
King's Walden SG4 .......48 A6
Crown Lodge SG15 ......11 A4
Crown Rd WD6 ........170 B8
Crown Rise WD25 .....154 D5
Crown Rose Ct HP23 ...100 A3
Crown St AL3 ..........106 B5
Crown Terr CM23 ........77 A7
Crown Wlk HP3 .......138 E7
Crown Yd AL3 .........106 D2
Crownfield EN10 .......135 A2
Croxdale Rd WD6 .....170 A7
Croxley Ctr WD18 .....166 D4
Croxley Sta WD3 ......166 B3
Croxley View WD18 ....166 E3
Croxton Cl 3 LU3 .......45 A7
Crozier Ave CM23 .......76 C8
Crunnell's Gn SG4 ......48 E5
Crusader Way WD18 ...166 F3
Cubbington Cl LU3 .....45 A7
Cubitt Cl SG4 ...........35 C7
Cubitts Cl AL6 ..........89 F3
Cublands SG13 .........114 B6
Cuckmans Dr AL2 .....141 A6
Cuckoo's Nest LU2 ......64 A7
Cucumber La AL9,SG13 .132 A1
Cuffley Ave WD25 .....154 D5
Cuffley Cl LU3 ..........44 F4
Cuffley Ct HP2 ........125 C8
Cuffley Hill EN7 .......147 B2
Cuffley Sch EN6 .......146 F1
Cuffley Sta EN6 .......146 F2
Cullera Cl HA6 ........174 F4
Cullings Ct EN9 ........163 F6
Culver Ct SG10 ..........74 F1
Culver Lo AL1 .........127 E5
Culver Rd AL1 .........127 E5
Culverden Rd WD19 ...175 B7
Culverhouse Rd LU3 ....45 C3
Culworth Cl LU1 ........62 E3
Cumberland Cl
Hertford SG14 .........113 C8
Pimlico HP3 ...........139 E7
Cumberland Ct
2 Hoddesdon EN11 .....135 A7
St Albans AL3 .........127 E4
Cumberland Dr AL3 ...106 B6
Cumberland St LU1 ....63 E6
Cumberlow Pl HP2 .....125 C2
Cumcum Hill AL9 ......131 E2
Cundalls Rd SG12 .......93 E2
Cunningham Ave
Enfield EN3 ...........162 E3
Hatfield AL10 ..........129 D6
St Albans AL1 .........127 F1
Cunningham Ct 3 EN8 .148 E3
Cunningham Hill Inf Sch
AL1 ..................128 A1
Cunningham Hill Jun Sch
AL1 ..................128 A1
Cunningham Hill Rd
AL1 ..................128 A1
Cunningham Rd EN8 ...148 E4
Cupid Green La
Flamstead HP2 .........104 E3
Hemel Hempstead HP2 ...105 A1
Curlew Cl
Berkhamsted HP4 .......122 C3
Letchworth SG6 ..........11 E1
Curlew Cres SG8 .........7 E8
Curlew Ct EN10 ........148 F8
Curlew Rd LU2 .........46 C5

**Curo Pk** AL2 . . . . . . . . . . .**141** E4
**Currie St** SG13 . . . . . . . .**113** E6
**Curteys** CM17 . . . . . . . . .**118** C5
**Curtis Cl** WD3 . . . . . . . . .**165** A1
**Curtis Rd** HP3 . . . . . . . .**125** D4
**Curtis Way** HP4 . . . . . . .**122** D3
**Curtiss Dr** WD25 . . . . . .**153** F5
**Curzon Gate Ct** [1]
　WD17 . . . . . . . . . . . . . . . .**167** A8
**Curzon Rd** LU3 . . . . . . . .**45** C1
**Cussans Ho** WD18 . . . . .**166** E3
**Cussons Cl** EN7 . . . . . . .**148** A2
**Cut Throat Ave** HP4,LU6 . .**81** E7
**Cutenhoe Rd** LU1 . . . . . .**63** E4
**Cutforth Rd** CM21 . . . . . .**97** E3
**Cuthbert Cl** EN7 . . . . . . .**147** F2
**Cutlers Gn** LU2 . . . . . . . . .**46** F2
**Cutmore Dr** AL4 . . . . . . .**129** B1
**Cutts La** SG4 . . . . . . . . . . .**66** D1
**Cuttsfield Terr** HP1 . . . .**123** F2
**Cuttys La** SG1 . . . . . . . . . .**50** E5
**Cwmbran Ct** HP2 . . . . . .**124** F7
**Cygnet Cl**
　Borehamwood WD6 . . . .**170** C8
　Northwood HA6 . . . . . . .**174** C4
**Cygnet Ct** [11] CM23 . . . . .**76** F6
**Cygnet Ho**
　Hemel Hempstead HP3 . .**138** F6
　[1] Stanmore HA7 . . . . . .**176** F4
**Cygnet Way** LU1 . . . . . . .**116** A1
**Cylers Thicket** AL6 . . . . .**89** C6
**Cymbeline Ct** AL3 . . . . . .**127** C4
**Cypress Ave**
　Crews Hill EN2 . . . . . . . .**161** A4
　Welwyn Garden City AL7 .**111** C5
**Cypress Cl** EN9 . . . . . . . .**163** D5
**Cypress Rd** HA3 . . . . . . .**176** D1
**Cypress Wlk** WD25 . . . . .**154** B4
**Cyrils Way** AL1 . . . . . . . .**141** D8

**D**

**Dacorum Way** HP1 . . . . .**124** C3
**Dacre Bldgs** EN8 . . . . . . .**148** F2
**Dacre Cres** SG4 . . . . . . . . .**66** C1
**Dacre Gdns** WD6 . . . . . . .**170** C4
**Dacre Gn** SG8 . . . . . . . . . . . .**7** F6
**Dacre Ind Est** EN8 . . . . . .**148** F3
**Dacre Rd** SG5 . . . . . . . . . . .**35** A8
**Daffodil Cl** AL10 . . . . . . .**109** F1
**Dagger La** WD6 . . . . . . . .**169** B4
**Daggs Dell Rd** HP1 . . . . .**123** E5
**Dagnall Rd**
　Great Gaddesden HP1 . . .**103** C5
　Whipsnade HP4,LU6 . . . . .**81** D8
**Dagnall Sch** HP4 . . . . . . . .**81** C5
**Dagnalls** SG6 . . . . . . . . . . . .**22** F2
**Dahlia Cl**
　Hammond Street EN7 . . . .**147** C6
　Luton LU2 . . . . . . . . . . . . .**46** B4
**Dailmead** EN6 . . . . . . . . .**157** F5
**Daintrees** SG12 . . . . . . . . .**95** E4
**Daintry Lodge** HA6 . . . . .**174** F3
**Dairy Cotts** SG5 . . . . . . . .**19** B2
**Dairy Mews** WD18 . . . . .**167** A4
**Dairy Way** WD25 . . . . . . .**139** F2
**Dairyglen Ave** EN8 . . . . .**162** A4
**Daisy Cl** SG6 . . . . . . . . . . . .**23** A8
**Daisy Dr** AL10 . . . . . . . . .**129** F8
**Dalby Cl** LU4 . . . . . . . . . . .**44** B3
**Dale Ave** AL4 . . . . . . . . . . .**87** B5
**Dale Cl**
　Hitchin SG4 . . . . . . . . . . .**34** F4
　Pinner HA5 . . . . . . . . . . .**175** B2
**Dale Ct** CM21 . . . . . . . . . . .**97** C1
**Dale Rd** LU1 . . . . . . . . . . . .**63** C7
**Dale The** Letchworth SG6 . .**22** C5
　Waltham Abbey EN9 . . . .**163** E5
**Dales Path** WD6 . . . . . . .**170** D4
**Dales Rd** WD6 . . . . . . . . .**170** D4
**Daleside Dr** EN6 . . . . . . .**158** F6
**Dalewood** Harpenden AL5 .**86** D1
　Welwyn Garden City AL7 .**111** D5
**Dalkeith Rd** AL5 . . . . . . . .**86** C1
**Dallow Prim Sch** LU1 . . .**63** C8
**Dallow Rd** LU1 . . . . . . . . .**63** B8
**Dalroad Ent Est** LU1 . . . .**63** B8
**Dalton Cl** LU3 . . . . . . . . . .**31** B1
**Dalton Gdns** CM23 . . . . . .**76** E4
**Dalton St** AL3 . . . . . . . . .**127** D4
**Dalton Way**
　Watford WD17 . . . . . . . .**167** D4
　Whitwell SG4 . . . . . . . . . .**66** C2
**Daltry Cl** SG1 . . . . . . . . . .**36** C2
**Daltry Rd** SG1 . . . . . . . . . .**36** C2
**Damask Cl** Tring HP23 . . .**100** C1
　Weston SG4 . . . . . . . . . . . .**37** B8
**Damask Gn** HP1 . . . . . . .**123** E2
**Damask Green Rd** SG4 . . .**37** B8
**Dame Alice Owen's Sch**
　EN6 . . . . . . . . . . . . . . . . .**158** E6
**Dammersey Cl** AL3 . . . . . .**83** F4
**Damson Way** AL4 . . . . . .**128** C5
**Dancers End La** HP23 . . . .**99** C2
**Dancers Hill Rd** EN5 . . . .**158** E3
**Dancers La** EN5 . . . . . . . .**158** C4
**Dancote** SG3 . . . . . . . . . . . .**68** F5
**Dane Acres** CM23 . . . . . . .**76** D8
**Dane Bridge La** SG10 . . . .**75** B2
**Dane Cl** Harpenden AL5 . . .**86** C4
　Stotfold SG5 . . . . . . . . . . . .**11** F8
**Dane Ct** AL1 . . . . . . . . . . .**128** B2
**Dane End** SG8 . . . . . . . . . .**16** B4
**Dane End Ho** SG1 . . . . . . .**36** C1
**Dane End La** SG4 . . . . . . . .**37** E5

**Dane End Rd** SG11 . . . . . .**72** E3
**Dane Pk** CM23 . . . . . . . . . .**76** D8
**Dane O'Coys Rd** CM23 . . .**58** E1
**Dane Pk** CM23 . . . . . . . . . .**76** D8
**Dane Rd** LU3 . . . . . . . . . . . .**45** C2
**Dane St** CM23 . . . . . . . . . . .**77** A7
**Danebridge Rd** SG10 . . . .**75** B2
**Danefield Rd** SG5 . . . . . . .**20** C4
**Danemead** EN11 . . . . . . .**115** A1
**Danes The** AL2 . . . . . . . . .**141** C3
**Danesbury La** AL6 . . . . . . .**89** D8
**Danesbury Park Rd** AL6 . .**89** D8
**Danesbury Pk**
　Hertford SG14 . . . . . . . .**113** D7
　Welwyn AL6 . . . . . . . . . . .**89** C7
**Danesbury Pk Cvn Site**
　AL6 . . . . . . . . . . . . . . . . . .**89** D8
**Danescroft** SG6 . . . . . . . . .**12** A1
**Danesgate** SG1 . . . . . . . . .**50** D4
**Danestrete** SG1 . . . . . . . . .**50** D5
**Daniel Ho** [4] HA5 . . . . . .**175** C1
**Daniells** AL10 . . . . . . . . . .**111** A7
**Danvers Croft** HP23 . . . .**100** C5
**Danvers Dr** LU3 . . . . . . . . .**31** C1
**Darblay Cl** AL4 . . . . . . . . .**108** F5
**Darby Dr**
　Waltham Abbey EN9 . . . .**163** C6
　Welwyn AL6 . . . . . . . . . . .**68** E3
**Darcy Cl** EN8 . . . . . . . . . .**162** C1
**Dark La**
　Cheshunt EN7 . . . . . . . . .**148** A1
　Codicote SG4 . . . . . . . . . . .**88** E8
　Harpenden AL5 . . . . . . . .**107** D7
　Sandon SG9 . . . . . . . . . . . .**15** B1
　Wingrave HP22 . . . . . . . . .**60** C3
**Darkes La** EN6 . . . . . . . . .**159** A8
**Darlands Dr** EN5 . . . . . . .**171** D4
**Darley Hall** LU2 . . . . . . . .**47** C1
**Darley Rd** LU2,SG4 . . . . . .**47** C2
**Darnhills** WD7 . . . . . . . . .**155** F4
**Darnicle Hill** EN7 . . . . . .**147** A6
**Darr's La** HP4 . . . . . . . . . .**121** D6
**Darrington Rd** WD6 . . . .**169** E8
**Dart The** HP2 . . . . . . . . . .**125** A8
**Dartmouth Mews** LU4 . . .**44** D3
**Darwin Cl**
　Hemel Hempstead HP2 . .**105** B1
　St Albans AL3 . . . . . . . . .**127** E2
**Darwin Gdns** WD19 . . . .**175** C5
**Darwin Rd** SG2 . . . . . . . . .**51** B6
**Dashes The** CM20 . . . . . .**117** E1
**Datchet Cl** HP2 . . . . . . . .**125** B8
**Dauphin Ct** [5] LU2 . . . . . .**45** D1
**Dauphine Ct** HA3 . . . . . .**176** E1
**Davenham Ave** HA6 . . . .**174** F5
**Daventer Dr** HA7 . . . . . . .**176** F3
**David Evans Ct** SG6 . . . . .**22** D7
**Davies St** SG13 . . . . . . . .**113** E6
**Davis Cres** SG5 . . . . . . . . .**20** D4
**Davis Ct** AL1 . . . . . . . . . . .**127** E3
**Davis Ho** [11] HP4 . . . . . .**122** C4
**Davis' Row** SG15 . . . . . . . .**11** A4
**Davison Cl** EN8 . . . . . . . .**148** D3
**Davison Dr** EN8 . . . . . . . .**148** D3
**Davys Cl** AL4 . . . . . . . . . .**108** E7
**Dawes La** Sarratt WD3 . . .**151** F3
　Wheathampstead AL4 . . . .**87** D1
**Dawley** AL7 . . . . . . . . . . . .**89** F1
**Dawley Ct** HP2 . . . . . . . .**125** A7
**Dawlish Cl** SG2 . . . . . . . . .**69** C7
**Dawlish Rd** LU4 . . . . . . . . .**44** F3
**Dawson Cl** SG16 . . . . . . . .**10** C5
**Day's Cl** SG8 . . . . . . . . . . . .**7** C5
**Dayemead** AL7 . . . . . . . .**111** B3
**Days Cl** AL10 . . . . . . . . . .**129** F5
**Days Mead** AL10 . . . . . . .**129** F5
**De Havilland Aircraft**
　**Heritage Mus The**★
　AL2 . . . . . . . . . . . . . . . . .**143** B2
**De Havilland Ct** WD7 . . .**156** E7
**De Havilland Way** WD5 . .**153** F7
**De Tany Ct** AL1 . . . . . . . .**127** C2
**De Vere Wlk** WD17 . . . . .**166** E7
**Deacon Cl** AL1 . . . . . . . . .**141** D7
**Deacons Cl**
　Borehamwood WD6 . . . .**170** A5
　Pinner HA5 . . . . . . . . . . .**175** B1
**Deacons Ct** [7] LU2 . . . . . .**63** D8
**Deacons Hill** WD19 . . . .**167** C3
**Deacons Hts** WD6 . . . . . .**170** A3
**Deacons Way** SG5 . . . . . . .**21** D1
**Deaconsfield Rd** HP3 . . .**138** E8
**Dead Woman's La** SG4 . . .**48** C7
**Deadman's Ash La**
　WD3 . . . . . . . . . . . . . . . .**152** B3
**Deakin Cl** WD18 . . . . . . .**166** E2
**Dean Ct** WD25 . . . . . . . . .**154** D6
**Dean Field** HP3 . . . . . . . .**137** A4
**Dean Moore Cl** AL1 . . . .**127** D2
**Dean The** HP22 . . . . . . . . .**60** B3
**Dean's Gdns** AL4 . . . . . . .**128** A7
**Deane Ct** HA6 . . . . . . . . .**174** E2
**Deans Cl**
　Abbots Langley WD5 . . . .**153** D7
　Tring HP23 . . . . . . . . . . .**100** A4
**Deans Furlong** HP23 . . . .**100** A4
**Deans Lawn** [8] HP4 . . . .**122** C4
**Deans Mdw** HP4 . . . . . . . .**81** C5
**Deanscroft** SG3 . . . . . . . . .**68** F5
**Deard's End La** SG3 . . . . . .**68** F6
**Deards Wood** SG3 . . . . . . .**68** F5
**Debenham Ct** EN5 . . . . . .**171** C4
**Debenham Rd** EN7 . . . . .**148** B4

**Dee The** HP2 . . . . . . . . . .**124** F8
**Deep Denes** LU2 . . . . . . . .**46** A2
**Deepdene** EN6 . . . . . . . . .**158** D8
**Deeping Cl** SG3 . . . . . . . . .**68** F4
**Deer Cl** SG13 . . . . . . . . . .**113** F6
**Deer Park Way** EN9 . . . .**163** B4
**Deerfield Cl** SG12 . . . . . . .**93** D2
**Deerings The** AL5 . . . . . .**107** A4
**Deerswood Ave** AL10 . . .**130** B3
**Deeves Hall La** EN6 . . . .**157** E6
**Deimos Dr** HP2 . . . . . . . .**125** A6
**Delahay Rise** HP4 . . . . . .**122** B6
**Delamare Rd** EN8 . . . . . .**148** F2
**Delamere Rd** WD6 . . . . . .**170** B8
**Delfcroft** SG12 . . . . . . . . .**93** C2
**Delfield Gdns** LU1 . . . . . .**62** E4
**Delius Cl** WD6 . . . . . . . . .**169** C3
**Dell Cl** AL5 . . . . . . . . . . . . .**86** B3
**Dell Cl** WD3 . . . . . . . . . . .**173** A8
**Dell Field Ave** HP4 . . . . .**122** B6
**Dell La**
　Bishop's Stortford, Hockerill
　　CM23 . . . . . . . . . . . . . . .**77** A7
　Bishop's Stortford,
　　Latchmore Bank CM22 . .**77** B1
　Spellbrook CM22 . . . . . . .**98** A8
**Dell Mdw** HP3 . . . . . . . . .**138** E7
**Dell Rd**
　Berkhamsted HP4 . . . . . .**121** D5
　Enfield EN3 . . . . . . . . . . .**162** C1
　Watford WD24 . . . . . . . .**154** A2
**Dell Rise** AL2 . . . . . . . . . .**141** B5
**Dell Side** WD24 . . . . . . . .**154** A2
**Dell Springs** SG9 . . . . . . . .**40** C5
**Dell The**
　Baldock SG7 . . . . . . . . . . .**23** C8
　Brickendon SG13 . . . . . .**113** C3
　Caddington LU1 . . . . . . . .**62** E3
　Luton LU2 . . . . . . . . . . . . .**46** F1
　Markyate AL3 . . . . . . . . . .**83** D5
　Moor Park HA6 . . . . . . . .**174** E4
　Pinner HA5 . . . . . . . . . . .**175** D1
　Radlett WD7 . . . . . . . . . .**156** A4
　Royston SG8 . . . . . . . . . . . .**7** C5
　St Albans AL1 . . . . . . . . .**128** A4
　Stevenage SG1 . . . . . . . . .**50** E5
　Waltham Abbey EN9 . . . .**163** C3
　Welwyn AL6 . . . . . . . . . . .**90** A4
**Dellcot Cl** LU2 . . . . . . . . . .**46** B4
**Dellcott Cl** AL8 . . . . . . . .**110** C7
**Dellcroft Way** AL5 . . . . .**107** A5
**Dellcut Rd** HP2 . . . . . . . .**125** A5
**Dellfield** St Albans AL1 . .**127** F2
　Thundridge SG12 . . . . . . .**93** D8
**Dellfield Cl**
　Berkhamsted HP4 . . . . . .**122** A6
　Radlett WD7 . . . . . . . . . .**155** F4
　Watford WD17 . . . . . . . .**167** A7
**Dellfield Ct**
　[1] Harlow CM17 . . . . . .**118** C4
　Luton LU2 . . . . . . . . . . . . .**46** D2
**Dellfield Rd** AL10 . . . . . .**130** A5
**Dellmeadow** WD5 . . . . . .**139** E1
**Dellors Cl** EN5 . . . . . . . . .**171** D4
**Dells The**
　[11] Bishop's Stortford CM23 .**76** F7
　Hemel Hempstead HP3 . .**125** B2
**Dells Wood Cl** EN11 . . . .**114** F1
**Dellsome La**
　Colney Heath AL4 . . . . . .**143** E6
　Welham Green AL9 . . . . .**144** B8
**Dellswood Cl** SG13 . . . . .**113** E5
**Dellwood** WD3 . . . . . . . .**165** B1
**Delmar Ave** HP2 . . . . . . .**125** D2
**Delmer Ct** WD6 . . . . . . . .**156** F1
**Delmerend La** AL3 . . . . . .**84** C1
**Delphine Cl** LU1 . . . . . . . .**63** B6
**Delrow Cotts** WD25 . . . .**168** C8
**Delta Gain** WD19 . . . . . .**175** D7
**Demontfort Rise** SG12 . . .**93** C3
**Denbigh Cl** [2] HP2 . . . .**124** E2
**Denbigh High Sch** LU3 . . .**45** C2
**Denbigh Inf Sch** LU3 . . . .**45** B2
**Denbigh Jun Sch** LU3 . . . .**45** B2
**Denbigh Rd** LU3 . . . . . . . .**45** B2
**Denby** SG6 . . . . . . . . . . . . .**23** B4
**Dencora Ctr The** AL1 . . .**128** A3
**Dencora Way** LU3 . . . . . . .**44** B8
**Dendridge Cl** EN1 . . . . . .**162** B2
**Dene La** SG2 . . . . . . . . . . . .**51** E2
**Dene Rd** HA6 . . . . . . . . . .**174** D4
**Denes The** HP3 . . . . . . . .**138** F7
**Denewood Cl** WD17 . . . .**153** F2
**Denham Cl**
　Hemel Hempstead HP2 . .**125** A8
　Luton LU3 . . . . . . . . . . . . .**44** E8
**Denham La** SL9 . . . . . . . .**172** A2
**Denham Way** WD6 . . . . .**170** C8
**Denham Way (North Orbital**
　**Rd)** WD3 . . . . . . . . . . .**172** E4
**Denmark Cl** LU3 . . . . . . . .**44** E8
**Denmark St** WD17 . . . . . .**167** B7
**Dennis Cl** HP2 . . . . . . . . . .**99** A4
**Dennis Ct** [1] AL3 . . . . . .**127** D4
**Denny Ave** EN9 . . . . . . . .**163** D5
**Denny Ct** CM23 . . . . . . . . .**59** B2
**Denny Gate** EN8 . . . . . . .**148** F4
**Denny's La** HP4 . . . . . . . .**121** F3
**Densley Cl** AL8 . . . . . . . . .**110** D8
**Denton Cl**
　Barnet EN5 . . . . . . . . . . .**171** C4
　Luton LU4 . . . . . . . . . . . . .**44** B3
**Denton Ho** [10]
　WD19 . . . . . . . . . . . . . . .**175** C7
**Denton Rd** SG1 . . . . . . . . .**50** E4
**Dents Cl** SG6 . . . . . . . . . . .**23** C3
**Derby Ave** HA3 . . . . . . . .**176** D2
**Derby Ho** HA5 . . . . . . . . .**175** D1

**Derby Rd**
　Hoddesdon EN11 . . . . . .**135** D5
　Luton LU4 . . . . . . . . . . . . .**44** C2
　Watford WD18 . . . . . . . .**167** C5
**Derby Way** SG1 . . . . . . . . .**51** B8
**Derry Leys** AL10 . . . . . . .**129** C7
**Derwent Ave** Luton LU3 . .**45** B7
　Pinner HA5 . . . . . . . . . . .**175** E4
**Derwent Cl** WD25 . . . . . .**154** C5
**Derwent Lower Sch** SG16 **10** B5
**Derwent Rd**
　Harpenden AL5 . . . . . . . . .**85** C4
　Hemel Hempstead HP3 . .**125** C2
　Lower Stondon SG16 . . . . .**10** B4
　Luton LU2 . . . . . . . . . . . . .**64** A8
**Des Fuller Ct** [3] LU1 . . . .**63** F6
**Desborough Cl**
　Hertford SG14 . . . . . . . . .**92** C1
　Welwyn Garden City AL7 .**111** B3
**Desborough Dr** AL6 . . . . .**90** D5
**Desborough Rd** SG4 . . . . .**35** C8
**Desmond Rd** WD24 . . . . .**153** F3
**Deva Cl** AL3 . . . . . . . . . . .**127** A1
**Devereux Dr** WD17 . . . . .**153** E1
**Devoils La** [9] CM23 . . . . . .**76** F7
**Devon Cl** AL1 . . . . . . . . . .**127** E2
**Devon Rd** Watford WD24 .**167** D8
**Devonshire Bsns Pk**
　WD6 . . . . . . . . . . . . . . . .**170** D6
**Devonshire Cl** SG2 . . . . . .**69** A8
**Devonshire Ct** HA5 . . . . .**175** F2
**Devonshire Rd**
　[5] Harpenden AL5 . . . . . .**86** B1
　Pinner HA5 . . . . . . . . . . .**175** F2
**Dewars Cl** AL6 . . . . . . . . . .**89** C6
**Dewes Green Rd** CM23 . . .**30** F1
**Dewgrass Gr** EN8 . . . . . .**162** D4
**Dewhurst Rd** EN8 . . . . . .**148** C2
**Dewhurst St Mary CE Prim**
　**Sch** EN8 . . . . . . . . . . . .**148** C2
**Dewpond Cl** SG1 . . . . . . . .**50** C8
**Dewsbury Rd** LU3 . . . . . . .**45** C6
**Dexter Cl** Luton LU3 . . . . .**31** B1
　St Albans AL1 . . . . . . . . .**128** A2
**Dexter Rd** Barnet EN5 . . .**171** D3
　Harefield UB9 . . . . . . . . .**173** C1
**Diamond Ind Ctr** SG6 . . . .**23** C7
**Diamond Rd** WD24 . . . . .**154** A1
**Dickens Cl** AL3 . . . . . . . . .**127** D4
**Dickens Ct** HP2 . . . . . . . .**105** B1
**Dickenson Way** [19] SG12 .**93** D6
**Dicker Mill** SG13 . . . . . . .**113** D7
**Dicket Mead** AL6 . . . . . . . .**89** C5
**Dickins Cl** EN7 . . . . . . . . .**148** A5
**Dickinson Ave** WD3 . . . .**166** A3
**Dickinson Quay** HP3 . . . .**138** F7
**Dickinson Sq** WD3 . . . . . .**166** A3
**Dickinsons Field** AL5 . . .**107** C5
**Dickson** EN7 . . . . . . . . . . .**147** F4
**Dig Dag Hill** EN7 . . . . . . .**147** F4
**Digswell Cl** WD6 . . . . . . .**157** A1
**Digswell Ct** AL8 . . . . . . . .**110** E8
**Digswell Hill** AL6 . . . . . . . .**89** B2
**Digswell Ho** AL8 . . . . . . . .**89** D2
**Digswell House Mews**
　AL8 . . . . . . . . . . . . . . . . . .**89** D2
**Digswell La** AL7 . . . . . . . . .**89** F2
**Digswell Park Rd**
　Welwyn Garden City AL8 . .**89** D3
　Welwyn Garden City AL8 . .**89** D3
**Digswell Pl** AL8 . . . . . . . . .**89** C1
**Digswell Rd** AL8 . . . . . . . .**89** E1
**Digswell Rise** AL8 . . . . . .**110** E8
**Dimmocks La** WD3 . . . . .**152** B3
**Dimsdale Cotts** SG9 . . . . .**29** B7
**Dimsdale Cres** CM23 . . . . .**77** B6
**Dimsdale St** SG14 . . . . . .**113** C6
**Dinant Link Rd** EN11 . . .**135** B7
**Dingle** EN5 . . . . . . . . . . . .**170** F3
**Dinmore** HP3 . . . . . . . . . .**136** F3
**Ditchfield Rd** EN11 . . . . .**115** A1
**Ditchling Cl** LU2 . . . . . . . .**46** C3
**Ditchling Ct** [1] AL1 . . . .**127** C3
**Ditchmore La** SG1 . . . . . . .**50** D6
**Ditton Gn** LU2 . . . . . . . . . .**46** E3
**Divine Saviour RC Prim Sch**
　WD5 . . . . . . . . . . . . . . . .**153** D7
**Divot Pl** SG13 . . . . . . . . . .**114** B7
**Dixies Cl** SG7 . . . . . . . . . . . .**4** D3
**Dixon Pl** SG9 . . . . . . . . . . .**40** E7
**Dixon Rd** SG12 . . . . . . . .**114** E8
**Dixons Hill Cl** AL9 . . . . . .**144** B6
**Dixons Hill Rd** AL9 . . . . .**144** C5
**Dobb's Weir Rd** EN11,
　CM19 . . . . . . . . . . . . . . .**135** D2
**Docklands** SG5 . . . . . . . . .**20** D4
**Doctor's Commons Rd**
　HP4 . . . . . . . . . . . . . . . . .**122** B4
**Dodds La** HP2 . . . . . . . . . .**104** E1
**Dodwood** AL7 . . . . . . . . .**111** B5
**Dog Kennel La**
　Chorleywood WD3 . . . . .**164** F5
　Hatfield AL10 . . . . . . . . .**130** A6
　Royston SG8 . . . . . . . . . . . .**7** D6
**Doggetts Way** AL1 . . . . .**127** C1
**Dognell Gn** AL8 . . . . . . . .**110** B7
**Dolesbury Dr** AL6 . . . . . . .**89** C6
**Dollimore Cl** SG4 . . . . . . . .**67** F1
**Dollis Brook Wlk** EN5 . . .**171** E3
**Dollis Valley Dr** EN5 . . . .**171** E4
**Dollis Valley Way** EN5 . . .**171** F3
**Dolphin Sq** HP23 . . . . . . .**100** A3
**Dolphin Way** CM23 . . . . . .**77** A8
**Dolphin Yd**
　[2] Hertford SG14 . . . . .**113** D6
　St Albans AL1 . . . . . . . . .**127** C3
　[7] Ware SG12 . . . . . . . . .**93** D1

**Dominic Ct** EN9 . . . . . . . .**163** B6
**Doncaster Cl** SG1 . . . . . . .**51** C8
**Doncaster Gn** WD19 . . . .**175** C5
**Donkey La** HP23 . . . . . . . .**99** E2
**Donne Cl** SG8 . . . . . . . . . . . .**7** C8
**Dorant Ho** AL3 . . . . . . . .**127** D7
**Dorcas Ct** AL1 . . . . . . . . .**127** E2
**Dorchester Ave** EN11 . . .**135** A8
**Dorchester Ct**
　Croxley Green WD3 . . . .**166** D4
　St Albans AL1 . . . . . . . . .**128** A2
　Watford WD17 . . . . . . . .**167** E3
**Dordans Rd** LU4 . . . . . . . .**44** F4
**Dorel Cl** LU2 . . . . . . . . . . . .**45** F2
**Dormans Cl** HA6 . . . . . . .**174** D3
**Dormer Cl** EN5 . . . . . . . . .**171** D4
**Dormie Cl** AL3 . . . . . . . . .**127** C5
**Dornan Ct** LU1 . . . . . . . . . .**63** E5
**Dorrien's Croft** HP4 . . . .**121** F7
**Dorrington Cl** LU3 . . . . . .**45** C1
**Dorrofield Cl** WD3 . . . . .**166** D4
**Dorset Cl** HP4 . . . . . . . . .**121** F5
**Dorset Ct** [4] LU1 . . . . . . .**63** F6
**Dorset Ho** [13] CM23 . . . .**76** F7
**Douglas Ave** WD24 . . . . .**154** E2
**Douglas Cl** AL6 . . . . . . . . .**89** C3
**Douglas Dr** SG1 . . . . . . . . .**51** A8
**Douglas Ho** [11] EN8 . . . .**148** D3
**Douglas Rd**
　Harpenden AL5 . . . . . . . . .**85** F2
　Luton LU4 . . . . . . . . . . . . .**45** A2
**Douglas Way** AL7 . . . . . .**111** C6
**Dove Cl**
　Bishop's Stortford CM23 . .**76** E3
　Stansted Mountfitchet
　　CM24 . . . . . . . . . . . . . . .**59** E8
**Dove Ct** AL10 . . . . . . . . . .**130** A3
**Dove La** EN6 . . . . . . . . . . .**159** C5
**Dove Pk**
　Chorleywood WD3 . . . . .**164** C4
　Pinner HA5 . . . . . . . . . . .**176** A3
**Dovecote The** SG7 . . . . . . . .**4** D4
**Dovedale**
　Luton LU2 . . . . . . . . . . . . .**45** E6
　Stevenage SG2 . . . . . . . . .**51** B4
　Ware SG12 . . . . . . . . . . . .**93** C3
**Dovedale Cl** UB9 . . . . . . .**173** C1
**Dovehouse Croft** CM20 . .**118** A2
**Dovehouse Hill** LU2 . . . . .**46** B1
**Dovehouse La** LU2 . . . . . . .**82** D8
**Dover Cl** Luton LU3 . . . . . .**45** A3
　Pitstone LU7 . . . . . . . . . . .**80** D2
**Dover Way** WD3 . . . . . . .**166** C5
**Doverfield** EN7 . . . . . . . .**147** C2
**Dowding Way** WD25 . . . .**153** F5
**Dower Ct** SG4 . . . . . . . . . .**34** F5
**Dower Mews** [5] HP4 . . .**122** C4
**Dowland Ho** EN1 . . . . . . .**161** F1
**Dowling Ct** HP3 . . . . . . . .**138** D8
**Down Edge** AL3 . . . . . . . .**105** F5
**Down Green La** AL4 . . . . .**108** B7
**Downalong** WD23 . . . . . .**168** D3
**Downedge** AL3 . . . . . . . . .**127** B4
**Downer Dr** WD3 . . . . . . .**152** A3
**Downes Rd** AL4 . . . . . . . .**128** B7
**Downfield Cl** SG13 . . . . . .**114** C4
**Downfield Ct** SG12 . . . . . .**93** B5
**Downfield Jun Mix Inf Sch**
　EN8 . . . . . . . . . . . . . . . . .**162** E8
**Downfield Rd**
　Cheshunt EN8 . . . . . . . . .**162** E8
　Hertford Heath SG13 . . .**114** C5
**Downfields** AL8 . . . . . . . .**110** B4
**Downhall Ley** SG8 . . . . . . .**40** F2
**Downings Wood** WD3 . . .**172** D5
**Downlands**
　Baldock SG7 . . . . . . . . . . .**13** A1
　Luton LU3 . . . . . . . . . . . . .**44** C7
　Royston SG8 . . . . . . . . . . . .**7** C6
　Stevenage SG2 . . . . . . . . .**51** D7
　Waltham Abbey EN9 . . . .**163** E5
**Downlands Cvn Pk**
　LU1 . . . . . . . . . . . . . . . . . .**84** C8
**Downs La** AL10 . . . . . . . .**130** A3
**Downs Rd** LU1 . . . . . . . . . .**63** C7
**Downs The** AL10 . . . . . . .**130** A3
**Downs View** LU4 . . . . . . . .**44** D4
**Downsfield** AL10 . . . . . . .**130** B2
**Downside** HP2 . . . . . . . . .**124** E4
**Downside Inf Sch** LU4 . . . .**44** E1
**Downside Jun Sch** LU4 . . .**44** E1
**Downsway** St Albans AL1 . .**128** A4
**Downton Ct** [3] LU3 . . . . .**63** D8
**Downview** LU4 . . . . . . . . . .**44** B2
**Dowry Wlk** WD17 . . . . . .**153** F1
**Dragon Moth Rd** AL10 . .**129** D6
**Drakes Cl** EN8 . . . . . . . . .**148** D3
**Drakes Dr**
　Northwood HA6 . . . . . . .**174** B2
　St Albans AL1 . . . . . . . . .**128** C1
　Stevenage SG2 . . . . . . . . .**51** B7
**Drakes Mdw** CM17 . . . . .**118** E4
**Drakes Way** AL10 . . . . . .**130** B3
**Drapers Mews** LU3 . . . . . .**45** C1
**Drapers Way** SG1 . . . . . . .**50** C7
**Drayman's Ct** CM23 . . . . .**76** B5
**Drayton Cl** EN9 . . . . . . . .**163** E7
**Drayton Ave** EN6 . . . . . . .**158** E7
**Drayton Rd**
　Borehamwood WD6 . . . .**170** A5
　Luton LU4 . . . . . . . . . . . . .**44** A3
**Driftway** SG8 . . . . . . . . . . .**16** E4
**Driftway The** HP2 . . . . . .**124** F3
**Driftwood Ave** AL2 . . . . .**141** B5
**Drive The**
　Barnet EN5 . . . . . . . . . . .**171** E4
　Brookmans Park AL9 . . . .**145** B6

**Drive The** *continued*
Cheshunt EN7 . . . . . . . . . 148 B3
Goff's Oak EN7 . . . . . . . . 147 B3
Harlow CM20 . . . . . . . . . . 117 E1
Harpenden AL5 . . . . . . . . . .86 A1
Hertford SG14 . . . . . . . . . 113 C8
Hoddesdon EN11 . . . . . . . 135 A8
Kimpton AL4 . . . . . . . . . . . .87 B7
London Colney AL2 . . . . . 142 A5
Northwood HA6 . . . . . . . . 174 E2
Oaklands AL4 . . . . . . . . . . .69 A1
Potters Bar EN6 . . . . . . . . 158 F7
Radlett WD7 . . . . . . . . . . 156 A5
Rickmansworth WD3 . . . . 165 C3
Sawbridgeworth CM21 . . . .97 C3
Watford WD17 . . . . . . . . . 153 E2
**Driver's End** SG4 . . . . . . . . .68 A4
**Driver's End La** SG4,SG3 .68 A4
**Driveway The**
Cuffley EN6 . . . . . . . . . . . 146 E3
Hemel Hempstead HP1 . . . 124 B1
**Dromey Gdns** HA3 . . . . . . 176 E2
**Drop La** AL2 . . . . . . . . . . . 155 C7
**Drovers Way**
Bishop's Stortford CM23 . . .76 C3
Hatfield AL10 . . . . . . . . . . 130 B8
St Albans AL1 . . . . . . . . . 127 D3
**Drummond Dr** HA7 . . . . . 176 F3
**Drummond Ride** HP23 . . . 100 A5
**Drummonds The** LU4 . . . . .44 C2
**Drury La** SG12 . . . . . . . . . .95 E1
**Drycroft** AL7 . . . . . . . . . . . 110 E2
**Dryden Cres** SG2 . . . . . . . .51 C8
**Dryden Rd** HA3 . . . . . . . . 176 F2
**Drysdale Cl** 7 HA6 . . . . . 174 E2
**Dubbs Knoll Rd** SG8 . . . . . . .1 F5
**Dubrae Cl** AL3 . . . . . . . . . 127 A1
**Duchess Cl** CM23 . . . . . . . .76 C7
**Duchy Rd** EN4 . . . . . . . . . 159 D1
**Duck End** CM23 . . . . . . . . .59 E1
**Duck La** SG2 . . . . . . . . . . . .52 E4
**Duck's Hill Rd** HA6 . . . . . 174 E4
**Ducketts La** SG10 . . . . . . . .75 D1
**Ducketts Mead** SG8 . . . . . 116 B1
**Ducketts Wharf** 10 CM23 . .76 F6
**Ducketts Wood** SG12 . . . . .93 E6
**Duckling La** CM21 . . . . . . . .97 E2
**Duckmore La** HP23 . . . . . . .99 E2
**Dudley Ave** EN8 . . . . . . . . 162 D7
**Dudley Hill Cl** AL6 . . . . . . . .89 E8
**Dudley St** LU2 . . . . . . . . . . .63 E8
**Dudswell La** HP4 . . . . . . . 121 D7
**Dugdale Ct** SG5 . . . . . . . . .21 C1
**Dugdale Hill La** EN6 . . . . 158 E7
**Dugdales** WD3 . . . . . . . . . 166 A5
**Duke St** Hoddesdon EN11 135 A7
Luton LU2 . . . . . . . . . . . . .63 E8
Watford WD17 . . . . . . . . . 167 C6
**Duke's La** SG5 . . . . . . . . . . .34 F8
**Dukes Ave** LU6 . . . . . . . . . .81 E8
**Dukes Ct** 4 LU1 . . . . . . . . .63 D6
**Dukes Ride**
Bishop's Stortford CM23 . . .76 C7
18 Luton LU2 . . . . . . . . . .45 D1
**Dukes Way** HP4 . . . . . . . . 122 A6
**Dulwich Way** WD3 . . . . . . 166 A4
**Dumbarton Ave** EN8 . . . . 162 D5
**Dumbletons** WD3 . . . . . . . 172 E6
**Dumfries Cl** WD19 . . . . . . 175 A7
**Dumfries Ct** 9 LU1 . . . . . . .63 D6
**Dumfries St** LU1 . . . . . . . . .63 D6
**Duncan Cl** AL7 . . . . . . . . . 110 E5
**Duncan Ct** AL1 . . . . . . . . . 127 F1
**Duncan Way** WD23 . . . . . 167 E2
**Duncombe Cl**
Hertford SG14 . . . . . . . . . 113 C8
Luton LU3 . . . . . . . . . . . . .45 C6
**Duncombe Rd**
Berkhamsted HP4 . . . . . . . 121 E6
Hertford SG14 . . . . . . . . . 113 C8
**Duncombe Sch** SG14 . . . . 113 C7
**Duncots** SG5 . . . . . . . . . . . .21 E3
**Dundale Prim Sch**
HP23 . . . . . . . . . . . . . . . 100 A5
**Dundale Rd** HP23 . . . . . . . 100 A4
**Dundas Mews** SG1 . . . . . . .37 D4
**Dunedin Ho** SG8 . . . . . . . . . .7 C6
**Dunfermline Ho** 9
WD19 . . . . . . . . . . . . . . 175 C7
**Dunford St** 7 HA5 . . . . . . 175 F3
**Dunham's La** SG6 . . . . . . . .23 C6
**Dunkirks Mews** SG13 . . . 113 D4
**Dunlin** SG6 . . . . . . . . . . . . .11 E1
**Dunlin Rd** HP2 . . . . . . . . . 124 E8
**Dunmow Ct** LU3 . . . . . . . . .45 D2
**Dunmow Rd** CM23 . . . . . . .77 C2
**Dunn Cl** SG2 . . . . . . . . . . . .50 E3
**Dunnock Cl** WD6 . . . . . . . 170 A5
**Dunny La** WD4 . . . . . . . . . 151 F7
**Dunraven Ave** LU1 . . . . . . .63 A8
**Dunsby Rd** LU3 . . . . . . . . . .45 A6
**Dunsley Pl** HP23 . . . . . . . 100 B3
**Dunsmore** WD19 . . . . . . . 175 D8
**Dunsmore Ct** WD23 . . . . . 168 D3
**Dunsmore Rd** LU1 . . . . . . .63 C6
**Dunsmore Way** WD23 . . . 168 D3
**Dunstable Cl** LU4 . . . . . . . .45 A1
**Dunstable Ct** LU4 . . . . . . . .44 F2
**Dunstable Pl** 5 LU1 . . . . . .63 D7
**Dunstable Rd**
Caddington LU1,LU6 . . . . . .62 C3
Dagnall HP4,LU6 . . . . . . . . .81 C7
Luton LU4 . . . . . . . . . . . . .44 D2
Luton,Bury Park LU1,LU4 . .45 B4
Redbourn AL3 . . . . . . . . . 106 A7
Studham LU6 . . . . . . . . . . .82 B6
**Dunster Cl** Barnet EN5 . . 171 D5
Harefield UB9 . . . . . . . . . 173 B2

**Dunster Ct** WD6 . . . . . . . 170 D6
**Dunster Rd** HP2 . . . . . . . . 105 B1
**Dunsters Mead** AL7 . . . . . 111 B4
**Dunston Hill** HP23 . . . . . . 100 A4
**Durban Rd E** WD18 . . . . . 167 A5
**Durban Rd W** WD18 . . . . 167 A5
**Durbar Rd** LU4 . . . . . . . . . .45 B1
**Durham Cl**
Sawbridgeworth CM21 . . . .97 C1
Stanstead Abbotts SG12 . . 115 B3
**Durham Ct** EN5 . . . . . . . . 171 F6
**Durham Ho** 14 WD6 . . . . . 170 A7
**Durham Rd**
Borehamwood WD6 . . . . . 170 C6
Luton LU2 . . . . . . . . . . . . .64 A7
Stevenage SG1 . . . . . . . . . .37 A1
**Durley Gdns** LU1 . . . . . . . .63 D5
**Durrant Ct** HA3 . . . . . . . . 176 E2
**Durrants Dr** WD3 . . . . . . . 166 C5
**Durrants Hill Rd** HP3 . . . 138 D8
**Durrants La** HP4 . . . . . . . 121 F5
**Durrants Rd** HP4 . . . . . . . 121 F5
**Dury Rd** EN5 . . . . . . . . . . 171 F7
**Duxford Cl** LU3 . . . . . . . . . .45 B7
**Duxons Turn** HP2 . . . . . . 125 B4
**Dwight Rd** WD18 . . . . . . . 166 D2
**Dyer Ct** EN3 . . . . . . . . . . . 163 A2
**Dyers Ct** CM23 . . . . . . . . . .76 C5
**Dyes La** SG4 . . . . . . . . . . . .49 F3
**Dyke La** AL4 . . . . . . . . . . . 108 E7
**Dylan Cl** WD6 . . . . . . . . . . 169 D2
**Dymoke Gn** AL4 . . . . . . . . 128 A7
**Dymokes Way** EN11 . . . . 115 A1
**Dyrham La** EN5 . . . . . . . . 158 A3
**Dyson Ct** WD17 . . . . . . . . 167 C5
**Dysons Cl** EN8 . . . . . . . . . 162 D6

## E

**Eagle Centre Way** LU4 . . .44 B7
**Eagle Cl** LU4 . . . . . . . . . . . .44 A4
**Eagle Ct** Baldock SG7 . . . . .12 E1
Hertford SG13 . . . . . . . . . 114 B7
**Eagle Way** AL10 . . . . . . . . 130 A3
**Ealing Cl** WD6 . . . . . . . . . 170 D8
**Earl St** WD17 . . . . . . . . . . 167 C6
**Earls Cl** CM23 . . . . . . . . . . .76 D6
**Earls Hill Gdns** SG8 . . . . . . .7 C6
**Earls La** EN6 . . . . . . . . . . 157 F6
**Earls Meade** LU2 . . . . . . . .45 D1
**Earlsmead** SG6 . . . . . . . . . .22 F3
**Easington Rd** SG8 . . . . . . . .71 E7
**Easingwold Gdns** LU1 . . . .62 F8
**East Burrowfield** AL7 . . . 110 D4
**East Cl**
Chiswell Green AL2 . . . . . 141 B6
Hitchin SG4 . . . . . . . . . . . .22 B1
Stevenage SG1 . . . . . . . . . .50 F5
**East Comm**
Harpenden AL5 . . . . . . . . 107 C7
Redbourn AL3 . . . . . . . . . 106 A4
**East Dr** Moor Park WD1 . . 174 E8
Sawbridgeworth CM21 . . . .97 E1
St Albans AL4 . . . . . . . . . 128 F4
Watford WD25 . . . . . . . . . 154 B3
**East End Way** HA5 . . . . . . 175 F1
**East Flint** HP1 . . . . . . . . . 123 F4
**East Gate** CM20 . . . . . . . . 117 D1
**East Gn** HP3 . . . . . . . . . . . 139 A6
**East Hertfordshire Sec Ctr**
**(PRU)** EN8 . . . . . . . . . . 162 D5
**East Hill** SG5 . . . . . . . . . . .45 B6
**East La**
Abbots Langley WD5 . . . . 140 A2
Wheathampstead AL4 . . . . .87 D1
**East Lodge La** EN2 . . . . . . 160 E4
**East Mead** AL7 . . . . . . . . . 111 B3
**East Mimms** 4 HP2 . . . . . 124 E4
**East Mount** AL4 . . . . . . . . .87 D1
**East Pk** Harlow CM17 . . . . 118 C3
Sawbridgeworth CM21 . . . .97 E1
**East Rd**
Bishop's Stortford CM23 . . .77 B7
Enfield EN3 . . . . . . . . . . . 162 C1
Harlow CM20 . . . . . . . . . . 118 B4
**East Reach** SG2 . . . . . . . . .51 A4
**East Ridgeway** EN6 . . . . . 146 E3
**East Riding** AL6 . . . . . . . . .90 D5
**East St**
Hemel Hempstead HP2 . . . 124 D3
Lilley SG12 . . . . . . . . . . . .32 D2
Ware SG12 . . . . . . . . . . . .93 D1
**East View** Barnet EN5 . . . 171 F6
Essendon AL9 . . . . . . . . . 131 F6
St Ippolyts SG4 . . . . . . . . .35 C2
**East Wlk** CM20 . . . . . . . . . 117 D1
**Eastbourne Ave** SG1 . . . . .50 A6
**Eastbrook Prim Sch**
HP2 . . . . . . . . . . . . . . . . 125 A8
**Eastbrook Rd** EN9 . . . . . . 163 E6
**Eastbrook Way** HP2 . . . . . 124 E3
**Eastbury Ave** HA6 . . . . . . 174 F5
**Eastbury Ct**
St Albans AL1 . . . . . . . . . 127 F4
Watford WD19 . . . . . . . . . 167 C2
**Eastbury Farm Jun Mix Inf**
**Sch** HA6 . . . . . . . . . . . 174 F5
**Eastbury Pl** HA6 . . . . . . . 174 F5
**Eastbury Rd**
Northwood HA6 . . . . . . . . 174 E4
Watford WD19 . . . . . . . . . 167 C3
**Eastcheap** SG6 . . . . . . . . . .22 F6
**Eastcote Dr** AL5 . . . . . . . . 107 D6
**Eastcott Cl** LU2 . . . . . . . . . .46 D1
**Eastend Cotts** CM19 . . . . 116 D1
**Eastern Ave**
Cheshunt EN8 . . . . . . . . . 162 F6

**Eastern Ave** *continued*
Lower Stondon SG16 . . . . . .10 C3
**Eastern Way** SG6 . . . . . . . .12 A1
**Eastfield Ave** WD24 . . . . 167 D8
**Eastfield Cl** LU2 . . . . . . . . .46 C4
**Eastfield Ct** AL4 . . . . . . . . 128 D6
**Eastfield Prim Sch** EN3 . 162 D1
**Eastfield Rd**
Cheshunt EN8 . . . . . . . . . 162 F7
Enfield EN3 . . . . . . . . . . . 162 D1
Royston SG8 . . . . . . . . . . . .7 E6
**Eastgate** SG1 . . . . . . . . . . .50 D5
**Eastglade** HA6 . . . . . . . . . 174 F5
**Easthall Cotts** SG4 . . . . . . .67 C8
**Easthall Ho** SG1 . . . . . . . . .36 C1
**Eastham Ct** EN5 . . . . . . . 171 F4
**Eastholm** SG6 . . . . . . . . . . .23 A8
**Eastholm Gn** SG6 . . . . . . . .23 A8
**Eastlea Ave** WD25 . . . . . . 154 E2
**Eastman Way** HP2 . . . . . . 125 A6
**Eastmoor Ct** AL5 . . . . . . . 107 C6
**Eastmoor Pk** AL5 . . . . . . . 107 C6
**Eastnor** HP3 . . . . . . . . . . . 137 A3
**Easton Gdns** WD6 . . . . . . 170 D5
**Eastor** AL7 . . . . . . . . . . . . . .90 A1
**Eastwick Cres** WD3 . . . . . 172 F8
**Eastwick Hall La** CM20 . . 117 A5
**Eastwick Rd**
Eastwick CM20 . . . . . . . . 117 B4
Gilston CM20 . . . . . . . . . . 117 E6
**Eastwick Row** HP2 . . . . . . 125 A2
**Eastwood Cl** HP2 . . . . . . . 125 A4
**Eaton Gate** HA6 . . . . . . . . 174 C4
**Eaton Green Ct** LU2 . . . . . .64 C8
**Eaton Green Rd** LU2 . . . . . .64 C8
**Eaton Ho** 5 CM23 . . . . . . . .77 B8
**Eaton Pl** LU2 . . . . . . . . . . . .46 D1
**Eaton Rd**
Hemel Hempstead HP2 . . . 125 B6
St Albans AL1 . . . . . . . . . 128 B3
**Eaton Valley Rd** LU2 . . . . . .64 B8
**Ebberns Rd** HP3 . . . . . . . . 138 E8
**Ebenezer St** 7 LU1 . . . . . . .63 D6
**Ebury App** WD3 . . . . . . . . 165 D1
**Ebury Cl** HA6 . . . . . . . . . . 174 C5
**Ebury Ct** WD3 . . . . . . . . . 165 D1
**Ebury Rd**
Rickmansworth WD3 . . . . 165 D1
Watford WD17 . . . . . . . . . 167 C5
**Ebury Rdbt** WD3 . . . . . . . 165 D1
**Echo Hill** SG8 . . . . . . . . . . . .7 C5
**Eddy St** HP4 . . . . . . . . . . . 122 A5
**Eden Cl** EN3 . . . . . . . . . . . 163 A1
**Edenhall Cl** HP2 . . . . . . . . 125 D2
**Edens Ct** CM23 . . . . . . . . . .77 B7
**Edens Mount** CM21 . . . . . . .97 F4
**Edenvale** EN7 . . . . . . . . . . 148 B2
**Edgars Ct** AL7 . . . . . . . . . 110 E5
**Edgbaston Dr** WD7 . . . . . 156 F2
**Edgbaston Rd** WD19 . . . . 175 B7
**Edgcott Cl** LU3 . . . . . . . . . .31 B1
**Edgecote Cl** LU1 . . . . . . . . .62 E3
**Edgehill Gdns** LU3 . . . . . . .44 C8
**Edgeworth Cl** SG2 . . . . . . .51 C1
**Edgware Way** HA8 . . . . . . 169 D1
**Edgwarebury La** WD6,
HA8 . . . . . . . . . . . . . . . 169 F1
**Edinburgh Ave** WD3 . . . . 165 A2
**Edinburgh Cres** EN8 . . . . 162 E6
**Edinburgh Dr** WD5 . . . . . 154 A7
**Edinburgh Gdns** CM23 . . . .76 E6
**Edinburgh Pl** CM20 . . . . . 118 A4
**Edinburgh Sq** SG8 . . . . . . . .2 A6
**Edinburgh Way** CM20 . . . 117 E3
**Edison Cl** AL4 . . . . . . . . . . 128 C2
**Edison Rd** SG2 . . . . . . . . . .51 B6
**Edkins Cl** LU2 . . . . . . . . . . .45 E5
**Edlyn Cl** HP4 . . . . . . . . . . 121 F5
**Edmonds Dr** SG2 . . . . . . . .51 D4
**Edmund Beaufort Dr**
AL3 . . . . . . . . . . . . . . . . 127 E5
**Edmund Mews** WD4 . . . . . 139 A2
**Edmunds Rd** SG14 . . . . . . 112 F7
**Edridge Cl** WD23 . . . . . . . 168 C4
**Edulf Rd** WD6 . . . . . . . . . . 170 C7
**Edward Amey Cl** WD25 . . 154 C3
**Edward Cl**
Abbots Langley WD5 . . . . 153 F7
St Albans AL1 . . . . . . . . . 127 F2
**Edward Cotts** SG11 . . . . . . .54 C3
**Edward Ct**
Hemel Hempstead HP3 . . . 138 D7
Waltham Abbey EN9 . . . . . 163 F6
**Edward St** LU2 . . . . . . . . . .45 F1
**Edwards Ho** 6 SG1 . . . . . . .50 E6
**Edwick Ct** EN8 . . . . . . . . . 148 D2
**Edwin Ware Ct** 1 HA5 . . . 175 C1
**Edwinstree CE Mid Sch**
SG9 . . . . . . . . . . . . . . . . .40 D8
**Edwy Cl** EN5 . . . . . . . . . . 171 D3
**Egdon Dr** LU2 . . . . . . . . . . .45 D6
**Egerton Rd** HP4 . . . . . . . . 122 B6
**Egerton-Rothesay Sch**
HP4 . . . . . . . . . . . . . . . . 121 E4
**Egg Farm La** WD4 . . . . . . 139 B1
**Egglesfield Cl** HP4 . . . . . . 121 E6
**Eggleton Dr** HP23 . . . . . . 100 A4
**Eight Acres** HP23 . . . . . . . 100 A4
**Eighth Ave** LU3 . . . . . . . . .44 D7
**Eisenberg Cl** SG7 . . . . . . . .13 B1
**Elaine Gdns** LU1 . . . . . . . .63 A1
**Elbow La**
Hertford Heath SG13 . . . . 134 B7
Stevenage SG2 . . . . . . . . . .51 B1
**Eldefield** SG6 . . . . . . . . . . .22 D7
**Elder Ct** WD23 . . . . . . . . . 176 E8
**Elder Rd** SG12 . . . . . . . . . .93 F3

**Elder Way** SG1 . . . . . . . . . .50 E3
**Elderbeck Cl** EN7 . . . . . . . 148 A2
**Elderberry Cl** LU2 . . . . . . .46 B4
**Elderberry Dr** SG4 . . . . . . .35 A4
**Elderberry Way** WD25 . . 154 B4
**Elderfield** CM17 . . . . . . . . 118 D4
**Eldon Ave** WD6 . . . . . . . . 170 B7
**Eldon Rd**
Hoddesdon EN11 . . . . . . . 135 D4
Luton LU4 . . . . . . . . . . . . .44 C1
**Eldrig Turn** HP2 . . . . . . . . 124 E7
**Eleanor Ave** AL3 . . . . . . . 127 D5
**Eleanor Cross Rd** EN8 . . 162 F5
**Eleanor Gdns** EN5 . . . . . . 171 D4
**Eleanor Rd** Cheshunt EN8 162 E6
Hertford SG14 . . . . . . . . . 113 C7
**Eleanor Way** EN8 . . . . . . 162 F5
**Electric Ave** EN3 . . . . . . . 162 F3
**Element Ho** EN3 . . . . . . . . 162 F3
**Eleni Ho** EN8 . . . . . . . . . . 162 D6
**Elfrida Rd** WD18 . . . . . . . 167 C4
**Elgar Cl** WD6 . . . . . . . . . . 169 D2
**Elgar Path** LU2 . . . . . . . . . .63 E8
**Elgin Dr** HA6 . . . . . . . . . . 174 E3
**Elgin Ho** SG4 . . . . . . . . . . .35 A6
**Elgin Rd** Cheshunt EN8 . . 148 C1
Hoddesdon EN10 . . . . . . . 148 C1
**Elgood Ave** HA6 . . . . . . . . 175 A3
**Eliot Rd** Royston SG8 . . . . . .7 D8
Stevenage SG2 . . . . . . . . . .51 C6
**Elizabeth Cl** Barnet EN5 . 171 D6
Lower Nazeing EN9 . . . . . 149 D8
Welwyn Garden City AL7 . 111 C6
**Elizabeth Ct** 10 Luton LU1 63 D6
St Albans AL4 . . . . . . . . . 128 D6
Watford WD17 . . . . . . . . . 153 F1
**Elizabeth Dr** HP23 . . . . . . 100 B6
**Elizabeth Ho**
7 Watford WD24 . . . . . . 167 C7
Welwyn Garden City AL7 . 111 C6
**Elizabeth Rd** CM23 . . . . . . .76 E5
**Elizabeth St** LU1 . . . . . . . .63 D6
**Elizabeth Way** CM20 . . . . 117 B2
**Ellen Cl** HP2 . . . . . . . . . . . 124 F4
**Ellenborough Cl** CM23 . . .76 D5
**Ellenbrook Cl** WD24 . . . . 167 C8
**Ellenbrook Cres** AL10 . . . 129 C8
**Ellenbrook La** AL10 . . . . . 129 C8
**Ellenhall Cl** LU3 . . . . . . . . .45 C1
**Ellerdine Cl** LU3 . . . . . . . . .45 B4
**Ellesborough Cl** WD19 . . 175 C5
**Ellesfield** AL6 . . . . . . . . . . .89 B5
**Ellesmere Gr** EN5 . . . . . . 171 F4
**Ellesmere Rd** HP4 . . . . . . 122 D4
**Ellice** SG6 . . . . . . . . . . . . . .23 B4
**Ellingham Cl** HP2 . . . . . . . 125 A5
**Ellingham Rd** HP2 . . . . . . 124 F4
**Elliott Cl** AL7 . . . . . . . . . . 110 D3
**Elliott Ct** CM23 . . . . . . . . . .77 A8
**Ellis Ave** SG1 . . . . . . . . . . .50 E8
**Ellis Fields** AL3 . . . . . . . . 127 E6
**Elliswick Rd** AL5 . . . . . . . .86 B2
**Ells Ct** LU2 . . . . . . . . . . . . .45 F1
**Ellwood Gdns** WD25 . . . . 154 C5
**Ellwood Terr** WD19 . . . . . 164 D4
**Elm Ave** Caddington LU1 . .62 E3
Watford WD19 . . . . . . . . . 167 E2
**Elm Cl** EN9 . . . . . . . . . . . . 163 D5
**Elm Cotts** Holdbrook EN9 163 D1
Meesden SG9 . . . . . . . . . . .29 F6
**Elm Dr** Cheshunt EN8 . . . 148 E3
Hatfield AL10 . . . . . . . . . 130 A4
St Albans AL4 . . . . . . . . . 128 C3
**Elm Gdns** Enfield EN2 . . . 161 D1
Welwyn Garden City AL8 . 110 B6
**Elm Gn** HP1 . . . . . . . . . . . 123 E5
**Elm Gr** Berkhamsted HP4 122 C4
Bishop's Stortford CM23 . . .77 B7
Watford WD24 . . . . . . . . . 154 A2
**Elm Hatch** HA5 . . . . . . . . 175 F3
**Elm Park Rd** HA5 . . . . . . . 175 D1
**Elm Pk** SG7 . . . . . . . . . . . .23 F8
**Elm Rd** Barnet EN5 . . . . . 171 F5
Bishop's Stortford CM23 . . .76 F5
**Elm Terr** HA3 . . . . . . . . . . 176 D2
**Elm Tree Wlk**
Chorleywood WD3 . . . . . . 164 F5
Tring HP23 . . . . . . . . . . . 100 A5
**Elm Way** WD3 . . . . . . . . . 165 B1
**Elm Wlk** Radlett WD7 . . . 155 F3
Royston SG8 . . . . . . . . . . . .7 F7
Stevenage SG2 . . . . . . . . . .51 B3
**Elmbank Ave** EN5 . . . . . . 171 C5
**Elmbridge** CM17 . . . . . . . 118 F3
**Elmbrook Dr** CM23 . . . . . . .76 E3
**Elmcote** HA5 . . . . . . . . . . 175 D1
**Elmcote Way** WD3 . . . . . . 165 F3
**Elmfield Cl** EN6 . . . . . . . . 158 E6
**Elmfield Ct** LU2 . . . . . . . . .46 A1
**Elmfield Rd** EN6 . . . . . . . 158 E6
**Elmhurst** EN10 . . . . . . . . . 135 A4
**Elmhurst Cl** WD23 . . . . . . 167 E5
**Elmhurst Rd** EN3 . . . . . . . 162 C2
**Elmoor Ave** AL6 . . . . . . . . .89 B5
**Elmoor Cl** AL6 . . . . . . . . . .89 B4
**Elmore Rd** Enfield EN3 . . 162 D1
Luton LU2 . . . . . . . . . . . . .46 A1
**Elmroyd Ave** EN6 . . . . . . 158 F6
**Elmroyd Cl** EN6 . . . . . . . . 158 F6
**Elms Cl** SG4 . . . . . . . . . . . .35 E3
**Elms Rd** Harrow HA3 . . . . 176 E3
Ware SG12 . . . . . . . . . . . .94 A2
**Elms The** Codicote SG4 . . .67 C8
Hertford SG13 . . . . . . . . . 114 A6
Stevenage SG2 . . . . . . . . . .69 B8
**Elmscroft Gdns** EN6 . . . . 158 F7
**Elmside** LU6 . . . . . . . . . . . .82 E8
**Elmside Wlk** SG5 . . . . . . . .34 F7

**Dri – Ess** **189**

**Elmswell Ct** SG14 . . . . . . 112 F7
**Elmtree Ave** LU2 . . . . . . . .46 E3
**Elmwood**
Sawbridgeworth CM21 . . . .97 F1
Welwyn Garden City AL8 . 110 B5
**Elmwood Ave** Baldock SG7 23 F7
Borehamwood WD6 . . . . . 170 B5
**Elmwood Cres** LU2 . . . . . . .45 E3
**Elmwood Ct** SG7 . . . . . . . . .23 F8
**Elppin Ct** EN10 . . . . . . . . . 134 F3
**Elsinge Rd** EN1 . . . . . . . . 162 C3
**Elstree & Borehamwood Sta**
WD6 . . . . . . . . . . . . . . . 170 A5
**Elstree Distribution Pk**
WD6 . . . . . . . . . . . . . . . 170 C6
**Elstree Hill N** WD6 . . . . . 169 D4
**Elstree Hill S** WD6 . . . . . 169 D2
**Elstree Pk** WD6 . . . . . . . . 170 D3
**Elstree Rd** Bushey WD23 . 168 E3
Elstree WD6 . . . . . . . . . . 169 A3
Hemel Hempstead HP2 . . . 105 A1
**Elstree Way** WD6 . . . . . . . 170 C7
**Elton Ave** EN5 . . . . . . . . . 171 F4
**Elton Ct** SG14 . . . . . . . . . . 113 C7
**Elton Pk** WD17 . . . . . . . . . 167 B7
**Elton Rd** SG14 . . . . . . . . . 113 C7
**Elton Way** WD25 . . . . . . . 168 B7
**Elvaston Ct** EN5 . . . . . . . . 171 C4
**Elveden Cl** LU2 . . . . . . . . . .45 E6
**Elvington Gdns** LU3 . . . . . .31 B1
**Ely Cl** Hatfield AL10 . . . . . 129 F6
Stevenage SG2 . . . . . . . . . .51 D7
**Ely Gdns** WD6 . . . . . . . . . 170 D4
**Ely Rd** AL1 . . . . . . . . . . . . 128 B2
**Ely Way** LU4 . . . . . . . . . . . .44 D4
**Embleton Rd** WD19 . . . . . 175 A7
**Emerald Ct** WD6 . . . . . . . 156 F3
**Emerald Rd** LU4 . . . . . . . . .44 A3
**Emerton Ct** HP4 . . . . . . . . 121 E7
**Emerton Garth** HP4 . . . . . 121 E7
**Emma Rothschild Ct**
HP23 . . . . . . . . . . . . . . . 100 A5
**Emma's Cres** LU2 . . . . . . 115 B4
**Emmanuel Lodge** EN8 . . 148 C1
**Emmanuel Rd** HA6 . . . . . . 174 F3
**Emmer Gn** LU2 . . . . . . . . . .46 F2
**Emmitt Cl** WD7 . . . . . . . . 156 E6
**Emperor Cl** HP4 . . . . . . . . 121 F7
**Emperors Gate** SG2 . . . . . .51 D8
**Empire Ctr** WD24 . . . . . . 167 C8
**Empire Pl** WD18 . . . . . . . 166 F5
**Empress Rd** LU3 . . . . . . . . .44 E4
**Endeavour Rd** EN8 . . . . . 148 E4
**Enderby Rd** LU3 . . . . . . . . .45 C6
**Enderley Cl** HA3 . . . . . . . 176 E2
**Enderley Rd** HA3 . . . . . . . 176 E2
**Endersby Rd** EN5 . . . . . . 171 C4
**Endymion Ct** AL10 . . . . . . 130 C6
**Endymion Mews** AL10 . . . 130 C6
**Endymion Rd** AL10 . . . . . 130 C6
**Enfield Cty Lower Sch**
EN2 . . . . . . . . . . . . . . . . 161 E1
**Enfield Lock Sta** EN3 . . . 162 E2
**Englefield** LU2 . . . . . . . . . .45 F3
**Englehurst** AL5 . . . . . . . . .86 D1
**Enid Cl** AL2 . . . . . . . . . . . 154 F8
**Enjakes Cl** SG2 . . . . . . . . . .69 B7
**Ennerdale Cl** AL1 . . . . . . 128 B1
**Ennis Cl** AL5 . . . . . . . . . . 107 D6
**Ennismore Cl** SG6 . . . . . . .23 C3
**Ennismore Gn** LU2 . . . . . . .46 F1
**Enslow Cl** LU2 . . . . . . . . . .62 D3
**Enterprise Ctr** Luton LU2 .64 B6
**1** Luton,High Town LU2 . .63 F8
**Enterprise Ctr The**
Potters Bar EN6 . . . . . . . 144 E1
Stevenage SG1 . . . . . . . . . .50 B7
**Enterprise Pk** SG4 . . . . . . .66 C2
**Enterprise Way**
Hemel Hempstead HP2 . . . 125 C5
Luton LU3 . . . . . . . . . . . . .45 B8
**Enville Ho** 8 WD19 . . . . . 175 C7
**Epping Forest District Mus**★
EN9 . . . . . . . . . . . . . . . . 163 F6
**Epping Gn** HP2 . . . . . . . . . 125 B8
**Epping Way** LU3 . . . . . . . . .44 C8
**Epsom Ct** WD3 . . . . . . . . . 165 B1
**Ereswell Rd** LU3 . . . . . . . . .45 A7
**Erin Cl** LU4 . . . . . . . . . . . . .45 A2
**Erin Ct** LU4 . . . . . . . . . . . . .45 A2
**Ermine Cl** Cheshunt EN7 . 162 B8
Royston SG8 . . . . . . . . . . . .7 D8
St Albans AL3 . . . . . . . . . 127 A2
**Ermine Ct** SG9 . . . . . . . . . .40 E8
**Ermine Pl** 8 LU2 . . . . . . . .45 D1
**Ermine Point Bsns Pk**
SG12 . . . . . . . . . . . . . . . .93 B3
**Ermine St** Buckland SG9 . .27 D6
Thundridge SG12 . . . . . . . .93 D7
**Erskine Ho** 5 WD19 . . . . 175 D7
**Escarpment Ave** HP4,LU6 81 D8
**Escot Way** EN5 . . . . . . . . 171 C4
**Esdaile La** EN11 . . . . . . . 135 A4
**Eskdale**
London Colney AL2 . . . . . 142 F4
Luton LU4 . . . . . . . . . . . . .44 C5
**Eskdale Ct** 3 HP2 . . . . . . 124 E7
**Essendon CE Prim Sch**
AL9 . . . . . . . . . . . . . . . . 131 F6
**Essendon Gdns** AL7 . . . . . 110 F6
**Essendon Hill** AL9 . . . . . . 131 F7
**Essex Cl** LU4 . . . . . . . . . . . .63 E6
**Essex Ct** AL3 . . . . . . . . . . 163 E6
**Essex La** WD4 . . . . . . . . . 153 D6
**Essex Mead** HP2 . . . . . . . 105 A1

**Essex Rd**
Borehamwood WD6 ......**170** A6
Hoddesdon EN11 ......**135** C6
Stevenage SG1 .........**50** B8
Watford WD17 .........**167** A7
Essex St AL1 .........**127** E4
Essex Yd HP22 .........**60** C3
Estcourt Rd WD17 .....**167** C6
Estfeld Cl 4 EN11 ....**115** B1
Ethelred Cl AL7 ......**110** F5
Etna Rd AL3 ..........**127** D4
Eton Ho 9 WD24 ......**167** C7
Etonbury Mid Sch SG15 ..**11** C7
Europa Rd HP2 ........**124** F6
Euston Ave WD18 .....**166** F4
Evan's Cl WD3 ........**166** A4
Evans Ave WD25 ......**153** F4
Evans Cl SG8 ............**7** D7
Evans Gr AL4 .........**128** C7
Evans Way HP2 .......**100** B4
Evans Wharf HP3 .....**138** C7
Evedon Cl LU3 .........**44** F6
Evelyn Dr HA5 .......**175** D3
Evelyn Rd LU5 .........**44** A1
Evelyn Sharp Ho HP2 ...**125** A2
Evensyde WD18 .......**166** D3
Everard Cl AL1 .......**127** D1
Everest Cl SG15 .......**11** B5
Everest Gdns CM23 .....**76** E6
Everest Way HP2 ......**125** A4
Everett Cl Bushey WD23 **168** E1
Hammond Street EN7 ..**147** C6
Everett Ct WD7 .......**156** A5
Evergreen Cl SG3 ......**69** A2
Evergreen Rd SG12 .....**93** F3
Evergreen Way LU3 .....**45** A8
Evergreen Wlk 2 HP3 **124** D1
Everlasting La AL3 ....**127** C5
Eversden Ct HP2 .....**105** B1
Eversley Lodge EN11 ..**135** A6
Evron Pl 4 SG14 ......**113** D6
Exchange Bldgs 7 EN5 **171** C4
**Exchange Rd**
Stevenage SG1 .........**50** F5
Watford WD18 ........**167** B5
**Executive Pk Ind Est**
AL1 ..................**128** B3
Exeter Cl Stevenage SG1 ..**37** B2
Watford WD24 ........**167** C7
Exeter Ho 7 WD4 .....**170** A7
Exhims Mews HP4 .....**121** E6
Explorer Dr WD18 .....**166** F3
Extension Rd SG13 .....**113** F6
Exton Ave LU2 .........**46** A1
Eynsford Ct SG4 .......**34** F6
Eynsford Rd LU4 ......**44** D3

**F**

Faggots Cl WD7 ......**156** C4
Faints Cl EN7 .......**147** F2
Fair Cl WD23 ........**168** B2
Fair Oak Ct LU2 .......**45** F3
Fair Oak Dr LU2 .......**45** F3
Fair View EN6 .......**145** B2
Fairacre HP3 ........**138** F7
Fairacre Ct 2 HA6 ...**174** E4
Fairacres Cl WD6 .....**158** F6
Fairburn Rd WD6 .....**170** A4
Faircross Ho 8 WD17 **167** B6
Faircross Way AL1 ....**128** A5
**Fairfield** Buntingford SG9 **40** F6
Northwood HA6 .......**175** A1
Pinner HA6 ..........**175** A1
Fairfield Ave WD19 ...**175** D7
**Fairfield Cl**
Harpenden AL5 ........**86** D1
Hatfield AL10 ........**130** C8
Northwood HA6 ......**174** B4
Radlett WD7 ........**155** E2
Fairfield Dr EN10 ....**148** F7
Fairfield Jun Sch WD7 **155** E3
Fairfield Rd EN11 ....**135** A8
**Fairfield Way** Hitchin SG4 **35** D8
Stevenage SG1 ........**37** C3
Fairfield Wlk 6 EN8 **148** E3
**Fairfields Prim Sch**
EN7 .................**148** A4
Fairfolds WD25 ......**154** E4
Fairford Ave LU2 ......**45** E4
Fairgreen Rd LU1 .....**62** F3
Fairhaven AL2 .......**141** D4
Fairhill HP3 .........**138** F7
Fairlands Lo WD6 ....**170** A6
Fairlands Lodge 6
WD6 .................**170** A6
Fairlands Prim Sch SG1 **50** D6
Fairlands Way SG1 ....**51** A7
**Fairlawns** Pinner HA5 **175** D1
Watford WD17 ........**153** F1
Fairley Way EN7 .....**148** B3
Fairmead Ave AL5 ....**107** C8
Fairoaks Gr EN3 .....**162** D2
Fairseat Cl WD23 ....**176** E8
Fairshot Ct AL4 ......**108** D2
Fairthorn Cl HP23 .....**99** E3
Fairview Dr WD17 ....**153** E3
Fairview Est EN11 ....**135** C4
Fairview Rd SG1 ......**50** B7
**Fairway**
Bishop's Stortford CM23 ..**77** C6

**Fairway** continued
Hemel Hempstead HP3 ..**138** F7
Sawbridgeworth CM21 ...**97** F2
Ware SG12 ...........**114** C8
Fairway Ave WD6 .....**170** B7
**Fairway Cl**
Chiswell Green AL2 ...**141** C4
Harpenden AL5 ......**107** A5
Fairway Ct HP3 ......**138** F7
Fairway Ho WD6 .....**170** B6
**Fairway The**
Abbots Langley WD5 ..**153** D7
Moor Park HA6 ......**174** E6
**Fairways** Cheshunt EN8 **148** D5
Waltham Abbey EN9 ..**163** C6
Faithfield WD19 .....**167** E3
**Falcon Cl** Hatfield AL10 **130** A3
Northwood HA6 ......**174** B4
Sawbridgeworth CM21 ..**97** C1
Stevenage SG2 .......**51** D2
Falcon Ct 2 SG12 ....**93** C3
Falcon Ridge HP4 ...**122** C3
**Falcon Way**
Watford WD25 .......**154** E5
Welwyn Garden City AL7 **110** E8
Falconer Rd WD23 ....**168** A3
Falconer Sch WD23 ...**168** A4
Falconer St CM23 .....**76** C5
Falconers Field AL5 ...**85** C3
Falconers Pk CM21 ....**97** D1
Falconers Rd LU2 .....**46** B1
Falkirk Gdns WD19 ...**175** D5
Falkland Rd EN5 .....**171** E7
Fallow End AL6 .......**68** D1
Fallow Rise SG13 ....**113** A6
**Fallowfield**
Stevenage SG2 .......**51** C3
Welwyn Garden City AL7 **89** F1
Fallowfield Cl WD3 ...**173** C2
Fallowfield Wlk HP1 ..**124** A6
Fallows Gn AL5 .......**86** B3
Falmouth Cl AL3 .....**127** D5
Falstaff Gdns AL1 ...**141** C8
Falstone Gn LU2 ......**46** E1
Fanhams Hall Rd SG12 **93** F3
Fanhams Rd SG12 .....**93** E2
Fanshaw Ct SG14 ....**113** C7
Fanshawe Cres SG12 ..**93** C2
Fanshawe St SG14 ...**113** B7
Fanshaws La SG13 ...**133** C5
Fantail La HP23 .......**99** F4
Far End AL10 ........**130** B2
Faraday Cl Luton LU4 ..**44** C1
Watford WD18 .......**166** D3
Faraday Rd SG2 ......**51** B6
Faringdon Rd LU4 .....**44** C3
Faringford Cl EN6 ...**159** D8
Farland Rd HP2 .....**125** B3
Farley Cl LU1 .........**63** C5
Farley Farm Rd LU1 ..**63** B5
Farley Hill LU1 ......**63** C5
Farley Jun Sch LU1 ...**63** C6
Farley Lodge LU1 ....**63** D5
**Farm Ave** AL5 ......**85** D4
**Farm Cl** Barnet EN5 **171** C4
Borehamwood WD6 ...**156** E1
Cheshunt EN8 ........**148** C1
Cuffley EN6 ........**146** E4
Harpenden AL5 .......**85** D4
Hertford SG14 ......**113** A6
Letchworth SG6 .....**12** A1
London Colney WD7 ..**142** E1
Roydon CM19 ........**116** B1
Shenleybury WD7 ...**156** E8
Stevenage SG1 ......**50** E4
Welwyn Garden City AL8 **110** C6
Farm Cotts SG12 ....**93** D5
Farm Cres AL2 ......**142** A4
Farm End AL6 .......**174** B2
Farm Field WD17 ...**153** E1
Farm Gn LU1 .........**63** C5
Farm Hill Rd EN9 ...**163** D6
Farm La Hoddesdon EN11 **135** C8
Rickmansworth WD3 ..**165** C6
Standon SG11 .......**73** A8
Farm Pl HP4 .......**121** F5
**Farm Rd**
Little Chalfont WD3 ...**164** A5
Northwood HA6 .....**174** C5
Slip End LU1 .......**85** B7
St Albans AL1 ......**127** E6
**Farm Way** Bushey WD23 **168** B5
Moor Park HA6 .....**174** F6
Farmbrook LU2 ......**45** D7
Farmers Cl WD25 ...**154** B6
Farmery Ct HP4 ....**122** B4
**Farmhouse Cl** EN10 **148** F6
Farmhouse La HP2 ...**125** A5
Farmhouse The HP2 **125** A5
Farmstead Rd HA3 ..**176** D1
Farne Ho 5 WD18 ..**166** F3
**Farnham CE Prim Sch**
CM23 ................**58** D6
**Farnham Cl**
Bovingdon HP3 .....**137** A3
Sawbridgeworth CM21 **97** C1
Farnham Gn CM23 ...**58** B7
Farnley Gr LU2 ......**64** A7
Farquhar St SG14 ...**113** C7
Farr's La LU2 .......**65** B1
Farraline Rd WD18 ..**167** B5
Farrant Way WD6 ...**169** E8
Farriday Cl AL3 .....**127** E5
Farrier Ct SG8 ........**7** C7
Farriers Cl Baldock SG7 **12** E1
Bovingdon HP3 .....**137** B3

**Farriers Cl** continued
Codicote SG4 ........**67** F1
Farriers End EN10 ...**148** F5
Farriers Way WD6 ...**170** D4
Farringford Cl AL2 ..**141** B5
Farrington Cotts EN5 **171** F6
Farrington Pl HA6 ...**174** F6
Farrow Cl LU3 .......**31** C1
Farthing Cl WD18 ...**167** C4
Farthing Dr SG6 ......**23** C3
Farthings The HP1 ..**124** B3
Faulkner Ct AL1 ....**127** E5
Faverolle Gn EN8 ...**148** D3
Faversham HP23 ....**100** A4
**Fawbert & Barnard Inf Sch**
CM21 ................**97** C3
**Fawbert & Barnard Sch**
CM17 ................**118** C3
Fawcett Rd SG2 .....**51** B8
Fawkon Wlk EN11 ...**135** A6
Fawn Ct AL9 ........**130** C7
Fay Gn WD5 .........**153** D6
Fayerfield EN6 ......**159** D8
Fayland Cotts SG9 ...**41** E7
Feacey Down HP1 ...**124** B5
Fearney Mead WD3 .**165** A1
Fearnhill Sch SG6 ....**22** C5
Fearnley Rd AL8 ....**110** C5
Fearnley St WD18 ...**167** B5
Feather Dell AL10 ...**130** A5
Featherbed La HP3 ..**138** B7
Featherston Rd SG2 .**51** C3
**Featherstone Gdns**
WD6 .................**170** C5
**Featherstone Wood Prim Sch**
SG2 ..................**51** C3
Federal Way WD24 ..**167** C8
Felbrigg Cl LU2 .....**46** F2
Felden Cl Pinner HA5 **175** E3
Watford WD25 ......**154** D5
Felden Dr HP3 ......**138** A7
Felden La HP3 ......**138** A7
Felden Lawns HP3 ..**138** A7
Felix Ave LU2 ......**46** A2
Fell Path WD6 .....**170** D4
Fellowes La AL4 ...**143** E8
Fellowes Way SG2 ..**51** A4
Fells Cl SG8 .........**34** F8
Felmersham Ct LU1 .**63** B7
Felmersham Rd LU1 .**63** A7
Felmongers CM20 ..**118** B2
Felstead Cl LU2 ....**45** F3
Felstead Rd EN8 ...**162** E7
Felstead Way LU2 ..**45** F3
**Felton Cl**
Borehamwood WD6 ..**156** E1
Cheshunt EN10 ....**148** F6
Luton LU2 .........**46** D1
Fen End SG1 ........**11** F8
Fennycroft Rd HP1 ..**124** A6
Fensom's Cl HP2 ...**124** D4
Fensomes Alley HP2 **124** D4
**Fenwick Cl** LU3 ...**45** B5
Fenwick Path WD6 **156** F1
Ferguson Gr EN8 ...**148** D2
Fermor Cres LU2 ...**46** C1
Fern Cl EN10 ......**148** F8
Fern Ct HP4 ......**122** B4
Fern Dells AL10 ...**129** F4
Fern Dr HP3 ......**124** C2
Fern Gr AL8 .......**89** D2
Fern Ho HA7 .....**176** F4
Fern Way WD25 ...**154** B4
**Ferndale**
7 Harpenden AL5 ..**86** A2
Much Hadham SG10 ..**74** F2
Ferndale Rd Enfield EN3 **162** E2
Luton LU1 .........**63** B7
Ferndene AL2 .....**154** F8
Ferndown HA6 ...**175** A1
Ferndown Cl HA5 .**175** A1
Ferndown Rd WD19 **175** C6
Fernecroft AL1 ...**141** D8
Ferney Rd EN7 ...**147** D5
Fernheath LU3 ....**31** A1
Fernhills WD4 ....**153** D6
Fernleigh Ct HA2 ..**176** B1
Fernleys AL4 ......**128** C5
Ferns Cl EN3 ......**162** E3
Fernville La HP2 ..**124** D3
Ferny Hill EN4 ...**159** F1
Ferrars Cl LU4 ....**44** B1
Ferrars Inf Sch LU4 **44** B3
Ferrars Jun Sch LU4 **44** B3
Ferrers La AL4 ...**108** B5
Ferrier Rd SG2 ...**51** C6
Ferryhills Cl WD19 **175** C7
Feryngs Cl CM17 ..**118** C4
Fesants Croft CM23 **118** B3
Fetherstone Cl EN6 **159** D7
**Fiddle Bridge La** AL10 **129** F6
**Fiddlebridge Ind Ctr**
AL10 ...............**129** F6
Fidler Pl WD23 ...**168** B3
**Field Cl** Harpenden AL5 **107** D7
St Albans AL4 .....**128** A7
Field Cres SG8 ......**7** F7
Field End EN5 ....**171** B5
Field End La Luton LU2 **46** C4
Watford WD19 ....**167** E2
Field Fare Gn LU4 ..**44** A5
Field Jun Sch WD18 **167** C4
Field La SG6 .......**22** F4
**Field Rd**
Hemel Hempstead HP2 **125** A3

**Field Rd** continued
Watford WD19 .....**167** E3
Field View Rd EN6 **159** A6
Field View Rise AL2 **140** E2
**Field Way** Bovingdon HP3 **137** A4
Hoddesdon EN11 ..**115** C2
Rickmansworth WD3 **165** B1
Field's Ct EN6 .....**159** D6
**Fielder Ctr (Univ of Herts)**
AL10 ...............**129** D8
Fielders Way WD7 **156** C6
**Fieldfare** Letchworth SG6 **11** C4
Stevenage SG2 .....**51** D3
Fieldfare Way SG8 ...**7** E8
Fieldfares AL2 ....**142** D4
Fieldgate Ho SG1 ..**50** F5
Fieldgate Rd LU4 ..**44** D2
Fieldings EN8 .....**148** F2
Fields End HP23 ...**100** A6
Fields End La HP1 **123** E5
**Fieldway**
Berkhamsted HP4 **122** A4
Stansted Abbotts SG12 **115** B4
Wigginton HP23 ...**100** D1
Fifth Ave Letchworth SG6 **23** C6
Watford WD25 ....**154** D5
**Fifth Avenue / Allende Ave**
CM20 ..............**117** C3
Figtree Hill HP2 ..**124** D4
Filey Cl SG1 .......**50** A7
Fillingham Way AL10 **129** C7
Filmer Rd LU4 ....**44** E4
Filton Ho 6 WD19 **175** D7
Finch Cl Hatfield AL10 **130** A3
Luton LU4 .........**44** A4
Finch Gn WD3 ....**164** F5
Finch La WD23 ...**168** A5
Finch Rd HP4 ....**122** A4
Finchdale HP1 ....**124** A3
Finche's End SG2 ..**52** B8
**Finches The**
Hertford SG13 ...**114** B6
Hitchin SG4 .......**35** A4
Finley Rd AL5 ....**86** D3
Finsbury Ct EN8 .**162** E5
Finsbury Rd LU4 .**44** D5
Finucane Rise WD23 **176** B3
Finway LU1 ......**63** A8
Finway Ct WD24 .**167** C8
Finway Rd HP2 ..**125** B7
Fir Cl SG2 .........**51** F1
Fir Tree Cl HP3 ..**125** B2
Fir Tree Ct WD6 **169** F5
Fir Tree Hill WD3 **153** A4
Firbank Dr WD19 **167** E2
Firbank Rd AL3 ..**127** F7
**Firbank Trad Est** LU1 **63** A8
**Fire Station Alley** EN5 **171** E7
Firecrest SG6 .....**11** C4
Firlands CM23 ....**76** E6
Firlands Ho CM23 **76** E6
Firs Cl Hatfield AL10 **130** B4
Hitchin SG5 .......**34** D8
Firs Dr AL4 ......**87** C5
Firs Jun Sch The CM23 **76** E6
Firs La EN6 .......**159** B6
**Firs The**
Hammond Street EN7 **147** C6
Harpenden AL5 ....**86** D2
St Albans AL1 ....**142** B7
Welwyn Garden City AL8 **89** C2
Wigginton HP23 ..**100** D1
Firs Wlk Northwood HA6 **174** D4
Tewin AL6 ........**90** E5
Firs Wood Cl EN6 **159** F7
First Ave WD25 ...**154** D4
**First Avenue / Mandela Ave**
CM20 ..............**117** C2
**First Garden City Heritage**
Mus ★ SG6 ........**23** A4
Firthesden Vinyard ★
HP4 .................**123** B8
Firway AL6 .......**89** F7
Firway Cl AL6 ....**89** F7
Firwood Ave AL4 .**128** C3
Fish Cl SG8 .........**7** C6
Fish Hill SG8 .......**7** C6
Fish St AL3 .......**106** B5
Fish Street Farm AL3 **106** B5
Fisher Cl Holdbrook EN3 **163** A2
Kings Langley WD4 **139** A2
Fisher Rd HA3 ....**176** F1
Fisher's Green Rd SG1 **50** B8
**Fisher's Ind Est** WD18 **167** C4
Fishermans Way EN11 **135** C4
**Fishers Cl** Holdbrook EN8 **163** A5
Standon SG11 .....**55** D3
Watford WD23 ....**167** E6
Fishers Gn SG1 ....**36** A1
Fishers Hatch CM20 **117** C1
Fishers Mead SG11 **55** D3
Fishery Cotts HP1 **124** A1
Fishery Pas HP1 ..**124** B1
Fishery Rd HP1 ...**124** A1
Fishponds Rd SG5 .**34** E8
Fishpool St AL3 ...**127** C3
Fitzjohn Ave EN5 **171** E5
Fitzroy Ave LU3 ..**45** B3
Fitzwarin Cl LU3 .**44** E8
Fitzwilliam Ct CM17 **118** E4
**Five Acres**
Kings Langley WD4 **138** F2
London Colney WD7 **142** D6
Stansted Mountfitchet
CM24 ..............**59** E8
Five Acres Ave AL2 **140** F2
Five Fields Cl WD19 **175** F7
Five Oaks Caddington LU1 **62** F4
Hatfield AL10 ....**130** B2

**Five Oaks Mid Sch** LU1 **62** F3
**Five Oaks Prim Sch**
AL10 ...............**130** A3
Five Springs LU3 ..**44** E6
Five Springs Ct LU3 **44** E6
Flackwell Ho WD18 **166** E3
Flags The HP2 ....**125** B3
Flagstaff Cl EN9 ..**163** B6
Flagstaff Rd EN9 .**163** B6
**Flamstead End Prim Sch**
EN7 .................**148** A4
Flamstead End Rd EN8 **148** A5
Flamstead Sch AL3 **84** B1
Flamsteadbury La AL3 **106** A4
Flandrian Cl EN3 .**163** B6
Flash La EN2 ......**161** C3
Flatfield Rd HP3 .**125** A1
**Flaunden Bottom** HP3, HP5 **150** E4
Flaunden Hill HP3 **151** A6
Flaunden Ho WD18 **166** E2
**Flaunden La**
Bovingdon HP3 ...**137** D3
Sarratt WD3 ......**151** E6
Flavian Cl AL3 ...**126** F1
Flax Mews AL3 ...**83** C4
Flecker Cl HA7 ..**176** F5
**Fleetville Inf Sch** AL1 **128** B3
Fleetville Jun Sch AL1 **128** B3
Fleetway SG6 .....**23** D4
Fleetwood Cres SG1 **50** B7
Fleetwood Way WD19 **175** C6
Fleming Cl EN7 ..**148** A5
Fleming Cres SG14 **113** A6
Fletcher Way HP2 **124** D6
Flete Ho WD18 ..**166** E3
Flexley Wood AL7 **90** A1
Flight Path SG16 **10** B3
Flinders Cl St Albans AL1 **128** A3
Stevenage SG2 ...**51** D5
Flint Cl LU3 ......**44** E7
Flint Copse AL3 .**106** C6
Flint Ct LU1 .....**63** D5
Flint Rd SG6 .....**23** C8
Flint Way AL3 ...**127** C7
Flintings The HP2 **103** F8
Flora Gr AL1 ....**127** F2
Floral Dr AL2 ...**142** D5
Florence Cl LU3 .**44** D6
Florence Cl WD25 **154** A4
Florence Ct HA6 **174** E4
Florence St SG1 .**34** F8
Florence Wlk 8 CM23 **76** F8
Florida Cl WD23 .**176** D8
Flowers Ind Est 11 LU1 **63** E6
Flowers Way LU1 **63** E7
Flowton Gr AL5 .**107** A7
Floyds Barns HP22 **60** C2
Fog Cotts HP23 ..**101** A5
Fogerty Cl EN3 .**163** B2
Fold Croft CM20 **117** A1
Foldingshott SG3 **69** D3
Follett Dr WD5 .**153** F8
Folly Ave AL3 ..**127** C4
Folly Cl Hitchin SG4 **35** A5
Radlett WD7 ....**155** F3
Folly Fields AL4 **87** B3
**Folly La** Caddington LU1 **62** E4
St Albans AL3 ...**127** C4
Folly Path SG4 .**35** A5
Folly Pathway WD7 **155** F3
**Folly The** Buntingford SG9 **40** F8
Hertford SG14 ..**113** D6
Folly View SG12 **115** B4
Fontmell Cl AL3 **127** E5
Fontwell Cl HA3 **176** E3
Football Cl SG7 .**12** E1
Forbes Ave EN6 **159** D7
Ford Cl WD23 ...**168** C5
Ford Cotts SG11 **75** B8
Ford Field SG11 **75** A8
Ford Hill SG11 ..**75** B8
Ford St SG11 ...**55** E6
Fordham Cl SG7 .**4** D4
Fordham Rd SG8 ..**7** E5
**Fordhams Wood (Nature Reserve) ★** SG8 **6** E4
Fordwich Cl SG14 **113** A6
Fordwich Hill SG14 **113** A6
Fordwich Rd AL8 **110** C5
Fordwich Rise SG14 **113** A6
**Fore St** Harlow CM17 **118** C4
Hatfield AL9 ....**130** C6
Hertford SG14 ..**113** D6
Weston SG4 .....**24** B1
Forebury Ave CM21 **97** F2
Forebury Cres CM21 **97** F2
Forebury The CM21 **97** F2
Forefield AL2 ...**141** A4
Forelands Pl CM21 **97** F2
Forest Ave 5 HP3 **124** D1
**Forest La** WD7 .....**156** B8
**Forest Rd** Cheshunt EN8 **148** D2
Enfield EN3 .....**162** E3
Watford WD25 ..**154** B6
Forest Row SG2 .**50** D1
Forest Wlk WD3 **167** F8
Foresters Cl EN7 **147** E4
Foresthall Rd CM24 **59** E4
Forfar Ho 7 WD19 **175** C7
**Forge Cl**
Chipperfield WD4 **152** A8
5 Hitchin SG5 ..**34** F8
**Forge Cotts**
Essendon AL9 ...**131** E6
Hatfield Heath CM22 **98** F3

Forge End AL2 .........141 A5
Forge La Northwood HA6 .174 E3
Welwyn AL6 ...........89 C5
Forres Cl EN11 .......135 A8
Forres Prim Sch EN11 ..115 B1
Forrest Cres LU2 ......46 A3
Forresters Dr AL7 ....111 C5
Fortnums Acre HA7 ...176 F4
Fortuna Cl SG1 ........51 C8
Fortune La WD6 ......169 D3
Forty Hall★ EN2 .......161 F2
Forty Hill EN2 ........161 F1
Forty Hill CE Prim Sch
   EN2 ...............162 A2
Forty Hill Ho EN2 ....161 F1
Forum The SG1 ........50 D5
Fosbery Ct EN3 .......163 E2
Fosman Cl 7 SG5 ......34 D8
Foster Cl Cheshunt EN8 .148 E1
   Stevenage SG1 .......36 D1
Foster Dr SG4 .........35 A5
Foster Rd HP1 .......124 B1
Foston Cl LU3 .........44 F6
Fotherley Rd WD3 ....172 F8
Foulds Sch EN5 ......171 D6
Founceley Ave LU2 ....71 F8
Founders Rd EN11 ...115 B1
Fountain Cl
   Borehamwood WD6 ...170 A7
   Cheshunt EN8 .......148 D1
Fountain Dr SG13 ....113 F7
Fountain Pl EN9 ......163 C5
Fountains Rd LU3 .....45 D3
Four Acres Stevenage SG1 50 D7
   Welwyn Garden City AL7 .110 F4
Four Acres The CM21 ..98 A4
Four Limes AL4 ......108 D8
Four Swannes Prim Sch
   EN8 ................162 E6
Four Tubs The WD23 ..168 D2
Fouracres SG6 ........23 A3
Fouracres Dr HP3 ....124 F1
Fouracres Wlk HP3 ..124 F1
Fourdrinier Way HP3 ..138 D8
Fourth Ave Harlow CM20 117 C1
   Letchworth SG6 ......23 C7
   Luton LU3 ...........44 D7
   Watford WD25 .......154 D4
Fourways SG13 ......133 A5
Fourways Ct 1 EN11 ...135 A7
Fourways Market AL9 .144 C7
Fovant SG1 ...........36 B1
Fovant Cl AL5 .......107 C6
Fowley Cl EN8 .......162 F5
Fowlmere Rd SG8 .....9 F8
Fox Cl Bushey WD23 ..168 B5
   Elstree WD6 .........169 D3
   Wigginton HP23 .....100 D1
Fox Cnr SG8 ...........1 F5
Fox Hill SG8 ...........1 F5
Fox Hill Rd SG8 .......1 F5
Fox La SG8 ...........15 F7
Fox Rd Stevenage SG1 ..50 E4
   Wigginton HP23 .....100 C2
Fox's La AL9 ........144 F7
Foxbury Cl LU2 .......45 D6
Foxcroft AL1 ........128 A1
Foxdell HA6 ........174 D4
Foxdell Inf Sch LU1 ...63 A8
Foxdell Jun Sch LU1 ...62 E8
Foxdells SG14 ......112 C3
Foxdells La CM23 .....58 F2
Foxes Cl SG13 ......114 B6
Foxes Dr EN7 .......148 A2
Foxes La EN6 .......146 E3
Foxes Par EN9 ......163 C6
Foxfield SG2 .........51 C3
Foxfield Cl HA6 ....174 F4
Foxglove Bank SG8 ....7 F5
Foxglove Cl
   Bishop's Stortford CM23 .76 C6
   Hatfield AL10 .......130 B4
   Hoddesdon EN11 ....115 C1
Foxglove Way Luton LU3 .45 D2
   Oaklands AL6 .......89 E8
Foxgloves The HP1 ...123 E2
Foxgrove Path WD19 ..175 D5
Foxhill Luton LU2 .....45 E5
   Watford WD24 .......154 A3
Foxholes Ave SG13 ...113 F6
Foxhollows AL3 .....130 B7
Foxlands Cl WD25 ...154 A5
Foxley Dr SG13 .......77 B8
Foxley Gr AL6 ........89 F4
Foxleys WD19 .......175 E2
Foxton Rd EN11 ....135 A6
Foxtree Ho WD25 ...154 E3
Foxwood Chase EN9 ..163 C4
Foyle Cl SG1 .........37 C3
Frampton Rd EN6 ...145 C1
Frampton St SG14 ...113 D6
Francis Ave AL3 ....127 D6
Francis Bacon Sch AL1 .142 B8
Francis Cl Hitchin SG4 ..35 A5
   Stotfold SG5 ........11 E6
Francis Combe Sch & Com
   Coll WD25 .........154 C7
Francis Cl Harlow CM20 .117 B2
   St Albans AL1 .......127 C2
Francis Green Ho EN9 .163 B6
Francis House Prep Sch
   HP23 ...............99 F3
Francis Rd Hinxworth SG7 .3 C6
   Ware SG12 ...........93 D2
   Watford WD18 ......167 B5
Francis St LU1 ........63 D8
Francis Wks EN11 ...135 A6
Frank Lester Way LU2 .64 D8

Frank Martin Ct EN7 ..148 B1
Frankland Cl WD3 ...166 A2
Frankland Rd WD3 ...166 B3
Franklin Ave EN7 ...148 B1
Franklin Cl
   Colney Heath AL4 ...129 E1
   Hemel Hempstead HP3 .138 E8
   Pirton SG5 ..........20 D4
Franklin Gdns SG4 ....22 B1
Franklin Rd WD17 ...167 B7
Franklin's Rd SG1 ....50 C8
Franks Cl SG16 ........10 B5
Franshams WD23 ....176 D3
Fraser Rd EN8 ......148 E3
Fred Millard Ct SG1 ...50 E5
Frederick St LU2 .....45 E1
Frederick Street Pas 45 E1
Freeman Ave LU3 .....45 B8
Freemans St SG1 .....21 D1
Freewaters Cl SG5 ....21 E4
Freezywater St George's
   Prim Sch EN3 ......162 D3
Freman Coll SG9 .....40 D8
Freman Dr SG9 .......40 D8
French Horn Ct 5 SG12 .93 D1
French Horn La AL10 .130 B6
French Lodge SG5 ....34 F8
French Row 4 AL3 ...127 D3
French's Cl SG12 ....115 C8
Frenches Yd 21 SG12 ..93 D1
Frensham EN7 ......148 A1
Frensham Dr SG4 .....22 C2
Frere Ct SG3 .........58 F1
Freshwater Cl LU3 ....44 F7
Freshwaters CM20 ..117 E1
Fretherne Rd AL8 ...110 D4
Friars Cl LU1 .........63 B5
Friars Ct LU1 .........63 B5
Friars Field HP4 ....121 E5
Friars Rd Braughing SG11 .56 A7
   Weston SG4 .........24 B1
Friars Way
   Kings Langley WD4 ..139 A1
   Luton LU1 ...........63 B5
   Watford WD23 ......167 F8
Friars Wlk HP23 .....100 A4
Friars Wood CM23 ....77 C8
Friarscroft EN10 ...135 A3
Friday Furlong SG5 ...34 C8
Friedberg Ave CM23 ..76 B2
Friendless La AL3 .....83 F2
Friends Ave EN8 ....162 D7
Friern Cl 6 EN7 ....147 E5
Friesian Cl LU4 .......44 A3
Frimley Rd HP1 .....123 E4
Fringewood Cl HA6 ..174 B2
Frinton Cl WD19 ....175 B6
Friston Gn LU2 .......46 D1
Frithsden Copse HP4 .122 B6
Frithwood Ave HA6 ..174 F4
Frithwood Prim Sch
   HA6 ...............174 F4
Frobisher Dr WD23 ..168 A3
Frobisher Dr SG2 .....51 B7
Frobisher Rd AL1 ...128 C1
Frobisher Way AL10 ..129 B3
Froghall Cotts WD6 ..170 D3
Froghall La SG2 ......38 B1
Frogmoor Ct WD3 ...173 B8
Frogmoor La WD3 ...173 D8
Frogmore AL2 ......141 D4
Frogmore Hill SG14 ...70 B7
Frogmore Ho SG1 .....36 C1
Frogmore Home Pk
   AL2 ...............141 D4
Frogmore Rd HP3 ...138 D8
Frogmore Road Ind Est
   HP3 ...............138 D8
Frogmore St HP23 ...100 A3
Frogs Hall La SG11 ...53 F3
Frome Cl WD23 .....168 A3
Frome Sq HP2 ......125 A8
Front St LU1 .........63 C1
Front The HP4 ......123 B7
Frost Ho HP4 .......122 C3
Frowick Cl AL1 .....144 B8
Frowyke Cres EN6 ...158 A7
Fry Rd SG2 ..........51 C5
Fryth Mead AL3 ....127 B4
Fulbeck Way HA2 ...176 C1
Fulbourne Cl LU4 .....44 E2
Fulford Gr WD19 ....175 B8
Fuller Cl 3 CM23 .....77 A7
Fuller Gdns WD24 ...154 B2
Fuller Rd WD24 ....154 B2
Fuller Way WD3 ....166 A4
Fuller's Almshouses
   CM24 ...............59 F6
Fullers Cl EN9 ......163 F6
Fullers Ct SG6 .......22 E7
Fulling Mill La AL6 ....89 B6
Fulmar Cres HP1 ....124 A3
Fulmore Cl AL5 ......86 D4
Fulton Cl SG1 .........50 C5
Fulton Cres CM23 ....77 C8
Fulton Ct
   Borehamwood WD6 ..156 F1
   Holdbrook EN3 ......163 A1
Furham Field HA5 ...176 A3
Furlay Cl SG6 ........22 D7
Furlong The HP23 ...100 A3
Furlong Way SG12 ...115 A7
Furlongs HP1 .......124 A4
Furmston Ct SG6 .....23 A7
Furneux Pelham CE Sch
   SG9 ...............43 A4
Furriers Cl CM23 .....76 C5
Furrowfield AL10 ...130 B7

Furrows The LU3 .....45 B7
Furse Ave AL4 ......128 A7
Furtherfield WD5 ...153 E7
Furtherground 1 HP2 .124 E2
Furze Cl Luton LU2 ...45 D7
   South Oxhey WD19 ..175 C5
Furze Gr SG8 .........7 E5
Furze Rd HP1 ......123 D2
Furze View WD3 ....164 C4
Furzebushes La AL2 .140 F6
Furzedown SG2 .....51 B4
Furzedown Ct 18 AL5 ..86 D3
Furzefield EN8 .....148 B3
Furzefield Ct EN6 ...158 B3
Furzefield Ctr The EN6 .158 D8
Furzefield Rd AL7 ...110 E4
Furzehill Par WD6 ...170 A6
Furzehill Mid Sch WD6 .170 A5
Furzehill Rd WD6 ...170 B5
Furzen Cres AL10 ...129 F2

## G

Gable Cl
   Abbots Langley WD5 .153 E7
   Pinner HA5 .........176 A3
Gables Ave WD6 ....169 F6
Gables Lodge EN4 ...159 C1
Gables The
   3 Hemel Hempstead HP1 124 D4
   Sawbridgeworth CM21 ..97 E2
   Watford WD3 .......167 B3
   Watford, Woodside WD25 .154 D6
Gaddesden Cres WD25 .154 E5
Gaddesden Gr AL7 ...111 B6
Gaddesden La AL3 ...105 C4
Gaddesden Row HP2 .104 C6
Gaddesden Row Jun Mix Inf
   Sch HP2 ...........104 B6
Gade Ave WD18 ....166 E5
Gade Bank WD1 ....166 D5
Gade Cl
   Hemel Hempstead HP1 .124 B6
   Watford WD18 ......166 E5
Gade Twr HP3 ......138 F6
Gade Valley Cl WD4 ..139 A3
Gade Valley Cotts HP1 .103 E4
Gade Valley Jun Inf Sch
   HP1 ...............124 D4
Gade View Gdns WD4 .153 C7
Gadebridge Ct HP1 ..124 C4
Gadebridge La
   Hemel Hempstead HP1 .124 B5
   Hemel Hempstead HP1 .124 C5
Gadebridge Rd HP1 ..124 B4
Gadeside WD24,WD25 .153 B4
Gadeview HP1 ......124 C3
Gadeview Rd HP3 ...138 D7
Gadmore La HP23 ...119 F7
Gadswell Cl WD25 ...154 E3
Gage Cl SG8 ..........7 D7
Gainsborough Ave AL1 .127 F8
Gainsford Cres SG4 ..22 C2
Gainswood AL7 .....110 E5
Gaitskell Ho AL10 ...130 D5
Gall End La CM24 ....59 F7
Galleria The AL10 ...129 F5
Gallery The
   Letchworth SG6 ....22 F6
   7 Luton LU1 ........63 E7
Galley Gn SG13 ....115 A2
Galley Hill HP1 ....124 B6
Galley La EN5 ......171 B7
Galleycroft Ct 4 AL10 .130 A6
Galleyhill Rd EN9 ...163 E2
Galleywood SG5 .....21 D4
Galliard Ct LU3 ......45 B4
Galloway Cl
   1 Bishop's Stortford CM23 76 F8
   Cheshunt EN10 .....148 F5
Galloway Rd CM23 ...58 F1
Gallows Hill WD4 ...153 C7
Gallows Hill La WD5 .153 D8
Galston Rd LU3 ......44 D8
Gammon Cl HP3 ....125 A2
Gammons La WD17,
   WD24 .............154 A2
Gamnel Mews HP23 ..100 B7
Ganders Ash WD25 ..154 A6
Gandhi Ct 1 WD24 ..167 D7
Gangies Hill CM21 ...97 A4
Gant Ct EN9 ........163 F5
Ganton Wlk WD19 ..175 E6
Ganymede Pl HP2 ...124 F6
Gaping La SG5 .......34 D7
Garden Ave AL10 ...130 A2
Garden Cl Barnet EN5 .171 C5
   Harpenden AL5 .....107 A5
   Royston SG8 ..........7 E7
   St Albans AL1 .......128 B4
   Watford WD17 ......166 F7
   Woolmer Green SG3 ..69 B2
Garden Cott AL2 ....141 E4
Garden Cotts SG11 ...73 A8
Garden Ct
   Hoddesdon EN10 ....134 F4
   Welwyn Garden City AL7 .110 E7
   Wheathampstead AL4 ..87 D1
Garden Field SG2 ....51 E2
Garden Field La HP4 .122 F2
Garden Fields Jun Mix Inf
   Sch AL3 ...........127 D6
Garden Ho AL9 .....131 E6
Garden Hos The CM21 .98 B3
Garden La SG8 .......7 D5
Garden Rd
   Abbots Langley WD5 .153 E8

Garden Rd continued
   Buntingford SG9 ....40 E8
   Woolmer Green SG3 ..69 B2
Garden Row 6 SG5 ...34 F8
Garden Terr SG12 ....92 E4
Garden Terrace Rd
   CM17 ..............118 C4
Garden Wlk Royston SG8 ..7 E7
   Stevenage SG1 .......50 E5
Gardenia Ave LU3 ....45 A4
Gardens of the Rose The★
   AL2 ................140 F5
Gardens The Baldock SG7 .23 E8
   Brookmans Park AL9 .144 A4
   Henlow SG16 ........10 D8
   Stotfold SG5 ........11 E6
   Watford WD17 ......166 F7
Gardiners La SG7 .....4 D4
Gardner Ct Luton LU1 ..63 E4
   Watford WD25 .....154 C4
Gareth Ct WD6 .....156 F1
Garfield Ct LU2 ......46 A3
Garfield St WD24 ...154 B1
Garland Cl Cheshunt EN8 162 E8
   Hemel Hempstead HP2 .124 D4
Garland Ct 4 AL1 ...127 E3
Garland Rd SG12 .....93 E1
Garnault Rd EN1 ...161 F1
Garner Dr EN10 ....148 E5
Garnett Cl WD24 ...154 D3
Garnett Dr AL2 ....140 F2
Garrard Way AL4 ...108 A2
Garratts Rd WD23 ..168 C2
Garretts Cl SG14 ...113 C6
Garretts Mead LU2 ..46 B3
Garrison Ct 2 SG4 ...34 F7
Garrowsfield EN5 ...171 F4
Garsmouth Way WD25 .154 D3
Garston Cres WD25 .154 C5
Garston Dr WD25 ...154 C5
Garston Inf Sch WD25 .154 D4
Garston La WD25 ...154 C5
Garston Manor Sch
   WD25 .............154 C7
Garston Park Par WD25 154 D5
Garston Sta WD25 ...154 D4
Garter Ct 10 LU2 ....45 D1
Garth Rd SG6 ........22 A3
Garth The WD5 ....153 D6
Garthland Dr EN5 ...171 C4
Gartlet Rd WD17 ...167 C6
Gas La SG8 ..........17 C3
Gascoyne Cl EN6 ...158 A7
Gascoyne Way SG13,
   SG14 .............113 D5
Gatcombe Ct AL1 ...128 A2
Gate Cl WD6 .......170 C8
Gate Cotts WD3 ...164 D5
Gate End HA6 ......175 A3
Gatecroft HP3 .....139 A8
Gatehill Gdns LU3 ....31 B1
Gatehill Rd HA6 ....175 A3
Gatehouse Mews SG9 .40 E8
Gates Way SG1 ......50 C6
Gatesbury Way SG11 ..55 D3
Gatesdene Cl HP4 ...102 C4
Gateshead Rd WD6 ..170 A8
Gateway Cl HA6 ....174 C4
Gateways The EN7 ..147 E3
Gatwick Cl CM23 .....59 B1
Gauldie Way SG1 ....55 D2
Gaumont App WD17 .167 B6
Gaunts Way SG6 .....12 A2
Gaveston Dr HP4 ...122 B6
Gayland Ave LU2 ....64 B8
Gayton Cl LU3 .......45 B4
Gaywood Ave EN8 ..148 C1
Gazelda Ind Est WD17 .167 D4
Gean Wlk 3 AL10 ...130 A2
Geddes Rd WD23 ...168 C5
Geddings Rd EN11 ..135 B6
Geddington Ct EN8 ..163 A5
Generals Wlk The EN3 .162 E2
Gentle Ct SG7 ........23 E8
Gentlemens Field SG12 .93 B3
George Field Ho 4
   WD3 ..............165 D2
George Gn CM22 .....77 B1
George Green Villas
   CM22 ...............98 B8
George La 3 SG5 .....34 F7
George Leighton Ct SG2 .51 B4
George Lovell Dr EN3 .163 A2
George St
   Berkhamsted HP4 ...122 D4
   Hemel Hempstead HP2 .124 D4
   Hertford SG14 ......113 C6
   Luton LU1 ...........63 E7
   Markyate AL3 .......83 E5
   St Albans AL3 ......127 D3
   Watford WD18 ......167 C5
George St W LU1 .....63 E7
George Street Prim Sch
   HP2 ..............124 D4
George V Ave HA5 ..175 F1
George V Way WD3 .152 B3
George Wlk 9 SG2 ...51 C6
George's Wood Rd AL9 .145 B5
Georges Mead WD6 .169 D3
Georgewood Rd HP3 .139 A7
Georgina Ct SG15 ...11 A3
Gerard Ave CM23 ....76 E4
Gerard Ct 2 AL5 .....86 A4
Gernon Rd SG6 ......22 F5
Gernon Wlk SG6 .....22 F5
Gew's Cnr EN8 .....148 C4
Giant Tree Hill WD23 .168 D1

Gibbons Cl
   Borehamwood WD6 ..169 E8
   Sandridge AL4 ......108 C1
Gibbons Way SG3 ....68 F5
Gibbs Cl EN8 .......148 D2
Gibbs Couch WD19 ..175 D3
Gibbs Field CM23 .....76 D5
Gibraltar Lodge AL5 ..86 D3
Gibson Cl SG4 ........35 B7
Gidian Ct AL2 ......141 D4
Gifford's La SG11 ....54 A2
Gilbert Ct AL5 .......86 B4
Gilbert Rd UB9 ....173 D1
Gilbert St EN3 .....162 C2
Gilbert Way HP4 ...122 A4
Gilbert's Hill HP23 ..119 E3
Gilbey Ave CM23 .....77 B6
Gilbey Cres CM24 ....59 E8
Gildea Cl HA5 ......176 A3
Gilden Cl CM17 ....118 E4
Gilden Way CM17 ...118 D3
Gilder Cl LU3 ........45 A8
Gilderdale LU4 .......44 B6
Gilders CM21 ........97 C2
Giles Cl AL4 .......108 C1
Giles Inf Sch The SG1 ..37 A1
Giles Jun Sch SG1 ...37 A1
Gill Cl WD18 .......166 C3
Gillam St LU2 .......63 E8
Gillan Gn WD23 ....176 C8
Gillian Ave AL1 ....141 C7
Gillian Ho HA3 ....176 E4
Gilliat's Gn WD3 ...164 D5
Gilliflower Ho EN11 .135 A5
Gillings Ct EN5 ....171 C5
Gillison Ct SG6 ......23 B5
Gills Hill WD7 ......155 F4
Gills Hill La WD7 ...155 F3
Gills Hollow WD7 ...155 F3
Gilmour Cl EN2 ....162 A4
Gilpin Gn AL5 .......86 C1
Gilpin Rd SG12 ....114 E8
Gilpin's Gallop SG12 .115 B4
Gilpin's Ride HP4 ...122 E5
Gilsland EN9 .......163 E4
Gilston Mews CM20 .117 C6
Gilston Pk CM20 ...117 C7
Ginns Rd SG9 ........43 D6
Gippeswyck Cl HA5 .175 D2
Gipsy La
   Bishop's Stortford
   CM24 ...............59 C4
   Knebworth AL6,SG3 ..68 E4
   Luton LU1 ...........64 A6
Girdle Rd SG4 .......22 A2
Girons Ct SG4 .......35 A7
Girtin Rd WD23 ....168 C5
Girton Ct EN8 ......148 E1
Girton Way WD3 ...166 C4
Gisburne Way WD24 .154 A2
Gladding Rd EN7 ...147 B6
Glade The Baldock SG7 .23 E7
   Letchworth SG6 .....22 F3
   Welwyn Garden City AL8 .110 C8
Glades The HP1 ....123 E4
Gladeside AL4 .....128 C6
Gladesmere Ct WD24 .154 B2
Gladeway The EN9 ..163 C6
Gladsmuir Rd EN5 ..171 E7
Gladstone Ave LU1 ...63 C7
Gladstone Ct SG2 ...69 A8
Gladstone Pl EN5 ...171 D5
Gladstone Rd
   Dane End SG12 ......71 F8
   Hoddesdon EN11 ...135 F1
   Ware SG12 ..........93 C2
   Watford WD17 ......167 C6
Glaisdale LU4 ........44 C5
Glamis Cl Cheshunt EN7 .148 A2
   Hemel Hempstead HP2 .105 B1
Glanfield HP2 ......124 E6
Glassmill Ho 6 HP4 .122 C4
Gleave Cl AL1 ......128 B4
Glebe Ave SG15 .....11 A7
Glebe Cl Essendon AL9 .131 F6
   Hemel Hempstead HP3 .138 E7
   Hertford SG14 ......113 D8
   Pitstone LU7 ........80 D5
   Watton at S SG14 ....70 D3
Glebe Cotts AL9 ...131 F6
Glebe Ct
   Bishop's Stortford CM23 .77 B8
   Hatfield AL10 ......130 C6
   Watford WD25 .....154 D6
   Watton at S SG14 ....70 E3
Glebe Ho AL9 ......131 F6
Glebe La EN5 ......171 A3
Glebe Rd Hertford SG14 .113 D8
   Letchworth SG6 ....23 B8
   Welwyn AL6 .........89 B5
Glebe The Ardeley SG2 .38 C3
   Harlow CM20 ......117 E1
   Kings Langley WD4 ..139 A2
   St Ippolyts SG4 .....35 C2
   Stevenage SG2 ......51 B2
   Watford WD25 .....154 D6
Glebe View SG2 .....38 C2
Glebeland AL10 ....130 C5
Glebelands CM20 ...117 F3
Gleed Ave WD23 ...176 D8
Glemsford Cl LU4 ....44 B6
Glemsford Dr AL5 ...86 C2
Glen Chess WD3 ...165 C5
Glen Faba Rd CM19 .135 F6
Glen The Caddington LU1 .62 E3

Glen The *continued*
Hemel Hempstead HP2 . . .124 F8
Northwood HA6 . . . . . . . .174 D3
**Glen Way** WD17 . . . . . . .153 E1
**Glenblower Ct** AL4 . . . . .128 D3
**Glenbourne** SG4 . . . . . . . .67 F1
**Glencoe Rd** WD23 . . . . .168 A3
**Glencorse Gn** WD19 . . .175 D6
**Glendale** HP1 . . . . . . . . . .124 B3
**Glendale Wlk** EN8 . . . . .148 E1
**Glendean Ct** EN3 . . . . . .162 F3
**Gleneagles Cl** WD19 . . .175 D6
**Gleneagles Dr** LU2 . . . . . .45 E6
**Glenester Cl** EN11 . . . . .115 A1
**Glenferrie Rd** AL1 . . . . .128 A3
**Glenfield Ct** SG14 . . . . . .112 F7
**Glenfield Rd** LU3 . . . . . . .45 C6
**Glengall Pl** AL1 . . . . . . . .141 E8
**Glenhaven Ave** WD6 . . .170 A6
**Glenlyn Ave** AL1 . . . . . . .128 B2
**Glenmire Terr** SG12 . . . .115 D4
**Glenmore Gdns** WD5 . . .154 A7
**Glenshee Cl** HA6 . . . . . .174 C4
**Glenview Gdns** HP1 . . . .124 B3
**Glenview Rd** HP1 . . . . . .124 B3
**Glenville Ave** EN2 . . . . . .161 D1
**Glenwood**
Hoddesdon EN10 . . . . . . . .134 F4
Welwyn Garden City AL7 . .111 D5
**Glenwood Cl** SG2 . . . . . . .51 C2
**Glevum Cl** AL3 . . . . . . . . .126 F1
**Globe Cl** AL5 . . . . . . . . . . .86 B1
**Globe Cres** CM23 . . . . . . .58 D6
**Globe Ct** Hertford SG14 . .113 C8
Hoddesdon EN10 . . . . . . . .148 F8
**Glossop Way** SG15 . . . . . . .11 B7
**Gloucester Ave** EN8 . . . .162 E6
**Gloucester Cl** SG1 . . . . . .36 C2
**Gloucester Ho** 6 WD6 . .170 A7
**Gloucester Rd**
Enfield EN2 . . . . . . . . . . . .161 C1
1 Luton LU1 . . . . . . . . . . . .63 F6
**Glover Cl** EN7 . . . . . . . . .147 F4
**Glovers Cl** SG13 . . . . . . .113 C4
**Glovers Ct** SG5 . . . . . . . . .21 F1
**Glynde The** SG2 . . . . . . . . .69 B8
**Goat La** EN1 . . . . . . . . . . .161 F1
**Gobions Way** EN6 . . . . . .145 B3
**Goblins Gn** AL7 . . . . . . . .110 D5
**Goddard End** SG2 . . . . . . .69 C8
**Goddards Cl** SG13 . . . . . .132 C4
**Godfrey Cl** SG2 . . . . . . . . .51 B3
**Godfreys Cl** LU1 . . . . . . . .63 B6
**Godfreys Ct** LU1 . . . . . . . .63 B6
**Godfries Cl** AL6 . . . . . . . . .90 E3
**Godsafe** CM17 . . . . . . . . .118 E4
**Godwin Cl** E4 . . . . . . . . . .163 C1
**Goff's La** EN7 . . . . . . . . . .147 E2
**Goff's Oak Ave** EN7 . . . .147 C3
**Goffs Cres** EN7 . . . . . . . .147 C2
**Goffs La** EN7 . . . . . . . . . .148 A2
Goffs Oak Jun Mix Inf Sch
EN7 . . . . . . . . . . . . . . . . .147 B3
Goffs Sch EN7 . . . . . . . . . .148 A2
**Gold Cl** EN10 . . . . . . . . . .134 E3
**Gold Crest Cl** LU4 . . . . . . .44 A5
**Golda Cl** EN5 . . . . . . . . . .171 D3
**Goldcrest Way** WD23 . . .168 C1
**Goldcroft** HP3 . . . . . . . . .125 A1
**Golden Dell** AL7 . . . . . . .110 F2
Goldfield Inf Sch HP23 . . . .99 F3
**Goldfield Rd** HP23 . . . . . .99 F3
**Goldfinch Way** WD6 . . . .170 A5
**Goldings**
Bishop's Stortford CM23 . . .77 B8
Hertford SG14 . . . . . . . . . .92 A1
**Goldings Cres** AL10 . . . . .130 B6
**Goldings Ho** AL10 . . . . . .130 B6
**Goldings La** SG14 . . . . . . .92 A2
**Goldington Cl** EN11 . . . . .114 F1
**Goldon** SG6 . . . . . . . . . . . .23 C4
**Goldring Way** AL2 . . . . . .142 B5
**Goldsmith Way** AL3 . . . .127 C4
**Goldstone Cl** SG12 . . . . . .93 D2
**Golf Cl** WD23 . . . . . . . . .167 D6
**Golf Club Rd** AL9 . . . . . .145 A6
**Golf Ride** EN2 . . . . . . . . .161 A4
**Gombards** AL3 . . . . . . . . .127 D4
**Gomer Cl** SG4 . . . . . . . . . .67 E2
**Gonnerston** AL3 . . . . . . .127 B4
**Gonville Ave** WD3 . . . . . .166 B3
**Gonville Cres** SG2 . . . . . . .51 C2
**Goodacre Cl** EN6 . . . . . . .159 C7
**Goodey Meade** SG2 . . . . . .52 F2
**Goodison Cl** WD23 . . . . . .168 C4
**Goodliffe Pk** CM23 . . . . . .59 B2
**Goodrich Cl** WD25 . . . . .154 A4
**Goodwin Ct** 4 EN8 . . . . .148 E3
**Goodwin Ho** WD18 . . . . .166 E3
**Goodwin Stile** CM23 . . . . .76 D5
**Goodwins Mead** LU7 . . . . .80 A7
**Goodwood Ave**
Enfield EN3 . . . . . . . . . . . .162 C2
Watford WD24 . . . . . . . . .153 E3
**Goodwood Cl** EN11 . . . . .135 A7
**Goodwood Par** WD24 . . .153 E3
**Goodwood Path** 2
WD6 . . . . . . . . . . . . . . . . .170 A7
**Goodwood Rd** SG8 . . . . . . . .7 F6
**Goodyers Ave** WD7 . . . . .155 F5
**Goose Acre** Botley HP5 . .136 A1
Cheddington LU7 . . . . . . . . .80 A7
**Goose La** CM22 . . . . . . . . .98 E7
**Gooseacre** AL7 . . . . . . . .110 F4
**Gooseberry Hill** LU3 . . . . .45 B7
**Goosecroft** HP1 . . . . . . . .123 F4
**Goosefields** WD3 . . . . . .165 C3
**Goral Mead** WD3 . . . . . .165 D1
**Gordian Way** SG2 . . . . . . .37 C1
**Gordon Ave** HA7 . . . . . . .176 F4
**Gordon Cl** AL1 . . . . . . . . .128 B2
**Gordon Ct** SG3 . . . . . . . . .69 A5
**Gordon Ho** AL1 . . . . . . . .128 B2
**Gordon Mans** EN5 . . . . . .171 F5
**Gordon Rd** EN9 . . . . . . . .163 A5
**Gordon St** LU1 . . . . . . . . .63 D7
**Gordon Way** EN5 . . . . . . .171 F5
**Gordon's Wlk** AL5 . . . . . .107 C8
**Gore La** SG11 . . . . . . . . . . .73 D3
**Gorelands La** HP8 . . . . . .172 A7
**Gorham Dr** AL1 . . . . . . . .141 E8
Gorhambury★ AL3 . . . . . .126 C4
**Gorle Cl** WD25 . . . . . . . . .154 A4
**Gorleston Cl** SG1 . . . . . . .36 A1
**Gorse Cl** AL10 . . . . . . . . .129 F2
**Gorse Cnr**
Harpenden AL5 . . . . . . . . .107 C8
St Albans AL3 . . . . . . . . . .127 D5
**Gorselands** AL5 . . . . . . . .107 B7
**Gorst Cl** SG6 . . . . . . . . . . .22 E5
**Gosford Ho** WD18 . . . . . .166 E3
**Gosforth La**
South Oxhey WD19 . . . . . .175 B7
5 South Oxhey WD19 . . . .175 C7
**Gosforth Path** WD19 . . . .175 A7
**Goshawk Cl** LU4 . . . . . . . .44 A4
**Goslett Ct** WD23 . . . . . . .168 A4
**Gosling Ave** SG5 . . . . . . . .33 C2
Gosling Ski Ctr★ AL8 . . .110 C4
**Gosmore** SG1 . . . . . . . . . . .36 C2
**Gosmore Ley Cl** SG4 . . . . .34 F3
**Gosmore Rd** SG4 . . . . . . . .34 F5
**Gossamers The** WD25 . . .154 E4
**Gosselin Ho** SG14 . . . . . .113 D8
**Gosselin Rd** SG14 . . . . . .113 C8
**Gossom's End** HP4 . . . . .122 A5
**Gossoms Ryde** HP4 . . . . .122 A5
Gothic Mede Lower Sch
SG15 . . . . . . . . . . . . . . . . . .11 A5
**Gothic Way** SG15 . . . . . . . .11 B5
**Gould Cl** AL9 . . . . . . . . . .144 B7
**Government Row** EN3 . . .163 A2
**Gowar Field** EN6 . . . . . . .158 A7
**Gower Rd** SG8 . . . . . . . . . . .7 C7
**Gowers The** CM20 . . . . . .118 B2
**Grace Ave** WD7 . . . . . . . .156 E6
**Grace Cl** WD6 . . . . . . . . .170 D8
**Grace Gdns** CM23 . . . . . . .76 F4
**Grace Way** SG1 . . . . . . . . .50 E7
**Graces Maltings** HP23 . . .100 A3
**Graemesdyke Rd** HP4 . . .122 A3
**Grafton Cl** AL4 . . . . . . . . .128 D2
**Grafton Pl** SG11 . . . . . . . . .55 F1
**Graham Ave** EN10 . . . . . .134 E2
**Graham Cl** AL1 . . . . . . . . .127 D1
**Graham Ct** 2 AL3 . . . . . .127 D4
**Graham Gdns** LU3 . . . . . . .45 A5
**Graham Rd** HA3 . . . . . . . .176 E1
**Grailands** CM23 . . . . . . . .76 D8
**Grammar School Wlk**
SG5 . . . . . . . . . . . . . . . . . . .34 E7
**Grampian Way** LU3 . . . . . .44 C8
**Granaries The** EN9 . . . . .163 E5
**Granary Cl** AL4 . . . . . . . .108 D8
**Granary Ct** CM21 . . . . . . . .97 E2
**Granary La** AL5 . . . . . . . . .86 C1
**Granary The**
Flamstead HP2 . . . . . . . . .104 F4
Roydon CM19 . . . . . . . . . .116 B1
Stanstead Abbotts SG12 . .115 C3
**Granby Ave** AL5 . . . . . . . . .86 D2
**Granby Ct** AL5 . . . . . . . . . .86 D2
**Granby Rd** Luton LU4 . . . . .44 E2
Stevenage SG1 . . . . . . . . . .36 C2
**Grandfield Ave** WD17 . . .167 A8
**Grange Ave** Luton LU4 . . . .44 D4
Totteridge N20 . . . . . . . . .171 E2
**Grange Bottom** SG8 . . . . . . .7 E5
**Grange Cl**
Hemel Hempstead HP2 . . .125 A2
Hertford SG14 . . . . . . . . . .113 B6
Hitchin SG4 . . . . . . . . . . . . .35 A4
Markyate AL3 . . . . . . . . . . .83 D6
Watford WD17 . . . . . . . . .167 A8
**Grange Court Rd** AL5 . . .107 C6
**Grange Ct** Hertford SG14 113 C7
Letchworth SG6 . . . . . . . . . .12 A1
3 St Albans AL3 . . . . . . . .127 D4
Waltham Abbey EN9 . . . . .163 C5
**Grange Dr** SG5 . . . . . . . . . .11 F5
**Grange Gdns** SG12 . . . . . .114 E8
**Grange Hill** AL6 . . . . . . . . .89 C6
Grange Jun Sch SG6 . . . . . .12 A2
**Grange La** WD25 . . . . . . .168 D8
**Grange Pk** CM23 . . . . . . . .58 F1
**Grange Rd**
Bishop's Stortford CM23 . . .77 A7
Borehamwood WD6 . . . . . .169 F4
Letchworth SG6 . . . . . . . . . .22 F8
Pitstone LU7 . . . . . . . . . . . .80 D5
Tring HP23 . . . . . . . . . . . .100 C5
Watford WD23 . . . . . . . . .167 F4
Wilstone HP23 . . . . . . . . . .79 D1
**Grange Rise** SG4 . . . . . . . .67 F1
**Grange St** AL3 . . . . . . . . .127 D4
**Grange The**
Abbots Langley WD5 . . . . .153 E8
Bishop's Stortford CM23 . . .58 F1
Hoddesdon EN11 . . . . . . . .135 A5
Rickmansworth WD3 . . . . .165 D2
Sewardstone EN9 . . . . . . .163 D2
Standon SG11 . . . . . . . . . . .55 D3
Therfield SG8 . . . . . . . . . . .15 F6
**Grange Wlk** CM23 . . . . . . .77 A7
**Grangedale Cl** HA6 . . . . .174 E2
**Grangeside** CM23 . . . . . . .59 A2
**Grangewood** EN6 . . . . . . .145 B1
**Gransden Cl** LU3 . . . . . . . .45 A7
**Grant Gdns** AL5 . . . . . . . . .86 B2
**Grantham Cl** SG8 . . . . . . . . .7 B8
**Grantham Gdns** SG12 . . . .93 E2
**Grantham Gn** WD6 . . . . .170 C4
**Grantham Mews** HP4 . . .122 D4
**Grantham Rd** LU4 . . . . . . .45 B1
**Granville Ct** AL1 . . . . . . .127 F3
**Granville Dene** HP3 . . . . .137 A4
**Granville Gdns** EN11 . . . .115 A2
**Granville Rd** Barnet EN5 .171 D6
Hitchin SG4 . . . . . . . . . . . . .22 C1
Luton LU1 . . . . . . . . . . . . . .63 B8
St Albans AL1 . . . . . . . . . .127 F3
Watford WD18 . . . . . . . . .167 C5
Berkhamsted HP4 . . . . . . .121 E6
**Grasmere** SG1 . . . . . . . . . .37 C3
**Grasmere Ave**
Harpenden AL5 . . . . . . . . . .86 C1
Luton LU3 . . . . . . . . . . . . . .45 B7
**Grasmere Cl**
Hemel Hempstead HP3 . . .125 B1
Watford WD25 . . . . . . . . .154 B7
**Grasmere Rd** Luton LU3 . . .45 C7
St Albans AL1 . . . . . . . . . .128 B1
Ware SG12 . . . . . . . . . . . . .93 E3
**Grass Mdws** SG2 . . . . . . . .51 D7
**Grass Warren** AL6 . . . . . . .90 E1
**Grassington Cl** AL2 . . . . .141 A1
**Grassy Cl** HP1 . . . . . . . . .124 A4
**Gravel Dr** HP23 . . . . . . . . .99 B3
**Gravel La** HP1 . . . . . . . . .124 A3
**Gravel Path**
Berkhamsted HP4 . . . . . . .122 E5
Hemel Hempstead HP1 . . .124 A3
**Graveley Ave** WD6 . . . . . .170 C4
**Graveley Cl** SG1 . . . . . . . .36 C2
**Graveley Dell** AL7 . . . . . .111 B5
**Graveley La** SG4 . . . . . . . .36 B5
Graveley Prim Sch SG4 . . .36 B5
**Graveley Rd** Graveley SG1 .36 B3
Great Wymondley SG4 . . . . .35 F6
**Gravelhill Terr** HP1 . . . . .124 A2
**Gravelly Dell** SG11 . . . . . .55 F8
**Gravelly La** SG11 . . . . . . . .55 F8
**Gravely Ct** HP2 . . . . . . . .125 C2
**Gray's La** SG5 . . . . . . . . . .34 D7
**Grayling Ct** HP4 . . . . . . .121 F6
**Graylings The** WD5 . . . . .153 D6
**Grays Cl** SG8 . . . . . . . . . . . .7 C8
**Grays Ct** CM23 . . . . . . . . .76 E8
**Graysfield** AL7 . . . . . . . .111 A3
**Grazings The** HP2 . . . . . .124 F5
**Great Ashby Way** SG1 . . .37 B3
**Great Braitch La** AL10 . . .109 F1
**Great Bramingham La**
LU3 . . . . . . . . . . . . . . . . . . .31 B2
**Great Break** AL7 . . . . . . .111 B5
**Great Cambridge Rd**
Cheshunt EN8 . . . . . . . . . .148 D4
Enfield EN1 . . . . . . . . . . . .162 C6
**Great Conduit** AL7 . . . . .111 C7
**Great Dell** AL8 . . . . . . . . . .89 D1
**Great Eastern Cl** CM23 . . .77 A6
**Great Elms Rd** HP3 . . . . .138 F7
Great Gaddesden CE Prim
Sch HP1 . . . . . . . . . . . . .103 D3
**Great Ganett** AL7 . . . . . . .111 C4
**Great Gn** SG5 . . . . . . . . . . .20 D4
**Great Gr** WD23 . . . . . . . .168 B5
**Great Groves** EN7 . . . . . .147 E3
**Great Hadham Rd** CM23 . .76 C5
**Great Heart** HP2 . . . . . . .124 E5
**Great Heath** AL10 . . . . . .130 B8
**Great Hyde Hall** CM21 . . . .98 B3
**Great Innings N** SG14 . . . .70 D4
**Great Innings S** SG14 . . . .70 D3
**Great Lawne** SG3 . . . . . . . .69 D2
**Great Ley** AL7 . . . . . . . . .110 E4
**Great Mdw** EN10 . . . . . . .135 A1
**Great Molewood** SG14 . . . .92 B1
**Great North Rd**
Barnet EN5 . . . . . . . . . . . .171 E6
Brookmans Park AL9,EN6 .145 B5
Hatfield AL9 . . . . . . . . . . .130 C5
Oaklands AL6 . . . . . . . . . . .89 E7
Radwell SG7 . . . . . . . . . . . .12 D3
Welwyn Garden City AL8 . .110 A7
**Great Palmers** HP2 . . . . .124 F8
**Great Pk** WD4 . . . . . . . . .139 A1
**Great Plumtree** CM20 . . . .117 F2
**Great Rd** HP2 . . . . . . . . . .124 F4
**Great Slades** EN6 . . . . . .158 F6
**Great Stockwood Rd**
EN7 . . . . . . . . . . . . . . . . .147 D5
**Great Sturgess Rd** HP1 . .123 F3
**Great Whites Rd** HP3 . . .124 F1
Great Wood Ctry Pk★
EN6 . . . . . . . . . . . . . . . . .146 B5
**Greatfield Cl** AL5 . . . . . . .85 C4
**Greatham Rd** WD23 . . . .167 D6
**Green Acres** Lilley LU2 . . .32 D2
Stevenage SG2 . . . . . . . . . . .51 C1
Welwyn Garden City AL7 . .110 F3
**Green Banks** AL1 . . . . . . .127 F1
**Green Bushes** LU4 . . . . . . .44 D6
**Green Cl**
Brookmans Park AL9 . . . . .144 E5
Cheshunt EN8 . . . . . . . . . .162 E8
Luton LU4 . . . . . . . . . . . . . .44 C5
Stevenage SG2 . . . . . . . . . . .50 F2
**Green Croft** AL10 . . . . . .130 A8
**Green Ct** 6 LU4 . . . . . . . . .44 C5
**Green Dell Way** HP3 . . . .125 C3
**Green Dragon Ct** LU1 . . . .63 F6
**Green Drift** SG8 . . . . . . . . . .7 C7
**Green Edge** WD25 . . . . . .154 A4
**Green End** Braughing SG11 55 E8
Welwyn AL6 . . . . . . . . . . . .89 B4
Green End Bsns Ctr
WD3 . . . . . . . . . . . . . . . . .152 A2
**Green End Gdns** HP1 . . . .124 A2
**Green End La** HP1 . . . . . .123 F3
**Green End Rd** HP1 . . . . . .124 A2
**Green Hill Cl** SG11 . . . . . .55 F7
**Green La** Ashwell SG7 . . . . . .4 E5
Bovingdon HP3 . . . . . . . . .137 A3
Bovingdon,Pudds Cross
HP3 . . . . . . . . . . . . . . . .136 F3
Braughing SG11 . . . . . . . . .55 F7
Croxley Green WD3 . . . . . .165 F4
Hemel Hempstead HP2 . . .125 D4
Hitchin SG4 . . . . . . . . . . . . .22 B1
Hoddesdon EN10 . . . . . . . .149 B8
Kensworth Common LU6 . . .82 E8
Latimer HP5 . . . . . . . . . . .150 C6
Letchworth SG6 . . . . . . . . . .23 C8
Luton LU2 . . . . . . . . . . . . . .46 C4
Markyate AL3 . . . . . . . . . . .83 F5
Northwood HA6 . . . . . . . . .174 E3
Pitstone LU7 . . . . . . . . . . . .80 E5
St Albans, New Greens
AL3 . . . . . . . . . . . . . . . . .127 D7
St Albans, Sopwell AL1 . . .142 A7
Watford WD19 . . . . . . . . .167 C2
Welwyn Garden City AL7 . .111 D5
**Green Lane Cl** AL5 . . . . . .107 E8
**Green Lanes** AL10 . . . . . .109 F2
Green Lanes Prim Sch
AL10 . . . . . . . . . . . . . . . .109 F1
**Green Leys Cotts** SG11 . . .55 F1
**Green Man Ct** CM20 . . . . .117 A4
**Green Mdw** EN6 . . . . . . . .145 A1
**Green Milverton** LU3 . . . . .45 A7
**Green Oaks** LU2 . . . . . . . .45 F3
**Green Path** HP22,HP23 . . . .99 D4
**Green St**
Chorleywood WD3 . . . . . .164 C6
Harlow CM17 . . . . . . . . . .118 D1
Royston SG8 . . . . . . . . . . . . .7 D8
Shenley WD6,WD7 . . . . . .157 A3
Stevenage SG1 . . . . . . . . . . .50 C7
**Green The**
Bishop's Stortford CM23 . . .76 F4
Cheddington LU7 . . . . . . . . .80 A7
Cheshunt EN8 . . . . . . . . . .148 C3
Codicote SG4 . . . . . . . . . . . .67 F1
Kimpton SG4 . . . . . . . . . . . .66 D1
Knebworth SG3 . . . . . . . . . .68 C5
London Colney AL2 . . . . . .142 D4
Luton LU4 . . . . . . . . . . . . . .44 C5
Mentmore LU7 . . . . . . . . . . .61 D4
Newnham SG7 . . . . . . . . . . .12 E7
Peters Green LU2 . . . . . . . .65 C3
Pitstone LU7 . . . . . . . . . . . .80 D4
Potten End HP4 . . . . . . . . .123 B6
Royston SG8 . . . . . . . . . . . . .7 D6
Sarratt WD3 . . . . . . . . . . .152 A3
Stotfold SG5 . . . . . . . . . . . .11 F7
Waltham Abbey EN9 . . . . .163 C5
Ware SG12 . . . . . . . . . . . . .93 D3
Welwyn AL6 . . . . . . . . . . . .89 B5
Welwyn Garden City AL7 . .111 A4
**Green Vale** AL7 . . . . . . . .111 A5
**Green View Cl** HP3 . . . . .137 A2
**Green Way Gdns** HA3 . . .176 E1
**Green Way The** HA3 . . . .176 E2
**Greenacre Cl** EN5 . . . . . .158 F1
**Greenacres**
Bushey WD23 . . . . . . . . . .176 D8
Hemel Hempstead HP2 . . .125 D2
Pitstone LU7 . . . . . . . . . . . .80 C4
**Greenall Cl** EN8 . . . . . . . .148 E1
**Greenbank** EN8 . . . . . . . .148 B3
**Greenbank Rd** WD17 . . . .153 D3
**Greenbury Cl** Barley SG8 . . .8 F1
Chorleywood WD3 . . . . . .164 C5
**Greencoates** SG13 . . . . . .113 E5
**Greene Field Rd** HP4 . . . .122 C4
**Greene Wlk** HP4 . . . . . . .122 D3
**Greener Ct** EN3 . . . . . . . .163 A2
**Greenes Ct** HP4 . . . . . . . .122 C5
**Greenfield** Hatfield AL9 . . .130 D8
Royston SG8 . . . . . . . . . . . . .7 B7
Welwyn Garden City AL8 . . .89 D1
**Greenfield Ave**
Ickleford SG5 . . . . . . . . . . .21 D4
South Oxhey WD19 . . . . . .175 E8
**Greenfield La** SG5 . . . . . . .21 E4
**Greenfield Rd** SG1 . . . . . . .50 E7
**Greenfield St** EN9 . . . . . .163 C5
**Greenfields** Cuffley EN6 . .146 E1
Stansted Mountfitchet
CM24 . . . . . . . . . . . . . . . . .59 E7
Greenfields Prim Sch
WD19 . . . . . . . . . . . . . . . .175 C5
**Greengate** LU3 . . . . . . . . . .44 C8
**Greenheys Cl** HA6 . . . . . .174 E2
**Greenhill Ave** LU2 . . . . . . .45 E3
**Greenhill Cres** WD18 . . . .166 E3
**Greenhill Ct** HP1 . . . . . . .124 B2
**Greenhill Pk** CM23 . . . . . .76 D5
**Greenhills** SG12 . . . . . . . .93 C3
**Greenhills Cl** WD3 . . . . . .165 B4
**Greenland Rd** EN5 . . . . . .171 C3
**Greenlands** WD6 . . . . . . .170 D3
Greenlane Ind Est SG6 . . . .23 C7
**Greenleas** EN9 . . . . . . . . .163 E5
**Greenriggs** LU2 . . . . . . . . .46 F2
**Greenside** WD6 . . . . . . . .157 A1
**Greenside Dr** SG5 . . . . . . .34 D8
**Greenside Pk** LU2 . . . . . . .45 E3
Greenside Sch SG2 . . . . . . .51 B2
**Greensleeves Cl** AL4 . . . .128 C2
**Greenstead** CM21 . . . . . . .97 E1
**Greensward** WD23 . . . . . .168 B3
**Greenway**
Berkhamsted HP4 . . . . . . .122 A4
Bishop's Stortford CM23 . . .77 C6
Harpenden AL5 . . . . . . . . .107 E8
Hemel Hempstead HP2 . . .125 B3
Letchworth SG6 . . . . . . . . . .23 A2
Pinner HA5 . . . . . . . . . . . .175 B1
Walkern SG2 . . . . . . . . . . . .52 B8
Greenway Fst Sch HP4 . .121 F4
**Greenway The**
Enfield EN3 . . . . . . . . . . . .162 D4
Potters Bar EN6 . . . . . . . .159 A6
Rickmansworth WD3 . . . . .165 A2
Tring HP23 . . . . . . . . . . . . .99 F5
**Greenways**
Abbots Langley WD5 . . . . .153 E7
Buntingford SG9 . . . . . . . . .40 D8
Goff's Oak EN7 . . . . . . . . .147 B2
Hertford SG14 . . . . . . . . . .113 B6
Luton LU2 . . . . . . . . . . . . . .46 B5
Stevenage SG1 . . . . . . . . . . .50 E6
Welwyn AL6 . . . . . . . . . . . .89 E3
**Greenwich Ct**
Cheshunt EN8 . . . . . . . . . .162 E5
St Albans AL1 . . . . . . . . . .128 A2
**Greenwich Way** EN9 . . . .163 C4
**Greenwood Ave** EN7 . . . .162 B8
**Greenwood Cl** EN7 . . . . .162 B8
**Greenwood Dr** WD25 . . . .154 B5
**Greenwood Gdns** WD7 . . .156 E6
**Greenyard** EN9 . . . . . . . .163 C6
**Greer Rd** HA3 . . . . . . . . .176 C2
**Gregories Cl** LU3 . . . . . . . .45 D1
**Gregory Ave** EN6 . . . . . . .159 C6
**Gregory Mews** EN9 . . . . .163 B7
**Gregson Cl** WD6 . . . . . . .170 C8
**Grenadier Cl** AL4 . . . . . . .128 C2
**Grenadine Cl** EN7 . . . . . .147 F4
**Grenadine Way** HP23 . . .100 A5
Greneway Sch The SG8 . . . .7 E7
**Grenfell Cl** WD6 . . . . . . .170 C8
**Grenville Ave** EN10 . . . . .134 F2
**Grenville Cl** EN8 . . . . . . .162 D7
**Grenville Ct** WD3 . . . . . . .164 C5
**Grenville Way** SG2 . . . . . .51 A1
**Gresford Cl** AL4 . . . . . . .128 D3
**Gresham Cl** LU2 . . . . . . . .64 D8
**Gresham Ct** HP4 . . . . . . .122 B3
**Gresley Cl** AL8 . . . . . . . .110 E8
**Gresley Ct** Enfield EN1 . . .162 C4
Potters Bar EN6 . . . . . . . .145 C1
**Gresley Way** SG2 . . . . . . . .51 D5
**Greville Cl** AL9 . . . . . . . .144 C7
**Grey House The** 4
WD17 . . . . . . . . . . . . . . . .167 A7
**Greycaine Rd** WD24 . . . .154 D2
**Greydells Rd** SG1 . . . . . . .50 E6
**Greyfriars** SG12 . . . . . . . .93 B3
**Greyfriars La** AL5 . . . . . .107 A7
**Greyhound La** EN6 . . . . . .158 A6
**Greystoke Cl** HP4 . . . . . .122 A3
**Griffiths Way** AL1 . . . . . .127 C1
**Griffon Way** WD25 . . . . .153 F5
**Grimsdyke Cres** EN5 . . . .171 C6
Grimsdyke Fst & Mid Sch
HA5 . . . . . . . . . . . . . . . . .175 F4
**Grimsdyke Lo** AL1 . . . . . .128 A3
**Grimsdyke Rd**
Pinner HA5 . . . . . . . . . . . .175 E3
Wigginton HP23 . . . . . . . .100 D1
**Grimston Rd** AL1 . . . . . . .127 F2
**Grimstone Rd** SG4 . . . . . . .35 E4
**Grimthorpe Cl** AL3 . . . . .127 D6
**Grindcobbe** AL1 . . . . . . .141 D8
**Grinders End** SG4 . . . . . . .36 B4
**Grinstead La** CM22 . . . . . .98 C6
**Groom Rd** EN10 . . . . . . . .148 F5
**Grooms Cotts** HP5 . . . . . .136 B1
**Groomsby Dr** LU7 . . . . . . .80 E5
**Grosvenor Ave** WD4 . . . .139 C3
**Grosvenor Cl** CM23 . . . . . .76 D4
**Grosvenor Ct**
Croxley Green WD3 . . . . . .166 D4
Stevenage SG1 . . . . . . . . . . .50 A7
**Grosvenor Ho** 4 CM23 . . . .77 B8
**Grosvenor Rd** Baldock SG7 12 F1
Borehamwood WD6 . . . . . .170 B6
Hoddesdon EN10 . . . . . . . .134 F3
Luton LU3 . . . . . . . . . . . . . .45 B5
Moor Park HA6 . . . . . . . . .174 F5
St Albans AL1 . . . . . . . . . .127 E2
Watford WD17 . . . . . . . . .167 C6
**Grosvenor Rd W** SG7 . . . . .12 F1
**Grosvenor Terr** HP1 . . . . .124 A2
**Grotto The** SG12 . . . . . . .114 D8
**Ground La** AL10 . . . . . . . .130 B7
**Grove Ave** AL5 . . . . . . . . .107 D7
**Grove Cotts** WD23 . . . . . .168 A3
**Grove Cres** WD3 . . . . . . .166 A5
**Grove Ct** Arlesey SG15 . . . . .11 A8
Barnet EN5 . . . . . . . . . . . .171 F6
Waltham Abbey EN9 . . . . .163 B6
**Grove Cvn Pk The** LU1 . . . .63 B3
**Grove End** LU1 . . . . . . . . . .63 B5
**Grove Farm Pk** HA6 . . . . .174 D5
**Grove Gdns** Enfield EN3 . .162 D1
Tring HP23 . . . . . . . . . . . .100 B5
**Grove Hall Rd** WD23 . . . .167 E5
**Grove Hill** CM24 . . . . . . . .59 E7
**Grove Ho** Bushey WD23 . . .167 F3
Cheshunt EN8 . . . . . . . . . .148 B1
Hitchin SG4 . . . . . . . . . . . . .22 A2
Grove Inf Sch The AL5 . . .107 D7
Grove Jun Sch The AL5 . .107 D7

**Grove La** HP5 ....136 B5
**Grove Lea** AL10 ....130 A2
**Grove Mdw** AL7 ....111 C6
**Grove Mead** AL10 ....129 F5
**Grove Mill La** WD3, WD17 ....153 C1
**Grove Park Rd** LU1 ....63 B3
**Grove Path** EN7 ....162 A8
**Grove Pk**
Bishop's Stortford CM23 ...76 C8
Tring HP23 ....100 C5
**Grove Pl**
19 Bishop's Stortford CM23 76 F7
Bushey WD25 ....168 B8
Welham Green AL9 ....144 C7
**Grove Rd**
Borehamwood WD6 ....170 A8
Harpenden AL5 ....107 D7
Hemel Hempstead HP1 ...124 A1
Hitchin SG4 ....21 F1
Luton LU1 ....63 D7
Northwood HA6 ....174 D5
Rickmansworth WD3 ....173 A8
Slip End LU1 ....63 B2
St Albans AL1 ....127 D2
Stevenage SG1 ....50 D7
Tring HP23 ....100 C5
Ware SG12 ....93 F2
**Grove Rd W** EN3 ....162 C2
Grove Road Prim Sch HP23 ....100 C5
**Grove The**
Brookmans Park AL9 ....145 A4
Chipperfield WD4 ....138 C1
Great Hallingbury CM22 ...77 F4
Latimer HP5 ....150 D3
Little Hadham SG11 ....75 E7
Luton LU1 ....63 B5
Potters Bar EN6 ....159 C7
Radlett WD7 ....156 A5
Tring HP23 ....100 C5
**Grove Way** WD3 ....164 B4
**Grove Wlk** SG14 ....113 C8
**Grovebury Gdns** AL2 ....141 C4
**Grovedale Cl** EN7 ....147 F1
**Groveland Way** SG5 ....12 A5
**Grovelands**
Chiswell Green AL2 ....141 B4
Hemel Hempstead HP2 ...125 C5
**Grovelands Ave** SG4 ....22 C2
Grovelands Bsns Ctr HP2 ....125 C5
**Grover Cl** HP2 ....124 D4
**Grover Rd** WD19 ....167 D3
**Grovewood Cl** WD3 ....164 B4
**Grubbs La** AL9 ....145 C8
Gryphon Ind Pk The AL3 ....127 F8
Guardian Ind Est LU1 ....63 C8
**Guernsey Cl** LU4 ....44 A3
**Guernsey Ho** Enfield EN3 162 D1
Watford WD18 ....167 A3
**Guessens Ct** AL8 ....110 C6
**Guessens Gr** AL8 ....110 C6
**Guessens Rd** AL8 ....110 C6
**Guessens Wlk** AL8 ....110 C7
Guilden Morden CE Prim Sch SG8 ....1 F5
**Guildford Cl** SG1 ....36 F2
**Guildford Rd** AL1 ....128 B2
**Guildford St** LU1 ....63 E7
**Guildhouse The** WD3 ....166 B3
**Guilfords** CM17 ....118 D5
**Guinevere Gdns** EN8 ....162 E8
**Gulland Cl** WD23 ....168 C4
**Gullbrook** HP1 ....124 A3
**Gullet Wood Rd** WD25 ....154 A4
**Gullicot Way** LU7 ....80 D4
**Gulphs The** SG13 ....113 D5
**Gun La** SG3 ....68 F4
**Gun Meadow Ave** SG3 ....69 A4
**Gun Rd** SG3 ....69 A4
**Gun Road Gdns** SG3 ....68 F4
Gunnels Wood Ind Est SG1 ....50 D3
**Gunnels Wood Rd** SG1 ..50 B5
**Gunner Dr** EN3 ....163 A2
**Gurney Court Rd** AL1 ...127 F5
**Gurney's La** SG5 ....21 B7
**Gwent Cl** WD25 ....154 D5
**Gwynfa Cl** AL6 ....89 D7
**Gwynne Cl** HP23 ....100 A5
**Gwynns Wlk** SG13 ....113 E6
**Gyfford Wlk** EN7 ....162 B8
**Gypsy Cl** SG12 ....114 F4
**Gypsy La**
Abbots Langley WD4 ....153 D5
Great Amwell SG12 ....114 F4
Welwyn Garden City AL7 ...110 F1
**Gypsy Moth Ave** AL10 ...129 E7

## H

Haberdashers' Aske's Sch for Boys WD6 ....169 B6
Haberdashers' Aske's Sch for Girls WD6 ....169 B5
**Hackforth Cl** EN5 ....171 B4
**Hackney Cl** WD6 ....170 D4
**Haddam Hall** SG11 ....57 E2
**Haddenham Ct** HP2 ....105 B1
**Haddestoke Gate** EN8 ...148 F5
**Haddon Cl**
Borehamwood WD6 ....170 A6
Hemel Hempstead HP3 ...125 A2
Stevenage SG2 ....69 C7
**Haddon Ct** 20 AL5 ....86 B1
**Haddon Rd**
Chorleywood WD3 ....164 C4
Luton LU2 ....63 F8
**Hadham Ct** CM23 ....76 E8
**Hadham Gr** CM23 ....76 C8
**Hadham Ho** CM23 ....76 D8
**Hadham Rd**
Bishop's Stortford CM23 ...76 D8
Little Hadham SG11 ....57 F1
Standon SG11 ....55 F1
**Hadland Cl** HP3 ....137 A5
**Hadleigh** SG6 ....23 B4
**Hadleigh Ct**
Hoddesdon EN10 ....134 F1
Wheathampstead AL5 ....107 E6
**Hadley Cl** WD6 ....169 F3
**Hadley Ct** LU3 ....45 D1
**Hadley Gn** EN5 ....171 F7
**Hadley Gn W** EN5 ....171 F7
**Hadley Gr** EN5 ....171 E7
**Hadley Green Rd** EN5 ...171 F7
**Hadley Highstone** EN5 ...171 F8
**Hadley Par** 6 EN5 ....171 E6
**Hadley Rd** EN2,EN4 ....160 C1
**Hadley Ridge** EN5 ....171 F6
Hadley Wood Prim Sch EN4 ....159 C1
Hadley Wood Sta EN4 ...159 C1
**Hadlow Down Cl** LU3 ....45 A5
**Hadrian Cl** AL3 ....127 A1
**Hadrian Way** SG7 ....23 D7
**Hadrians Wlk** SG1 ....51 C8
**Hadwell Cl** SG2 ....51 A3
**Hagdell Rd** LU1 ....63 C5
**Hagden La** WD18 ....167 A4
**Haggerston Rd** WD6 ...156 E1
**Hagsdell Rd** SG13 ....113 D5
**Haig Cl** AL1 ....128 B2
**Haig Ho** AL1 ....128 B2
**Hailey Ave** EN11 ....115 A2
**Hailey Cl** SG13 ....114 E2
Hailey Hall Sch SG13 ...114 F2
**Hailey La** SG13 ....114 E2
Haileybury & Imperial Service Coll SG13 ....114 D2
**Haines Way** WD25 ....154 A5
**Haldane Cl** EN3 ....163 B1
**Haldens** AL7 ....89 F1
**Haldens Ho** 3 AL7 ....89 F1
**Hale Ct** SG13 ....113 D5
**Hale Ho** EN3 ....162 D2
**Hale La** HP22 ....119 A3
**Hale Rd** SG13 ....113 D5
**Hales Mdw** AL5 ....86 A2
**Hales Park Cl** HP2 ....125 C4
**Hales Pk** HP2 ....125 C4
**Haleswood Rd** HP2 ....125 B4
**Half Acre** SG5 ....34 D6
**Half Acres** CM23 ....76 F8
**Half Moon Cotts** CM21 ...97 B1
**Half Moon La** LU1 ....84 C8
**Half Moon Mdw** HP2 ...125 C8
**Half Moon Mews** 5 AL1 ....127 D3
**Halfhide La** EN8 ....148 D5
**Halfhides** EN9 ....163 D6
**Halfway Ave** LU4 ....44 D1
**Halifax Cl**
Bricket Wood AL2 ....154 F8
Watford WD25 ....153 F5
**Halifax Rd** WD3 ....164 C2
**Halifax Way** AL7 ....111 E6
**Hall Barns** SG9 ....42 F4
**Hall Cl** WD3 ....165 A1
**Hall Cotts** SG9 ....29 A1
**Hall Dr** UB9 ....173 C2
**Hall Gdns** AL4 ....143 D8
**Hall Gr** AL7 ....111 B4
**Hall Heath Cl** AL1 ....128 B5
**Hall La** Great Chishill SG8 ...9 F2
Great Hormead SG9 ....29 A1
Kimpton SG4 ....87 C8
Woolmer Green SG3 ....69 A2
**Hall Mead** SG6 ....22 D6
**Hall Park Gate** HP4 ....122 E3
**Hall Park Hill** HP4 ....122 E3
**Hall Pk** HP4 ....122 E3
**Hall Place Cl** AL1 ....127 E4
**Hall Place Gdns** AL1 ...127 E4
**Hall Rd** HP2 ....125 B5
**Hallam Cl** WD24 ....167 C7
**Hallam Gdns** HA5 ....175 E3
**Halland Way** HA6 ....174 D4
**Halley Rd** EN9 ....163 B3
**Halleys Ridge** SG14 ....113 A5
**Halliday Cl** WD7 ....156 E7
**Halling Hill** CM20 ....117 F2
**Hallingbury Cl** CM22 ....77 B1
**Hallingbury Rd**
Bishop's Stortford CM22 ...77 B4
Sawbridgeworth CM21 ....98 A4
**Hallmores** EN10 ....135 A4
**Hallowell Rd** HA6 ....174 E3
**Hallowes Cres** WD19 ...175 A7
**Halls Cl** AL6 ....89 C4
**Hallside Rd** EN1 ....161 F1
**Hallwicks Rd** LU2 ....46 B3
**Hallworth Dr** SG5 ....11 E6
**Hallworth Ho** SG5 ....11 E6
**Halsey Dr**
Hemel Hempstead HP1 ...123 F5
Hitchin SG4 ....35 B7
**Halsey Pk** AL2 ....142 F4
**Halsey Pl** WD24 ....154 B1
**Halsey Rd** WD18 ....167 B6
**Halstead Hill** EN7 ....147 E1
**Halter Cl** WD6 ....170 D4
**Halton Cl** AL2 ....141 C3
Halton Wood (Forest Wlks)★ HP23 ....119 A5
**Haltside** AL10 ....129 E4
**Halwick Cl** HP1 ....124 B1
**Halyard Cl** LU3 ....45 B6
Halyard High Sch LU4 ...44 A3
**Hamberlins La** HP4 ....121 C7
**Hamble Ct** WD18 ....167 A5
**Hambleden Pl** WD7 ....155 F4
**Hambledon Ct** EN4 ....159 D1
**Hamblings Cl** WD7 ....156 D6
**Hambridge Way** SG5 ....20 D4
**Hambro Cl** LU2 ....85 F7
**Hamburgh Ct** EN8 ....148 D3
**Hamels Dr** SG13 ....114 B7
**Hamels La** SG9 ....55 B7
**Hamer Cl** HP3 ....137 A3
**Hamer Ct** LU2 ....45 D8
**Hamilton Ave** EN11 ....135 A8
**Hamilton Cl**
Bricket Wood AL2 ....155 A8
Dagnall HP4 ....81 C5
South Mimms EN6 ....158 A6
**Hamilton Ct** 3 AL10 ...130 B3
**Hamilton Mead** HP3 ...137 A4
**Hamilton Rd**
Abbots Langley WD4 ....153 C6
Berkhamsted HP4 ....122 B4
South Oxhey WD19 ....175 B7
St Albans AL1 ....128 A4
**Hamilton St** WD18 ....167 C4
**Hamlet Cl** AL2 ....140 F1
**Hamlet The** HP4 ....123 A7
**Hammarskjold Rd** CM20 ....117 D2
**Hammer La** HP2 ....124 F4
**Hammer Par** WD25 ....154 A6
**Hammerdell** SG6 ....22 D7
**Hammers Gate** AL2 ....141 A5
**Hammond Cl** Barnet EN5 171 E4
Hammond Street EN7 ....147 F5
Stevenage SG1 ....50 D6
**Hammond Ct** LU1 ....63 C1
**Hammond End La** AL5 ...106 F5
Hammond Prim Sch The HP2 ....124 F6
**Hammonds Hill** AL5 ....106 F4
**Hammonds La** AL10 ....109 B3
**Hammondstreet Rd** EN7 ....147 D5
**Hammondswick** AL5 ....106 F4
**Hamonte** SG6 ....23 C4
**Hampden** SG4 ....66 C1
**Hampden Cl** SG6 ....23 B8
**Hampden Cres** EN7 ....162 B8
**Hampden Hill** SG12 ....93 F2
**Hampden Hill Cl** SG12 ...93 F2
**Hampden Pl** AL2 ....141 E2
**Hampden Rd**
Harrow HA3 ....176 C1
Hitchin SG4 ....22 C1
**Hampden Rise** SG8 ....7 D4
**Hampden Way** WD17 ....153 E3
**Hampermill La** WD19 ...167 A1
**Hampton Cl** SG2 ....69 C7
**Hampton Gdns** CM21 ...118 C7
**Hampton Rd** LU4 ....63 B8
**Hamstel Rd** CM20 ....117 C1
**Hamsworth Ct** SG14 ....112 F7
**Hanaper Dr** SG8 ....8 F2
**Hanbury Cl** Cheshunt EN8 148 E2
Ware SG12 ....93 E1
**Hanbury Cotts** AL9 ....131 E6
**Hanbury Dr** SG12 ....93 C6
**Hanbury Mews** SG12 ....93 C5
**Hancock Ct** WD6 ....170 C8
**Hancock Dr** LU2 ....45 E5
**Hancroft Rd** HP3 ....124 F1
**Hand La** CM21 ....97 C1
**Handa Cl** HP3 ....139 B8
**Handcross Rd** LU2 ....46 D2
**Handley Gate** AL2 ....140 F2
**Handpost Lodge Gdns** HP2 ....125 D2
**Handside Cl** AL8 ....110 C6
**Handside Gn** AL8 ....110 C7
**Handside La** AL8 ....110 C6
**Handsworth Way** WD19 175 A7
**Hangar Ruding** WD19 ...175 F7
**Hanger Cl** HP1 ....124 B2
**Hangmans La** AL6 ....89 F8
**Hanover Cl** SG2 ....50 F1
**Hanover Ct**
Croxley Green WD3 ....166 A4
Hoddesdon EN11 ....135 A7
Luton LU4 ....44 D5
9 Pinner HA5 ....175 F3
Waltham Abbey EN9 ....163 C6
**Hanover Gdns** WD5 ....139 F1
**Hanover Gn** HP1 ....124 A1
**Hanover Ho** AL7 ....110 F4
**Hanover Wlk** AL10 ....129 F2
**Hanross Cl** AL2 ....140 E1
**Hanscombe End Rd** SG5 .19 D7
**Hanselin Cl** HA7 ....176 F5
**Hanswick Cl** LU2 ....46 B2
**Hanworth Cl** LU2 ....45 D7
**Hanyards End** EN6 ....146 E3
**Hanyards La** EN6 ....146 D3
Happy Valley Ind Pk WD4 ....139 B3
**Harbert Gdns** AL2 ....141 C2
**Harborne Cl** WD19 ....175 C5
**Harbour Ct** WD23 ....168 B4
**Harbury Dell** LU3 ....45 B7
**Harcourt Rd**
Bushey WD23 ....168 C4
Tring HP23 ....100 C4
**Harcourt St** LU1 ....63 E5
**Hardenwick Ct** 4 AL5 ...86 A2
**Harding Cl** Luton LU3 ....44 E7
Redbourn AL3 ....106 B5
Watford WD25 ....154 C6
**Harding Ct** AL5 ....86 B4
**Harding Par** 8 AL5 ....86 B1
**Hardings** AL7 ....111 C7
**Hardingstone Ct** EN8 ...162 F5
**Hardwick Cl** SG2 ....69 C7
**Hardwick Gn** LU3 ....45 B7
**Hardwicke Pl** AL2 ....142 D4
**Hardy Cl** Barnet EN5 ....171 E4
Hitchin SG4 ....35 C7
**Hardy Dr** SG8 ....7 D8
**Hardy Rd** HP2 ....124 F4
**Hare Cres** WD25 ....154 A7
**Hare La** AL10 ....130 B3
**Hare Street Rd** SG9 ....41 B8
**Harebell** AL7 ....110 E3
**Harebell Cl** SG13 ....114 B6
**Harebreaks The** WD24 ..154 B2
**Harefield** Harlow CM20 ..118 A1
Stevenage SG2 ....51 C3
**Harefield Ct** LU1 ....62 F8
Harefield Hospl UB9 ....173 C2
Harefield Inf Sch UB9 ..173 C2
Harefield Jun Sch UB9 .173 C2
**Harefield Pl** AL4 ....128 D6
**Harefield Rd** Luton LU1 ...62 F8
Rickmansworth WD3 ....173 D7
Harefield Road Ind Est WD3 ....173 E6
**Harepark Cl** HP1 ....123 F4
Haresfoot Sch HP4 ....122 B1
**Harewood** WD3 ....165 C4
**Harewood Ct** HA3 ....176 E2
**Harewood Rd** WD19 ....175 B7
**Harford Dr** WD17 ....166 E8
Harforde Ct SG13 ....114 A6
**Hargrave Cl** CM24 ....59 E8
**Hargreaves Ave** EN7 ....162 B8
**Hargreaves Cl** EN7 ....162 B8
**Hargreaves Rd** SG8 ....7 D5
**Harkett Cl** HA3 ....176 F1
**Harkett Ct** HA3 ....176 F1
**Harkness** EN7 ....148 B2
**Harkness Ct** SG4 ....22 B1
Harkness Ind Est WD6 .170 A5
**Harkness Way** SG4 ....22 C2
**Harland Ct** UB9 ....173 C1
**Harlech Rd** WD5 ....154 A8
Harlequin The WD17 ....167 C5
**Harlesden Rd** AL1 ....128 A3
**Harlestone Cl** LU3 ....31 A1
**Harley Ct** AL4 ....128 D7
**Harlings The** SG13 ....114 C2
Harlow Coll CM20 ....117 D1
**Harlow Ct** HP2 ....125 A7
Harlow Mill Sta CM20 ..118 C5
**Harlow Rd** Roydon CM19 .116 C1
Sawbridgeworth CM21 ....118 C8
Harlow Sports Ctr CM20 ....117 D2
Harlow Stad (Greyhounds) CM19 ....116 E1
Harlow Town Sta CM20 .117 D3
Harlowbury Prim Sch CM17 ....118 D4
**Harlton Ct** EN9 ....163 F5
**Harmer Dell** AL6 ....89 F4
**Harmer Green La** AL6 ....90 B5
**Harmony Cl** AL10 ....130 A7
**Harmsworth Way** N20 ..171 F1
**Harness Way** AL4 ....128 D6
**Harold Cres** EN9 ....163 C7
**Harold Ct** EN8 ....162 F5
Harpenden Hospl (private) AL5 ....86 A4
**Harpenden La** AL3 ....106 B6
Harpenden Meml Hospl AL5 ....86 B2
Harpenden Prep Sch AL5 85 F2
**Harpenden Rd**
Wheathampstead AL5,AL4 .108 B8
St Albans AL3 ....127 E6
**Harpenden Rise** AL5 ....85 F3
Harpenden Sta AL5 ....86 B1
**Harper Ct** SG1 ....50 F5
**Harper La** WD7 ....156 B8
Harperbury Hospl WD7 .156 C8
**Harps Hill** AL3 ....83 E5
**Harpsfield Broadway** AL10 ....129 F6
**Harptree Way** AL1 ....128 A5
**Harriet Walker Way** WD3 ....164 F2
**Harriet Way** WD23 ....168 D2
**Harrington Cl** 8 CM23 ..77 A7
**Harrington Ct** SG13 ....114 C3
**Harriot Hts** AL3 ....127 C4
**Harris Ho** 14 WD18 ....166 F3
**Harris La** Great Offley SG5 33 D2
Shenley WD7 ....157 A6
**Harris Rd** WD25 ....154 A4
**Harris's La** SG12 ....93 C1
**Harrison Cl** Hitchin SG4 ....34 F7
Northwood HA6 ....174 C4
**Harrison Rd** EN9 ....163 C4
**Harrison Wlk** EN8 ....148 D1
**Harrisons** CM23 ....59 D2
**Harrogate Rd** 2 WD19 ..175 C7
Harrow Coll, Harrow Weald Campus HA3 ....176 E4
**Harrow Ct** SG1 ....50 E5
**Harrow View** HA2 ....176 C1
**Harrow Way** WD19 ....175 E6
**Harrow Weald Pk** HA3 .176 D4
**Harrow Yd** HP23 ....100 A3
**Harrowbond Rd** CM17 ..118 C1
**Harrowden Ct** LU2 ....64 C8
**Harrowden Rd** LU2 ....64 B8
**Harrowdene** SG2 ....51 C4
**Harry Scott Ct** LU4 ....44 C6
**Harston Dr** EN3 ....163 A1
**Hart Hill Dr** LU2 ....63 F8
**Hart Hill La** LU2 ....63 F8
**Hart Hill Path** LU2 ....63 F8
Hart Hill Prim Sch LU2 ..63 F8
**Hart La** LU2 ....64 A8
**Hart Lodge** 10 EN5 ....171 E6
**Hart Rd** Harlow CM17 ...118 C6
St Albans AL1 ....127 D2
**Hart Wlk** LU2 ....46 A1
**Hartcran Ho** 7 WD19 ...175 D7
**Hartfield Ave** WD6 ....170 A4
**Hartfield Cl** WD6 ....170 A4
**Hartfield Ct** 6 SG12 ....93 D2
**Hartforde Rd** WD6 ....170 B8
**Harthall La** WD4,HP3 ....139 D4
**Hartham La** SG14 ....113 D6
**Hartham Villas** SG14 ....113 C7
**Hartland Ct** SG5 ....34 D7
**Hartland Rd** EN8 ....148 D1
**Hartley Rd** LU2 ....63 F8
**Hartmoor Mews** EN3 ....162 D2
**Harts Cl** WD23 ....168 A8
**Hartsbourne Ave** WD23 .176 D8
**Hartsbourne Cl** WD23 ..176 D8
**Hartsbourne Pk** WD23 ..176 E8
Hartsbourne Prim Sch WD23 ....176 D8
**Hartsbourne Rd** WD23 ..176 D8
**Hartsbourne Way** HP2 ..125 C2
Hartsfield Jun Mix Inf Sch SG7 ....12 F1
**Hartsfield Rd** LU2 ....46 B2
**Hartspring La** WD23, WD25 ....168 A8
**Hartswood Gn** WD23 ...176 D8
**Hartwell Gdns** AL5 ....85 E1
**Hartwood** 3 LU2 ....63 F8
**Harvest Cl** LU4 ....44 A3
**Harvest Ct** Letchworth SG6 23 A2
Oaklands AL6 ....89 E7
St Albans AL4 ....128 D7
**Harvest End** WD25 ....154 D3
**Harvest La** SG2 ....51 D7
**Harvest Mead** AL10 ....130 B7
**Harvest Rd** WD23 ....168 B5
**Harvey Rd**
Croxley Green WD3 ....166 A3
London Colney AL2 ....142 C5
Stevenage SG2 ....51 B6
Harvey Road Prim Sch WD3 ....166 A3
**Harvey's Hill** LU2 ....45 F5
**Harveyfields** EN9 ....163 C5
**Harvingwell Pl** HP2 ....125 B5
**Harwood Cl** Tewin AL6 ....90 E2
Welwyn Garden City AL8 ...89 E2
**Harwood Hill** AL8 ....89 E1
Harwood Hill Jun Mix Inf Sch AL8 ....89 E2
**Harwoods Rd** WD18 ....167 A5
**Hasedines Rd** HP1 ....124 A4
**Haseldine Mdws** AL10 ...129 F4
**Haseldine Rd** AL2 ....142 D5
**Haselfoot** SG6 ....22 E6
**Hasketon Dr** LU4 ....44 B6
**Haslemere** CM23 ....77 A4
Haslemere Est The EN11 ....135 D6
Haslemere Ind Est AL7 .110 F7
**Haslewood Ave** EN11 ...135 A6
**Haslingden Cl** AL5 ....85 D3
**Hastings Cl** SG1 ....50 A8
**Hastings St** LU1 ....63 D6
**Hastings Way**
Croxley Green WD3 ....166 C5
Watford WD23 ....167 E5
**Hastoe Farm Barns** HP23 ....119 F7
**Hastoe La** HP23 ....100 A2
Hatch End High Sch HA3 ....176 B2
Hatch End Sta HA5 ....176 A3
**Hatch Gn** CM22 ....98 B8
**Hatch La** SG4 ....24 A3
**Hatching Gn** AL5 ....107 A6
**Hatching Green Cl** AL5 .107 A6
**Hatfield Ave** AL10 ....129 E8
Hatfield Bsns Ctr AL10 .129 D8
**Hatfield Cres** HP2 ....124 F7
Hatfield House & Gdns★ AL9 ....130 D5
**Hatfield Rd**
Essendon AL9 ....111 E1
Potters Bar EN6 ....159 C8
St Albans AL1,AL4 ....128 C3
Watford WD24 ....167 B8
Hatfield Sta AL9 ....130 C6
**Hatfield Tunnel** AL10 ....129 F6
**Hathaway Cl** LU4 ....44 B2
**Hathaway Ct** AL4 ....128 E3
**Hatherleigh Gdns** EN6 .159 D7
**Hatters La** WD18 ....166 D3
**Hatters Way** LU1,LU4 ....44 D1
**Hatton Rd** EN8 ....148 D2
**Havelock Rd**
Kings Langley WD4 ....138 F3
Luton LU2 ....45 E1
**Havelock Rise** LU2 ....45 E1

Haven Cl AL10 .........129 F6
Haven The SG5 ...........11 F6
Havensfield WD4 ........152 B8
Havercroft Cl AL3 .......127 C1
Haverdale LU4 ...........44 C4
Havers Inf Sch CM23 .....76 E5
Havers La CM23 ..........76 F5
Havers Par CM23 .........76 F5
Haward Rd EN11 .........135 C8
Hawbush Cl AL6 ..........89 B4
Hawbush Rise AL6 ........89 B5
Hawes Cl HA6 ...........174 C1
Hawes La E4 .............163 C1
Haweswater Dr WD25 ....154 C6
Hawfield Gdns AL2 ......141 D5
Hawkesworth Cl HA6 ....174 E3
Hawkfield SG6 ...........22 E8
Hawkfields LU2 ..........45 E6
Hawkings Way HP3 ......137 C7
Hawkins Cl WD6 ........170 C7
Hawkins Hall La SG3 ......69 E2
Hawkshead Ct EN8 ......162 F5
Hawkshead La A19 ......144 D3
Hawkshead Rd EN6 ......145 B2
Hawkshill AL1 ...........128 A2
Hawkshill Dr HP3 .......137 F8
Hawksmead Cl EN3 ......162 D3
Hawksmoor WD7 ........157 A6
Hawksmoor Sch WD6 ...170 C8
Hawkwell Dr HP23 ......100 C4
Hawridge & Cholesbury CE
Sch HP5 ...............120 E2
Hawridge La HP5 ........120 F1
Hawridge Vale HP5 ......120 F1
Hawsley Rd AL5 ........107 A4
Hawthorn Ave LU2 .......46 B4
Hawthorn Cl
  Abbots Langley WD5 ...154 A7
  Harpenden AL5 ........107 D7
  Hertford SG14 ........113 A4
  Hitchin SG5 ...........34 E6
  Royston SG8 ...........7 C5
  Watford WD17 ........153 F1
Hawthorn Cres LU1 .......62 E3
Hawthorn Gr Barnet EN5 170 E3
  Enfield EN2 ...........161 D1
Hawthorn Hill SG6 .......22 F7
Hawthorn La HP1 .......123 F4
Hawthorn Rd EN11 ......135 B8
Hawthorn Rise CM23 .....76 F3
Hawthorn Way
  Chiswell Green AL2 ....141 A7
  Royston SG8 ...........7 F7
Hawthorne Ave EN7 ....162 B8
Hawthorne Cl EN7 ......162 B8
Hawthorne Ct HA6 ......175 A1
Hawthorne Rd WD7 .....156 A5
Hawthornes AL8 ........110 D8
Hawthorns The
  Berkhamsted HP4 ......122 A5
  Hemel Hempstead HP3 .137 F7
  Maple Cross WD3 .....172 D5
  Ridge EN6 ............157 E6
  Stevenage SG1 .........51 A4
  Ware SG12 ............93 C3
Hawtrees WD7 .........155 F4
Hay Cl WD6 ............170 C4
Hay Gn SG8 .............15 F6
Hay La AL5 .............86 A1
Hay Wains SG3 ..........69 B2
Haybourn Mead HP1 ...124 B2
Haycroft
  Bishop's Stortford CM23 .77 C7
  Luton LU2 .............45 E4
Haycroft Rd SG1 .........50 E2
Hayden Rd EN9 .........163 C4
Haydon Dell WD23 ......167 F3
Haydon Hill Ho WD23 ..167 F2
Haydon Rd WD19 ......167 E3
Hayes Cl LU2 ...........46 C5
Hayes Hill Farm* EN9 ..149 C3
Hayes Wlk
  Cheshunt EN10 ........148 F6
  Potters Bar EN6 .......159 B6
Hayfield SG2 ...........51 D7
Hayfield Cl WD23 ......168 B5
Haygarth SG3 ..........69 A4
Hayhurst Rd LU4 ........44 B1
Hayley Bell Gdns CM23 ..76 F3
Hayley Comm SG2 .......51 C3
Hayling Dr LU2 ..........46 D3
Hayling Rd WD19 ......175 B8
Haymeads AL8 ..........89 E1
Haymeads La CM23 ......77 C6
Haymoor SG6 ..........22 E7
Haynes Cl AL7 .........111 A5
Haynes Mead HP4 .....122 A6
Haysman Cl SG6 ........23 B7
Hayton Cl LU3 ..........31 D1
Haywood Cl HA5 .......175 D1
Haywood Ct EN9 .......163 F5
Haywood Dr WD3 ......164 F4
Haywood La SG8 ........16 A6
Haywood Pk WD3 .....164 F4
Haywoods Dr HP3 ......137 F8
Haywoods La SG8 .......7 F5
Hazel Cl
  **3** Hammond Street EN7 .147 F5
  Welwyn AL6 ...........89 E3
Hazel Ct Hitchin SG4 ....35 A7
  Shenley WD7 .........156 A6
Hazel End CM23 ........59 A5
Hazel Gdns CM21 ........97 F1

Hazel Gr Hatfield AL10 ..129 F2
  Stotfold SG5 ...........11 E5
  Watford WD25 ........154 B4
  Welwyn Garden City AL7 .111 C7
Hazel Grove Ho AL10 ...129 F3
Hazel Mead EN5 ........171 B4
Hazel Rd
  Berkhamsted HP4 ......122 D3
  Chiswell Green AL2 ....141 B3
Hazel Tree Rd WD24 ...154 B3
Hazelbury Ave WD5 ....153 C7
Hazelbury Cres LU1 ......63 C8
Hazelbury **3** LU1 .....63 C8
Hazelcroft HA5 .........176 B4
Hazeldell SG14 ..........70 D3
Hazeldell Link HP1 ......123 E2
Hazeldell Rd HP1 .......123 F2
Hazeldene EN8 .........162 E7
Hazelend Rd CM23 ......59 B4
Hazelgrove Prim Sch
  AL10 ................129 F2
Hazelmere Rd
  St Albans AL4 .........128 C6
  Stevenage SG2 ........69 A8
Hazels The AL6 ..........90 E2
Hazelwood Cl Hitchin SG5 .34 F8
  Luton LU2 .............46 B4
Hazelwood Dr
  Pinner HA5 ...........175 B1
  St Albans AL4 ........128 C4
Hazelwood La WD5 .....153 D7
Hazelwood Rd WD3 ....166 C3
Hazely HP2 ............100 C4
Heacham Cl LU4 .........44 B4
Headingley Cl
  Hammond Street EN7 ..147 F5
  Shenley WD7 .........156 F7
  Stevenage SG1 .........50 E8
Headlands Dr HP4 ......122 E5
Headstone La HA3 ......176 B2
Headstone Lane Sta
  HA3 .................176 B2
Healey Rd WD18 .......166 F3
Healy Ct EN5 ..........171 D3
Hearle Way AL10 .......129 E7
Hearn's Way AL11 .....127 B3
Heath Ave Royston SG8 ...7 C6
  St Albans AL3 ........127 D5
Heath Brow HP1 .......124 C1
Heath Cl Harpenden AL5 .107 C7
  Hemel Hempstead HP1 .124 C2
  Luton LU1 .............63 B6
  Potters Bar EN6 .......145 B2
Heath Cotts EN6 ......145 B1
Heath Dr Potters Bar EN6 145 A1
  Ware SG12 ............93 D3
Heath Farm Ct WD7 ...153 D2
Heath Farm La AL1,AL3 127 E5
Heath Hall SG7 ..........23 F7
Heath Hill SG4 ..........67 D1
Heath La Codicote SG4 ...67 E1
  Hemel Hempstead HP1 .124 C2
  Hertford Heath SG13 ..114 C2
Heath Lodge WD23 .....167 F7
Heath Mount Sch SG14 ..71 B2
Heath Rd
  Breachwood Green SG4 ..47 D1
  Oaklands AL6 ..........68 F1
  Potters Bar EN6 ......145 B1
  St Albans AL1 ........127 E5
  Watford WD17 ........167 E2
Heath Row CM23 ........59 B1
Heath The
  Breachwood Green SG4 ..47 D2
  Radlett WD7 .........156 A6
Heath Way WD7 .......156 C8
Heathbourne Rd WD23 168 F1
Heathbrow Rd AL6 ......89 F8
Heathcote Ave AL10 ...130 A7
Heathcote Sch The SG2 ..51 A2
Heathcroft AL7 ........111 C6
Heathdene Manor
  WD17 ...............166 F8
Heather Cl
  Abbots Langley WD5 ...154 A7
  Bishop's Stortford CM23 ..76 D6
Heather Ct AL2 ........142 D4
Heather Gdns EN9 .....163 C3
Heather Rd AL8 ........110 C4
Heather Rise WD23 ....167 F7
Heather Way
  Harrow HA7 ..........176 F4
  Hemel Hempstead HP2 124 D4
  Potters Bar EN6 ......158 F7
Heathermere SG6 .......11 F1
Heathfield SG8 ..........7 B6
Heathfield Cl
  Caddington LU1 ........62 F4
  Potters Bar EN6 ......145 B1
  Watford WD19 ........167 C2
Heathfield Ct **2** AL1 ..127 C4
Heathfield Lower Sch
  LU1 .................62 E4
Heathfield Rd Hitchin SG5 21 F1
  Luton LU3 ............45 C4
  Watford WD23 .......167 F5
Heathgate SG13 ........114 B2
Heathlands AL6 .........68 F1
Heathlands Dr AL3 ....127 E5
Heathlands Sch AL3 ...127 E6
Heathside
  Colney Heath AL4 .....143 B8
  St Albans AL1 ........127 E5
Heathside Cl HA6 ......174 D5
Heathside Rd HA6 .....174 D6
Heathview AL5 ........107 B8
Heaton Ct EN8 ........148 D2
Heaton Dell LU2 ........46 E1
Heay Fields AL7 .......111 C7

Hebden Cl LU4 ..........44 B4
Hebing End SG2 ........52 F2
Heckford Cl WD18 .....166 C3
Hedge Row HP1 .......124 A5
Hedgebrooms AL7 .....111 C7
Hedgerow Cl SG2 .......51 D8
Hedgerow La EN5 .....171 B4
Hedgerow The LU4 ......44 D6
Hedgerow Wlk EN8 ...148 D1
Hedgerows CM21 .......97 F2
Hedgerows The
  Bishop's Stortford CM23 ..77 B6
  Stevenage SG2 ........51 D8
Hedges Cl AL10 .......130 B6
Hedges The AL3 ......127 C7
Hedgeside HP1 ........123 A4
Hedgeside Rd HA6 ....174 C5
Hedley Cl HP22 .........99 A4
Hedley Rd AL1 ........128 B3
Hedley Rise LU2 ........46 F2
Hedley Villas AL1 ......128 B3
Hedworth Ave EN8 ....162 D6
Heights The
  Hemel Hempstead HP2 124 F6
  Luton LU3 .............44 E5
Helena AL1 ............159 D1
Helena Pl **5** HP2 ....124 D5
Helens Gate EN8 ......148 F5
Helham Gn SG12 .......94 A4
Hellards Rd SG1 ........50 D7
Hellebore Ct SG1 .......51 B8
Helmsley Cl LU4 ........44 C5
Helston Cl HA5 ........175 F3
Helston Gr HP2 ........124 D8
Helston Pl WD7 .......153 F7
Hemel Hempstead General
  Hospl HP2 ............124 D3
Hemel Hempstead Rd
  Great Gaddesden HP4 ...81 F1
  Hemel Hempstead HP2,
  HP3 .................125 E1
  Redbourn AL3,HP2 ....105 C2
  St Albans HP3,AL2,AL3 126 D1
Hemel Hempstead Sch The
  HP1 .................124 C2
Hemel Hempstead Sta
  HP3 .................138 A8
Hemingford Dr LU2 .....45 D9
Hemingford Rd WD17 ..153 E3
Hemming Way WD25 ...154 A4
Hemmings The HP4 ....121 F3
Hemp La HP23 ........100 F1
Hempstall AL7 ........111 B4
Hempstead La HP4 ....123 C6
Hempstead Rd
  Bovingdon HP3 ......137 B5
  Kings Langley WD4 ...139 A3
  Watford WD17 .......153 E2
Henbury Way WD19 ...175 D7
Henderson Cl AL3 ....127 C7
Henderson Pl
  Bedmond WD5 ......139 F4
  Little Berkhamsted SG13 132 C2
Hendon Wood La NW7 171 A1
Hendren SG1 ...........51 A8
Henge Way LU3 ........44 E7
Henlow Ind Est SG16 ...10 B4
Henry Cl EN2 ..........161 E1
Henry St
  Hemel Hempstead HP3 138 D7
  Tring HP23 ...........100 A3
Hensley Cl Hitchin SG4 ..35 B6
Henstead Pl LU2 ........46 D1
Hepburn Ct EN6 ......158 A7
Heracles Cl AL2 .......141 C3
Herald Cl CM23 ........76 D6
Herbert St HP2 .......124 D4
Hereford Rd LU4 ........44 A3
Hereward Cl EN9 .....163 C7
Herga Ct WD17 .......167 A4
Heritage Cl AL3 ......127 D3
Heritage Wlk WD3 ....164 E6
Herkomer Cl WD23 ...168 B3
Herkomer Rd WD23 ..168 A3
Herm Ho EN3 .........162 D1
Hermitage Ct
  Potters Bar EN6 ......159 C6
  Stansted Mountfitchet
  CM24 ................59 D7
Hermitage Ho CM24 ...59 D7
Hermitage Rd SG5 ......34 F7
Hermitage The SG15 ...11 B8
Herne Ct WD23 ......168 C2
Herne Rd Bushey WD23 168 B3
  Stevenage SG1 ........36 B1
Herneshaw AL10 ......129 F3
Herns La AL7 .........111 B8
Herns Way AL7 ......111 A7
Heron Cl
  Hemel Hempstead HP3 138 F6
  Rickmansworth WD3 ..173 D8
  Sawbridgeworth CM21 ..97 D1
Heron Ct CM23 .........77 A7
Heron Dr Luton LU2 .....45 E6
  Stanstead Abbotts SG12 115 C3
Heron Mead EN3 ......163 A1
Heron Pl UB9 .........173 A4
Heron Trad Est LU3 .....44 C7
Heron Way Hatfield AL10 130 A3
  Stotfold SG5 ..........11 E6
Heron Wlk HA6 .......174 C6
Heronfield EN6 .......145 C1
Herongate Rd EN8 ....148 E4
Herons Elm HP4 ......121 E7
Herons Way AL1 .....142 B8
Herons Wood CM20 ..117 B2
Heronsgate Rd WD3 ..164 B3

Heronslea WD25 ......154 C3
Heronswood EN9 .....163 E5
Heronswood Pl AL7 ...111 A5
Heronswood Rd AL7 ..111 A5
Hertford Castle* SG14 .113 C5
Hertford County Hospl
  SG14 ...............113 B6
Hertford East Sta SG13 113 B6
Hertford Heath Jun Mix Inf
  Sch SG13 ...........114 C4
Hertford Mews EN6 ...159 C8
Hertford Mus* SG14 ..113 D6
Hertford North Sta
  SG14 ...............113 B6
Hertford Rd Enfield EN3 162 D3
  Great Amwell SG12 ...114 C4
  Hatfield AL9 .........111 B1
  Hoddesdon EN11 .....134 E3
  Stevenage SG2 ........69 B7
  Tewin AL6 ............90 F2
  Welwyn AL6 ...........89 D3
Hertford Regional Coll
  Cheshunt EN10 ......148 F6
  Ware SG12 ...........114 D8
Hertford St Andrew CE Prim
  Sch SG14 ...........112 F7
Hertfordshire & Essex High
  Sch The CM23 .......77 B7
Hertfordshire Bsns Ctr
  AL2 .................142 D5
Hertfordshire Theatre Sch
  SG4 .................34 F2
Hertingfordbury Prim Sch
  SG14 ...............112 C4
Hertingfordbury Rd
  Hertford SG14 .......113 B5
  Hertingfordbury SG14 112 F4
Herts & Essex Com Hospl
  CM23 ...............77 B6
Hertsmere Ind Pk WD6 170 D6
Hertswood Ct **1** EN5 171 E5
Hertswood Sch WD6 ..170 C7
Hester Ho CM20 ......117 C2
Heswall Ct **5** LU1 ....63 F6
Heswall Gn WD19 ....175 A7
Hetchleys HP1 .......124 C1
Hever Cl LU7 ..........80 D2
Hewins Cl EN9 .......163 E1
Hewitt Cl AL4 ........108 D7
Hewlett Rd LU3 ........44 E5
Hexton Jun Mix Inf Sch
  SG5 .................19 A1
Hexton Rd
  Great Offley SG5 ......33 C3
  Lilley LU2 ............32 C3
Heybridge Ct SG14 ...112 F7
Heydon Rd SG8 ........9 E3
Heydons Cl AL3 ......127 D5
Heyford Rd WD7 .....155 F2
Heyford Way AL10 ...130 C7
Heysham Dr WD19 ...175 D5
Heywood Dr LU2 .......45 F2
Hibbert Ave WD24 ...154 D1
Hibbert Rd HA3 ......176 F1
Hibbert St LU1 ........63 E6
Hibbert Street Almshouses **13**
  LU1 .................63 E6
Hibberts Ct SG6 .......22 E7
Hickling Cl LU2 ........46 D1
Hickling Way AL5 ......86 C3
Hickman Cl EN10 .....134 D3
Hickman Ct LU3 ........44 D8
Hickman's Hill SG7 .....24 D4
Hicks Rd AL3 ..........83 F6
Hidalgo Ct HP2 ......124 F6
Hideaway The WD3 ...153 F8
Hides The CM20 ......117 C1
Higgins Rd EN7 ......147 D4
Higgins Wlk SG1 ......36 C1
High Acres WD5 ......153 D7
High Ash Rd AL4 .....108 C7
High Ave SG6 ..........22 E4
High Barnet Sta EN5 ..171 F5
High Beech Rd LU3 .....44 D7
High Beeches Prim Sch
  AL5 .................86 D1
High Canons WD6 ....157 D2
High Cl WD3 ..........165 C4
High Cross WD25 ....155 D2
High Dane SG2 ........22 A2
High Dells AL10 ......129 C6
High Elms
  Harpenden AL5 .......107 A6
  Watford WD25 .......154 B8
High Elms Cl HA6 ....174 D4
High Elms La
  Abbots Langley WD25,
  WD5 ................154 C8
  Benington SG2 ........52 F1
High Firs Radlett WD7 ..155 F4
  Radlett WD7 .........156 A4
High Firs Cres AL5 ...107 D8
High Gr St Albans AL3 .127 D5
  Welwyn Garden City AL8 110 C2
High House Est CM17 .118 F4
High La CM24 ..........59 F8
High Mead SG12 .......93 E3
High Meads AL4 ......108 C8
High Oak Rd SG12 .....93 E3
High Oaks Enfield EN2 ..160 F1
  **4** Northwood HA6 ..174 F5
  St Albans AL3 ........127 D7
High Oaks Rd AL8 ....110 B7
High Pastures CM22 ...98 D1
High Plash SG1 .......50 E5
High Point **15** LU1 ...63 D6
High Rd Bushey WD23 .168 D1

High Rd continued
  Essendon AL9 .........131 E5
  Harrow HA3 .........176 E3
  Hoddesdon EN10 .....134 F4
  Shillington SG5 .......19 E8
  Stapleford SG14 ......92 A2
  Watford WD25 .......154 A7
High Ridge Cuffley EN6 146 E3
  Harpenden AL5 .......85 E3
  Luton LU2 ............46 C1
High Ridge Cl HP3 ....138 D6
High Ridge Rd HP3 ...138 D7
High Road Broxbourne
  EN10 ...............134 F1
High Road Turnford
  EN10 ...............148 E6
High Road Wormley
  EN10 ...............148 F8
High St
  Abbots Langley WD5 ..139 F1
  Arlesey SG15 ..........11 A5
  Ashwell SG7 ...........4 D3
  Baldock SG7 ..........23 F8
  Barkway SG8 ..........17 C3
  Barley SG8 ............8 F2
  Barnet EN5 ..........171 E5
  Bedmond WD5 ......139 F4
  Berkhamsted HP4 ....122 B4
  Berkhamsted, Northchurch
  HP4 ................121 E6
  Bishop's Stortford CM23 ..76 F7
  Bovingdon HP3 ......137 D6
  Buntingford SG9 ......40 E8
  Bushey WD23 .......168 A3
  Cheddington LU7 ......80 A7
  Cheshunt EN8 .......148 D2
  Cheshunt, Theobald's Grove Sta
  EN8 ................162 D3
  Cheshunt, Waltham Cross
  EN8 ................162 C6
  Codicote SG4 ..........67 F3
  Colney Heath AL4 ....129 B1
  Elstree WD6 .........169 D3
  Eyeworth SG19 ........1 A8
  Flamstead AL3 ........84 B2
  Graveley SG4 .........36 C4
  Great Offley SG5 ......33 C3
  Guilden Morden SG8 ...1 F4
  Harefield UB9 ........173 C1
  Harlow CM17 ........118 D4
  Harpenden AL5 .......86 A1
  Harrow HA3 .........176 F1
  Hemel Hempstead HP1,
  HP3 ................124 D4
  Hinxworth SG7 ........3 D6
  Hitchin SG5 ..........34 E7
  Hitchin, Gosmore SG4 ..34 F3
  Hoddesdon EN11 .....135 A5
  Hunsdon SG12 ........95 D1
  Kimpton SG4 .........66 C1
  Kings Langley WD4 ...139 A2
  London Colney AL2 ...142 D5
  Luton LU4 ...........44 C4
  Markyate AL3 ........83 E5
  Much Hadham SG10 ..74 F3
  Northwood HA6 ......174 F2
  Pirton SG5 ...........20 D4
  Pitstone LU7 .........80 E5
  Potters Bar EN6 ......159 C7
  Redbourn AL3 .......106 B5
  Reed SG8 ............16 E5
  Rickmansworth WD3 ..165 E1
  Roydon CM19 ........116 B1
  Royston SG8 ..........7 D6
  Sandridge AL4 .......108 C2
  St Albans AL3 ........127 D3
  Standon SG11 ........55 E1
  Standon, Puckeridge SG11 55 D3
  Stanstead Abbotts SG12 115 C4
  Stevenage SG1 .......50 C7
  Stotfold SG5 ..........11 F6
  Tring HP23 ..........100 A3
  Walkern SG2 .........38 B1
  Ware SG12 ...........93 D1
  Watford WD17 .......167 B6
  Watford WD17 .......167 C5
  Watton at S SG14 .....70 E3
  Welwyn AL6 ..........89 C5
  Wheathampstead AL4 ..87 D1
  Whitwell SG4 .........66 F7
  Widford SG12 ........95 E5
High Street Bsns Pk
  EN8 ................162 E7
High Street Gn HP2 ...125 A3
High Town Rd LU2 .....45 F1
High Tree Cl CM21 .....97 D1
High View
  Birchanger CM23 ......59 D3
  Chorleywood WD3 ...165 A5
  Hatfield AL10 ........130 A2
  Hitchin SG5 ...........34 D7
  Markyate AL3 ........83 E5
  Watford WD18 ......166 F3
High View Ct HA3 .....176 E3
High Wickfield AL7 ...111 C5
High Wood Cl LU1 .....62 F7
High Wood Rd EN11 ..114 F1
High Wych CE Prim Sch
  CM21 ...............97 A1
High Wych La CM21 ....97 A2
High Wych Rd
  Gilston CM21 ........117 C7
  High Wych CM21 .....97 B1
High Wych Way HP2 ..105 A1
Higham Dr LU2 .........46 D1
Highbanks Rd HA5 ....176 B4
Highbarns HP3 ......139 A6
Highbridge Ct EN9 ...163 B6

Highbridge Ho EN9 . . . . . . . . .163 B6
Highbridge Ret Pk EN9 .163 B5
Highbridge St EN9 . . . . . . .163 B6
Highbury Ho (North Herts
  Music Sch) SG4 . . . . . . .35 A7
Highbury Inf Sch SG4 . . . . .34 F6
Highbury Rd Hitchin SG4 . .35 A7
  Luton LU3 . . . . . . . . . . . .45 C1
Highbush Rd SG5 . . . . . . . .11 E5
Highclere Ct 4 AL1 . . . . . .127 E4
Highclere Dr HP3 . . . . . . . .139 B7
Highcroft 2 SG2 . . . . . . . . .50 F1
Highcroft Rd HP3 . . . . . . . .138 B6
Highfield Bushey WD23 . . .176 E8
  Kings Langley WD4 . . . . .138 E3
  Letchworth SG6 . . . . . . . .22 E4
  Little Hadham SG11 . . . . .57 C3
  Sawbridgeworth CM21 . . .97 E3
  South Oxhey WD19 . . . . .175 F7
  Watford WD25 . . . . . . . . .153 F5
Highfield Ave
  Bishop's Stortford CM23 . . .77 C6
  Harpenden AL5 . . . . . . . .107 C8
Highfield Cl HA6 . . . . . . . .174 E2
Highfield Cres HA6 . . . . . .174 E2
Highfield Ct
  Hertford SG13 . . . . . . . . .113 D4
  Stevenage SG1 . . . . . . . . .50 F7
Highfield Dr EN10 . . . . . . . .134 E2
Highfield Hall AL4 . . . . . . .142 E7
Highfield Ho HP2 . . . . . . . .124 F5
Highfield La
  Colney Heath AL4 . . . . . .142 E8
  Hemel Hempstead HP2 . . .124 F5
Highfield Oval AL5 . . . . . . . .86 A4
Highfield Park Dr AL4 . . . .142 C8
Highfield Rd
  Berkhamsted HP4 . . . . . .122 D4
  Hammond Street EN7 . . . .147 E5
  Hertford SG13 . . . . . . . . .113 D4
  Luton LU4 . . . . . . . . . . . .45 B1
  Northwood HA6 . . . . . . . .174 E2
  Sandridge AL4 . . . . . . . . .108 B1
  Tring HP23 . . . . . . . . . . . .99 E3
  Watford WD23 . . . . . . . . .167 E4
  Wigginton HP23 . . . . . . .100 D1
Highfield Sch The SG6 . . .22 D4
Highfield Way WD3 . . . . . .165 B3
Highfields Cuffley EN6 . . .146 E3
  Radlett WD7 . . . . . . . . . .155 F4
Highfields Cl LU5 . . . . . . . .44 A2
Highfield Way EN6 . . . . . .159 B7
Highgate Gr CM21 . . . . . . . .97 D2
Highgrove Ct EN8 . . . . . . .162 D5
Highland Dr
  Bushey WD23 . . . . . . . . .168 C2
  Hemel Hempstead HP3 . . .125 B3
Highland Rd
  Bishop's Stortford CM23 . . .76 F3
  Lower Nazeing EN9 . . . . .135 E1
  Northwood HA6 . . . . . . . .175 A1
Highlands Hatfield AL9 . . .130 C8
  Royston SG8 . . . . . . . . . . .7 E6
  Watford WD19 . . . . . . . . .167 C1
Highlands The
  Potters Bar EN6 . . . . . . . .145 C1
  Rickmansworth WD3 . . . .165 B2
Highmead CM24 . . . . . . . . .59 E8
Highmill SG12 . . . . . . . . . . .93 D3
Highmoor AL5 . . . . . . . . . . .86 A4
Highover Cl LU2 . . . . . . . . .46 B1
Highover Jun Mix Inf Sch
  SG4 . . . . . . . . . . . . . . . . .22 C1
Highover Rd SG6 . . . . . . . . .22 D5
Highover Way SG4 . . . . . . .22 B1
Highridge Pl EN2 . . . . . . . .160 F1
Highview Cl EN6 . . . . . . . .159 C6
Highview Gdns
  Potters Bar EN6 . . . . . . . .159 C6
  St Albans AL4 . . . . . . . . .128 C8
Highway The HA7 . . . . . . . .176 F2
Highwood Ave WD23 . . . . .167 F8
Highwood Prim Sch
  WD23 . . . . . . . . . . . . . . .167 F8
Highwoodhall La HP3 . . . .139 C7
Hilbury AL10 . . . . . . . . . . .129 F4
Hilfield La WD25 . . . . . . . .168 D6
Hilfield La S WD23 . . . . . .168 F3
Hill Cl Barnet EN5 . . . . . . .171 C4
  Harpenden AL5 . . . . . . . . .86 C4
  Luton LU3 . . . . . . . . . . . .45 C7
Hill Comm HP3 . . . . . . . . .139 A8
Hill Crest
  Potters Bar EN6 . . . . . . . .159 C5
  Whitwell SG4 . . . . . . . . . .66 E6
Hill Crest Lodge WD6 . . . .169 F5
Hill Croft Cl LU4 . . . . . . . . .44 C6
Hill Ct EN6 . . . . . . . . . . . .159 C5
Hill Dyke Rd AL4 . . . . . . . .108 E7
Hill End La AL4 . . . . . . . . .128 C2
Hill End Rd UB9 . . . . . . . . .173 C3
Hill Farm Ave WD25 . . . . .154 A6
Hill Farm Cl WD25 . . . . . .154 A6
Hill Farm La
  Ayot St Lawrence AL6 . . . .88 C5
  Redbourn AL3 . . . . . . . . .106 C1
Hill Head Cotts SG10 . . . .75 B1
Hill Ho Harefield UB9 . . . .173 C1
  Hertford SG13 . . . . . . . . .113 C5
Hill House Ave HA7 . . . . . .176 F3
Hill Ley AL10 . . . . . . . . . . .129 F5
Hill Leys EN6 . . . . . . . . . . .146 E3
Hill Mead HP4 . . . . . . . . . .122 A3
Hill Milford AL5 . . . . . . . . .86 D3
Hill Pickford AL5 . . . . . . . .86 D4
Hill Rd Codicote SG4 . . . . .67 E1
  Northwood HA6 . . . . . . . .174 D4
Hill Rise Cuffley EN6 . . . . .146 E3

Hill Rise continued
  Luton LU3 . . . . . . . . . . . .44 D7
  Potters Bar EN6 . . . . . . . .159 C5
  Rickmansworth WD3 . . . .165 B2
Hill Side LU7 . . . . . . . . . . . .79 F7
Hill St AL3 . . . . . . . . . . . .127 C3
Hill The Harlow CM17 . . . .118 C4
  Wheathampstead AL4 . . . .108 D8
Hill Top SG7 . . . . . . . . . . . .23 E7
Hill View
  Berkhamsted HP4 . . . . . .122 A6
  Buckland SG9 . . . . . . . . . .27 D8
  Whitwell SG4 . . . . . . . . . .66 E6
Hillary Cl LU3 . . . . . . . . . . .44 D7
Hillary Cres LU1 . . . . . . . . .63 C6
Hillary Ho WD6 . . . . . . . . .170 B6
Hillary Rd HP2 . . . . . . . . . .125 A4
Hillary Rise SG15 . . . . . . . .11 B5
Hillberry Ct WD23 . . . . . . .168 B2
Hillborough Inf Sch LU1 .63 C6
Hillborough Jun Sch LU1 63 D6
Hillborough Rd LU1 . . . . . .63 D6
Hillbrow SG6 . . . . . . . . . . . .22 D5
Hillcrest Baldock SG7 . . . . .23 F7
  Hatfield AL10 . . . . . . . . . .130 A5
  St Albans AL3 . . . . . . . . . .127 B1
  Stevenage SG1 . . . . . . . . .50 F5
Hillcrest Ave LU2 . . . . . . . . .45 C8
Hillcrest Cl EN7 . . . . . . . . .147 C2
Hillcrest Rd WD7 . . . . . . . .157 A6
Hillcroft Cres WD19 . . . . .175 B8
Hilldown Rd HP1 . . . . . . . .124 A5
Hille Bsns Ctr WD24 . . . . .167 B8
Hillfield AL10 . . . . . . . . . . .130 C8
Hillfield Ave HA6 . . . . . . . . .22 A2
Hillfield Ct HP2 . . . . . . . . .124 E3
Hillfield Rd HP2 . . . . . . . . .124 D3
Hillgate SG4 . . . . . . . . . . . .22 A3
Hillgrove Bsns Pk EN9 . . .135 C1
Hillhouse EN9 . . . . . . . . . .163 F6
Hilliard Rd HA6 . . . . . . . . .174 F2
Hillingdon Rd WD25 . . . .154 B5
Hillmead SG1 . . . . . . . . . . .51 A6
Hillmead Prim Sch CM23 76 C7
Hillpath SG6 . . . . . . . . . . . .23 B6
Hillpoint WD3 . . . . . . . . . .165 C4
Hillrise Ave WD24 . . . . . . .154 D2
Hills La HA6 . . . . . . . . . . . .174 E2
Hillsborough Gn WD19 .175 A7
Hillshott SG6 . . . . . . . . . . . .23 A6
Hillshott Inf Sch SG6 . . . . .23 A6
Hillside Codicote SG4 . . . . .67 F1
  Hatfield AL10 . . . . . . . . . .130 A5
  Hoddesdon EN11 . . . . . . .134 F7
  Royston SG8 . . . . . . . . . . .7 D5
  St Albans AL4 . . . . . . . . .128 C2
  Stevenage SG1 . . . . . . . . .50 F5
  Ware SG12 . . . . . . . . . . .114 D8
  Welwyn Garden City AL7 . .111 B3
Hillside Ave
  Bishop's Stortford CM23 . . .77 A7
  Borehamwood WD6 . . . . .170 B5
  Cheshunt EN8 . . . . . . . . .162 D8
Hillside Cl WD5 . . . . . . . . .153 E7
Hillside Cotts
  Birchanger CM23 . . . . . . .59 C3
  Wareside SG12 . . . . . . . . .94 F4
Hillside Cres Enfield EN2 161 D1
  Northwood HA6 . . . . . . . .175 A2
  Stanstead Abbotts SG12 . .115 B4
  Watford WD19 . . . . . . . . .167 D3
Hillside Ct Cheshunt EN8 162 D8
  8 St Albans AL1 . . . . . . .127 E4
Hillside End CM23 . . . . . . .59 C3
Hillside Gate 6 AL1 . . . . .127 E4
Hillside Gdns
  Barnet EN5 . . . . . . . . . . .171 E5
  Berkhamsted HP4 . . . . . .122 D3
  Pinner HA6 . . . . . . . . . . .175 B2
Hillside Ho SG1 . . . . . . . . . .50 F5
Hillside Jun & Inf Schs
  HA6 . . . . . . . . . . . . . . . . .175 A3
Hillside La SG12 . . . . . . . .115 A5
Hillside Mans EN5 . . . . . . .171 F5
Hillside Rd
  Chorleywood WD3 . . . . . .164 C4
  Harpenden AL5 . . . . . . . . .85 F3
  Luton LU3 . . . . . . . . . . . .45 D1
  Pinner HA5 . . . . . . . . . . .175 B3
  Radlett WD7 . . . . . . . . . .156 B4
  St Albans AL1 . . . . . . . . .127 E4
  Watford WD23 . . . . . . . . .167 E4
Hillside Rise HA6 . . . . . . . .175 A4
Hillside Sch The WD6 . . . .170 C5
Hillside Terr SG13 . . . . . . .113 C4
Hillside Way AL6 . . . . . . . . .90 A8
Hilltop AL3 . . . . . . . . . . . .105 F6
Hilltop Cl EN7 . . . . . . . . . .147 F5
Hilltop Cotts
  Great Munden SG11 . . . . .54 D4
  Great Offley SG5 . . . . . . .33 C3
Hilltop Ct LU1 . . . . . . . . . . .63 C7
Hilltop Rd Bedmond WD4 139 D4
  Berkhamsted HP4 . . . . . .122 C3
Hilltop View AL4 . . . . . . . .108 C7
Hilltop Wlk AL5 . . . . . . . . .107 D8
Hillview Cl HA5 . . . . . . . . .175 F4
Hillview Cres LU2 . . . . . . . .45 C8
Hillview Gdns EN8 . . . . . . .148 E4
Hillview Rd HA5 . . . . . . . . .175 F4
Hilly Fields AL7 . . . . . . . . .111 C7
Hilmay Dr HP1 . . . . . . . . . .124 A3
Hilton Cl SG1 . . . . . . . . . . . .50 B7
Himalayan Way WD18 . . .166 F3
Hindhead Gn WD19 . . . . .175 C5
Hine Ho AL4 . . . . . . . . . . . .128 D2

Hine Way SG5 . . . . . . . . . . .21 C1
Hinwick Cl SG15 . . . . . . . . .11 B7
Hinxworth Rd Ashwell SG7 . .4 A4
  Hinxworth SG7 . . . . . . . . .3 C3
Hipkins CM23 . . . . . . . . . . .76 E4
Hipkins Pl EN10 . . . . . . . .134 E3
Hispano Mews EN3 . . . . . .163 A2
Hitchen Mews EN3 . . . . . .163 A2
Hitchin British Schools Mus★
  SG4 . . . . . . . . . . . . . . . . .34 F6
Hitchin Bsns Ctr The
  SG4 . . . . . . . . . . . . . . . . .22 A3
Hitchin Girls' Sch SG4 . . . .34 A3
Hitchin Hill SG4 . . . . . . . . .34 F5
Hitchin Hospl SG5 . . . . . . .34 D8
Hitchin Mus★ SG5 . . . . . .34 E7
Hitchin Rd Arlesey SG15 . . .11 A2
  Great Wymondley SG4 . . . .35 D6
  Hexton SG5 . . . . . . . . . . .19 E1
  Hitchin SG4 . . . . . . . . . . .34 F3
  Kimpton SG4 . . . . . . . . . .66 D2
  Letchworth SG6 . . . . . . . .22 E3
  Lower Stondon SG16 . . . . .10 C6
  Luton LU2 . . . . . . . . . . . .46 A4
  Pirton SG5 . . . . . . . . . . . .20 C2
  Stevenage SG1 . . . . . . . . .36 B1
  Stotfold SG5 . . . . . . . . . . .11 E5
  Weston SG4 . . . . . . . . . . .24 B1
Hitchin Road Ind & Bsns Ctr
  SG15 . . . . . . . . . . . . . . . .11 A3
Hitchin St SG7 . . . . . . . . . . .23 E8
Hitchin Sta SG4 . . . . . . . . .35 A8
Hitchwood Cotts SG4 . . . .48 F5
Hither Field SG12 . . . . . . . .93 E3
Hitherbaulk AL7 . . . . . . . .110 E4
Hitherfield La AL5 . . . . . . . .86 A2
Hitherway AL8 . . . . . . . . . . .89 D2
Hitherwell Dr HA3 . . . . . . .176 D2
Hive Cl WD23 . . . . . . . . . .176 D8
Hive Rd WD23 . . . . . . . . . .176 E8
Hixberry La AL4 . . . . . . . . .128 C1
Hobart Wlk AL3 . . . . . . . . .127 F7
Hobbs Cl Cheshunt EN8 . .148 D2
  St Albans AL4 . . . . . . . . .128 E2
Hobbs Cross Rd CM17 . . .118 F3
Hobbs Ct SG1 . . . . . . . . . . .51 A8
Hobbs Hayes SG8 . . . . . . . .16 E5
Hobbs Hill AL6 . . . . . . . . . .89 C4
Hobbs Hill Rd HP3 . . . . . .138 F8
Hobbs Hill Wood Prim Sch
  HP3 . . . . . . . . . . . . . . . .125 B1
Hobbs Way AL8 . . . . . . . . .110 C5
Hobby Horse Cl EN7 . . . . .147 C5
Hobletts Manor Inf Sch
  HP2 . . . . . . . . . . . . . . . .125 A4
Hobletts Manor Jun Sch
  HP2 . . . . . . . . . . . . . . . .125 A4
Hobletts Rd HP2 . . . . . . . .124 F4
Hobsons Cl EN11 . . . . . . . .114 F1
Hobsons Wlk HP23 . . . . . . .99 F5
Hobtoe Rd CM20 . . . . . . . .117 A1
Hockerill La AL4 . . . . . . . . . .4 D1
Hockerill Anglo-European
  Coll CM23 . . . . . . . . . . . .77 B7
Hockerill Ct 7 CM23 . . . . .77 A7
Hockerill St CM23 . . . . . . .77 A7
Hocklands AL7 . . . . . . . . . .111 C7
Hockwell Ring LU4 . . . . . . .44 C4
Hoddesdon Ind Ctr
  EN11 . . . . . . . . . . . . . . .135 C7
Hoddesdon Rd SG12 . . . .115 C3
Hodges Way WD18 . . . . . .167 A3
Hodings Rd CM20 . . . . . . .117 C2
Hodson Pl EN3 . . . . . . . . . .163 A1
Hodwell SG7 . . . . . . . . . . . .4 D4
Hoe La Enfield EN1,EN3 . .162 B1
  Lower Nazeing EN9 . . . . .135 F1
  Ware SG12 . . . . . . . . . . .114 D7
Hoe The WD19 . . . . . . . . . .175 D8
Hoecroft EN9 . . . . . . . . . . .135 F1
Hoecroft Ct EN3 . . . . . . . . .162 C1
Hoestock Rd CM21 . . . . . . .97 D2
Hog Hall La HP4 . . . . . . . . .81 A5
Hog La HP5 . . . . . . . . . . . .121 C1
Hogarth Ct WD23 . . . . . . .168 B2
Hogg End La AL3 . . . . . . . .126 D6
Hogg La HA6 . . . . . . . . . . .169 A5
Hogges Cl EN11 . . . . . . . . .135 A6
Hogpits Bottom HP3 . . . . .151 A7
Hogsdell La SG13 . . . . . . .114 B4
Holbeck La EN7 . . . . . . . . .147 F5
Holbein Gate HA6 . . . . . . .174 E5
Holborn Cl AL4 . . . . . . . . .128 D8
Holbrook Cl EN1 . . . . . . . .162 A1
Holcroft Rd AL5 . . . . . . . . .86 D3
Holdbrook AL4 . . . . . . . . . .35 B7
Holdbrook Ct EN8 . . . . . . .162 F5
Holdbrook Prim Sch
  EN8 . . . . . . . . . . . . . . . .162 F5
Holden Cl Hertford SG13 .113 E7
  Hitchin SG4 . . . . . . . . . . .35 C7
Holders La SG2 . . . . . . . . . .51 E5
Holdings The AL9 . . . . . . .130 D7
Holecroft EN9 . . . . . . . . . .163 E5
Holford Way LU3 . . . . . . . . .31 B1
Holgate Dr LU4 . . . . . . . . . .44 B3
Holkham Cl LU4 . . . . . . . . .44 A4
Holkham Ho 11 EN5 . . . . .171 E6
Holland Cl AL3 . . . . . . . . . .45 C2
Holland Gdns WD25 . . . . .154 C4
Holland Rd LU3 . . . . . . . . . .45 B2
Holland Way CM17 . . . . . .118 C1
Holland's Croft SG12 . . . . .95 D1
Holliday St HP4 . . . . . . . . .122 D4
Hollier Ct AL10 . . . . . . . . .130 B6
Holliers Way AL10 . . . . . . .130 A5

Hollies Cl SG8 . . . . . . . . . . .7 E6
Hollies The
  Bovingdon HP3 . . . . . . . .137 A2
  St Albans AL3 . . . . . . . . .127 E4
  St Albans, Townsend AL3 .127 C5
  Watford WD18 . . . . . . . . .166 F5
  Welwyn Garden City AL8 . .110 B3
  Wigginton HP23 . . . . . . .100 D1
Hollies Way EN6 . . . . . . . .159 C8
Hollow La SG4 . . . . . . . . . . .34 F7
Holloway La WD3 . . . . . . .151 C2
Holloway The HP23,HP22 .99 C4
Holloways La AL9 . . . . . . . .144 F3
Holly Cl AL10 . . . . . . . . . . .129 F4
Holly Copse SG14 . . . . . . .113 A7
Holly Croft SG14 . . . . . . . .113 A7
Holly Dell SG13 . . . . . . . . .113 C4
Holly Dr
  Berkhamsted HP4 . . . . . .122 D3
  Potters Bar EN6 . . . . . . . .159 B6
Holly Farm Cl LU1 . . . . . . .62 E3
Holly Gr HA5 . . . . . . . . . . .175 E2
Holly Grove Rd SG14 . . . . .91 C3
Holly Hall Ct AL6 . . . . . . . .89 C5
Holly Hedges La HP3 . . . .151 C8
Holly Ind Est WD24 . . . . .167 C8
Holly La AL5 . . . . . . . . . . . .86 E6
Holly Leys SG2 . . . . . . . . . .69 C8
Holly Rd Enfield EN3 . . . . .162 D3
  Woolmer Green SG3 . . . . .69 B1
Holly Shaws SG2 . . . . . . . .51 B1
Holly St LU1 . . . . . . . . . . . .63 E6
Holly Street Trad Est 12
  LU1 . . . . . . . . . . . . . . . . .63 E6
Holly Tree Ct HP2 . . . . . . .125 B3
Holly Wlk Harpenden AL5 .86 D1
  Welwyn Garden City AL8 . .89 C2
Hollybush Ave AL2 . . . . . .141 A7
Hollybush Cl
  Harrow HA3 . . . . . . . . . .176 E2
  Oaklands AL6 . . . . . . . . . .89 E8
  Potten End HP4 . . . . . . . .123 D7
  Watford WD19 . . . . . . . . .167 C2
Hollybush Hill LU2,SG5 . . .32 F1
Hollybush Ho AL7 . . . . . . .110 E4
Hollybush La
  Datchworth SG3 . . . . . . . .69 C3
  Flamstead AL3 . . . . . . . . .84 B3
  Harpenden AL5 . . . . . . . . .86 A3
  Hemel Hempstead HP1 . . .123 F4
  Welwyn Garden City AL7 . .110 E3
  Whitwell SG4 . . . . . . . . . .66 B8
Hollybush Prim Sch
  SG14 . . . . . . . . . . . . . . .113 A6
Hollybush Rd LU2 . . . . . . . .46 C1
Hollybush Row EN3 . . . . . .120 D8
Hollybush Way EN7 . . . . . .148 A3
Hollycross Rd SG12 . . . . .115 B7
Hollyfield Hatfield AL10 . .130 A2
  Tring HP23 . . . . . . . . . . .100 C5
Hollyfield Cl HP23 . . . . . . .100 C5
Hollyfields EN10 . . . . . . . .148 E5
Hollygrove WD23 . . . . . . .168 D2
Hollyhock Cl HP1 . . . . . . . .123 E4
Hollytree Cl HP5 . . . . . . . .150 B8
Hollytree Ho WD24 . . . . . .153 E3
Hollywood Ct WD6 . . . . . .169 F5
Holm Oak Pk WD18 . . . . .167 A4
Holmbrook Ave LU3 . . . . . .45 C5
Holmbury Cl WD23 . . . . . .176 E8
Holmbury St Mary Ct
  AL1 . . . . . . . . . . . . . . . . .128 B2
Holmdale SG6 . . . . . . . . . . .23 B5
Holmdale Cl WD6 . . . . . . .169 F7
Holme Cl Cheshunt EN8 . .162 E8
  Hatfield AL10 . . . . . . . . .129 E8
Holme Lea WD25 . . . . . . . .154 C5
Holme Pk WD6 . . . . . . . . .169 F7
Holme Pl HP2 . . . . . . . . . .125 C4
Holme Rd AL10 . . . . . . . . .129 E8
Holme Way HA7 . . . . . . . . .176 F4
Holmes Ct AL3 . . . . . . . . .127 C4
Holmesdale EN8 . . . . . . . .162 D4
Holmfield Cl LU1 . . . . . . . .63 D5
Holmscroft Rd LU3 . . . . . . .44 F6
Holmshill La EN5,WD6 . . .157 F2
Holmside Rise WD19 . . . .175 B7
Holmwood Rd EN3 . . . . . .162 D3
Holroyd Cres SG7 . . . . . . . .23 F7
Holt Cl WD6 . . . . . . . . . . .169 F5
Holt Cotts The SG4 . . . . . . .66 C4
Holt Ho EN8 . . . . . . . . . . .148 B3
Holt The
  Hemel Hempstead HP2 . . .124 E2
  Welwyn Garden City AL7 . .111 D5
Holts Mdw AL3 . . . . . . . . .100 B6
Holtsmere Cl Luton LU2 . . .46 C1
  Watford WD25 . . . . . . . . .154 C4
Holtsmere End Inf Sch
  HP2 . . . . . . . . . . . . . . . .125 B8
Holtsmere End Jun Sch
  HP2 . . . . . . . . . . . . . . . .125 B8
Holtsmere End La HP2 . . .105 C1
Holwell SG1 . . . . . . . . . . . .36 C7
Holwell Ct AL9 . . . . . . . . .111 F1
Holwell Hyde AL7 . . . . . . .111 C4
Holwell Hyde La AL7 . . . .111 C3
Holwell La AL9 . . . . . . . . .131 F8
Holwell Prim Sch AL7 . . .110 F5
Holwell Rd Holwell SG5 . . .21 C7
  Pirton SG5 . . . . . . . . . . . .20 E6
  Welwyn Garden City AL7 . .110 F5
Holy Acre CM19 . . . . . . . .116 A1
Holy Cross Hill EN10 . . . .148 A8
Holy Family RC Jun Mix Inf
  Sch AL7 . . . . . . . . . . . . . .90 A1
Holy Rood RC Inf Sch
  WD17 . . . . . . . . . . . . . . .153 D3

Holy Rood RC Jun Sch
  WD17 . . . . . . . . . . . . . . .153 D3
Holy Trinity CE Prim Sch
  Cheshunt EN8 . . . . . . . . .162 D7
  Northwood HA6 . . . . . . . .174 C4
Holyfield Hall Farm★
  EN9 . . . . . . . . . . . . . . . .149 C4
Holyfield Rd EN9 . . . . . . . .149 D2
Holyrood Cres AL1 . . . . . . .141 D7
Holyrood Ct WD18 . . . . . .167 B5
Holywell Cl LU6 . . . . . . . . .82 C6
Holywell Ct LU3 . . . . . . . . .45 B4
Holywell Hill AL1 . . . . . . .127 D2
Holywell Jun Mix Inf Sch
  WD18 . . . . . . . . . . . . . . .166 F3
Holywell Rd Studham LU6 .82 D6
  Watford WD18 . . . . . . . . .167 A4
Home Cl Cheshunt EN10 . .148 F7
  Luton LU1 . . . . . . . . . . . .44 C4
  Stotfold SG5 . . . . . . . . . . .11 F7
Home Farm Cotts
  Newgate Street SG13 . . . .146 F8
  Slip End LU1 . . . . . . . . . . .85 A8
Home Farm Ct
  Bovingdon HP3 . . . . . . . .136 F1
  Cockernhoe LU2 . . . . . . . .46 D5
  Standon SG11 . . . . . . . . . .55 D3
Home Farm Ind Pk
  SG12 . . . . . . . . . . . . . . .115 F5
Home Farm Rd
  Berkhamsted HP4 . . . . . .121 D7
  Rickmansworth WD3 . . . .174 A6
Home Field EN5 . . . . . . . .171 F4
Home Ley AL7 . . . . . . . . . .110 E6
Home Mdw AL7 . . . . . . . . .110 E6
Home Park Ind Est
  WD4 . . . . . . . . . . . . . . .139 B1
Home Park Mill Link Rd
  WD4 . . . . . . . . . . . . . . .139 B1
Home Way WD3 . . . . . . . .164 F1
Homedale Dr LU4 . . . . . . . .44 D2
Homedell Ho AL5 . . . . . . . .85 E3
Homefield
  Bovingdon HP3 . . . . . . . .137 B3
  Hinxworth SG7 . . . . . . . . .3 D6
  Potten End HP4 . . . . . . . .123 B7
Homefield La SG4 . . . . . . . .49 F2
Homefield Rd
  Bushey WD23 . . . . . . . . .168 A4
  Chorleywood WD3 . . . . . .164 D5
  Hemel Hempstead HP2 . . .125 A2
  Radlett WD7 . . . . . . . . . .155 F2
  Ware SG12 . . . . . . . . . . . .93 E2
Homeleigh Ct EN8 . . . . . . .148 B1
Homeleigh St EN8 . . . . . . .148 B1
Homepark Cotts WD4 . . . .139 B1
Homerfield AL8 . . . . . . . . .110 C7
Homerswood La AL6 . . . . . .89 A2
Homerswood Prim Sch
  AL8 . . . . . . . . . . . . . . . . .89 D2
Homerton Rd LU3 . . . . . . . .45 A6
Homestead Cl AL2 . . . . . . .141 C4
Homestead Ct AL7 . . . . . . .110 F4
Homestead La AL7 . . . . . . .110 F4
Homestead Moat SG1 . . . .50 E4
Homestead Rd
  Hatfield AL10 . . . . . . . . .130 B8
  Rickmansworth WD3 . . . .165 D2
Homestead Way LU1 . . . . .63 C5
Homesteads The SG12 . . .116 D8
Homewood Ave EN6 . . . . .146 E4
Homewood Ct WD3 . . . . . .164 F5
Homewood Ind Sch AL2 141 B3
Homewood La EN6 . . . . . .146 C4
Homewood Rd AL1 . . . . . .128 B5
Honey Brook EN9 . . . . . . .163 D4
Honey La
  Brent Pelham CB11 . . . . . .30 D3
  Buntingford SG9 . . . . . . . .40 E8
  5 Hertford SG14 . . . . . . .113 D6
  Waltham Abbey EN9 . . . . .163 E5
Honeybourne CM23 . . . . . .76 E4
Honeycroft AL8 . . . . . . . . .110 C5
Honeycroft Dr AL4 . . . . . .142 C8
Honeycross Rd HP1 . . . . . .123 E2
Honeygate LU2 . . . . . . . . . .45 E4
Honeymead AL6 . . . . . . . . .89 F3
Honeymeade CM21 . . . . . .118 C7
Honeysuckle Cl
  Bishop's Stortford CM23 . .76 C6
  Hertford SG13 . . . . . . . . .114 A6
Honeysuckle Gdns AL10 130 B4
Honeyway SG8 . . . . . . . . . . .7 E6
Honeywood Cl EN6 . . . . . .159 C6
Honilands Prim Sch
  EN1 . . . . . . . . . . . . . . . .162 B3
Honiton Mews LU3 . . . . . . .44 E6
Honours Mead HP3 . . . . . .137 A4
Hoo Cotts SG5 . . . . . . . . . .33 D1
Hoo Farm Cotts SG5 . . . . .33 D1
Hoo St LU1 . . . . . . . . . . . . .63 E5
Hoo The CM17 . . . . . . . . .118 C5
Hook Gate EN1 . . . . . . . . .162 B3
Hook La Northaw EN6 . . . .159 F7
  Northaw EN6 . . . . . . . . . .160 A8
Hook's Cross SG14 . . . . . . .69 C6
Hoopers Mews WD23 . . . .168 B1
Hoops La SG8 . . . . . . . . . . .15 F6
Hop Garden Way WD25 . .154 C8
Hope Gn WD25 . . . . . . . . .154 A6
Hopewell Rd SG7 . . . . . . . .23 D8
Hopground Cl AL1 . . . . . . .128 A1
Hopkins Cres AL4 . . . . . . .108 B1
Hopkins Yd AL1 . . . . . . . . .127 E2
Hoppit Rd EN9 . . . . . . . . .163 B7

Hopton Rd SG1 .........50 A8
Hopwood Cl WD17 .....153 E3
Horace Brightman Cl
LU3 ..................45 A7
Horace Gay Gdns SG6 ...22 E6
Horbeam Cl WD6 .......170 A8
Hordle Gdns AL1 .......127 F2
Horizon Ho EN3 ........162 F3
Hormead CE Prim Sch
SG9 ...................41 F8
Horn Hill SG4 ..........66 E6
Hornbeam Cl SG14 .....113 B7
Hornbeam Ct SG4 .......35 E5
Hornbeam La AL9 ......131 E2
Hornbeam Spring SG3 ...68 F4
Hornbeam Way EN7 ....147 F2
Hornbeams
Bricket Wood AL2 .....140 F1
Welwyn Garden City AL7 .111 F4
Hornbeams Ave EN1 ....162 C4
Hornbeams The
Harlow CM20 ..........117 C2
Stevenage SG2 ..........51 B4
Hornets The WD18 .....167 E5
Hornhill Rd WD3 .......172 D5
Horns Cl SG13 .........113 C4
Horns Mill Rd SG13 ....113 C3
Horns Rd SG13 ........113 C5
Hornsby Cl LU2 .........46 C1
Hornsfield AL7 ........111 C7
Horrocks Cl SG12 .......93 D3
Horsa Gdns AL10 ......129 E7
Horse Cross SG11 .......56 D3
Horse Hill HP5 ........150 D7
Horsecroft Rd HP1 ....124 A1
Horselers HP3 ........139 A4
Horsemans Dr AL2 ....141 B6
Horseshoe Bsns Pk AL2 141 B1
Horseshoe Cl Barley SG8 .8 F1
Cheddington LU7 .......80 A7
Stanstead Abbotts SG12 .115 D4
Horseshoe Ct Hitchin SG4 .34 E6
Horseshoe Hill SG9 ....42 A8
Horseshoe La
Great Hormead SG9 ....42 A8
Totteridge N20 .......171 D1
Watford WD25 ........154 C1
Horseshoe The HP3 ...125 C1
Horsham AL2 ..........46 D2
Horsleys WD3 .........172 D5
Horton Gdns HP2 .....105 A1
Horwood WD3 .........165 A2
Horwood Cotts WD25 .168 E8
Horwood Dr WD24 .....154 E2
Hospital Rd SG15 ......11 A4
Houghton Mews 12 LU1 .63 D6
Housden Cl AL4 .......108 E7
House La Arlesey SG15 ...11 A7
Sandridge AL4 ........108 C1
St Albans AL4 ........128 D7
House On The Hill Toy Mus★
CM24 .................59 F6
Housefield Way AL4 ...142 C8
Housewood End HP1 ..124 B6
Housman Ave SG8 ......2 C1
How Field AL5 .........85 B2
How Wood AL2 ........141 B3
How Wood Prim Sch
AL2 ..................141 C4
How Wood Sta AL2 ....141 C3
Howard Agne Cl HP3 ..137 A4
Howard Cl Bushey WD23 .168 E2
Luton LU3 .............45 A4
St Albans AL1 ........128 C1
Stotfold SG5 ...........11 E5
Waltham Abbey EN9 ...163 D5
Watford WD24 .........154 A2
Howard Ct Enfield EN1 .161 E1
Letchworth SG6 ........23 B4
Howard Ctr The AL8 ..110 D6
Howard Dr
Borehamwood WD6 ...170 D5
Letchworth SG6 ........23 B3
Howard Gate SG6 ......23 B4
Howard Park Cnr SG6 ..23 A6
Howard Way Barnet EN5 171 D4
Harlow CM20 .........117 F2
Howards Cl HA5 .......175 B1
Howards Dr HP1 ......124 A5
Howards Wood SG6 ....23 B3
Howardsgate AL8 .....110 D6
Howberry Gn SG15 .....11 A3
Howe Cl WD7 .........156 E7
Howe Dell AL10 .......130 B5
Howe Dell Prim Sch
AL10 .................130 B5
Howe Green House Sch
CM22 .................77 D2
Howe Rd HP3 .........125 A1
Howell Hill Cl LU7 .....61 D5
Howfield Gn EN11 ....115 A1
Howicks Gn AL7 ......111 A3
Howland Garth AL1 ...141 C7
Howlands AL7 ........111 B3
Howlands Ho AL7 .....111 A3
Howse Rd EN9 ........163 D4
Howton Pl WD17 ......168 D1
Hoylake Ct LU1 ........63 F5
Hoylake Gdns WD19 ..175 D6
Hubbards Rd WD3 ....164 D4
Huckleberry Cl LU3 ....45 A8
Hudnall La HP4 .......111 A3
Hudson Cl St Albans AL1 .141 D8
Watford WD24 ........153 F3
Hudson Rd SG2 .........51 B7

Hudsons Ct EN6 ......159 A8
Huggins La AL9 .......144 C8
Hugh Villas CM23 ......77 A5
Hughenden Rd AL4 ...128 C6
Hugo Gryn Way WD7 ..156 E8
Hull Cl EN7 ..........147 D5
Hull La SG11 ..........55 E7
Humber Ct SG1 ........36 F3
Humberstone Cl LU4 ...44 E2
Humberstone Rd LU4 ..44 E2
Humphrey Talbot Ave
LU6 ...................81 F7
Hunsdon AL7 .........111 D6
Hunsdon Jun Mix Inf Sch
SG12 .................95 D1
Hunsdon Rd
Stanstead Abbotts SG12 .115 E5
Widford SG12 ..........95 E3
Hunsdon Road Cotts
SG12 .................115 E5
Hunston Cl LU4 ........44 B5
Hunt Cl AL4 ..........128 D6
Hunter Cl
Borehamwood WD6 ...170 C4
Potters Bar EN6 ......159 B6
Hunter Wlk WD6 .....170 D4
Hunter's La WD25 ....153 F6
Huntercrombe Gdns
WD19 ................175 C5
Hunters Cl
Bovingdon HP3 .......137 A2
Stevenage SG2 .........51 D7
Stotfold SG5 ...........11 E6
Tring HP23 ...........100 B5
Hunters Gate WD25 ..154 A6
Hunters Oak HP2 .....125 B8
Hunters Pk HP4 ......122 E5
Hunters Reach EN7 ...147 F2
Hunters Ride AL2 ....155 A8
Hunters Way Royston SG8 .7 E3
Welwyn Garden City AL7 .110 F3
Hunting Gate
Hemel Hempstead HP2 .124 E7
Hitchin SG4 ...........22 A3
Hunting Hall LU2 ......64 C8
Huntingdon Cl EN10 ..148 E7
Huntingdon Ct EN5 ...171 F6
Huntingdon Rd SG1 ...50 B8
Hunton Bridge Hill
WD4 .................153 C6
Hunts Cl LU1 ..........63 C6
Huntsman Cl SG11 .....55 D3
Huntsmans Cl HP4 .....81 C5
Huntsmill Rd HP1 ....123 E2
Hurlock Way LU4 ......44 C5
Hurn Gr CM23 .........59 C1
Hurricane Way WD5 ..154 A7
Hurst Cl Baldock SG7 ..13 A1
Bishop's Stortford CM23 ...76 E7
Welwyn Garden City AL7 .111 C5
Hurst Dr AL2 .........162 D5
Hurst Drive Prim Sch
EN8 ..................162 D5
Hurst Pl HA6 .........174 B2
Hurst Way LU3 ........44 F5
Hurstlings AL7 .......111 B5
Hutchings Lo WD3 ...165 E1
Hutton Cl Hertford SG14 .113 A6
Luton LU4 .............44 E3
Hutton Gdns HA3 ....176 C3
Hutton La HA3 .......176 D3
Hutton Wlk HA3 .....176 C3
Hyatt Ind Est SG1 .....50 A5
Hyburn Cl
Bricket Wood AL2 ....140 F1
Hemel Hempstead HP3 .125 B2
Hyde Ave
Potters Bar EN6 ......159 B6
Stotfold SG5 ...........11 E5
Hyde Cl Barnet EN5 ...171 F6
Harpenden AL5 ........86 B4
Hyde Ct EN8 .........162 E5
Hyde Gn E SG2 ........51 B3
Hyde Gn N SG2 ........51 B3
Hyde Gn S SG2 ........51 B3
Hyde Ho 5 LU2 ........63 F8
Hyde La Bedmond HP3 .139 D5
Bovingdon HP3 .......137 A3
Park Street AL2 ......141 D3
Peters Green LU2 ......65 C2
Hyde Mdws HP3 .....137 A4
Hyde Mead EN9 ......149 E8
Hyde Mead Ho EN9 ..149 E8
Hyde Rd Caddington LU1 .62 F4
Watford WD17 .......167 A7
Hyde Terr HP3 .......139 E7
Ware SG12 .............93 B2
Hyde The Stevenage SG2 .51 C3
Ware SG12 .............93 B2
Hyde Valley AL7 .....110 F4
Hyde View Rd AL5 .....86 B4
Hyde Way AL7 ........110 E6
Hydean Way SG2 ......51 B3
Hyperion Ct HP2 .....124 F6
Hyver Hill NW7 ......170 D2

Ibberson Way SG4 .....35 A7
Iceni Ct SG6 ...........23 B7
Ickleford Bury SG5 ....21 E5
Ickleford Gate SG5 ....21 D3
Ickleford Prim Sch SG5 .21 E4
Ickleford Rd SG5 ......34 F8
Ickley Ct LU4 ..........44 A4
Icknield Cl Ickleford SG5 .21 E4
St Albans AL3 ........126 F1

Icknield Gn
Letchworth SG6 .......22 E6
Tring HP23 ...........100 A6
Icknield High Sch LU3 ..45 C5
Icknield Inf Sch SG6 ...22 D6
Icknield Prim Sch LU3 ..45 B5
Icknield Rd LU3 ........44 F4
Icknield Walk Fst Sch SG8 7 E7
Icknield Way Baldock SG7 .12 E1
Dagnall LU6 ...........81 A8
Letchworth SG6 ........22 E6
Luton LU3 .............45 B7
Tring HP23 ............99 E4
Icknield Way E SG7 ....12 F1
Icknield Wlk SG8 ......7 F7
Idenbury Ct LU1 .......63 C7
Ilex Ct HP4 ..........122 B4
Ilford Cl LU2 ..........46 D3
Ilkley Rd WD19 ......175 D5
Imberfield LU4 .........44 C3
Immanuel Coll WD23 ..168 E2
Imperial Pk SG4 ......167 C8
Imperial Way
Hemel Hempstead HP3 .138 E7
Watford WD24 .......167 C8
Impresa Pk EN11 .....135 C7
Indells AL10 .........129 F4
Ingelheim Ct SG1 .....50 D7
Ingersoll Rd EN3 ....162 C1
Inglefield EN6 .......145 A1
Ingles AL8 ............89 E2
Ingleside Dr SG1 ......36 B3
Ingram Gdns LU2 ......45 D7
Inkerman Rd AL1 ....127 E2
Inkerman St LU1 ......63 D7
Inn's Cl SG1 ..........50 D6
Innes Ct HP3 ........138 D8
Innova Way Enfield EN3 .162 F3
Holdbrook EN3 .......163 A3
Inskip Cres SG1 .......50 E5
Iona Cl SG1 ...........36 F2
Iredale View SG1 ......13 A1
Irene Stebbings Ho AL4 128 C4
Iron Dr SG13 .........114 B7
Irving Cl CM23 ........76 D4
Irving Cres LU7 ........80 A8
Isabel Gate EN8 ......148 F5
Isabella Ho EN8 ......163 A5
Isabelle Cl EN7 ......147 C2
Isenburg Way HP2 ...124 D8
Isherwood Cl SG8 ......7 C8
Island Centre Way EN3 .163 A2
Island Ct CM23 ........77 A5
Islay Ho 4 WD18 .....166 F3
Islington Way SG1 .....36 F2
Italstyle Bldgs CM20 ..118 C6
Itaska Cotts WD23 ...168 E1
Ivatt Ct SG4 ..........35 C7
Iveagh Cl HA6 .......174 B2
Iveagh Ct HP2 .......124 D4
Ivel Cl SG6 ...........23 C4
Ivel Rd SG1 ...........50 C7
Ivel Way Baldock SG7 ..24 A6
Stotfold SG5 ...........11 F8
Ives Rd SG14 ........113 B7
Ivinghoe Cl
St Albans AL4 ........128 C8
Watford WD25 .......154 D4
Ivinghoe Rd
Bushey WD23 ........168 D2
Rickmansworth WD3 .165 A2
Ivory Cl AL4 .........128 C1
Ivory Ct HP3 ........138 E8
Ivy Ct LU1 ............63 B8
Ivy Ho WD19 ........167 D3
Ivy House La HP4 ....122 E4
Ivy Lea WD3 .........165 A1
Ivy Rd LU1 ............63 C8
Ivy Terr EN11 .......135 C8
Ivy Wlk AL10 ........129 F8
Ivybridge EN10 ......135 A4

J Ct CM20 ............117 F1
Jackdaw Cl SG2 .......51 D4
Jackdaws AL7 ........111 C6
Jackets La HA6 ......174 B3
Jacketts Field WD5 ..153 F8
Jackman's Pl SG6 .....23 B5
Jacks La UB9 .........173 A2
Jackson Sq 10 CM23 ..76 F7
Jackson St SG7 .......12 E1
Jackson's La SG8 ......16 E5
Jacksons Dr EN7 ....148 A3
Jacob Ct EN3 ........163 A2
Jacobs Ladder AL9 ...130 C5
James Bedford Cl HA5 .175 C1
James Cl WD23 ......167 E4
James Ct Luton LU4 ...44 B2
14 Luton, New Town LU1 .63 E6
James Foster Ho SG5 ..21 E1
James Lee Sq EN3 ...163 A1
James Marshall Commercial
Ctr AL5 ...............86 A1
James Way
South Oxhey WD19 ...175 D6
Stevenage SG1 ........50 C7
Jameson Ct AL1 .....127 F4
Jameson Rd AL5 ......86 B3
Jane Cl HP2 .........125 B8
Jansel Ho LU2 ........46 B4
Jarden SG6 ...........23 C4
Jardine Ct SG1 ........51 A8
Jarman Cl HP3 ......124 E1
Jarman Way
Hemel Hempstead HP2 .124 F2

Jarman Way continued
Royston SG8 ...........7 B7
Jarvis Cl EN5 ........171 D4
Jarvis Cleys EN7 ....147 F5
Jasmin Cl
Bishop's Stortford CM23 ..76 C6
Northwood HA6 ......174 F2
Jasmin Way HP1 .....123 E4
Jasmine Ct SG5 .......11 F7
Jasmine Dr SG13 ....114 A6
Jasmine Gdns AL10 ..130 A7
Jasons Hill HP5 .....136 B2
Jasper Cl EN3 .......162 C1
Jay Cl SG6 ............22 E8
Jaywood LU2 .........46 C6
Jeans La CM23 ........76 D3
Jeans Way LU5 .......44 A1
Jeeves Yd 6 SG4 ......34 F6
Jeffrey Cl SG8 .........7 C8
Jeffries Rd SG12 ......93 E1
Jellicoe Gdns HA7 ...176 F4
Jellicoe Rd WD18 ....167 A3
Jenkins Ave AL2 ....140 E1
Jenkins Ct HP22 .......60 C3
Jenkins La
Bishop's Stortford CM22 ..77 C5
St Leonards HP23 ....119 C3
Jenning Wood AL6 ....89 F7
Jennings Cl SG1 ......50 E3
Jennings Rd AL1 ....128 A4
Jennings Way
Barnet EN5 ..........171 C6
Hemel Hempstead HP3 .124 E1
Jenningsbury Ct SG13 .114 A4
Jenyns St SG11 .......55 F7
Jepps Cl EN7 ........147 E4
Jepps La SG8 ..........7 D6
Jerome Dr AL3 .......127 A1
Jersey Cl EN11 ......135 A7
Jersey Ho Enfield EN3 .162 D1
9 Watford WD18 ....166 F3
Jersey La
St Albans, Marshalswick
AL4 ..................128 B5
St Albans, Sandridge AL4 128 C8
Jersey Rd LU4 ........44 A3
Jervis Ave EN3 ......162 E4
Jervis Rd CM23 .......76 F6
Jessop Rd SG1 ........37 A1
Jeve Cl SG7 ...........13 A1
Jewell Ct WD25 .....154 D5
Jill Grey Pl SG4 ......34 F6
Jillifer Rd LU4 ........44 A2
Jim Desormeaux Bglws
CM20 .................117 E2
Jinnings The AL7 ....111 B3
Jocelyns CM17 ......118 C4
Jocketts Hill HP1 ....123 F3
Jocketts Rd HP1 ....123 F2
Jodies Ct AL4 .......128 C5
Joel St HA6 ..........175 A1
John Barker Pl SG5 ...21 A1
John Ct EN11 ........115 A1
John Eliot Cl EN9 ...135 E2
John F Kennedy RC Sch
HP1 ..................123 F4
John Henry Newman RC Sch
The SG1 ..............36 B1
John Lamb Ct HA3 ..176 E2
John Penrose Sch UB9 .173 D2
John Sale Cl SG7 ......4 C3
John St Luton LU1 ....63 E7
3 Royston SG8 .......7 D6
John Tate Rd SG13 ..113 F6
John Warner Sch The
EN11 .................115 B1
Johnby Cl EN3 ......162 E2
Johns La HP5 ........121 E1
Johns Rd CM23 .......59 A1
Johnson Ct HP3 .....124 E1
Joiner's Cl HP5 .....136 B1
Joint The SG8 .........16 E6
Jones Rd EN7 .......147 B1
Jonquil Cl AL7 .......111 B4
Jordan Cl WD25 ....153 F4
Jordan's Way AL2 ...140 F1
Jordans AL7 .........111 C7
Jordans Rd WD3 ....165 A1
Joslyn Cl EN3 .......163 A1
Jowitt Ho 1 SG1 .....50 E6
Joyce Ct EN9 ........163 D5
Jubilee Ave
London Colney AL2 ...142 D5
Ware SG12 .............93 F2
Jubilee Cl
Lower Stondon SG16 ...10 B3
Pinner HA5 ...........175 C1
Jubilee Cotts
Aspenden SG9 .........40 D5
Great Hormead SG9 ...42 A8
Jubilee Cres SG15 .....11 A2
Jubilee Ct Harpenden AL5 .86 C3
Hatfield AL10 ........130 B8
Waltham Abbey EN9 ..163 F6
Jubilee Meml Ave SG1 .50 D8
Jubilee Rd
Letchworth SG6 ......23 D7
Stevenage SG1 .......50 B8
Watford WD24 ......154 A1
Jubilee Trad Ctr SG6 ..23 D7
Jubilee Wlk WD4 ...139 A1
Judge St WD24 .....154 B1
Judge's Hill EN6 ....145 F2
Julia Ct LU3 ..........45 B4
Julia Gate SG2 ........51 C8
Julian's Ct SG1 .......50 C8
Julian's Rd SG1 ......50 B8

Julie Ho EN11 .......135 C8
Julius Gdns LU3 ......44 F7
Junction Cl AL8 .....110 D7
Juniper Ave AL2 ....155 A8
Juniper Cl Barnet EN5 .171 D4
Chesham EN10 ......148 F6
Luton LU4 .............44 F4
Rickmansworth WD3 .173 D7
Juniper Ct HA3 .....176 F2
Juniper Gate WD3 ..173 D8
Juniper Gdns
Oaklands AL4 .........89 C7
Shenley WD7 ........156 E6
Juniper Gn HP1 .....123 E3
Juniper Gr WD17 ...154 A1
Juniper Ho EN10 ....148 F6
Juno Rd HP2 ........124 F6
Jupiter Dr HP2 ......124 F5
Jupiter Drive Jun Mix & Inf
Sch HP2 .............124 F5
Jupiter Gate SG2 .....51 D8
Juxon Cl HA3 .......176 B2

Kaida Ho 6 WD3 .....165 D2
Kardwell Cl SG4 ......35 A6
Karen Ho SG16 .......10 A4
Karens Ct EN3 ......162 D2
Katemon Ct SG12 ...115 D4
Kates Cl EN5 ........171 A4
Katescroft AL7 ......110 C2
Katherine Cl HP3 ...138 E8
Katherine Pl WD5 ..154 A7
Katrine Sq HP2 .....124 E7
Kay Cl HP23 .........100 A5
Kay Wlk AL4 ........128 D3
Keats Cl
Hemel Hempstead HP2 .105 B1
Royston SG8 ..........7 B7
Stevenage SG2 .......51 C7
Keats Ho 15 AL5 ......86 B1
Keats Way SG4 .......35 C7
Keble Terr WD5 ....153 F7
Kecksy's CM21 .......97 F4
Keeble Cl LU2 ........46 E1
Keele Ct WD24 ......167 C7
Keepers Cl
Cheddington LU7 .....80 A7
Luton LU2 .............46 C2
Keiths Rd HP3 ......125 A2
Keiths Wood SG3 .....68 F5
Kelbys AL7 ...........111 C7
Keller Cl SG2 .........51 B4
Kelling Cl LU2 ........45 C8
Kelly Cl WD6 .......170 D7
Kelly Ct WD6 .......170 C7
Kelman Ct EN8 ......162 D8
Kelmscott Wlk WD18 .167 A4
Kelmscott Cres WD18 .167 A4
Kelshall WD25 ......154 E3
Kelshall St SG8 ......15 E5
Kelvin Cl LU1 .........63 E6
Kelvin Cres HA3 ....176 E3
Kemble Cl EN6 .....159 D6
Kemble Ho HA7 ....176 F5
Kemp Pl WD23 .....168 A3
Kempe Cl AL1 ......141 C7
Kempe Rd EN1 .....162 C3
Kemprow WD25 ....155 D3
Kemps Dr HA6 .....174 F3
Kempsey Cl LU2 ......46 D2
Ken Davies Ct AL3 ..127 F7
Kendal Cl LU3 ........44 D7
Kendal Rd EN9 .....163 C4
Kendale HP3 ........125 A2
Kendale Rd 3 Hitchin SG4 34 F6
Luton LU4 .............44 B2
Kendall Cl AL7 ......110 F2
Kendall Ct WD6 ....170 C8
Kendals Cl WD7 ....155 E3
Kenerne Dr EN5 ....171 E4
Kenford St WD25 ...154 B7
Kenilworth Cl
Borehamwood WD6 ..170 C6
Hemel Hempstead HP2 .124 C2
Stevenage SG2 .......69 C7
Kenilworth Cres EN1 .161 E1
Kenilworth Ct WD17 .167 A8
Kenilworth Dr
Borehamwood WD6 ..170 D6
Croxley Green WD3 ..166 B5
Kenilworth Gdns WD19 .175 C5
Kenilworth Ho WD6 .170 C6
Kenilworth Prim Sch
WD6 .................170 D6
Kenilworth Rd LU1 ...63 C8
Kenmare Cl SG1 ......36 F3
Kennedy Ave EN11 ..134 F6
Kennedy Cl
Cheshunt EN8 .......148 E3
London Colney AL2 ..142 D5
Pinner HA5 ..........175 F4
Kennedy Rd SG12 ....71 E7
Kennel La AL5 ........85 A5
Kennelwood La AL10 .130 B6
Kennesbourne Ct AL5 ..85 D4
Kenneth Gdns 4 HA7 .176 F4
Kenneth Rd LU2 ......46 A1
Kennett Way SG1 .....36 F3
Kenning Rd EN11 ...135 B8
Kennington Rd LU3 ...45 B3
Kensington Ave WD18 .166 F5
Kensington Cl AL1 ...128 A1
Kensington Ct EN1 ..161 E1
Kensington Mews
WD18 ...............167 A5

Kensington Way WD6 ..170 D6
Kensworth Lower Sch
  LU6 ............82 F8
Kensworth Rd LU6 ....82 D4
Kent Cl WD6 ........157 D1
Kent Cres CM23 ......76 E4
Kent Pl SG5 ........34 D8
Kent Rd LU1 ........62 F8
Kentish La AL9 ......145 C7
Kenton Gdns AL1 ....127 F2
Kenton La HA3 ......176 F3
Kents Ave HP3 ......138 D7
Kents La SG11 ......55 E2
Kenwood Dr WD3 ....172 F8
Kenworth Cl EN8 ....162 D6
Kenyon Pl AL1 ......110 E3
Kerdistone Cl EN6 ..145 B1
Kernow Ct LU2 ......46 A1
Kerr Cl SG3 ........68 F5
Kerri Cl EN5 ........171 C5
Kerril Croft CM20 ..117 A1
Kershaw Cl LU3 ......45 A8
Kershaw's Hill SG4 ..34 F6
Kessingland Ave SG1 ..36 A1
Keston Mews WD17 ..167 B7
Kestrel Cl
  Berkhamsted HP4 ....122 C3
  Stevenage SG2 ......51 D2
  Watford WD25 ......154 E5
Kestrel Ct 4 SG12 ..93 C3
Kestrel Gdns CM23 ..76 C6
Kestrel Gn AL10 ....130 A4
Kestrel Way Luton LU4 ..44 A5
  Royston SG8 ........7 E8
  Welwyn Garden City AL7 ..110 F8
Kestrel Wlk SG6 ....23 B3
Kestrels The AL2 ....154 F8
Keswick Cl AL1 ......128 B1
Keswick Dr EN3 ......162 C3
Kettering Rd EN3 ....162 D2
Kettle Green Rd SG10 ..74 E2
Ketton Cl LU2 ......64 A7
Ketton Ct LU2 ......64 A7
Kevere Ct HA6 ......174 B5
Kewferry Dr HA6 ....174 C5
Kewferry Rd HA6 ....174 C5
Keyfield AL1 ........127 D2
Keymer Cl LU2 ......46 C3
Keynton Cl LU2 ......112 F7
Keysers Rd EN10 ....135 B1
Kibes La SG12 ......93 E1
Kidner Cl LU2 ......45 E5
Kilby Cl WD25 ......154 D4
Kilbride Ct HP2 ....124 F7
Kildonan Cl WD17 ..166 F8
Kilfillan Gdns HP4 ..122 A4
Kilfillan Pk HP4 ....122 A4
Killigrew Inf Sch AL2 ..141 B6
Killigrew Jun Sch AL2 ..141 B6
Kilmarnock Dr LU2 ..45 E5
Kilmarnock Rd WD19 ..175 D6
Kiln Ave HP6 ........150 C1
Kiln Cl HP4 ........123 B6
Kiln Cotts HP2 ......125 B4
Kiln Ground HP3 ....125 A1
Kiln House Cl SG12 ..93 E2
Kiln House Yd SG8 ....7 C6
Kiln La HP5 ........150 B8
Kiln Way HA6 ......174 E4
Kilncroft HP3 ......125 B1
Kilnfield AL7 ......89 F1
Kilsmore La EN8 ....148 D2
Kilvinton Dr EN2 ..161 D1
Kilworth Cl AL7 ....111 B4
Kimberley Cl SG1 ....11 F2
Kimberley Cl CM23 ..77 A5
Kimberley Rd AL3 ..127 D4
Kimble Cl WD18 ....166 E2
Kimble Ct LU2 ......168 C2
Kimblewick WD19 ..167 E1
Kimbolton Cres SG2 ..69 A7
Kimbolton Gn WD6 ..170 C5
Kimps Way HP3 ....139 A8
Kimpton Bottom AL5,SG4 ..86 E7
Kimpton Cl HP2 ....125 B8
Kimpton Pl WD25 ..154 D5
Kimpton Prim Sch SG4 ..66 C1
Kimpton Rd
  Ayot St Peter AL6 ....89 A6
  Codicote SG4 ......67 B1
  Kimpton SG4,AL4 ....87 C7
  Luton LU1,LU2 ......64 A6
  Peters Green LU2,SG4 ..65 E2
Kimptons Cl EN6 ....158 D7
Kimptons Mead EN6 ..158 D7
Kinderscout HP3 ....125 A1
Kindersley Cl AL6 ..89 C6
Kindersley Way WD5 ..153 D8
Kinetic Bsns Ctr WD6 ..170 A6
King Arthur Ct EN3 ..162 B4
King Charles Rd WD7 ..156 E7
King Edward Rd
  Cheshunt EN8 ......162 E6
  Shenley WD7 ......156 F6
  Watford WD17 ......167 D3
King Edward St HP3 ..138 D7
King Edward's Rd SG12 ..93 E2
King George Ave WD23 ..168 B3
King George Cl SG1 ..50 E6
King George Rd
  Waltham Abbey EN9 ..163 C5
  Ware SG12 ........93 E2
King George's Way SG4 ..66 E6
King Georges Ave
  WD18 ............166 E5
King Georges Cl SG5 ..21 D1
King Harold Ct EN9 ..163 C6
King Harold Sch EN9 ..163 E6

King Harry La AL3 ....127 B1
King Harry St HP2 ..124 D2
King Henry Ct LU3 ..45 B2
King Henry's Mews
  EN3 ..............163 A2
King Henrys Ct EN9 ..163 C3
King James Ave EN6 ..146 E2
King James Way SG8 ..7 D6
King St
  Bishop's Stortford CM23 ..76 F7
  Luton LU1 ........63 E7
  Markyate AL3 ......83 E5
  2 Royston SG8 ....7 D6
  Tring HP23 ........100 A3
  Watford WD18 ......167 C5
King Street Mews 1
  CM23 ............76 F7
King Williams Ct EN9 ..163 C4
King's Cotts CM23 ....77 A6
King's La WD4 ......152 B8
King's Mews 7 HP2 ..124 D4
King's Rd Cheshunt EN8 ..162 E5
  Hertford SG13 ......114 A7
  Hitchin SG5 ........34 F8
  London Colney AL2 ..142 C5
  St Albans AL3 ......127 C3
King's Walden Rd SG5 ..33 D2
King's Wlk SG8 ......7 D5
Kingcroft Rd AL5 ..107 D7
Kingfisher Cl
  Harrow HA3 ......176 F3
  Northwood HA6 ....174 B2
  Stanstead Abbotts SG12 ..115 C3
  Wheathampstead AL4 ..87 D1
Kingfisher Ct Enfield EN2 ..160 F1
  Hitchin SG5 ........35 A6
Kingfisher Dr HP3 ..138 F6
Kingfisher Lure
  Kings Langley WD4 ..139 B2
  Rickmansworth WD3 ..165 B5
Kingfisher Rise SG2 ..51 D2
Kingfisher Way
  Bishop's Stortford CM23 ..77 A4
  Roydon CM19 ......116 A1
Kingham Rd SG12 ....94 C5
Kinghamway LU2 ....45 E1
Kings Ave
  Hemel Hempstead HP3 ..138 F7
  Watford WD18 ......167 A5
Kings Cl
  Chipperfield WD4 ..152 B8
  Northwood HA6 ....174 F4
  5 Watford WD18 ..167 C5
Kings Ct
  Berkhamsted HP4 ..122 C5
  Bishop's Stortford CM23 ..77 A8
  Harpenden AL5 ....107 B8
Kings Farm Rd WD3 ..164 D3
Kings Field Cotts WD5 ..153 F8
Kings Heath Pk AL5 ..86 C6
Kings Hedges SG5 ....34 C8
Kings Langley Prim Sch
  WD4 ............138 F3
Kings Langley Sch WD4 ..138 E3
Kings Langley Sta WD4 ..139 C1
Kings Mdw WD4 ....139 A3
Kings Oak WD3 ......166 A5
Kings Oak Private Hospl The
  EN2 ..............161 A4
Kings Park Ind Est WD4 ..139 B2
Kings Rd Barnet EN5 ..171 C5
Kings Sch The AL5 ..85 F4
Kings Walden Rise SG2 ..51 C8
Kingsbridge Rd CM23 ..77 A8
Kingsbury Ave AL3 ..127 C4
Kingsbury Watermill★
  AL3 ..............127 B4
Kingscroft AL7 ......111 B7
Kingsdale Ho AL6 ..89 B3
Kingsdale Rd HP4 ..122 A4
Kingsdown SG4 ......35 B6
Kingsdown Ave LU2 ..45 D5
Kingsfield EN11 ....135 A5
Kingsfield Ct WD19 ..167 D2
Kingsfield Dr EN3 ..162 D4
Kingsfield Rd
  Dane End SG12 ......71 E8
  Watford WD19 ......167 D3
Kingsfield Way EN3 ..162 D4
Kingsgate AL3 ......127 B1
Kingshill Ave AL4 ..128 B6
Kingshill Ct 6 EN5 ..171 E5
Kingshill Inf Sch SG12 ..93 D3
Kingshill Way HP4 ..122 B2
Kingshott Sch SG4 ..35 B5
Kingsland Ct 7 LU1 ..63 F6
Kingsland Rd
  Hemel Hempstead HP1 ..124 A1
  Luton LU1 ........63 F6
Kingsland Way SG7 ....4 C3
Kingsley Ave
  Borehamwood WD6 ..169 F7
  Cheshunt EN8 ......148 C2
Kingsley Ct AL7 ......110 F2
Kingsley Rd LU3 ......45 A5
Kingsley Wlk HP23 ..100 A4
Kingsmead
  Cheshunt EN8 ......148 D3
  Cuffley EN6 ......146 E3
  Lower Nazeing EN9 ..135 C1
  Sawbridgeworth CM21 ..97 E1
  St Albans AL4 ......128 A8
Kingsmead Rd CM23 ..77 A8
Kingsmill Ct 1 AL10 ..130 B3
Kingston Pl HA3 ....176 F3
Kingston Rd LU2 ....45 F1

Kingston Vale SG8 ....7 E5
Kingsway Cuffley EN6 ..146 E1
  Luton LU4 ........45 A1
  Royston SG8 ........7 C8
  Stotfold SG5 ......11 F7
  Ware SG12 ........93 D3
Kingsway Gdns SG5 ..11 F7
Kingsway Ind Est LU1 ..63 A8
Kingsway Inf Sch WD25 ..154 A5
Kingsway Jun Sch
  WD25 ............154 A5
Kingsway North Orbital Rd
  WD25 ............154 B5
Kingswell Ride EN6 ..146 E1
Kingswood Ave SG4 ..35 D8
Kingswood Rd WD25 ..154 B5
Kingwell Rd EN4 ....159 D1
Kinloch Ct 6 AL5 ..86 B1
Kinross Ct LU3 ......44 D8
Kinsbourne Cl AL5 ..85 C4
Kinsbourne Cres AL5 ..85 D4
Kinsbourne Ct AL5 ..85 F3
Kinsbourne Green La
  AL5 ..............85 B3
Kintyre Ho 2 WD18 ..166 F3
Kipling Cl AL5 ......35 C7
Kipling Gr HP2 ......105 B3
Kipling Pl HA7 ......176 F4
Kipling Rd LU2 ........2 E1
Kipling The LU3 ....45 B6
Kipling Way AL5 ....86 B1
Kirby Cl HA6 ......174 F4
Kirby Dr LU3 ......45 A8
Kirkcaldy Gn 1 WD19 ..175 C7
Kirkdale Ct 8 LU1 ..63 E6
Kirkdale Rd AL5 ....86 A2
Kirklands AL8 ......89 D2
Kirkwick Ave AL5 ..86 A1
Kit's La SG7 ........25 C8
Kitchener Cl AL1 ..128 B2
Kitcheners La SG2 ..38 B1
Kitching St
  St Ippolyts SG4 ......49 F5
  Stevenage SG1 ......50 A5
Kite Field HP4 ......121 E7
Kite Way SG6 ......22 E8
Kitsbury Ct HP4 ....122 B4
Kitsbury Rd HP4 ....122 B4
Kitsbury Terr HP4 ..122 B4
Kitson Way CM20 ..117 C1
Kitswell Rd AL7 ....156 A6
Kitswell Way WD7 ..155 F6
Kitt's End Rd EN5 ..158 E2
Kiwi Ct SG5 ........21 F1
Klondyke AL5 ......85 D4
Knap Cl SG2 ........23 D8
Knebworth Ct CM23 ..76 D6
Knebworth Ctry Pk★
  SG3 ..............68 C7
Knebworth Ho★ SG3 ..68 B6
Knebworth Path WD6 ..170 D5
Knebworth Prim Sch
  SG3 ..............69 A5
Knebworth Sta SG3 ..68 F5
Kneesworth House Hospl
  SG8 ..............2 C5
Kneesworth Rd SG8 ..2 E8
Kneesworth St SG8 ..7 C6
Knella Gn AL7 ......111 A6
Knella Rd AL7 ......111 A6
Knella Road Workshops
  AL7 ..............111 A6
Knight St CM21 ......97 E2
Knight's Ct CM21 ..97 E2
Knights Cl
  Bishop's Stortford CM23 ..76 C8
  Buntingford SG9 ....40 E6
  Watton at S SG14 ..70 D4
Knights Ct
  Standon SG11 ......55 F1
Knights Field LU2 ..45 D1
Knights Orch
  Hemel Hempstead HP1 ..123 F5
  St Albans AL3 ......127 C3
Knights Templar Sch The
  SG7 ..............23 E8
Knights Templars Gn
  SG2 ..............51 D4
Knightsbridge Way HP2 ..124 E4
Knightscote Cl UB9 ..173 D1
Knightsfield AL8 ....89 D2
Knightsfield Sch AL8 ..89 D3
Knoll Cres HA6 ......174 F2
Knoll Gn HP2 ......124 E5
Knoll Rise LU2 ......45 E4
Knoll The SG13 ....114 B7
Knolles Cres AL9 ..144 B7
Knolls Cl HP22 ......60 B3
Knowl Piece SG4 ....22 A3
Knowl Pk WD6 ......169 E4
Knowl Way WD6 ....169 F4
Knowle SG1 ........36 F6
Knowle Cl AL5 ......107 D7
Knowle Ho EN11 ....135 A5
Knowle The EN11 ..135 A5
Knutsford Ave WD24 ..154 D1
Knutsford Sch WD24 ..154 D1
Koh-I-Noor Ave WD3 ..168 A3
Kristiansand Way SG6 ..23 C8
Kymswell Rd SG2 ....51 C3
Kynance Cl LU2 ......46 A2
Kynaston Cl HA3 ..176 D3
Kynaston Wood HA3 ..176 D3
Kyrkeby SG6 ........23 C4
Kytes Dr WD25 ......154 D6

L

Laburnum Cl
  Cheshunt EN8 ......162 D8
  Luton LU3 ........45 C7
Laburnum Gr
  Chiswell Green AL2 ..141 B6
  Luton LU3 ........45 B7
Laburnum Rd EN11 ..135 B8
Lachbury Cl LU1 ....63 A6
Lackmore Rd EN1 ..162 C4
Lacre Way SG6 ......23 C7
Ladbrooke Cl EN6 ..159 A7
Ladbrooke Dr EN6 ..159 A7
Ladbrooke JMI Sch EN6 ..159 A7
Ladies Gr AL3 ......127 C3
Lady Cooper Ct HP4 ..122 E6
Lady Gr AL7 ........110 E2
Lady Spencer's Gr AL1 ..127 C2
Lady Zia Wernher Sch
  LU2 ..............46 B3
Lady's Cl WD18 ....167 C5
Ladygrove Cotts SG4 ..48 F5
Ladygrove Ct SG4 ..48 F5
Ladyhill LU4 ......44 B6
Ladymeadow HP3 ..138 D4
Ladyshot CM20 ....118 B1
Ladysmith Rd
  Harrow HA3 ......176 E1
  Pitstone LU7 ......80 C5
  St Albans AL3 ......127 C4
Ladywalk WD3 ......172 E6
Ladywell Prospect CM21 ..98 A1
Ladywood Cl WD3 ..165 D6
Ladywood Rd SG14 ..112 F6
Laguna Ct 2 AL1 ..127 E3
Laidon Sq HP2 ......124 D7
Lake Dr WD23 ......176 D8
Lake Rd EN9 ......135 E2
Lake The WD23 ....168 D1
Lake View
  Bishop's Stortford CM23 ..76 B3
  Potters Bar EN6 ....159 C6
Lake Villas SG9 ......43 B4
Lakeland Cl HA3 ....176 D4
Lakes Ct SG12 ......115 B4
Lakeside
  Borehamwood WD6 ..170 A4
  Tring HP23 ........100 A5
Lakeside Pl AL2 ....142 D4
Lakeside Rd EN8 ..148 C3
Lakeside Sch AL8 ..110 B4
Lalleford Rd LU2 ..46 D1
Lalsham Ho 4 WD19 ..175 C7
  Watford WD25 ......154 C5
Lamb Cl AL4 ........108 E7
Lamb Ct AL3 ......106 B5
Lamb La AL3 ......106 B5
Lamb Mdw SG15 ....11 A3
Lambert Ct WD6 ..170 D8
Lambourn Chase WD7 ..155 F3
Lambourn Dr LU2 ..45 E5
Lambourn Gdns AL5 ..85 F3
Lambs Cl Cuffley EN6 ..146 F2
  Dunstable LU5 ....44 A1
Lambs Gdns SG12 ..95 D4
Lambton Ave EN8 ..162 D6
Lamer La AL4 ......87 D3
Lamers Rd LU2 ......46 B2
Lammas Mead SG5 ..21 C7
Lammas Path SG2 ..51 B4
Lammas Rd
  Cheddington LU7 ....80 A7
  Watford WD17 ......167 C4
  Watton at S SG14 ..70 D4
Lammas Way LU2 ....22 F8
Lammasmead EN10 ..148 B1
Lamorna Cl Luton LU3 ..44 F6
  Radlett WD7 ......156 B5
Lamorna Ct HA3 ....176 E1
Lampits HP1 ......135 B6
Lamsey Rd HP3 ....124 D1
Lancaster Ave
  Hadley Wood EN4 ..159 D1
  Hitchin SG5 ........34 E8
  Luton LU2 ........45 C8
Lancaster Cl SG1 ..36 E2
Lancaster Dr HP3 ..136 F4
Lancaster Rd Hitchin SG5 ..34 E8
  St Albans AL1 ......127 F5
Lancaster Way
  Abbots Langley WD5 ..153 F8
  Bishop's Stortford CM23 ..76 C8
  Welwyn AL6 ......89 C3
Lancing Ho 5 WD24 ..167 C7
Lancing Rd LU2 ....46 D1
Lancing Way WD3 ..166 B4
Landau Way EN10 ..148 F5
Landford Cl WD3 ..173 E8
Landmead Rd EN8 ..148 E2
Landridge Dr EN1 ..162 B1
Lands' End WD6 ....169 D3
Lane End
  Berkhamsted HP4 ..121 F4
  Hatfield AL10 ......129 D2
Lane Gdns WD23 ..168 E2
Lanefield Wlk AL8 ..110 C6
Lanercost Cl AL6 ..90 A7
Langbridge Cl SG4 ..35 A4
Langdale Ave AL5 ..86 D2
Langdale Cl 2 HP2 ..124 E6
Langdale Gdns EN3 ..162 C4
Langdale Terr WD6 ..170 C6
Langdon St HP23 ..100 A3
Langfield Cl EN9 ..135 E1

Langford Cl AL4 ....128 C3
Langford Dr LU2 ....46 A3
Langham Cl Luton LU2 ..45 D7
  St Albans AL4 ......128 D8
Langham Ho 9 LU1 ..63 D8
Langholme WD23 ..168 C1
Langland Ct HA6 ..174 D3
Langland Dr HA5 ..175 E3
Langleigh SG6 ......11 F1
Langley Ave HP3 ..138 F8
Langley Cres
  Kings Langley WD4 ..139 A1
  St Albans AL3 ......127 C5
Langley Ct EN7 ....147 C3
Langley Gn EN9 ....135 D1
Langley Gr AL4 ....108 C2
Langley Hill WD4 ..138 F2
Langley Hill Cl WD4 ..139 A2
Langley La
  Abbots Langley WD5 ..153 F7
  Langley SG4 ......49 C3
Langley Lodge La WD4 ..153 A8
Langley Rd
  Abbots Langley WD5 ..153 F8
  Chipperfield WD4 ..138 B1
  Watford WD17 ......167 A8
Langley Row EN5 ..171 E8
Langley St LU1 ....63 E6
Langley Terrace Ind Pk 10
  LU1 ..............63 E6
Langley Way WD17 ..166 F8
Langley Wharf WD4 ..139 A4
Langleybury La WD4 ..153 A4
Langmead Dr WD23 ..168 D1
Langstone Ley AL7 ..111 B5
Langthorne Ave SG1 ..50 E6
Langton Gr HA6 ....174 C5
Langton Ho EN11 ..134 F6
Langton Rd Harrow HA3 ..176 C3
  Hoddesdon EN11 ..134 F6
Langwood 6 WD17 ..167 A8
Langwood Gdns WD17 ..167 A8
Langworthy HA5 ..176 A4
Lankester Rd SG8 ....7 C5
Lannock SG6 ......23 D4
Lannock Hill SG4 ..23 D3
Lannock Prim Sch SG6 ..23 C4
Lanrick Copse HP4 ..122 E5
Lansdowne Cl WD25 ..154 D4
Lansdowne Ct EN10 ..135 A3
Lansdowne Rd LU3 ..45 D1
Lanterns La SG2 ....51 D5
Lanthony Ct SG15 ..11 A4
Lanthorn Cl EN10 ..134 E4
Laporte Way LU4 ..44 F1
Lapwing Cl HP2 ....124 E6
Lapwing Dell SG6 ..23 B3
Lapwing Rd LU4 ....44 A4
Lapwing Rise SG2 ..51 D5
Lapwing Way WD5 ..154 A8
Larch Ave
  Bricket Wood AL2 ..140 E1
  Hitchin SG4 ........35 A4
Larch Cl EN7 ......147 E4
Larch La AL6 ......89 F8
Larch Rise HP4 ....122 A5
Larch View HP4 ....124 B2
Larches Ave EN1 ..162 C4
Larches The
  Berkhamsted HP4 ..121 D5
  Little Chalfont HP6 ..150 B1
  Luton LU2 ........45 D1
  Northwood HA6 ....174 C4
  St Albans AL4 ......128 D7
  Ware SG12 ........93 C3
  Watford WD23 ......167 E4
Larchwood CM23 ..76 D5
Lark Rise AL10 ....130 A3
Larken Cl WD23 ..168 C1
Larken Dr WD23 ..168 C1
Larkens Cl SG11 ..55 D3
Larkin Pl SG8 ......2 D1
Larkins Cl SG7 ....12 F1
Larkinson SG1 ....50 C7
Larks Ridge AL2 ..141 A4
Larksfield SG12 ..93 E3
Larkspur Cl
  Bishop's Stortford CM23 ..76 D6
  Hemel Hempstead HP1 ..123 E4
Larkspur Gdns LU4 ..44 F2
Larksway CM23 ....76 C6
Larkswood Rise AL4 ..128 C8
Larmans Rd EN3 ..162 B3
Larsen Dr EN9 ......163 D5
Larwood Gr SG1 ....51 A8
Larwood Sch SG1 ..50 F7
Latchford Mews 8 AL4 ..87 F2
Latchford Pl HP1 ..124 A2
Latchmore Bank CM22 ..77 B2
Latchmore Cl SG4 ..34 F5
Latimer Cl
  Hemel Hempstead HP2 ..125 B8
  Pinner HA5 ......175 C2
  Watford WD18 ....166 E2
Latimer Ct EN8 ....162 F5
Latimer Gdns
  Pinner HA5 ......175 C2
  Welwyn Garden City AL7 ..111 B6
Latimer Rd
  Little Chalfont HP6,HP5 ..150 C2
  Luton LU1 ........63 E6
Latium Cl AL1 ......127 D2
Lattimore Rd
  St Albans AL1 ......127 E3
  Wheathampstead AL4 ..108 C8

Latton Hall Cl CM20 ....118 A1
Lauderdale Rd WD4 ....153 C6
Laughton Ct WD6 ......170 D7
Launceston WD3 ........164 B3
Launton LU3 ..............31 B1
Laura Ct HA2 ............176 C1
Laural Ct EN6 ..........146 E2
Laurance Haines Prim Sch
The WD18 ..............167 A3
Laureate Way HP1 ......124 B5
Laurel Ave EN6 ........158 F7
Laurel Bank HP3 ........137 F8
Laurel Cl
Hemel Hempstead HP2 ..124 F4
Watford WD19 ..........167 C4
Laurel Ct EN6 ..........146 F1
Laurel Fields EN6 ......158 F8
Laurel Mews SG7 ........12 E1
Laurel Pk HA3 ..........176 F3
Laurel Rd AL1 ..........127 F3
Laurel Way SG5 ..........21 E3
Laureldene LU4 ..........74 F1
Laurels Cl AL3 ..........141 B8
Laurels The
Bushey WD23 ............176 E8
Hammond Street EN7 ....147 E5
Potten End HP4 ........123 C6
Laurelside Wlk LU5 ......44 A2
Lauries Cl HP1 ..........123 C1
Laurino Pl WD23 ........176 C8
Lavender Cl
Bishop's Stortford CM23 ..76 D6
Hammond Street EN7 ....147 F4
Harlow CM20 ............117 C1
Hatfield AL10 ..........129 F8
Luton LU2 ..............45 E7
Lavender Cres AL3 ......127 C5
Lavender Ct Baldock SG7 ..12 E1
Hitchin SG4 ..............35 B6
Lavender Gdns
Enfield EN2 ............161 B1
Harrow HA3 ............176 E4
Lavender Prim Sch EN2 161 B1
Lavender Rd EN2 ........161 D1
Lavender Way SG4 ........34 D7
Lavender Wlk HP2 ......124 D6
Lavinia Ave WD25 ......154 D5
Lavrock La WD3 ........165 F2
Law Hall La SG4 ..........66 A8
Law Hall Lane Cotts SG4 66 A8
Lawford Ave WD3 ......164 C3
Lawford Cl
Chorleywood WD3 ......164 C3
Luton LU1 ..............63 C7
Lawn Ave SG4 ............66 C1
Lawn Gdns LU1 ..........63 D5
Lawn La HP3 ............138 D8
Lawn Mans EN5 ..........171 F5
Lawn The CM20 ........118 B3
Lawn Vale HA5 ..........175 E1
Lawns Cl SG5 ............33 C2
Lawns Ct SG8 ............7 D5
Lawns Dr The EN10 ....134 F2
Lawns The Harrow HA5 ..176 B3
Hemel Hempstead HP1 ..123 E4
Shenley WD7 ............156 E6
St Albans AL3 ..........127 C4
Stevenage SG2 ..........51 D4
Welwyn Garden City AL8 ..89 D1
Lawnswood EN5 ........171 E4
Lawrance Gdns EN8 ....148 D3
Lawrance Rd AL3 ......127 C7
Lawrence Ave
Letchworth SG6 ..........23 A4
Sawbridgeworth CM21 ....97 E4
Stansted Abbotts SG12 ..115 C3
Stevenage SG1 ..........50 E7
Lawrence Cl SG14 ......112 E7
Lawrence Ct 4 WD19 ...175 D7
Lawrence End Rd LU2 ....65 D4
Lawrence Hall End AL7 ..110 E3
Lawrence Moorings
CM21 ..................97 F2
Lawrie Ct HA3 ..........176 F3
Laxton Cl LU2 ..........46 E1
Laxton Gdns Baldock SG7 ..24 A7
Shenley WD7 ............156 E7
Lay Brook AL4 ..........128 A7
Layard Rd EN1 ..........161 F1
Layham Dr LU2 ..........46 E1
Layhill HP2 ............124 D5
Layston CE Fst Sch SG9 ..40 F6
Layston Mdw SG9 ........40 F6
Layston Pk SG8 ..........7 D5
Layton St AL7 ..........110 E2
Le Corte Cl WD4 ........138 F2
Lea Bank LU3 ............44 E6
Lea Bank Ct LU3 ........44 E6
Lea Bushes WD25 ......154 E4
Lea Cl
Bishop's Stortford CM23 ..59 B1
Bushey WD23 ..........168 B4
Lea Ct AL5 ..............86 A3
Lea Farm Jun Sch
WD25 ..................154 D4
Lea Gn AL9 ............130 E8
Lea Gr CM23 ............59 B1
Lea Manor High Sch LU3 44 F8
Lea Manor Recn Ctr LU3 ..44 F8
Lea Mount EN1 ..........147 E3
Lea Prim Sch The AL5 ...86 A4
Lea Rd Harpenden AL5 ....86 A3
Hoddesdon EN11 ........135 C8
Holdbrook EN9 ..........163 A5

Lea Rd continued
Luton LU1 ................63 F7
Watford WD24 ..........154 B1
Lea Road Ind Pk EN9 ...163 A5
Lea Valley High Sch
EN3 ..................162 C4
Lea Valley Park Visitor Ctr★
EN9 ..................163 C2
Lea Wlk AL5 ............86 C4
Leacroft AL5 ............86 D3
Leaders Cl HP22 ........60 B3
Leaf Cl HA6 ............174 D3
Leaf Way AL1 ..........141 D8
Leafield LU3 ............44 F4
Leaford Cres WD24 ....153 E2
Leaford Ct WD24 ......153 F3
Leaforis Rd EN7 ........148 A3
Leafy La HP23 ..........99 E1
Leagrave High St LU4 ....44 B3
Leagrave Prim Sch LU4 ..44 C4
Leagrave Rd LU4 ........45 B2
Leagrave Sta LU4 ........44 E5
Leahoe Gdns SG13 ......113 C5
Leamington Rd LU3 ......45 A7
Leander Gdns WD25 ....154 E2
Leas The Baldock SG7 ....23 E7
Hemel Hempstead HP3 ..139 A7
Watford WD23 ..........167 F7
Leasey Bridge La AL4 ....87 A1
Leasey Dell Dr AL4 ......87 A2
Leaside HP2 ............125 C2
Leaside Ct AL5 ..........86 C3
Leaside Wlk 6 SG12 ....93 D1
Leat Cl LU2 ..............97 F3
Leathersellers Cl 12
EN5 ..................171 E6
Leathwaite Cl LU3 ......45 A6
Leaves Spring SG2 ......51 A2
Leavesden Ct WD5 ......154 A8
Leavesden Film Studios
WD4 ..................153 E5
Leavesden Green Jun Mix Inf
Sch WD25 ............154 A5
Leavesden Rd WD24 ....154 B1
Leaview EN9 ............163 B6
Lebanon Cl WD17 ......153 D3
Lectern La AL1 ..........141 E7
Leda Ave LU3 ..........162 D1
Ledgemore La HP1,HP2 ..103 F3
Ledwell Rd LU1 ..........62 F3
Lee Bridge Cnr LU2 ......85 F7
Lee Cl Hertford SG13 ...113 C4
Stansted Abbotts SG12 ..115 C4
Lee Farm Cl HP5 ......136 A1
Lee The HA6 ............174 F5
Lee Valley Ctry Pk★
EN10 ..................135 B2
Leeches Way LU7 ........80 A7
Leecroft Rd EN5 ........171 E5
Leefe Way EN6 ..........146 D3
Leeming Rd WD6 ......169 F8
Lees Ave HA6 ............174 F2
Leeside Barnet EN5 ....171 E3
Potters Bar EN6 ........159 D7
Leeswood Ct SG14 ......112 F7
Leete Pl SG8 ............7 D7
Leeway Ct HA5 ........175 F3
Leggatts Cl WD24 ......153 B2
Leggatts Rise WD25 ....154 A4
Leggatts Way WD24 ....154 A3
Leggatts Wood Ave
WD24 ................154 B3
Leggett Gr SG1 ..........50 E8
Leggfield Terr HP1 ......123 F4
Leghorn Cres LU4 ........44 A3
Legions Way CM23 ......77 A8
Legra Ave EN11 ........135 A6
Leicester Rd LU4 ........44 E1
Leigh Comm AL7 ......110 F4
Leigh Ct WD6 ..........170 D7
Leigh Rodd WD19 ......175 F1
Leighton Buzzard Rd
Great Gaddesden HP1 ..103 E2
Hemel Hempstead HP1 ..124 D5
Leighton Ct EN8 ........148 D2
Leighton Gr Harrow HA3 176 D1
Wingrave HP22 ..........60 C3
Lemonfield Dr WD25 ...154 E6
Lemsford Ct WD6 ......170 C5
Lemsford La AL8 ........110 B4
Lemsford Rd
Hatfield AL10 ..........130 A6
St Albans AL1 ..........127 F4
Lemsford Springs (Nature
Reserve)★ AL8 ........110 A3
Lemsford Village AL8 ...109 F5
Lennon Cl LU1 ..........63 D7
Lennox Gn LU2 ..........46 F2
Lensbury Cl EN8 ........148 E3
Leonard Ct HA3 ........176 E3
Leonard's Cl AL6 ........89 E8
Lesbury Cl LU2 ..........46 E1
Leslie Cl SG2 ............51 C2
Letchfield HP5 ........150 B8
Letchmore Inf Sch SG1 ..50 D7
Letchmore Rd
Radlett WD7 ..........156 A3
Stevenage SG1 ..........50 D7
Letchworth Bsns & Ret Pk
SG6 ..................23 C6
Letchworth Cl WD19 ...175 D5
Letchworth Gate SG6 ...23 B4
Letchworth La SG6 ......22 F5
Letchworth Mus & Art Gall★
SG6 ..................22 F5

Letchworth Rd
Baldock SG7 ..............23 D7
Luton LU3 ................45 A4
Letchworth Sta SG6 ......22 F6
Letter Box Row SG4 ......34 F3
Level's Gn CM23 ..........58 C5
Leven Cl Cheshunt EN8 ..162 D6
South Oxhey WD19 ......175 D5
Leven Dr EN8 ..........162 D6
Leven Way HP2 ........124 D7
Levenage La SG12 ......95 E3
Levendale LU4 ..........44 C5
Leventhorpe Sch The
CM21 ..................97 E4
Leveret Cl WD25 ......154 A5
Leverstock Green CE Prim
Sch HP2 ..............125 D2
Leverstock Green Rd
Hemel Hempstead HP2, ..125 B3
Hemel Hempstead HP2,
125 C2
Leverstock Green Way
HP2,HP3 ..............125 C3
Leverton Jun & Inf Sch The
EN9 ..................163 F5
Leverton Way EN9 ......163 C6
Lewes Way WD3 ........166 C5
Lewington Ct EN3 ......162 D2
Lewis Cl UB9 ..........173 C1
Lewis Ho 3 WD18 ......166 F3
Lewis La SG15 ..........11 A6
Lewsey Park Ct LU4 ....44 A4
Lewsey Rd LU4 ..........44 B2
Lexington Cl WD6 ......169 F6
Lexington Ct HA6 ......174 B6
Lexington Way EN5 ....171 D5
Ley Hill Rd HP3 ........136 E2
Ley Hill Sch HP5 ......136 B1
Ley Ho AL7 ............111 C6
Ley Park Prim Sch
EN10 ..................134 F1
Ley Wlk AL7 ............111 C6
Leyburne Cl LU7 ........61 C8
Leyburne Rd LU3 ........45 B6
Leycroft Way AL5 ......107 E7
Leyden Rd SG1 ..........50 D2
Leygreen Cl LU2 ........64 A8
Leyhill Dr LU1 ..........63 B4
Leyland Ave AL1 ......127 D1
Leyland Cl EN8 ........148 C2
Leys Ave SG6 ..........22 F6
Leys Cl UB9 ..........173 D2
Leys Prim Sch The SG1 ..37 A2
Leys Rd HP3 ..........124 F1
Leys The St Albans AL4 ..128 D6
Tring HP23 ............100 B4
Leysdown AL7 ..........111 D6
Leyton Gn AL5 ..........86 A1
Leyton Rd AL5 ..........86 A1
Liberty Cl SG13 ........113 C3
Liberty Wlk AL1 ......128 C2
Library Rd LU1 ..........63 E7
Lichfield Ho 4 HA6 ....170 A7
Lichfield Rd HA6 ......175 A1
Lichfield Way EN10 ....134 F1
Liddel Cl LU3 ..........45 B3
Lidgate Cl AL4 ..........44 B6
Lieutenant Ellis Way
EN7,EN8 ..............162 A7
Lighthorne Rise LU3 ....45 A7
Lightswood Cl EN7 ....147 D4
Lilac Ave EN1 ..........162 C3
Lilac Gr LU3 ............44 C8
Lilac Rd EN11 ..........135 B8
Lilac Way AL5 ..........107 D6
Lilbourne Dr SG13 ....114 A1
Lilley Bottom LU2,SG4 ..47 C5
Lilley Bottom Rd SG4 ....48 B1
Lilleyhoo La LU2,SG5 ...32 F2
Lilliard Ct EN11 ......115 B2
Lilly La HP2 ..........125 D7
Limberlost The AL6 ......89 B7
Limbrick Al AL5 ........107 C6
Limbury Rd LU3 ........44 F4
Lime Ave Kimpton AL4 ..87 B7
Luton LU4 ..............44 C3
Lime Cl Aston SG2 ......51 D4
Harrow HA3 ............176 F1
Ware SG12 ............93 E2
Lime Gr Royston SG8 ....7 E8
Totteridge N20 ........171 F1
Lime Tree Pl AL1 ......127 F2
Lime Tree Wlk
Bushey WD23 ..........176 E8
Enfield EN2 ............161 C1
Rickmansworth WD3 ...165 B4
Lime Walk Prim Sch
HP2 ..................124 F1
Lime Way WD7 ........156 C8
Lime Wlk HP3 ........124 F1
Limedene Cl HA5 ......175 D2
Limekiln Cl SG8 ........7 E5
Limekiln La Baldock SG7 ..23 F7
Stansted Mountfitchet
CM24 ..................59 C5
Limes Cres 4 CM23 .....77 A7
Limes Ct Cheshunt EN8 ..162 E7
Hoddesdon EN11 ......135 A6
Limes Rd EN8 ........162 E7
Limes The Buckland SG9 ..27 D8
Cheshunt EN8 ..........148 C7
Hertford SG14 ........113 C6
Hitchin SG5 ............34 D6
Luton LU1 ..............63 E5
2 Northwood HA6 ....174 E5
St Albans AL1 ........127 E5

Limes The continued
Welwyn Garden City AL7 ..111 A4
Limetree Ave LU1 ......85 A7
Limetree Ct HA5 ......176 A3
Limit Home Pk HP4 ....121 D7
Linacres LU4 ............44 D4
Linbridge Way LU2 ......46 E2
Linces Way AL7 ........111 B4
Lincoln Cl
Bishop's Stortford CM23 ..76 D5
Welwyn Garden City AL7 ..111 D6
Lincoln Ct
Berkhamsted HP4 ....122 B4
Borehamwood WD6 ....170 D4
Lincoln Dr
Croxley Green WD3 ....166 B6
South Oxhey WD19 ....175 C7
Lincoln Hill SG9 ........29 A5
Lincoln Mews HP2 ....124 C2
Lincoln Rd Luton LU4 ....45 B1
Stevenage SG1 ..........37 B2
Lincoln Way WD3 ......166 B5
Lincoln's Cl AL4 ......128 D8
Lincot La SG4 ..........67 C2
Lindbergh AL7 ........111 C6
Linden Ave WD18 ......166 F5
Linden Cl EN7 ........148 B1
Linden Cres AL1 ......128 A3
4 Luton LU2 ............63 F8
Linden Glade HP1 ....124 C2
Linden Gn SG6 ..........23 A8
Linden Lea SG4 ........154 A6
Linden Rd Luton LU4 ....44 E4
Redbourn AL3 ..........106 A6
Linden Sq UB9 ........173 A4
Lindencroft SG6 ........12 A1
Lindens The
Bishop's Stortford CM23 ..76 F6
Hatfield AL10 ..........129 F6
Hemel Hempstead HP3 ..137 F8
Stevenage SG1 ..........50 E4
Lindley Cl AL5 ..........86 A4
Lindlings HP1 ........123 E2
Lindrick Ho 11 WD19 ...175 C7
Lindsay Ave SG4 ........35 B5
Lindsay Cl SG8 ..........2 C1
Lindsay Pl EN7 ........148 B1
Lindsay Rd LU2 ........46 D1
Lindsey Cl CM23 ......58 F1
Lindsey Rd CM23 ......58 F1
Lindum Pl AL3 ........127 A1
Linfield Ct SG14 ......112 F7
Linford Cl HA6 ........174 E3
Lingfield Rd Royston SG8 ..7 F6
Stevenage SG1 ..........37 C1
Lingfield Way WD17 ...153 F1
Lingholm Way EN5 ....171 D4
Lingmoor Dr WD25 ....154 C6
Lington Ave HP5 ......136 A1
Link Cl AL10 ..........130 B5
Link Dr AL10 ..........130 B5
Link Rd
Bishop's Stortford CM23 ..76 F8
Hemel Hempstead HP1 ..124 C6
Oaklands AL6 ..........89 D7
Watford WD24 ........167 D7
Link The SG6 ..........12 A1
Link Way CM23 ........76 E6
Link Wlk AL10 ........130 B6
Linkfield AL7 ..........110 E2
Links Ave WD3 ........127 C5
Links Bsns Ctr The CM23 77 C7
Links Dr
Borehamwood WD6 ....169 F5
Radlett WD7 ..........155 F6
Links The Cheshunt EN8 ..148 D5
Welwyn Garden City AL8 ..110 B6
Links View AL3 ........127 C5
Links Way
Croxley Green WD3 ....166 C5
Luton LU2 ..............45 D8
Linkside Rd CM23 ......77 C6
Linksway HA6 ........174 C2
Linkway HA5 ..........175 D2
Linkways E SG1 ........50 F5
Linkways W SG1 ........50 F5
Linley Ct AL3 ..........127 F6
Linley Dell LU2 ........46 D2
Linnet Cl Bushey WD23 ..168 C1
Letchworth SG6 ........22 E8
Luton LU4 ..............44 A4
Linnet Rd WD5 ........154 A8
Linning Pond AL3 ......84 B1
Linsey Cl HP3 ........139 A7
Linster Gr WD6 ........170 C4
Linten Cl SG4 ..........35 C6
Linton Ave WD6 ......169 F7
Lintott Cl SG1 ........50 D6
Linwood CM21 ........97 E2
Linwood Rd
Harpenden AL5 ........107 C7
Ware SG12 ............93 F3
Lion Ct WD6 ..........170 C8
Lion Yd SG4 ..........66 D1
Liphook Rd WD19 ....175 D6
Lippitts Hill LU2 ......45 E5
Lismirrane Ind Pk WD6 ..169 B3
Lismore
Hemel Hempstead HP3 ..125 C1
Stevenage SG1 ..........51 C1
Lister Ave SG4 ..........34 F5
Lister Cl SG3 ............36 C2
Lister Cotts WD6 ......169 A4
Lister Hospl SG1 ......36 B2
Liston Cl LU4 ..........44 B5
Little Acre AL3 ........127 C6

Little Acres SG12 ......114 D8
Little Beechill EN2 ....160 D3
Little Berkhamsted La
AL9,SG13 ............132 B3
Little Berries LU3 ......44 E7
Little Bridge Rd 17 HP4 122 D4
Little Burrow AL7 ....110 D4
Little Bushey La WD23 ..168 C5
Little Catherells HP1 ..123 F5
Little Chishill Rd SG8 ...18 C8
Little Dell AL8 ........110 D8
Little Furze Jun Mix & Inf
Sch WD19 ............175 B7
Little Gaddesden CE Prim
Sch HP4 ..............102 C8
Little Gaddesden Ho
HP4 ..................102 E6
Little Ganett AL7 ......111 C4
Little Gr WD23 ........168 B5
Little Graylings WD5 ...153 E6
Little Green Jun Sch
WD3 ..................166 B6
Little Green La WD3 ...166 B6
Little Grove Ave EN7 ..147 E4
Little Hadham Prim Sch
SG11 ..................57 C2
Little Hardings AL7 ....111 C7
Little Hayes WD4 ......139 A2
Little Heath CM22 ......98 F3
Little Heath La HP4 ...123 B4
Little Heath Prim Sch
EN6 ..................145 C1
Little Heath Spinney
AL3 ..................127 E5
Little Henleys SG12 ....95 D1
Little Hill WD3 ........164 C3
Little Hoo HP23 ........99 F4
Little How Croft WD5 ..153 C8
Little Hyde SG2 ........51 B4
Little La Harpenden AL5 107 C6
Pirton SG5 ............20 D5
Little Lake AL7 ........111 B3
Little Larkins EN5 ....171 E3
Little Ley AL7 ........110 E3
Little Martins WD23 ..168 B4
Little Mead AL10 ....130 B8
Little Mimms 2 HP2 ...124 E4
Little Mollards HP22 ...60 A3
Little Moss La HA5 ....175 E1
Little Mundells AL7 ...110 F8
Little Munden CE Prim Sch
SG12 ..................71 E8
Little Orch HP2 ........125 A5
Little Orchard Cl
Abbots Langley WD5 ...153 D7
Pinner HA5 ............175 E1
Little Oxhey La WD19 ..175 E6
Little Parndon Sch
CM20 ..................117 B1
Little Piper's Cl EN7 ...147 B2
Little Pk WD3 ..........137 A3
Little Potters WD23 ...168 B5
Little Rd HP2 ..........124 F4
Little Reddings Prim Sch
WD23 ..................168 B4
Little Ridge AL7 ......111 A6
Little Rivers AL7 ......111 A7
Little St EN9 ..........163 C3
Little Stock Rd EN7 ...147 D5
Little Stream Cl HA6 ..174 E5
Little Thistle AL7 ......111 C4
Little Tring Rd HP23 ...99 F6
Little Twye HP23 ......119 F3
Little Twye Rd HP23 ...119 F3
Little Wade AL7 ......110 F3
Little Widbury SG12 ...93 F1
Little Widbury La SG12 ..93 F1
Little Windmill Hill
WD4 ..................151 F7
Little Wood Croft LU3 ..44 E7
Little Youngs AL8 ....110 C6
Littlebrook Gdns EN8 ..148 D1
Littlebury Cl SG5 ......12 A5
Littlechurch Rd LU2 ...46 B3
Littlecote Pl HA5 ......175 E2
Littlecote Rd LU1 ......46 B2
Littlegreen La LU1 ......62 E3
Liverpool Rd Luton LU1 ..63 D7
St Albans AL1 ........127 E3
Watford WD18 ........167 B4
Livingstone Ct EN5 ...171 E7
Livingstone Link SG2 ...51 B8
Livingstone Wlk HP2 ..124 F7
Lloyd Mews EN3 ......163 A1
Lloyd Way SG4 ..........66 C1
Lloyd-Taylor Cl SG11 ..57 B2
Loates La WD17 ......167 C6
Loates Pasture CM24 ..59 D8
Local Board Rd WD17 ..167 D4
Locarno Ave LU4 ......44 C6
Lochinver House Sch
EN6 ..................145 B1
Lochnell Rd HP4 ......121 F6
Lock Ho HP3 ..........138 E7
Lock View LU1 ..........97 F2
Lockers Park La HP1 ..124 B3
Lockers Park Sch HP1 ..124 B3
Locket Rd HA3 ........176 F1
Lockley Cres AL10 ....130 B7
Lockleys Dr AL6 ........89 C5
Lockyer Cl EN3 ......163 B1
Lodge Ave WD6 ......170 B4
Lodge Cl Cheddington LU7 ..80 A7
Hertford SG14 ........113 C8
Lodge Cres EN8 ......162 D5

**Lodge Ct**
Abbots Langley WD25 . . . . .154 A7
Ickleford SG5 . . . . . . . . . .21 E3
**Lodge Dr** Hatfield AL9 . . . .130 D8
Rickmansworth WD3 . . . . .165 C5
**Lodge End**
Croxley Green WD3 . . . . . .166 D5
Radlett WD7 . . . . . . . . . .156 B5
**Lodge Farm** SG4 . . . . . . .67 E1
**Lodge Farm Prim Sch**
SG2 . . . . . . . . . . . . . . . .51 C7
**Lodge Gdns** AL5 . . . . . . .86 A2
**Lodge La** EN9 . . . . . . . . .163 D4
**Lodge The** Harefield UB9 173 C3
Watford WD24 . . . . . . . . .167 C7
**Lodge Way** SG2 . . . . . . . .51 A1
**Lodgefield** AL7 . . . . . . . . .89 E1
**Loftus Cl** LU4 . . . . . . . . . .44 B3
**Logans** EN5 . . . . . . . . . .171 D6
**Loire Mews** AL5 . . . . . . .107 C7
**Lombardy Cl** HP4 . . . . . .125 D2
**Lombardy Dr** HP4 . . . . . .122 D3
**Lombardy Way** WD6 . . . .169 E7
**Lomond Rd** HP2 . . . . . . .124 D7
**Lomond Way** SG1 . . . . . . .37 C3
**London Bible Coll** HA6 .174 D4
**London Coll of Professional
Studies** LU1 . . . . . . . . . .63 E7
**London Colney Jun Mix Inf
Sch** AL2 . . . . . . . . . . . .142 D6
**London Luton Airport**
LU2 . . . . . . . . . . . . . . . .64 D7
**London Rd**
Aston Clinton HP22 . . . . . .99 A4
Baldock SG7 . . . . . . . . . . .23 F6
Barkway SG8 . . . . . . . . . .17 D1
Barley SG8 . . . . . . . . . . . .8 F1
Berkhamsted HP4 . . . . . . .122 E3
Bishop's Stortford CM23 . . .77 A5
Buntingford SG9 . . . . . . . .40 F6
Bushey WD23 . . . . . . . . .167 F3
Harlow CM17 . . . . . . . . . .118 C2
Hemel Hempstead HP1,
HP3 . . . . . . . . . . . . . . .124 A1
Hertford SG13 . . . . . . . . .113 E5
Hertford Heath SG13 . . . .114 B3
Hitchin SG4 . . . . . . . . . . .34 F5
Knebworth SG3 . . . . . . . . .69 A3
Langley SG4 . . . . . . . . . . .49 D5
Luton LU1 . . . . . . . . . . . .84 F7
Luton,New Town LU1 . . . . .63 E4
Markyate AL3 . . . . . . . . . .83 F5
Rickmansworth WD3 . . . .173 E8
Royston SG8 . . . . . . . . . . .7 D5
Sawbridgeworth CM21 . . . .97 E2
Shenley WD7 . . . . . . . . . .157 A5
St Albans AL1 . . . . . . . . .142 C7
Stevenage SG1,SG2 . . . . . .50 D3
Stotfold SG5 . . . . . . . . . . .3 A2
Tring HP23 . . . . . . . . . . .100 C3
Ware SG12 . . . . . . . . . . .114 E7
Welwyn AL6 . . . . . . . . . . .89 C4
**London Row** SG15 . . . . . .11 A3
**Londrina Ct** 14 HP4 . . . . .122 C4
**Londrina Terr** 15 HP4 . . .122 C4
**Long Arrotts** HP1 . . . . . .124 B5
**Long Barn Cl** WD25 . . . .154 A7
**Long Buftlers** SG5 . . . . .107 F8
**Long Chaulden** HP1 . . . .123 E3
**Long Cl** LU2 . . . . . . . . . . .46 C3
**Long Croft** CM24 . . . . . . .59 D8
**Long Croft Dr** EN8 . . . . .163 A6
**Long Croft Rd** Luton LU1 . .63 A7
Maple Cross WD3 . . . . . . .172 D5
**Long Cutt** AL3 . . . . . . . . .106 A6
**Long Elmes** HA3 . . . . . . .176 C2
**Long Elms** WD5 . . . . . . .153 D6
**Long Elms Cl** WD5 . . . . .153 D6
**Long Fallow** AL2 . . . . . . .141 A4
**Long Grove Cl** EN10 . . . .134 E4
**Long Hale** LU7 . . . . . . . . .80 C3
**Long Hedge** LU7 . . . . . . .80 C4
**Long Hyde** SG2 . . . . . . . .51 B4
**Long John** HP3 . . . . . . . .124 F1
**Long La** Aston SG2 . . . . . .51 E5
Bovingdon HP3 . . . . . . . .150 F8
Chorleywood WD3 . . . . . .164 D2
Rickmansworth WD3 . . . .172 F8
Whitwell SG4 . . . . . . . . . .66 A7
**Long Leaves** SG2 . . . . . . .51 A2
**Long Ley** Cheddington LU7 .80 A7
Harlow CM20 . . . . . . . . .117 F1
Welwyn Garden City AL7 . .111 C6
**Long Marston CE Prim Sch**
HP23 . . . . . . . . . . . . . . .79 B4
**Long Marston Rd**
Cheddington HP23,LU7 . . . .79 E7
Marsworth HP23 . . . . . . . .79 F2
**Long Mdw**
Bishop's Stortford CM23 . . .76 D4
Markyate AL3 . . . . . . . . . .83 F5
Watton at S SG14 . . . . . . .70 D4
**Long Mimms** 3 HP2 . . . .124 E4
**Long Moor** EN8 . . . . . . . .148 E2
**Long Pightle Mobile Home
Pk** WD3 . . . . . . . . . . . .152 F2
**Long Ridge** SG2 . . . . . . . .51 B3
**Long Room** UB9 . . . . . . .173 A3
**Long Row** SG5 . . . . . . . . .19 D1
**Long Spring** AL3 . . . . . . .127 F7
**Long View** HP4 . . . . . . . .122 A6
**Longacre** CM17 . . . . . . . .118 B4
**Longacres** AL4 . . . . . . . .128 D3
**Longbridge Cl** HP23 . . . .100 A6
**Longcliffe Path** WD19 . . .175 A7
**Longcroft** WD19 . . . . . . .167 B2
**Longcroft Ave** AL5 . . . . . .85 F1
**Longcroft Gdns** AL8 . . . .110 D5

**Longcroft Gn** AL8 . . . . . .110 D5
**Longcroft La**
Bovingdon HP3 . . . . . . . .137 D5
Welwyn Garden City AL8 . .110 D5
**Longcroft Rd** SG1 . . . . . . .50 E7
**Longcrofts** EN9 . . . . . . . .163 E5
**Longdean Pk** HP3 . . . . . .139 A7
**Longdean Sch** HP3 . . . . .139 B8
**Longfield** HP3 . . . . . . . . .125 B1
**Longfield Ave** EN3 . . . . . .162 C4
**Longfield Cl** SG6 . . . . . . . .22 D7
**Longfield Dr** LU4 . . . . . . . .44 D1
**Longfield Gdns** HP23 . . . .99 E3
**Longfield La** EN7 . . . . . . .148 A4
**Longfield Rd**
Harpenden AL5 . . . . . . . .107 C7
Tring HP23 . . . . . . . . . . . .99 F3
**Longfields** SG2 . . . . . . . . .51 C1
**Longlands** HP2 . . . . . . . . .125 A3
**Longlands Cl** EN8 . . . . . .162 D7
**Longlands Prim Sch**
EN10 . . . . . . . . . . . . . . .148 F6
**Longlands Rd** AL7 . . . . . .110 F5
**Longlees** WD3 . . . . . . . . .172 D5
**Longman Ct** HP3 . . . . . . .138 E6
**Longmans** SG1 . . . . . . . . .55 F7
**Longmans Cl** WD18 . . . . .166 C3
**Longmead**
Buntingford SG9 . . . . . . . .40 D7
Hatfield AL10 . . . . . . . . .130 B8
Letchworth SG6 . . . . . . . . .22 E7
Woolmer Green SG3 . . . . . .69 A2
**Longmeadow Dr** SG5 . . . .21 F5
**Longmeadow Gn** SG2 . . . .51 C1
**Longmeadow Jun & Inf Schs**
SG2 . . . . . . . . . . . . . . . .51 B1
**Longmore Cl** WD3 . . . . . .172 F6
**Longmore Gdns** AL7 . . . .110 F6
**Longridge** WD7 . . . . . . . .156 B5
**Longspring** WD24 . . . . . .154 B2
**Longstanton Ct** HP2 . . . .105 B1
**Longwood Rd** SG14 . . . . .112 F8
**Longwood Sch** WD23 . . .167 F5
**Loning The** EN3 . . . . . . . .162 C1
**Lonsdale** HP2 . . . . . . . . .124 E6
**Lonsdale Cl** Luton LU3 . . .45 B5
Pinner HA5 . . . . . . . . . . .175 E2
**Lonsdale Ct** SG1 . . . . . . . .50 F7
**Lonsdale Rd** SG1 . . . . . . . .50 F7
**Lonsdale Sch** SG1 . . . . . . .50 F7
**Loom La** WD7 . . . . . . . . .156 A2
**Loom Pl** WD7 . . . . . . . . . .156 A3
**Loop Rd** EN9 . . . . . . . . . .163 B7
**Loppys Hill** CM24 . . . . . . .59 E6
**Lorane Ct** WD17 . . . . . . .167 A7
**Lord Mead La** AL6,SG4 . . .88 C7
**Lord St** Hoddesdon EN11 .134 D6
Watford WD17 . . . . . . . . .167 C6
**Lords Ave** CM23 . . . . . . . .76 B7
**Lords Cl** WD7 . . . . . . . . .156 E7
**Lords Mdw** AL3 . . . . . . . .106 A5
**Lords Pl** 12 LU2 . . . . . . . .45 D1
**Lords Wood** AL7 . . . . . . .111 C6
**Lordship Ctr** SG6 . . . . . . .23 A3
**Lordship Farm** SG6 . . . . .23 B2
**Lordship Farm Prim Sch**
SG6 . . . . . . . . . . . . . . . .23 A3
**Lordship La** SG6 . . . . . . . .23 B4
**Lordship Rd** EN7 . . . . . . .148 B1
**Loreto Coll** AL1 . . . . . . . .127 E3
**Loring Rd** HP4 . . . . . . . . .122 C3
**Lorne Rd** HA3 . . . . . . . . .176 F1
**Lorraine Pk** HA3 . . . . . . .176 E3
**Lorrimer Cl** LU2 . . . . . . . .45 E6
**Louisa Cotts** HP23 . . . . .100 A3
**Louise Wlk** HP3 . . . . . . . .137 A3
**Louisville Cl** SG12 . . . . . .115 C4
**Louvain Way** WD25 . . . . .154 B7
**Lovatts** WD3 . . . . . . . . . .166 A5
**Love La**
Abbots Langley WD5 . . . . .139 F1
Ashwell SG7 . . . . . . . . . . .4 A4
Kings Langley WD4 . . . . . .138 E3
Pinner HA5 . . . . . . . . . . .175 E1
**Lovel Cl** HP1 . . . . . . . . . .124 A3
**Lovell Cl** SG4 . . . . . . . . . .35 A6
**Lovell Rd** EN1 . . . . . . . . .162 B3
**Lovering Rd** EN7 . . . . . . .147 C6
**Lovett Rd** AL2 . . . . . . . . .142 A5
**Low Hill Rd** CM19 . . . . . .135 F6
**Low Rd** LU1 . . . . . . . . . . .131 F8
**Lowbell La** AL2 . . . . . . . .142 E4
**Lower Adeyfield Rd**
HP2 . . . . . . . . . . . . . . . .124 D4
**Lower Barn** HP3 . . . . . . .138 F8
**Lower Bourne Cl** 5
SG12 . . . . . . . . . . . . . . . .93 C3
**Lower Bourne Gdns**
SG12 . . . . . . . . . . . . . . . .93 C3
**Lower Clabdens** SG12 . . .93 F1
**Lower Cotts** SG9 . . . . . . . .30 B2
**Lower Dagnall St** AL3 . . .127 C3
**Lower Derby Rd** 4
WD17 . . . . . . . . . . . . . . .167 C5
**Lower Emms** HP2 . . . . . .125 C8
**Lower End** HP22 . . . . . . . .60 D8
**Lower Farm Cotts** SG7 . . .3 B7
**Lower Gn** AL6 . . . . . . . . . .90 C7
**Lower Gower Rd** SG8 . . . .7 D8
**Lower Harpenden Rd**
LU1,LU2 . . . . . . . . . . . . .64 C3

**Lower Hatfield Rd** SG13 .112 F1
**Lower High St** WD17 . . . .167 D4
**Lower Icknield Way**
Marsworth HP23 . . . . . . . .80 A1
Wilstone HP22,HP23 . . . . .99 C7
**Lower Innings** SG4 . . . . . .34 D8
**Lower King St** SG8 . . . . . .7 D6
**Lower Kings Rd** HP4 . . . .122 C5
**Lower Luton Rd** AL4,AL5 . .86 C3
**Lower Mardley Hill** AL6 . .89 F8
**Lower Mdw** EN8 . . . . . . .148 D4
**Lower Paddock Rd**
WD19 . . . . . . . . . . . . . . .167 E3
**Lower Park Cres** CM23 . . .76 F5
**Lower Paxton Rd** AL1 . . .127 E2
**Lower Plantation** WD3 . .165 C6
**Lower Rd**
Breachwood Green SG4 . . . .47 F1
Chorleywood WD3 . . . . . .164 D5
Great Amwell SG12 . . . . .114 F6
Hemel Hempstead HP3 . . .139 A5
Little Hallingbury CM22 . . .98 C7
**Lower Sales** HP1 . . . . . . .123 F2
**Lower Sean** SG2 . . . . . . . .51 A3
**Lower Shott** EN7 . . . . . . .147 F5
**Lower St** CM24 . . . . . . . . .59 F7
**Lower Tail** WD19 . . . . . . .175 E4
**Lower Tub** WD23 . . . . . . .168 D2
**Lower Yott** HP2 . . . . . . . .124 F2
**Lowerfield** AL7 . . . . . . . . .111 A5
**Lowes Cl** SG1 . . . . . . . . . .37 C2
**Lowestoft Rd** WD24 . . . .167 B8
**Loweswater Cl** WD25 . . .154 C6
**Lowfield** CM21 . . . . . . . . .97 E1
**Lowfield Ct** EN11 . . . . . . .135 A6
**Lowfield La** EN11 . . . . . . .135 A6
**Lowgate La**
Dane End SG12 . . . . . . . . .72 C5
Thundridge SG12 . . . . . . . .72 C5
**Lowlands** AL9 . . . . . . . . .130 C8
**Lowson Gr** WD19 . . . . . . .167 E2
**Lowswood Cl** HA6 . . . . . .174 C2
**Lowther Cl** WD6 . . . . . . . .169 F4
**Loxley Cl** SG12 . . . . . . . . .93 E1
**Loxley Rd** HP4 . . . . . . . . .121 F6
**Loxwood Cl** HP3 . . . . . . .137 F8
**Lucan Rd** EN5 . . . . . . . . .171 E6
**Lucas Ct** EN9 . . . . . . . . . .163 F6
**Lucas Gdns** LU3 . . . . . . . .45 B8
**Lucas La** Ashwell SG7 . . . .4 E4
Hitchin SG5 . . . . . . . . . . .34 D7
**Lucern Cl** EN7 . . . . . . . . .147 E4
**Lucerne Way** LU3 . . . . . . .45 C4
**Lucks Hill** HP1 . . . . . . . . .123 E3
**Ludgate** HP23 . . . . . . . . . .99 F4
**Ludlow Ave** LU1 . . . . . . . .63 E4
**Ludlow Mead** WD19 . . . .175 B6
**Ludlow Way** WD3 . . . . . .166 C5
**Ludwick Cl** AL7 . . . . . . . .110 F4
**Ludwick Gn** AL7 . . . . . . .110 F5
**Ludwick Way** AL7 . . . . . .110 F5
**Luffenham Ho** 1 WD19 .175 D7
**Lukes La** WD3 . . . . . . . . . .79 D3
**Lukes Lea** HP23 . . . . . . . .80 A1
**Lullington Cl** LU2 . . . . . . .46 C3
**Lullington Garth** WD6 . . .170 A4
**Lulworth Ave** EN7 . . . . . .147 B2
**Lumbards** AL7 . . . . . . . . . .90 A1
**Lumen Rd** SG8 . . . . . . . . .7 D7
**Lunardi Ct** SG11 . . . . . . . .55 C3
**Lundin Wlk** WD19 . . . . . .175 D6
**Lundy Ho** WD18 . . . . . . .166 F4
**Luton & Dunstable Hospl**
LU4 . . . . . . . . . . . . . . . .44 C2
**Luton & Dunstable Hospl
(Faringdon Wing)** LU4 . .44 C3
**Luton Airport Parkway Sta**
LU1 . . . . . . . . . . . . . . . .64 B5
**Luton Dr The** LU1 . . . . . . .64 B3
**Luton Ent Pk** LU3 . . . . . . .44 B8
**Luton La** Harpenden AL3 . .85 B1
Redbourn AL3 . . . . . . . . . .85 B1
**Luton Maternity Hospl**
LU1 . . . . . . . . . . . . . . . .44 C2
**Luton Mus & Art Gall**★
LU3 . . . . . . . . . . . . . . . .45 D2
**Luton Rd** Caddington LU1 . .63 A4
Cockernhoe LU2 . . . . . . . .46 E3
Dunstable LU5 . . . . . . . . .44 A1
Great Offley SG5 . . . . . . . .33 B2
Harpenden AL5 . . . . . . . . .85 D4
Kimpton SG4 . . . . . . . . . .66 B2
Luton LU4 . . . . . . . . . . . .44 A7
Markyate AL3 . . . . . . . . . .83 F7
Streatley LU3 . . . . . . . . . .31 A6
**Luton Regional Sports Ctr**
LU2 . . . . . . . . . . . . . . . .46 A5
**Luton Ret Pk** LU1 . . . . . . .64 A6
**Luton Sixth Form Coll**
LU2 . . . . . . . . . . . . . . . .45 E4
**Luton Sta** LU2 . . . . . . . . . .63 E8
**Luton Town FC** LU1 . . . . .63 C8
**Luton Univ** LU1 . . . . . . . .63 F7
**Luton Univ, Putteridge Bury**
LU2 . . . . . . . . . . . . . . . .46 D6
**Luton White Hill**
Great Offley SG5 . . . . . . . .33 B2
Lilley LU2 . . . . . . . . . . . . .46 F8
**Luxembourg Cl** LU3 . . . . .44 D8
**Luxford Pl** CM21 . . . . . . . .97 F1
**Luynes Rise** SG9 . . . . . . . .40 E6
**Lybury La** AL3 . . . . . . . . .105 F7
**Lycaste Cl** AL1 . . . . . . . . .128 A2
**Lych Gate** WD25 . . . . . . .154 D6
**Lychgate Cotts** HP3 . . . .137 B4
**Lydekker Mews** 1 AL5 . . .86 A2
**Lydia Cl** AL9 . . . . . . . . . . .144 C7
**Lydia Mews** AL9 . . . . . . . .144 C7

**Lye Hill** SG4 . . . . . . . . . . .65 D7
**Lye La** AL2 . . . . . . . . . . . .141 A2
**Lye The** HP4 . . . . . . . . . . .102 D6
**Lygean Ave** SG12 . . . . . . .93 E1
**Lygetun Dr** LU3 . . . . . . . . .44 F7
**Lygrave** SG2 . . . . . . . . . . .69 C8
**Lyle's Row** SG4 . . . . . . . . .34 F6
**Lyles La** AL8 . . . . . . . . . .110 E8
**Lymans Rd** SG15 . . . . . . . .11 A6
**Lyme Ave** HP4 . . . . . . . . .121 D7
**Lymington Ct** WD25 . . . .154 A5
**Lymington Rd** SG1 . . . . . .50 B8
**Lynbury Ct** WD18 . . . . . .167 A6
**Lynch Cl** AL4 . . . . . . . . . .128 C2
**Lynch Hill** LU6 . . . . . . . . .83 A8
**Lynch The** EN11 . . . . . . . .135 B6
**Lyndale** SG1 . . . . . . . . . . .50 E4
**Lyndhurst Ave** HA5 . . . . .86 C2
**Lyndhurst Cl** AL5 . . . . . . .86 C2
**Lyndhurst Dr** AL5 . . . . . . .86 C2
**Lyndhurst Gdns** HA5 . . .175 B2
**Lyndhurst Rd** LU1 . . . . . . .63 C7
**Lyndon Ave** HA5 . . . . . . .175 E4
**Lyndon Mead** AL4 . . . . . .108 C2
**Lyne Way** HP1 . . . . . . . . .123 F5
**Lyneham Rd** LU2 . . . . . . . .46 C1
**Lynford Cl** EN5 . . . . . . . .170 F4
**Lynmouth Rd** AL7 . . . . . .110 F6
**Lynn Cl** HA3 . . . . . . . . . . .176 D1
**Lynsey Cl** AL3 . . . . . . . . .109 A4
**Lynton Ave** Arlesey SG15 . .11 A5
St Albans AL1 . . . . . . . . .128 C2
**Lynton Crest** EN6 . . . . . . .159 A7
**Lynton Ct** CM23 . . . . . . . .76 E4
**Lynton Par** EN6 . . . . . . . .148 D1
**Lynwood Ave** LU2 . . . . . . .46 A3
**Lynwood Dr** HA6 . . . . . . .174 F2
**Lynwood Hts** WD3 . . . . . .165 C4
**Lyon Way** AL4 . . . . . . . . .129 A3
**Lyrical Way** HP1 . . . . . . . .124 B5
**Lys Hill Gdns** SG14 . . . . .113 B8
**Lysander Cl** HP3 . . . . . . . .137 A4
**Lysander Way**
Abbots Langley WD5 . . . . .153 C5
Welwyn Garden City AL7 . .111 D7
**Lysley Pl** AL9 . . . . . . . . . .145 C4
**Lytham Ave** WD19 . . . . . .175 E5
**Lytton Ave** Enfield EN3 . .162 E1
Letchworth SG6 . . . . . . . .22 F5
**Lytton Fields** SG3 . . . . . . .68 F5
**Lytton Gdns** AL8 . . . . . . .110 D6
**Lytton Rd** HA5 . . . . . . . . .175 E3
**Lytton Way** SG1 . . . . . . . .50 C6
**Lyttons Way** EN11 . . . . . .115 A1

## M

**Mabbutt Cl** AL2 . . . . . . . .140 E1
**Mabey's Wlk** CM21 . . . . . .97 B1
**Macaulay Rd** LU4 . . . . . . .44 A2
**Macdonnell Gdns** WD25 .153 E4
**Macer's La** EN10 . . . . . . .148 F7
**Macers Ct** EN10 . . . . . . . .148 F7
**Macfadyen Webb Ho**
SG6 . . . . . . . . . . . . . . . .23 A7
**Macintosh Cl** EN7 . . . . . .147 D5
**Macintyre Sch** HP22 . . . . .60 C3
**Mackenzie Sq** SG2 . . . . . .51 B3
**Mackerel Hall** SG8 . . . . . .7 B6
**Maddesfield Ct** WD7 . . . .156 E6
**Maddison Hts** WD18 . . . .166 F5
**Maddles** SG6 . . . . . . . . . .23 D4
**Maddox Rd** Harlow CM20 .117 E1
Hemel Hempstead HP2 . . .125 B3
**Made Feld** SG1 . . . . . . . . .50 F5
**Madford Ret Pk** LU4 . . . . .44 F2
**Madgeways Cl** SG12 . . . .114 F5
**Madgeways La** SG12 . . . .114 F5
**Magdalene Ct** SG7 . . . . . .12 F1
**Magellan Cl** SG2 . . . . . . . .51 D5
**Magisters Lodge** WD3 . . .166 A4
**Magna Cl** AL5 . . . . . . . . .107 D6
**Magnaville Rd**
Bishop's Stortford CM23 . . .76 E4
Bushey WD23 . . . . . . . . .168 F2
**Magnolia Ave** WD5 . . . . .154 A7
**Magnolia Cl**
Hertford SG13 . . . . . . . . .114 A6
Park Street AL2 . . . . . . . .141 D5
**Magpie Cl** EN1 . . . . . . . . .162 A1
**Magpie Cres** SG2 . . . . . . .51 D5
**Magpie Hall Rd** WD23 . . .176 E8
**Magpie Wlk** 2 AL10 . . . .130 C3
**Magpies The** LU2 . . . . . . .45 E6
**Maiden St** SG4 . . . . . . . . .24 C1
**Maidenhall Inf Sch** LU4 . .45 A2
**Maidenhall Jun Sch** LU4 .45 A2
**Maidenhall Rd** LU4 . . . . . .45 A2
**Maidenhead St** 3 SG14 .113 D6
**Maidenhead Yd** SG14 . . .113 D6
**Main Ave** HA6 . . . . . . . . .174 C7
**Main Par** WD3 . . . . . . . . .164 C5
**Main Rd** SG14 . . . . . . . . . .91 D3
**Main Rd N** HP4 . . . . . . . . .81 A6
**Main Rd S** HP4 . . . . . . . . .81 D4
**Maison Alfont** HA3 . . . . . .176 E2
**Maitland Rd** CM24 . . . . . .59 E6
**Major Haddock Cl** SG8 . . .7 C7
**Malden Fields** WD23 . . . .167 D4
**Malden Ho** 15 WD19 . . . .175 C7
**Malden Lodge** 2 WD7 . . .167 A7
**Malden Rd**
Borehamwood WD6 . . . . .170 A6
Watford WD17 . . . . . . . . .167 D4
**Maldon Ct** AL5 . . . . . . . . .86 B2
**Malham Cl** LU4 . . . . . . . . .44 F2
**Malins Cl** EN5 . . . . . . . . .171 C4

**Mall The** AL2 . . . . . . . . . .141 C4
**Mallard Gdns** LU3 . . . . . .45 A5
**Mallard Rd** Royston SG8 . . .7 C6
Stevenage SG2 . . . . . . . . .51 D2
Watford WD5 . . . . . . . . . .154 A8
**Mallard Way**
Northwood HA6 . . . . . . . .174 C3
Roydon CM19 . . . . . . . . .116 A1
Watford WD25 . . . . . . . . .154 E3
**Mallards Ct** WD19 . . . . . .175 F7
**Mallards The** HP3 . . . . . .138 F6
**Mallion Ct** EN9 . . . . . . . .163 F6
**Mallories** CM20 . . . . . . . .117 F2
**Mallow The** LU3 . . . . . . . .44 F3
**Mallow Wlk**
Goff's Oak EN7 . . . . . . . .147 D3
Royston SG8 . . . . . . . . . . .7 E5
**Malm Cl** WD3 . . . . . . . . . .173 D8
**Malmes Croft** HP3 . . . . . .125 C1
**Malmsdale** AL8 . . . . . . . . .89 D2
**Maltby Dr** EN1 . . . . . . . . .162 B1
**Malthouse Ct** 5 AL1 . . . .127 D2
**Malthouse La** LU2 . . . . . . .46 F1
**Malthouse La** SG5 . . . . . .12 A7
**Malthouse Pl** WD7 . . . . . .156 E8
**Malthouse The** 16 SG14 .113 D6
**Malting Cotts** SG9 . . . . . .40 F6
**Malting La** Aldbury HP23 .101 D5
Braughing SG11 . . . . . . . .55 E7
Dagnall HP4 . . . . . . . . . . .81 C5
Much Hadham SG10 . . . . .74 F2
**Malting Mead** AL10 . . . . .130 C6
**Maltings Cl** Baldock SG8 . .13 B1
Royston SG8 . . . . . . . . . . .7 C7
**Maltings Ct** 2 SG7 . . . . . .23 F8
**Maltings Dr** AL4 . . . . . . . .108 C8
**Maltings Ind Est The**
SG12 . . . . . . . . . . . . . . .115 D4
**Maltings La** SG8 . . . . . . . .9 E2
**Maltings Mews** SG13 . . . .113 C5
**Maltings Orch** SG5 . . . . . .20 D3
**Maltings The**
Abbots Langley WD4 . . . .153 C5
Hemel Hempstead HP2 . . .124 D4
Letchworth SG6 . . . . . . . .12 C1
Royston SG8 . . . . . . . . . . .7 C7
St Albans AL1 . . . . . . . . .127 D3
Walkern SG2 . . . . . . . . . . .52 B8
**Malus Cl** HP2 . . . . . . . . . .125 A4
**Malvern Cl** Bushey WD23 .168 C3
Hatfield AL10 . . . . . . . . .129 F6
St Albans AL4 . . . . . . . . .128 C7
**Malvern Rd** Enfield EN3 . .162 E2
Luton LU1 . . . . . . . . . . . .63 B7
**Malvern Way**
Croxley Green WD3 . . . . .166 B4
Hemel Hempstead HP2 . . .124 F6
**Malvern Way Inf Sch**
WD3 . . . . . . . . . . . . . . .166 C4
**Malzeard Ct** 17 LU3 . . . . .45 D1
**Malzeard Rd** LU3 . . . . . . .45 D1
**Manan Cl** HP3 . . . . . . . . .125 C1
**Manchester Cl** SG1 . . . . . .36 F3
**Manchester St** LU1 . . . . . .63 E7
**Mancroft Rd** LU1 . . . . . . .62 E2
**Mandela Pl** 4 WD24 . . . .167 D7
**Mandelyns** HP4 . . . . . . . .121 E7
**Mandeville** SG2 . . . . . . . .69 C8
**Mandeville Cl**
Hertford SG13 . . . . . . . . .113 C3
Hoddesdon EN10 . . . . . . .134 F3
Watford WD17 . . . . . . . . .153 F1
**Mandeville Dr** AL1 . . . . . .141 D8
**Mandeville Prim Sch**
Sawbridgeworth CM21 . . . .97 D3
St Albans AL1 . . . . . . . . .141 D8
**Mandeville Rd**
Enfield EN3 . . . . . . . . . . .162 E3
Hertford SG13 . . . . . . . . .113 C3
Potters Bar EN6 . . . . . . . .159 C7
**Mandeville Rise** AL8 . . . .110 D8
**Mangrove Dr** SG13 . . . . .113 E4
**Mangrove Gn** LU2 . . . . . . .46 E4
**Mangrove La** SG13 . . . . . .113 E2
**Mangrove Rd**
Cockernhoe LU2 . . . . . . . .46 E4
Hertford SG13 . . . . . . . . .113 E5
Luton LU2 . . . . . . . . . . . .46 C2
**Manhattan Ave** WD18 . . .166 F5
**Manland Ave** AL5 . . . . . . .86 B3
**Manland Prim Sch** AL5 . .86 B3
**Manland Way** AL5 . . . . . .86 C3
**Manley Highway** SG5 . . . .34 B7
**Manley Highway Cotts**
SG5 . . . . . . . . . . . . . . . .34 A7
**Manley Rd** HP2 . . . . . . . .124 E4
**Manly Dixon Dr** EN3 . . . .162 E2
**Mannicotts** AL8 . . . . . . . .110 B6
**Manning Cl** WD19 . . . . . .167 D3
**Manning Pl** LU2 . . . . . . . .46 E2
**Manor Ave** HP3 . . . . . . . .138 D8
**Manor Cl** Barnet EN5 . . . .171 E5
Berkhamsted HP4 . . . . . .122 C4
Hatfield AL10 . . . . . . . . .129 F8
Hertford SG14 . . . . . . . . .113 D8
Ickleford SG5 . . . . . . . . . .21 E3
Letchworth SG6 . . . . . . . .22 F3
**Manor Cotts**
Chorleywood WD3 . . . . . .164 B3
Northwood HA6 . . . . . . . .174 F2
**Manor Cres** SG4 . . . . . . . .35 B8
**Manor Ct** Caddington LU1 .62 F4
Cheshunt EN8 . . . . . . . . .162 D8
Enfield EN1 . . . . . . . . . . .162 B3
Harefield UB9 . . . . . . . . .173 C1

**Manor Ct** *continued*
Potters Bar EN6 . . . . . . . . . .158 F7
Radlett WD7 . . . . . . . . . .155 F1
Waltham Abbey EN9 . . . .163 D6
**Manor Dr** AL2 . . . . . . . . . .141 A4
**Manor Farm Bsns Pk**
SG5 . . . . . . . . . . . . . . . . . . .19 A6
**Manor Farm Cl** LU4 . . . . .44 C3
**Manor Farm La** LU7 . . . . .61 C8
**Manor Farm Rd** EN1 . . . .162 B4
**Manor Farm Stables** SG8 68 C5
**Manor Fields Prim Sch**
CM23 . . . . . . . . . . . . . . . . .76 D5
**Manor Ho The 2** HA6 . .174 B4
**Manor House Dr**
Northwood HA6 . . . . . . .174 B3
Stevenage SG2 . . . . . . . . .51 D7
**Manor House Gdns**
WD5 . . . . . . . . . . . . . . . . .153 D8
**Manor Links** CM23 . . . . . .77 C7
**Manor Lodge Sch** WD7 .143 C1
**Manor Par** AL10 . . . . . . .129 F8
**Manor Place Ind Est**
WD6 . . . . . . . . . . . . . . . . .170 C6
**Manor Pound Rd** LU7 . . .80 A7
**Manor Rd** Barnet EN5 . . .171 E5
Bishop's Stortford CM23 . .77 A7
Caddington LU1 . . . . . . . . .62 F2
Cheddington LU7 . . . . . . . .79 F7
Harlow CM17 . . . . . . . . . .118 C5
Hatfield AL10 . . . . . . . . . .129 F8
Hoddesdon EN11 . . . . . . .135 A7
Lea Valley AL4 . . . . . . . . . .86 A7
London Colney AL2 . . . . .142 C5
Luton LU1 . . . . . . . . . . . . . .63 F6
Potters Bar EN6 . . . . . . . .159 A8
St Albans AL1 . . . . . . . . . .127 E4
Stansted Mountfitchet
CM24 . . . . . . . . . . . . . . . .59 E5
Tring HP23 . . . . . . . . . . . .100 A4
Waltham Abbey EN9 . . . .163 D6
Watford WD17 . . . . . . . . .167 B8
**Manor St** HP4 . . . . . . . . .122 D4
**Manor View** SG2 . . . . . . .51 B1
**Manor Way**
Borehamwood WD6 . . . .170 C6
Cheshunt EN8 . . . . . . . . .148 E1
Croxley Green WD3 . . . . .166 B5
Letchworth SG6 . . . . . . . . .22 F3
Potters Bar EN6 . . . . . . . .145 A1
**Manorcroft Par 6** EN8 .148 D1
**Manorside** EN5 . . . . . . . .171 E5
**Manorville Rd** HP3 . . . . .138 C7
**Mansard Cl** HP23 . . . . . .100 B3
**Mansards The** AL1 . . . . .127 F4
**Manscott Ho 8** WD19 . .175 D7
**Manscroft Rd** HP1 . . . . .124 B5
**Mansdale Rd** AL3 . . . . . .105 C4
**Manse Ct** AL3 . . . . . . . . . .83 F5
**Mansells La** SG4 . . . . . . . .67 F3
**Mansfield** CM21 . . . . . . . .97 A1
**Mansfield Ct** SG14 . . . . .113 C8
**Mansfield Gdns** SG14 . . .113 C8
**Mansfield Mews 1** SG7 . .23 E8
**Mansfield Rd** Baldock SG7 .23 E8
Luton LU4 . . . . . . . . . . . . .45 B1
**Mansion Dr** HP23 . . . . . .100 B3
**Mansion The** HP4 . . . . . .122 E6
**Manston Cl** EN8 . . . . . . .148 C1
**Manston Ct** CM23 . . . . . . .59 B1
**Manston Way** AL4 . . . . . .128 D2
**Manton Dr** LU2 . . . . . . . . .45 D3
**Manton Rd** Hitchin SG4 . . .35 B6
Holdbrook EN3 . . . . . . . .163 A1
**Manx Cl** LU4 . . . . . . . . . . .45 A2
**Maple Ave**
Bishop's Stortford CM23 . .76 D8
St Albans AL3 . . . . . . . . . .127 C7
**Maple Cl**
Bishop's Stortford CM23 . .76 D8
Hatfield AL10 . . . . . . . . . .130 A4
Watford WD23 . . . . . . . . .167 E7
**Maple Cotts** AL5 . . . . . . .107 B5
**Maple Cross Jun Mix Inf Sch**
WD3 . . . . . . . . . . . . . . . .172 E5
**Maple Ct**
5 Borehamwood WD6 . .170 A5
16 Luton LU1 . . . . . . . . . .63 D6
5 Pinner HA5 . . . . . . . . .175 C1
Stansted Abbotts SG12 . .115 D3
Watford WD25 . . . . . . . . .154 D3
**Maple Flats** AL5 . . . . . . . .86 A3
**Maple Gn** HP1 . . . . . . . . .123 E5
**Maple Gr**
Bishop's Stortford CM23 . .76 D8
Watford WD17 . . . . . . . . .167 A8
Welwyn Garden City AL7 . .89 F1
**Maple Leaf Cl** WD5 . . . . .154 A7
**Maple Lodge** SG14 . . . . .113 C5
**Maple Lodge Cl** WD3 . . .172 E6
**Maple Pk** EN11 . . . . . . . .135 C6
**Maple Rd** AL5 . . . . . . . . . .85 F1
**Maple Rd E** LU4 . . . . . . . .63 B8
**Maple Rd W** LU4 . . . . . . .63 B8
**Maple River Ind Est**
CM20 . . . . . . . . . . . . . . . .118 B6
**Maple Sch** AL1 . . . . . . . .127 E4
**Maple Spring** CM23 . . . .76 D8
**Maple Way**
Kensworth Common LU6 . .82 E8
Royston SG8 . . . . . . . . . . . . .7 E8
**Maplecroft La** EN9 . . . . .135 E2
**Maplefield** AL2 . . . . . . . .141 C2
**Mapleleaf Villas** EN8 . . .148 D4
**Maples Ct 1** SG5 . . . . . . .34 E7

**Maples The**
Goff's Oak EN7 . . . . . . . .147 E3
Hitchin SG4 . . . . . . . . . . . .34 F5
**Maplethorpe Ct** SG12 . . . .93 C1
**Mapleton Cres** EN3 . . . . .162 C1
**Maplewood** SG12 . . . . . . .93 C3
**Maplewood Ct 3** HA6 . .174 F5
**Maran Ave** AL6 . . . . . . . . .89 C4
**Marbury Rd** LU3 . . . . . . . .44 F4
**Marchmont Gn** HP2 . . . .124 D5
**Marconi Way** AL4 . . . . . .128 D3
**Marcus Cl 1** SG1 . . . . . . .51 C8
**Marden Hill Ho** AL6 . . . .111 F8
**Mardle Cl** LU1 . . . . . . . . . .62 E2
**Mardlebury Rd** SG3 . . . . .69 B1
**Mardley Ave** AL6 . . . . . . .90 A8
**Mardley Dell** AL6 . . . . . . .68 F1
**Mardley Hill** AL6 . . . . . . . .69 A1
**Mardley Hts** AL6 . . . . . . . .69 A1
**Mardley Wood** AL6 . . . . . .68 F1
**Mardleybury Ct** SG3 . . . . .69 A1
**Mardon 1** HA5 . . . . . . . . .175 F3
**Mardyke Rd** CM20 . . . . . .118 A2
**Marford Rd**
Hatfield AL1,AL6 . . . . . . .109 C7
Wheathampstead AL4 . . .108 E8
**Margaret Ave** AL3 . . . . . .127 D5
**Margaret Ct**
Abbots Langley WD5 . . . .153 F7
Potters Bar EN6 . . . . . . . .159 C6
Waltham Abbey EN9 . . . .163 D6
**Margaret Cotts** WD7 . . . .156 D8
**Margaret Wix Prim Sch**
AL3 . . . . . . . . . . . . . . . . .127 C7
**Margeholes** WD19 . . . . . .175 E8
**Margery Wood** AL7 . . . . . .90 A1
**Margherita Pl** EN9 . . . . .163 F5
**Margrave Gdns 4** CM23 .76 E5
**Marguerite Way** CM23 . . .76 C6
**Marian Gdns** WD25 . . . .154 B6
**Marigold Pl** CM17 . . . . . .118 B4
**Marina Gdns** EN8 . . . . . .148 C1
**Mariner Way 2** HP2 . . . .125 A2
**Marion Cl** AL3 . . . . . . . . .167 F8
**Marion Wlk 4** HP2 . . . . .124 F8
**Mark Hall Comp Sch**
CM17 . . . . . . . . . . . . . . . .118 C3
**Mark Hall Cycle Mus &
Gdns** ★ CM20 . . . . . . . .118 B3
**Mark Hall Moors** CM20 .118 B3
**Mark Rd** HP2 . . . . . . . . . .125 B5
**Markab Rd** HA6 . . . . . . . .175 A5
**Markeston Gr** WD19 . . . .175 D6
**Market Hill**
Buntingford SG9 . . . . . . . .40 E7
6 Royston SG8 . . . . . . . . . .7 D6
Royston SG8 . . . . . . . . . . . . .7 D5
**Market Ho** CM20 . . . . . . .117 D1
**Market Oak La** HP3 . . . . .139 A7
**Market Pl** Hatfield AL10 . .130 B6
6 Hertford SG14 . . . . . . .113 D6
Hitchin SG5 . . . . . . . . . . . .34 E7
St Albans AL3 . . . . . . . . . .127 D3
Stevenage SG1 . . . . . . . . .50 D5
Watford WD17 . . . . . . . . .167 C5
**Market Sq**
6 Bishop's Stortford CM23 76 F7
6 Luton LU1 . . . . . . . . . . .63 B6
Stevenage SG1 . . . . . . . . .50 D5
Waltham Abbey EN9 . . . .163 C6
**Market St**
7 Bishop's Stortford CM23 76 F7
Harlow CM17 . . . . . . . . . .118 C4
Hertford SG14 . . . . . . . . .113 D6
Watford WD18 . . . . . . . . .167 B5
**Markfield Cl** LU3 . . . . . . . .45 C7
**Markham Rd**
Hammond Street EN7 . . . .147 C6
Luton LU3 . . . . . . . . . . . . .45 C8
**Markyate Rd** LU1 . . . . . . .63 B1
**Markyate Village Sch**
AL3 . . . . . . . . . . . . . . . . . .83 D6
**Marlborough Cl**
Bishop's Stortford CM23 . .76 F5
Oaklands AL6 . . . . . . . . . .89 F8
Weston SG4 . . . . . . . . . . .37 B8
**Marlborough Ct**
Luton LU1 . . . . . . . . . . . . .63 D7
Northwood HA6 . . . . . . . .174 F3
**Marlborough Gate** AL1 . .127 E3
**Marlborough Ho** HP4 . . .122 B3
**Marlborough Pk** AL5 . . . .107 C7
**Marlborough Rd**
Luton LU3 . . . . . . . . . . . . .45 D1
St Albans AL1 . . . . . . . . . .127 E3
Stevenage SG2 . . . . . . . . .51 C5
Watford WD18 . . . . . . . . .167 B5
**Marlborough Rise** HP2 . .124 E6
**Marlborough Sch** AL1 . . .141 C8
**Marle Gdns** EN9 . . . . . . .163 C7
**Marley Ct** EN10 . . . . . . . .148 F8
**Marley Rd** AL7 . . . . . . . . .111 A4
**Marlin Cl** HP4 . . . . . . . . . .121 F5
**Marlin Copse** HP4 . . . . . .122 A3
**Marlin Hill** HP23 . . . . . . .120 A8
**Marlin Sq** WD5 . . . . . . . .153 F8
**Marlins Cl** WD3 . . . . . . . .164 E7
**Marlins End** HP4 . . . . . . .121 F3
**Marlins Mdw** WD18 . . . .166 D3
**Marlins The** HA6 . . . . . . .174 F5
**Marlins Turn** HP1 . . . . . .124 B6
**Marlow Ave** LU1 . . . . . . . .63 A8
**Marlowe Cl** SG2 . . . . . . . .51 C8
**Marlowes** HP1 . . . . . . . . .124 D3
**Marmet Ave** SG6 . . . . . . . .22 E6
**Marnham Rise** HP1 . . . . .124 A5

**Marquis Cl**
Bishop's Stortford CM23 . .76 B7
Harpenden AL5 . . . . . . . . .86 D2
**Marquis Cl 9** LU2 . . . . . . .45 D1
**Marquis La** AL5 . . . . . . . . .86 D2
**Marrilyne Ave** EN3 . . . . .162 F1
**Marriott Rd** Barnet EN5 . .171 D6
Luton LU3 . . . . . . . . . . . . .45 B6
**Marriott Terr** WD3 . . . . . .164 F5
**Marriotts** CM17 . . . . . . . .118 C5
**Marriotts Sch** SG2 . . . . . . .51 A6
**Marriotts Way** HP3 . . . . .124 D1
**Marryat Rd** EN1 . . . . . . . .162 B4
**Marschefield** SG5 . . . . . . .11 E6
**Marsden Cl** AL8 . . . . . . . .110 B4
**Marsden Gn** AL8 . . . . . . .110 B4
**Marsden Rd** AL8 . . . . . . .110 C5
**Marsh Cl** EN6 . . . . . . . . . .162 F6
**Marsh Hill** EN9 . . . . . . . .149 A6
**Marsh Ho** LU3 . . . . . . . . . .44 F4
**Marsh La** Harlow CM17 . . .118 E5
Stanstead Abbotts SG12 . .115 C4
Ware EN11 . . . . . . . . . . . .114 E8
**Marsh Rd** LU3 . . . . . . . . . .44 F4
**Marshal's Dr** AL1 . . . . . . .128 A6
**Marshall Ave** AL3 . . . . . .127 F6
**Marshall Rd** LU2 . . . . . . . .46 C2
**Marshall's La** SG2,SG1 . .72 C2
**Marshalls Heath La** AL4,
AL5 . . . . . . . . . . . . . . . . .87 A4
**Marshalls Way** AL4 . . . . . .86 F2
**Marshals Ct** AL1 . . . . . . .128 B5
**Marshalswick La** AL1 . . .128 B6
**Marshbarns** CM23 . . . . . . .76 C8
**Marshcroft Dr** EN8 . . . . .148 F1
**Marshcroft La** HP23 . . . .100 D6
**Marshe Cl** EN6 . . . . . . . . .159 D7
**Marshgate** Harlow CM20 .117 E3
Stevenage SG1 . . . . . . . . .50 D5
**Marshgate Dr** SG13 . . . .113 E7
**Marshgate Trad Est**
SG13 . . . . . . . . . . . . . . . .113 E7
**Marshmoor Cres** AL9 . . .130 D1
**Marshmoor La** AL9 . . . . .144 D8
**Marsom Gr** LU3 . . . . . . . . .45 B8
**Marston Cl** HP3 . . . . . . . .125 A2
**Marston Ct** HP23 . . . . . . . .79 B4
**Marston Gdns** LU2 . . . . . .45 D4
**Marston Rd** EN11 . . . . . .135 B7
**Marsworth Ave** HA5 . . . .175 D2
**Marsworth CE Inf Sch**
HP23 . . . . . . . . . . . . . . . . .80 A2
**Marsworth Rd** WD18 . . .166 E2
**Marsworth Rd** LU7 . . . . . .80 C5
**Marsworth Resr Nature
Reserve** ★ HP23 . . . . . .100 A8
**Marten Gate** AL4 . . . . . . .128 A7
**Martham Ct** AL5 . . . . . . . .86 C3
**Marthorne Cres** HA3 . . . .176 D1
**Martian Ave** HP2 . . . . . . .124 F6
**Martin Cl** AL10 . . . . . . . . .130 A3
**Martin Way** SG6 . . . . . . . .22 D5
**Martindale Ct** SG7 . . . . . .23 F6
**Martindale Prim Sch**
HP1 . . . . . . . . . . . . . . . . .123 F4
**Martindale Rd** HP1 . . . . .123 F4
**Martindales The** LU2 . . . .63 F7
**Martinfield** AL7 . . . . . . . .110 F7
**Martinfield Bsns Ctr**
AL7 . . . . . . . . . . . . . . . . .110 F7
**Martingale Rd** SG8 . . . . . . .7 E6
**Martini Dr** EN3 . . . . . . . .163 A2
**Martins Cl** WD7 . . . . . . . .155 E3
**Martins Dr** Cheshunt EN8 148 E3
Hertford SG13 . . . . . . . . .114 B6
**Martins Way** SG1 . . . . . . .36 E1
**Martins Wlk** WD6 . . . . . .170 A5
**Martins Wood Prim Sch**
SG1 . . . . . . . . . . . . . . . . . .37 B1
**Martlesham** AL7 . . . . . . . .111 E6
**Martyr Cl** AL1 . . . . . . . . . .141 D7
**Marwood Cl** WD4 . . . . . . .138 F2
**Mary Brash Ct** LU2 . . . . . .46 C3
**Mary Cross** HP23 . . . . . . .100 A4
**Mary Exton Jun Mix Inf Sch**
SG4 . . . . . . . . . . . . . . . . . .35 C7
**Mary McArthur Pl** CM24 .59 E8
**Mary Park Gdns** CM23 . . .76 F4
**Mary Proud Ct** AL6 . . . . . .89 C7
**Maryland** AL10 . . . . . . . . .129 F5
**Marymead Cl** SG2 . . . . . . .69 A8
**Marymead Dr** SG2 . . . . . .69 A8
**Marymead Ind Est** SG2 . .69 B8
**Maryport Rd** LU4 . . . . . . .45 A2
**Masefield** SG4 . . . . . . . . . .35 C7
**Masefield Ave**
Borehamwood WD6 . . . .170 B4
Stanmore HA7 . . . . . . . . .176 F5
**Masefield Ct** AL5 . . . . . . . .86 B4
**Masefield Rd** AL5 . . . . . . .86 B4
**Masefield Way** SG8 . . . . . . .2 B1
**Maslen Rd** AL4 . . . . . . . . .128 C1
**Mason Cl** WD6 . . . . . . . . .170 D7
**Mason Way** EN9 . . . . . . .163 F6
**Mason's Rd 2** HP4 . . . . .122 D4
**Masons Ct** CM23 . . . . . . . .76 E7
**Masons Rd** Enfield EN1 . .162 C3
Hemel Hempstead HP2 . .125 B4
**Masterman Wharf 12**
CM23 . . . . . . . . . . . . . . . .76 F7
**Masters Cl** LU1 . . . . . . . . .63 B5
**Matching La** CM23 . . . . . .76 B8
**Mathams Dr** CM23 . . . . . .76 D5
**Mathews Cl** SG1 . . . . . . . .36 D1
**Matlock Cl** EN5 . . . . . . . .171 D4
**Matlock Cres** Luton LU4 . .44 C1
South Oxhey WD19 . . . . .175 C7
**Matthew Gate** SG4 . . . . . .35 A5

**Mattocke Rd** SG5 . . . . . . .21 C1
**Maud Jane's Cl** LU7 . . . . .80 E5
**Maude Cres** WD24 . . . . . .154 B1
**Maulden Cl** LU2 . . . . . . . . .46 C1
**Maxted Cl** HP2 . . . . . . . . .125 C5
**Maxted Cnr** HP2 . . . . . . . .125 B6
**Maxted Rd** HP2 . . . . . . . .125 C6
**Maxwell Cl** WD3 . . . . . . . .173 A8
**Maxwell Rd**
Borehamwood WD6 . . . .170 B6
Northwood HA6 . . . . . . . .174 E3
St Albans AL1 . . . . . . . . . .128 B2
Stevenage SG1 . . . . . . . . .50 B5
**Maxwell Rise** WD19 . . . .167 E2
**Maxwell's Path** SG5 . . . . .34 D8
**May Cl** AL3 . . . . . . . . . . . .127 D5
**May Cotts** WD18 . . . . . . .167 C4
**May Gdns** WD6 . . . . . . . .169 D3
**May St** Great Chishill SG8 . . .9 E2
Luton LU1 . . . . . . . . . . . . .63 E5
**Mayall Cl** EN3 . . . . . . . . .163 A1
**Maybury Ave** EN8 . . . . . .148 B3
**Maybury Cl** EN1 . . . . . . . .162 B1
**Maycock Gr** HA6 . . . . . . .174 F4
**Maycroft** Letchworth SG6 . .12 A1
Pinner HA5 . . . . . . . . . . . .175 B1
**Maycroft Rd** EN7 . . . . . . .147 E5
**Maydencroft La** SG4 . . . . .34 E3
**Maydwell Lodge** WD6 . . .169 F7
**Mayer Rd** EN9 . . . . . . . . .163 B3
**Mayes Cl** CM23 . . . . . . . . .77 D8
**Mayfair** WD3 . . . . . . . . . .166 D4
**Mayfield**
Waltham Abbey EN9 . . . .163 D5
Welwyn Garden City AL8 . .89 C2
**Mayfield Cl** Harlow CM17 .118 F4
Harpenden AL5 . . . . . . . . .85 E3
**Mayfield Inf Sch** EN8 . . .148 A4
**Mayfield Pk** CM23 . . . . . .76 D3
**Mayfield Rd** LU2 . . . . . . . .46 B4
**Mayflower Ave** HP2 . . . .124 D3
**Mayflower Cl**
Codicote SG4 . . . . . . . . . .67 F1
Hertingfordbury SG14 . . .112 E4
Lower Nazeing EN9 . . . . .149 E8
**Mayflower Gdns** CM23 . .76 B6
**Mayflower Rd** AL2 . . . . . .141 B4
**Mayhill Rd** EN5 . . . . . . . .171 E3
**Maylands Ave** HP2 . . . . . .125 B5
**Maylands Ct** HP2 . . . . . . .125 B4
**Maylands Rd** WD19 . . . . .175 C6
**Mayles Cl** SG1 . . . . . . . . . .50 B7
**Maylin Cl** SG4 . . . . . . . . . .35 C8
**Maylins Dr** CM21 . . . . . . .97 D2
**Maynard Cl**
Holdbrook EN3 . . . . . . . .163 A1
Waltham Abbey EN9 . . . .163 F5
**Maynard Dr** AL1 . . . . . . . .141 D8
**Maynard Pl** EN6 . . . . . . . .146 E2
**Maynard Rd** HP2 . . . . . . .124 D2
**Mayne Ave** Luton LU4 . . . .44 C4
St Albans AL3 . . . . . . . . . .127 A2
**Mayo Cl** EN8 . . . . . . . . . .148 C3
**Mayo Gdns** HP1 . . . . . . . .124 B2
**Maypole St** CM17 . . . . . .118 C1
**Mays La** EN5 . . . . . . . . . .171 D3
**Mayshades Cl** SG3 . . . . . .69 A2
**Maythorne Cl** WD18 . . . .166 E5
**Maytree Cres** WD24 . . . .153 F4
**Maytree La** HA7 . . . . . . . .176 F3
**Maytrees** Hitchin SG4 . . . .35 A6
Radlett WD7 . . . . . . . . . . .156 A2
**Maze Green Hts** CM23 . . .76 D7
**Maze Green Rd** CM23 . . . .76 D7
**Mazoe Cl** CM23 . . . . . . . . .76 F5
**Mazoe Rd** CM23 . . . . . . . .76 F5
**McAdam Cl** EN11 . . . . . . .135 A8
**Mcclintock Pl** EN3 . . . . . .163 B2
**McDonald Ct** AL10 . . . . . .130 A3
**McDougall Rd 13** HP4 . .122 D4
**McGredy** EN7 . . . . . . . . . .148 B3
**McKellar Cl** WD23 . . . . . .176 C8
**McKenzie Rd** EN10 . . . . .135 A3
**Mead Bsns Ctr** SG13 . . . .113 E7
**Mead Cl** Harrow HA3 . . . .176 D2
Stevenage SG1 . . . . . . . . .50 F6
**Mead Ct**
Stansted Mountfitchet
CM24 . . . . . . . . . . . . . . . .59 D7
Waltham Abbey EN9 . . . .163 B5
**Mead Ho** AL10 . . . . . . . . .130 B8
**Mead La** SG13 . . . . . . . . .113 E7
**Mead Park Ind Est**
CM20 . . . . . . . . . . . . . . . .117 F4
**Mead Pl** WD3 . . . . . . . . . .165 B1
**Mead Rd** WD7 . . . . . . . . .157 A6
**Mead The** Cheshunt EN8 .148 C2
Hitchin SG5 . . . . . . . . . . . .21 F2
Hoddesdon EN10 . . . . . . .135 B2
South Oxhey WD19 . . . . .175 C7
**Mead View** SG9 . . . . . . . . .43 E6
**Mead Way** WD23 . . . . . . .167 E5
**Meadgate Rd** EN9 . . . . . .135 C3
**Meadow Ave** WD7 . . . . . .156 C8
**Meadow Cl** Barnet EN5 . .171 F3
Bricket Wood AL2 . . . . . .141 A2
Datchworth SG3 . . . . . . . .69 D1
Enfield EN3 . . . . . . . . . . .162 E1
Hertford SG13 . . . . . . . . .113 F7
London Colney AL2 . . . . .142 D4
St Albans AL4 . . . . . . . . . .128 C6
Tring HP23 . . . . . . . . . . . .100 A4
Welham Green AL9 . . . . .144 D7
**Meadow Croft**
Caddington LU1 . . . . . . . . .62 F4
Hatfield AL10 . . . . . . . . . .129 F5
**Meadow Dell** AL10 . . . . . .129 F5

**Meadow Gn** AL8 . . . . . . .110 C6
**Meadow La** LU7 . . . . . . . . .80 E3
**Meadow Rd**
Berkhamsted HP4 . . . . . .122 B6
Borehamwood WD6 . . . .170 B7
Bushey WD23 . . . . . . . . .168 B4
Hemel Hempstead HP3 . .139 A7
Luton LU3 . . . . . . . . . . . . .45 A4
Watford WD25 . . . . . . . . .154 B5
**Meadow The**
Hertford Heath SG13 . . . .114 E2
Welwyn Garden City AL7 .111 C6
**Meadow View**
Buntingford SG9 . . . . . . . .40 D6
Whitwell SG4 . . . . . . . . . . .66 E6
**Meadow Way**
Bedmond WD5 . . . . . . . .139 F4
Caddington LU1 . . . . . . . . .62 E4
Codicote SG4 . . . . . . . . . .67 E1
Great Offley SG5 . . . . . . . .33 C3
Hitchin SG5 . . . . . . . . . . . .34 D6
Kings Langley WD4 . . . . .139 A1
Letchworth SG6 . . . . . . . . .22 F5
Potters Bar EN6 . . . . . . . .159 A5
Rickmansworth WD3 . . . .165 C2
Sawbridgeworth CM21 . . .98 A1
Stevenage SG1 . . . . . . . . .50 F5
Stotfold SG5 . . . . . . . . . . .11 F6
Therfield SG8 . . . . . . . . . .16 A6
**Meadow Way The** HA3 . .176 E2
**Meadow Wlk**
Harpenden AL5 . . . . . . . .107 C8
Standon SG11 . . . . . . . . . .55 C8
**Meadow Wood Sch**
WD23 . . . . . . . . . . . . . . .168 C4
**Meadowbank** Hitchin SG4 .22 B1
Kings Langley WD4 . . . . .139 A1
Watford WD19 . . . . . . . . .167 C2
**Meadowbanks** EN5 . . . . .171 A4
**Meadowbrook** HP23 . . . .100 B6
**Meadowcroft**
Berkhamsted HP4 . . . . . .121 D7
Bushey WD23 . . . . . . . . .168 B3
St Albans AL1 . . . . . . . . . .142 A8
Stansted Mountfitchet
CM24 . . . . . . . . . . . . . . . .59 E7
**Meadowcross** EN9 . . . . . .163 F5
**Meadowlands** CM23 . . . . .59 A2
**Meadows The**
Bishop's Stortford CM23 . .76 E5
Breachwood Green SG4 . . .47 C1
Hemel Hempstead HP1 . .123 E4
Sawbridgeworth CM21 . . .98 A2
**Meadows View Cotts**
SG12 . . . . . . . . . . . . . . . . .94 C7
**Meadowside** WD25 . . . . .154 B8
**Meadowsweet Cl** CM23 . .76 C6
**Meads La** AL4 . . . . . . . . . .87 D1
**Meads Prim Sch The**
LU3 . . . . . . . . . . . . . . . . . .45 A6
**Meads The**
Berkhamsted HP4 . . . . . .121 F6
Bricket Wood AL2 . . . . . .140 F2
Letchworth SG6 . . . . . . . . .22 E6
Luton LU3 . . . . . . . . . . . . .45 A3
Stansted Mountfitchet CM24 59 F4
Tring HP23 . . . . . . . . . . . .100 B4
**Meadview Rd** SG12 . . . . .114 D8
**Meadway** Barnet EN5 . . . .171 F5
Berkhamsted HP4 . . . . . .122 E6
Colney Heath AL4 . . . . . .143 D8
Enfield EN3 . . . . . . . . . . .162 D3
Harpenden AL5 . . . . . . . .107 E8
Hoddesdon EN11 . . . . . . .135 A4
Knebworth SG3 . . . . . . . . .68 F3
Stevenage SG1 . . . . . . . . .50 A6
Welwyn Garden City AL7 .110 F4
Stevenage SG1 . . . . . . . . .50 B7
**Meadway Cl** HA5 . . . . . . .176 B4
**Meadway The** EN6 . . . . . .146 F2
**Meautys** AL3 . . . . . . . . . . .127 A1
**Medalls Link** SG2 . . . . . . .51 A3
**Medalls Path** SG2 . . . . . . .51 A3
**Medcalf Rd** EN3 . . . . . . . .162 F2
**Medina Rd** LU4 . . . . . . . . .45 A1
**Medlows** AL5 . . . . . . . . . . .85 E2
**Medow Mead** WD7 . . . . .155 F4
**Medway Cl** WD25 . . . . . . .154 C5
**Medway Rd** HP2 . . . . . . . .124 D2
**Medwick Mews** HP2 . . . .125 B8
**Mees Cl** LU3 . . . . . . . . . . . .31 A1
**Meeting Alley** WD17 . . . .167 C5
**Meeting House La**
Baldock SG7 . . . . . . . . . . .12 E1
Buntingford SG9 . . . . . . . .40 E7
**Megg La** WD4 . . . . . . . . . .138 B1
**Melbourn Rd** SG8 . . . . . . . .7 D7
**Melbourn St** SG8 . . . . . . . .7 D6
**Melbourne Cl**
St Albans AL3 . . . . . . . . . .127 F7
Stotfold SG5 . . . . . . . . . . .11 F6
**Melbourne Ct**
Cheshunt EN8 . . . . . . . . .162 F5
Welwyn Garden City AL8 .110 B5
**Melbourne Rd** WD23 . . . .168 B3
**Melford Cl 3** LU2 . . . . . . .46 D1
**Melings Ho** HP2 . . . . . . . .125 B8
**Melne Rd** SG2 . . . . . . . . . .69 B8
**Melrose Ave**
Borehamwood WD6 . . . .170 B4
Potters Bar EN6 . . . . . . . .159 B7
**Melrose Ct** EN8 . . . . . . . .148 D2
**Melrose Pl** WD17 . . . . . . .153 F1
**Melson Sq 8** LU1 . . . . . . .63 E7
**Melson St** LU1 . . . . . . . . . .63 E7
**Melsted Rd** HP1 . . . . . . . .124 B3
**Melvern Cl** SG2 . . . . . . . . .69 B7
**Melvyn Cl** EN7 . . . . . . . . .147 B3

Memorial Rd LU3 .......44 F4
Mendip Cl AL4 .......128 C8
Mendip Rd WD23 .......168 C3
Mendip Way
Hemel Hempstead HP2 ..124 E6
Luton LU3 ...........44 C8
Mendlesham AL7 .......111 E6
Mentley La SG11 .......54 E4
Mentley La E SG11 .......55 D4
Mentley La W SG11 .......55 C4
Mentmore★ LU7 .......61 C4
Mentmore Cross Rds
LU7 ...........60 F6
Mentmore Rd
Cheddington LU7 .......79 F8
St Albans AL1 .......127 E1
Mentmore View HP3 .......99 F5
Mepham Cres HA3 .....176 C3
Mepham Gdns HA3 .....176 C3
Mercer Pl HA5 .......175 C1
Mercers HP2 .......124 E5
Mercers Ave CM23 .......76 B4
Mercers Row AL1 .......127 C1
Merchant Dr SG13 .......113 F7
Merchant Taylors' Sch
HA6 .......166 E1
Merchants Wlk SG7 .......13 B1
Mercia Rd SG7 .......24 A8
Mercury Ho WD18 .....166 E5
Mercury Wlk ▌ HP2 ..124 F6
Mereden Ct AL1 .......141 C8
Meredews SG6 .......23 B7
Meredith Cl HA5 .....175 D3
Meredith Rd SG1 .......51 A8
Merefield CM21 .......97 E1
Meriden Ho ▐ EN5 .....171 E5
Meriden Prim Sch
WD25 .......154 D3
Meriden Way WD25 .....154 E2
Meridian Sch SG8 .......7 E4
Meridian Way SG12 .....115 B5
Merle Ave UB9 .......173 C1
Merlin Way WD25 .....153 F5
Merling Croft HP4 .....121 E7
Mermaid Cl SG4 .......35 B7
Merrill Pl ▐ CM23 .......76 E5
Merrow Dr HP1 .......123 E4
Merrows Cl HA6 .......174 C4
Merry Hill Inf Sch
WD23 .......168 B2
Merry Hill Mount WD23 168 B1
Merry Hill Rd WD23 ...168 B1
Merryfield WD17 .......154 A1
Merryfields AL4 .......128 E3
Mersey Pl
Hemel Hempstead HP2 ..124 F8
▌ Luton LU1 .......63 D7
Merton Rd Enfield EN2 .161 D1
Watford WD18 .......167 B5
Meryfield Cl WD6 .....169 F7
Meryfield Prim Sch
WD6 .......169 F8
Metford Cres EN3 .....163 A1
Metro Ctr St Albans AL4 .127 F7
Watford WD18 .......166 D2
Metropolis Ctr WD6 ...170 A6
Metropolitan Mews
WD18 .......166 F5
Metropolitan Pl WD18 .166 F5
Metropolitan Station App
WD18 .......166 F5
Meux Cl EN7 .......162 A8
Mews The
Bishop's Stortford CM22 ..77 A3
▐ Harpenden AL5 .......86 B1
Letchworth SG6 .......12 C1
Sawbridgeworth CM21 ...97 E3
Stansted Mountfitchet CM24 59 F7
Meyer Gn EN1 .......162 A1
Meyrick Ave LU1 .......63 C6
Meyrick Ct LU1 .......63 D6
Mezen Cl HA6 .......174 D5
Michael Muir Ho SG5 ..21 D1
Michaels Rd CM23 .......59 A2
Micklefield Rd HP2 ...125 C3
Micklefield Way WD6 .156 E1
Micklem Dr HP1 .......123 F4
Micklem Prim Sch HP1 .124 A4
Midcot Way HP4 .......121 F6
Middle Drift SG8 .......7 C6
Middle Furlong WD23 .168 B5
Middle Hill HP1 .......123 E3
Middle La HP3 .......137 A1
Middle Ope WD24 .....154 B2
Middle Rd
Berkhamsted HP4 .......122 B4
Waltham Abbey EN9 .....163 B7
Middle Row
▌ Bishop's Stortford CM23 76 F6
▌ Stevenage SG1 .......50 C7
Middle St EN9 .......149 F8
Middle Way WD24 .....154 B2
Middle Way The HA3 ..176 F1
Middlefield
Hatfield AL10 .......130 A4
Welwyn Garden City AL7 .110 E3
Middlefield Ave EN11 .135 A8
Middlefield Cl
Hoddesdon EN11 .......135 A8
St Albans AL4 .......128 C6
Middlefield La SG16 ...10 C7
Middlefield Rd EN11 ...135 A8
Middlefields SG6 .......11 F1
Middlefields Ct SG6 ...11 F1
Middleknights Hill HP1 .124 A6
Middlesborough Cl SG1 .36 F2

Middleton Mid Sch
SG12 .......114 D7
Middleton Rd Luton LU2 ..46 D4
Rickmansworth WD3 .....165 A1
Midhurst SG6 .......22 F8
Midhurst Gdns LU3 .......45 C4
Midland Cotts SG5 .......22 A1
Midland Ho ▐ AL1 .....127 E3
Midland Rd
Hemel Hempstead HP2 ..124 D3
Luton LU2 .......63 E8
Midland Way SG16 .......10 B3
Midway AL3 .......141 B8
Mike Mably Ho AL10 ...129 F7
Milburne Ct ▌ WD17 ...167 A7
Milburn Cl LU3 .......31 B1
Milby Ct WD6 .......169 F8
Mildmay Rd SG1 .......37 B1
Mildred Ave
Borehamwood WD6 .......170 B5
Watford WD18 .......167 A5
Mile Cl EN9 .......163 C6
Mile House Cl AL1 .....142 A8
Mile House La AL1 .....142 A8
Milestone Cl SG2 .......51 D4
Milestone Rd Hitchin SG4 .21 D2
Knebworth SG3 .......69 A5
Milford Cl AL4 .......128 D7
Milford Hill AL5 .......86 D4
Milksey La SG4 .......36 C5
Mill Bridge Barnet EN5 .171 F3
Hertford SG14 .......113 C6
Mill Cl Buntingford SG9 ..40 E7
Hatfield AL8 .......110 A5
Hemel Hempstead, Nash Mills
HP3 .......139 A6
Hemel Hempstead, Piccotts End
HP1 .......124 B7
Hitchin SG4 .......35 C8
Stotfold SG5 .......12 A6
Ware SG12 .......93 D1
Wingrave HP22 .......60 A3
Mill Cnr EN5 .......171 F8
Mill Cotts LU7 .......60 D8
Mill End SG11 .......55 F7
Mill Farm Cl HA5 .....175 C1
Mill Gdns HP3 .......100 A4
Mill Green La AL9 .....110 E1
Mill Green Mus & Mill★
AL9 .......130 E8
Mill Green Rd AL7 .....110 E5
Mill Ground Cotts SG4 ..24 C1
Mill Hill Farnham CM23 ..58 E5
Royston SG8 .......7 E4
Stansted Mountfitchet
CM24 .......59 E6
Mill La Albury SG11 .......57 C6
Arlesey SG15 .......10 F4
Cheshunt EN8 .......148 E1
Flamstead AL3 .......84 A1
Harlow CM17 .......118 E4
Hatfield Heath CM22 .....98 F3
Hexton SG5 .......19 C3
Hitchin SG4 .......34 F3
Hoddesdon EN10 .......135 A2
Kings Langley WD4 .....139 A2
Meesden SG9 .......30 A5
Sawbridgeworth CM21 ...97 F3
Stotfold SG5 .......12 A6
Therfield SG8 .......15 E8
Welwyn AL6 .......89 C5
Weston SG4 .......24 C1
Wingrave HP22 .......60 C2
Mill Lane Cl EN10 .....134 F2
Mill Mead Prim Sch
SG14 .......113 C6
Mill Race SG12 .......115 D4
Mill Rd Hertford SG14 ..113 D6
Royston SG8 .......7 D7
St Ippolyts SG4 .......35 A3
Mill Side CM24 .......59 E6
Mill St Ashwell SG7 .......4 D4
Berkhamsted HP4 .......122 C4
Bishop's Stortford CM23 ..77 A5
Hemel Hempstead HP3 ..138 D8
Luton LU1 .......63 D8
Mill Stream Lodge WD3 173 A8
Mill View AL2 .......141 D4
Mill View Rd HP23 .......99 F4
Mill Way
Breachwood Green SG4 ..47 D2
Rickmansworth WD3 .....164 F1
Watford WD23 .......167 E8
Millacres ▌ SG12 .......93 E1
Milland Ct WD6 .......170 D8
Millard Way SG4 .......22 C1
Millbank HP3 .......138 D7
Millbridge Mews ▐
SG14 .......113 C6
Millbrook Ct SG12 .......93 D4
Millbrook Rd WD23 ...167 F8
Millbrook Sch EN8 .....148 E2
Millcrest Rd EN7 .....147 B3
Millcroft CM23 .......59 A1
Millennium Ct WD3 ...165 E2
Millennium Wharf WD3 .165 E1
Miller Ave EN3 .......163 A1
Miller Cl HA5 .......175 C1
Millers Cl CM23 .......76 C5
Millers Ct SG14 .......113 D5
Millers La SG12 .......115 C4
Millers Rise AL1 .......127 E2
Millers View SG10 .......74 E1
Millfield
Berkhamsted HP4 .......122 D5
Harlow CM17 .......118 C4
Thundridge SG12 .......93 E8

Millfield continued
Welwyn Garden City AL7 .111 C7
Millfield Fst Sch SG9 ...40 E7
Millfield Ho WD18 .....166 D3
Millfield La
Caddington LU1 .......62 D2
Hitchin SG4 .......34 F4
Little Hadham SG11 .......75 D8
Millfield Rd LU3 .......45 B3
Millfield Way LU1 .......62 D2
Millfield Wlk HP3 .....139 A8
Millfields
Sawbridgeworth CM21 ...97 C3
Stansted Mountfitchet
CM24 .......59 E6
Millgreen Cotts AL9 ...131 F8
Millhoo Ct EN9 .......163 F5
Millhouse La AL4 .......140 A4
Millhurst Mews CM17 ..118 E4
Milliners Ct AL1 .......127 E3
Milliners Way
Bishop's Stortford CM23 ..76 C4
Luton LU3 .......45 C1
Millmead Way SG14 ...113 B6
Millside CM23 .......77 A5
Millstream Cl
Hertford SG14 .......113 B6
Hitchin SG4 .......22 A1
Millthorne Cl WD3 ...165 F4
Millwards AL10 .......130 B2
Millwood Ct SG5 .......11 F6
Millwright Wlk HP3 ...138 F6
Milne Cl SG6 .......23 B3
Milne Field HA5 .......176 A3
Milner Cl WD25 .......154 B6
Milner Ct Bushey WD23 .168 B3
Luton LU2 .......63 E8
Milneway UB9 .......173 B2
Milton Ave EN5 .......171 F4
Milton Cl SG8 .......2 C1
Milton Ct
Hammond Street EN7 ...147 F5
▌ Harpenden AL5 .......86 B1
Hemel Hempstead HP2 ..105 B1
Waltham Abbey EN9 .....163 C5
Milton Dene HP2 .......125 B8
Milton Dr WD6 .......170 B4
Milton Rd Harpenden AL5 .86 B1
Luton LU1 .......63 C6
Ware SG12 .......93 D2
Milton St
Waltham Abbey EN9 .....163 C5
Watford WD24 .......167 B8
Milton View SG4 .......35 C7
Milverton Gn LU3 .......45 A7
Mimms Hall Rd EN6 ...158 D7
Mimms La EN6,WD7 ...157 C6
Mimram Cl SG4 .......66 E7
Mimram Pl AL6 .......89 C5
Mimram Rd
Hertford SG14 .......113 B5
Welwyn AL6 .......89 C5
Mimram Wlk AL6 .......89 C5
Minchen Rd CM20 .......118 A3
Minderhall Ct SG1 .......50 C7
Minehead Way SG1 .......50 A7
Minerva Cl ▐ SG1 .......51 C8
Minerva Dr WD24 .....153 E3
Minims The AL10 .......130 A3
Minister Cl AL2 .......141 E3
Minoan Dr HP3 .......138 E7
Minorca Way LU4 .......44 A3
Minsden Rd SG2 .......51 D3
Minster Cl AL10 .......130 A3
Minster Ho AL10 .......130 A3
Minster Rd SG8 .......7 C8
Minstrel Cl HP1 .......124 B4
Minstrel Ct HA3 .......176 E1
Miss Joans Ride HP4,LU6 81 E7
Missenden Ho WD18 ...166 E2
Mistletoe Ct LU2 .......64 C8
Mistletoe Hill LU2 .......64 C8
Mistley Rd CM20 .......118 A2
Miswell La HP23 .......99 F3
Mitchell Cl
Abbots Langley WD5 ...154 A7
Bovingdon HP3 .......136 F4
St Albans AL1 .......141 D7
Welwyn Garden City AL7 .111 C6
Mitre Bldgs CM20 .......117 C1
Mitre Ct ▐ SG14 .......113 D6
Mitre Gdns CM23 .......77 A4
Mixes Hill Ct LU2 .......46 A4
Mixes Hill Rd LU2 .......45 F4
Mixies The SG5 .......11 E6
Moakes The LU3 .......44 E7
Moat Cl WD3 .......168 A4
Moat La Luton LU3 .......45 B4
Wingrave HP22 .......60 B2
Moat The SG11 .......55 D3
Moatfield Rd WD23 ...168 B4
Moatside SG9 .......29 B7
Moatview Ct WD23 ...168 B4
Moatwood Gn AL7 .....110 C5
Mobbsbury Way SG2 ...51 C7
Mobley Gn LU2 .......46 B3
Moffats Cl AL9 .......145 A5
Moffats La AL9 .......144 F5
Moira Cl LU3 .......44 D7
Moles La SG9 .......28 A3
Molescroft AL5 .......85 D4
Molesworth EN11 .......115 A2
Molewood Rd SG14 ...113 B7
Mollison Ave EN3 .....163 A6
Molteno Rd WD17 .....167 A8
Molyneaux Ave HP3 ...136 F4
Momples Rd CM20 .....118 B1

Monarch Hall LU2 .......64 C8
Monarch Wlk WD7 .....156 F6
Monarch's Way EN8 ...162 E6
Monastery Cl AL3 .....127 C3
Money Hole La AL6 ...111 E7
Moneyhill Ct WD3 .....165 B1
Moneyhill Par WD3 ...165 C1
Moneyhill Rd WD3 .....165 C1
Monica Cl WD3 .......93 D2
Monkhams Hall EN9 ...149 C2
Monklands SG6 .......22 D6
Monks Cl
Hoddesdon EN10 .......135 A3
Letchworth SG6 .......22 C6
Redbourn AL3 .......106 B5
St Albans AL1 .......127 E4
Monks Horton Way AL1 128 A4
Monks Rise AL8 .......89 D2
Monks Row ▐ SG12 ....93 E8
Monks View SG2 .......50 F2
Monks Walk Sch AL8 ...89 C3
Monks Wlk SG9 .......40 E7
Monksmead WD6 .......170 C5
Monksmead Sch WD6 .170 C6
Monkswick Rd CM20 ...117 F1
Monkswood AL8 .......89 C2
Monkswood Ave AL1 ..163 D6
Monkswood Dr CM23 ...76 F5
Monkswood Gdns WD6 .170 D5
Monkswood Ret Pk SG1 .50 E3
Monkswood Way SG1 ...50 E3
Monmouth Rd WD17 ...167 B6
Monmouth St SG8 .......7 E7
Monro Gdns HA3 .......176 E3
Monro Ind Est EN8 ...162 E5
Mons Ave SG7 .......23 F6
Mons Cl AL5 .......107 D6
Monson Rd EN10 .......134 F3
Montacute Rd WD23 ...168 E2
Montague Ave LU4 .......44 A6
Montague Hall Pl WD23 168 A3
Montague Rd HP4 .......122 B4
Montayne Rd EN7 .....148 C2
Monterey Lodge HA6 ...174 E4
Montesole Ct ▐ HA5 ..175 C1
Montessori At Little
Cheverells (Sch) AL3 ...83 D4
Montfitchet Wlk SG2 ...51 D7
Montgomerie Cl HP4 ..122 A6
Montgomery Ave HP2 .125 A4
Montgomery Dr EN8 ...148 E3
Monton Cl LU3 .......44 F6
Montrose Ave LU3 .......45 C3
Montrose Rd HA3 .......176 F1
Monument Pl AL3 .....127 D4
Moon La EN5 .......171 F6
Moor End Rd HP1 .......124 C2
Moor Hall La CM23 .......76 B3
Moor Hall Rd CM17 ...118 E4
Moor La Moor Park WD3 .174 A8
Sarratt WD3 .......151 E3
Moor Lane Crossing
WD18 .......166 C2
Moor Mill La AL2 .......141 E2
Moor Park Rd HA6 .....174 D4
Moor Park Sta HA6 ...174 D7
Moor Pk Ind Ctr WD18 .166 C2
Moor St LU1 .......63 C8
Moor View WD18 .......167 A3
Moore Rd HP4 .......121 F6
Moorend AL7 .......111 A3
Moorfields SG9 .......41 E8
Moorhen Way WD19 ...116 A1
Moorhurst Ave EN7 ...147 B2
Moorings The
Bishop's Stortford CM23 ..77 A5
St Albans AL1 .......127 F4
Watford WD23 .......167 E5
Moorland Gdns LU2 ...63 D8
Moorland Rd
Harpenden AL5 .......86 B4
Hemel Hempstead HP1 ..124 A1
Moorlands
Park Street AL2 .......141 E3
Welwyn Garden City AL7 .111 A3
Moorlands Reach CM21 .98 A1
Moorlands Sch LU4 .......44 C3
Moormead Cl SG5 .......34 D6
Moormead Hill SG5 .....34 D6
Moors Farm Cotts HP5 .136 B4
Moors Ley SG2 .......38 B1
Moors The AL7 .......111 A4
Moors Wlk AL7 .......111 C6
Moorside
Hemel Hempstead HP3 ..138 B8
Welwyn Garden City AL7 .111 A3
Moortown Rd WD19 ...175 C6
Moorymead Cl SG14 ...70 D3
Moran Cl AL2 .......154 F4
Morecambe Cl Luton LU4 .44 B3
Stevenage SG1 .......50 F2
Morefields HP23 .......100 A6
Moremead EN9 .......163 D6
Moreton Ave AL5 .......85 F2
Moreton Cl EN7 .......148 B4
Moreton End Cl AL5 ...85 F2
Moreton End La AL5 ...85 F2
Moreton Pk Ind Est LU2 .46 A2
Moreton Pl AL5 .......85 F3
Moreton Rd N LU2 .......46 A2
Moreton Rd S LU2 .......46 A2
Morgan Cl
Northwood HA6 .......174 F4
Stevenage SG1 .......36 D1
Morgan Gdns WD25 ...155 B2
Morgan's Rd SG13 .....113 D4
Morgan's Wlk SG13 ...113 D3
Morgans SG13 .......113 D4

Morgans Jun Mix Inf Sch
SG13 .......113 D4
Morice Rd EN11 .......134 F8
Morland Way EN8 .....148 E3
Morley Gr CM20 .......117 C2
Morley Hill EN2 .......161 D1
Morley La SG11 .......73 F5
Morningside WD3 .....165 C1
Mornington AL6 .......90 A4
Mornington Rd WD7 ...156 B5
Morpeth Ave WD6 .....156 F1
Morpeth Ct ▐ HP2 .....124 E2
Morrell Cl LU3 .......45 A7
Morrell Ct AL7 .......110 F7
Morrello Gdns SG4 .....35 A5
Morris Cl
Lower Stondon SG16 ...10 C5
Luton LU3 .......44 E8
Morris Ct Holdbrook EN3 .163 A2
Waltham Abbey EN9 .....163 F5
Morris Way AL2 .......142 D5
Morrison Ct ▐ EN5 ...171 E5
Morriston Cl WD19 ...175 C5
Morse Cl UB9 .......173 C1
Mortain Dr HP4 .......121 F6
Mortimer Cl
Bushey WD23 .......168 B3
Luton LU1 .......63 A7
Mortimer Gate EN8 ...148 F4
Mortimer Hill HP23 ...100 B4
Mortimer Rd SG8 .......7 E7
Mortimer Rise HP23 ...100 B4
Morton Cl LU7 .......80 C4
Morton St SG8 .......7 D7
Morven Cl EN6 .......159 C8
Mosquito Way AL10 ...129 E2
Moss Bury Prim Sch SG1 51 A7
Moss Cl Pinner HA5 .....175 F1
Rickmansworth WD3 .....173 D8
Moss Gn AL7 .......110 E4
Moss La HA5 .......175 E1
Moss Rd WD25 .......154 B5
Moss Side AL2 .......140 F1
Moss Way SG5 .......21 C1
Mossbank Ave LU2 .......64 C8
Mossdale Ct ▌ LU4 .......44 C5
Mossendew Cl UB9 ...173 D2
Mossman Dr LU1 .......62 E4
Mostyn Rd Bushey WD23 168 C4
Luton LU3 .......44 E4
Mott St E4 .......163 D1
Motts Cl SG14 .......70 D4
Moulton Rise LU2 .......63 F8
Mount Cl HP1 .......123 F7
Mount Dr
Park Street AL2 .......141 D6
Stansted Mountfitchet
CM24 .......59 E5
Mount Garrison SG4 ...34 F7
Mount Grace Rd EN6 ..159 B8
Mount Grace Sch EN6 .159 B8
Mount Keen SG1 .......37 C3
Mount Pleasant
Harefield UB9 .......173 A2
Hertford Heath SG13 ...114 D4
Hitchin SG5 .......34 D6
St Albans AL3 .......127 B2
Mount Pleasant Cl AL9 .130 D8
Mount Pleasant Flats
SG1 .......50 E8
Mount Pleasant La
Bricket Wood AL2 .......140 E1
Hatfield AL9 .......130 C8
Mount Pleasant Lane Jun Mix
& Inf Sch AL2 .......140 E1
Mount Pleasant Rd LU3 .44 E5
Wheathampstead AL4 ...87 D1
Mount Rd Hertford SG14 .113 A5
Wheathampstead AL4 ...87 D1
Mount The Barley SG8 ...8 F1
Hammond Street EN7 ...147 D5
▌ Luton LU3 .......63 D8
Potters Bar EN6 .......145 B1
Rickmansworth WD3 .....165 C3
Mount Vernon Hospl
HA6 .......174 B4
Mount View Enfield EN2 .160 F1
London Colney AL2 .......142 F4
Rickmansworth WD3 .....165 B1
Mount Way AL7 .......110 F3
Mountbatten Cl AL1 ...142 B8
Mounteagle SG8 .......7 D5
Mountfield Rd
Hemel Hempstead HP2 ..124 E3
Luton LU2 .......45 F2
Mountfitchet Castle &
Norman Village★ CM24 .59 F6
Mountfitchet High Sch
CM24 .......59 F4
Mountfitchet Rd CM24 ..59 E5
Mountgrace Rd LU2 .....46 C6
Mountjoy SG4 .......22 C1
Mountside HA7 .......176 F2
Mountsorrel SG13 .....113 F6
Mountview HA6 .......174 F4
Mountview EN7 .......147 F5
Mountway EN6 .......145 A1
Mountway AL7 .......110 F3
Mowat Ind Est WD24 ...154 C1
Mowbray Cres SG5 .......11 F7
Mowbray Gdns SG4 .....35 A5
Mowbray Rd CM20 .....118 A3
Mowbrays The SG5 .......11 F7
Moxes Wood LU3 .......44 F2
Moxom Ave EN8 .......148 E1
Moxon St EN5 .......171 F6

Mozart Ct SG1 .........50 C5
Muddy La SG6 .........22 F3
Muirfield LU2 .........45 E6
Muirfield Cl WD19 ...175 C6
Muirfield Gn WD19 ...175 C6
Muirfield Rd WD19 ...175 B6
Muirhead Way SG3 ...68 F3
Mulberry Cl
  Cheshunt EN10 ......148 F7
  Chiswell Green AL2 ..141 B3
  Luton LU1 ...........63 B7
  Stotfold SG5 .........11 F5
  Tring HP23 .........100 A5
  Watford WD17 ......153 A5
Mulberry Ct
  Bishop's Stortford CM23 ..77 A5
  5 Hemel Hempstead HP1 124 D4
  Royston SG8 ..........7 D5
Mulberry Gdns WD7 ..156 E6
Mulberry Gn CM17 ...118 D4
Mulberry Lodge WD19 167 D3
Mulberry Mead AL10 .109 F1
Mulberry Pl AL3 .....106 B4
Mulberry Terr CM17 .118 B4
Mulberry Way SG5 ....21 D2
Mull Ho WD18 .......166 F4
Mullion Cl Harrow HA3 ..176 B2
  Luton LU2 ...........46 B5
Mullion Wlk WD19 ...175 D6
Mullway SG6 .........22 C6
Mulready Wlk HP3 ...138 E7
Mundells
  Hammond Street EN7 ..148 A4
  Welwyn Garden City AL7 ..111 A8
Mundells AL7 ........110 F8
Munden Gr WD24 ....154 D1
Munden Rd SG12 .....71 E7
Munden View WD25 ..154 D3
Mundesley Cl
  South Oxhey WD19 ...175 C6
  Stevenage SG1 .......36 B1
Mungo-Park Cl WD23 176 B1
Munro Rd WD23 .....168 C4
Muntings The SG2 ....51 A3
Munts Mdw SG4 ......24 C1
Murchison Rd EN11 ..115 B1
Muriel Ave WD18 ....167 C4
Murray Cres HA5 ....175 D2
Murray Rd
  Berkhamsted HP4 ....122 C6
  Northwood HA6 .....174 E3
Murrell La SG5 .......12 A5
Murton Ct AL1 ......127 E4
Museum Ct HP23 ....100 A3
Museum of St Albans *
  AL1 ...............127 E3
Musgrave Ct EN7 ....147 F4
Musk Hill HP1 ......123 D2
Muskalls Cl EN7 ....148 A4
Muskham Rd CM20 ..118 B3
Musleigh Manor SG12 ..93 F1
Musley Hill SG12 .....93 E2
Musley Inf Sch SG12 ..93 E2
Musley La SG12 ......93 E2
Mussons Path LU2 ...45 E1
Muswell Cl LU3 ......45 B6
Mutchetts Cl WD25 ..154 E6
Mutford Croft 2 LU2 ..46 D1
Mutton La EN6 ......158 E8
Myddelton Ave EN1 ..161 C1
Myddelton House Gdns *
  EN2 ...............162 A3
Myddleton Path EN7 .162 B8
Myddleton Rd SG12 .114 D8
Myers Cl WD7 .......156 E7
Myles Ct WD17 ......147 C2
Mylne Ct EN8 ......148 C4
Mylne Ct EN11 ......115 A1
Mymms Dr AL9 .....145 B4
Mymwood Cl AL9 ...145 C4
Myrtle Cotts
  Sarratt WD3 ........152 A3
  Tring HP23 .........100 C8
Myrtle Gn HP1 ......123 E1
Myrtle Gr EN2 ......161 D1
Myrtleside Cl HA6 ..174 D3
Myson Way CM23 ....77 B7

**N**

Nags Head Cl SG13 ..114 B7
Nails La 15 CM23 .....76 F7
Nairn AL5 ..........107 D6
Nairn Gn WD19 .....175 A7
Nan Aires HP22 ......60 A3
Nancy Downs WD19 .167 C2
Nap The WD4 .......139 A2
Napier Ct ...........142 D6
Napier Ct Cheshunt EN8 ..148 B3
  Luton LU1 ..........63 D7
Napier Dr WD25 ....167 E5
Napier Hall LU2 .....64 C8
Napier Rd LU1 ......63 D7
Nappsbury Rd LU4 ..44 D5
Napsbury Ave AL2 ..142 C5
Napsbury La AL1 ....142 A7
Nascot Pl WD17 ....167 B7
Nascot Rd WD17 ....167 B7
Nascot St WD17 ....167 B7
Nascot Wood Inf Sch
  WD17 ..............154 A1
Nascot Wood Jun Sch
  WD17 ..............154 A1
Nascot Wood Rd WD17 .153 F1

Naseby Rd LU1 .......63 B7
Nash Cl
  Borehamwood WD6 ..169 F5
  Datchworth SG3 .....69 E2
  Stevenage SG2 .......51 B6
  Welham Green AL9 ..144 D8
Nash Gn HP3 .......138 F6
Nash Mills CE Prim Sch
  HP3 ...............138 F6
Nash Mills La HP3 ..138 F5
Nash Rd SG3 .........7 D5
Nathaniel Wlk HP23 .100 A5
Nathans Cl AL6 ......89 C6
Nayland Cl LU2 ......46 A1
Nazeing New Rd EN10 135 B2
Nazeing Prim Sch EN9 135 D1
Nazeing Rd EN9 .....135 D1
Nazeingbury Cl EN9 .135 D1
Nazeingbury Par EN9 135 D1
Neagh Cl SG1 ........37 C3
Neagle Cl WD6 .....170 C8
Neal Cl HA6 ........175 A2
Neal Ct Hertford SG14 ..113 C6
  Waltham Abbey EN9 ..163 F6
Neal St WD18 ......167 C4
Necton Rd AL4 .....108 E8
Needham Rd LU4 ....44 B6
Neild Way WD3 ....164 F2
Nell Gwynn Cl WD7 .156 E7
Nelson Ave AL1 ....142 B8
Nelson Rd
  Bishop's Stortford CM23 ..77 A5
  Dagnall HP4 .........81 C5
Nelson St SG14 .....113 B7
Nene Rd LU6 .........10 B4
Neptune Ct WD6 ...170 A6
Neptune Dr HP2 ...124 E5
Neptune Gate SG2 ..51 D8
Neston Rd WD24 ...154 C2
Nether St SG12 ......95 E4
Netherby Cl HP23 ..100 C6
Nethercott Cl LU2 ..46 C1
Netherfield Ct SG12 .115 D3
Netherfield La SG12 .115 D3
Netherfield Rd AL5 .107 B4
Netherhall Rd CM19 135 F5
Netherstones SG5 ...11 F7
Netherway AL3 .....141 A8
Netley Dell SG2 .....23 B3
Nettleswell Cross CM20 ..117 D2
Nettleswell Orch CM20 ..117 D1
Nettleswell Rd CM20 ..117 F3
Nettleswell Twr CM20 ..117 D1
Nettlecroft
  Hemel Hempstead HP1 ..124 B2
  Welwyn Garden City AL7 ..111 B7
Nettleden Rd
  Little Gaddesden HP4 ..102 E4
  Nettleden HP1 ......103 C1
  Potten End HP4 .....123 B8
Nevell's Gn SG6 .....22 F6
Nevells Rd SG6 ......22 F6
Nevil Cl HA6 .......174 D5
Nevill Gr WD24 ....167 B8
Neville Cl EN6 ......158 F8
Neville Rd LU3 ......45 A5
Neville Road Pas LU3 ..45 A5
Neville's Ct SG6 .....23 B7
New Barn La CM22 ..77 D1
New Barnes Ave AL1 ..142 A8
New Barns La SG10 ..74 E4
New Bedford Rd
  Luton LU3 ..........45 D3
  Luton,High Town LU1 ..63 D8
New Briars Prim Sch
  AL10 ...............130 A5
New Cl SG3 .........68 F6
New Cotts
  Brookmans Park AL9 ..144 D3
  Cheshunt EN8 ......162 C5
  Markyate AL3 ........83 E6
  Whitwell SG4 ........66 A7
New Ct SG3 .........69 A2
New England Cl SG4 ..34 F4
New England St AL3 ..127 C3
New Farm La HA6 ..174 D2
New Farm Traveller's Site
  SG8 ................2 A8
New Ford Bsns Pk EN8 .162 F5
New Ford Rd EN8 ..162 F5
New Forge Pl AL3 ..106 B5
New Greens Ave AL3 .127 D7
New Hall Cl HP3 ...137 A4
New House Pk AL1 ..142 B7
New Inn Rd SG7 .....3 D5
New Kent Rd AL1 ...127 D3
New Mill Terr HP23 .100 B6
New Park Dr HP2 ..125 B3
New Park La SG2 ....51 D8
New Park Rd
  Harefield UB9 ......173 C2
  Newgate Street SG13 ..146 D7
New Path CM23 .....76 F6
New Pl AL6 .........89 B4
New Provident Pl 7
  HP4 ...............122 D4
New Rd
  Berkhamsted HP4 ..122 D6
  Berkhamsted, Northchurch
    HP4 .............121 F7
  Chipperfield WD4 ...137 F1
  Croxley Green WD3 .166 A4
  Elstree WD6 ........169 D3
  Great Chishill SG8 ...9 D6
  Harlow CM17 ......118 D4
  Hatfield AL8 .......110 A3
  Hertford SG14 .....113 D8

New Rd continued
  Hoddesdon EN10 ...135 A4
  Little Hadham SG11 ..75 A7
  Lower Stondon SG17 .10 A8
  Radlett WD7 .......155 E2
  Radlett, Letchmore Heath
    WD25 ............168 A5
  Sarratt WD3 .......151 F1
  Shenley WD7 ......157 A5
  South Mimms EN6 ..158 A6
  Tring HP23 ........100 B6
  Ware SG12 .........93 D1
  Watford WD17 .....167 C5
  Welwyn AL6 .........89 F3
  Woolmer Green SG3 ..69 B3
New River Ave SG12 ..115 B4
New River Cl EN11 ..135 B7
New River Ct EN7 ..162 B8
New River Trad Est
  EN8 ...............148 D5
New St Berkhamsted HP4 122 D4
  Cheddington LU7 ....79 F7
  5 Luton LU3 ........63 D6
  Sawbridgeworth CM21 ..97 E3
  Slip End LU1 ........63 C1
  Watford WD17 .....167 C5
New Station Cotts EN10 135 A3
New Town SG4 .......67 F1
New Town Rd 9 LU1 ..63 E6
New Town St LU1 ....63 E6
New Wood AL7 .....111 C7
Newark Cl SG8 .......7 C8
Newark Gn WD6 ...170 D6
Newark Rd LU4 .....45 A2
Newberries Ave WD7 ..156 B4
Newberries Prim Sch
  WD7 ...............156 C4
Newbold Rd LU3 ....45 B7
Newbolt SG8 .........7 D8
Newbolt Rd HA7 ...176 F5
Newbury Ave EN3 ..162 F2
Newbury Cl
  Bishop's Stortford CM23 ..76 E8
  Luton LU4 ..........44 E2
  Stevenage SG1 ......36 D1
Newcastle Cl SG1 ....36 F2
Newcombe Rd LU1 ..63 C7
Newcome Path WD7 .157 A5
Newcome Rd WD7 ..157 A5
Newdigate Gn UB9 .173 D2
Newdigate Rd UB9 .173 C2
Newdigate Rd E UB9 .173 D2
Newell La SG2 .......38 D7
Newell Rd HP3 .....138 E8
Newell Rise HP3 ...138 E8
Newells SG6 .........23 D4
Newells Hedge LU7 ..80 D5
Newfield La HP2 ...124 F3
Newfield Way AL4 ..128 D1
Newfields AL8 ......110 B5
Newford Cl HP2 ....125 D3
Newgate SG2 .........51 A4
Newgate Cl AL4 ....128 D6
Newgate St SG13 ...146 E7
Newgate Street Village
  SG13 .............146 E6
Newgatestreet Rd EN7 147 B4
Newground Rd HP23 .101 B3
Newhall Ct EN9 ....163 F6
Newhouse Cres WD25 ..154 B6
Newhouse Rd HP3 ..137 A4
Newland Cl Pinner HA5 ..175 F4
  St Albans AL1 ......142 A8
Newland Gdns SG13 .113 E6
Newlands Hatfield AL9 ..130 C7
  Letchworth SG6 .....23 A3
Newlands Ave WD7 ..155 F5
Newlands Cl E SG4 ..34 F4
Newlands Cl W SG4 ..34 F4
Newlands Cvn Site WD5 139 F5
Newlands La SG4 ....34 F4
Newlands Pl EN5 ...171 A4
Newlands Way
  Hemel Hempstead HP1 ..123 D4
  Luton LU1 ..........63 C3
Newlands Way EN6 .145 B1
Newlyn Wlk WD25 ..154 D6
Newlyn Cl
  Bricket Wood AL2 ..140 E1
  Stevenage SG1 ......50 A6
Newlyn Rd EN5 ....171 F5
Newman Ave SG8 ....7 E6
Newmans Ct SG14 ...70 D3
Newmans Dr AL5 ....85 F2
Newmarket Ct AL3 .127 C4
Newmarket Rd
  Royston SG8 .........7 E6
  Royston SG8 .........7 F6
Newnham Cl LU2 ....46 D1
Newnham Par 5 EN8 .148 D1
Newnham Rd SG7 ...12 E6
Newnham Way SG7 ..4 B2
Newport Cl EN3 ....162 E2
Newport Mead WD19 .175 D6
Newports CM21 .....97 C1
Newquay Gdns WD19 .175 B8
Newstead AL10 ....129 F2
Newstead Ho UB9 ..173 C1
Newteswell Dr EN9 .163 D7
Newton Cl
  Harpenden AL5 ....107 D6
  Hoddesdon EN11 ...115 B3
Newton Cres WD6 .170 C5
Newton Dr CM21 ...97 C1
Newton Rd Harrow HA3 .176 E1
  Stevenage SG2 ......51 B6
Newtondale LU4 ....44 C5

Newtons Way SG4 ...34 F6
Newtown Rd CM23 ..76 F6
Niagara Cl EN8 .....148 D2
Nicholas Breakspear RC Sch
  AL4 ...............128 E2
Nicholas Cl
  St Albans AL3 ......127 D6
  Watford WD24 .....154 B2
Nicholas La SG14 ...113 C6
Nicholas Pl SG1 .....36 D1
Nicholas Rd WD6 ..169 F4
Nicholas Way
  Hemel Hempstead HP2 ..124 F5
  Northwood HA6 ....174 C2
Nicholls Cl Luton LU2 ..46 C2
  Redbourn AL3 ......105 F5
Nicholson Court Ind Ctr
  EN11 .............135 B6
Nicola Cl HA3 ......176 D1
Nicoll Way WD6 ...170 D5
Nicolson Dr WD23 .176 C8
Nidderdale HP2 ....124 F6
Nightingale Ave SG8 ..2 A5
Nightingale Cl Luton LU2 ..46 C6
  Radlett WD7 .......155 F3
  Watford WD5 ......154 A8
Nightingale Ct
  Hertford SG14 .....113 C6
  Hitchin SG5 ........35 A8
  1 Luton LU3 ........63 C8
  Radlett WD7 .......156 A4
  Rickmansworth WD3 .165 C2
Nightingale Lane AL1,AL4 ..142 C7
Nightingale Lodge HP4 .122 B4
Nightingale Pl WD3 .165 D2
Nightingale Rd
  Bushey WD23 ......168 A4
  Hammond Street EN7 ..147 C6
  Hitchin SG5 ........34 F8
  Rickmansworth WD3 .165 C2
Nightingale Terr SG15 ..11 A3
Nightingale Way
  Baldock SG7 ........23 F6
  Royston SG8 .........7 E8
Nightingale Wlk
  Hemel Hempstead HP2 ..105 C1
  Stevenage SG2 ......51 C5
Nightingales EN9 ..163 E5
Nimbus Way SG4 ...35 C7
Nimmo Dr WD23 ..168 D2
Nimrod Cl AL4 ....128 C5
Nimrod Dr AL10 ...129 D6
Nine Ashes SG12 ...116 D7
Ninefields EN9 .....163 F6
Ninesprings Way SG4 ..35 B6
Ninfield Ct LU2 .....46 C3
Ninian Rd HP2 .....124 E8
Ninning's La LG6 ...68 D2
Ninnings Cotts AL5 .107 A8
Ninth Ave LU3 ......44 D7
Niton Cl EN5 ......171 D3
Niven Cl WD6 .....170 C8
Noake Mill La HP1 ..124 A8
Nobel Sch The SG2 ..51 C7
Nobel Villas SG4 ...163 D5
Nobles The CM23 ...76 D3
Node Way Gdns AL6 ..89 C3
Nodes Dr SG2 ......51 A1
Noke Cl AL2 .......140 F4
Noke Lane Bsns Ctr AL2 140 F4
Noke Shot AL5 ......86 C4
Noke Side AL2 .....141 A4
Noke The SG2 ......69 B8
Nokes The HP1 ....124 A5
Nokeside SG2 ......69 B8
Nook The SG12 ....115 B4
Norbury Ave WD24 ..167 C2
Norfolk Ave WD24 .154 C1
Norfolk Cl 4 EN5 ..171 E5
Norfolk Gdns WD6 .170 D5
Norfolk Rd
  Buntingford SG9 ....40 E8
  Luton LU2 .........64 A7
  Rickmansworth WD3 .165 E1
Norfolk Way CM23 ..76 F5
Norman Ave CM23 ..76 D6
Norman Cl St Albans AL1 141 E8
  Waltham Abbey EN9 ..163 D6
Norman Cres HA5 ..175 C2
Norman Ct
  Potters Bar EN6 ....145 C1
  Stansted Mountfitchet
    CM24 ............59 E7
  Stevenage SG1 ......36 F1
Norman Rd Luton LU3 ..45 B2
  Welwyn AL6 .........89 B3
Norman's La SG8 .....7 D5
Norman's Way CM24 ..59 E7
Normandy Ave EN5 ..171 F5
Normandy Ct HP1 ..124 D4
Normandy Dr HP4 ..122 B6
Normandy Rd AL3 ..127 D4
Normandy Way EN11 .135 D6
Normans Cl SG6 ....11 F1
Normans La AL6 ....68 E2
Normansfield Cl WD23 .168 B2
Norris Cl CM23 .....77 C2
Norris Gr EN10 ....134 E3
Norris La EN11 ....135 A7
Norris Rd EN11 ....135 A6
Norris Rise EN11 ...134 F7
North App
  Moor Park HA6 ....174 C8
  Watford WD25 .....154 A5
North Area Pupil Referral
  Unit SG6 ...........22 D3
North Ave Letchworth SG6 .23 B8
  Shenley WD7 ......156 E7

North Barn EN10 ..135 B1
North Cl Barnet EN5 ..171 C4
  Chiswell Green AL2 ..141 C4
  Royston SG8 .........7 C7
North Comm AL3 ..106 A4
North Common Rd AL3 .106 A4
North Cotts AL2 ....142 A6
North Ct AL3 ........83 C6
North Dr St Albans AL4 .128 E5
  Thundridge SG11 ...72 E1
North Drift Way LU1 .63 B6
North End SG8 ......15 D6
North Gate CM20 ..117 C1
North Hertfordshire Coll
  Letchworth SG6 ....22 F5
  Stevenage SG1 ......50 D4
North Hertfordshire Coll
  (Hitchin Ctr) SG4 ..35 B8
North Hill HP3 ....164 E8
North Luton Ind Est LU4 .44 B7
North Orbital Commercial Pk
  AL1 ...............142 A5
North Orbital Rd
  Bricket Wood AL2 ..140 E2
  Chiswell Green AL2 ..141 B5
  Colney Heath AL4 ..129 C2
  London Colney AL1,AL2,
    AL4 ..............142 D6
  Park Street AL2 ....141 D6
  Watford WD25 .....154 D7
North Pl Harlow CM20 ..118 B5
  Hitchin SG5 ........21 D1
  Waltham Abbey EN9 ..163 B6
North Rd Baldock SG7 ..12 C3
  Berkhamsted HP4 ..122 B4
  Cheshunt EN8 ......162 E6
  Chorleywood WD3 .164 D4
  Hertford SG14 .....113 A7
  Hertford SG14 .....113 C6
  Hoddesdon EN11 ...135 A7
  Stevenage SG1 ......36 C2
North Ride AL6 .....89 C6
North Riding AL2 ..141 A1
North Road Ave SG14 .113 A7
North Road Gdns SG14 .113 B6
North St
  4 Bishop's Stortford CM23 76 F7
  Lower Nazeing EN9 ..135 E1
  Luton, Hart Hill LU2 ..45 E1
  Luton,High Town LU2 ..63 E8
North Terr 5 CM23 ..76 F7
North View Cotts SG12 ..95 D4
North Western Ave
  Stanmore WD6 .....169 A2
  Watford,Garston WD24 ..154 C3
  Watford,Leavesden Green
    WD2 .............153 D4
Northaw CE Prim Sch
  EN6 ...............146 A1
Northaw Cl HP2 ...125 B8
Northaw Pk EN6 ...159 F7
Northaw Rd E EN6 ..146 E1
Northaw Rd W EN6 .160 C8
Northbridge Rd HP4 .122 A6
Northbrook Dr HA6 ..174 E3
Northbrook Rd EN5 .171 E3
Northchurch La HP4,
  HP5 ...............121 D2
Northchurch St Mary's CE
  Fst Sch HP4 .......121 E6
Northcliffe Dr N20 ..171 F1
Northcote 3 HA5 ..175 C1
Northcotts AL9 ....130 C6
Northcourt WD3 ...165 A1
Northdown Rd AL10 .130 A2
Northend HP3 .....125 C1
Northern Ave SG16 ..10 C3
Northern Ho SG4 ...35 B7
Northfield Braughing SG11 55 F7
  Hatfield AL10 ......130 B8
  Standon SG11 .......55 E2
Northfield Gdns WD24 .154 C2
Northfield Rd
  Aldbury HP23 ......100 F7
  Borehamwood WD6 ..170 B8
  Cheshunt EN8 ......162 E7
  Guilden Morden SG7 ..1 C2
  Harpenden AL5 .....86 C4
  Sawbridgeworth CM21 ..97 E4
Northfields SG15 ...11 F1
Northfields Inf Sch SG6 ..11 F1
Northgate HA6 .....174 C3
Northgate End CM23 ..76 F8
Northgate Ho EN8 ..148 D2
Northgate Path WD6 ..169 F8
Northgate Prim Sch
  CM23 .............76 E8
Northlands EN6 ....159 D8
Northolt Ave CM23 ..59 B1
Northridge Way HP1 .124 A3
Northside AL4 .....108 B1
Northumberland Ave
  EN1 ...............162 B1
Northview Rd LU2 ...45 F2
Northway
  Rickmansworth WD3 .165 A1
  1 Welwyn Garden City AL7 89 F1
Northwell Dr LU3 ..44 F7
Northwick Rd WD19 .175 C6
Northwood AL7 ....111 D6
Northwood & Pinner District
  Hospl HA6 .........175 A2
Northwood Cl EN7 ..147 F4
Northwood Coll HA6 .174 D3
Northwood Hills Cir
  HA6 ...............175 A2

Northwood Hills Sta
HA6 . . . . . . . . . . . . . .175 A1
Northwood Prep Sch
WD3 . . . . . . . . . . . . . .174 C8
Northwood Sch HA6 . .173 E3
Northwood Sta HA6 . .175 B2
Northwood Sta HA6 . .174 E3
Northwood Way
Harefield UB9 . . . . . . .173 C8
Northwood HA6 . . . . . .175 A3
Norton Bury La SG6 . . . .12 C2
Norton Cl WD6 . . . . . .170 A8
Norton Cres SG7 . . . . . .23 E8
Norton Gn SG1 . . . . . . . .50 B3
Norton Green Rd SG1 . .50 C4
Norton Mill La SG6 . . . .12 D3
Norton Rd
Letchworth SG5,SG6,SG7 . .12 C2
Luton LU3 . . . . . . . . . . .44 F4
Stevenage SG1 . . . . . . .50 D4
Norton Road Prim Sch
LU3 . . . . . . . . . . . . . . .44 F4
Norton Way N SG6 . . . .23 A7
Norton Way S SG6 . . . .23 A5
Nortonstreet La SG4 . . .67 B7
Norvic Rd HP23 . . . . . . .80 A1
Norwich Cl SG1 . . . . . . .37 B1
Norwich Ho 5 WD6 . . .170 A7
Norwich Way WD3 . . . .166 B5
Norwood Cl SG14 . . . . .112 F7
Norwood Rd EN8 . . . . .148 E1
Nottingham Cl WD25 . .154 A6
Nottingham Rd WD3 . . .164 C1
Novello Way WD6 . . . .170 D8
Nugent's Pk HA5 . . . . .175 F2
Nugents Ct HA5 . . . . . .175 E2
Numbers Farm WD4 . . .139 C2
Nun's Cl SG5 . . . . . . . . .34 E7
Nunfield WD4 . . . . . . . .152 B8
Nunnery Cl AL1 . . . . . . .127 E1
Nunnery La LU3 . . . . . . .45 B5
Nunnery Stables AL1 . .127 D1
Nuns La AL1 . . . . . . . . .141 E8
Nunsbury Dr EN10 . . . .148 E6
Nunsbury Drive Cotts
EN10 . . . . . . . . . . . . . .148 E6
Nup End Cl HP22 . . . . . .60 B3
Nup End La HP22 . . . . . .60 B3
Nupton Dr SG5 . . . . . . .171 C3
Nurseries Rd AL4 . . . . .108 E7
Nursery Cl
Bishop's Stortford CM23 . .76 F6
Stevenage SG2 . . . . . . . .69 A8
Nursery Cotts SG1 . . . . .50 A6
Nursery Fields CM21 . . .97 D2
Nursery Gdns
Goff's Oak EN7 . . . . . . .147 D3
Tring HP23 . . . . . . . . . .100 B4
Ware SG12 . . . . . . . . . . .93 E1
Welwyn Garden City AL7 . .89 E1
Nursery Hill AL7 . . . . . . .89 E1
Nursery Par LU3 . . . . . . .44 E5
Nursery Rd
Bishop's Stortford CM23 . .76 F6
Cheshunt EN10 . . . . . . .148 F6
Hoddesdon EN11 . . . . . .115 B1
Lower Nazeing EN9 . . . .135 D2
Luton LU3 . . . . . . . . . . . .44 F5
Nursery Row 5 EN5 . . .171 E6
Nursery Terr HP4 . . . . .123 B7
Nut Gr AL8 . . . . . . . . . . .89 D1
Nut Slip SG9 . . . . . . . . . .40 E6
Nutcroft SG3 . . . . . . . . .69 D2
Nutfield AL7 . . . . . . . . . .90 A1
Nuthampstead Rd SG8 . .17 E2
Nutleigh Gr SG5 . . . . . . .21 D1
Nuttfield Cl WD3 . . . . . .166 B3
Nutwood Gdns 5 EN7 .147 E5
Nye Way HP3 . . . . . . . .137 A3
Nymans Cl LU2 . . . . . . .46 D3

O

Oak Ave
Bricket Wood AL2 . . . . .141 A1
Enfield EN2 . . . . . . . . . .160 F1
Oak Cl
Hemel Hempstead HP3 . .138 F7
Waltham Abbey EN9 . . . .163 D5
Oak Ct HA6 . . . . . . . . . .174 D4
Oak Dr Berkhamsted HP4 .122 D3
Sawbridgeworth CM21 . .118 C8
Oak End SG9 . . . . . . . . . .40 D7
Oak Glade HA6 . . . . . . .174 B2
Oak Gn WD5 . . . . . . . . .153 E7
Oak Gr Hatfield AL10 . . .129 F5
Hertford SG13 . . . . . . . .113 C4
Oak Green Way WD5 . . .153 E7
Oak Hall CM23 . . . . . . . .76 E8
Oak La Cholesbury HP23 .120 B2
Cuffley EN6 . . . . . . . . . .146 F3
Graveley SG4 . . . . . . . . .36 C4
Oak Path SG4 . . . . . . . .168 B3
Oak Piece AL6 . . . . . . . . .89 E7
Oak Piece Ct AL6 . . . . . . .89 E7
Oak Pk SG12 . . . . . . . . . .95 B1
Oak Rd Luton LU4 . . . . . .63 C8
Woolmer Green SG3 . . . .69 B1
Oak St
Bishop's Stortford CM23 . .76 F6
Hemel Hempstead HP3 . .138 F7
Oak Tree Cl
Abbots Langley WD5 . . .153 D7
Benington SG2 . . . . . . . .52 F4
Hatfield AL10 . . . . . . . . .130 A6
Hertford Heath SG13 . . .114 C3

Oak Tree Cl continued
Letchworth SG6 . . . . . . . .22 E4
Oak Tree Ct Elstree WD6 .169 D3
Oaklands AL6 . . . . . . . . .89 E8
Oak Way AL5 . . . . . . . . .107 A5
Oakbank WD7 . . . . . . . .156 B3
Oakcroft Cl HA5 . . . . . .175 B1
Oakdale AL8 . . . . . . . . . .89 D1
Oakdale Ave HA6 . . . . .175 A1
Oakdale Cl WD19 . . . . .175 C6
Oakdale Rd WD19 . . . . .175 C6
Oakdene EN8 . . . . . . . . .148 E1
Oakdene Cl HA5 . . . . . .175 F3
Oakdene Rd
Hemel Hempstead HP3 . .138 F7
Watford WD24 . . . . . . . .154 B3
Oakdene Way AL1 . . . . .128 C3
Oaken Gr AL7 . . . . . . . .110 E3
Oakfield WD3 . . . . . . . .165 A2
Oakfield Ave SG4 . . . . . .35 B5
Oakfield Cl EN6 . . . . . . .158 F8
Oakfield Rd AL5 . . . . . .107 A5
Oakfields SG2 . . . . . . . . .51 C1
Oakfields Ave SG3 . . . . .69 A6
Oakfields Cl SG2 . . . . . . .51 C1
Oakfields Rd SG3 . . . . . .69 A6
Oakhill SG6 . . . . . . . . . . .23 D4
Oakhill Ave HA5 . . . . . .175 E1
Oakhill Cl WD3 . . . . . . .172 E6
Oakhill Ct EN5 . . . . . . . .171 D5
Oakhill Dr AL6 . . . . . . . .89 A6
Oakhill Rd WD3 . . . . . . .172 D6
Oakhurst Ave AL5 . . . . .107 A5
Oakhurst Pl WD18 . . . . .166 F5
Oakhurst Rd EN3 . . . . . .162 D3
Oakington AL7 . . . . . . . .111 D6
Oaklands HP4 . . . . . . . .122 A4
Oaklands (Herts Coll of
Agriculture & Hort)
AL4 . . . . . . . . . . . . . . .128 A4
Oaklands Ave
Brookmans Park AL9 . . .144 E4
Watford WD19 . . . . . . . .167 B4
Oaklands Cl CM23 . . . . .59 B2
Oaklands Coll
St Albans AL1 . . . . . . . .127 E3
St Albans,The Camp AL4 .128 D1
Oaklands Coll (Boreham
Wood Campus) WD6 . .170 C7
Oaklands Coll (Harpenden
Campus) AL5 . . . . . . . .86 B1
Oaklands Coll (Lemsford
Lane Campus) AL8 . . . .110 B4
Oaklands Coll (Welwyn
Garden City Campus)
AL8 . . . . . . . . . . . . . . .110 D7
Oaklands Ct Oaklands AL6 89 E7
Watford WD17 . . . . . . . .167 A8
Oaklands Dr CM23 . . . . .59 B2
Oaklands Gate HA6 . . . .174 E4
Oaklands Gr EN10 . . . . .148 E2
Oaklands La Arkley EN5 .171 B5
St Albans AL4 . . . . . . . .128 F5
Oaklands Pk CM23 . . . . .59 B2
Oaklands Prim Sch AL6 .89 E7
Oaklands Rd
Hammond Street EN7 . . .147 E5
Totteridge N20 . . . . . . . .171 F2
Oaklands Rise AL6 . . . . .89 F7
Oaklands Wood AL10 . . .130 A5
Oaklawn HP23 . . . . . . . .100 A3
Oaklea AL6 . . . . . . . . . . .89 E7
Oaklea Cl AL6 . . . . . . . . .89 E8
Oaklea Wood AL6 . . . . . .89 E7
Oakleigh Ct CM23 . . . . . .76 D8
Oakleigh Dr WD3 . . . . . .166 C3
Oakleigh Rd HA5 . . . . . .175 F4
Oakley Cl LU4 . . . . . . . . .44 D4
Oakley Ct SG8 . . . . . . . . .7 D7
Oakley Rd
Harpenden AL5 . . . . . . .107 D7
Luton LU4 . . . . . . . . . . . .44 E4
Oakmeade HA5 . . . . . . .176 A4
Oakmede 6 HA5 . . . . .171 D5
Oakmere EN6 . . . . . . . . .159 C6
Oakmere Cl EN6 . . . . . .159 D8
Oakmere La EN6 . . . . . .159 C7
Oakmere Prim Sch EN6 .159 D7
Oakridge AL2 . . . . . . . . .140 F2
Oakridge Ave WD7 . . . .155 F6
Oakridge La WD7 . . . . . .155 E5
Oakroyd Ave EN6 . . . . . .158 F6
Oakroyd Cl EN6 . . . . . . .158 F6
Oaks Hitchin SG4 . . . . . .34 F5
Radlett WD7 . . . . . . . . .155 F4
Oaks Cross SG2 . . . . . . .51 B1
Oaks Ret Pk CM20 . . . . .117 F3
Oaks The
Berkhamsted HP4 . . . . . .122 A4
Slip End LU1 . . . . . . . . . .63 C1
Watford WD19 . . . . . . . .167 C1
Oaktree Cl
14 Bishop's Stortford CM23 76 F7
Goff's Oak EN7 . . . . . . . .147 B3
Oaktree Cotts SG12 . . . .114 F6
Oaktree Garth AL7 . . . . .110 E5
Oakview Cl Cheshunt EN7 148 B3
Harpenden AL5 . . . . . . .106 F5
Oakway LU6 . . . . . . . . . .82 B7
Oakway Pl WD7 . . . . . . .156 A5
Oakwell Cl SG2 . . . . . . . .69 D7
Oakwell Dr EN6 . . . . . . .160 B7
Oakwood
Berkhamsted HP4 . . . . . .121 E7
Waltham Abbey EN9 . . . .163 E5
Oakwood Ave WD6 . . . .170 B5
Oakwood Cl SG2 . . . . . . .51 C2

Oakwood Dr
Harpenden AL5 . . . . . . .106 F5
Luton LU3 . . . . . . . . . . . .44 C8
St Albans AL4 . . . . . . . .128 C4
Oakwood Est CM20 . . . .118 B4
Oakwood Prim Sch AL4 128 C4
Oakwood Rd
Bricket Wood AL2 . . . . .140 F2
Pinner HA5 . . . . . . . . . .175 B1
Oban Terr LU1 . . . . . . . . .63 B8
Oberon Cl WD6 . . . . . . .170 C8
Obrey Way CM23 . . . . . .76 E3
Occupation Rd WD18 . . .167 B4
Octagan The SG12 . . . . .93 D2
Octavia Ct WD24 . . . . . .167 C7
Oddfellows 10 SG14 . . . .113 D6
Oddy Hill Tring HP23 . . . .100 C3
Wigginton HP23 . . . . . . .100 C2
Odeon Par AL4 . . . . . . .154 B3
Odyssey Rd WD6 . . . . . .170 B8
Offa Rd AL3 . . . . . . . . . .127 C3
Offas Way AL4 . . . . . . . .108 D8
Offerton Ho 18 WD19 . . .175 C7
Offley Cross SG5 . . . . . . .34 B5
Offley Endowed Prim Sch
SG5 . . . . . . . . . . . . . . . .33 C3
Offley Hill SG5 . . . . . . . .33 C3
Offley Rd SG5 . . . . . . . . .34 D6
Ogard Rd EN11 . . . . . . .135 C6
Okeford Cl HP23 . . . . . . .99 F4
Okeford Dr HP23 . . . . . . .99 F4
Okeley La HP23 . . . . . . . .99 E3
Old Bakery SG5 . . . . . . . .34 E7
Old Barn La WD3 . . . . . .165 A4
Old Barn Mews WD3 . . .165 A4
Old Bedford Rd Luton LU2 45 E4
Luton, Warden Hill LU2 . . .45 D5
Old Bell Cl CM24 . . . . . . .59 D6
Old Bourne Way SG1 . . . .37 A3
Old Brewery Cl SG5 . . . .11 F7
Old Brewery Pl SG4 . . . . .66 D1
Old Chantry La SG4 . . . . .35 F2
Old Charlton Rd SG5 . . . .34 E6
Old Chorleywood Rd
WD3 . . . . . . . . . . . . . . .165 D3
Old Church La SG12 . . . .93 E7
Old Coach Rd The SG14 .112 C4
Old Common The SG9 . . .43 B4
Old Crabtree La HP2 . . . .124 E2
Old Cross SG14 . . . . . . .113 C6
Old Dean HP3 . . . . . . . .137 A4
Old Dr The AL8 . . . . . . . .110 B5
Old Farm LU7 . . . . . . . . .80 D4
Old Fishery La
Hemel Hempstead HP1 . .123 F1
Hemel Hempstead HP1 . .137 F8
Old Fold Cl EN5 . . . . . . .171 F8
Old Fold La EN5 . . . . . . .171 F8
Old Fold View EN5 . . . . .171 C6
Old Forge Cl
Abbots Langley WD25 . . .154 A6
Welwyn Garden City AL7 . .89 F2
Old Forge Rd EN1 . . . . . .161 F1
Old Forge Row SG13 . . .114 B3
Old Forge The HP23 . . . .79 B4
Old French Horn La
AL10 . . . . . . . . . . . . . . .130 B6
Old Gannon Cl WD3 . . . .174 C5
Old Garden Ct AL3 . . . . .127 C3
Old Gorhanbury Ho★
AL3 . . . . . . . . . . . . . . .126 C4
Old Granary The SG7 . . . .4 D4
Old Grove Ct EN7 . . . . . .147 D5
Old Hale Way SG5 . . . . . .21 E2
Old Hall Cl HA5 . . . . . . .175 E2
Old Hall Dr HA5 . . . . . . .175 E2
Old Harpenden Rd AL3 .127 E6
Old Hat Factory The 1
LU2 . . . . . . . . . . . . . . . .45 D1
Old Herns La AL7 . . . . . .111 C8
Old Hertford Rd AL9 . . .130 C7
Old Highway EN11 . . . . .135 C8
Old House Ct HP2 . . . . . .124 F3
Old House La
Lower Nazeing EN9 . . . . .149 F8
Sarratt WD4 . . . . . . . . . .152 F4
Old House Rd HP2 . . . . . .124 F3
Old Knebworth La SG3,
SG2 . . . . . . . . . . . . . . . .68 D8
Old La SG3 . . . . . . . . . . .69 B5
Old Leys AL10 . . . . . . . .130 A4
Old London Rd
Hertford SG13 . . . . . . . .113 C6
St Albans AL1 . . . . . . . .127 E2
Old Maltings The 2
CM23 . . . . . . . . . . . . . . .77 A7
Old Maple HP2 . . . . . . . .104 F1
Old Meadow Cl HP4 . . . .122 A2
Old Mill Gdns HP4 . . . . .122 D4
Old Mill La CM22 . . . . . . .98 B6
Old Mill Rd WD4 . . . . . .153 C5
Old Nazeing Rd EN9,
EN10 . . . . . . . . . . . . . . .135 C1
Old North Rd
Kneesworth SG8 . . . . . . . .2 B4
Royston SG8 . . . . . . . . . . .7 C8
Old Oak AL1 . . . . . . . . . .141 E8
Old Oak Cl SG15 . . . . . . .11 A8
Old Oak Close Ind Est
SG15 . . . . . . . . . . . . . . .11 A8
Old Oak Gdns HP4 . . . . .121 E7
Old Oaks EN9 . . . . . . . . .163 E7
Old Orch Luton LU1 . . . . .63 D5
Park Street AL2 . . . . . . . .141 D5
Old Orchard Cl EN4 . . . .159 D1
Old Park Rd SG5 . . . . . . .34 E7
Old Parkbury La AL2 . . . .141 F1

Old Parkway Sch AL8 . . .110 C5
Old Priory Pk AL1 . . . . . .127 E2
Old Rd CM17 . . . . . . . . .118 D5
Old Rectory Cl AL5 . . . . . .86 A1
Old Rectory Dr AL10 . . . .130 B5
Old Rectory Gdns AL4 . .108 D8
Old Redding HA3 . . . . . .176 C6
Old River La CM23 . . . . . .76 F7
Old School Cl SG4 . . . . . .67 F1
Old School Cotts HP5 . . .136 D5
Old School Flats The
HP23 . . . . . . . . . . . . . . .99 D8
Old School Gn SG2 . . . . .52 E5
Old School Orch SG14 . . .70 E3
Old School The
Hertford Heath SG13 . . .114 C4
Shillington SG5 . . . . . . . .19 E8
Old School Wlk
Arlesey SG15 . . . . . . . . . .11 A4
Slip End LU1 . . . . . . . . . .63 C1
Old Shire La WD3 . . . . .164 A2
Old Solesbridge La
WD3 . . . . . . . . . . . . . . .165 A6
Old Sopwell Gdns AL1 . .127 E1
Old South Cl HA5 . . . . . .175 D2
Old Uxbridge Rd WD3 . .172 C3
Old Vicarage Gdns AL3 . .83 D6
Old Waddling La 5 AL4 . .87 D1
Old Walled Gdn The SG1 .36 C1
Old Watford Rd AL2 . . . .140 E2
Old Watling St AL1 . . . . .84 B3
Old Works The AL1 . . . . .127 E2
Old's App WD18 . . . . . . .166 C1
Old's Cl WD18 . . . . . . . .166 B1
Olde Ct HA4 . . . . . . . . . .174 E4
Olde Swann Ct SG1 . . . . .50 C8
Olden Mead SG6 . . . . . . .23 B3
Oldfield Cl EN8 . . . . . . . .148 E3
Oldfield Ct AL1 . . . . . . . .127 E3
Oldfield Dr EN8 . . . . . . .148 E3
Oldfield Farm Rd
Lower Stondon SG16 . . . .10 A3
Lower Stondon SG16 . . . .10 C4
Oldfield Rd
Hemel Hempstead HP1 . .123 E2
London Colney AL2 . . . . .142 D6
Oldfield Rise SG4 . . . . . . .66 E7
Oldhall Ct SG4 . . . . . . . . .66 E7
Oldhall St SG14 . . . . . . .113 D6
Oldhams Trad Est
WD24 . . . . . . . . . . . . . .154 C2
Oldhill Wood LU6 . . . . . .82 D6
Oldhouse Croft CM20 . . .117 E2
Oldings Cnr AL9 . . . . . . .110 B1
Oldpark Ride EN7 . . . . . .161 D7
Oldwood AL6 . . . . . . . . . .89 D7
Olive Taylor Ct HP2 . . . .124 F7
Oliver Cl
Hemel Hempstead HP3 . .138 E7
Park Street AL2 . . . . . . . .141 D4
Oliver Ct SG12 . . . . . . . . .92 E4
Oliver Rd HP3 . . . . . . . . .138 E7
Oliver Rise HP3 . . . . . . .138 E7
Oliver's La SG5 . . . . . . . .11 F7
Olivers Cl HP4 . . . . . . . .123 C7
Olivia Gdns UB9 . . . . . . .173 C2
Olleberrie La HP3,WD3 . .151 D7
Olwen Mews HA5 . . . . .175 D1
Olyard Ct LU1 . . . . . . . . .63 B6
Olympus Rd SG1 . . . . . . .10 B4
Omega Ct 4 SG12 . . . . . .93 E1
Omega Maltings 2 SG12 .93 E1
On The Hill WD19 . . . . .175 E8
Onslow Cl AL10 . . . . . . .130 B5
Onslow Rd LU4 . . . . . . . .44 D5
Onslow St Audrey's Sch
AL10 . . . . . . . . . . . . . . .130 B5
Ontario Cl EN10 . . . . . . .148 E6
Opening The SG4 . . . . . . .88 F8
Openshaw Way SG6 . . . .23 A6
Optima Bsns Pk EN11 . .135 C7
Opus Ct WD6 . . . . . . . . .170 A6
Oram Pl HP3 . . . . . . . . . .138 D8
Orbital Cres WD25 . . . . .153 F4
Orchard Ave
Berkhamsted HP4 . . . . . .122 A4
Harpenden AL5 . . . . . . . .85 F1
Watford WD25 . . . . . . . .154 B8
Orchard Cl
Borehamwood WD6 . . . .169 E5
Bushey WD23 . . . . . . . . .168 D1
Caddington LU1 . . . . . . . .62 E4
Chorleywood WD3 . . . . .164 D5
Cuffley EN6 . . . . . . . . . .146 E3
Hemel Hempstead HP2 . .124 F5
Kneesworth SG8 . . . . . . . .2 A5
Letchworth SG6 . . . . . . . .22 B5
Little Berkhamsted SG13 .132 C4
Radlett WD7 . . . . . . . . .155 E3
St Albans AL1 . . . . . . . .127 F2
St Ippolyts SG4 . . . . . . . .34 F2
Stanstead Abbotts SG12 .115 C4
Ware SG12 . . . . . . . . . . .93 D2
Watford WD17 . . . . . . . .166 F7
Wingrave HP22 . . . . . . . .60 B3
Orchard Cres SG1 . . . . . .50 C7
Orchard Croft CM20 . . . .118 A2
Orchard Ct HP9 . . . . . . .137 A4
Orchard Dr
Chiswell Green AL2 . . . . .141 B5
Chorleywood WD3 . . . . .164 D5
Standon SG11 . . . . . . . . .55 E2
Watford WD17 . . . . . . . .166 F7
Orchard Gdns EN9 . . . . .163 C5
Orchard Ho SG11 . . . . . .55 F7
Orchard House La AL1 . .127 D2
Orchard Lea CM21 . . . . . .97 C1
Orchard Mead AL10 . . . .129 F5

Orchard On The Green The
WD3 . . . . . . . . . . . . . . .165 A2
Orchard Pl EN8 . . . . . . .148 D1
Orchard Prim Sch The
WD24 . . . . . . . . . . . . . .153 F3
Orchard Rd Baldock SG7 . .12 E1
Barnet EN5 . . . . . . . . . .171 F5
Bishop's Stortford CM23 . .59 B1
Hitchin SG4 . . . . . . . . . .22 B1
Royston SG8 . . . . . . . . . . .7 B7
Stevenage SG1 . . . . . . . .50 C7
Tewin AL6 . . . . . . . . . . . .90 C5
Welwyn AL6 . . . . . . . . . .89 C5
Orchard Sq EN10 . . . . . .148 F7
Orchard St
Hemel Hempstead HP3 . .138 D7
St Albans AL3 . . . . . . . .127 C2
Orchard The Baldock SG7 . .23 F8
Codicote SG4 . . . . . . . . .67 F1
Hertford SG14 . . . . . . . .92 C1
Kings Langley WD4 . . . . .139 A2
Radlett WD6 . . . . . . . . .168 F7
Tonwell SG12 . . . . . . . . .92 E7
Welwyn Garden City AL8 .110 D8
Orchard View AL6 . . . . . .89 F7
Orchard Way
Bovingdon HP3 . . . . . . .137 A3
Breachwood Green SG4 . .47 E5
Goff's Oak EN7 . . . . . . .147 B3
Knebworth SG3 . . . . . . . .68 E5
Letchworth SG6 . . . . . . . .22 F8
Lower Stondon SG16 . . . .10 C4
Luton LU4 . . . . . . . . . . . .44 A3
Pitstone LU7 . . . . . . . . . .80 E5
Potters Bar EN6 . . . . . . .145 B2
Rickmansworth WD3 . . . .165 A2
Royston SG8 . . . . . . . . . . .7 C8
Orchards The
Sawbridgeworth CM21 . . .97 E3
Slip End LU1 . . . . . . . . . .63 C2
Tring HP23 . . . . . . . . . . .99 F3
Orchid Cl
Goff's Oak EN7 . . . . . . .147 C1
Hatfield AL10 . . . . . . . . .109 F1
Orchid Ho AL1 . . . . . . . .127 F3
Ordelmere SG6 . . . . . . . .11 F1
Ordnance Rd EN3 . . . . . .162 C2
Oregon Way LU3 . . . . . . .45 A8
Organ Hall Rd WD6 . . . .169 E2
Orient Cl AL1 . . . . . . . . .127 E1
Orient Ctr The WD24 . . .154 D2
Oriole Cl WD5 . . . . . . . .154 A8
Oriole Way CM23 . . . . . .76 C6
Orion Gate SG1 . . . . . . . .50 F5
Orion Way HA6 . . . . . . .175 A6
Orkney Ho WD18 . . . . . .166 F4
Orlando Cl SG4 . . . . . . . .35 A6
Ormesby Dr EN6 . . . . . .158 D2
Ormonde Rd HA6 . . . . . .174 D6
Ormsby Cl LU1 . . . . . . . .63 E5
Ormskirk Rd WD19 . . . .175 D5
Oronsay HP4 . . . . . . . . .125 B1
Orphanage Rd WD17,
WD24 . . . . . . . . . . . . . .167 C7
Orpington Cl LU4 . . . . . .44 A3
Orton Cl AL4 . . . . . . . . .128 A7
Orwell Ave SG1 . . . . . . . .36 F3
Orwell Ct 5 WD24 . . . . .167 D7
Orwell View SG7 . . . . . . .13 B1
Osborn Way AL8 . . . . . .110 D6
Osborne Ct 9 Luton LU1 . .63 F6
Potters Bar EN6 . . . . . . .145 B1
Osborne Gdns EN6 . . . . .145 B1
Osborne Rd
Cheshunt EN8 . . . . . . . .148 E4
Hoddesdon EN10 . . . . . .135 A4
Luton LU1 . . . . . . . . . . . .63 E5
Potters Bar EN6 . . . . . . .145 B1
Watford WD24 . . . . . . . .154 C1
Osborne Way HP23 . . . .100 D1
Osbourne Ave WD4 . . . .138 F3
Osbourne Gdns 5 CM23 .76 E5
Osier Ct 8 SG5 . . . . . . . .34 F8
Osiers The WD3 . . . . . . .166 C3
Osmington Pl HP23 . . . . .99 F4
Osprey Cl WD25 . . . . . . .154 E5
Osprey Gdns SG2 . . . . . .51 D2
Osprey Ho 3 SG12 . . . . .93 C3
Osprey Wlk LU4 . . . . . . . .44 A5
Ostell Cres EN3 . . . . . . .163 A1
Oster St AL3 . . . . . . . . . .127 C4
Ostler Cl CM23 . . . . . . . .76 C4
Oswald Rd AL1 . . . . . . . .127 E2
Otley Way WD19 . . . . . .175 C7
Otter Gdns AL10 . . . . . .130 B4
Otterpool La WD25 . . . . .154 E1
Otterspool Way WD25 . .154 F1
Otterton Cl AL5 . . . . . . . .85 F3
Ottoman Terr WD17 . . . .167 C6
Ottway Wlk AL6 . . . . . . . .89 C4
Otway Gdns WD23 . . . . .168 E2
Otways Cl EN6 . . . . . . . .159 B6
Oudle La SG10 . . . . . . . .74 F2
Oughton Cl SG5 . . . . . . . .34 C8
Oughton Head Way SG5 . .34 D8
Oughton Prim Sch SG5 . .21 C1
Oughtonhead La SG5 . . . .34 C8
Oughtonhead Prim Sch
SG5 . . . . . . . . . . . . . . . .34 C8
Oulton Cres EN6 . . . . . . .158 D2
Oulton Rise AL5 . . . . . . . .86 C5
Oulton Way WD19 . . . . .175 F6
Oundle Ave WD23 . . . . .168 C3
Oundle Ct SG2 . . . . . . . . .69 C8

Oundle Path SG2 ......69 C8
Oundle The SG2 ......69 C8
Our Lady RC Prim Sch
AL7 ......110 E4
Our Lady's RC Prim Sch
SG5 ......21 E2
Ousden Cl EN8 ......148 E1
Ousden Dr EN8 ......148 E1
Ouseley Cl LU4 ......44 D3
Outlook Ho EN3 ......162 F3
Oval The Cheshunt EN10 .148 E7
Lower Stondon SG16 ......10 C3
Stevenage SG1 ......37 A1
Overfield Rd LU2 ......46 C1
Overlord Cl EN10 ......134 E3
Overstone Rd
Harpenden AL5 ......86 C1
Luton LU4 ......44 D1
Overstream WD3 ......165 B5
Overtrees AL5 ......85 F3
Oving Cl LU2 ......46 D2
Owen Dr SG8 ......2 D1
Owen Jones Cl SG16 ......10 C5
Owens Way WD3 ......166 A3
Owles La SG9 ......41 A6
Ox La AL5 ......86 B3
Oxcroft CM23 ......76 F3
Oxen Ind Est LU2 ......45 F1
Oxen Rd LU2 ......45 F1
Oxendon Dr EN11 ......135 A5
Oxfield Cl HP4 ......122 A3
Oxford Ave AL1 ......128 C2
Oxford Cl Cheshunt EN8 .148 C2
Kneesworth SG8 ......2 A7
Moor Park HA6 ......174 D6
Oxford Ho [8] WD6 ......170 A4
Oxford Pl AL10 ......129 E7
Oxford Rd
Breachwood Green SG4 ......47 E1
[2] Luton LU1 ......63 E6
Oxford St WD18 ......167 B4
Oxhey Ave WD19 ......167 D2
Oxhey Dr S WD19 ......175 B7
Oxhey Inf Sch WD19 ......167 E4
Oxhey La Pinner HA5 ......176 A5
South Oxhey WD19 ......175 F7
Watford WD19 ......167 D2
Oxhey Rd WD19 ......167 D2
Oxhey Ridge Cl HA6 ......175 B5
Oxhey Wood Prim Sch
WD19 ......175 C7
Oxlease Dr AL10 ......130 B4
Oxleys Rd SG2 ......51 B3
Oxleys The CM17 ......118 E4
Oysterfields AL3 ......127 C4

**P**

Pacatian Way SG1 ......51 C8
Packhorse Cl AL4 ......128 C6
Packhorse La EN6 ......157 D8
Paddick Cl EN11 ......134 F7
Paddock Cl Hunsdon SG12 95 D1
Letchworth SG6 ......23 A5
Watford WD19 ......167 E3
Paddock Ho AL7 ......111 B6
Paddock Rd SG9 ......40 E8
Paddock The
Bishop's Stortford CM23 ..76 D3
Hatfield AL10 ......130 A6
Hitchin SG4 ......35 A5
Hoddesdon EN10 ......135 A3
Paddock Way HP3 ......123 E3
Paddock Wood AL5 ......107 C2
Paddocks Cl SG2 ......51 B4
Paddocks The
Chorleywood WD3 ......164 F5
Codicote SG4 ......68 A1
Hertford Heath SG13 ......114 B3
Kimpton AL4 ......87 B6
Stevenage SG2 ......51 B3
Welwyn Garden City AL7 .111 B7
Padgate Ho [12] WD19 ..175 D7
Padgets The EN9 ......163 E5
Page Cl SG7 ......23 F6
Page Hill SG12 ......93 C2
Page Rd SG13 ......114 A6
Pageant Rd AL1 ......127 D2
Pages Cl CM23 ......76 D5
Pages Croft HP4 ......122 A6
Paget Cotts SG12 ......71 F7
Paignton Cl LU4 ......44 D4
Paine's La HA5 ......175 E1
Paines Orch LU7 ......80 A8
Painters La EN3 ......162 E4
Palace Cl WD4 ......139 A1
Palace Gdns
Bishop's Stortford CM23 ..76 E5
Royston SG8 ......7 C6
Palfrey Cl AL3 ......127 C5
Pallas Rd HP2 ......124 F5
Pallett Ct EN11 ......135 B4
Palmer Ave WD23 ......168 B4
Palmer Cl SG14 ......113 C4
Palmer Ct SG12 ......92 E4
Palmer Gdns EN5 ......171 D4
Palmer Rd SG14 ......113 D4
Palmers Gr EN9 ......135 F1
Palmers La [8] CM23 ......76 F7
Palmers Rd WD6 ......170 B8
Palmers Way EN8 ......148 E2
Palmerston Cl AL8 ......110 C6
Palmerston Cl SG2 ......51 B7
Palmerston Dr [7] AL4 ..87 D1

Pamela Ave HP3 ......138 F8
Pamela Gdns CM23 ......76 F3
Pams La SG4 ......66 D1
Pancake La HP2 ......125 D2
Pankhurst Cres SG4 ......51 C5
Pankhurst Pl WD24 ......167 C6
Pankridge WD19 ......175 D8
Panshanger Aerodrome
AL6,AL7 ......111 D7
Panshanger Dr AL7 ......111 C6
Panshanger Prim Sch
AL7 ......111 A7
Pantiles The WD23 ......168 D1
Panxworth Rd [1] HP3 ..124 D1
Paper Mill La SG11 ......55 E1
Par Cl SG13 ......114 B7
Parade The
Hatfield AL10 ......130 C7
Letchworth SG6 ......11 F1
Luton LU3 ......44 C7
South Oxhey WD19 ......175 D7
South Oxhey WD19 ......175 E7
Watford WD17 ......167 B6
Paradise HP2 ......124 D2
Paradise Cl EN7 ......148 B3
Paradise Rd EN9 ......163 C5
Paradise Wildlife Pk★
EN10 ......133 F2
Paramount Ind Est
WD24 ......154 C1
Parish Cl WD25 ......154 C5
Parishes Mead SG2 ......51 D4
Park Ave
Bishop's Stortford CM23 ..76 F3
Luton LU3 ......44 C7
Potters Bar EN6 ......159 D6
Radlett WD7 ......156 B6
Rickmansworth WD3 ......165 A5
St Albans AL1 ......128 A4
Watford WD23 ......167 D6
Watford,West Watford
WD18 ......167 A5
Park Ave N AL5 ......85 F1
Park Ave S AL5 ......85 F1
Park Avenue Maisonettes
WD23 ......167 F7
Park Avenue Trad Est
LU3 ......44 C7
Park Cl Baldock SG7 ......23 F7
Brookmans Park AL9 ......145 A5
Harrow HA3 ......176 E2
Hatfield AL9 ......130 C6
Markyate AL3 ......83 D5
Rickmansworth WD3 ......174 B6
Stevenage SG2 ......51 B1
Watford WD23 ......167 D6
Park Cnr AL4 ......143 B8
Park Cres Baldock SG7 ......23 E7
Borehamwood WD6 ......169 F6
Harrow HA3 ......176 E2
Park Ct Harlow CM20 ......117 D2
Letchworth SG6 ......23 A6
Luton LU2 ......45 D1
Northwood HA6 ......174 F4
Park Dr Baldock SG7 ......23 E7
Potters Bar EN6 ......159 B8
Standon SG11 ......55 D3
Stanmore HA3 ......176 E4
Park Farm Cl SG16 ......10 D8
Park Farm Ind Est SG9 ..40 D8
Park Farm Ind Pk SG8 ..18 F2
Park Farm La SG8 ......18 C2
Park Gate SG4 ......34 F6
Park Gdns SG7 ......23 E7
Park Hill Harlow CM17 ..118 B4
Harpenden AL5 ......85 F2
Park Hill Rd HP1 ......124 B3
Park Ho
Berkhamsted HP4 ......122 B5
Welwyn Garden City AL8 .110 D7
Park Ind Est AL2 ......141 E4
Park La
Bishop's Stortford CM23 ..76 F4
Cheshunt EN7 ......162 D6
Colney Heath AL4 ......129 C5
Hammond Street EN7 ......148 A4
Harefield UB9 ......173 B2
Harlow CM20 ......117 D2
Hemel Hempstead HP2 ..124 D2
Hoddesdon EN10 ......134 F3
Kimpton SG4 ......66 C1
Knebworth SG3 ......68 D5
Standon SG11 ......55 D3
Park Lane Paradise
EN7 ......148 A6
Park Lodge WD25 ......154 D5
Park Mans HA6 ......174 C7
Park Mdw AL7 ......130 C6
Park Mead CM20 ......117 B1
Park Mews AL7 ......130 C6
Park Mount AL5 ......85 F3
Park Nook Gdns EN2 ......161 D2
Park Pl Park Street AL2 ..141 D4
Stevenage SG1 ......50 D5
Park Place Chambers
SG1 ......50 D5
Park Rd Barnet EN5 ......171 F5
Bushey WD23 ......168 A3
Cheshunt EN8 ......162 D6
Enfield EN3 ......162 E3
Hemel Hempstead HP1 ..124 C1
Hertford SG13 ......113 C6
Hoddesdon EN11 ......135 A6
Northaw EN6 ......146 A1
Radlett WD7 ......156 A4
Rickmansworth WD3 ......165 E2
Stansted Mountfitchet
CM24 ......59 E6

Park Rd continued
Tring HP23 ......100 A3
Ware SG12 ......93 B2
Watford WD17 ......167 B8
Park Rise
Berkhamsted HP4 ......121 E6
Harpenden AL5 ......85 E3
Harrow HA3 ......176 E2
Park Rise Cl AL5 ......85 E3
Park Sq LU1 ......63 E7
Park St Baldock SG7 ......23 E8
Berkhamsted HP4 ......122 B5
Hatfield AL9 ......130 C6
Hitchin SG4 ......34 E6
Luton LU1 ......63 F6
Park Street AL2 ......141 D5
Tring HP23 ......100 A3
Park St W LU1 ......63 E7
Park Street CE Sch AL2 141 D4
Park Street La ......141 C3
Park Street Sta AL2 ......141 D5
Park Terr Enfield EN3 ..162 E1
[2] Luton LU1 ......63 F6
Much Hadham SG10 ......74 F3
Park The Redbourn AL3 .106 B5
St Albans AL1 ......128 A5
Park Viaduct LU1 ......63 F6
Park View
Great Hormead SG9 ......42 A7
Hatfield AL10 ......130 C7
Hoddesdon EN11 ......135 A5
Pinner HA5 ......175 F2
Potters Bar EN6 ......159 C6
Stevenage SG2 ......51 B1
Park View Cl Luton LU3 ..44 D6
St Albans AL1 ......128 A2
Park View Cotts CM23 ..76 F3
Park View Ct HP4 ......122 B4
Park View Dr AL3 ......83 D6
Park View Rd
Berkhamsted HP4 ......122 B4
Pinner HA5 ......175 B3
Park Way Hitchin SG5 ..34 E6
Rickmansworth WD3 ......165 C1
Parker Ave SG14 ......113 D8
Parker Cl SG6 ......22 E4
Parker St WD6 ......168 B8
Parker's Field SG2 ......51 C4
Parkers La SG7 ......3 D5
Parkfield
Chorleywood WD3 ......164 F5
Letchworth SG6 ......23 D4
Markyate AL3 ......83 D5
Parkfield Ave HA2 ......176 C1
Parkfield Cres
Harrow HA2 ......176 C1
Kimpton SG4 ......66 D1
Parkfield Ho HA2 ......176 B2
Parkfield View EN6 ......159 B7
Parkfields AL8 ......110 D6
Parkgate Inf Sch AL4 ..154 C2
Parkgate Jun Sch
WD24 ......154 C2
Parkgate Rd WD24 ......154 C2
Parkhurst Rd SG14 ......113 C7
Parkins Cl SG11 ......73 A6
Parkinson Cl AL4 ......108 D8
Parkland Cl [3] EN11 ..115 B1
Parkland Dr LU1 ......63 D5
Parklands Bushey WD23 .168 C3
Hemel Hempstead HP1 ..123 F5
Royston SG8 ......7 E6
Waltham Abbey EN9 ......163 D7
Parklands Cl EN4 ......159 D1
Parklands Dr AL3 ......127 A2
Parkmead [6] LU1 ......63 F6
Parkside Cheshunt EN8 .162 E5
Potters Bar EN6 ......159 C7
Watford WD19 ......167 C3
Welwyn AL6 ......89 C5
Wyddial SG9 ......27 D2
Parkside Com Prim Sch
WD6 ......156 F1
Parkside Ct EN7 ......148 B3
Parkside Dr WD17 ......166 F7
Parkside Rd HA6 ......174 F5
Parkview Ct HA3 ......176 E3
Parkview Ho WD19 ......167 D3
Parkway
Sawbridgeworth CM21 ..97 F1
Stevenage SG2 ......51 A1
Welwyn Garden City AL8 .110 C6
Parkway Cl AL8 ......110 C6
Parkway Ct AL1 ......142 B8
Parkway Gdns AL8 ......110 D5
Parkway Rd LU1 ......64 B5
Parkwood Cl EN10 ......134 F4
Parkwood Dr HP1 ......123 F3
Parliament Sq SG14 ......113 C6
Parmiter's Sch WD23 ..154 C8
Parndon Mill La CM20 ..117 B3
Parnel Rd SG12 ......93 D2
Parnell Cl WD5 ......139 F1
Parr Cres HP2 ......125 B8
Parrott's La HP23 ......120 A4
Parrotts Cl WD3 ......166 A4
Parrotts Field EN11 ......135 B7
Parson's Cl AL3 ......84 B1
Parsonage Cl
Abbots Langley WD5 ......139 E1
Tring HP23 ......100 A3
Parsonage La HP3 ......100 A3
Parsonage Farm
Rickmansworth WD3 ......165 C2
Wingrave HP22 ......60 B3
Parsonage Farm Trad Est
CM24 ......59 F3
Parsonage La Albury SG11 57 A6

Parsonage La continued
Bishop's Stortford CM23 ..77 C8
Spellbrook CM21 ......97 D6
Stansted Mountfitchet CM24 59 F4
Welham Green AL9 ......144 B8
Parsonage Pl HP23 ......100 A3
Parsonage Rd
Rickmansworth WD3 ......165 D2
Welham Green AL9 ......144 B8
Parsons Green Est SG1 ..37 C2
Parthia Cl SG8 ......7 E6
Partridge Cl Barnet EN5 .171 C8
Bushey WD23 ......168 C1
Luton LU4 ......44 A5
Partridge Hill SG7 ......4 C3
Partridge Rd AL3 ......127 D7
Parva Cl AL5 ......107 D6
Parvills EN9 ......163 D7
Parys Rd LU3 ......45 B6
Pascal Way SG6 ......23 B8
Pasfield EN9 ......163 D6
Passfield Cotts SG11 ......72 F1
Passingham Ave SG4 ......35 A6
Paston Rd HP2 ......124 E5
Pasture Cl WD23 ......168 C2
Pasture La SG4 ......65 E8
Pasture Rd SG6 ......22 E3
Pastures Ct LU4 ......44 A3
Pastures The
Chiswell Green AL2 ......141 A7
Hatfield AL10 ......130 B4
Hemel Hempstead HP1 ..123 E4
Stevenage SG2 ......51 D8
Totteridge N20 ......171 F1
Ware SG12 ......93 C3
Watford WD19 ......167 C2
Welwyn Garden City AL7 .111 B4
Pastures Way LU4 ......44 A4
Pat Larner Ho [9] AL1 ..127 D2
Paternoster Cl EN9 ......163 F6
Paternoster Hill EN9 ..163 F7
Pathway The
Radlett WD7 ......155 F3
Watford WD19 ......167 D1
Patmore Cl CM23 ......76 C8
Patmore Heath (Nature
Reserve)★ SG11 ......57 D8
Patmore Link Rd HP2 ..125 C2
Patmore Rd EN9 ......163 E5
Patricia Gdns CM23 ......76 E5
Patrick Gr EN9 ......163 B6
Paul's Gn EN8 ......162 E6
Pauls La EN11 ......135 A6
Paxton Rd
Berkhamsted HP4 ......122 D4
St Albans AL1 ......127 E2
Payne End SG9 ......15 B1
Payne's Pk SG5 ......34 E7
Paynes Cl SG6 ......12 A1
Paynes Field Cl HP4 ......121 D7
Paynes La EN9 ......149 C2
Paynesfield Rd WD23 ..168 F2
Pea La HP4 ......121 D7
Peabody Ct EN3 ......163 A2
Peace Cl EN7 ......148 B2
Peace Dr WD17 ......167 A6
Peace Gr AL6 ......90 A7
Peace Prospect WD17 ..167 A6
Peach Cl LU1 ......63 F6
Peacock Wlk WD5 ......154 A8
Peacocks Cl HP4 ......121 F6
Peakes La EN7 ......147 F4
Peakes Pl AL1 ......127 F3
Peakes Way EN7 ......147 F4
Pear Tree Cl SG16 ......10 B3
Pear Tree Dell SG6 ......23 B3
Pear Tree Wlk EN7 ......147 E5
Pearces Wlk [4] AL1 ..127 D2
Pearl Ct Baldock SG7 ......12 F1
Pearman Dr SG12 ......71 E7
Pearsall Ct SG6 ......23 B5
Pearson Ave SG13 ......113 C4
Pearsons Ct SG13 ......113 C4
Peartree Cl
Hemel Hempstead HP1 ..124 A4
Welwyn Garden City AL7 .110 E6
Peartree Ct
Watford WD24 ......154 C2
Welwyn Garden City AL7 .110 E5
Peartree Farm AL7 ......110 E6
Peartree La AL7 ......110 E6
Peartree Prim Sch AL7 .110 E5
Peartree Rd
Hemel Hempstead HP1 ..124 A4
Luton LU2 ......46 C4
Peartree Spring Inf Sch
SG2 ......51 B3
Peartree Spring Jun Sch
SG2 ......51 B3
Peartree Way SG2 ......51 A3
Peascroft Rd HP3 ......125 B1
Peasecroft SG9 ......39 C7
Peasmead SG9 ......40 E6
Pebbles The SG7 ......12 C4
Peck's Hill EN9 ......135 E2
Peckworth Ind Est SG16 ..10 A4
Pedlars La SG9 ......15 E7
Pedley Hill HP4,LU6 ......82 C1
Peel Cres SG14 ......113 C8
Peel Pl [6] LU1 ......63 D7
Peel St LU1 ......63 D7
Peerglow Ctr SG12 ......114 E8
Peerless Ind Est WD18 166 B1
Peg's La SG13 ......113 D5
Pegasus Ct WD5 ......153 F7
Pegasus Pl AL3 ......127 D5
Pegmire La WD25 ......168 C8

Pegrum Dr AL2 ......142 B5
Pegs La HP3 ......95 D5
Pegsdon Cl LU3 ......45 B7
Pegsdon Way SG5 ......19 E1
Peitley Cotts AL3 ......84 A1
Pelham Ct
Hemel Hempstead HP2 ..125 C3
Welwyn Garden City AL7 .111 C5
Pelham Rd SG11 ......55 F7
Pelhams The WD25 ......154 D4
Pelican Way SG6 ......11 F1
Pemberton Almshouses [4]
AL3 ......127 D4
Pemberton Cl AL1 ......141 D8
Pembridge Chase HP3 ..137 A3
Pembridge La EN10 ......133 E2
Pembridge Rd HP3 ......137 A3
Pembroke Ave
Enfield EN1 ......162 B1
Luton LU4 ......44 F3
Pembroke Cl EN10 ......148 E8
Pembroke Dr EN7 ......147 B2
Pembroke Ho [3] WD6 ..170 A5
Pembroke Rd Baldock SG7 23 F8
Moor Park HA6 ......174 C7
Pemsel Ct HP3 ......124 C1
Penda Cl LU3 ......44 F7
Pendennis Ct AL5 ......107 D7
Penfold Cl SG7 ......24 A7
Penfold Trad Est WD24 ..167 C8
Pengelly Cl EN7 ......148 B1
Penhill LU3 ......44 E6
Penhill Cl LU3 ......44 E6
Penman Cl AL2 ......141 A4
Penn Cl WD3 ......164 D3
Penn Ho Moor Park HA6 .174 C7
[14] South Oxhey WD19 ..175 C2
Penn Pl [1] WD3 ......165 D2
Penn Rd
Chiswell Green AL2 ......141 C4
Rickmansworth WD3 ......165 A1
Stevenage SG1 ......50 E4
Penn Way
Chorleywood WD3 ......164 D3
Letchworth SG6 ......23 B3
Pennard Ho [3] WD19 ..175 D7
Penne Cl WD7 ......156 A5
Pennine Ave LU3 ......44 D8
Pennine Way HP2 ......125 A2
Pennington La CM24 ......59 D8
Penningtons CM23 ......76 C5
Penns The SG8 ......17 E6
Penny Croft AL5 ......107 A4
Penny Ct WD17 ......167 B7
Pennyfather Cl SG3 ......69 E2
Pennyfathers La AL6 ......90 B4
Pennymead CM20 ......118 A1
Penray EN5 ......171 E6
Penrose Ave WD19 ......175 E8
Penrose Ct HP2 ......124 E7
Penscroft Gdns WD6 ..170 D5
Penshurst CM17 ......118 C3
Penshurst Cl AL5 ......85 D4
Penshurst Rd EN6 ......159 D7
Penta Ct WD6 ......170 A5
Pentagon Pk HP2 ......125 C5
Pentland HP2 ......124 F6
Pentland Rd WD23 ......168 C3
Pentland Rise SG1 ......37 C3
Pentley Cl AL8 ......89 D1
Pentley Pk AL8 ......89 D1
Penton Dr EN8 ......148 D2
Pentrich Ave EN1 ......162 A1
Penzance Cl UB9 ......173 D1
Peplins Cl AL9 ......144 E5
Peplins Way AL9 ......144 E5
Peppard Cl AL3 ......106 A6
Pepper Cl SG7 ......23 F8
Pepper Hill SG12 ......114 F4
Peppercorn Wlk SG4 ......35 B7
Peppett's Gn HP5 ......120 D1
Pepsal End SG2 ......69 B8
Pepsal End Rd LU1 ......84 C7
Pepys Cres EN5 ......171 C4
Pepys Way SG7 ......23 E8
Percheron Dr LU4 ......44 A3
Percheron Rd WD6 ......170 D3
Percival Ct EN8 ......148 E1
Percival Way LU2 ......64 C7
Percy Rd WD18 ......167 B5
Peregrine Cl
Bishop's Stortford CM23 ..76 D6
Watford WD25 ......154 E5
Peregrine Ho [1] SG12 ..93 C3
Peregrine Rd LU4 ......44 A4
Perham Way AL2 ......142 D6
Perivale Gdns WD25 ..154 B5
Periwinkle Cl SG8 ......17 C5
Periwinkle La SG5 ......21 F1
Permain Cl WD7 ......156 E6
Perowne Way SG11 ......55 E3
Perram Cl EN10 ......148 E5
Perriors Cl EN7 ......148 A4
Perry Dr SG8 ......7 E7
Perry Gn HP2 ......105 A1
Perry Hill EN9 ......149 F8
Perry Mead WD23 ......168 C3
Perrycoste Cl AL4 ......128 A8
Perrymead LU2 ......46 F2
Perrysfield Rd EN8 ......148 E5
Perrywood AL8 ......110 D8
Perrywood La SG14 ......91 B7
Perspective Ho EN3 ......162 E4
Pescot Hill HP1 ......124 B5
Petard Cl LU4 ......44 A2
Peter's Pl HP4 ......121 E6
Peterborough Ho [9]
WD6 ......170 A7

Peterlee Ct **2** HP2 . . . . .124 F7
Peters Ave AL2 . . . . . . .142 C5
Peters Way SG3 . . . . . . . .68 F6
Peters Wood Hill SG12 .114 E7
Petersfield AL3 . . . . . . . .127 E7
Peterslea WD4 . . . . . . . .139 B2
Pettys Cl EN8 . . . . . . . . .148 D3
Petunia Cl LU3 . . . . . . . . .45 C1
Petworth Cl SG2 . . . . . . . .69 C7
Pevensey Cl LU2 . . . . . . . .46 D4
Pewterers Ave CM23 . . . .76 C4
**Pheasant Cl**
　Berkhamsted HP4 . . . . .122 C3
　Tring HP23 . . . . . . . . . .100 B6
Pheasants Way WD3 . . . .165 B2
Phillimore Ct WD7 . . . . .155 E3
Phillimore Pl WD7 . . . . .155 E3
Phillipers WD25 . . . . . . .154 E4
Phillips Ave AL5 . . . . . . . . .7 C8
Phipps Hatch La EN2 . . .161 C1
Phoenix Cl HA6 . . . . . . .174 F6
Phoenix Ct EN3 . . . . . . .162 C1
**Phyllis Courtnage Ho** **4**
HP2 . . . . . . . . . . . . . . . .124 D5
Piccotts End La HP2 . . . .124 D7
Piccotts End Rd HP1 . . . .124 C7
Pick Hill EN9 . . . . . . . . .163 F7
Pickets Cl WD23 . . . . . . .168 E1
Picketts AL8 . . . . . . . . . . .89 D1
Pickford Hill AL5 . . . . . . .86 C3
Pickford Rd Markyate AL3 83 D5
　St Albans AL1 . . . . . . . .128 B2
Picknage Cnr SG8 . . . . . . .9 A2
Picknage Rd SG8 . . . . . . . .9 A2
Pie Cnr AL3 . . . . . . . . . . .84 C1
Pie Gdn AL3 . . . . . . . . . . .84 C1
Pierian Spring HP1 . . . .124 B5
Pietley Hill AL3 . . . . . . . .84 A1
Pig La CM22 . . . . . . . . . . .77 A3
Pigeonwick AL5 . . . . . . . .86 B3
Piggotts La LU4 . . . . . . . .44 D4
Piggotts Way CM23 . . . . .76 E5
Piggottshill La AL5 . . . . .107 D8
Pightle Cl SG8 . . . . . . . . . .7 D7
Pightle The LU7 . . . . . . . .80 D3
Pike End SG1 . . . . . . . . . .50 D6
Pikes Cotts EN5 . . . . . . .171 C5
Pikes Leap **6** AL4 . . . . . .87 D1
**Pilgrim Cl**
　Chiswell Green AL2 . . . .141 C4
　Watford WD25 . . . . . . .154 D6
Pilgrims Row SG9 . . . . . . .40 F3
Pilgrims Way SG1 . . . . . . .37 B2
Piltdown Rd WD19 . . . . .175 D3
Pin Green Ind Est SG1 . . .37 C2
Pin Green Prim Sch SG1 . .50 F6
Pinchfield WD3 . . . . . . . .172 D5
Pindar Rd EN11 . . . . . . .135 C7
**Pine** Berkhamsted HP4 122 B4
　Cheshunt EN8 . . . . . . . .148 D3
Pine Crest AL6 . . . . . . . . .89 E8
**Pine Gr**
　Bishop's Stortford CM23 . .77 B6
　Bricket Wood AL2 . . . . .140 F1
　Brookmans Park AL9 . . .145 B6
　Totteridge N20 . . . . . . .171 F1
　Watford WD23 . . . . . . .167 F8
Pine Ridge AL3 . . . . . . . .142 A8
Pine Tree Cl HP2 . . . . . .124 D4
Pine Wlk HP4 . . . . . . . . .121 D7
Pinecroft HP3 . . . . . . . . .138 F7
Pinecroft Cres EN5 . . . . .171 E5
Pinecroft Ct HP3 . . . . . . .138 F7
Pinehill Hospl SG4 . . . . . .35 A7
Pinehurst Cl WD5 . . . . . .153 E7
Pinelands CM23 . . . . . . . .58 F1
Pineridge Ct **4** EN5 . . .171 D5
Pines Ave SG1 . . . . . . . .162 B3
Pines Cl HA6 . . . . . . . . . .174 E4
Pines Hill CM24 . . . . . . . .59 D5
**Pines The**
　Borehamwood WD6 . . . .169 F7
　Hemel Hempstead HP3 . .137 F7
Pinetree Gdns **5** HP2 . .124 E2
Pinetree Ho WD25 . . . . .154 E3
**Pinewood** AL7 . . . . . . . .110 E4
Pinewood Ave HA5 . . . . .176 B4
**Pinewood Cl**
　Borehamwood WD6 . . . .170 D7
　Pinner HA5 . . . . . . . . . .176 B4
　South Oxhey WD19 . . . .175 B5
　St Albans AL4 . . . . . . . .128 C3
　Watford WD17 . . . . . . .167 A8
Pinewood Dr EN6 . . . . . .158 F8
Pinewood Gdns HP1 . . . .124 B3
**Pinewood Lodge** **1**
WD23 . . . . . . . . . . . . . .168 D1
Pinewood Sch WD23 . . .114 D7
Pinewoods **4** SG2 . . . . . .50 F1
Pinfold Rd WD23 . . . . . .167 F7
Pinford Dell **4** LU2 . . . . .46 D1
Pinks Farm WD7 . . . . . . .157 C8
Pinnacles EN9 . . . . . . . . .163 E5
Pinnate Pl AL7 . . . . . . . .110 E2
Pinner Gn HA5 . . . . . . . .175 C1
Pinner Hill HA5 . . . . . . . .175 B3
Pinner Hill Rd HA5 . . . . .175 C1
Pinner Park Ave HA2 . . .176 C1
Pinner Park Gdns HA2 . .176 C1
**Pinner Rd**
　Northwood HA6 . . . . . . .175 A1
　Watford WD19 . . . . . . .167 E2
**Pinner Wood Fst & Mid Schs**
HA5 . . . . . . . . . . . . . . . .175 C2
Pinnocks Cl SG7 . . . . . . . .23 F7
Pinnocks La SG7 . . . . . . . .23 F8
Pinto Cl WD6 . . . . . . . . .170 D3
Pioneer Way WD18 . . . . .166 F3

Pipers Ave AL5 . . . . . . . .107 D7
Pipers Cl AL3 . . . . . . . . .106 A6
Pipers Hill HP1 . . . . . . . .103 D3
**Pipers La**
　Caddington AL3,LU1 . . . . .62 F1
　Wheathampstead AL5 . . .107 F7
Pipit Cl SG8 . . . . . . . . . . . .7 E8
Pippens AL8 . . . . . . . . . . .89 E1
Pippin Cl WD7 . . . . . . . .156 E6
Pippin Gr SG8 . . . . . . . . . .7 C7
Pippins The WD25 . . . . .154 C5
Pirton Cl Hitchin SG5 . . . .34 D6
　St Albans AL4 . . . . . . . .128 C8
Pirton Cross SG5 . . . . . . .34 A7
Pirton Ct HP2 . . . . . . . . .124 F4
**Pirton Hill Inf Sch** LU4 .44 B6
**Pirton Hill Jun Sch** LU4 .44 B6
Pirton Rd Hitchin SG5 . . . .34 C6
　Holwell SG5 . . . . . . . . . .21 A7
　Luton LU4 . . . . . . . . . . . .44 D5
Pirton Sch SG5 . . . . . . . . .20 D4
Pishiobury Dr CM21 . . . .118 D3
Pitfield AL8 . . . . . . . . . . . .89 D1
Pitsford Terr LU2 . . . . . . .46 A1
Pitstone Cl AL4 . . . . . . . .128 C8
**Pitstone Common Forest**
**Trails**✲ HP4 . . . . . . . .101 F1
**Pitstone Green Farm Mus**✲
LU7 . . . . . . . . . . . . . . . . .80 D4
**Pitstone Windmill**✲ LU7 .80 F4
Pitt Cl SG2 . . . . . . . . . . . .51 B1
Pitt Dr AL4 . . . . . . . . . . .142 C8
Pitteway Wlk SG14 . . . . .113 C6
Pittmans Field CM20 . . .117 F1
Pix Cl SG5 . . . . . . . . . . . .11 A8
Pix Farm La HP1 . . . . . . .123 C2
Pix Rd Letchworth SG6 . . .23 A6
　Stotfold SG5 . . . . . . . . . .11 E5
Pixies Cl HP1 . . . . . . . . .123 C2
**Pixies Hill Cres** HP1 . . .123 F2
**Pixies Hill Jun Mix Inf Sch**
HP1 . . . . . . . . . . . . . . . .123 F2
Pixies Hill Rd HP1 . . . . . .123 F2
Pixmore Ave SG6 . . . . . . .23 B6
Pixmore Ind Est SG6 . . . .23 A6
Pixmore Jun Sch SG6 . . . .23 A5
Pixmore Way SG6 . . . . . . .23 A5
Plaistow Way SG8 . . . . . . .9 E2
Plaiters Cl HP2 . . . . . . . .100 B4
Plaitford Cl WD3 . . . . . . .173 E8
Plantaganet Pl EN9 . . . .163 B6
Plantation Rd LU3 . . . . . .44 D7
Plantation Wlk HP1 . . . .124 A6
Plash Dr SG1 . . . . . . . . . .50 E5
Plashes Cl SG11 . . . . . . . .55 D2
Plashes Dr SG9 . . . . . . . . .40 F4
Plashets CM22 . . . . . . . . .98 D1
Platt Cl LU4 . . . . . . . . . . .44 D4
Plawsfield WD3 . . . . . . . .173 E8
**Plaw Hatch Cl** CM23 . . .77 B8
**Plaw Hatch Cnr** CM23 . .77 D8
Playford Sq LU4 . . . . . . . .44 D5
Pleasance The AL5 . . . . . .85 D4
Pleasant Pl WD3 . . . . . . .172 E3
Pleasant Rd CM23 . . . . . .76 E8
Pleasant Rise AL9 . . . . . .130 C8
Plewes Cl LU6 . . . . . . . . . .82 E8
Plough Cl SG8 . . . . . . . . . .5 B8
Plough Hill EN6 . . . . . . .146 E2
**Plough La** Harefield UB9 .173 C4
　King's Walden SG4 . . . . .48 A5
　Potten End HP4 . . . . . . .123 B7
　Sarratt WD3 . . . . . . . . .151 F1
Ploughmans Cl CM23 . . .76 C5
Ploughmans End AL7 . . .111 C5
Plover Cl HP4 . . . . . . . . .122 C3
Plum Tree Rd SG16 . . . . .10 B2
Plummers La LU2 . . . . . . .65 C2
Plumpton Cl LU2 . . . . . . .46 D3
Plumpton Rd EN11 . . . . .135 C8
Pluto Rise HP2 . . . . . . . .124 F5
Plymouth Cl LU2 . . . . . . .46 B1
Poets Chase HP1 . . . . . . .124 B5
Poets Cl HP1 . . . . . . . . . .124 B4
Poets Ct AL5 . . . . . . . . . . .86 B1
**Poets Gate**
　Goff's Oak EN7 . . . . . . .147 E3
　Widford SG12 . . . . . . . . .95 D4
Poets Gn LU4 . . . . . . . . . .44 A2
Polayn Garth AL8 . . . . . .110 C7
Polegate LU2 . . . . . . . . . . .46 D2
Polehanger La HP1 . . . . .123 E5
Poles Hill WD3 . . . . . . . .151 E6
**Poles La** Thundridge SG12 .93 C6
　Ware SG12 . . . . . . . . . . .93 C3
Poles Pk SG12 . . . . . . . . .93 C6
Police Row SG8 . . . . . . . .15 F7
Police Station La WD23 168 B2
Pollard Gdns SG1 . . . . . . .50 F8
Pollards WD3 . . . . . . . . .172 D5
Pollards Cl EN7 . . . . . . . .147 C2
Pollards Way SG5 . . . . . . .20 D4
Pollicott Cl AL4 . . . . . . . .128 C8
Pollywick Rd HP23 . . . . .100 D1
Polsten Mews EN3 . . . . .163 A2
Polzeath Cl LU2 . . . . . . . .64 C8
Pomeroy Cres WD24 . . .154 B3
Pomeroy Gr LU2 . . . . . . . .45 E6
Pomfret Ave LU2 . . . . . . .45 F1
**Pond Cl** Harefield UB9 . .173 C1
　Luton LU4 . . . . . . . . . . . .44 B5
　Stevenage SG1 . . . . . . . .50 C7
　Tring HP23 . . . . . . . . . .100 A4
Pond Croft Hatfield AL10 .129 F5
　Welwyn Garden City AL7 .110 E5
Pond Ct SG4 . . . . . . . . . . .67 F1
Pond Field AL7 . . . . . . . . .90 A1
**Pond La** Baldock SG7 . . .23 B8
　Little Gaddesden HP4 . . .102 E7

**Pond La** continued
　Stansted Mountfitchet
　CM24 . . . . . . . . . . . . . . .59 D7
Pond Rd HP3 . . . . . . . . .139 A6
Pondcroft Rd SG3 . . . . . . .69 A4
Pondfield Cres AL4 . . . . .128 B7
Pondside SG4 . . . . . . . . . .36 C4
Pondsmeade AL3 . . . . . .106 B5
Pondwick Rd AL5 . . . . . . .85 E2
Pondwicks Cl AL1 . . . . . .127 C2
Pondwicks Rd LU1 . . . . . .63 F7
**Ponsbourne St Mary's CE**
**Prim Sch** SG13 . . . . . .146 E7
Pooleys La AL9 . . . . . . . .144 C8
**Pope Paul RC Prim Sch**
EN6 . . . . . . . . . . . . . . . .158 F6
Pope's Rd WD5 . . . . . . . .153 E8
Popes Ct LU2 . . . . . . . . . .45 D1
Popes La CM24 . . . . . . . .154 B1
Popes Row SG12 . . . . . . .93 D3
Popis Gdns SG12 . . . . . . .93 E2
**Poplar Ave** Hatfield AL10 129 D5
　Luton LU3 . . . . . . . . . . . .45 C8
**Poplar Cl** Hitchin SG4 . . .35 B6
　Royston SG8 . . . . . . . . . . .7 E7
　Thundridge SG11 . . . . . .72 F2
Poplar Rd LU6 . . . . . . . . .82 E8
Poplar Shaw EN9 . . . . . .163 F6
Poplar View SG12 . . . . . . .92 E4
Poplars AL7 . . . . . . . . . . .90 A1
**Poplars Cl** Hatfield AL10 .129 D5
　Luton LU2 . . . . . . . . . . . .46 B3
　Watford WD25 . . . . . . .154 B7
**Poplars The** Arlesey SG15 .11 A8
　Borehamwood WD6 . . . .170 A8
　Great Hallingbury CM22 . .77 F4
　**2** Hammond Street EN7 .147 E5
　Harefield UB9 . . . . . . . .173 C2
　Hemel Hempstead HP1 . .124 B2
　Ickleford SG5 . . . . . . . . .21 F5
　St Albans AL1 . . . . . . . .142 B7
Popple Way SG1 . . . . . . . .50 E6
**Poppy Cl**
　Hemel Hempstead HP1 . .123 D4
　Luton LU3 . . . . . . . . . . . .45 D2
Poppy Mead SG1 . . . . . . .50 F4
Poppy Wlk
　Goff's Oak EN7 . . . . . . .147 D3
　Hatfield AL10 . . . . . . . .129 F8
Poppyfields AL7 . . . . . . .111 C5
Porlock Dr LU2 . . . . . . . . .46 C1
Port Hill SG14 . . . . . . . . .113 C7
Port La CM22 . . . . . . . . . .98 C4
Port Vale SG14 . . . . . . . .113 C6
Porter's Mews SG4 . . . . . .67 F1
Porters Cl SG9 . . . . . . . . .40 E8
Porters Hill AL5 . . . . . . . .86 C4
Porters Park Dr WD7 . . .156 E7
Porters Wood AL3 . . . . . .127 F7
Portland Ct LU4 . . . . . . . .45 A1
**Portland Dr**
　Cheshunt EN7 . . . . . . . .162 A8
　Enfield EN2 . . . . . . . . . .161 E1
Portland Hts HA6 . . . . . .174 F6
Portland Ind Est SG15 . . .11 A3
**Portland Pl**
　**17** Bishop's Stortford CM23 76 F7
　Hertford Heath SG13 . . .114 C4
**Portland Rd**
　Bishop's Stortford CM23 . .76 F7
　Luton LU4 . . . . . . . . . . . .45 A1
Portland St AL3 . . . . . . . .127 C4
Portman Cl Hitchin SG5 . .21 C7
　St Albans AL4 . . . . . . . .128 C7
Portman Ho AL3 . . . . . . .127 D6
Portmill La SG5 . . . . . . . .34 F7
**Post Office Cotts** CM22 . .98 C8
**Post Office Rd** CM20 . . .117 D1
**Post Office Row** SG4 . . . .24 B1
**Post Office Wlk** **8**
SG14 . . . . . . . . . . . . . . .113 D6
Post Wood Rd SG12 . . . .114 C3
Postfield AL7 . . . . . . . . . . .90 A1
Posting Ho HP3 . . . . . . . .101 A5
Postwood Gn SG13 . . . . .114 C3
Potash La SG12 . . . . . . . . .79 A5
**Potten End CE Fst Sch**
HP4 . . . . . . . . . . . . . . . .123 B6
Potten End Hill HP1 . . . .123 E8
**Potter St**
　Bishop's Stortford CM23 . .76 F7
　Pinner HA5 . . . . . . . . . .175 B2
Potter Street Hill HA5 . .175 B3
**Potters Bar Com Hospl**
EN6 . . . . . . . . . . . . . . . .159 C5
Potters Bar Mus✲ EN6 . .158 F4
Potters Bar Sta EN6 . . . .158 F7
Potters Ct EN6 . . . . . . . .159 A7
Potters Field AL3 . . . . . . .127 C7
Potters Heights Cl HA5 . .175 B3
**Potters La**
　Borehamwood WD6 . . . .170 C8
　Stevenage SG1 . . . . . . . .50 B4
Potters Mews WD6 . . . . .169 D3
**Potterscrouch La** CM23,
AL3 . . . . . . . . . . . . . . . .140 E7
Pottersheath Rd AL6 . . . .68 D1
Pottery Cl LU3 . . . . . . . . .44 F7
Potton Rd SG8 . . . . . . . . . .1 F6
Pouchen End La HP1 . . . .123 D3
Poulteney Rd CM24 . . . . .59 E8
Poultney Cl WD7 . . . . . . .156 F7
**Pound Ave** SG1 . . . . . . . .50 D6
**Pound Cl**
　Lower Nazeing EN9 . . . .149 E8

**Pound Cl** continued
　Sandridge AL4 . . . . . . . .108 C2
Pound Gn SG8 . . . . . . . . . .1 F5
Pound La WD7 . . . . . . . .156 F5
Poundfield WD25 . . . . . .153 F4
Poundwell AL7 . . . . . . . .111 A5
Powdermill La EN9 . . . . .163 B6
Powdermill Mews EN9 . .163 B6
Powdermill Way EN9 . . .163 B6
Power Cl LU1 . . . . . . . . . .63 F7
Power Dr EN3 . . . . . . . . .162 F3
Powis Ct Bushey WD23 . .168 C1
　Potters Bar EN6 . . . . . .159 C5
Powys Ct WD6 . . . . . . . .170 D6
Poynders Hill HP2 . . . . . .125 C3
Poynders Mdw SG4 . . . . .88 F8
Poynings Cl AL5 . . . . . . .107 F8
Poynters Rd LU5 . . . . . . . .44 A2
Prae Cl AL3 . . . . . . . . . . .127 B3
**Prae Wood Prim Sch**
AL3 . . . . . . . . . . . . . . . .127 A1
Praetorian Ct AL1 . . . . . .141 C8
Prebendal Dr LU1 . . . . . . .63 B2
Precinct The EN10 . . . . . .134 F3
Premier Ct EN3 . . . . . . . .162 D1
Premier Pl WD18 . . . . . .166 F4
Prentice Way LU2 . . . . . . .64 D7
Prescott Rd EN8 . . . . . . .148 E4
Presdales Ct SG12 . . . . .114 D8
Presdales Dr SG12 . . . . .114 D8
Presdales Sch SG12 . . . .114 D7
**Presentation Ct** LU1 . . . .63 F6
President Way LU2 . . . . . .64 D8
Prestatyn Cl SG1 . . . . . . .50 B8
Preston Cl HA6 . . . . . . . .175 A1
**Preston Gdns**
　Enfield EN3 . . . . . . . . . .162 E2
　Luton LU2 . . . . . . . . . . . .45 F2
Preston Path LU2 . . . . . . .45 F2
**Preston Prim Sch** SG4 . .48 D7
Preston Rd Preston SG4 . .48 E7
　St Ippolyts SG4 . . . . . . . .34 F1
Prestwick Cl LU2 . . . . . . .45 E5
Prestwick Dr CM23 . . . . .59 B1
Prestwick Rd WD19 . . . .175 D6
Prestwood **2** WD19 . . . .175 E8
Prestwood Gate AL1 . . . .127 E5
Pretoria Rd WD18 . . . . . .167 A5
Pretty Cnr HA6 . . . . . . . .175 A5
Priestland Gdns HP4 . . . .122 E6
Priestleys LU1 . . . . . . . . . .63 A7
Primary Way SG15 . . . . . .11 A4
Primett Rd SG1 . . . . . . . . .50 C7
Primley La LU2 . . . . . . . . .45 F2
**Primrose Cl** Arlesey SG15 .11 A4
　Bishop's Stortford CM23 . .59 B1
　Hatfield AL10 . . . . . . . .130 B4
　Hemel Hempstead HP1 . .123 E2
　Luton LU3 . . . . . . . . . . . .45 D2
Primrose Cotts WD7 . . . .156 A4
Primrose Ct SG1 . . . . . . . .50 D7
Primrose Dr SG13 . . . . . .114 B6
**Primrose Gdns**
　Bushey WD23 . . . . . . . .168 B2
　Radlett WD7 . . . . . . . . .156 A4
Primrose Hill WD4 . . . . . .139 B3
Primrose Hill Rd SG1 . . . .50 D7
Primrose La Arlesey SG15 .11 A4
　Radlett WD25 . . . . . . . .155 C1
Primrose Path EN7 . . . . .162 A8
Primrose View SG8 . . . . . .7 F5
**Prince Andrew's Cl** SG8 . .7 D5
**Prince Edward St** **6**
HP4 . . . . . . . . . . . . . . . .122 C4
Prince Eugene Pl AL1 . . .141 C8
**Prince of Wales Prim Sch**
EN3 . . . . . . . . . . . . . . . .162 F2
Prince Pk HP1 . . . . . . . . .124 A2
Prince St WD17 . . . . . . . .167 C6
Prince Way LU2 . . . . . . . .64 D8
Prince's St SG5 . . . . . . . . .11 F7
Princes Ave Enfield EN3 . .162 F4
　Watford WD18 . . . . . . .167 A5
Princes Cl HP4 . . . . . . . .122 A6
**Princes Ct**
　Bishop's Stortford CM23 . .76 C7
　Hemel Hempstead HP3 . .138 B8
**Princes Gate**
　Bishop's Stortford CM23 . .76 C7
　Harlow CM20 . . . . . . . .117 E3
Princes Mews SG8 . . . . . . .7 C6
Princes Pl **15** LU2 . . . . . .45 D1
Princes St SG12 . . . . . . . .93 D2
**Princess Alexandra Hospl**
CM20 . . . . . . . . . . . . . .117 C1
Princess Diana Dr AL4 . .128 C2
**Princess Helena Coll The**
SG4 . . . . . . . . . . . . . . . . .48 E6
Princess St LU1 . . . . . . . . .63 D7
Printers Cl AL1 . . . . . . . .127 D2
Printers Way CM20 . . . . .118 A5
Priors **9** CM23 . . . . . . . .77 A7
Priors Cl SG13 . . . . . . . .114 B3
Priors Ct CM22 . . . . . . . . .98 C4
Priors Hill SG5 . . . . . . . . .20 C4
**Priors Wood Prim Sch**
SG12 . . . . . . . . . . . . . . . .94 A3
Priors Wood Rd SG13 . . .114 C3
Priory Ave CM17 . . . . . . .118 C5
**Priory Ct** Cheshunt EN10 .148 E7
　Hoddesdon EN11 . . . . . .135 A5
　Royston SG8 . . . . . . . . . . .7 E6
　Stanmore HA7 . . . . . . . .176 D1
　Totteridge N20 . . . . . . .171 F2
**Priory Ct**
　**9** Berkhamsted HP4 . . . .122 C4
　Bishop's Stortford CM23 . .76 C7
　Bushey WD23 . . . . . . . .168 C1

**Pet – Qua** **205**

**Priory Ct** continued
　**13** Hertford SG14 . . . . . .113 D6
　Hitchin SG4 . . . . . . . . . . .34 F5
　St Albans AL1 . . . . . . . .127 E2
Priory Dell SG1 . . . . . . . . .50 F5
Priory Dr Stanmore HA7 .176 F1
　Stansted Mountfitchet
　CM24 . . . . . . . . . . . . . . .59 E5
Priory End SG4 . . . . . . . . .34 F5
Priory Gate EN8 . . . . . . .148 F4
**Priory Gdns**
　Berkhamsted HP4 . . . . .122 C4
　Luton LU2 . . . . . . . . . . . .45 D4
**Priory La**
　Great Wymondley SG4 . . .35 F4
　Royston SG8 . . . . . . . . . . .7 D6
Priory Lo WD3 . . . . . . . . .165 D2
Priory Orch AL3 . . . . . . . .84 B2
Priory Row SG12 . . . . . . .95 E4
**Priory Sch The** SG5 . . . . .21 E2
Priory St Hertford SG14 . .113 D6
　Ware SG12 . . . . . . . . . . .93 C1
**Priory View**
　Bushey WD23 . . . . . . . .168 E2
　Little Wymondley SG4 . . .35 E4
Priory Way SG4 . . . . . . . .34 F4
Priory Wharf **12** SG14 . .113 D6
Priory Wlk AL1 . . . . . . . .141 E8
Pritchett Cl EN3 . . . . . . .163 A2
Proctor Way LU2 . . . . . . .64 C7
Proctors Way CM23 . . . . .77 A4
Progress Way LU4 . . . . . . .44 B7
**Progression Ctr** HP2 . . . .125 A6
Prospect La AL5 . . . . . . . .107 A4
Prospect Pl AL6 . . . . . . . .89 C5
**Prospect Rd**
　Cheshunt EN8 . . . . . . . .148 C2
　St Albans AL1 . . . . . . . .127 D1
Prospect Way LU2 . . . . . .64 C7
Protea Way SG6 . . . . . . . .23 B6
Providence Gr SG1 . . . . . .50 E8
Providence Pl **17** SG14 . .113 D6
Providence Way SG7 . . . .23 F7
Provost Way LU2 . . . . . . .64 C8
Prowse Ave WD23 . . . . .176 C8
Pryor Cl WD5 . . . . . . . . .153 F7
Pryor Rd SG7 . . . . . . . . . .23 F6
Pryor Way SG6 . . . . . . . . .23 D5
Pryors Cl CM23 . . . . . . . .77 A6
Pryors Ct SG7 . . . . . . . . . .12 F1
Puddephat's La AL3 . . . .104 D7
Pudding La Barley SG8 . . . .9 A1
　Hemel Hempstead HP1 . .124 A5
Puddingstone Dr AL4 . . .128 C1
Pudgell The SG8 . . . . . . . .9 E2
Pulham Ave EN10 . . . . . .134 C7
**Pullar Meml Prim Sch**
SG11 . . . . . . . . . . . . . . . .72 E2
Puller Rd Barnet EN5 . . .171 E7
　Hemel Hempstead HP1 . .124 A2
Pulleys Cl HP1 . . . . . . . .123 F4
Pulleys La HP1 . . . . . . . .123 F4
Pullman Cl AL1 . . . . . . . .127 E1
Pullman Dr SG4 . . . . . . . .35 B7
Pulter's Way SG4 . . . . . . .35 A6
Pump Hill SG9 . . . . . . . . .30 A2
Pump Ho The **12** CM23 . .77 A7
**Pumphouse The** SG8 . . . .7 D7
Punch Bowl La AL3 . . . . .126 B8
Punchard Cres EN3 . . . . .163 B1
Purbeck Ho **8** WD18 . . .166 F5
Purbrock Ave WD25 . . . .154 C3
Purcell Cl Datchworth AL6 .90 E6
　Radlett WD6 . . . . . . . . .169 D8
Purcell Ct SG1 . . . . . . . . .50 C8
Purcell Sch WD23 . . . . . .168 A7
Purkiss Rd SG13 . . . . . . .113 C3
Purley Ctr LU3 . . . . . . . . .44 E7
Purlings Rd WD23 . . . . . .168 B4
Pursley Gdns WD6 . . . . .157 A1
Purway Cl LU3 . . . . . . . . .44 E7
Purwell La SG4 . . . . . . . . .35 C8
**Purwell Prim Sch** SG4 . . .35 D8
Putney Rd EN3 . . . . . . . .162 D3
Puttenham Cl WD19 . . . .175 D8
Puttenham Ct HP23 . . . . .78 F2
**Putteridge High Sch** LU2 .46 C5
**Putteridge Inf Sch** LU2 . .46 C5
**Putteridge Jun Sch** LU2 . .46 B4
Putteridge Par LU2 . . . . . .46 B4
Putteridge Rd LU2 . . . . . .46 C4
**Putteridge Recn Ctr** LU2 46 C5
Putterills The AL5 . . . . . . .86 A1
Putters Croft HP2 . . . . . .124 F5
Puttocks Cl AL9 . . . . . . . .144 C8
Puttocks Dr AL9 . . . . . . .144 C8
Pye Cnr CM20 . . . . . . . . .117 D5
Pyghtle Ct LU1 . . . . . . . . .63 A7
**Pyghtle The**
　Buntingford SG9 . . . . . . .40 D7
　Luton LU1 . . . . . . . . . . . .63 A7
Pyms Cl SG6 . . . . . . . . . .23 B8
Pynchbek CM23 . . . . . . . .76 C5
Pynchon Paddocks CM22 98 D7
Pynefield Ho WD3 . . . . . .164 F2
Pytchley Cl LU2 . . . . . . . .45 E5

**Q**

Quadrangle The AL8 . . . .110 C7
**Quadrant The**
　Letchworth SG6 . . . . . . . .22 F6
　Royston SG8 . . . . . . . . . . .7 C8
　St Albans AL4 . . . . . . . .128 B6

**Quadrant The** *continued*
Stevenage SG1 .........**50** D4
**Quail Wlk** SG8 .........**7** E8
**Quaker La** EN9 .......**163** C5
**Quaker Rd** SG12 .......**93** E3
**Quakers La** EN6 .....**159** B8
**Quantock Cl** Luton LU3 ...**45** B8
St Albans AL4 .........**128** C7
Stevenage SG1 .........**37** D3
**Quantock Rise** LU3 .....**31** B3
**Quantocks** HP2 .......**124** F6
**Quartermass Cl** HP1 ...**124** A4
**Quartermass Rd** HP1 ...**124** A4
**Queen Anne's Cl** SG5 ...**11** F7
**Queen Elizabeth Ct**
Barnet EN5 ..........**171** F5
Waltham Abbey EN9 .....**163** C3
**Queen Elizabeth II Hospl**
AL7 .............**111** A2
**Queen Elizabeth's Girls Sch**
EN5 ............**171** F5
**Queen Elizabeth's Sch**
EN5 ............**171** D6
**Queen Hoo La** AL6 .....**90** F4
**Queen Mary's Ave**
WD18 ...........**166** E5
**Queen Marys Ct** EN9 ...**163** C4
**Queen St**
Chipperfield WD4 ......**152** A7
Hitchin SG4,SG5 ......**34** F7
Pitstone LU7 .........**80** D4
St Albans AL3 ........**127** C3
Stotfold SG5 .........**12** A6
Tring HP23 ..........**100** A3
**Queen Victoria Meml Hospl**
AL6 ............**89** B4
**Queen's Cl** CM21 .......**97** F4
**Queen's Ct**
Aspenden SG9 ........**40** D5
Hertford SG13 ........**113** D5
St Albans AL1 ........**128** B3
**Queen's Dr** EN8 .......**163** A5
**Queen's Dr The** WD3 ...**165** A3
**Queen's Pl** WD17 ......**167** C6
**Queen's Rd**
Cheshunt EN8 ........**162** E6
Harpenden AL5 .......**107** B7
Hertford SG13 ........**113** D5
Watford WD17 .......**167** C6
**Queen's Sq The** HP2 ...**124** F4
**Queens Ave** WD18 .....**166** F5
**Queens Cl** 4 Luton LU1 ...**63** E6
Stansted Mountfitchet
CM24 ............**59** E8
**Queens Cres**
Bishop's Stortford CM23 ...**76** B4
St Albans AL4 .........**128** B6
**Queens Ct** Cheshunt EN8 ...**162** F5
14 Luton LU2 .........**45** D1
Watford WD17 .......**167** C6
**Queens Dr** WD5 .......**153** F7
**Queens Head Wlk** EN4 ...**148** E8
**Queens Rd** Barnet EN5 ...**171** E6
Berkhamsted HP4 ......**122** A5
Royston SG8 .........**7** D7
Ware SG12 ..........**93** F2
**Queens Road Est** EN5 ...**171** D6
**Queens Silver Ct** HA6 ...**174** E4
**Queens Way**
Cheshunt EN8 ........**162** F5
Shenley WD7 .........**156** E7
**Queens' Sch** WD23 .....**168** A6
**Queensgate** EN8 .......**162** F5
**Queensgate Ctr** CM20 ...**117** F4
**Queensway**
Hemel Hempstead HP1,
HP2 ............**124** E4
Royston SG8 .........**7** D7
Stevenage SG1 .......**50** D5
**Queensway Ho** 1 AL10 ...**130** A4
**Queenswood Cres**
WD25 ...........**154** A6
**Queenswood Dr** SG4 ...**22** C1
**Queenswood Sch** AL9 ...**145** D3
**Quendell Wlk** HP2 .....**124** E3
**Quendon Dr** EN9 ......**163** D6
**Quickbeams** AL7 .......**90** A1
**Quickbury Farm** CM21 ...**98** B2
**Quickley La** WD3 ......**164** C4
**Quickley Rise** WD3 ....**164** C3
**Quickly Brow** WD3 ....**164** B3
**Quickmoor La** WD4 ....**152** C6
**Quickswood** LU3 .......**45** A7
**Quickwood** Cl WD3 ....**165** A3
**Quills** SG6 ...........**23** D4
**Quilter Cl** LU3 ........**44** F4
**Quin Ct** SG11 .........**55** F7
**Quinces Croft** HP1 .....**124** A5
**Quincey Rd** SG12 ......**93** C4
**Quinn Way** SG6 .......**23** C5
**Quinta Dr** EN5 ........**171** C4

**R**

**Raans Rd** HP6 .......**150** A1
**Raban Cl** SG2 ........**51** C1
**Raban Ct** SG7 ........**12** F1
**Rabley Heath Rd** AL6 ...**68** B2
**Rackman Dr** LU3 ......**45** C5
**Radburn Cnr** SG6 ......**23** C5
**Radburn Prim Sch** SG6 ...**23** C5
**Radburn Way** SG6 .....**23** C4
**Radcliffe Rd** SG5 ......**35** A8
**Radlett Inf Sch** WD7 ...**156** B3

**Radlett La**
London Colney AL2 .....**141** E2
Watford WD24 .......**167** D7
**Radlett Lodge Sch** WD7 ...**156** B8
**Radlett Park Rd** WD7 ...**156** A4
**Radlett Prep Sch** WD7 ...**156** C1
**Radlett Rd**
Aldenham WD7 .......**156** E6
Radlett WD7 .........**156** A4
**Radlett Sta** WD7 ......**156** A4
**Radnor Ct** HA3 .......**176** F2
**Radnor Rd** HA3 .......**176** F2
**Radstone Pl** LU2 ......**46** E1
**Radwell La** SG7 .......**12** C4
**Raebarn Gdns** EN5 ....**171** B4
**Raffin Cl** SG3 ........**69** E4
**Raffin Green La** SG3 ...**69** F4
**Raffin Pk** SG3 ........**69** E3
**Ragged Hall La** AL2 ...**140** E7
**Raglan Ave** EN8 ......**162** D5
**Raglan Gdns** WD19 ...**167** B1
**Raglan Ho** HP4 .......**122** A4
**Rags La** EN7 .........**147** E4
**Railway Pl** SG13 ......**113** E6
**Railway Rd** SG8 ......**162** F6
**Railway St** SG13,SG14 ...**113** D6
**Railway Terr** HP4 .....**139** A4
**Rainbow Cl** AL3 ......**105** F6
**Rainbow Ct** WD19 ....**167** C3
**Rainer Cl** EN8 .......**148** D2
**Rainsborough Ct** SG13 ...**114** A7
**Rainsford Rd** CM24 ...**59** E8
**Raleigh Cres** SG2 .....**51** B8
**Raleigh Gr** LU4 .......**44** D1
**Rally The** SG15 .......**11** A7
**Ralph Sadleir Mid Sch**
SG11 ............**55** E3
**Ralston Way** WD19 ...**175** D8
**Ram Gorse** CM20 .....**117** B2
**Ram Yard (Ind Est)** SG15 ...**11** A4
**Ramblers Way** AL7 ....**111** C5
**Rambling Way** HP4 ...**123** C6
**Ramerick Gdns** SG15 ...**11** A2
**Ramney Dr** EN3 ......**162** E2
**Ramridge Prim Sch** LU2 ...**46** B2
**Ramridge Rd** LU2 .....**46** A2
**Ramryge Ct** AL1 ......**127** D1
**Ramsay Cl** EN10 .....**134** E2
**Ramsbury Rd** AL1 ....**127** E2
**Ramsdell** SG1 ........**50** F5
**Ramsey Cl**
Brookmans Park AL9 ...**145** D4
St Albans AL1 ........**128** A1
**Ramsey Lodge Ct** 7
AL1 ............**127** E4
**Ramson Rise** HP1 .....**123** E2
**Rand's Cl** SG5 ........**21** B7
**Rand's Cotts** SG5 .....**21** B7
**Rand's Mdw** SG5 .....**21** B7
**Randalls Ride** HP2 ....**124** E5
**Randalls Wlk** AL2 .....**140** F1
**Randolph Ct** 3 HA5 ...**176** A3
**Randon Cl** HA2 .......**176** B1
**Ranelagh Rd** HP2 .....**125** B3
**Ranleigh Wlk** AL5 ....**107** D6
**Rannoch Wlk** HP2 ....**124** D7
**Ranock Cl** LU3 .......**44** D8
**Ranskill Rd** WD6 .....**170** A8
**Ransom Cl** Hitchin SG4 ...**34** F4
Watford WD19 .......**167** C2
**Rant Mdw**
Hemel Hempstead HP3 ...**125** A1
Hemel Hempstead HP3 ...**125** A2
**Ranulf Cl** CM17 ......**118** C6
**Ranworth Ave**
Hoddesdon EN11 .....**115** B2
Stevenage SG2 .......**69** C7
**Ranworth Cl** 2 HP3 ...**124** D1
**Ranworth Gdns** EN6 ...**158** D8
**Raphael Cl** WD7 ......**156** E7
**Raphael Dr** WD24 ....**167** D7
**Rapper Ct** LU3 .......**63** D8
**Rasehill Cl** WD3 ......**165** C4
**Rathlyn** HP3 .........**139** B8
**Ratty's La** EN11,CM19 ...**135** D6
**Raven Cl** WD3 .......**165** D2
**Raven Ct** AL10 .......**130** A4
**Ravenbank Rd** LU2 ...**46** C5
**Ravenfield Rd** AL7 ...**110** F6
**Ravenhill Way** LU4 ...**44** B4
**Ravens Cl** HP4 .......**122** E6
**Ravens La** HP4 .......**122** D4
**Ravens Wharf** 5 HP4 ...**122** D4
**Ravenscroft** Barnet EN5 ...**171** E5
Harpenden AL5 .......**107** D6
Hoddesdon EN10 .....**134** D1
Watford WD25 .......**154** E4
**Ravenscroft Pk** EN5 ...**171** D5
**Ravenscroft Sch & Tech Coll**
The N20 ............**171** F2
**Ravensdell** HP1 ......**123** F4
**Ravensthorpe** LU2 ....**46** B4
**Ravenswood Pk** HA6 ...**175** A4
**Rawdon Dr** EN11 .....**135** A5
**Ray's Hill** HP5 .......**120** C2
**Rayburn Rd** HP1 .....**124** A5
**Raydon Rd** EN8 ......**162** D7
**Rayfield** AL8 ........**89** D1
**Rayleigh Ho** WD5 ....**153** F7
**Raymer Cl** AL1 ......**127** E4
**Raymer Ct** 1 AL1 ....**127** E4
**Raymond Cl** WD5 ....**153** D7
**Raymond Cotts** SG5 ...**21** E4
**Raymond Ct** EN6 .....**159** C5
**Raymonds Cl** AL7 ....**110** E4
**Raymonds Plain** AL7 ...**110** E4
**Raynham Cl** CM23 ....**77** C8
**Raynham Rd** CM23 ...**76** B8
**Raynham St** SG13 ....**113** E6

**Raynham Way** LU2 ....**46** D1
**Raynsford Rd** SG12 ...**93** E1
**Raynton Rd** EN3 ......**162** D2
**Readings The** WD3 ...**164** F6
**Recreation Ground** CM24 **59** E6
**Rectory Cl**
Bishop's Stortford CM23 ...**76** D3
Essendon AL9 ........**131** F6
Hunsdon SG12 .......**116** D8
**Rectory Dr** CM23 .....**58** D6
**Rectory Gdns** AL10 ...**130** B5
**Rectory La**
Berkhamsted HP4 .....**122** C4
Datchworth SG3 ......**69** C2
Farnham CM23 .......**58** D6
Kings Langley WD4 ...**139** A3
Lilley LU2 ..........**32** D2
Rickmansworth WD3 ...**165** D1
Shenley WD7 ........**157** B7
Stevenage SG1 .......**36** D3
Watton at S SG14 .....**70** D3
**Rectory Rd**
Rickmansworth WD3 ...**165** D2
Welwyn Garden City AL8 ...**89** B1
**Rectory Wood** CM20 ...**117** C1
**Red Brick Cotts** SG11 ...**57** B1
**Red Cottage** HP23 ....**100** D1
**Red Cow Cotts** LU6 ...**83** C8
**Red House Cl** SG12 ...**114** E8
**Red Lion** WD25 ......**155** C2
**Red Lion Cotts** SG5 ...**33** C2
**Red Lion Ct** 5 CM23 ...**77** A7
**Red Lion La**
Hemel Hempstead HP3 ...**139** A5
Sarratt WD3 .........**152** A4
**Red Lodge** WD6 ......**169** F6
**Red Lodge Gdns** HP4 ...**122** A3
**Red Rails** LU1 .......**63** C5
**Red Rails Ct** LU1 .....**63** C5
**Red Rd** WD6 .........**169** F6
**Redan Rd** SG12 ......**93** E3
**Redbrick Row** CM22 ...**98** B8
**Redcar Dr** SG1 .......**50** A6
**Redcote La** AL5 ......**107** A7
**Redding Ho** WD18 ...**166** E5
**Redding La** AL3 ......**105** F8
**Reddings**
Hemel Hempstead HP3 ...**125** A1
Welwyn Garden City AL8 ...**110** C7
**Reddings Ave** WD23 ...**168** B4
**Reddings Prim Sch The**
HP3 ............**125** A1
**Redditch Ct** HP2 ......**124** F7
**Redferns Cl** LU1 ......**63** A6
**Redferns Ct** LU1 ......**63** A6
**Redgrave Gdns** LU3 ...**44** F7
**Redhall Cl** AL10 ......**129** F1
**Redhall Dr** AL10 ......**129** F1
**Redhall La**
Colney Heath AL4 .....**129** E1
Sarratt WD3 .........**165** E8
**Redheath Cl** WD25 ...**153** F4
**Redhoods Way E** SG6 ...**22** E7
**Redhoods Way W** SG6 ...**22** E6
**Redhouse The** EN10 ...**134** F1
**Redlands Rd** EN3 .....**162** E1
**Redmire Cl** LU4 ......**44** B6
**Redoubt** Cl SG4 ......**22** A1
**Redpole Ct** WD3 .....**165** E1
**Redricks La** CM21 ....**118** A6
**Redvers Cl** CM23 .....**59** A2
**Redwell St** EN8 ......**162** F5
**Redwing Cl** SG2 ......**51** D4
**Redwing Gr** WD5 ....**154** A8
**Redwing Rise** SG8 ....**7** E8
**Redwood Cl** WD19 ...**175** D6
**Redwood Dr**
Hemel Hempstead HP3 ...**124** E1
Luton LU3 ..........**44** C8
**Redwood Rise** WD6 ...**157** B2
**Redwood Way** EN5 ...**171** D4
**Redwoods** Hertford SG14 **113** C7
Welwyn Garden City AL8 ...**89** D4
**Reed Cl** AL2 .........**142** E4
**Reed Fst Sch** SG8 .....**16** E5
**Reed Pl** AL5 .........**85** F3
**Reedham Cl** AL2 .....**141** A2
**Reedings Jun Sch** CM21 **97** E3
**Reedings Way** CM21 ...**97** F4
**Reeds Chapel** 12 WD24 ...**167** C7
**Reeds Cres** WD24 ....**167** C7
**Reeds Dale** LU2 ......**46** C2
**Reeds The** AL7 .......**110** D5
**Reeves Ave** LU3 ......**45** B4
**Reeves Pightle** SG8 ...**9** F3
**Regal Cl** SG11 .......**55** E2
**Regal Ct** 4 Hitchin SG5 ...**34** F8
Tring HP23 ..........**100** A3
**Regal Way** WD24 ....**154** C1
**Regency Cl** CM23 .....**76** E7
**Regency Ct**
Hemel Hempstead HP2 ...**124** D3
Hoddesdon EN10 .....**148** F8
St Albans AL1 ........**128** B3

**Regency Ct** *continued*
Watford WD17 .......**167** A8
**Regency Ho** WD7 .....**156** A4
**Regent Cl**
Kings Langley WD4 ...**139** A3
St Albans AL4 ........**128** C7
Welwyn Garden City AL7 ...**110** E5
**Regent Ct** SG5 .......**11** F7
**Regent Gate** EN8 .....**162** E5
**Regent St** Luton LU1 ...**63** F7
Stotfold SG5 .........**11** F7
Watford WD24 .......**154** B1
**Regent's Ct** HA5 .....**175** D1
**Regents Cl** WD7 ......**156** A5
**Regina Cl** EN5 .......**171** D6
**Reginald Mews** CM17 ...**118** C1
**Reginald Rd** LU2 .....**174** F3
**Reginald St** LU2 .....**45** E1
**Regis Ave** AL1 .......**141** D7
**Remus Ct** AL1 .......**141** D7
**Rendlesham Ave** WD7 ...**155** F2
**Rendlesham Cl** SG12 ...**93** B2
**Rendlesham Rd** EN2 ...**161** B1
**Rendlesham Way** WD3 ...**164** C3
**Rennie** EN3 .........**163** A1
**Rennison Cl** EN7 .....**147** A1
**Renshaw Cl** LU2 .....**46** E2
**Repton Cl** LU3 .......**44** F6
**Repton Gn** AL3 ......**127** D6
**Repton Way** WD3 ....**166** A4
**Reson Way** HP1 .....**124** B2
**Reston Path**
Borehamwood WD6 ...**157** A1
Luton LU2 ..........**46** E2
**Retford Cl** WD6 ......**157** A1
**Retreat The** WD5 ....**153** C8
**Revels Cl** SG14 ......**113** D8
**Revels Rd** SG14 .....**113** D8
**Reynard Copse** CM23 ...**58** F1
**Reynard Way** SG13 ...**114** B6
**Reynard's Way** AL2 ...**140** F3
**Reynards Rd** AL6 ....**89** C7
**Reynolds** SG6 .......**11** F1
**Reynolds Cl** HP1 .....**124** A4
**Reynolds Cres** AL3 ...**128** B8
**Rhee Spring** SG7 .....**13** B1
**Rhodes Ave** CM23 ....**76** F5
**Rhodes Meml Mus &**
**Commonwealth Ctr**★
CM23 ...........**77** A6
**Rhodes Way** WD24 ...**167** D8
**Rhymes** HP1 ........**124** B5
**Rib Cl** SG11 .........**55** E2
**Rib Vale** SG14 ......**92** D1
**Rib Way** SG9 ........**40** C2
**Ribbledale** AL2 ......**142** F4
**Ribblesdale** HP2 ....**124** E6
**Ribocon Way** LU4 ...**44** B7
**Ribston Ct** WD7 .....**156** D6
**Riccat La** SG1 ......**36** F3
**Rice Cl** HP2 ........**124** F4
**Richard Ct** 1 EN5 ...**171** E6
**Richard Hale Sch** SG13 ...**113** D6
**Richard Stagg Cl** AL1 ...**128** C1
**Richard Wittington Prim Sch**
The CM23 .........**76** E4
**Richards Cl**
Bushey WD23 .......**168** D2
Luton LU1 ..........**63** B6
**Richards Ct** LU1 ....**63** B5
**Richards St** AL10 ...**129** E7
**Richardson Cl** AL2 ...**142** E4
**Richardson Cres** EN7 ...**147** B4
**Richardson Pl** AL4 ...**129** B1
**Richfield Rd** WD23 ...**168** C2
**Richmond Cl**
Bishop's Stortford CM23 ...**76** C7
Borehamwood WD6 ...**170** D4
Cheshunt EN8 .......**148** C2
Ware SG12 ..........**93** B3
**Richmond Ct**
4 Hatfield AL10 ......**130** B3
Hoddesdon EN10 .....**134** F3
Luton LU2 ..........**45** F1
Potters Bar EN6 .....**159** C8
St Albans AL1 ........**128** A3
**Richmond Dr** WD17 ...**166** E7
**Richmond Gdns** HA3 ...**176** F1
**Richmond Hill** LU2 ...**45** E2
**Richmond Hill Sch** LU2 ...**45** E2
**Richmond Rd** EN6 ...**159** C8
**Richmond Way** WD3 ...**166** C5
**Richmond Wlk** AL4 ...**128** D7
**Rickfield Cl** AL10 ....**130** A3
**Rickmansworth La** SL9 ...**172** A5
**Rickmansworth Park Jun Mix**
**Inf Sch** WD3 ......**165** D2
**Rickmansworth Rd**
Chorleywood WD3 ...**164** F6
Harefield UB9 .......**173** D3
Northwood HA6 .....**174** D3
Pinner HA5 .........**175** C1
Watford WD18 .......**166** E5
**Rickmansworth Sch**
WD3 ............**165** D3
**Rickmansworth Sta**
WD3 ............**165** D2
**Rickyard The** Ashwell SG7 ...**4** D3
Letchworth SG6 .....**12** C1
**Rickyard Mdw** AL3 ...**106** A5
**Riddell Gdns** SG7 ....**23** F8
**Riddy Hill Cl** SG4 ...**35** A6
**Riddy La** Hitchin SG4 ...**35** A6
Luton LU3 ..........**45** C5
**Riddy The** SG4 ......**88** F8
**Ridge Ave** Harpenden AL5 **85** E4
St Albans AL1 ........**128** B3

**Ridge Ct** LU2 .......**46** A1
**Ridge La** WD17 ......**153** F2
**Ridge Lea** HP1 .......**123** F2
**Ridge Rd** SG6 .......**23** A6
**Ridge St** WD24 ......**154** B1
**Ridge The** Barnet EN5 ...**171** F4
Letchworth SG6 .....**23** A6
Northwood HA6 .....**174** F3
**Ridge View** HP23 ....**100** C5
**Ridge Way** WD3 .....**165** B2
**Ridgedown** AL3 .....**106** A5
**Ridgefield** WD17 ....**153** F5
**Ridgehurst Ave** WD25 ...**153** F5
**Ridgeleigh Ct** 3 EN5 ...**171** E6
**Ridgeview** EN5 ......**171** D3
**Ridgeway**
Berkhamsted HP4 ....**121** F4
Harpenden AL5 ......**85** E4
Kensworth Common LU6 ...**82** E8
Little Hadham SG11 ...**57** F3
London Colney WD7 ...**156** C8
Stevenage SG1 .......**50** F5
Welwyn Garden City AL7 ...**111** B6
**Ridgeway Cl** HP3 ....**138** F5
**Ridgeway Ct** HA5 ...**176** A3
**Ridgeway The**
Codicote SG4 ........**67** F1
Cuffley EN6 .........**146** A4
Hadley Wood EN2,EN4 ...**160** D3
Hertford SG14 .......**112** F7
Hitchin SG5 .........**34** D6
Radlett WD7 ........**155** F2
St Albans AL4 ........**128** C7
Ware SG12 ..........**93** C3
Watford WD17 .......**153** E2
**Ridgewood Dr** AL5 ...**85** E4
**Ridgewood Gdns** AL5 ...**85** E4
**Ridgmont Rd** AL1 ...**127** E2
**Ridgway Rd** LU2 ....**45** F1
**Ridings The**
Bishop's Stortford CM23 ...**76** D4
Hertford SG14 ......**113** A6
Latimer HP5 ........**150** D3
Luton LU3 ..........**45** C1
Markyate AL3 .......**83** E6
Stevenage SG2 ......**51** B3
**Ridler Rd** EN1 ......**161** C1
**Ridlins End** SG2 ....**51** C2
**Rigby Pl** EN3 ......**163** A2
**Rigery La** SG11 .....**73** A7
**Riley Rd** EN3 ......**162** C1
**Ringmer Ct** LU2 ....**46** C3
**Ringshall Dr** HP4 ...**102** C8
**Ringshall Rd** HP4 ...**81** B3
**Ringtale Pl** SG7 .....**13** B1
**Ringway Rd** AL2 ....**141** C4
**Ringwood Rd** LU2 ...**45** D7
**Ripley Rd** Enfield EN2 ...**161** C1
Luton LU4 ..........**44** B4
**Ripley Way** Cheshunt EN7 **148** B1
Hemel Hempstead HP1 ...**123** E4
**Ripon Rd** SG1 .......**37** A2
**Ripon Way**
Borehamwood WD6 ...**170** D4
St Albans AL4 ........**128** D7
**Rise Cotts** SG12 .....**95** D2
**Rise The** Baldock SG7 ...**23** E7
Borehamwood WD6 ...**169** F4
Harrow HA3 ........**176** C1
Park Street AL2 ......**141** D6
**Risedale Cl** HP3 .....**138** E8
**Risedale Hill** HP3 ...**138** E8
**Risedale Rd** HP3 ....**138** E8
**Rising Hill Cl** HA6 ...**174** C4
**Risingholme Cl**
Bushey WD23 .......**168** B2
Harrow HA3 ........**176** E1
**Risingholme Rd** HA3 ...**176** E1
**Ritcroft Cl** HP3 .....**125** B2
**Ritcroft Dr** HP3 .....**125** B2
**Ritcroft St** HP3 .....**125** B2
**Ritz Ct** EN6 ........**159** A8
**Rivenhall End** AL7 ...**111** C6
**River Ave** EN11 .....**135** B7
**River Cl** EN8 ........**163** A5
**River Ct** Ickleford SG5 ...**21** F4
Sacombe SG12 .......**92** E4
Sawbridgeworth CM21 ...**97** F3
**River Gn** Gn SG9 .....**40** E8
**River Hill** AL3 ......**84** B2
**River Lee Ctry Pk**★ EN9 **149** B1
**River Mead** SG5 .....**21** C2
**River Meads** SG12 ...**115** C4
**River Park Ind Est** HP4 ...**122** A5
**River Pk** HP1 .......**124** A1
**River St** SG12 ......**93** E1
**River View** AL7 .....**89** F2
**River Way** Harlow CM20 **118** B5
Luton LU4 ..........**44** E5
**Riverbank** HP1 ......**124** B7
**Riverbanks Cl** AL5 ...**86** C4
**Riverfield La** CM21 ...**97** E3
**Riverford Cl** AL5 ....**86** B4
**Rivermill** CM20 .....**117** C2
**Rivermill Ct** SG8 .....**7** C7
**Rivers Hospl The** CM21 **97** C1
**Riversend Rd** HP3 ...**138** C8
**Rivershill** SG11 .....**70** E3
**Riverside**
Bishop's Stortford CM23 ...**76** F7
Buntingford SG9 .....**40** E7
Hemel Hempstead HP3 ...**138** F6
Hertford SG14 ......**113** D6
London Colney AL2 ...**142** E4
Welwyn AL6 .........**89** B5
**Riverside Ave** EN10 ...**135** A1
**Riverside Bsns Pk** CM24 **59** E6

**Riverside Cl**
Kings Langley WD4 ....**139** B2
St Albans AL1 ...........**127** E1
**Riverside Club** (Tennis Ctr)
The HA6 ................**174** B3
**Riverside Cotts** SG12 ...**115** C4
**Riverside Ct**
Harlow CM20 ...........**118** C6
St Albans AL1 ...........**127** E1
**Riverside Dr** WD3 .......**165** D1
**Riverside Est** AL5 .......**86** C4
**Riverside Gdns** HP4 ....**122** A5
**Riverside Mews**
Hoddesdon EN10 .......**148** E8
**10** Ware SG12 ...........**93** D1
**Riverside Path** EN8 ....**148** C2
**Riverside Rd** Luton LU3 ...**45** A5
St Albans AL1 ...........**127** E2
Watford WD19 ..........**167** B3
**Riverside Wlk 16** CM23 ...**76** F7
**Riversmead** EN11 ......**135** A5
**Riversmeet** SG14 .......**113** B5
**Rivett Cl** SG7 ...........**13** A1
**Roan Wlk** SG8 ............**7** E6
**Roaring Meg Ret Pk** SG1 **50** E3
**Robbery Bottom La** AL6 ...**90** A8
**Robbs Cl** HP1 ...........**124** A5
**Robe End** HP1 ...........**123** F5
**Robert Allen Ct 3** LU1 ...**63** E6
**Robert Ave** AL1 ........**141** C7
**Robert Cl** EN6 ...........**92** A5
**Robert Humbert Ho** SG6 ...**23** A5
**Robert Saunders Ct** SG6 ...**22** E4
**Robert Tebbutt Ct** SG5 ...**34** E6
**Robert Wallace Cl** CM23 ...**58** F1
**Roberts Cl** EN8 .........**148** E1
**Roberts La** SL9 .........**172** B5
**Roberts Rd** WD18 .......**167** C4
**Roberts Way** AL10 ......**129** F3
**Roberts Wood Dr** SL9 ...**172** A5
**Robertson Cl** EN10 .....**148** E5
**Robertson Rd 11** HP4 ...**122** D4
**Robeson Way** WD6 ......**170** C8
**Robin Cl** SG12 ..........**115** C3
**Robin Ct** AL5 ............**86** B4
**Robin Hill** HP4 ..........**122** C4
**Robin Hood Dr**
Harrow HA3 .............**176** F3
Watford WD17 ...........**167** F8
**Robin Hood La** AL10 .....**130** A6
**Robin Hood Mdw** HP2 ....**124** F8
**Robin Mead** AL7 ..........**90** A1
**Robin Way** EN6 .........**146** E3
**Robina Cl** HA6 ..........**174** F2
**Robins Cl** AL2 ..........**142** E4
**Robins Nest Hill** SG13 ...**132** C6
**Robins Rd** HP3 ..........**125** A1
**Robins The** CM17 .......**118** C6
**Robins Way** AL10 .......**129** F2
**Robinsfield** HP1 ........**124** A3
**Robinson Ave** EN7 ......**147** B3
**Robinson Cl** CM23 .......**76** F5
**Robinson Cres** WD23 ...**168** C1
**Robinsway** EN9 .........**163** E5
**Robinswood** LU2 ........**45** E5
**Robsons Ct** EN8 ........**148** C2
**Rochdale Ct 6** LU1 ......**63** E6
**Rochester Ave** LU2 ......**46** C4
**Rochester Dr** WD25 .....**154** C4
**Rochester Way**
Croxley Green WD3 ......**166** B5
Royston SG8 .............**7** D8
**Rochford Ave** EN9 ......**163** D5
**Rochford Cl**
Cheshunt EN8 ..........**148** E5
Stansted Mountfitchet
CM24 ..................**59** E5
**Rochford Dr** LU2 .........**46** E2
**Rochford Ho** EN9 .......**163** D6
**Rochford Rd** CM23 .......**59** C1
**Rock Rd** SG8 .............**7** C8
**Rockfield Ave** SG12 .....**93** D3
**Rockingham Gate**
WD23 ..................**168** C3
**Rockingham Way** SG1 ...**50** E4
**Rockleigh** SG14 ........**113** C6
**Rockley Rd** LU1 .........**63** A7
**Rockliffe Ave** WD4 .....**139** A1
**Rockways** EN5 ..........**170** F3
**Rodeheath** LU4 .........**44** D3
**Roden Cl** CM17 .........**118** F4
**Rodgers Cl** WD6 ........**169** D3
**Rodings Row** EN5 ......**171** E5
**Rodney Ave** AL1 ........**128** A1
**Rodney Cres** EN11 ......**135** A8
**Rodwell Yd** HP23 .......**100** A3
**Roe Cl** SG5 .............**11** E5
**Roe End La** AL3 ..........**83** B4
**Roe Green Cl** AL10 ......**129** F4
**Roe Green Ctr** AL10 .....**129** F4
**Roe Green La** AL10 ......**129** F5
**Roe Hill Cl** AL10 ........**129** F4
**Roebuck**
Hertford SG13 ..........**114** A6
Luton LU1 ...............**63** B6
**Roebuck Ct 1** SG2 ......**50** F1
**Roebuck Gate** SG2 ......**50** F1
**Roebuck Prim Sch** SG2 ...**50** F2
**Roebuck Ret Pk** SG1 .....**50** E2
**Roecroft Lower Sch** SG5 ...**11** F6
**Roedean Ave** EN3 .......**162** C1
**Roedean Cl** LU2 .........**46** D3
**Roedean Ho 3** WD24 ...**167** C7
**Roefields Cl** HP3 .......**138** A7
**Roehyde Way** AL10 ......**129** E1
**Roestock Gdns** AL4 .....**129** E1
**Roestock La** AL4 ........**129** E1
**Rofant Rd** HA6 ..........**174** E4

**Rogate Rd** LU2 ..........**46** C5
**Roger de Clare Sch** SG11 **55** E2
**Roger's La** SG9 ..........**29** A5
**Rogers Cl** EN7 .........**147** D4
**Rogers Ruff** HA6 .......**174** C2
**Rokewood Mews 3**
SG12 ...................**93** D2
**Roland St** AL1 ..........**128** B2
**Rolleston Cl** SG12 .......**93** C3
**Rollswood** AL7 .........**110** E3
**Rollswood Rd** AL6 .......**89** B8
**Rollys La** SG7 .............**4** D4
**Roman Cl** UB9 ..........**173** B2
**Roman Gdns** WD4 ......**139** B1
**Roman Ho**
London Colney AL2 .....**142** D4
Watford WD18 ..........**166** E5
**Roman La** SG7 ..........**24** D4
**Roman Mews 7** EN11 ...**135** A7
**Roman Rd** LU4 ..........**44** E3
**Roman Rise** CM21 .......**97** D2
**Roman St 8** EN11 ......**135** A7
**Roman Vale** CM17 ......**118** C5
**Roman Way** Markyate AL3 **83** E6
Standon SG11 ...........**55** D5
Waltham Abbey EN9 ....**163** B4
Welwyn AL6 .............**89** C6
**Roman Way Fst Sch** SG8 ...**7** D4
**Romans End** AL3 .......**127** C1
**Romany Cl** SG6 ..........**22** C6
**Romany Ct** HP2 .........**125** C4
**Romeland** Elstree WD6 ...**169** D1
St Albans AL3 ...........**127** C3
Waltham Abbey EN9 ....**163** C4
**Romeland Hill** AL3 .....**127** C3
**Romilly Dr** WD19 .......**175** D4
**Rondini Ave** LU3 ........**45** B3
**Ronsons Way** AL4 ......**127** F7
**Rook Tree Cl** SG5 .......**12** A6
**Rook Tree La** SG5 .......**12** A6
**Rookery Dr** LU2 .........**45** C4
**Rookery The**
Hatfield AL9 ............**144** D8
Stansted Mountfitchet
CM24 ..................**59** E8
Westmill SG9 ...........**40** F1
**Rookery Yd** SG1 .........**50** C7
**Rookes Cl** AL8 .........**110** D5
**Rooks Hill**
Rickmansworth WD3 ....**165** D5
Welwyn Garden City AL8 ...**110** C5
**Rooks Nest Cotts** SG1 ...**36** E2
**Rooks Nest Farm** SG1 ...**36** E2
**Rooks Nest La** SG8 ......**16** A5
**Rookwood Dr** SG2 .......**51** B1
**Rosary Ct** EN6 .........**145** B1
**Rosary Gdns** WD23 .....**168** E6
**Rose Acre** Pimlico HP3 ...**139** E6
Redbourn AL3 ..........**105** F6
**Rose Cotts** Arlesey SG15 ...**11** A6
Bricket Wood AL2 .......**141** B1
Meesden SG9 ...........**30** A5
Wyddial SG9 ............**28** A3
**Rose Ct**
Hammond Street EN7 ...**148** A4
St Albans AL4 ..........**128** C5
**Rose Garden Mews**
WD3 ...................**165** B5
**Rose Gdns** WD18 .......**167** A4
**Rose La** Essendon AL9 ...**131** C5
Wheathampstead AL4 ...**87** C2
**Rose Lawn** WD23 .......**168** C1
**Rose Mdw** SG11 ........**41** E4
**Rose Mead** EN6 ........**145** C1
**Rose Vale** EN11 ........**135** A6
**Rose Wlk** Royston SG8 ....**7** C7
St Albans AL4 ..........**128** C5
**Rose Wlk The** WD7 .....**156** B3
**Rose Wood Cl** LU2 .......**45** F3
**Roseacre Gdns** AL7 .....**111** D6
**Roseacres** CM21 ........**97** D3
**Rosebank** EN9 .........**163** E6
**Rosebarn La** HP23 ......**79** D1
**Roseberry Ct** WD17 .....**167** A8
**Rosebery** CM23 .........**77** C6
**Rosebery Ave** AL5 ......**85** F1
**Rosebery Mews** LU7 ....**61** D4
**Rosebery Rd** WD23 .....**168** B2
**Rosebery Way** HP23 ....**100** B5
**Rosebriar Wlk** WD24 ...**153** F3
**Rosecroft Ct** HA6 ......**174** C4
**Rosecroft Dr** WD17 .....**153** E3
**Rosecroft La** AL6 .......**90** A8
**Rosedale** AL7 ...........**89** F2
**Rosedale Ave** EN7 .....**147** F2
**Rosedale Cl**
Bricket Wood AL2 .......**140** E1
Luton LU3 ..............**44** C7
**Rosedale Way** EN7 .....**148** A3
**Rosehatch** HP1 .........**123** E4
**Rosehill** HP4 ...........**122** B4
**Rosehill Cl** EN11 .......**134** F6
**Rosehill Ct** HP1 ........**124** A1
**Rosehill Gdns** WD5 .....**153** C7
**Roselands Ave** EN11 ....**114** F1
**Roselands Prim Sch**
EN11 ..................**114** F1
**Roseley Cotts** CM20 ....**117** B4
**Rosemary Cl 3** CM17 ...**118** C4
**Rosemary Ct 2** HA5 ....**176** A3
**Rosemont Cl** SG6 .......**22** E6
**Rosemoor Cl** AL7 .......**110** F5
**Rosewood Ct** HP1 ......**123** E4
**Rosewood Dr** EN2 ......**161** A4
**Roslyn Cl** EN10 ........**134** E2
**Ross Cl** Hatfield AL10 ...**130** A8
Luton LU1 ...............**63** B6

**Ross Cl** continued
Stanmore HA3 ..........**176** C3
**Ross Cres** WD25 ........**154** A4
**Ross Ct** SG2 ............**51** B7
**Ross Haven Pl** HA6 .....**174** F2
**Ross Rd** WD25 ..........**154** C4
**Ross Way** HA6 .........**174** F6
**Rossdale Cl** EN2 .......**161** B3
**Rossendale Prim Sch** HP1 **124** A5
**Rossfold Rd** LU3 ........**44** D8
**Rossgate** HP1 ..........**124** A5
**Rossgate Prim Sch** HP1 **124** A5
**Rossington Ave** WD6 ...**156** E1
**Rossington Cl** EN1 .....**162** B1
**Rossiter Fields** EN5 ....**171** F3
**Rosslyn Cres** LU3 .......**45** C5
**Rosslyn Rd** WD18 ......**167** B6
**Rossway** LU1 ...........**63** B1
**Rossway Dr** WD23 .....**168** D4
**Rossway La** HP4 .......**121** A7
**Roswell Cl** EN8 .........**148** E1
**Rotham Rd** WD25 .......**154** C5
**Rother Cl** WD25 ........**154** C5
**Rotheram Ave** LU1 ......**63** B5
**Rotherfield** LU2 .........**46** D3
**Rotherfield Rd** EN3 .....**162** D2
**Rothesay Ct** HP4 .......**122** A4
**Rothesay Rd** LU1 .......**63** D7
**Roughdown Ave** HP3 ...**138** A8
**Roughdown Rd** HP3 .....**138** B8
**Roughdown Villas** HP3 ...**138** A8
**Roughdown Villas Rd**
HP3 ...................**138** A8
**Roughs The** HA6 .......**174** B2
**Roughwood Cl** WD17 ...**153** E1
**Round Diamond Prim Sch**
SG1 ...................**37** B3
**Round Mead** SG2 .......**51** D3
**Roundabout Ho** HA6 ....**175** A2
**Roundabout La** AL6 .....**89** F8
**Roundcroft** EN7 ........**147** F5
**Roundhaye** SG1 ........**50** C7
**Roundhedge Way** EN2 ...**160** F1
**Roundhills** SG13 .......**163** E4
**Roundings The** SG13 ...**114** C2
**Roundmoor Dr** EN8 .....**148** E2
**Roundway The** WD18 ...**166** F2
**Roundwood** HP3 .......**138** E4
**Roundwood Cl**
Hitchin SG4 ............**22** C2
Oaklands AL6 ...........**89** D8
**Roundwood Ct** AL5 .....**85** F3
**Roundwood Dr** AL8 .....**110** C7
**Roundwood Gdns** AL5 ...**85** E2
**Roundwood La** AL5 .....**85** D3
**Roundwood Park Sch**
AL5 ...................**85** E2
**Roundwood Pk** AL5 .....**85** E3
**Roundwood Prim Sch**
AL5 ...................**85** E2
**Rounton Rd** EN9 .......**163** E6
**Rousebarn La** WD3 .....**166** C7
**Row The** HP5 ..........**120** D2
**Rowan Cl**
Bricket Wood AL2 ......**155** A8
Harrow HA7 ............**176** F4
Luton LU1 ...............**63** B7
Shenley WD7 ..........**156** E6
St Albans AL4 ..........**128** E3
Weston SG4 ............**37** B8
**Rowan Cres**
Letchworth SG6 ........**22** E7
Stevenage SG1 .........**50** E2
**Rowan Dr** EN10 ........**148** F6
**Rowan Gr** SG4 ..........**35** A4
**Rowan Way** AL5 .......**107** C8
**Rowan Wlk**
**2** Hatfield AL10 .......**130** A2
Sawbridgeworth CM21 ...**97** E2
**Rowans** AL7 ............**90** A1
**Rowans Prim Sch The**
AL7 ...................**90** A1
**Rowans The** Baldock SG7 ...**23** E7
Hemel Hempstead HP1 ...**124** A3
Hoddesdon EN10 .......**134** F4
**Rowbeech Cotts** LU6 ....**83** C8
**Rowbourne Pl** EN6 ......**146** D3
**Rowcroft** HP1 ..........**123** E2
**Rowel Field** LU2 ........**46** C1
**Rowington Cl** LU2 ......**46** E2
**Rowland Pl** HA6 ........**174** E3
**Rowland Rd** SG1 ........**50** F4
**Rowland Way** SG6 ......**22** F6
**Rowlands Ave** HA5 .....**176** B4
**Rowlands Cl** EN8 ......**148** D1
**Rowlands Ct 3** EN8 ....**148** D1
**Rowlatt Cl** AL1 .........**127** E4
**Rowlatt Dr** AL3 ........**127** A1
**Rowley Cl** WD19 .......**167** E3
**Rowley Gdns** EN8 .....**148** D3
**Rowley Green Rd** EN5 ...**171** A4
**Rowley La** Barnet EN5 ...**170** F5
Borehamwood WD6 ....**170** D4
**Rowley Wlk** HP2 .......**125** C8
**Rowley's Rd** SG13 .....**113** F7
**Rowney Gdns** CM21 ....**118** C8
**Rowney La** SG2 .........**72** B5
**Rowney Wood** CM21 ...**97** C1
**Rows The** CM20 ........**117** D1
**Roxley Cotts** SG6 ......**23** B2
**Roxley Manor** SG6 ......**36** B8
**Roy Rd** HA6 ...........**174** F3
**Royal Ave** EN8 ........**162** E6
**Royal Cl** Aldbury HP23 ...**101** A5
Hemel Hempstead HP3 ...**138** E8

**Royal Masonic Sch for Girls**
WD3 ...................**165** D4
**Royal National Orthopaedic**
Hospl HA7 ..............**169** B1
**Royal Oak Cl** SG9 .......**27** D5
**Royal Oak Gdns 6** CM23 **76** F6
**Royal Oak La** SG5 .......**20** D4
**Royal Rd** AL1 ..........**128** B3
**Royal Veterinary Coll**
AL9 ...................**144** D3
**Royce Cl** EN10 .........**134** F2
**Royce Gr** WD25 ........**153** F5
**Roydon Cl** LU4 .........**44** A4
**Roydon Ct** HP2 ........**105** A1
**Roydon Lodge Chalet Est**
CM19 ..................**116** C1
**Roydon Mill** CM19 ......**116** A1
**Roydon Mill Leisure Pk**
CM19 ..................**116** A1
**Roydon Rd** Harlow CM19 ...**116** E1
Stanstead Abbotts SG12 ...**115** E4
**Roydon Sta** CM19 ......**116** B2
**Royse Gr** SG8 ...........**7** D4
**Roysia Mid Sch** SG8 .....**7** D7
**Royston & District Mus** ✱
SG8 ....................**7** C6
**Royston Cl** SG14 ......**113** B6
**Royston Gr** HA5 .......**176** A4
**Royston Hospl** SG8 ......**7** D4
**Royston Park Rd** HA5 ...**176** A5
**Royston Rd** Baldock SG7 ...**13** D2
Barkway SG8 ...........**17** C5
Barley SG8 .............**8** F3
St Albans AL1 ..........**128** B2
Royston Sta SG8 ........**7** C7
**Rubin Pl** EN3 ..........**163** A4
**Rucklers La** WD4 ......**138** C4
**Ruckles Ct** SG1 ........**50** E5
**Rudd Cl** SG2 ...........**51** B3
**Rudham Gr** SG6 ........**23** C3
**Rudolf Steiner Sch**
WD4 ...................**138** E2
**Rudolph Rd** WD23 ......**168** A3
**Rudyard Cl** LU4 ........**44** D3
**Rue de St Lawrence**
EN9 ...................**163** C5
**Rueley Dell Rd** LU2 .....**32** D2
**Rufford Cl** WD17 .......**153** F2
**Rugby Way** WD3 .......**166** B4
**Ruins The** AL3 .........**106** B5
**Rumballs Cl** HP3 .......**139** A8
**Rumballs Ct** CM23 ......**76** C4
**Rumballs Rd** HP3 .......**139** A8
**Rumbold Rd** EN11 .....**135** C8
**Rumsley** EN7 ..........**148** A4
**Runcie Cl** AL4 .........**128** A7
**Runcorn Cres** HP2 .....**124** F7
**Rundells** SG6 ..........**23** D4
**Runfold Ave** LU3 .......**45** A5
**Runham Rd** HP3 .......**124** E1
**Runley Rd** LU1 .........**62** F7
**Runnalow** SG6 ........**22** E7
**Runsell Rise** LU1 .......**63** D6
**Runsley** AL7 ...........**90** A1
**Runswick Ct** SG1 .......**50** A7
**Runway The** AL10 .....**129** E7
**Ruscombe Dr** AL2 .....**141** C5
**Rush Cl** SG12 .........**115** C4
**Rush Dr** EN9 ..........**163** C3
**Rushall Gn** LU2 ........**46** E2
**Rushby Mead** SG6 ......**23** A5
**Rushby Pl** SG6 .........**23** A5
**Rushby Wlk** SG6 .......**23** A6
**Rushden Rd** SG9 .......**26** A3
**Rushen Dr** SG13 .......**114** C2
**Rushendon Furlong** LU7 ...**80** E5
**Rushes Ct** CM23 ........**77** A5
**Rushfield**
Potters Bar EN6 ........**158** E6
Sawbridgeworth CM21 ...**97** C2
**Rushfield Rd** SG12 ......**93** F3
**Rushleigh Ave** EN8 ....**148** D1
**Rushleigh Gn** CM23 ....**76** C4
**Rushmead Villas** CM20 **117** C3
**Rushmere Ct** HP3 ......**138** E7
**Rushmere La** HP5 ......**136** B3
**Rushmoor Cl** WD3 .....**173** D8
**Rushmore Cl** LU1 ......**62** E4
**Rushton Ave** WD25 .....**154** A4
**Rushton Ct** EN8 .......**148** D2
**Ruskin Ave** EN9 .......**163** E5
**Ruskin Cl** EN7 .........**147** E5
**Ruskin La** SG4 .........**35** C7
**Rusper Gn** LU2 .........**46** D3
**Russell Ave** AL3 .......**127** D3
**Russell Cl**
Kensworth Common LU6 ...**82** E8
Moor Park HA6 .........**174** C6
Stevenage SG2 .........**51** B2
**Russell Cres** WD25 .....**153** F4
**Russell Ct** AL2 ........**141** A1
**Russell La** WD17 .......**153** D3
**Russell Mead** HA3 .....**176** F2
**Russell Pl** HP3 ........**138** B8
**Russell Rd** Enfield EN1 ...**161** F1
Moor Park HA6 .........**174** C6
**Russell St** Hertford SG14 **113** C6
Luton LU1 ...............**63** D6
**Russell Way** WD19 .....**167** E3
**Russell's Ride** EN8 .....**162** E8
**Russell's Slip** SG5 ......**34** D6
**Russellcroft Rd** AL8 ....**110** C7
**Russet Ct** EN7 .........**147** E5
**Russet Dr** Shenley WD7 ...**156** E7
St Albans AL3 ..........**128** C2
**Russett Ho** AL7 .......**111** D6

Riv – St A **207**

**Russett Wood** AL7 .....**111** D5
**Russettings 2** HA5 .....**175** F3
**Rutherford Cl**
Borehamwood WD6 ....**170** C7
Stevenage SG1 .........**50** A6
**Rutherford Way** WD23 **168** E1
**Ruthin Cl** LU1 ..........**63** D5
**Ruthven Ave** EN8 ......**162** D6
**Rutland Cres** LU2 .......**64** A7
**Rutland Ct** LU2 .........**64** A7
**Rutland Gdns** HP2 .....**124** F4
**Rutland Hall** LU2 .......**64** A7
**Rutland Pl** WD23 ......**168** D1
**Rutland The** WD23 .....**168** D1
**Rutts The** WD23 .......**168** D1
**Ryall Cl** AL2 ...........**140** E2
**Ryan Way** WD24 .......**167** C8
**Ryans Ct** LU2 ..........**45** F1
**Rydal Ct** WD25 ........**154** B7
**Rydal Mount** EN6 ......**158** E6
**Rydal Way** LU3 .........**44** F5
**Ryde Sch The** AL9 .....**130** C8
**Ryde The** AL9 .........**130** C8
**Ryder Ave** SG5 .........**21** D3
**Ryder Cl** Bovingdon HP3 **137** A4
Bushey WD23 ..........**168** B3
Hertford SG13 .........**114** B7
**Ryder Seed Mews 3**
AL1 ...................**127** D2
**Ryder Way** SG5 ........**21** D3
**Ryders Ave** AL4 .......**129** E3
**Ryders Hill** SG1 ........**37** C3
**Rye Cl** Harpenden AL5 ...**86** B4
Stevenage SG1 .........**36** F3
**Rye Gdns** SG7 ..........**13** B1
**Rye Hill** Harpenden AL5 ...**86** B4
**2** Luton LU2 ...........**45** D1
**Rye House Gatehouse** ✱
EN11 ..................**135** D8
**Rye House Sta** EN11 ...**135** C8
**Rye Mead Cotts** EN11 ...**135** C8
**Rye Rd** EN11 ..........**135** C8
**Rye St** CM23 ...........**58** F1
**Ryecroft** Hatfield AL10 **129** E8
Stevenage SG1 .........**50** E7
**Ryecroft Cl** HP2 .......**125** C2
**Ryecroft Cres** EN5 .....**171** B4
**Ryecroft Ct** AL4 .......**128** E3
**Ryecroft Way** LU2 ......**46** A4
**Ryefeld Cl** EN11 .......**115** B3
**Ryefield** LU3 ..........**31** A1
**Ryefield Cres** HA6 .....**175** A1
**Ryelands** AL7 .........**110** F3
**Ryelands Prim Sch**
EN11 ..................**135** B7
**Rylands Heath** LU2 .....**46** F2
**Ryley Cl** SG8 ...........**10** B5
**Ryman Ct** WD3 ........**164** C3
**Rymill Cl** HP3 .........**137** A3
**Ryton Cl** LU1 ..........**63** B6

**S**

**Saberton Cl** AL3 .......**105** F4
**Sabine Ho** WD5 ........**153** F7
**Sacombe Gn** LU3 .......**31** B1
**Sacombe Green Rd** SG12 **71** E4
**Sacombe Pound** SG12 ...**71** E3
**Sacombe Rd**
Hemel Hempstead HP1 ...**123** F5
Hertford SG14 .........**92** C1
Stapleford SG14 ........**92** B4
**Sacombs Ash La** CM21 ...**96** E7
**Sacred Heart Language Coll**
The HA3 ...............**176** F1
**Sacred Heart Prim Sch**
LU2 ...................**46** A3
**Sacred Heart RC Prim Sch**
Bushey WD23 ..........**167** F3
Ware WD12 ............**93** D1
**Saddlers Cl** Arkley EN5 ...**171** B4
Baldock SG7 ...........**23** E8
Bishop's Stortford CM23 ...**76** C4
Borehamwood WD6 ....**170** D6
Pinner HA5 ............**176** A4
**Saddlers Mews** AL3 .....**83** E5
**Saddlers Path** WD6 .....**170** D4
**Saddlers Pl** SG8 .........**7** C7
**Saddlers Wlk** WD4 .....**139** A2
**Sadleir Rd** AL1 .........**127** E1
**Sadler Cl** EN7 .........**147** C6
**Sadlers Way** SG14 .....**113** A6
**Sadlier Rd** SG11 ........**55** E2
**Saffron Cl** Arlesey SG15 ...**11** A7
Hoddesdon EN11 .......**134** F7
Luton LU2 ..............**45** D7
**Saffron Green Prim Sch**
WD6 ...................**170** E5
**Saffron Hill** SG6 .......**22** E6
**Saffron La** HP1 ........**124** B4
**Saffron Mdw** SG11 .....**55** E2
**Saffron St** SG8 ..........**7** F5
**Sainfoin End** HP2 ......**125** C3
**St Adrian's RC Prim Sch**
AL1 ...................**141** C8
**St Agnell's Farm Mews**
HP2 ...................**105** A1
**St Agnells Ct** HP2 ......**125** A1
**St Agnells La** HP2 ......**125** A1
**St Alban & St Stephen RC Inf**
Sch AL1 ...............**127** E2
**St Alban & St Stephen RC**
Jun Sch AL1 ..........**128** A3
**St Alban's RC Prim Sch**
CM20 ..................**117** F2

**St Albans City Hospl**
AL3 . . . . . . . . . . . . **127** C5
**St Albans Dr** SG1 . . . . . **36** E1
**St Albans Girls' Sch**
AL3 . . . . . . . . . . . . **127** E7
**St Albans High Sch for Girls**
AL1 . . . . . . . . . . . . **127** E4
**St Albans Hill** HP3 . . . **124** F1
**St Albans La** WD5 . . . . **140** A5
**St Albans Link** SG1 . . . **36** E1
**St Albans Music Sch**
AL3 . . . . . . . . . . . . **127** D6
**St Albans Rd** Barnet EN5 **171** E7
Codicote SG4 . . . . . . . .**88** F7
Dancers Hill EN5 . . . . **158** C3
Harpenden AL5 . . . . . .**107** B6
Hemel Hempstead HP2,
HP3 . . . . . . . . . . . .**124** E2
Redbourn AL3 . . . . . .**106** C3
Ridge EN6 . . . . . . . .**157** F8
Sandridge AL4 . . . . . .**108** B3
St Albans AL4 . . . . . .**128** A8
**St Albans Rd E** AL10 . . **130** B6
**St Albans Rd W** AL10 . .**129** D5
**St Albans Ret Pk** AL1 . .**127** E7
**St Albans Roman Theatre**★
AL3 . . . . . . . . . . . .**127** A3
**St Albans Sch** AL3 . . . .**127** C3
**St Albans Sta** AL1 . . . .**127** F3
**St Albert the Great RC Prim
Sch** HP3 . . . . . . . . .**125** A4
**St Aldates Ct** LU3 . . . . .**45** B3
**St Andrew Mews 1**
SG14 . . . . . . . . . . .**113** C6
**St Andrew St** SG14 . . . .**113** C6
**St Andrew's Ave** AL5 . . .**85** F1
**St Andrew's CE Prim Sch**
SG4 . . . . . . . . . . . . .**35** A4
**St Andrew's CE Prim Sch**
SG10 . . . . . . . . . . . .**74** C2
**St Andrew's Cl** LU1 . . . .**63** B1
**St Andrew's Ho** CM20 . .**117** F7
**St Andrew's Pl 2** SG4 . .**34** F6
**St Andrew's Rd** HP3 . . .**138** D7
**St Andrews CE Prim Sch**
SG12 . . . . . . . . . . .**115** D4
**St Andrews Dr** SG1 . . . .**36** F2
**St Andrews Mews** LU3 . .**45** A4
**St Andrews Montessori Prep
Sch** WD25 . . . . . . . .**154** C8
**St Andrews Rd 2**
WD19 . . . . . . . . . . .**175** D7
**St Andrews Terr** WD19 .**175** C5
**St Andrews Wlk** LU1 . . .**63** C1
**St Ann's La** LU1 . . . . . .**63** F7
**St Ann's Rd** LU1 . . . . . .**63** F7
**St Anna Rd** LU1 . . . . . **171** D4
**St Anne's Cl** EN7 . . . . .**148** A3
**St Anne's Ct 7** SG5 . . .**34** F8
**St Anne's Pk** EN10 . . . **135** A4
**St Anne's Rd** Hitchin SG5 .**34** F8
London Colney AL2 . . . .**142** D4
**St Annes Cl** WD19 . . . .**175** C6
**St Anthonys Ave** HP3 . .**125** B1
**St Anthonys RC Prim Sch**
WD18 . . . . . . . . . . .**166** E4
**St Audreys Cl** AL10 . . . **130** B2
**St Audreys Gn** AL7 . . . **110** F5
**St Augusta Ct** AL3 . . . .**127** D5
**St Augustine Ave** LU3 . .**45** C3
**St Augustine Cl 1** SG5 . .**34** F8
**St Augustine RC Prim Sch**
EN11 . . . . . . . . . . . **135** B6
**St Augustines Cl** EN10 .**134** F3
**St Augustines Dr** EN10 .**134** F3
**St Barnabas Ct**
Harrow HA3 . . . . . . . **176** C2
Hemel Hempstead HP2 .**125** A3
**St Bartholomew's CE Prim
Sch** HP23 . . . . . . . .**100** D1
**St Barts Cl** AL4 . . . . . .**128** D2
**St Bernadette RC Prim Sch**
AL2 . . . . . . . . . . . .**142** D4
**St Bernard's Cl** LU3 . . . .**45** C3
**St Bernard's Rd** AL3 . . .**127** E4
**St Brelades Pl** AL4 . . . .**128** D7
**St Catharine's Rd**
EN10 . . . . . . . . . . . **135** A4
**St Catherine of Siena RC
Prim Sch** WD25 . . . .**154** D4
**St Catherine's CE Prim Sch**
SG12 . . . . . . . . . . . .**93** B2
**St Catherines Ave** LU3 . .**45** B3
**St Catherines Ct** CM23 . .**76** E7
**St Christopher Sch** SG6 . .**22** F3
**St Christophers Ct** WD3 **164** D5
**St Clement Danes Sch**
WD3 . . . . . . . . . . . .**164** D7
**St Clement's CE Jun Sch**
EN8 . . . . . . . . . . . .**148** E4
**St Clements Ct** EN9 . . . **163** C6
**St Columba's Coll** AL3 . .**127** C1
**St Cross Chambers**
EN11 . . . . . . . . . . . **135** A4
**St Cross Ct** EN11 . . . . **135** A4
**St Cross RC Prim Sch**
EN11 . . . . . . . . . . . **135** A4
**St Cuthbert Mayne RC Jun
Sch** HP1 . . . . . . . . **124** B4
**St Cuthberts Gdns 3**
HA5 . . . . . . . . . . . .**175** F3
**St Cuthberts Rd** EN11 . .**115** C1
**St David's La** HP2 . . . . **125** D2
**St David's Dr** EN10 . . . **134** F4
**St Davids Cl** SG1 . . . . . .**36** F2

**St Dominic RC Prim Sch**
AL5 . . . . . . . . . . . .**107** B8
**St Dunstan's Rd** SG12 . .**116** D8
**St Edmund's Coll** SG11 . .**55** A1
**St Edmund's Way**
CM17 . . . . . . . . . . .**118** C4
**St Edmunds** HP4 . . . . .**122** C3
**St Edmunds Wlk** AL4 . . **128** D2
**St Elizabeth's Sch & Home**
SG10 . . . . . . . . . . . .**96** C6
**St Elmo Ct** SG4 . . . . . .**34** F5
**St Ethelbert Way** AL5 . . .**45** C4
**St Etheldreda's Dr**
AL10 . . . . . . . . . . . **130** C5
**St Evroul Ct 5** SG12 . . .**93** D2
**St Faiths Cl** SG4 . . . . . .**22** B1
**St Francis Cl**
Buntingford SG9 . . . . . .**40** F6
Potters Bar EN6 . . . . .**159** C5
Watford WD19 . . . . . .**167** B1
**St Francis' Coll** SG6 . . . .**22** E4
**St George's Dr** WD19 . .**175** E6
**St George's Rd**
Enfield EN1 . . . . . . . .**161** F1
Hemel Hempstead HP3 .**138** C7
Watford WD24 . . . . . .**154** B1
**St George's Sch** AL5 . . .**86** B2
**St George's Way** SG1 . . .**36** B2
**St Georges End** SG9 . . . .**29** A6
**St Georges Works** EN8 .**148** F1
**St Giles Ct** EN8 . . . . . .**162** C4
**St Giles Rd** SG4 . . . . . .**67** F2
**St Giles' Ave** EN6 . . . . **158** B7
**St Giles' CE Prim Sch**
EN6 . . . . . . . . . . . .**158** A7
**St Helen's CE Prim Sch**
AL4 . . . . . . . . . . . .**108** D8
**St Helen's Cl** AL4 . . . . **108** D8
**St Helen's Sch** HA6 . . . **174** E4
**St Heliers Rd** AL4 . . . . **128** B8
**St Hilda's Sch**
Bushey WD23 . . . . . .**168** B2
Harpenden AL5 . . . . . .**85** F2
**St Hugh's Sch** SG11 . . . .**73** A8
**St Ignatius Coll** EN1 . . **162** B3
**St Ippolyts CE Prim Sch**
SG4 . . . . . . . . . . . . .**35** B3
**St Ives Cl** Luton LU3 . . . .**45** B3
Welwyn AL6 . . . . . . . .**89** F3
**St James Ctr** CM20 . . . **118** A4
**St James Rd**
Harpenden AL5 . . . . . .**86** B4
Watford WD18 . . . . . .**167** B4
**St James Way** CM23 . . .**76** C3
**St James's Rd** LU3 . . . . .**45** B3
**St James's Ct** AL5 . . . . .**86** B3
**St James's Rd** EN7 . . . .**147** D3
**St Joan of Arc RC Sch**
WD3 . . . . . . . . . . . .**165** E2
**St John Cl** LU1 . . . . . . .**63** B5
**St John Fisher RC Prim Sch**
AL4 . . . . . . . . . . . .**128** C6
**St John RC Prim Sch**
SG7 . . . . . . . . . . . . .**23** F7
**St John The Baptist CE Prim
Sch** SG12 . . . . . . . .**115** A5
**St John's Ave** CM17 . . .**118** D4
**St John's CE Prim Sch**
Crews Hill EN2 . . . . . **161** B2
Hatfield AL8 . . . . . . . **109** F5
Welwyn Garden City AL6 .**89** F2
**St John's Cl** EN6 . . . . . **159** B7
**St John's Cres** CM24 . . .**59** E7
**St John's Ct**
Harpenden AL5 . . . . . **107** C7
**21** Hertford SG13 . . . . **113** D6
**6** Northwood HA6 . . . .**174** E3
**St John's La** CM24 . . . . .**59** E7
**St John's Path** SG4 . . . .**34** F5
**St John's RC Prim Sch**
WD3 . . . . . . . . . . . .**165** B1
**St John's Rd**
Arlesey SG15 . . . . . . . **11** A4
Harpenden AL5 . . . . . **107** C7
Hemel Hempstead HP1 .**124** B1
Hitchin SG4 . . . . . . . .**34** F4
Stansted Mountfitchet
CM24 . . . . . . . . . . . .**59** E7
Watford WD17 . . . . . .**167** B7
**St John's Sch** HA6 . . . . **175** B4
**St John's St** SG13 . . . . **113** D6
**St John's Terr** EN2 . . . **161** D1
**St John's Well Ct** HP4 . .**122** B5
**St John's Well La** HP4 . .**122** B5
**St Johns** SG11 . . . . . . .**55** E3
**St Johns CE Inf Sch**
WD7 . . . . . . . . . . . .**155** F4
**St Johns Cl** AL6 . . . . . .**89** C6
**St Johns Ct** Luton LU1 . . .**63** C6
Rickmansworth WD3 . . **165** B1
St Albans AL1 . . . . . .**128** B5
**St Johns La** SG12 . . . . **115** A6
**St Johns Wlk** CM17 . . . **118** C4
**St Joseph RC Prim Sch**
WD19 . . . . . . . . . . .**175** C2
**St Joseph's Cl** LU3 . . . . .**45** A4
**St Joseph's in the Park Sch**
SG14 . . . . . . . . . . .**113** A4
**St Joseph's RC Inf Sch**
LU3 . . . . . . . . . . . . .**45** A4
**St Joseph's RC Jun Sch**
LU3 . . . . . . . . . . . . .**45** A4
**St Joseph's RC Prim Sch**
Bishop's Stortford CM23 . .**76** E6
Cheshunt EN8 . . . . . .**162** E7
Hertford SG14 . . . . . .**113** A7
**St Joseph's Rd** EN8 . . . **162** E6

**St Josephs Court La**
AL5 . . . . . . . . . . . .**107** B8
**St Julian's Rd** AL1 . . . . **127** D1
**St Katharines Cl** SG5 . . .**21** D3
**St Katherine's Way**
HP4 . . . . . . . . . . . .**121** F7
**St Laurence Dr** EN10 . .**148** F8
**St Lawrence Cl**
Abbots Langley HP3 . . .**139** E1
Bovingdon HP3 . . . . . **137** A4
**St Lawrence Way** AL2 . .**140** F1
**St Lawrences Ave** LU3 . .**45** C3
**St Leonard's Ct** AL4 . . .**108** C1
**St Leonard's Rd** SG14 . .**113** D8
**St Leonards Cl**
Hertford SG13 . . . . . **113** E8
Watford WD23 . . . . . .**167** E5
**St Leonards Cres** AL4 . .**108** C1
**St Leonards Rd** EN9 . . .**149** D6
**St Luke's Ave** EN2 . . . . **161** D1
**St Luke's Cl** LU4 . . . . . .**44** E2
**St Luke's Sch** AL3 . . . . **106** A6
**St Magnus St** HP3 . . . . **125** C1
**St Margaret Clitheroe RC
Prim Sch** SG2 . . . . . .**50** F2
**St Margaret of Scotland Jun
Sch** LU1 . . . . . . . . .**63** B5
**St Margaret of Scotland RC
Inf Sch** LU1 . . . . . . .**63** B5
**St Margaret's Cl** HP4 . . **122** D3
**St Margaret's Rd** SG12 .**115** B2
**St Margaret's Sch**
WD3 . . . . . . . . . . . .**168** A2
**St Margarets** SG2 . . . . .**50** F2
**St Margarets Ave** LU3 . .**45** B3
**St Margarets Cl** LU3 . . .**31** A6
**St Margarets Sta** SG12 .**115** C4
**St Margarets Way** HP2 .**125** D3
**St Mark's Cl** SG5 . . . . . .**21** D1
**St Marks Cl** AL4 . . . . . **129** B1
**St Martha's Convent Jun
Sch** HP4 . . . . . . . . .**171** E5
**St Martin de Porres RC Prim
Sch** LU4 . . . . . . . . .**44** A4
**St Martin's Ave** LU2 . . . .**45** F2
**St Martin's Rd** SG3 . . . .**69** A5
**St Martin's Sch** HA6 . . .**174** D5
**St Martins** HA6 . . . . . **174** D5
**St Martins Ct**
Harpenden AL5 . . . . . .**86** C4
South Oxhey WD19 . . . **175** C6
**St Mary RC Prim Sch** SG8 . **7** D7
**St Mary's Ave**
Berkhamsted UB2 . . . .**121** D4
Moor Park HA6 . . . . . **174** E5
Stotfold SG5 . . . . . . . .**11** F4
**St Mary's CE High Sch**
EN8 . . . . . . . . . . . .**148** B1
**St Mary's CE Jun Sch**
SG12 . . . . . . . . . . . .**93** D3
**St Mary's CE Prim Sch**
WD3 . . . . . . . . . . . .**173** D7
**St Mary's CE Prim Sch**
Stansted Mountfitchet
CM24 . . . . . . . . . . . .**59** E7
Welham Green AL9 . . . **144** B8
**St Mary's Cl**
Letchworth SG6 . . . . . .**22** F2
Pirton SG5 . . . . . . . . .**20** D4
Redbourn AL3 . . . . . .**106** A4
**St Mary's Ct**
**8** Hemel Hempstead HP2 **124** D4
Potters Bar EN6 . . . . .**159** B7
Welwyn AL6 . . . . . . . .**89** C4
**St Mary's Ctyd 3** SG12 . .**93** D1
**St Mary's Dr** CM24 . . . .**59** E7
**St Mary's Inf Sch** SG7 . .**23** E6
**St Mary's Jun Mix Sch**
SG7 . . . . . . . . . . . . .**23** E6
**St Mary's La** SG14 . . . .**112** F3
**St Mary's Lower Sch**
SG5 . . . . . . . . . . . . .**12** A6
**St Mary's Prim Sch** AL6 . .**89** B4
**St Mary's RC Sch** CM23 . .**76** E7
**St Mary's Rd**
Cheshunt EN8 . . . . . .**148** C2
Hemel Hempstead HP2 .**124** D4
Luton LU1 . . . . . . . . .**63** F7
Standon SG11 . . . . . . .**55** D2
Watford WD18 . . . . . .**167** B5
**St Mary's Rise** SG4 . . . .**47** D1
**St Mary's Way** SG7 . . . .**23** E6
**St Marys Cl** SG2 . . . . . .**51** E2
**St Marys Pk** SG8 . . . . . . .**7** D6
**St Marys Rd** AL6 . . . . . .**89** C5
**St Marys Wlk** AL4 . . . . **128** B7
**St Matthew's Inf Sch**
LU2 . . . . . . . . . . . . .**45** E1
**St Matthews** Luton LU2 .**63** E8
Watford WD19 . . . . . .**167** D3
**St Meryl Sch** WD19 . . .**175** E7
**St Michael's CE Prim Sch**
Bishop's Stortford CM23 . .**76** F7
St Albans AL3 . . . . . .**127** B3
**St Michael's Cres** LU3 . .**45** D3
**St Michael's La** AL3 . . .**127** B3
**St Michael's Mount** SG4 .**35** A8
**St Michael's RC High Sch**
WD25 . . . . . . . . . . .**154** D7
**St Michael's Rd** EN10 . .**135** A3
**St Michael's St** AL3 . . . **127** B3
**St Michael's Woolmer Green
CE Prim Sch** Woolmer
Green SG3 . . . . . . . . .**69** A1
**St Michaels Ave** HP3 . . **125** B1

**St Michaels Cl**
Harlow CM20 . . . . . . .**117** E1
Harpenden AL5 . . . . . **107** D7
**St Michaels Ct** SG1 . . . .**51** B8
**St Michaels Dr** WD25 . .**154** B6
**St Michaels Rd** SG4 . . . .**35** B7
**St Michaels View** AL10 . .**130** B7
**St Michaels Way** EN6 . .**145** B1
**St Mildreds Ave** LU3 . . .**45** C3
**St Monicas Ave** LU3 . . . .**45** B3
**St Neots Cl** WD6 . . . . .**157** A1
**St Nicholas CE Prim Sch**
Harpenden AL5 . . . . . .**86** A1
Letchworth SG6 . . . . . .**12** C1
Stevenage SG2 . . . . . .**50** F4
**St Nicholas Cl** WD6 . . .**169** D3
**St Nicholas Ct** AL5 . . . .**85** D7
**St Nicholas Elstree CE Prim
Sch** WD6 . . . . . . . .**169** D3
**St Nicholas Gn** CM17 . .**118** C1
**St Nicholas House Prep Sch**
HP3 . . . . . . . . . . . .**139** E2
**St Nicholas Mount** HP1 .**123** F3
**St Nicholas Sch** CM17 . .**118** F3
**St Ninian's Ct 8** LU2 . . .**63** D8
**St Olam's Ct** LU3 . . . . . .**45** B6
**St Olives** SG5 . . . . . . . .**11** C5
**St Pancras Ho** SG8 . . . . .**2** D1
**St Paul's CE Prim Sch**
WD4 . . . . . . . . . . . .**152** A8
**St Paul's Gdns** LU1 . . . .**63** E5
**St Paul's Rd**
Hemel Hempstead HP2 .**124** E4
Luton LU1 . . . . . . . . .**63** E5
**St Paul's Walden Prim Sch**
SG4 . . . . . . . . . . . . .**66** D7
**St Pauls CE Prim Sch**
WD4 . . . . . . . . . . . .**153** C5
**St Pauls Cl** AL5 . . . . . .**107** D8
**St Pauls Ct 3** SG2 . . . . .**50** F1
**St Pauls Pl** AL1 . . . . . .**128** A3
**St Pauls RC Prim Sch**
EN7 . . . . . . . . . . . .**148** B4
**St Pauls Way**
Waltham Abbey EN9 . . **163** D6
Watford WD24 . . . . . .**167** C2
**St Peter's Ave** SG15 . . . .**11** A4
**St Peter's CE Prim Sch**
WD3 . . . . . . . . . . . .**165** B1
**St Peter's Cl**
Barnet EN5 . . . . . . . **171** B4
Bushey WD23 . . . . . .**168** D1
Rickmansworth WD3 . . **165** B1
St Albans AL1 . . . . . .**127** D1
**St Peter's Rd** AL1 . . . . . **127** E4
**St Peter's Sch** AL1 . . . . **127** E2
**St Peter's St** AL1 . . . . . **127** D4
**St Peters Cl** AL10 . . . . **130** A6
**St Peters Hill** HP23 . . . **100** A4
**St Peters Rd** LU1 . . . . . .**63** B7
**St Peters Way** WD3 . . .**164** B5
**St Philip Howard RC Prim
Sch** AL10 . . . . . . . .**130** B5
**St Raphaels Ct 5** AL1 . .**127** E4
**St Ronans Cl** EN4 . . . . .**159** D1
**St Rose's RC Inf Sch**
HP1 . . . . . . . . . . . .**124** A1
**St Saviors View** AL1 . . .**127** F4
**St Saviours's Cres** LU1 . .**63** D6
**St Stephen's Ave** AL3 . .**141** B8
**St Stephen's Cl** AL3 . . .**141** B8
**St Stephen's Hill** AL1 . . **127** C1
**St Stephen's Rd** EN3 . . **162** D2
**St Stephens Rd** EN5 . . .**171** D4
**St Teresa RC Prim Sch**
WD6 . . . . . . . . . . . .**170** B7
**St Teresa's RC Fst & Mid
Sch** HA3 . . . . . . . . .**176** C2
**St Thomas Ct** HA5 . . . .**175** E2
**St Thomas More RC Prim Sch**
Berkhamsted HP4 . . . .**122** A4
Letchworth SG6 . . . . . .**22** D4
**St Thomas of Canterbury RC
Prim Sch** SG11 . . . . .**55** C3
**St Thomas Pl** AL4 . . . . **108** D8
**St Thomas' Dr** HA5 . . . .**175** E2
**St Thomas's Cl** LU2 . . . .**46** A4
**St Thomas's Rd** LU2 . . . .**46** A4
**St Vincent de Paul RC Prim
Sch** SG1 . . . . . . . . .**51** A6
**St Vincent Dr** AL1 . . . . **128** A1
**St Vincent Gdns** LU4 . . .**44** D3
**St Vincent's Way** EN6 . .**159** C6
**St Winifreds Ave** LU3 . . .**45** C3
**St Yon Ct** AL4 . . . . . . .**128** E3
**Sale Dr** SG7 . . . . . . . . .**12** F1
**Salisbury Ave**
Harpenden AL5 . . . . . .**86** A1
St Albans AL1 . . . . . .**128** B4
**Salisbury Cl**
Bishop's Stortford CM23 . .**76** F5
Potters Bar EN6 . . . . .**159** C7
**Salisbury Cres** EN8 . . . **162** D7
**Salisbury Gdns** AL7 . . .**110** F5
**Salisbury Hall Dr** AL10 . .**129** E7
**Salisbury Ho** AL3 . . . . **127** C2
**Salisbury Rd** Baldock SG7 . .**12** F1
Barnet EN5 . . . . . . . **171** E6
Enfield EN3 . . . . . . . .**162** F2
Harpenden AL5 . . . . . .**86** D3
Hoddesdon EN11 . . . .**135** C8
Luton LU1 . . . . . . . . .**63** D6
Stevenage SG1 . . . . . .**37** A2
Watford WD24 . . . . . .**154** A1
Welwyn Garden City AL7 .**111** A5
**Salisbury Sq**
Hatfield AL9 . . . . . . .**130** C6

**Salisbury Sq** continued
**7** Hertford SG14 . . . . **113** D6
**Sally Deards La** AL6 . . . .**68** B3
**Salmon Cl** AL7 . . . . . . .**90** A1
**Salmons Cl** SG12 . . . . . .**93** D4
**Saltdean Cl** LU2 . . . . . .**46** C4
**Salter's Cl** HP4 . . . . . . **121** F6
**Salters** CM23 . . . . . . . .**76** C4
**Salters Cl** WD3 . . . . . . **165** E1
**Salters Gdns** WD17 . . . **167** A8
**Saltfield Cres** LU4 . . . . .**44** C4
**Salusbury La** SG5 . . . . . .**33** C2
**Salvatorian Coll** HA3 . . .**176** E1
**Salwey Cres** EN10 . . . . **134** F3
**Samian Gate** AL3 . . . . **126** C1
**Sampson Ave** EN5 . . . .**171** D4
**Samuel Lucas Jun Mix Inf
Sch** SG5 . . . . . . . . .**34** D7
**Samuel Sq 2** AL1 . . . . **127** D2
**Sancroft Rd** HA3 . . . . . **176** E1
**Sanctuary Cl** UB9 . . . . **173** C3
**Sandalls Spring** HP1 . . . **123** F5
**Sandalwood Cl** LU3 . . . .**45** B7
**Sanday Cl** HP3 . . . . . . **125** D3
**Sandbrook La** HP23 . . . .**79** C1
**Sandeman Gdns** SG12 . . .**93** E2
**Sander's Cnr** EN2 . . . . .**161** B5
**Sanderling Cl** SG6 . . . . .**22** E8
**Sanders Cl**
Hemel Hempstead HP3 .**138** F7
London Colney AL2 . . . **142** D4
Stansted Mountfitchet
CM24 . . . . . . . . . . . .**59** D6
**Sanders Rd** WD3 . . . . .**139** A7
**Sandfield Rd** AL1 . . . . .**128** A3
**Sandgate Rd** LU4 . . . . . .**44** D2
**Sandhurst Ct** AL5 . . . . **107** D6
**Sandifield** AL10 . . . . . . **130** B2
**Sandle Rd** CM23 . . . . . .**77** A7
**Sandmere Cl** HP2 . . . . **125** A2
**Sandon Cl** HP23 . . . . . .**99** F4
**Sandon Jun Mix Inf Sch**
SG9 . . . . . . . . . . . . .**15** C1
**Sandon Rd** EN8 . . . . . .**148** C1
**Sandover Cl** SG4 . . . . . .**35** B6
**Sandown Rd**
Stevenage SG1 . . . . . .**37** C1
Watford WD24 . . . . . .**154** C1
**Sandown Road Ind Est**
WD24 . . . . . . . . . . .**154** C2
**Sandpit Hill Cotts** HP23 **120** B3
**Sandpit La** AL1,AL4 . . . .**128** C5
**Sandpit Rd** AL7 . . . . . . **110** E4
**Sandridge Cl** HP2 . . . . .**105** A1
**Sandridge Ct** AL4 . . . . **128** D7
**Sandridge Gate Bsns Ctr**
AL1 . . . . . . . . . . . .**127** F7
**Sandridge Pk** AL3 . . . . **127** F8
**Sandridge Rd** AL1 . . . . **127** F5
**Sandridge Rd** SG4 . . . . **108** D1
**Sandridgebury La**
Sandridge AL3,AL4 . . .**108** A2
St Albans AL3 . . . . . .**127** E8
**Sandringham Cres** AL4 .**128** C8
**Sandringham Gdns 6**
CM23 . . . . . . . . . . . .**76** E5
**Sandringham Rd**
Potters Bar EN6 . . . . .**145** B1
Watford WD24 . . . . . .**154** C1
**Sandringham Sch** AL4 . .**128** B7
**Sandringham Way** EN8 .**162** D5
**Sandy Cl** SG14 . . . . . . .**113** B6
**Sandy Gr** SG4 . . . . . . . .**34** F6
**Sandy La** Bushey WD25 . .**168** C6
Moor Park HA6 . . . . . **175** A5
**Sandy Lane Cvn Site**
WD25 . . . . . . . . . . .**168** C6
**Sandy Lodge** HA6 . . . . **174** E8
**Sandy Lodge Ct** HA6 . . .**174** E5
**Sandy Lodge La** HA6 . . .**174** E8
**Sandy Lodge Rd** WD3 . .**174** E7
**Sandy Lodge Way** HA6 . .**174** E4
**Sandycroft Rd** HP6 . . . .**150** C1
**Sanfoin Rd** LU4 . . . . . . .**44** A4
**Sanfoine Cl** SG4 . . . . . .**35** C8
**Santers La** EN6 . . . . . . **158** E6
**Santingfield N** LU1 . . . . .**63** B6
**Santingfield S** LU1 . . . . .**63** B6
**Sappers Cl** CM21 . . . . . .**97** F2
**Saracen Est** HP2 . . . . . **125** B5
**Saracens Head** HP2 . . . **125** A4
**Saracens Head Yd 1**
AL1 . . . . . . . . . . . .**127** D2
**Sargents** SG11 . . . . . . . .**55** F1
**Sarita Cl** HA3 . . . . . . . **176** D1
**Sark Ho** Enfield EN3 . . . **162** D1
**10** Watford WD18 . . . .**166** F3
**Sarratt Ave** HP2 . . . . . **125** A8
**Sarratt CE Prim Sch**
WD3 . . . . . . . . . . . .**152** A3
**Sarratt La**
Rickmansworth WD3 . . **165** C3
Sarratt WD3 . . . . . . .**165** D8
**Sarratt Rd** WD3 . . . . . **165** C8
**Sarum Pl** HP2 . . . . . . .**124** E7
**Sarum Rd** LU3 . . . . . . . .**44** F4
**Satinwood Cl 1** HP3 . . .**124** E1
**Saturn Way** HP2 . . . . . **124** F6
**Saucey Ave** AL5 . . . . . .**86** B3
**Sauncey Wood** AL5 . . . .**86** E4
**Sauncey Wood La** AL5 . . .**86** E6
**Sauncey Wood Prim Sch**
AL5 . . . . . . . . . . . . .**86** D4
**Saunders Cl**
Cheshunt EN8 . . . . . .**148** D4
Letchworth SG6 . . . . . .**23** C7
**Savanna Ct** WD18 . . . . **166** F5

Savill Cl EN7 ..........147 C6
Savoy Cl UB9 ..........173 D1
**Sawbridgeworth Rd**
  Hatfield Heath CM22 ....98 E3
  Little Hallingbury CM22 ..98 B6
**Sawbridgeworth Sta**
  CM21 .................98 A3
Sawells EN10 ..........134 F2
Sawtry Cl LU3 ..........45 A6
Sawtry Way WD6 .......157 A1
Sawyers La EN6 .......158 D5
Sawyers Way HP2 ......124 F3
Sax Ho SG6 ...........11 E1
Saxon Ave HA3 ........11 F8
Saxon Cl Harpenden AL5 ..86 C4
  Letchworth SG6 .......11 F1
**Saxon Ct**
  Borehamwood WD6 .....169 E8
  6 Hitchin SG4 ........34 F6
Saxon Rd Luton LU3 ....45 C2
  Welwyn AL6 ..........89 B3
  Wheathampstead AL4 ..108 D7
Saxon Way Baldock SG7 ..13 B1
  Waltham Abbey EN9 ...163 C6
Saxted Cl LU2 .........46 D1
Saxton Mews WD17 ....167 A7
Sayer Way SG3 ........68 F4
Sayers Gdns HP4 .....122 A6
Sayers Rd LU2 .........46 B1
Scammell Way WD18 ..166 F3
Scarborough Ave SG1 ..50 B7
Scatterdells La WD4 ..138 C2
Scholar's Hill SG12 ....95 A4
Scholars Ct AL4 .......143 C8
Scholars Mews AL8 ....110 D8
Scholars The WD17 ....167 C4
Scholars Wlk 4 AL10 ..130 C4
School Essendon AL9 ..131 F6
  Stevenage SG2 ........51 B4
School Cotts SG4 ......47 F6
School Gdns HP4 ......123 B6
School Ho The 1 SG7 ..23 F7
School La Ardeley SG2 ..38 F3
  Aston SG2 ...........51 A2
  Barley SG8 ...........9 A1
  Bricket Wood AL2 .....155 A7
  Bushey WD23 .........168 B2
  Essendon AL9 ........131 F6
  Great Offley SG5 ......33 C3
  Harlow CM20 .........117 E2
  Hatfield AL10 ........130 C6
  Luton LU4 ...........44 D4
  Preston SG4 ..........48 E5
  Tewin AL6 ...........90 E2
  Watton at S SG14 .....70 E3
  Welwyn AL6 ..........89 B4
  Weston SG4 ..........24 C1
School Mead WD5 .....153 D7
School Rd EN6 ........145 C1
School Row HP1 .......123 F2
School Wlk SG6 .......23 B6
Schoolfields SG6 ......23 C5
Schubert Rd WD6 .....169 D3
Scot Gr HA5 ..........175 D3
Scotfield Ct LU2 ......46 D3
Scots Hill Cl WD3 .....165 F3
Scots Hill WD3 .......165 F3
Scots Mill La WD3 ....165 F3
Scotscraig WD7 ......155 F4
Scotswood EN5 .......171 B4
Scott Ave SG12 .......115 B4
Scott Cl SG8 ..........2 D1
**Scott Rd**
  Bishop's Stortford CM23 ..76 E6
  Luton LU3 ...........44 C7
  Stevenage SG2 ........51 B6
Scott's Grotto ★ SG12 ..114 D8
Scott's Rd SG12 ......114 D8
Scotts Cl SG12 .......114 D8
Scotts View AL4 ......110 C5
Scottswood Cl WD23 ..167 E7
Scottswood Rd WD23 ..167 E7
**Scratchwood Nature Trail★**
  NW7 ................170 D2
Scriveners Cl HP2 .....124 C3
Scrubbits Sq WD7 ....156 A4
**Scrubbits Park Rd**
  WD7 ................156 A4
Seabrook LU4 .........44 B3
Seabrook Rd WD4 .....139 D4
Seacroft Gdns WD19 ..175 D7
Seaford Cl LU2 ........46 C3
Seaforth Ct EN11 .....135 B4
Seaforth Dr EN8 ......162 D5
Seal Cl LU4 ...........44 D3
Seaman Cl AL2 .......141 D6
Searches La WD5 .....140 C4
**Seaton Rd**
  Hemel Hempstead HP3 ..124 E1
  London Colney AL2 ....142 D5
  Luton LU4 ...........44 F3
Sebright Rd Barnet EN5 ..171 E6
  Hemel Hempstead HP1 ..124 A1
  Markyate AL3 .........83 E5
Secker Cres HA3 ......176 C2
**Second Ave**
  Letchworth SG6 .......23 C6
  Watford WD25 ........154 D4
Sedbury Cl LU3 ........45 A6
Sedge Gn EN9,CM19 ...135 E3
Sedgewick Ct HP2 .....105 B1
Sedgwick Rd LU4 ......44 B7
Sedley Cl EN1 ........162 B1
Seebohm Cl SG5 ......21 C1

Seeleys The CM17 .....118 C4
Sefton Ave HA3 .......176 D2
Sefton Cl AL1 .........127 F4
Sefton Rd SG1 ........37 B1
Selbourne Rd LU4 .....45 A2
Selby Ave AL3 ........127 D3
Selden Hill HP2 .......124 D2
Sele Mill SG14 .......113 B6
Sele Rd SG14 .........113 B6
Sele Sch The SG14 ....112 F6
Selina Cl LU3 .........44 C7
Sell Ct EN7 ...........147 B5
Sellers Cl WD6 .......170 C8
Sells Rd SG12 ........93 F2
Sellwood Dr EN5 .....171 D4
Selsey Dr LU2 .........46 D4
Selwyn Ave LU1 .......129 E4
Selwyn Cres AL10 .....129 E5
Selwyn Dr AL10 .......129 E5
Sempill Rd HP3 .......124 C1
Senate Pl SG1 ........37 B3
Sentis Ct HA6 .........174 F4
Sequoia Cl WD23 .....168 D1
Sequoia Pk HA5 ......176 B4
Serby Ave SG8 ........7 D8
Sergehill La WD5 ......140 A5
Serpentine Cl SG1 ....37 C2
**Service Industry Bays**
  SG20 ...............117 F2
Service Rd The EN6 ...159 A7
Seven Acres HA6 .....175 A4
Seven Roe's Malting SG7 ..23 E8
Sevenoaks Ct HA6 ....174 C3
Severalls The LU2 .....46 B3
Severn Dr EN1 ........162 A1
**Severn Way**
  Stevenage SG1 .......36 F3
  Watford WD25 ........154 C5
Severnmead HP2 .....124 C6
Severnvale AL2 .......142 F4
Sewardstone Rd EN9 ..163 D3
Sewardstone St EN9 ..163 C5
Sewell Cl AL4 .........128 C3
Sewell Harris Cl CM20 ..117 F1
Sewells AL8 ..........89 E2
Sexton Cl EN7 ........147 B6
Seymour Ave LU1 .....63 F5
Seymour Cl HA5 ......175 F2
Seymour Cres HP2 ....124 E3
Seymour Ct HP4 ......121 E6
Seymour Mews CM21 ..118 E7
**Seymour Rd**
  Berkhamsted HP4 .....121 E6
  Luton LU1 ...........63 F5
  St Albans AL3 ........127 E4
Shackledell SG2 ......50 F2
Shacklegate La SG4 ...66 E5
Shackleton Gdns CM23 ..76 E6
Shackleton Spring SG2 ..51 A3
**Shackleton Way**
  Abbots Langley WD5 ..154 A7
  Welwyn Garden City AL7 ..111 D6
Shady Bush Cl WD23 ..168 C2
Shady La WD17 .......167 B7
**Shafford Cotts**
  Hemel Hempstead HP3 ..139 A5
  St Albans AL3 ........126 F6
**Shaftenhoe End Rd**
  Barley SG8 ...........9 A1
  Nuthampstead SG8 ....18 B8
**Shaftesbury Ct**
  Croxley Green WD3 ...166 C4
  Stevenage SG1 ........50 E4
**Shaftesbury High Sch**
  HA3 ................176 B2
Shaftesbury Ind Ctr SG6 ..23 B7
**Shaftesbury Quay 11**
  SG14 ...............113 D6
Shaftesbury Rd Luton LU4 ..45 B1
  Watford WD17 ........167 C6
**Shaftesbury Way**
  Bedmond WD4 .......139 C3
  Royston SG8 ..........7 E5
Shakespeare SG8 ......7 D8
Shakespeare Ct EN11 ..115 A2
**Shakespeare Ind Est**
  WD24 ...............154 A1
**Shakespeare Rd**
  Harpenden AL5 .......86 C1
  Luton LU4 ...........44 B2
Shakespeare St WD24 ..154 B1
Shalcross Dr EN8 .....148 F1
Shallcross Cres 6 AL10 ..130 A2
Shambrook Rd EN7 ....147 B6
Shangani Rd CM23 ....76 F5
**Shanklin Cl**
  Goff's Oak EN7 .......147 F2
  Luton LU3 ...........45 A7
Shanklin Gdns WD19 ..175 C6
Shantock Hall La HP3 ..136 E1
Shantock La HP3 .....136 E1
Sharmans Cl AL6 .....89 F4
Sharose Ct AL3 .......83 E5
Sharpcroft 1 HP2 .....124 D5
Sharpenhoe Rd LU3 ..31 A5
Sharpes La HP1 ......123 B1
Sharples Gn LU3 .....45 B8
Sharps Way Hitchin SG4 ..22 A1
  Hitchin SG4 ..........35 A8
Shaw Cl Bushey WD23 ..176 E8
  Cheshunt EN8 ........148 C3
Shaw's Cnr★ AL6 .....88 A6
Shaws The AL7 .......111 C5
Shearers The CM23 ...76 C4
Sheares Hoppit SG12 ..95 D2
Shearwater Cl SG2 ....51 D4
Sheepcot Dr WD25 ...154 C5
Sheepcot La WD25 ...154 B6

Sheepcot Villas WD25 ..154 C5
Sheepcote AL7 .......111 A3
Sheepcote La AL4 .....87 F1
Sheepcote Rd HP2 ....124 F3
Sheepcroft Hill SG2 ...51 D3
Sheephouse Rd HP3 ..124 F1
**Sheering CE Prim Sch**
  CM22 ...............98 D1
Sheering Dr CM17 ....118 E4
**Sheering Lower Rd**
  CM21 ...............98 A2
Sheering Mill La CM21 ..97 F2
**Sheering Rd**
  Harlow CM17 .........118 F4
  Harlow CM17 .........118 F5
Sheethanger La HP4 ..138 A7
Shefton Rise HA6 .....175 A3
Sheldon Cl EN7 .......147 E5
Shelford Rd EN5 .....171 C3
Shelley Cl Hitchin SG4 ..35 C7
  Moor Park HA6 .......174 F5
  Royston SG8 ..........2 D1
Shelley Ct Cheshunt EN7 ..148 A3
  16 Harpenden AL5 ....86 B1
  Waltham Abbey EN9 ..163 F6
Shelley La UB9 .......173 A3
Shelley Rd LU4 .......44 B2
Shelton Way LU2 .....46 A3
Shendish Edge HP3 ..138 F6
Shenley Ct HP2 ......125 B8
Shenley Hill WD7 ....156 B4
Shenley La AL2 ......142 C4
Shenley Prim Sch WD7 ..156 F5
**Shenley Rd**
  Borehamwood WD6 ...170 B6
  Hemel Hempstead HP2 ..105 B1
  Radlett WD7 .........156 C4
Shenleybury WD7 ....156 E8
Shenleybury Cotts WD7 ..156 E8
Shenleybury Villas WD7 ..156 E8
Shenstone Hill HP4 ...122 E5
Shenval Ho CM20 ....118 A4
Shephall Gn SG2 .....51 B2
**Shephall Green Inf Sch**
  SG2 ................51 B2
Shephall La SG2 ......50 F1
Shephall View SG1 ...51 A5
Shephall Way SG2 ....51 C3
**Shepherd Cl**
  Abbots Langley WD5 ..153 F8
  Royston SG8 ..........7 E5
Shepherd Inf Sch WD3 ..165 A1
**Shepherd Prim Sch**
  WD3 ................165 A1
Shepherd's La WD3 ..164 E2
Shepherd's Row AL3 ..106 B5
Shepherds Cl CM23 ...76 C4
Shepherds Ct SG14 ...92 C1
Shepherds Gn HP1 ...123 E2
Shepherds La SG1 ....50 A6
Shepherds Mead SG5 ..21 F2
Shepherds Rd WD18 ..166 F5
**Shepherds Way**
  Brookmans Park AL9 ..145 D4
  Harpenden AL5 .......85 D4
  Rickmansworth WD3 ..165 B2
Shepherds Wlk WD23 ..176 D8
Shepley Mews EN3 ...163 A2
Sheppard Cl EN1 .....162 B1
Sheppards Cl AL3 ....127 E6
Sheppards Yd 4 HP1 ..124 D4
Shepperton Cl WD6 ..170 D8
Sheppey's La WD5 ...139 E3
Sheraton Cl WD6 .....169 F4
Sheraton Ho WD3 ....164 C5
Sheraton Mews WD18 ..166 F5
Sherborne Ave LU2 ...45 D6
Sherborne Cotts WD18 ..167 C4
Sherborne Pl HA6 ....174 D4
Sherborne Way WD6 ..166 B5
Sherbourne Cl HP2 ...124 E2
Sherbourne Ct AL1 ...127 F3
Sherd Cl LU3 .........44 F7
Sheredes Dr EN11 ....134 F4
**Sheredes Prim Sch**
  EN11 ...............134 F5
Sheredes Sch EN11 ..134 F5
Sherfield Ave WD3 ...173 E8
Sheridan Cl HP1 .....124 B2
Sheridan Rd Luton LU3 ..45 C2
  Watford WD7 ........167 D2
Sheriden Wlk EN10 ..134 E3
Sheriff Way WD25 ...154 A5
Sheringham Ave SG1 ..36 B1
Sheringham Cl LU2 ...45 C7
Sherington Ave HA5 ..176 A3
Sherland Ct WD7 ....156 A4
Shernbroke Rd EN9 ..163 F5
Sherrards Mans AL8 ..89 B1
Sherrards Mews AL8 ..89 B1
Sherrardspark Rd AL8 ..110 D8
Sherrardswood Sch AL6 ..89 D4
Sherwood SG6 .......22 F8
**Sherwood Ct**
  20 Bishop's Stortford CM23 ..76 F7
  Watford WD25 ........154 A5
Sherwood Ho WD5 ...153 F8
Sherwood Pl 1 HP2 ...124 F7
Sherwood Rd LU4 ....45 A2
Sherwoods Rd WD19 ..167 E2
Sherwoods Rise AL5 ..107 D8
Shetland Cl WD6 .....170 D3
Shetland Ho 13 WD18 ..166 F3
Shillington Rd SG5 ...20 B5
Shillitoe Ave EN6 ....158 E7

Shingle Cl LU3 ........45 A8
Ship La LU7 ..........80 D3
Shire Cl EN10 ........148 F5
Shire Ct HP2 .........125 A4
**Shire La**
  Chalfont St Peter,Horn Hill
  WD3 ...............172 B6
  Chalfont St Peter,West Hyde
  WD3 ...............172 C4
  Chorleywood WD3 ...164 C4
  Maple Cross WD3 ....172 B5
  Tring HP23 ..........120 B4
Shiremeade WD6 .....169 F4
Shires The Luton LU2 ..45 D1
  Royston SG8 ..........7 E6
  Watford WD25 ........154 C8
Shirley Cl Cheshunt EN8 ..148 C2
  Cheshunt,Wormley EN10 ..148 F7
  Stevenage SG1 .......51 C8
**Shirley Rd**
  Abbots Langley WD5 ..153 F7
  Luton LU1 ...........63 C8
  St Albans AL1 .......127 F2
Shootersway HP4 .....121 D4
Shootersway La HP4 ..121 D4
Shootersway Pk HP4 ..121 F3
Shoplands AL8 .......89 D2
Shoreham Cl SG1 ....50 A8
Short Hale LU7 .......80 D3
Short La Aston SG2 ...51 E4
  Bricket Wood AL2 ....140 E2
Shortcroft CM23 .....77 D7
Shortlands Gn AL7 ...110 F5
Shortlands Pl CM23 ..76 F8
Shortmead Dr EN8 ...162 E8
Shothanger Way HP3 ..137 D6
Shott La SG2 .........23 A5
Shottfield Cl AL4 ....108 D2
Shrevington Gr LU3 ..45 C3
Shrubbery Gr SG8 ....7 D4
Shrubbery The HP1 ...123 E4
Shrubhill Rd HP1 ....123 F2
Shrublands AL9 .....145 B5
Shrublands Ave HP4 ..122 A4
Shrublands Rd HP4 ..122 A5
Shrublands The EN6 ..158 E6
Shrubs UB9 .........173 F4
Shrubs Rd UB9 ......173 F4
Shugars Gn HP23 ....100 B5
Sibley Ave AL5 ......107 E7
Sibley Cl LU2 ........46 B3
Sibthorpe Rd AL9 ...144 D7
Siccut Rd SG4 .......35 E4
Sicklefield Cl EN7 ...147 F5
Siddons Rd SG2 .....51 C6
Sidford Cl HP1 ......123 F3
Sidings Ct SG14 .....113 C7
**Sidings The**
  Hatfield AL10 ........129 E4
  Hemel Hempstead HP2 ..124 D3
  Hoddesdon EN10 .....135 A1
Sidmouth Cl WD19 ..175 B8
Sidney Ct EN8 .......162 F5
Sidney Terr CM23 ....76 F6
Signal Cl SG16 ......10 B3
Silam Rd SG1 .......50 C5
Silecroft Rd LU2 .....64 B8
Silk Mill WD17 ......167 B2
**Silk Mill Rd**
  Redbourn AL3 .......106 B4
  Watford WD19 .......167 B1
Silk Mill Way HP23 ..100 A5
Silkin Ct SG2 ........51 D3
Silver Birch Ct EN8 ..162 D8
Silver Cl HA3 ........176 D3
Silver Ct Ashwell SG7 ..4 D4
  Hitchin SG5 ..........34 F8
Silver Dell WD24 ....153 F4
Silver Hill WD6,WD7 ..157 B3
Silver Pl WD18 ......166 F5
Silver St Anstey SG9 ..29 A5
  Ashwell SG7 .........4 D4
  Goff's Oak EN7 ......147 D1
  Guilden Morden SG8 ..1 F4
  Luton LU1 ...........63 E7
Silver Trees AL2 .....140 F1
Silverbirch Ave SG5 ..11 F8
Silverdale Ho HA6 ...174 F4
Silverdale Rd WD23 ..167 E4
Silverfield EN10 ....134 F1
Silverthorn Dr HP3 ..139 B7
Silverwood Cl HA6 ..174 C2
Simmonds Rise HP3 ..124 D1
Simon Balle Sch SG13 ..113 E5
Simon Dean HP3 ....137 A4
Simpson Cl LU4 .....44 D2
Simpson Dr SG7 ....23 E8
Simpsons Ct 3 SG7 ..23 F8
Sinderby Cl SG1 ....169 E8
Sinfield Cl SG1 .....51 A5
Singlets La AL3 .....84 C2
**Sir Frederic Osborn Sch**
  AL7 ................111 B7
**Sir Herbert Janes Village The**
  LU4 ................44 D4
Sir John Lawes Sch AL5 ..86 C3
**Sir John Newsom Way**
  AL7 ................110 E3
Sir Joseph's Wlk AL5 ..107 A8
Sir Peter's Way HP4 ..81 E6
Sirus Rd HA6 .......175 A5
Sish Cl LU4 .........50 D6
Sish La SG1 .........50 D6
**Siskin Cl**
  Borehamwood WD6 ..170 A5

**Siskin Cl** continued
  Royston SG8 .........7 E8
  Watford WD23 .......167 E5
Sisson Cl SG2 .......51 C2
Sitwell Gr HA7 ......176 F5
Six Acres HP3 .......139 A8
Six Cotts SG11 ......57 C6
Six Hills Way SG1,SG2 ..50 C4
Sixth Ave Letchworth SG6 ..23 C6
  Watford WD25 .......154 C4
Skegness Rd SG1 ....50 A8
Skegsbury La SG4 ...65 F1
Skelton Cl LU3 ......31 B1
Skidmore Way WD3 ..165 E1
Skimpans Cl AL9 ....144 D7
Skimpot Rd LU4 .....44 A1
Skinners St CM23 ...76 C4
Skipton Cl SG2 ......68 F8
Skua Cl LU4 .........44 A5
Skye Ho 11 WD18 ...166 F3
Skylark Cnr SG2 .....51 D3
Skylark Pl SG8 ......7 E8
Skys Wood Rd AL4 ..128 B7
**Skyswood Prim Sch**
  AL4 ................128 C6
Slade Ct WD7 .......156 A4
Sleaford Gn WD19 ..175 D7
Sleapcross Gdns AL4 ..129 C2
Sleaps Hyde SG2 ....51 C1
Sleapshyde La AL4 ..129 C2
Sleddale HP2 .......124 E6
Sleets End HP1 .....124 B5
Slimmons Dr AL4 ...128 A4
Slip End 2 .........14 B6
Slip End Lower Sch LU1 ..63 B1
Slip La SG3,AL6 .....68 C4
Slipe La EN10 ......148 F7
Slipe The LU7 ......80 A7
Slippers Hill HP2 ...124 D4
Sloan Ct SG1 .......50 F6
Sloansway AL7 .....90 A1
Slowmans Cl AL2 ...141 C3
Slype The AL4 ......87 B3
Small Acre HP1 ....123 F3
Smallcroft AL7 .....111 B7
Smallford La AL4 ...129 B2
Smallwood Cl AL4 ..108 E7
Smarts Gn EN7 .....147 F5
Smeaton Cl EN9 ....163 E4
Smeaton Rd EN3 ...163 A2
Smith St WD18 .....167 C5
**Smith's End La**
  Barley SG8 ..........17 F8
  Nuthampstead SG8 ...18 A8
Smithfield HP2 .....124 D5
Smiths Cres AL4 ....129 C2
Smiths La EN7 .....147 D5
Smiths Lane Mall 5 LU1 ..63 E7
Smiths Sq 6 LU1 ....63 E7
**Smithy The**
  Little Hadham SG11 ..57 B2
  Sawbridgeworth CM21 ..97 E3
Smug Oak Bsns Ctr AL2 ..141 B1
Smug Oak La AL2 ...141 D1
Snailswell La SG5 ...21 C5
Snatchup AL3 ......106 A5
Snells Mead SG9 ....40 F7
Snipe The SG4 .....24 B1
Snowdrop Cl CM23 ..76 C6
Snowford Cl 1 LU3 ..45 A7
Snowley Par CM23 ..59 B1
Soham Rd EN3 .....162 F2
Solar Ct WD18 .....166 F4
Solar Way EN3 .....162 F3
Solesbridge Cl WD3 ..164 C6
Solesbridge La WD3 ..165 B7
Sollershott E SG6 ...22 F5
Sollershott Hall SG6 ..22 F4
Sollershott W SG6 ..22 E4
Solomon's Hill WD3 ..165 D2
Solway HP2 ........124 F5
Solway Rd N LU3 ...45 A4
Solway Rd S LU3 ...45 A3
Somerford Cl EN10 ..135 A2
Someries Inf Sch LU2 ..46 C3
Someries Jun Sch LU2 ..46 C3
**Someries Rd**
  Harpenden AL5 ......86 C4
  Hemel Hempstead HP1 ..123 F5
Somers Rd SG1 .....144 C7
Somers Sq AL9 .....144 C8
Somers Way WD23 ..168 C2
Somersby Cl LU1 ...63 E5
Somerset Ave LU2 ..46 A1
Somerset Rd EN3 ...163 A1
Somersham AL7 ....111 D6
Sommer's Ct SG12 ..114 E8
Sonia Cl WD19 .....167 C2
Soothouse Spring AL3 ..127 F7
Soper Mews EN3 ....163 A1
Soper Sq CM17 ....118 C3
Sopers Rd EN6 .....146 F2
Sopwell La AL1 .....127 C2
Sorrel Cl Luton LU3 ..45 B8
  Royston SG8 .........7 F5
Sorrel Garth SG4 ...35 A6
Sotheron Rd WD17 ..167 C6
Souberie Ave SG6 ..22 F5
Souldern St WD18 ..167 B4
South App HA6 ....174 D7
South Bank Rd HP4 ..121 F6
South Block CM21 ..97 C3
**South Charlton Mead La**
  EN11 ..............135 D5
South Cl Baldock SG7 ..23 F7

**South Cl** *continued*
Barnet EN5 . . . . . . . . . . . .**171** F6
Chiswell Green AL2 . . . . . .**141** B6
Royston SG8 . . . . . . . . . . . . .**7** B7
**South Comm** AL3 . . . . . . . .**106** B5
**South Cottage Dr** WD3 .**164** F4
**South Cottage Gdns**
WD3 . . . . . . . . . . . . . . . . . . .**164** F4
**South Dene** HP2 . . . . . . . .**104** A4
**South Dr** Cuffley EN6 . . . .**146** E1
St Albans AL4 . . . . . . . . . .**128** E4
**South Drift Way** LU1 . . . .**63** B5
**South Farm Cotts** AL2 . .**142** C3
**South Hill Cl** SG4 . . . . . . .**35** A6
**South Hill Prim Sch**
HP1 . . . . . . . . . . . . . . . . . . .**124** C2
**South Hill Rd** HP1 . . . . . .**124** C3
**South Ley** AL7 . . . . . . . . . .**110** E3
**South Ley Ct** AL7 . . . . . . .**110** E3
**South Lodge Mews** ☑
SG7 . . . . . . . . . . . . . . . . . . . .**23** F7
**South Luton High Sch**
LU1 . . . . . . . . . . . . . . . . . . . .**63** F5
**South Ordnance Rd**
EN3 . . . . . . . . . . . . . . . . . .**163** A2
**South Park Ave** WD3 . .**164** F4
**South Park Gdns** HP4 .**122** B5
**South Pl** Harlow CM20 . .**118** A4
Hitchin SG5 . . . . . . . . . . . . .**34** D8
Waltham Abbey EN9 . . . .**163** C6
**South Rd** Baldock SG7 . .**24** A7
Bishop's Stortford CM23 . .**77** A5
Chorleywood WD3 . . . . . .**164** C4
Harlow CM20 . . . . . . . . . .**118** A4
Luton LU1 . . . . . . . . . . . . . . .**63** D6
Standon SG11 . . . . . . . . . . .**55** D2
**South Riding** AL2 . . . . . .**141** A4
**South St**
Bishop's Stortford CM23 . .**76** F6
Hertford SG14 . . . . . . . . .**113** D6
Stanstead Abbotts SG12 . .**115** C4
**South Street Commercial Ctr**
☑ CM23 . . . . . . . . . . . . . . . .**76** F6
**South View** SG6 . . . . . . . . .**22** F5
**South View Rd** HA5 . . . .**175** B4
**South Way**
Abbots Langley WD5,
WD25 . . . . . . . . . . . . . . . .**153** E6
Hatfield AL10 . . . . . . . . . .**130** A2
Waltham Abbey EN9 . . . .**163** C3
**South Weald Dr** EN9 . .**163** D6
**Southacre Way** HA5 . . .**175** C2
**Southall Cl** SG12 . . . . . . . .**93** D2
**Southbrook** CM21 . . . . . . .**97** E1
**Southbrook Dr** ☑ EN8 .**148** D3
**Southdown Ct** AL10 . . . .**130** A4
**Southdown Ho** AL5 . . . .**107** C8
**Southdown Ind Est** AL5 .**107** C8
**Southdown Rd**
Harpenden AL5 . . . . . . . .**107** B8
Hatfield AL10 . . . . . . . . . .**130** A2
**Southend Cl** SG1 . . . . . . . .**50** D7
**Southern Ave** SG16 . . . . .**10** C3
**Southern Gn** SG9 . . . . . . . .**26** A4
**Southern Rise** LU2 . . . . . .**85** F7
**Southern Terr** ☑ EN11 . .**115** B1
**Southern Way**
Letchworth SG6 . . . . . . . . .**22** E8
Studham LU6 . . . . . . . . . . .**82** C4
**Southernwood Cl** HP2 . .**125** A4
**Southerton Way** WD7 . .**156** E6
**Southfern Ct** AL7 . . . . . . .**110** D4
**Southfield** Barnet EN5 . .**171** D3
Braughing SG11 . . . . . . . . .**55** F7
Welwyn Garden City AL7 .**110** D4
**Southfield Ave** WD24 . .**154** C1
**Southfield Rd**
Cheshunt EN8 . . . . . . . . . .**162** E7
Hoddesdon EN11 . . . . . . .**135** A7
**Southfield Sch** AL10 . . .**130** B1
**Southfield Way** AL4 . . . .**128** D6
**Southfields**
Letchworth SG6 . . . . . . . . .**11** F1
Standon SG11 . . . . . . . . . . .**55** E2
**Southgate** SG1 . . . . . . . . . .**50** D4
**Southgate Cotts** WD3 . .**165** E2
**Southgate Ct** ☑ AL5 . . . .**86** D1
**Southgate Ho** ☑ EN8 . .**148** D1
**Southgate Rd** EN6 . . . . . .**159** C6
**Southhill** HA6 . . . . . . . . . .**174** E4
**Southlynn Ho** ☑ LU2 . . . .**63** F8
**Southmead Cres** EN8 . .**148** F1
**Southmill Cl** CM23 . . . . . . .**77** A6
**Southmill Rd** CM23 . . . . . .**77** A5
**Southmill Trad Ctr** CM23 .**77** A6
**Southsea Ave** WD18 . . . .**167** A5
**Southsea Rd** SG1 . . . . . . . .**50** B8
**Southside** SG9 . . . . . . . . . . .**28** A3
**Southview Cl** ☑ EN7 . . . .**147** E5
**Southview Rd** AL5 . . . . . . .**86** D3
**Southwark Cl** SG1 . . . . . . .**37** B2
**Southwark Ho** ☑ WD6 . .**170** A7
**Southwold Cl** SG1 . . . . . . .**50** A6
**Southwold Rd** WD24 . . .**154** C2
**Soval Ct** HA6 . . . . . . . . . . .**174** D3
**Sovereign Ct** WD18 . . . .**167** A5
**Sovereign Pk**
Hemel Hempstead HP2 . .**125** B5
Luton LU4 . . . . . . . . . . . . . . .**44** F1
St Albans AL4 . . . . . . . . . .**128** D2
**Sowerby Ave** LU2 . . . . . . .**46** C3
**Sparhawke** SG6 . . . . . . . . .**12** A1
**Sparrow Cl** LU4 . . . . . . . . .**44** A4
**Sparrow Dr** SG2 . . . . . . . . .**51** D4
**Sparrows Herne** WD23 .**168** C2
**Sparrows Way** WD23 . . .**168** C1

**Sparrowswick Ride** AL3 .**127** C8
**Spayne Cl** LU3 . . . . . . . . . . .**45** B8
**Spear Cl** LU3 . . . . . . . . . . . .**44** E6
**Spectrum Ho** EN3 . . . . . .**162** E3
**Speedwell Cl**
Hemel Hempstead HP1 . .**123** E2
Luton LU3 . . . . . . . . . . . . . . .**45** A8
**Speke Cl** SG2 . . . . . . . . . . . .**51** D5
**Spellbrook La E** CM22 . . .**97** F8
**Spellbrook La W** CM23 . .**97** E7
**Spellbrook Prim Sch**
CM23 . . . . . . . . . . . . . . . . . . .**97** F7
**Spellbrooke** ☑ SG5 . . . . .**34** D8
**Spencer Ave** EN7 . . . . . . .**147** E5
**Spencer Cl** CM24 . . . . . . . .**59** E6
**Spencer Gate** AL1 . . . . . .**127** E5
**Spencer Jun Sch** AL3 . . .**127** E6
**Spencer Ho** SG5 . . . . . . . . .**11** F6
**Spencer Mews** AL1 . . . . .**127** E4
**Spencer Pl** AL4 . . . . . . . . .**108** C2
**Spencer Rd** Harrow HA3 .**175** F7
Luton LU3 . . . . . . . . . . . . . . .**45** C2
**Spencer St**
Hertford SG13 . . . . . . . . .**113** E7
St Albans AL3 . . . . . . . . . .**127** D3
**Spencer Way** HP1 . . . . . .**124** A6
**Spencer Wlk** WD3 . . . . . .**165** C4
**Spenser Cl** SG8 . . . . . . . . . . .**2** D1
**Spenser Rd** AL5 . . . . . . . . .**86** C1
**Sperberry Hill** SG4 . . . . . .**35** B2
**Speyhawk Pl** EN6 . . . . . . .**145** B1
**Sphere Ind Est The** AL1 .**128** B2
**Spicer St** AL3 . . . . . . . . . . .**127** C3
**Spicersfield** EN7 . . . . . . . .**148** A4
**Spindleberry Cl** AL6 . . . . .**90** A7
**Spinney Cl** SG4 . . . . . . . . . .**35** B6
**Spinney Jun & Inf Schs The**
CM20 . . . . . . . . . . . . . . . . .**118** A4
**Spinney La** AL6 . . . . . . . . . .**68** E3
**Spinney Rd** LU3 . . . . . . . . . .**44** D7
**Spinney The** Baldock SG7 .**23** E7
Berkhamsted HP4 . . . . . . .**121** F3
Cheshunt EN7 . . . . . . . . . .**148** B1
Harpenden AL5 . . . . . . . . .**85** E3
Hertford SG13 . . . . . . . . .**113** F6
Hoddesdon EN10 . . . . . . .**134** F4
Potters Bar EN6 . . . . . . . .**159** D8
Radlett WD25 . . . . . . . . . .**155** D1
Stansted Mountfitchet
CM24 . . . . . . . . . . . . . . . . .**59** E6
Stevenage SG2 . . . . . . . . . .**51** D7
Welwyn Garden City AL7 .**110** E5
**Spinneys Dr** AL3 . . . . . . . .**127** E6
**Spires Sh Ctr The** EN5 .**171** E6
**Spires The**
Bishop's Stortford CM23 . .**76** D7
Hemel Hempstead HP2 . .**124** D2
**Spittlesea Rd** LU2 . . . . . . .**64** C7
**Spooners Dr** AL2 . . . . . . .**141** C4
**Spratts La** LU6 . . . . . . . . . .**82** F8
**Spreckley Cl** SG16 . . . . . . .**10** B5
**Spring Cl** Barnet EN5 . . .**171** D4
Borehamwood WD6 . . . . .**170** A8
Harefield UB9 . . . . . . . . . .**173** D2
Latimer HP5 . . . . . . . . . . .**150** D3
**Spring Court Rd** EN2 . . .**161** A1
**Spring Crofts** WD23 . . . .**168** A4
**Spring Dr** SG2 . . . . . . . . . . .**69** B8
**Spring Field Rd** HP4 . . . .**122** A6
**Spring Gdns** WD25 . . . . .**154** C3
**Spring Glen** AL10 . . . . . . .**129** F4
**Spring Hills** CM20 . . . . . .**117** B1
**Spring Hills Twr** CM20 . .**117** A1
**Spring La** Cottered SG9 . . .**39** C5
Hemel Hempstead HP1 . .**124** A4
**Spring Mews** CM21 . . . . . .**97** E2
**Spring Pl** ☑ LU1 . . . . . . . . .**63** D6
**Spring Rd** Harpenden AL5 .**85** A4
Letchworth SG6 . . . . . . . . .**22** E4
Letchworth SG6 . . . . . . . . .**22** E6
**Spring Valley Ent Ctr**
AL3 . . . . . . . . . . . . . . . . . . .**127** E7
**Spring View Rd** SG12 . . .**114** C8
**Spring Way** HP2 . . . . . . . .**125** C5
**Spring Wlk** EN10 . . . . . . .**134** C2
**Springfield** WD23 . . . . . . .**168** D1
**Springfield Cl**
Croxley Green WD3 . . . . .**166** B4
Potters Bar EN6 . . . . . . . .**159** E8
**Springfield Cres** AL5 . . . .**86** B5
**Springfield Ct**
Bishop's Stortford CM23 . . .**76** E8
Rickmansworth WD3 . . . .**165** B1
**Springfield Lodge** SG13 .**113** E5
**Springfield Rd**
Cheshunt EN8 . . . . . . . . . .**162** E7
Hemel Hempstead HP2 . .**124** F4
Luton LU3 . . . . . . . . . . . . . . .**45** C6
St Albans AL1 . . . . . . . . . .**128** A2
St Albans, The Camp AL1 .**128** A2
Watford WD25 . . . . . . . . .**154** B6
**Springfields**
Hoddesdon EN10 . . . . . . .**134** F4
Waltham Abbey EN9 . . . .**163** E5
Welwyn Garden City AL8 .**110** B4
**Springfields Ho** AL8 . . . .**110** C4
**Springhall Ct** CM21 . . . . . .**97** E2
**Springhall La** CM21 . . . . . .**97** E1
**Springhall Rd** CM21 . . . . . .**97** E2
**Springhead** SG7 . . . . . . . . . .**4** D4
**Springle La** SG13 . . . . . . .**114** D4
**Springmead Jun Mix Inf Sch**
AL7 . . . . . . . . . . . . . . . . . . .**111** C7
**Springs Cotts** EN10 . . . .**148** E7

**Springs The**
Cheshunt EN10 . . . . . . . . .**148** E6
Hertford SG13 . . . . . . . . .**113** F7
**Springshott** SG6 . . . . . . . . .**22** E5
**Springwell Ave** WD3 . . .**173** A8
**Springwell Ct**
Rickmansworth WD3 . . . .**173** A8
Stanstead Abbotts SG12 . .**115** C4
**Springwell La** WD3 . . . . .**173** A6
**Springwood** EN7 . . . . . . .**148** A5
**Springwood Cl** UB9 . . . . .**173** D2
**Springwood Wlk** AL4 . . .**128** D6
**Spruce Way** AL2 . . . . . . . .**141** B4
**Spur The** WD5 . . . . . . . . . .**153** D6
**Spur The**
☑ Cheshunt EN8 . . . . . . . .**148** D3
Stevenage SG1 . . . . . . . . . .**50** E4
**Spurcroft** LU3 . . . . . . . . . . .**31** C1
**Spurrs Cl** SG4 . . . . . . . . . . .**35** B7
**Square St** CM17 . . . . . . . .**118** C1
**Square The**
Braughing SG11 . . . . . . . . .**55** F7
Buckland SG9 . . . . . . . . . . .**27** D5
Hemel Hempstead HP1 . .**124** C3
Hoddesdon EN10 . . . . . . .**148** E8
Much Hadham SG10 . . . . .**74** F3
Potten End HP4 . . . . . . . .**123** B7
Redbourn AL3 . . . . . . . . . .**105** F6
Sawbridgeworth CM21 . . .**97** E2
Watford WD24 . . . . . . . . .**154** B2
**Squires Cl** CM23 . . . . . . . . .**76** C8
**Squires Ct** EN11 . . . . . . . .**135** A5
**Squires Ride** HP2 . . . . . . .**104** F1
**Squirrel Chase** HP1 . . . .**123** E4
**Squirrels** ☑ CM23 . . . . . . . .**76** F8
**Squirrels The**
Bushey WD23 . . . . . . . . . .**168** D3
Hertford SG13 . . . . . . . . .**114** B6
Welwyn Garden City AL7 .**111** C5
**Stable Block The** AL6 . . . .**90** B2
**Stable Cotts** SG11 . . . . . . .**57** E2
**Stable Ct** AL1 . . . . . . . . . . .**127** E5
**Stable Mews**
Northaw AL9 . . . . . . . . . . .**145** E3
St Albans AL1 . . . . . . . . . .**127** E4
**Stables The** CM21 . . . . . . .**98** B3
**Stacey Ct** ☑ CM23 . . . . . . .**76** F6
**Stackfield** CM20 . . . . . . . .**118** A3
**Stacklands** AL8 . . . . . . . . .**110** B4
**Staddles** CM22 . . . . . . . . . . .**98** B8
**Stadium Est The** LU4 . . . . .**44** B1
**Stadium Way** CM19 . . . . .**116** F1
**Staff Cotts** UB9 . . . . . . . . .**173** B2
**Stafford Cl** EN8 . . . . . . . . .**148** B2
**Stafford Ct** EN10 . . . . . . .**135** A3
**Stafford Dr** EN10 . . . . . . .**135** A3
**Stafford Ho**
Bishop's Stortford CM23 . . .**76** F5
Hoddesdon EN10 . . . . . . .**135** A4
**Stafford Rd** HA3 . . . . . . . .**176** C3
**Staffords** CM17 . . . . . . . . .**118** E4
**Stag Ct** WD3 . . . . . . . . . . . .**164** C5
**Stag Green Ave** AL9 . . . .**130** C7
**Stag La** Berkhamsted HP4 .**122** B5
Chorleywood WD3 . . . . . .**164** C3
**Stagg Hill** EN4 . . . . . . . . . .**159** E3
**Stainer Rd**
Borehamwood WD6 . . . . .**156** D1
Radlett WD6 . . . . . . . . . . .**169** D8
**Stainers** CM23 . . . . . . . . . . .**76** C5
**Stains Cl** EN8 . . . . . . . . . . .**148** F3
**Stake Piece Rd** SG8 . . . . . .**7** C5
**Stakers Cl** AL5 . . . . . . . . . . .**86** B1
**Stamford Ave** SG8 . . . . . . . .**7** D7
**Stamford Cl** Harrow HA3 .**176** E3
Potters Bar EN6 . . . . . . . .**159** D7
**Stamford Ct** SG8 . . . . . . . . .**7** D7
**Stamford Rd** WD17 . . . . .**167** B7
**Stamford Yd** SG8 . . . . . . . . .**7** C6
**Stanborough Ave** WD6 .**157** B1
**Stanborough Cl**
Borehamwood WD6 . . . . .**157** A1
Welwyn Garden City AL8 .**110** C5
**Stanborough Gn** AL8 . . . .**110** C4
**Stanborough La** AL8 . . . .**110** C4
**Stanborough Mews**
AL8 . . . . . . . . . . . . . . . . . . .**110** D4
**Stanborough Prim Sch**
WD25 . . . . . . . . . . . . . . . .**154** C4
**Stanborough Rd** AL8 . . .**110** C4
**Stanborough Sch** AL8 . .**110** B4
**Stanborough Sec Sch**
WD25 . . . . . . . . . . . . . . . .**154** B4
**Stanbury Ave** WD17 . . . .**153** C2
**Standalone Farm**★ SG6 . .**22** D8
**Standard Rd** EN3 . . . . . . .**162** E4
**Standfield** WD5 . . . . . . . . .**139** E1
**Standhill Cl** SG4 . . . . . . . . .**34** F6
**Standhill Rd** SG4 . . . . . . . .**34** F6
**Standon Bsns Pk** SG11 . .**55** E1
**Standon Cl** SG11 . . . . . . . . .**55** F1
**Standon Hill** SG11 . . . . . . .**55** D2
**Standon Rd** SG11 . . . . . . . .**56** E3
**Standring Rise** HP3 . . . . .**138** B8
**Stane Cl** CM23 . . . . . . . . . . .**58** F1
**Stane Field** SG6 . . . . . . . . .**23** B3
**Stane St** SG7 . . . . . . . . . . . .**13** A1
**Stanelow Cres** SG11 . . . . .**55** D2
**Stanfields Ct** CM20 . . . . .**117** E1
**Stanford Rd** LU2 . . . . . . . . .**46** A1
**Stangate Cres** WD6 . . . . .**170** E4
**Stanhope Ave** HA3 . . . . . .**176** D2
**Stanhope Rd** Barnet EN5 .**171** D3
Cheshunt EN8 . . . . . . . . . .**162** E6
St Albans AL1 . . . . . . . . . .**127** C3
**Stanier Rise** HP4 . . . . . . . .**121** F7
**Stanley Ave** AL2 . . . . . . . .**141** A6
**Stanley Dr** AL10 . . . . . . . . .**130** B3

**Stanley Gdns**
Borehamwood WD6 . . . . .**169** E8
Tring HP23 . . . . . . . . . . . . . .**99** F3
**Stanley Livingstone Ct** ☑
LU1 . . . . . . . . . . . . . . . . . . . .**63** D6
**Stanley Rd** Hertford SG13 .**113** E5
Northwood HA6 . . . . . . . .**175** A2
Stevenage SG2 . . . . . . . . . .**51** B4
Streatley LU3 . . . . . . . . . . .**31** A5
Watford WD18 . . . . . . . . .**167** C5
**Stanley St** LU1 . . . . . . . . . .**63** D6
**Stanmore Chase** AL4 . . .**128** D2
**Stanmore Cres** LU3 . . . . .**44** F4
**Stanmore Rd**
Stevenage SG1 . . . . . . . . . .**50** D7
Watford WD24 . . . . . . . . .**167** B8
**Stanmount Rd** AL2 . . . . .**141** A6
**Stannington Path** WD6 .**170** A8
**Stansted Dr** EN11 . . . . . .**135** B8
**Stansted Rd**
Hertford SG13 . . . . . . . . .**114** A6
Hertford Heath SG13 . . .**114** A5
Hoddesdon EN11 . . . . . . .**115** B1
**Stansted Hill** SG10 . . . . . .**75** A1
**Stansted Mountfitchet Sta**
CM24 . . . . . . . . . . . . . . . . .**59** E6
**Stansted Mountfitchet**
**Windmill**★ CM24 . . . . . . .**59** D6
**Stansted Rd**
Birchanger CM23,CM24 . .**59** C4
Bishop's Stortford CM23 . .**59** B2
**Stanton Cl** AL4 . . . . . . . . .**128** D7
**Stanton Rd** LU4 . . . . . . . . . .**44** C1
**Stantons** CM20 . . . . . . . . .**117** B1
**Staplefield Cl** HA5 . . . . . .**175** E3
**Stapleford** AL7 . . . . . . . . .**111** D6
**Stapleford Prim Sch**
SG14 . . . . . . . . . . . . . . . . . .**92** A6
**Stapleford Rd** LU2 . . . . . . .**46** C4
**Stapleton Cl** EN6 . . . . . . .**159** D8
**Stapleton Rd** WD6 . . . . . .**157** A2
**Stapley Rd** AL3 . . . . . . . . .**127** D4
**Staplyton Rd** EN5 . . . . . .**171** E6
**Star Holme Ct** SG12 . . . . .**93** E1
**Star St** SG12 . . . . . . . . . . . .**93** E1
**Starkey Cl** EN7 . . . . . . . . .**147** C6
**Starlight Way** AL4 . . . . . .**128** C1
**Starling La** EN6 . . . . . . . . .**146** F3
**Startpoint** LU1 . . . . . . . . . . .**63** C7
**Stately Ct** LU3 . . . . . . . . . . .**45** D1
**Statham Cl** LU3 . . . . . . . . . .**31** B1
**Stathams Ct** AL3 . . . . . . . .**106** A3
**Station App**
Cheshunt EN8 . . . . . . . . . .**162** E5
Chorleywood WD3 . . . . . .**164** D5
Harlow CM20 . . . . . . . . . .**118** C5
Harpenden AL5 . . . . . . . . .**86** B1
Hitchin SG4 . . . . . . . . . . . .**35** A8
Kings Langley WD4 . . . . .**139** B1
Knebworth SG3 . . . . . . . . .**68** F5
Northwood HA6 . . . . . . . .**174** E3
Radlett WD7 . . . . . . . . . . .**156** A4
South Oxhey WD19 . . . . .**175** D7
**Station Cl**
Brookmans Park AL9 . . . .**144** E5
Potters Bar EN6 . . . . . . . .**158** F8
**Station Ct** ☑ SG13 . . . . . . .**93** D1
**Station Footpath** WD4 . .**139** B1
**Station Mews** EN6 . . . . . .**159** A8
**Station Par** SG6 . . . . . . . . .**22** F6
**Station Pl** SG6 . . . . . . . . . . .**22** F6
**Station Rd** Aldbury HP23 .**101** B5
Arlesey SG15 . . . . . . . . . . .**11** A4
Ashwell SG7 . . . . . . . . . . . . .**4** F4
Baldock SG7 . . . . . . . . . . . .**12** F1
Berkhamsted HP4 . . . . . . .**122** D4
Bishop's Stortford CM23 . .**77** A7
Borehamwood WD6 . . . . .**170** A5
Braughing SG11 . . . . . . . . .**55** E5
Bricket Wood AL2 . . . . . .**155** A8
Brookmans Park AL9 . . . .**144** D6
Buntingford SG9 . . . . . . . .**40** E7
Cheddington LU7 . . . . . . . .**79** F8
Cuffley EN6 . . . . . . . . . . . .**146** F2
Harlow CM17 . . . . . . . . . .**118** C4
Harpenden AL5 . . . . . . . . .**86** C2
Hemel Hempstead HP1 . .**124** D2
Hoddesdon EN10 . . . . . . .**135** A3
Holdbrook EN9 . . . . . . . . .**163** A5
Kings Langley WD4 . . . . .**139** B1
Knebworth SG3 . . . . . . . . .**69** A5
Letchworth SG6 . . . . . . . . .**22** F6
Letty Green SG14 . . . . . . .**112** B3
Long Marston HP23 . . . . .**79** B4
Lower Stondon SG16 . . . .**10** A4
Luton, Leagrave LU4 . . . . .**44** E5
Luton,High Town LU1 . . . .**63** E8
Much Hadham SG10 . . . . .**74** E1
Pitstone LU7 . . . . . . . . . . . .**80** E5
Radlett WD7 . . . . . . . . . . .**156** A4
Rickmansworth WD3 . . . .**165** D2
Sawbridgeworth CM21 . . .**97** F3
St Albans AL4 . . . . . . . . . .**129** B3
Standon SG11 . . . . . . . . . . .**55** E2
Stanstead Abbotts SG12 . .**115** C4
Stansted Mountfitchet
CM24 . . . . . . . . . . . . . . . . .**59** E6
Steeple Morden SG7,SG8 . .**5** C5
Tring HP23 . . . . . . . . . . . .**100** D4
Ware SG12 . . . . . . . . . . . . .**93** C1
Watford WD17 . . . . . . . . .**167** B7
Watton at Stone SG14 . . .**70** D3
Welwyn AL6 . . . . . . . . . . . .**89** E3
Wheathampstead AL4 . . .**87** F2
**Station Rdbt** WD3 . . . . . .**165** D2
**Station Terr** Hitchin SG4 . .**35** A8
Park Street AL2 . . . . . . . .**141** D5

**Station Way**
Letchworth SG6 . . . . . . . . .**22** E6
St Albans AL1 . . . . . . . . . .**127** F3
**Stationers Pl** HP3 . . . . . .**138** E6
**Staveley Rd** LU4 . . . . . . . . .**44** C1
**Steeplands** WD23 . . . . . . .**168** B2
**Steeple View** CM23 . . . . . .**76** F8
**Sten Cl** EN3 . . . . . . . . . . . . .**163** A2
**Stephens Cl** LU2 . . . . . . . . .**46** A3
**Stephens Gdns** LU2 . . . . . .**46** A3
**Stephens Way** AL3 . . . . .**105** F5
**Stephenson Cl** SG8 . . . . . . .**7** B7
**Stephenson Way** WD23,
WD24 . . . . . . . . . . . . . . . . .**167** D7
**Stephenson Wharf** HP3 .**138** F6
**Stephyns Chambers**
HP1 . . . . . . . . . . . . . . . . . . .**124** C2
**Stepnells** HP23 . . . . . . . . . .**80** A1
**Stepping Stones The**
LU3 . . . . . . . . . . . . . . . . . . . .**44** E5
**Sterling Ave** EN8 . . . . . . .**162** D5
**Sterling Rd** EN2 . . . . . . . .**161** D1
**Stevenage Cres** WD6 . . .**169** E8
**Stevenage Mus**★ SG1 . . . .**50** E5
**Stevenage Rd** Hitchin SG4 .**34** F5
Knebworth SG2,SG3 . . . . .**68** D7
Little Wymondley SG4 . . .**35** E3
Little Wymondley, Titmore Green
SG4 . . . . . . . . . . . . . . . . . . . .**35** E2
St Ippolyts SG4 . . . . . . . . .**35** C2
Walkern SG2 . . . . . . . . . . . .**51** E8
**Stevenage Rise** HP2 . . . .**124** F7
**Stevenage Sta** SG1 . . . . . .**50** C5
**Stevens Cl** EN6 . . . . . . . . .**158** D6
**Stevens Gn** WD23 . . . . . .**168** C1
**Steward Cl** EN8 . . . . . . . . .**148** E1
**Stewart Cl** WD5 . . . . . . . .**154** A7
**Stewart Rd** AL5 . . . . . . . . . .**86** B2
**Stewarts The** CM23 . . . . . .**76** E6
**Stile Plantation** SG8 . . . . .**7** E6
**Stilton Path** WD6 . . . . . . .**157** A1
**Stirling Bsns Pk** EN8 . . .**162** F5
**Stirling Cl** Hitchin SG4 . . .**35** C7
Stevenage SG2 . . . . . . . . . .**69** D7
**Stirling Cnr** EN5 . . . . . . . .**170** D3
**Stirling Ho** WD6 . . . . . . . .**170** C5
**Stirling Way**
Borehamwood WD6 . . . . .**170** D4
Watford WD5 . . . . . . . . . .**154** A7
Welwyn Garden City AL7 .**111** E6
**Stirling Way Ret Pk**
WD6 . . . . . . . . . . . . . . . . . .**170** D3
**Stoat Cl** SG13 . . . . . . . . . .**114** A6
**Stobarts Cl** SG3 . . . . . . . . .**68** F6
**Stock Bank** SG8 . . . . . . . . . .**8** D1
**Stockbreach Cl** AL10 . . . .**130** A6
**Stockbreach Rd** AL10 . . .**130** A6
**Stockens Dell** SG3 . . . . . . .**68** F4
**Stockens Gn** SG3 . . . . . . . .**68** F4
**Stockers Farm Rd** WD3 .**173** D8
**Stockfield Ave** EN11 . . . .**135** B8
**Stockholm Way** LU3 . . . . .**44** E8
**Stocking Hill** SG9 . . . . . . . .**39** E8
**Stocking La** SG6 . . . . . . . . .**18** C1
**Stockings La** SG13 . . . . . .**132** D6
**Stockingstone Rd** LU2 . . .**45** E3
**Stockmen Field** CM23 . . . .**76** C5
**Stockport Rd** WD3 . . . . . .**164** C2
**Stocks Mdw** HP2 . . . . . . .**125** A4
**Stocks Rd** HP23 . . . . . . . . .**101** D7
**Stockwell Cl** EN7 . . . . . . .**148** E3
**Stockwell La** EN7 . . . . . . .**148** E3
**Stockwood Craft Mus &**
**Gdns**★ LU1 . . . . . . . . . . . .**63** D4
**Stockwood Cres** LU1 . . . .**63** D6
**Stockwood Ct** ☑ LU1 . . . .**63** D6
**Stockwood Pk**★ LU1 . . . . .**63** D3
**Stone Cross** CM20 . . . . . .**117** D1
**Stonecroft** SG3 . . . . . . . . . .**68** F5
**Stonecroft Cl** EN5 . . . . . .**171** B5
**Stonecross** AL1 . . . . . . . . .**127** E4
**Stonecross Rd** AL10 . . . .**130** B7
**Stonehill Jun Mix Inf Sch**
SG6 . . . . . . . . . . . . . . . . . . . .**11** E1
**Stonehills** AL8 . . . . . . . . . .**110** D7
**Stonelea Rd** HP3 . . . . . . . .**138** F8
**Stoneleigh** CM21 . . . . . . . .**97** D3
**Stoneleigh Ave** EN1 . . . .**162** B1
**Stoneleigh Cl**
Cheshunt EN8 . . . . . . . . . .**162** D6
Luton LU1 . . . . . . . . . . . . . . .**45** B7
**Stoneleigh Dr** EN11 . . . . .**115** B1
**Stoneley** SG6 . . . . . . . . . . . .**11** F1
**Stonemason Cl** AL5 . . . . . .**86** A3
**Stonemead** AL8 . . . . . . . . . .**89** D3
**Stonesdale** LU4 . . . . . . . . . .**44** C4
**Stoneways Cl** LU4 . . . . . . .**44** C6
**Stoney Brook** CM24 . . . . .**59** E5
**Stoney Cl** HP4 . . . . . . . . . .**121** F6
**Stoney Comm** CM24 . . . . .**59** E5
**Stoney Common Rd**
CM24 . . . . . . . . . . . . . . . . .**59** D5
**Stoney La** Bovingdon HP3 .**137** C5
Chipperfield WD4 . . . . . . .**137** E1
Hemel Hempstead HP1 . .**137** B8
**Stoney Pl** CM24 . . . . . . . . . .**59** E5
**Stoneycroft**
Aldbury HP23 . . . . . . . . . .**101** C5
Hemel Hempstead HP1 . .**124** A3
Welwyn Garden City AL7 .**111** A7
**Stoneyfield Dr** CM24 . . . .**59** E6
**Stoneygate Rd** LU4 . . . . . .**44** D3
**Stonnells Cl** SG6 . . . . . . . . .**22** F8
**Stony Croft** SG1 . . . . . . . . .**50** E6
**Stony Hills** SG12 . . . . . . . .**92** C7
**Stony La**
Chenies HP5,HP6 . . . . . . .**150** E1
Great Offley LU2,SG4 . . . .**47** C4

Stonyshotts EN9 . . . . . . .163 E6
Stookslade HP22 . . . . . . .60 A3
Stopsley High Sch LU2 . .45 F4
Stopsley Prim Sch LU2 . .46 A4
Stopsley Way LU2 . . . . . .46 A3
Storehouse La SG4 . . . . .34 F6
Storey Ct WD23 . . . . . . .168 B4
Storey St HP3 . . . . . . . . .138 D7
Stormont Rd SG5 . . . . . . .21 F1
Stormont Sch EN6 . . . . . .159 D8
Stornoway HP3 . . . . . . . .125 B1
Stort Lodge CM23 . . . . . .76 D8
Stort Mill CM20 . . . . . . . .118 B6
Stort Rd CM23 . . . . . . . . .76 F6
Stort Valley Ind Pk CM23 .59 B2
Stortford Hall Ind Pk
   CM23 . . . . . . . . . . . . . .77 B7
Stortford Hall Pk CM23 . .77 B8
Stortford Hall Rd ▤
   CM23 . . . . . . . . . . . . . .77 B8
Stortford Rd
   Hatfield Heath CM22 . . . . .98 E4
   Hoddesdon EN11 . . . . . .135 C7
   Little Hadham SG11 . . . . .57 C2
   Standon SG11 . . . . . . . . .55 F2
Stotfold Ho SG5 . . . . . . .11 F6
Stotfold Rd Arlesey SG15 .11 C7
   Hinxworth SG7 . . . . . . . . .3 C1
   Hitchin SG4,SG6 . . . . . . .22 C4
   Letchworth SG6 . . . . . . . .11 D1
Stow The CM20 . . . . . . . .117 F2
Stox Mead HA3 . . . . . . . .176 D2
Strafford Cl EN6 . . . . . . .159 A7
Strafford Ct SG3 . . . . . . .69 A5
Strafford Gate EN6 . . . . .159 A7
Strafford Rd EN5 . . . . . . .171 E6
Straits The EN9 . . . . . . . .163 B7
Strandburgh Pl HP3 . . . .125 B1
Strangers Way LU4 . . . . .44 C4
Strangeways WD17 . . . . .153 E3
Stratfield Dr EN10 . . . . . .134 E4
Stratfield Rd WD6 . . . . . .170 A7
Stratford Lodge WD17 . . .167 B8
Stratford Rd Luton LU4 . . .45 B1
   Watford WD17 . . . . . . . .167 A7
Stratford Way
   Bricket Wood AL2 . . . . . .140 F2
   Hemel Hempstead HP3 . . .138 B8
   Watford WD17 . . . . . . . .167 A7
Strathmore Ave
   Hitchin SG5 . . . . . . . . . . .21 F1
   Luton LU1 . . . . . . . . . . . .63 F5
Strathmore Ct SG5 . . . . . .21 F1
Strathmore Inf Sch SG5 . .21 E2
Strathmore Rd SG4 . . . . .66 E6
Strathmore Wlk LU1 . . . . .63 F6
Stratton Ave EN2 . . . . . .161 D2
Stratton Ct ▤ HA5 . . . . .175 F3
Stratton Gdns LU2 . . . . .45 D4
Straw Plait Way SG15 . . .10 F4
Strawberry Field
   ▤ Hatfield AL10 . . . . . . .130 A2
   Luton LU3 . . . . . . . . . . . .44 E7
Strawberry Fields SG12 . .93 B2
Strawfields AL7 . . . . . . . .111 B7
Strawmead AL10 . . . . . . .130 B7
Strawplaiters Cl SG3 . . . .69 A2
Straws Hadley Ct HP22 . .60 E3
Strayfield Rd EN2 . . . . . .161 B2
Stream Woods Jun & Inf Sch
   AL10 . . . . . . . . . . . . . .130 B4
Street The Braughing SG11 55 F7
   Chipperfield WD4 . . . . . .152 A8
   Dane End SG11 . . . . . . . .53 F3
   Furneux Pelham SG9 . . . . .43 A4
   Sheering CM22 . . . . . . . .98 E1
   Wallington SG7 . . . . . . . .25 C8
Stretton Way WD6 . . . . .156 F1
Stringers La SG2 . . . . . . .51 E2
Stripling Way WD18 . . . .167 A3
Stroma LU3 . . . . . . . . . .125 C1
Stronnell Cl LU2 . . . . . . .46 B3
Stronsay Cl HP3 . . . . . . .125 C1
Stroud Wood Bsns Ctr
   AL2 . . . . . . . . . . . . . . .141 E4
Stuart Ct WD6 . . . . . . . .169 D3
Stuart Dr Hitchin SG4 . . . .35 B7
   Royston SG8 . . . . . . . . . . .7 D8
Stuart Ho EN9 . . . . . . . .163 F6
Stuart Rd AL6 . . . . . . . . .89 B3
Stuart St LU1 . . . . . . . . .63 D7
Stuart St Pas ▤ LU1 . . . .63 D7
Stuart Way HP2 . . . . . . .162 B8
Stuarts Cl ▤ HP3 . . . . . .124 D1
Stud Gn SG4 . . . . . . . . .154 B7
Studham CE Lower Sch
   LU6 . . . . . . . . . . . . . . . .82 B4
Studham La Dagnall HP4 .81 D4
   Whipsnade LU6 . . . . . . . .82 A7
Studio Way WD6 . . . . . .170 C8
Studios The WD23 . . . . .168 A3
Studlands Rise SG7 . . . . .7 E6
Studlands Rise Fst Sch
   SG8 . . . . . . . . . . . . . . . .7 E5
Studley Rd LU3 . . . . . . . .45 D1
Stump Cross SG8 . . . . . .15 C6
Sturgeon's Way SG4 . . . .22 B2
Sturla Cl SG14 . . . . . . . .113 B7
Sturlas Way EN8 . . . . . .162 D6
Sturmer Cl AL4 . . . . . . . .128 C2
Sturrock Way SG4 . . . . . .35 C6
Styles Cl LU2 . . . . . . . . .46 C2
Such Cl SG6 . . . . . . . . . .23 B7
Sudbury Cl AL1 . . . . . . .127 E2
Sudbury Rd LU4 . . . . . . .44 B6
Suffolk Cl
   Borehamwood WD6 . . . . .170 D4
   London Colney AL2 . . . . .142 C6

Suffolk Cl continued
   Luton LU4 . . . . . . . . . . . .44 A3
Suffolk Rd
   Potters Bar EN6 . . . . . . . .158 E7
   Royston SG8 . . . . . . . . . . .7 E6
Sugar La HP1 . . . . . . . . .123 B1
Sulgrave Cres HP23 . . . .100 C5
Sullivan Cres UB9 . . . . . .173 D1
Sullivan Way WD6 . . . . . .169 C3
Summer Ct HP2 . . . . . . .124 D5
Summer Dale AL8 . . . . . .89 C1
Summer Gr WD6 . . . . . . .169 D3
Summer Hill WD6 . . . . . .170 A4
Summer St LU1 . . . . . . . .63 C1
Summer Wlk AL3 . . . . . . .83 E5
Summercroft Jun & Inf Schs
   CM23 . . . . . . . . . . . . . .77 C8
Summerfield AL10 . . . . . .130 A2
Summerfield Cl AL2 . . . . .142 C5
Summerfield Rd
   Luton LU1 . . . . . . . . . . . .62 F8
   Watford WD25 . . . . . . . .154 A4
Summerhill Ct AL1 . . . . . .127 F4
Summerhouse La
   Harefield UB9 . . . . . . . . .173 A3
   Radlett WD8 . . . . . . . . . .168 C8
Summerhouse Way
   WD5 . . . . . . . . . . . . . . .139 F1
Summerlands Rd AL4 . . .128 C7
Summers Lodge SG6 . . . .22 D6
Summers Rd LU2 . . . . . . .46 C1
Summers Way AL2 . . . . . .142 E4
Summerswood La EN6,
   WD6 . . . . . . . . . . . . . .157 C3
Summerswood Prim Sch
   WD6 . . . . . . . . . . . . . .170 B5
Summit Cl EN5 . . . . . . . .171 F6
Summit Rd EN6 . . . . . . .144 E1
Sumpter Yd AL1 . . . . . . .127 D3
Sun Hill SG7 . . . . . . . . . . .7 C5
Sun La AL5 . . . . . . . . . . .86 A2
Sun Sq ▤ HP1 . . . . . . . .124 D4
Sun St Baldock SG7 . . . . .23 E8
   Hitchin SG5 . . . . . . . . . . .34 E6
   Sawbridgeworth CM21 . . . .97 F1
   Waltham Abbey EN9 . . . . .163 C6
Sunbury Ct
   ▤ Barnet EN5 . . . . . . . . .171 E5
   St Albans AL1 . . . . . . . . .128 B2
Sunderland Ave AL1 . . . .128 A4
Sunderland St WD4 . . . . .139 B2
Sunderland Gr WD25 . . . .153 F5
Sundew Rd HP1 . . . . . . .123 C2
Sundon Park Jun Sch
   LU3 . . . . . . . . . . . . . . . .44 C8
Sundon Park Rd LU3 . . . .44 C7
Sunmead Rd HP2 . . . . . .124 D5
Sunningdale
   Bishop's Stortford CM23 . .76 E6
   Luton LU1 . . . . . . . . . . . .63 F3
Sunningdale Mews AL7 . .89 F2
Sunnybank Prim Sch
   EN6 . . . . . . . . . . . . . . .159 A5
Sunny Hill SG9 . . . . . . . .40 F7
Sunnybank LU7 . . . . . . . .79 F7
Sunnybank Rd EN6 . . . . .159 A6
Sunnydell AL2 . . . . . . . .141 B5
Sunnyfield AL9 . . . . . . . .130 D8
Sunnyhill Rd
   Hemel Hempstead HP1 . . .124 B3
   Maple Cross WD3 . . . . . .172 D4
Sunnyside
   Lower Nazeing EN9 . . . . .135 F1
   Stansted Mountfitchet
   CM24 . . . . . . . . . . . . . .59 E6
Sunnyside Cotts HP5 . . . .136 A5
Sunnyside Rd SG4 . . . . . .35 A5
Sunridge Ave LU2 . . . . . .45 E2
Sunrise Cres HP3 . . . . . .138 F8
Sunrise Ind Est LU2 . . . . .46 A2
Sunset Dr LU2 . . . . . . . . .45 F3
Sunset View EN5 . . . . . .171 E7
Sunshine House Sch
   HA6 . . . . . . . . . . . . . . .174 D4
Surrey Pl HP23 . . . . . . . .100 A3
Surrey St LU1 . . . . . . . . .63 E6
Surrey Street Prim Sch
   LU1 . . . . . . . . . . . . . . . .63 F6
Sursham Ct AL3 . . . . . . . .83 E5
Sussex Cl EN11 . . . . . . .135 A7
Sussex Pl LU2 . . . . . . . . .46 D2
Sussex Rd WD24 . . . . . .154 A1
Sutcliffe Cl
   Bushey WD23 . . . . . . . . .168 C5
   Stevenage SG1 . . . . . . . .51 A8
Sutherland Ave EN6 . . . .146 D3
Sutherland Cl EN5 . . . . . .171 D5
Sutherland Ct
   Watford WD18 . . . . . . . .166 C2
   Welwyn Garden City AL7 . .110 F7
Sutherland Pl LU1 . . . . . .63 D5
Sutherland Way EN6 . . . .146 E3
Sutton Acres CM22 . . . . .98 D7
Sutton Cl
   Hoddesdon EN10 . . . . . .134 E4
   Tring HP23 . . . . . . . . . . .100 B6
Sutton Cres EN5 . . . . . . .171 D4
Sutton Ct SG12 . . . . . . .114 E8
Sutton Gdns
   Caddington LU1 . . . . . . . .62 E3
   Luton LU3 . . . . . . . . . . . .44 D6
Sutton Path WD6 . . . . . .170 A6
Sutton Rd St Albans AL1 . .128 B3
   Watford WD17 . . . . . . . .167 C6
Swale Cl SG1 . . . . . . . . .37 A3
Swallow Cl
   Bushey WD23 . . . . . . . . .168 C1
   Luton LU4 . . . . . . . . . . . .44 A4

Swallow Cl continued
   Rickmansworth WD3 . . . . .165 C2
Swallow Ct Enfield EN3 . .162 C2
   Hertford SG14 . . . . . . . . .113 C6
   Welwyn Garden City AL7 . .110 F6
Swallow Dell Prim Sch
   AL7 . . . . . . . . . . . . . . . .111 A5
Swallow End AL7 . . . . . .110 F6
Swallow Gdns AL10 . . . . .130 A3
Swallow La AL1 . . . . . . . .142 B8
Swallow Oaks AL5 . . . . . .153 F7
Swallow Pk HP2 . . . . . . .125 B7
Swallowdale La HP2 . . . .125 B6
Swallowfields AL7 . . . . . .110 F6
Swallows CM17 . . . . . . .118 C4
Swallows The AL7 . . . . . .89 F2
Swan & Pike Rd EN3 . . . .163 A1
Swan Cl WD3 . . . . . . . . .165 D2
Swan Ct
   ▤ Bishop's Stortford CM23 76 F6
Swan Field Ho ▤ WD3 . .165 D2
Swan La SG8 . . . . . . . . . .1 F4
Swan Mead
   Hemel Hempstead HP3 . . .138 F6
   Luton LU4 . . . . . . . . . . . .44 B4
Swan Rd AL6 . . . . . . . . .162 E5
Swan St SG7 . . . . . . . . . .4 D4
Swanfield Rd EN8 . . . . . .162 E6
Swangley's La SG3 . . . . .69 B4
Swanhill AL1 . . . . . . . . . .90 A1
Swanland Rd AL9,EN6 . . .144 B3
Swanley Bar La AL9 . . . .145 B3
Swanley Cres EN6 . . . . . .145 B2
Swanley Ct WD24 . . . . . .154 C2
Swannells Wood LU6 . . . .82 C4
Swans Cl AL4 . . . . . . . . .128 C2
Swans Ct EN8 . . . . . . . . .162 E5
Swanstand SG6 . . . . . . . .23 D4
Swanston Grange LU4 . . .44 B2
Swanston Path ▤
   WD19 . . . . . . . . . . . . . .175 C7
Swasedale Rd LU3 . . . . . .45 A6
Sweet Briar
   Bishop's Stortford CM23 . .76 B6
   Welwyn Garden City AL7 . .111 A3
Sweetbriar Cl HP1 . . . . . .124 A6
Sweyns Mead SG2 . . . . . .51 C7
Swift Cl Letchworth SG6 . .22 E8
   Royston SG8 . . . . . . . . . . .2 D1
   Stansted Abbotts SG12 . . .115 C3
Swiftfields AL7 . . . . . . . .111 A7
Swifts Green Cl LU2 . . . . .46 B5
Swifts Green Rd LU2 . . . .46 B5
Swinburne Ave SG5 . . . . .21 C1
Swinburne Cl SG8 . . . . . . .2 D1
Swing Gate Fst Sch
   HP4 . . . . . . . . . . . . . . .122 D3
Swing Gate La HP4 . . . . .122 D2
Swingate SG1 . . . . . . . . .50 D5
Swinnell Cl SG8 . . . . . . . .2 B5
Swiss Ave WD18 . . . . . .166 E6
Swiss Cl WD18 . . . . . . . .166 E6
Sword Cl EN10 . . . . . . . .134 D3
Sworders Yd ▤ CM23 . . .76 F7
Sycamore App WD3 . . . .166 C5
Sycamore Ave AL10 . . . . .130 A4
Sycamore Cl
   Hammond Street EN7 . . . .147 F4
   Hitchin SG4 . . . . . . . . . . .35 A4
   Watford WD23 . . . . . . . .167 A4
   Watford,Garston WD25 . . .154 B4
Sycamore Dr
   Park Street AL2 . . . . . . . .141 D4
   Tring HP23 . . . . . . . . . . .100 B4
Sycamore Ho HP2 . . . . . .124 E4
Sycamore Rd WD3 . . . . . .166 C4
Sycamore Rise HP4 . . . . .122 D3
Sycamores The
   Baldock SG7 . . . . . . . . . .23 E8
   Bishop's Stortford CM23 . .77 B6
   Hemel Hempstead HP3 . . .137 F8
   Radlett WD7 . . . . . . . . . .156 B5
   ▤ St Albans AL1 . . . . . . .127 C2
Sydney Rd WD18 . . . . . .166 F4
Sylam Cl LU3 . . . . . . . . .44 E7
Sylvan Cl HP3 . . . . . . . . .125 A4
Sylvan Hts AL1 . . . . . . . .128 A1
Sylvan Way AL7 . . . . . . .111 C5
Sylvandale AL7 . . . . . . . .111 C5
Sylvia Ave HA5 . . . . . . . .175 F4
Symonds Ct ▤ EN8 . . . . .148 D3
Symonds Green La SG1 . .50 A6
Symonds Green Rd SG1 . .50 A7
Symonds Rd SG5 . . . . . . .34 D8

T

Tabbs Cl SG6 . . . . . . . . .23 B7
Tacitus Cl ▤ SG1 . . . . . . .51 E4
Tailors CM23 . . . . . . . . . .76 B5
Takeley Cl EN9 . . . . . . . .163 D6
Talbot Ave WD19 . . . . . .167 E2
Talbot Ct HP3 . . . . . . . . .124 D1
Talbot Rd Harrow HA3 . . .176 F1
   Hatfield AL10 . . . . . . . . .130 A8
   Luton LU2 . . . . . . . . . . . .45 F2
   Rickmansworth WD3 . . . . .165 L1
Talbot St Hertford SG13 . .113 D6
   Hitchin SG5 . . . . . . . . . . .34 C8
Talbot Way SG6 . . . . . . . .12 B1
Talisman St SG4 . . . . . . .35 C4
Tall Trees Hitchin SG4 . . .35 A4
   Royston SG8 . . . . . . . . . . .7 E5
Tallack Cl HA3 . . . . . . . .176 E3
Tallents Cres AL5 . . . . . . .86 D3
Tallis Way WD6 . . . . . . .169 E8

Tamar Cl SG1 . . . . . . . . .37 A3
Tamar Gn HP2 . . . . . . . .124 F8
Tamarisk Cl AL3 . . . . . . .127 C7
Tameton Cl LU2 . . . . . . . .46 F2
Tamworth Rd SG13 . . . . .113 F7
Tancred Rd LU2 . . . . . . . .46 A4
Tanfield Cl EN7 . . . . . . . .148 A4
Tanfield Gn LU2 . . . . . . . .46 E1
Tanglewood
   Harpenden AL5 . . . . . . . .85 F2
   Welwyn AL6 . . . . . . . . . .90 A7
Tanglewood Cl HA7 . . . . .176 E8
Tankerfield Pl AL3 . . . . . .127 C3
Tanner Ho WD19 . . . . . . .167 A1
Tanners Cl AL3 . . . . . . . .127 C4
Tanners Cres SG13 . . . . .113 C4
Tanners Hill WD5 . . . . . .154 A8
Tanners Way LU2 . . . . . . .45 F1
Tanners Wood Cl WD5 . . .153 E7
Tanners Wood Ct WD5 . . .153 E7
Tanners Wood Jun Mix Inf
   Sch WD5 . . . . . . . . . . .153 E7
Tanners Wood La WD5 . . .153 E7
Tannery Cl SG8 . . . . . . . . .7 C6
Tannery Drift SG8 . . . . . . .7 C6
Tannery Drift Sch SG8 . . . .7 C6
Tannery The SG9 . . . . . . .40 E7
Tannery Yd SG4 . . . . . . .66 F6
Tannsfield Dr ▤ HP2 . . . .124 F5
Tannsmore Cl ▤ HP2 . . . .124 F5
Tansycroft AL7 . . . . . . . .111 B7
Tanworth Cl HA6 . . . . . . .174 C4
Tanworth Gdns HA5 . . . . .175 C1
Tany's Dell CM20 . . . . . .118 A3
Tany's Dell Com Prim Sch
   CM20 . . . . . . . . . . . . . .118 A3
Tanyard La AL3,SG4 . . . . .88 B2
Tapster St EN5 . . . . . . . .171 F6
Taransay HP3 . . . . . . . . .125 B1
Tarlings CM20 . . . . . . . .117 F3
Tarpan Way EN10 . . . . . .148 F6
Tarrant . . . . . . . . . . . . . .36 B1
Tarrant Dr AL5 . . . . . . . .107 D7
Tassell Hall AL3 . . . . . . .105 F6
Tate Gdns WD23 . . . . . . .168 E2
Tates Way SG1 . . . . . . . .36 B2
Tatlers La SG2 . . . . . . . . .51 E4
Tatsfield Ave EN9 . . . . . .149 E8
Tatsford Villas EN9 . . . . .135 C1
Tattershall Dr HP2 . . . . . .105 B1
Tattle Hill SG14 . . . . . . . .91 E2
Tatton St CM17 . . . . . . . .118 C1
Tauber Cl WD6 . . . . . . . .169 F5
Taunton Ave LU2 . . . . . . .46 B1
Taverners HP2 . . . . . . . .124 E5
Taverners Way EN11 . . . .135 A6
Tavistock Ave AL1 . . . . . .141 D8
Tavistock Cl
   Potters Bar EN6 . . . . . . . .159 D8
   St Albans AL1 . . . . . . . . .141 D8
Tavistock Cres LU1 . . . . . .63 E5
Tavistock Rd WD24 . . . . .167 D8
Tavistock St LU1 . . . . . . .63 E6
Taylers Cotts EN6 . . . . . .159 E7
Taylor Cl Harefield UB9 . .173 C1
   St Albans AL4 . . . . . . . . .128 A8
Taylor St LU2 . . . . . . . . .63 F8
Taylor Trad Est SG13 . . .114 B7
Taylor's Hill SG4 . . . . . . .34 F6
Taylor's La EN5 . . . . . . . .171 F8
Taylor's Rd SG5 . . . . . . . .11 F8
Taylors Ave EN11 . . . . . .135 A5
Taylors La HP23 . . . . . . .119 C3
Taywood Cl SG2 . . . . . . . .51 B2
Teal Dr HA6 . . . . . . . . . .174 C3
Teal Ho WD25 . . . . . . . .154 E3
Teal Way HP3 . . . . . . . . .138 F6
Teasdale Cl SG8 . . . . . . . .2 D1
Teasel Cl SG8 . . . . . . . . . .7 E5
Tedder Ave SG16 . . . . . . .10 B5
Tedder Rd HP2 . . . . . . . .125 A4
Tee Side SG13 . . . . . . . .114 B7
Tees Cl SG1 . . . . . . . . . .36 F3
Teesdale
   Hemel Hempstead HP2 . . .124 E6
   Luton LU4 . . . . . . . . . . . .44 C5
Telford Ave SG2 . . . . . . . .51 B6
Telford Cl WD25 . . . . . . .154 D4
Telford Ct Hatfield AL10 . .129 F3
   St Albans AL4 . . . . . . . . .127 E2
Telford Rd AL2 . . . . . . . .142 C4
Telford Way LU1 . . . . . . . .63 E6
Telmere Ind Est ▤ LU1 . . .63 E6
Telscombe Way LU2 . . . . .46 C3
Tempest Ave EN6 . . . . . .159 D7
Templar Ave SG7 . . . . . . .23 F6
Templars Dr HA3 . . . . . . .176 D4
Templars La SG4 . . . . . . .48 D6
Temple Bank CM20 . . . . .118 B5
Temple Cl Cheshunt EN7 . .162 A8
   Luton LU2 . . . . . . . . . . . .45 D5
   Preston SG5 . . . . . . . . . . .34 B4
   Watford WD17 . . . . . . . .166 F7
Temple Ct Hertford SG14 . .92 D1
   Potters Bar EN6 . . . . . . . .158 D8
Temple Fields SG14 . . . . .92 D1
Temple Gdns
   Letchworth SG6 . . . . . . . .23 C8
   Moor Park WD3 . . . . . . . .174 B6
Temple Ho EN7 . . . . . . . .162 A6
Temple La SG12 . . . . . . . .92 F8
Temple Mead
   Hemel Hempstead HP2 . . .124 D5
   Roydon CM19 . . . . . . . . .116 B1
Temple View AL3 . . . . . . .127 C5

Sto – Tho  211

Templefields Ent Ctr
   CM20 . . . . . . . . . . . . . .118 A3
Templepan La WD3 . . . . .152 E2
Templewood AL8 . . . . . . .89 D1
Templewood Prim Sch
   AL8 . . . . . . . . . . . . . . .110 D8
Tempsford AL7 . . . . . . . .111 D6
Tempsford Ave WD6 . . . .170 D5
Temsford Cl HA2 . . . . . . .176 C1
Tenby Dr LU4 . . . . . . . . .44 F3
Tenby Mews LU4 . . . . . . .44 E3
Tene The SG2 . . . . . . . . .23 F8
Tennand Cl EN7 . . . . . . .147 F5
Tennison Ave WD6 . . . . . .170 B4
Tennyson Ave Hitchin SG4 .35 C7
   Waltham Abbey EN9 . . . . .163 E5
Tennyson Cl SG8 . . . . . . . .2 E1
Tennyson Ho LU1 . . . . . . .63 E5
Tennyson Rd
   Chiswell Green AL2 . . . . . .141 B5
   Harpenden AL5 . . . . . . . .86 A2
   Luton LU1 . . . . . . . . . . . .63 E5
Tennyson Road Prim Sch
   LU1 . . . . . . . . . . . . . . . .63 E5
Tenterfield Ho AL6 . . . . . .89 C4
Tenth Ave LU3 . . . . . . . . .44 C7
Tenzing Gr LU1 . . . . . . . .63 C6
Tenzing Rd HP2 . . . . . . . .125 A3
Teresa Gdns EN8 . . . . . .162 D5
Terminus St CM20 . . . . . .117 D1
Terrace Gdns WD17 . . . .167 B7
Terrace The
   Essendon AL9 . . . . . . . . .131 E6
   Redbourn AL3 . . . . . . . . .106 A5
   Tring HP23 . . . . . . . . . . .100 A3
   Westmill SG9 . . . . . . . . . .40 F2
Tethys Rd HP2 . . . . . . . .124 F6
Tewin Cl St Albans AL4 . .128 C2
   Tewin AL6 . . . . . . . . . . . .90 C5
Tewin Cowper CE Prim Sch
   AL6 . . . . . . . . . . . . . . . .90 E2
Tewin Ct AL7 . . . . . . . . .110 F7
Tewin Hill AL6 . . . . . . . . .90 F5
Tewin Rd
   Hemel Hempstead HP2 . . .125 C3
   Welwyn Garden City AL7 . .110 F7
Thackeray Cl SG8 . . . . . . .2 D1
Thames Ave HP2 . . . . . . .124 F8
Thames Cl LU3 . . . . . . . .45 B3
Thamesdale AL2 . . . . . . .142 F4
Thanet Ho ▤ WD18 . . . . .166 F3
Thatchers Croft HP2 . . . .124 E7
Thatchers End SG4 . . . . .35 D8
Thatchers The CM23 . . . .76 C5
Thaxted Cl LU2 . . . . . . . .46 F2
Thaxted Way EN9 . . . . . .163 D6
Thaynesfield EN6 . . . . . .159 D8
Theabald's Grove Sta
   EN8 . . . . . . . . . . . . . . .162 D7
Thelby Cl LU3 . . . . . . . . .44 F6
Thele Ave SG12 . . . . . . .115 D4
Thele Est SG12 . . . . . . . .115 L4
Theleway Cl EN11 . . . . . .115 B1
Thellusson Way WD3 . . . .165 A2
Thelusson Ct WD7 . . . . . .156 A3
Theobald Bsns Ctr SG4 . .22 A3
Theobald Cres HA3 . . . . .176 C2
Theobald Ct WD6 . . . . . .170 A6
Theobald St
   Borehamwood WD6 . . . . .169 D5
   Radlett WD6,WD7 . . . . . .156 D2
Theobald's La
   Cheshunt EN8 . . . . . . . . .162 B7
   Cheshunt EN8 . . . . . . . . .162 D7
Theobald's Rd EN6 . . . . .146 F1
Theobalds Ct EN6 . . . . . .146 F1
Theobalds Park Camp Site
   EN7 . . . . . . . . . . . . . . .162 A6
Theobalds Park Coll
   EN7 . . . . . . . . . . . . . . .162 A6
Theobalds Park Rd EN2 .161 B3
Therfield Fst Sch SG8 . . .15 F7
Therfield Heath Nature
   Reserve ✳ SG8 . . . . . . . .7 A5
Therfield Rd AL3 . . . . . . .127 C6
Thetford Gdns LU2 . . . . . .45 E6
Thieves' La SG14 . . . . . .112 F7
Third Ave Letchworth SG6 .23 C7
   Luton LU3 . . . . . . . . . . . .44 D7
   Watford WD25 . . . . . . . .154 D4
Thirlestane AL1 . . . . . . . .127 C4
Thirlestone Rd LU4 . . . . . .44 D1
Thirlmere SG1 . . . . . . . . .37 C2
Thirlmere Dr AL1 . . . . . . .128 B1
Thirlmere Gdns HA6 . . . .174 C4
Thirsk Rd WD6 . . . . . . . .157 A1
Thirston Path ▤ WD6 . . . .170 A7
Thistle Cl HP1 . . . . . . . . .123 E2
Thistle Dr AL10 . . . . . . . .129 F8
Thistle Gr AL7 . . . . . . . . .111 C3
Thistle Rd LU1 . . . . . . . . .63 F7
Thistlecroft HP1 . . . . . . . .124 B2
Thistles The HP1 . . . . . . .124 B4
Thistley La SG4 . . . . . . . .34 F1
Thomas Alleyne Sch The
   SG1 . . . . . . . . . . . . . . . .50 C8
Thomas Bourne Ho ▤
   HP4 . . . . . . . . . . . . . . .122 D4
Thomas Coram CE Mid Sch
   The HP4 . . . . . . . . . . . .122 D2
Thomas Ct HP4 . . . . . . . .122 D1
Thomas Heskin Ct ▤
   CM23 . . . . . . . . . . . . . .77 A7
Thomas Rochford Way
   EN8 . . . . . . . . . . . . . . .148 F4

Thomas Watson Cottage Homes The EN5 .......171 E4
Thomas Way SG8 ........2 D1
Thompson Way WD3 ...165 A1
Thompsons Cl
Goff's Oak EN7 .........147 F2
Harpenden AL5 ..........86 A1
Thompsons Mdw SG8 ....1 F4
Thorley Ctr The CM23 ...76 D4
Thorley High CM23 ......76 F2
Thorley Hill CM23 .......76 F5
Thorley Hill Prim Sch CM23 ..................76 F4
Thorley La CM23 ........76 F3
Thorley La E CM23 ......76 D3
Thorley La W CM23 .....76 B4
Thorley Park Rd CM23 ...76 F4
Thorn Ave WD23 .......168 C1
Thorn Gr CM23 ..........77 B6
Thorn Grove Prim Sch CM23 ..................77 B6
Thorn Tree Dr HP23 .....99 F4
Thornage Cl LU2 ........45 D7
Thornbera Cl CM23 ......76 F4
Thornbera Gdns CM23 ...76 F4
Thornbera Rd CM23 .....76 F4
Thornbury AL5 ..........86 D1
Thornbury Cl
Hoddesdon EN11 .......115 B2
Stevenage SG2 ..........69 A8
Thornbury Gdns WD6 ..170 C5
Thorncroft HP3 ........125 B1
Thorndyke Ct HA5 ......175 F3
Thorne Cl HP1 .........124 B1
Thorne Ho AL1 .........127 E4
Thorne Way HP22 .......99 B4
Thorneycroft Cl LU3 .....44 F4
Thorneycroft Dr EN3 ...163 A2
Thornfield Rd CM23 .....76 E8
Thornhill Rd Luton LU4 ...44 F2
Moor Park HA6 .........174 C6
Thornton Gr HA5 ......176 A4
Thornton Rd Barnet EN5 171 E6
Potters Bar EN6 ........145 C1
Thornton St
Hertford SG14 .........113 D6
St Albans AL3 ..........127 C4
Thorntondale 5 LU4 ....44 C5
Thorpe Cres WD19 .....167 C2
Thorpe Rd AL1 .........127 D2
Thorpefield Cl AL4 .....128 D6
Thrales Cl LU3 ..........44 E7
Three Cherry Trees La HP2 ..................125 B7
Three Close La HP4 ....122 C4
Three Closes SG5 .......20 C4
Three Corners HP3 ....125 A1
Three Houses La SG4 ...67 D5
Three Meadows Mews HA3 ..................176 F2
Three Rivers Mus of Local History* WD3 ........165 E2
Three Star Cvn Pk SG16 .10 A3
Three Stiles SG2 ........52 E4
Three Valleys Way WD23 ..................167 E4
Thremhall Ave CM23 ....77 F8
Thresher Cl CM23 .......76 C5
Thricknells Cl LU3 ......44 E7
Thrift Farm La WD6 ....170 C7
Thriftfield HP2 .........124 D5
Thrimley La CM23 .......58 C6
Thristers Cl SG6 ........23 B3
Throcking La SG9 .......27 C1
Throcking Rd SG9 .......39 D8
Thrums WD24 ..........154 B2
Thrush Ave AL10 .......130 A3
Thrush Gn WD3 ........165 C2
Thrush La EN6 .........146 F3
Thumbswood AL7 ......111 A3
Thumpers HP2 .........124 E5
Thunder Hall 1 SG12 ....93 D2
Thundercourt SG12 .....93 D2
Thundridge Bsns Pk SG12 ..................93 D7
Thundridge CE Prim Sch SG12 ..................93 D7
Thundridge Cl AL7 .....111 B5
Thurgood Rd EN11 .....135 A8
Thurlow Cl SG1 .........36 D2
Thurnall Ave SG8 ........7 D5
Thurnall Cl SG7 .........23 F8
Thyme Cl LU2 ..........45 E7
Tibbles Cl WD25 .......154 E4
Tibbs Hill Rd WD5 .....139 F1
Tiberius Rd LU3 .........44 F6
Tichborne WD3 ........172 D5
Tile Kiln Cl HP3 ........125 B2
Tile Kiln Cres HP3 .....125 B2
Tile Kiln La HP3 .......125 B2
Tilecroft AL8 ............89 D1
Tilehouse Cl WD6 ......169 F6
Tilehouse La UB9 ......172 E2
Tilehouse St SG5 .......34 E6
Tilekiln Cl EN7 ........147 F2
Tilgate LU2 .............46 D3
Tillers Link SG2 .........51 A2
Tillotson Rd HA3 .......176 B3
Tilsworth Wlk AL4 .....128 C8
Timber Orch SG14 .......92 A2
Timbercroft AL7 .........89 F1
Timberidge WD3 .......165 D5
Timbers Ct AL5 ..........85 F2
Times Cl SG5 ............21 D2
Timplings Row HP1 ....124 B5
Timworth Cl LU2 ........46 D1
Tingeys Cl AL3 ........106 A5
Tinkers La HP23 .......121 A6
Tinsley Cl LU1 ..........63 B5
Tintagel Cl
Hemel Hempstead HP2 ...124 D8
Luton LU3 ..............45 B4
Tintern Cl Harpenden AL5 .85 C4
Stevenage SG2 ..........69 A7
Tinwell Mews WD6 .....170 D4
Tippendell La AL2 .....141 C5
Tippet Ct SG1 ...........50 D3
Tiree Cl HP3 ...........125 B1
Titan Ct LU4 ............44 F1
Titan Rd HP2 ..........124 F6
Titchfield Rd EN3 ......162 E2
Tithe Barn Cl AL1 ......141 C8
Tithe Barn Ct WD5 .....139 F2
Tithe Cl SG4 ............67 F1
Titian Ave WD23 .......168 E2
Titmore Ct SG4 ..........35 E2
Titmus Cl SG1 ...........50 E6
Tiverton Ct AL5 ........107 E6
Tiverton Rd EN6 .......159 E8
Toddington Rd LU4 .....44 C6
Toland Cl LU4 ...........44 C1
Tolcarne Dr HA5 .......175 A1
Tollgate Cl WD3 .......164 F5
Tollgate Rd
Colney Heath AL4,AL9 ...143 E7
Enfield EN3 ............162 D4
Welham Green AL9 ......144 A6
Tollpit End HP1 ........124 A6
Tollsworth Way SG11 ....55 D3
Tolmers Ave EN6 ......146 E3
Tolmers Gdns EN6 .....146 F2
Tolmers Mews SG13 ...146 E6
Tolmers Rd EN6 .......146 E3
Tolpits Cl WD18 .......166 F4
Tolpits La WD18 .......166 E2
Tom's Hill WD3 ........152 E3
Tomkins Cl WD6 .......169 E8
Tomlins Cl SG8 ...........8 F1
Toms Croft HP2 ........124 E2
Toms Field AL10 .......129 E4
Toms Hill Cl HP23 .....101 D5
Toms Hill Rd HP23 ....101 D5
Toms La WD4,WD5 .....139 D3
Tonwell St Mary's CE Prim Sch SG12 ..............92 E7
Tooke Cl HA5 ..........175 E2
Toorack Rd HA3 ........176 D1
Tooveys Mill Cl WD4 ...139 A2
Topstreet Way AL5 .....107 C8
Tormead HA6 ..........174 D4
Toronto Ho EN8 ........162 D8
Torquay Cres SG1 .......50 B7
Torquay Dr LU4 .........44 D4
Torridge Wlk 2 HP2 ...124 F8
Torrington Dr EN6 .....159 D7
Torrington Rd HP4 .....122 B4
Tortoiseshell Way HP4 .121 F6
Torwood Cl HP4 .......121 F4
Torworth Rd WD6 ......157 A1
Tot La CM23,CM24 ......59 D4
Totteridge Comm N20 ..171 D1
Totteridge Pk N20 .....171 C1
Totteridge Rd EN3 .....162 D2
Totteridge Village N20 ..171 F1
Totton Mews AL3 ......106 B5
Totts La SG2 ............38 C1
Toulmin Dr AL3 ........127 C7
Tovey Cl
London Colney AL2 .....142 D5
Lower Nazeing EN9 .....149 F8
Tower Cl
Berkhamsted HP4 .......122 A3
Hertford Heath SG13 ....114 C2
Kneesworth SG8 ..........2 A5
Little Wymondley SG4 ....35 F3
Tower Ct LU2 ...........46 A1
Tower Ctr EN11 ........135 A6
Tower Hill
Chipperfield WD4 .......137 F1
Much Hadham SG10 ......74 F2
Tower Hill La AL4 ......108 F4
Tower Hts EN11 .......135 A6
Tower Prim Sch SG12 ...93 E3
Tower Rd Codicote SG4 ...67 F2
Luton LU2 ..............64 A8
Ware SG12 .............93 F2
Tower St SG14 .........113 C8
Tower View SG4 .........66 D6
Tower Way LU2 .........64 A8
Towers Rd
Hemel Hempstead HP2 ...124 E4
Pinner HA5 ............175 E2
Stevenage SG1 ..........50 D4
Towers The SG1 ........50 D4
Town Ctr AL10 ........130 A6
Town Farm
Cheddington LU7 .........80 A7
Wheathampstead AL4 ....108 D8
Town Farm Cl SG8 .......1 F4
Town Farm Cres SG11 ...55 F2
Town Fields AL10 ......130 A6
Town La SG2 ............52 E4
Town Mead Rd EN9 ....163 C5
Town Mill Mews 3 SG14 ..................113 C6
Town Sq SG1 ...........50 D5
Towne Rd SG8 ...........7 D5
Townfield WD3 ........165 C2
Townley SG6 ............23 D4
Townsend HP2 .........124 D5
Townsend Ave AL1 .....127 E4
Townsend CE Sch AL3 ..127 C8
Townsend Cl
Barkway SG8 ............17 C3
Harpenden AL5 ..........85 F1
St Ippolyts SG4 ..........35 A3
Townsend Dr AL3 ......127 D5
Townsend La AL5 .......85 F1
Townsend Rd AL5 .......86 A2
Townsend Way HA6 ....175 A3
Townshend St SG13 ...113 E6
Townsley Cl LU1 ........63 E6
Tracey Ct 15 LU1 .......63 E6
Trafalgar Ave EN10 ....134 F2
Trafford Cl Shenley WD7 .156 E7
Stevenage SG1 ..........36 E1
Traherne Cl SG4 ........34 F5
Trajan Gate SG2 ........37 D1
Trapstyle Rd SG12 ......93 A2
Travellers Cl AL9 ......144 C8
Travellers La
Hatfield AL10 ..........130 B2
Welham Green AL9 ......130 C1
Treacle La SG9 ..........25 F3
Treacy Cl WD23 .......176 C8
Trebellan Dr HP2 ......124 F4
Treeby Ct EN3 .........163 A2
Treehanger Cl HP23 ...100 B4
Treetops AL6 ............89 E7
Treetops Cl HA6 .......174 D5
Trefoil Cl LU4 ...........44 A4
Trefusis Wlk WD17 ....166 E8
Tremaine Gr HP2 ......124 E7
Trent Cl Shenley WD7 ...156 E7
Stevenage SG1 ..........50 E8
Trent Rd LU3 ............45 B4
Tresco Rd HP4 .........121 F5
Trescott Cl LU2 .........46 E2
Tresilian Sq HP2 .......125 A8
Treslian Sq 1 HP2 ....124 F8
Trevalga Way HP2 .....124 E7
Trevellance Way WD25 .154 D6
Trevelyan Pl AL1 ......127 C1
Trevelyan Way HP4 ...122 B6
Trevera Ct Cheshunt EN8 .162 E6
Hoddesdon EN11 ........135 A7
Trevor Cl HA3 .........176 F3
Trevor Rd SG4 ..........35 A8
Trevose Way WD19 ....175 C7
Trewenna Dr EN6 ......159 D7
Triangle The SG4 ........34 F6
Trident Ctr WD24 ......167 C8
Trident Ind Est EN11 ..135 C7
Trident Rd WD25 ......153 F5
Trigg Terr SG1 ..........50 E6
Triggs Way LU2 .........46 E3
Trimley Cl LU4 ..........44 B5
Trinder Rd EN5 ........171 C4
Tring Bsns Ctr HP23 .....99 E4
Tring Ford Rd HP23 ...100 A7
Tring Hill HP23 ..........99 C3
Tring Ho WD18 ........166 E2
Tring Rd
Berkhamsted HP4 .......121 D7
Long Marston HP23 ......79 C3
Wingrave HP22 ..........60 C1
Tring Sch HP23 ........100 B4
Tring Sta HP23 ........101 A5
Trinity Cl
Bishop's Stortford CM23 ...76 F6
Northwood HA6 .........174 E4
Trinity Ct SG14 ........113 C8
Trinity Gr SG14 .......113 C8
Trinity Hall Cl WD24 ...167 C6
Trinity Ho
2 Borehamwood WD6 ...170 A5
Cheshunt EN8 ..........162 E7
Trinity La EN8 .........162 E7
Trinity Mews HP2 ......125 D2
Trinity Pl SG1 ..........50 D6
Trinity Rd
Hertford Heath SG13 ....114 C3
Luton LU3 ..............45 A4
Stevenage SG1 ..........50 C6
Stotfold SG5 ............11 F7
Ware SG12 .............93 E2
Trinity St CM23 .........76 F6
Trinity Way CM23 .......76 F6
Trinity Wlk
Hemel Hempstead HP2 ...125 D2
Hertford Heath SG13 ....114 C3
Tristram Rd SG4 ........22 B2
Triton Way HP2 .......124 F5
Trojan Terr CM21 .......97 E3
Troon Gdns LU2 ........45 E7
Trooper Rd HP23 ......101 C5
Trotter's Gap SG12 ....115 E4
Trotters Bottom EN5 ...158 B2
Trotts Hill Prim Sch SG1 .36 F1
Trout Rise WD3 .......165 B6
Troutstream Way WD3 .165 B5
Trouvere Pk HP1 ......124 B5
Trowbridge Gdns LU2 ...45 E3
Trowley Bottom AL3 ....105 B8
Trowley Hts AL3 .........84 B2
Trowley Rise WD5 .....153 F8
Truemans Rd SG5 .......21 D2
Trumper Rd SG1 ........36 F1
Trumpington Dr AL1 ...141 D8
Truncals LU1 ............63 D5
Trundlers Way WD23 ..168 E1
Truro Gdns LU3 .........45 C5
Trust Cotts HP4 .........81 A1
Trust Rd EN8 ..........162 E5
Tucker St WD18 .......167 C4
Tucker's Row 4 CM23 ...76 F6
Tudor Ave Cheshunt EN7 .162 B8
Watford WD24 ..........154 D2
Tudor Cl Cheshunt EN7 ..162 B8
Hatfield AL10 ..........129 F2
Tudor Cl *continued*
Hunsdon SG12 ..........116 D8
Stevenage SG1 ..........36 C1
Tudor Cres EN2 .......161 C1
Tudor Ct Barnet EN5 ...171 F5
Borehamwood WD6 ......169 E7
Hitchin SG5 .............34 D6
Kneesworth SG8 ..........2 B4
Rickmansworth WD3 .....165 A1
Sawbridgeworth CM21 ....97 E3
Tudor Dr WD24 ........154 D2
Tudor Gdns HA3 ......176 D1
Tudor Jun Mix & Inf Sch HP3 ..................124 E1
Tudor Lodge 3 HA6 ...174 E3
Tudor Manor Gdns WD25 ..................154 D7
Tudor Par WD3 ........165 A2
Tudor Rd Harrow HA3 ...176 D1
Luton LU3 ..............45 B2
Pinner HA5 ............175 C1
St Albans AL3 ..........127 E7
Welwyn AL6 .............89 B3
Wheathampstead AL4 ....108 E8
Tudor Rise EN10 ......134 E2
Tudor Sq 18 SG12 .......93 D1
Tudor Way
Hertford SG14 .........113 A7
Rickmansworth WD3 .....165 A2
Waltham Abbey EN9 .....163 D6
Tudor Wlk 17 Ware SG12 .93 D1
Watford WD24 ..........154 D2
Tuffnells Way AL5 ......85 D4
Tunfield Rd EN11 ......115 B1
Tunnel Wood Cl WD17 ..153 F2
Tunnel Wood Rd WD17 .153 F2
Tunnmeade CM20 ......118 A1
Turf La SG4 .............36 B4
Turkey St EN1,EN3 .....162 C2
Turkey Street Sta EN3 ..162 C2
Turmore Dale AL8 .....110 C5
Turnberry Ct WD19 ....175 C7
Turnberry Dr AL2 ......140 E1
Turner Cl SG1 ...........36 C2
Turner Rd WD23 .......168 C5
Turners Cl Bramfield SG14 91 C4
Harpenden AL5 ..........86 C4
Turners Cres CM23 ......76 C4
Turners Ct EN8 ........162 D8
Turners Hill
Cheshunt EN8 ..........148 D1
Hemel Hempstead HP2 ...124 E2
Turners Rd N LU2 .......46 A2
Turners Rd S LU2 .......46 A2
Turneys Orch WD3 .....164 D4
Turnford Sch EN8 ......148 E3
Turnford Villas EN8 ....148 F5
Turnpike Dr LU3 .........31 C1
Turnpike Gn HP2 ......124 F7
Turnpike La SG5 ........21 E3
Turnstones The WD25 ..154 E3
Turpin Cl EN3 .........163 A2
Turpin's Ride SG8 ........7 D5
Turpin's Rise SG2 .......50 F1
Turpin's Way SG7 .......23 F7
Turpins Chase AL6 ......89 F7
Turpins Cl SG14 .......112 F6
Turpins Ride AL6 .......89 F7
Tussauds Cl WD3 ......166 A4
Tuthill Ct SG8 ...........15 E7
Tuxford Cl WD6 .......156 E1
Tweed Cl HP4 .........122 B5
Twelve Acres AL7 ......110 E4
Twelve Leys HP22 .......60 B3
Twickenham Gdns HA3 .176 E3
Twigden Ct LU3 .........44 E5
Twin Foxes SG3 .........69 A1
Twinwoods SG1 .........50 F4
Twist The HP23 ........100 D2
Twitchell The SG7 .......23 F8
Two Acres AL7 ........110 F3
Two Beeches HP2 .....124 F8
Two Dells La HP5 ......136 A4
Two Oaks Dr AL6 .......90 C6
Two Waters Prim Sch HP3 ..................138 D6
Two Waters Rd
Hemel Hempstead HP3 ...124 C1
Hemel Hempstead HP3 ...138 D8
Twyford Bsns Ctr The CM23 ..................77 A4
Twyford Bury La CM22, CM23 ..................77 A4
Twyford Cl CM23 .......77 A5
Twyford Dr LU2 .........46 D1
Twyford Gdns CM23 ....76 F4
Twyford Mews CM22 ....77 A3
Twyford Mill CM22 .....77 A3
Twyford Rd
Bishop's Stortford CM23 ...77 A5
St Albans AL4 ..........128 D7
Twysdens Terr AL9 .....144 C7
Tye End SG2 ............69 B8
Tyfield Cl EN8 .........148 C1
Tylers AL5 ..............86 D1
Tylers Cl Buntingford SG9 .40 D7
Kings Langley WD4 ......138 F3
Tylers Cswy SG13 .....132 C1
Tylers Hill Rd HP5 ....150 A8
Tylers Mead LU2 ........45 E5
Tylers Way WD23,WD25 .168 E4
Tylers Wood AL6 .......90 C6
Tylersfield WD5 .......154 A8
Tynedale AL2 ..........142 F4
Tynemouth Dr EN1 ....162 A1
Typleden Cl HP2 ......124 D5
Tysoe Ave EN3 ........162 F2
Tythe Rd LU4 ...........44 C6
Tyttenhanger Gn AL4 ...142 E8


## U


Uckfield Rd EN3 .......162 D2
Ufford Cl HA3 .........176 B3
Ufford Rd HA3 .........176 B3
Ullswater Cl SG1 ........37 C2
Ullswater Rd HP3 ......125 C1
Ulverston Cl AL1 .......127 F3
Underacres Cl HP2 .....125 A4
Underhill Jun & Inf Schs EN5 ..................171 E4
Underwood Rd SG1 .....36 C2
Union Chapel Ho 1 LU1 .63 E6
Union Ct 19 HP4 .......122 D4
Union Gn HP2 .........124 D4
Union St Barnet EN5 ...171 E6
Luton LU1 ..............63 E6
Union Terr SG9 ..........40 E7
Unity Rd EN3 ..........162 D2
Univ of Hertfordshire AL10 ..................129 F3
Univ of Hertfordshire (Hertford Campus) SG13 ..................113 E4
University Cl WD23 ....168 A5
Unwin Cl SG6 ...........22 E4
Unwin Pl SG2 ...........51 C3
Unwin Rd SG2 ..........51 C3
Updale Cl EN6 .........158 E6
Upland Dr AL9 ........145 B6
Uplands Braughing SG11 ..55 F6
Croxley Green WD3 ......165 F3
Luton LU3 ..............44 D8
Stevenage SG2 ..........51 D7
Ware SG12 .............93 F2
Welwyn Garden City AL8 ...89 C2
Uplands Ave SG4 ........35 B6
Uplands Ct
3 Bushey WD23 .........168 D1
Luton LU1 ..............63 E4
Uplands The
Bricket Wood AL2 .......140 E1
Harpenden AL5 .........107 A4
Upper Ashlyns Rd HP4 .122 B3
Upper Barn HP3 .......138 F8
Upper Bourne End La HP1 ..................137 B8
Upper Clabdens SG12 ...93 F2
Upper Culver Rd AL1 ...127 F5
Upper Dagnall St AL3 ..127 D3
Upper George St LU1 ...63 D7
Upper Gn AL6 ...........90 D3
Upper Green Rd AL6 ....90 E3
Upper Hall Pk HP4 .....122 E2
Upper Heath Rd AL1 ...127 F5
Upper Highway WD5 ...153 D6
Upper Hill Rise WD3 ...165 B3
Upper Hitch WD19 .....167 E1
Upper Icknield Way
Aldbury LU7 .............80 E1
Aston Clinton HP22 ......99 A3
Tring HP23 ............100 D8
Upper King St SG8 .......7 D6
Upper Lattimore Rd AL1 ..................127 E3
Upper Marlborough Rd AL1 ..................127 E3
Upper Marsh La EN11 ..135 A5
Upper Maylins SG6 .....23 C3
Upper Paddock Rd WD19 ..................167 E3
Upper Pk CM20 ........117 B1
Upper Sales HP1 .......123 F2
Upper Sean SG2 ........51 A3
Upper Shot AL7 ........111 A7
Upper Shott EN7 ......147 F5
Upper Station Rd WD7 .156 A4
Upper Tail WD19 ......175 E7
Upper Tilehouse St SG5 .34 E7
Upperfield Rd AL7 .....110 F5
Upperstone Cl SG5 ......11 F6
Upshire Rd EN9 .......163 F7
Upton Ave AL3 ........127 D4
Upton Cl Luton LU2 ......45 D6
Park Street AL2 ........141 D6
Upton Lodge Cl WD23 ..168 C2
Upton Rd WD18 .......167 B6
Upwell Rd LU2 ..........46 B2
Uranus Rd HP2 ........124 F5
Urban Hive LU3 .........44 C8
Urban Rd CM23 .........77 B7
Uxbridge Rd WD3 .....173 A8
Uxbridge Rd (Harrow Weald) HA3 ..................176 D3
Uxbridge Rd (Hatch End) HA5 ..................175 F3
Uxbridge Rd (Pinner) HA5 ..................175 D2
Uxbridge Rd (Stanmore) HA7 ..................176 F4


## V


Vadis Cl LU3 ...........44 E7
Vale Ave WD6 .........170 B4
Vale Cl AL5 .............85 D4
Vale Cotts SG11 .........54 D5
Vale Ct AL4 ...........108 D7
Vale Dr EN5 ...........171 F5
Vale Ind Pk WD18 .....166 C1
Vale Rd WD23 .........167 E4
Valence Dr EN7 .......148 A3
Valency Cl HA6 ........174 F6
Valerian Way SG2 .......51 D8

Valerie Cl AL1 .........128 B3
Valerie Ct WD23 .......168 C2
Valeside SG14 .........113 A5
Vallance Pl AL5 .......107 C7
Vallans Cl SG12 .......93 D3
Vallansgate SG2 ......51 B1
Valley Cl Hertford SG13 ..113 D5
  Pinner HA5 ..........175 B1
  Studham LU6 .........82 B4
  Waltham Abbey EN9 ..163 C7
  Ware SG12 ...........93 B2
  Whipsnade HP4 .......81 E7
Valley Ct CM23 ........76 E5
Valley Gn HP2 .........105 B1
Valley Gn The AL8 ....110 C7
Valley Ho EN8 .........162 D8
Valley La AL3 .........83 E1
Valley Rd
  Berkhamsted HP4 .....121 F6
  Codicote SG4 ........67 F1
  Letchworth SG6 ......22 D7
  Rickmansworth WD3 ...165 B3
  St Albans AL3 .......127 F7
  Studham LU6 .........82 B3
  Welwyn Garden City AL8 ..110 B6
Valley Rise Lea Valley AL4 ..86 E7
  Royston SG8 .........7 E6
  Watford WD25 ........154 B6
Valley Road S SG4 ....88 F8
Valley Sch The SG2 ...50 F2
Valley The SG4 ........66 E7
Valley View Barnet EN5 ..171 E3
  Goff's Oak EN7 ......147 C3
Valley Way SG2 .......51 A3
Valley Wlk WD3 .......166 C4
Valleyside HP1 .......123 F3
Valpy Cl HP23 ........100 D1
Vancouver Rd EN10 ...148 E6
Vanda Cres AL1 .......127 F2
Vantorts Cl CM21 .....97 E2
Vantorts Rd CM21 .....97 E2
Vardon Rd SG1 .......50 F8
Varna Cl LU3 .........45 A3
Varney Cl
  Hammond Street EN7 ..148 A4
  Hemel Hempstead HP1 ..123 F3
Varney Rd HP1 ........123 F3
Vaughan Mead AL3 ....106 A4
Vaughan Rd
  Harpenden AL5 .......86 B1
  Stotfold SG5 ........11 E7
Vauxhall Rd
  Hemel Hempstead HP2 ..125 B3
  Luton LU1,LU2 ...........64 B5
Vauxhall Way LU2 ....46 B1
Vega Cres HA6 .......175 A5
Vega Rd WD23 ........168 C2
Velizy Ave CM20 .....117 D1
Venetia Rd LU2 ......46 A4
Ventnor Gdns LU3 ....45 A7
Ventura Pk AL2 ......141 F2
Venus Hill HP3 ......151 A8
Ver Mdw Cvn Site AL3 ..106 C6
  St Albans AL3 .......127 C3
Vera Ct WD19 ........167 D2
Vera La AL6 .........90 B4
Verdure Cl WD25 .....154 E7
Verity Way SG1 ......51 B8
Veritys AL10 ........130 A5
Verney Cl
  Berkhamsted HP4 ....121 F5
  Tring HP23 .........100 C5
Vernon Ave EN3 .....162 E3
Vernon Ct CM23 .....76 E4
Vernon Dr UB9 ......173 C2
Vernon Rd Luton LU1 ..63 C8
  Watford WD23 .......167 E4
Vernon's Cl .........127 E2
Veronica Ho AL7 ....111 B4
Verulam Cl AL7 .....110 F6
Verulam Gdns LU3 ...44 F6
Verulam Ind Est AL1 ..127 E1
Verulam Rd Hitchin SG5 ..34 F8
  St Albans AL3 ......127 C4
Verulam Sch AL3 ...128 A4
Verulamium Mus★ AL3 ..127 B3
Verulamium Roman City
  Walls★ AL3 ........127 B2
Verulamium Roman Town★
  AL3 ...............127 A3
Verwood Rd HA2 ....176 C1
Vespers Cl LU4 .....44 A2
Vesta Ave AL1 .....141 C8
Vesta Rd HP2 ......124 F5
Vestry Cl LU1 .....63 D7
Veysey Cl HP1 .....124 B1
Viaduct Cotts LU1 ..85 F8
Viaduct Rd SG12 ...114 E8
Viaduct Way AL7 ...89 F2
Vian Ave EN3 ......162 E4
Vicarage Cl Arlesey SG15 ..11 A8
  18 Bishop's Stortford CM23 76 F7
  Hemel Hempstead HP1 ..124 C2
  Northaw EN6 ........145 F1
  Shillington SG5 ....19 F8
  St Albans AL1 ......141 C8
  Standon SG11 .......55 E2
Vicarage Cswy SG13 ..114 E8
Vicarage Gdns
  Flamstead AL3 .....84 B1
  Marsworth HP23 ....80 A2
  Potten End HP4 ....123 B7
Vicarage La
  Bovingdon HP3 .....137 B4
  Kings Langley WD4 ..138 F2
  Pitstone LU7 ......80 F5
  Stapleford SG14 ...92 B2

Vicarage Rd
  Buntingford SG9 ...40 E8
  Marsworth HP23 ...80 A2
  Pitstone LU7 .....80 D3
  Potten End HP4 ...123 A7
  Ware SG12 ........93 E1
  Watford WD18 .....167 A4
  Wigginton HP23 ...100 D1
Vicarage Road Prec
  WD18 ............167 B5
Vicarage St LU1 ...63 F7
Vicarage Wood CM20 ..118 A4
Vicerons Pl CM23 ..76 D4
Victoria CE Fst Sch
  HP4 .............122 C4
Victoria Cl
  Rickmansworth WD3 ..165 D2
  Stevenage SG1 ....50 D7
Victoria Cres SG8 ..7 D7
Victoria Ct Harlow CM20 ..117 E1
  Watford WD17 ......167 C6
Victoria Dr SG5 ....12 A5
Victoria La AL5 ....171 F5
Victoria Mews SG13 ..113 A1
Victoria Pl HP2 ....124 D3
Victoria Rd
  Berkhamsted HP4 ...122 C4
  Bushey WD23 ......168 B1
  7 Harpenden AL5 ..86 B1
  Waltham Abbey EN9 ..163 C5
  Watford WD24 .....154 B1
Victoria Sq AL1 ...127 F2
Victoria St Luton LU1 ..63 E6
  St Albans AL1 ....127 E3
Victoria Way SG5 ..34 D8
Victors Way EN5 ...171 F6
Victory Ct SG8 ....7 E5
Victory Rd HP4 ....122 A5
View Point SG1 ....50 A5
View Rd EN6 ......159 C7
Vigors Croft AL10 ..129 F4
Villa Ct 6 LU2 ....63 D8
Villa Rd LU2 .....63 D8
Village Cl EN11 ...135 D8
Village Ct AL4 ....128 D7
Village Mews HP3 ..137 A4
Village St SG4 ....49 F1
Villiers Cl LU4 ...44 D3
Villiers Cres AL4 ..128 D6
Villiers Rd WD19 ..167 E3
Villiers St SG13 ..113 C6
Villiers-Sur-Marne Ave
  CM23 ............76 D4
Vincent SG6 ......23 C4
Vincent Cl EN8 ...148 E3
Vincent Ct HA6 ...174 F2
Vincent Rd LU4 ...44 D5
Vincenzo Cl AL9 ..144 C8
Vine Cl AL8 ......110 E8
Vine Gr CM20 .....117 C5
Vine Tree Ct WD3 ..173 B8
Vines The SG5 ....11 E6
Vineyard The
  Hertford SG14 ....113 D8
  Ware SG12 ........94 A2
  Welwyn Garden City AL8 ..110 E8
Vineyards Hill EN6 ..146 B2
Vineyards Rd EN6 ..146 A2
Vinters Ave SG1 ...50 F5
Violet Ave EN2 ....161 D1
Violet Way WD3 ...165 C5
Violets La SG9 ....43 B5
Virgil Dr EN10 ...148 F8
Virginia Cl LU2 ..45 F3
Viscount Cl LU3 ..45 A5
Viscount Ct 11 LU2 ..45 D1
Vivian Cl WD19 ...167 A1
Vivian Gdns WD19 ..167 A1
Vixen Dr SG13 ....114 A6
Vyse Cl EN5 ......171 C5

## W

Wacketts EN7 ......148 A4
Waddesdon Cl LU2 ..46 D2
Waddesdon Ct EN2 ..161 E1
Waddington Rd 1 AL3 ..127 D3
Waddling La AL4 ...87 D1
Wade The AL7 .....111 A3
Wades The AL10 ...130 A2
Wadesmill Rd
  Tonwell SG12,SG14 ..92 D3
  Ware SG12 ........93 D2
Wadham Rd WD5 ...153 F8
Wadhurst Ave LU3 ..45 C4
Wadley Cl 1 HP2 ..124 F2
Wadnall Way SG3 ..68 F3
Waggon Rd EN4 ...159 E2
Waggoners Yd 4 SG12 ..93 D2
Wagon Mead CM22 ..98 F3
Wagon Rd EN4 ....159 B2
Wagon Way WD3 ...165 C6
Waight Cl AL10 ...129 E7
Wain Cl EN6 ......145 B2
Wainwright St CM23 ..76 C5
Wakefields Wlk EN8 ..162 E8
Walace Ct EN3 ....163 A2
Walcot Ave LU2 ...46 B1
Waldeck Rd LU3 ...63 C8
Waldegrave Pk AL5 ..86 D1
Walden End SG1 ...50 E4
Walden Pl AL8 ....110 D8
Walden Rd AL8 ...110 D8
Waleran Cl HA7 ...176 F4
Waleys Cl LU3 ....44 E8
Walk The Hertford SG14 ..113 A5

Walk The continued
  Potters Bar EN6 ...159 B7
Walkern Prim Sch SG2 ..52 B8
Walkern Rd
  Benington SG2 ....52 D5
  Stevenage SG1 ....50 D8
  Watton at S SG14 ..70 C6
Walkers Cl AL5 ....107 C7
Walkers Rd AL5 ...107 B7
Walkers' Ct SG7 ..23 F8
Wall Hall (Univ Campus)
  WD25 ............155 B3
Wallace Way SG4 ..22 A2
Walled Gdn The AL6 ..90 B2
Waller Ave LU4 ...44 F3
Waller Dr HA6 ....175 A2
Waller Street Mall 3
  LU1 .............63 E7
Waller's Cl SG8 ...9 F2
Wallers Way EN11 ..115 B1
Wallingford Wlk AL1 ..141 D8
Wallis St EN9 ....163 B4
Walnut Ave SG7 ...24 A7
Walnut Cl
  Chiswell Green AL2 ..141 B4
  Hitchin SG4 ......35 A6
  Luton LU2 ........46 A4
  Much Hadham SG10 ..74 F2
  Royston SG8 ......7 D6
  Stotfold SG5 .....11 F6
Walnut Cotts SG8 ..97 E3
Walnut Ct
  Welwyn Garden City AL7 ..110 E3
  Wheathampstead AL4 ..108 D8
Walnut Dr CM23 ...76 D3
Walnut Gr
  Hemel Hempstead HP2 ..124 D3
  Welwyn Garden City AL7 ..110 E3
Walnut Ho AL7 ....110 F3
Walnut Tree Ave CM21 ..97 E4
Walnut Tree Cl Aston SG2 ..51 D4
  Cheshunt EN8 .....162 D8
  Hoddesdon EN11 ...135 A6
Walnut Tree Cres CM21 ..97 E3
Walnut Tree Rd SG5 ..20 D3
Walnut Tree Wlk SG12 ..114 E6
Walnut Way SG5 ...21 E4
Walpole Bldg WD3 ..165 E1
Walpole Cl HA5 ...176 A4
Walpole Ct SG2 ...69 C7
Walsh Cl SG5 .....34 D7
Walsham Cl SG2 ...69 C7
Walshford Way WD6 ..157 A1
Walsingham Cl
  Hatfield AL10 ....129 F6
  Luton LU2 ........45 D7
Walsingham Way AL2 ..142 C4
Walsworth Rd SG1 ..35 A8
Walter Rothschild Zoological
  Mus The★ HP23 ...100 A3
Walters Cl EN7 ...147 B6
Waltham Abbey★ EN9 ..163 C6
Waltham Cross Sta EN8 ..162 F5
Waltham Ct LU2 ...46 C3
Waltham Gate EN8 ..148 F5
Waltham Gdns EN3 ..162 C2
Waltham Holy Cross Inf Sch
  EN9 .............163 B6
Waltham Holy Cross Jun Sch
  EN9 .............163 D6
Waltham Rd
  4 Hitchin SG4 ....34 F6
  Waltham Abbey EN9 ..149 F5
Walton Cl EN11 ...135 C8
Walton Gdns EN9 ..163 B6
Walton Rd
  Hoddesdon EN11 ...135 C4
  Ware SG12 ........114 D8
  Watford WD23 ....167 E5
Walton St AL1 ....127 F5
Walverns Cl WD19 ..167 C3
Wandon Cl LU2 ....46 C4
Wannions Cl HP5 ..136 A1
Wansbeck Cl LU2 ..37 A3
Wansford Pk WD6 ..170 E5
Warburton Cl HA3 ..176 D4
Ward Cl
  Hammond Street EN7 ..148 A4
  Ware SG12 ........93 C2
Ward Cres CM23 ...76 E6
Ward Hatch CM20 ..118 A3
Warden Ct 5 LU2 ..63 E8
Warden Hill Cl LU2 ..45 C8
Warden Hill Gdns LU2 ..45 C8
Warden Hill Inf Sch LU2 ..45 C7
Warden Hill Jun Sch LU3 ..45 C7
Warden Hill Rd LU2 ..45 C8
Wardown Cres LU2 ..45 E2
Wardown Ct LU3 ...45 D2
Wards Cotts WD6 ..168 F7
Ware Mus★ SG12 ...93 D1
Ware Park Rd SG12,
  SG14 ............113 B4
Ware Rd Hertford SG13 ..113 E6
  Hoddesdon EN11 ...115 A1
  Tonwell SG12 .....92 F6
  Watton at S SG14,SG12 ..71 C3
  Widford SG12 .....95 D4
Ware Sta SG12 ....114 E8
Wareham's La SG14 ..113 C5
Warenford Way WD6 ..170 A8
Wareside HP2 .....105 A1
Wareside CE Prim Sch
  SG12 ............94 E3
Wareside Cl AL7 ..111 B5
Warham Rd HA3 ...176 F1

Warlow Cl EN3 ....163 A2
Warmark Rd HP1 ..123 E6
Warminster Cl LU2 ..46 F1
Warneford Pl WD19 ..167 E3
Warner Rd SG12 ...114 D8
Warners Ave EN11 ..134 F4
Warners Cl SG2 ...51 C3
Warners End Rd HP1 ..124 B4
Warren Cl Hatfield AL10 ..130 B8
  Letchworth SG6 ...22 D7
Warren Cotts SG8 ..9 A1
Warren Ct SG8 ....7 D5
Warren Dale AL8 ..89 D1
Warren Dell Prim Sch
  WD19 ............175 C7
Warren Dr The LU1 ..64 C1
Warren Gn AL10 ...130 B8
Warren Gr WD6 ...170 D5
Warren La Clothall SG7 ..24 D7
  Cottered SG9 .....39 B6
  Stanmore HA7 ....176 F8
Warren Park Rd SG14 ..113 D7
Warren Pl 16 LU2 ..63 D7
Warren Rd Bushey WD23 ..168 D1
  Luton LU1 ........62 F8
  St Albans AL1 ....141 C7
Warren Terr SG14 ..113 D8
Warren The
  Harpenden AL5 ...107 A6
  Radlett WD7 ......156 B6
  Royston SG8 .....7 D5
Warren Way AL6 ...89 E4
Warren Wood Ind Est
  SG14 ............91 F6
Warrenfield Cl EN7 ..162 A8
Warrengate La EN6 ..158 C8
Warrengate Rd AL9 ..144 C4
Warrensgreen La SG4 ..37 D5
Warton Gn LU2 ....46 E2
Warwick Ave EN6 ..146 D4
Warwick Cl
  Bushey WD23 .....168 E2
  Cuffley EN6 ......146 D4
  Hertford SG13 ....113 C4
Warwick Ct
  Chorleywood WD3 ..164 F6
  Luton LU4 ........63 B8
Warwick Dr EN8 ..148 D3
Warwick Rd
  Bishop's Stortford CM23 ..77 B6
  Borehamwood WD6 ..170 D6
  Enfield EN3 ......162 F2
  Pitstone LU7 .....80 D3
  St Albans AL1 ....127 F5
  Stevenage SG2 ...51 C6
Warwick Rd E LU4 ..63 B8
Warwick Rd W LU4 ..63 B8
Warwick Way WD3 ..166 C5
Wash La Dancers Hill EN6 ..158 C3
  South Mimms EN6 ..158 C5
Wash The
  Furneux Pelham SG9 ..43 D5
  Hertford SG14 ....113 D6
Washington Ave HP2 ..124 E8
Watchlytes AL7 ...111 C6
Watchlytes Jun Mix Inf Sch
  AL7 .............111 C6
Watchmead AL7 ...111 A6
Water End HP1 ....103 F2
Water End Cl WD6 ..169 F7
Water End Rd HP4 ..123 C7
Water Hall Farm & Craft
  Ctr★ SG4 ........66 F7
Water La
  Abbots Langley WD4 ..139 B2
  Berkhamsted HP4 ..122 C4
  Bishop's Stortford CM23 ..76 F8
  Bovingdon HP3 ...137 B1
  Hertford SG14 ...113 C5
  Hitchin SG5 ......21 F1
  Stansted Mountfitchet
  CM24 ............59 E6
  Watford WD17 ....167 B5
Water Row 11 SG12 ..93 D1
Waterbeach AL7 ...111 D6
Watercress Cl SG2 ..51 D5
Watercress Rd EN7 ..147 D5
Waterdale SG13 ...113 C4
Waterdell La SG4 ..35 A2
Waterdell Pl WD3 ..173 D8
Waterend
  Ayot St Peter AL4,AL6 ..88 E1
  Redbourn AL3 ....106 B5
Waterfield
  Chorleywood WD3 ..164 C2
  Welwyn Garden City AL7 ..111 B7
Waterfields Ret Pk
  WD17 ............167 D5
Waterfields Way WD17,
  WD23 ............167 D4
Waterford Comm SG14 ..92 B2
Waterford Gn AL7 ..111 B6
Watergate The WD19 ..175 D8
Waterhall Cotts SG13 ..132 D7
Waterhouse St HP1 ..124 C3
Waterhouse The HP1 ..124 C3
Waterloo La SG5 ..21 A6
Waterlow Mews SG4 ..35 E3
Waterman Cl WD19 ..167 B3
Watermark Way SG13 ..113 F6
Watermead Rd LU3 ..44 F6
Watermeadow AL2 ..141 E3
Watermill Ind Est SG9 ..40 E6
Watermill La
  Hertford SG14 ...113 D8
  Stansted Mountfitchet
  CM24 ............59 C6
Waters Dr WD3 ...165 E1

Waters End SG5 ...11 E6
Waterside
  Berkhamsted HP4 ..122 D4
  Kings Langley WD4 ..139 A2
  London Colney AL2 ..142 E4
  Radlett WD7 ......156 B5
  Stansted Mountfitchet
  CM24 ............59 E6
  Welwyn Garden City AL7 ..90 B1
Waterside Cotts AL9 ..130 E8
Waterside Ct WD4 ..139 B2
Waterside Ind Est EN11 ..135 D5
Waterside Mews UB9 ..173 A4
Waterside Pl CM22 ..98 A2
Waterslade Gn LU3 ..45 B6
Watersplash Ct AL2 ..142 E4
Waterways Bsns Ctr
  EN3 .............163 A1
Watery La
  Flamstead AL3,AL5 ..84 E3
  Hatfield AL10 ....129 E4
  Marsworth HP23 ..79 F1
Watford Arches Ret Pk
  WD17 ............167 D4
Watford By-pass WD6 ..169 C2
Watford Coll (annex)
  WD23 ............167 D6
Watford County Ct
  WD18 ............167 C5
Watford Ent Ctr WD18 ..166 F4
Watford Field Rd WD18 ..167 C4
Watford Football Gd &
  Saracens RFC WD18 ..167 B4
Watford General Hospl
  (Shrodells Wing)
  WD18 ............167 B4
Watford Gram Sch for Boys
  WD18 ............166 F5
Watford Gram Sch for Girls
  WD18 ............167 B5
Watford Heath WD19 ..167 D2
Watford Heath Farm
  WD19 ............167 D2
Watford High Street Sta
  WD17 ............167 C5
Watford Junction Sta
  WD17 ............167 C7
Watford Mus★ WD17 ..167 C5
Watford North Sta
  WD24 ............154 C2
Watford Rd
  Abbots Langley WD4 ..153 C6
  Chiswell Green AL2 ..141 A6
  Croxley Green WD3 ..166 B3
  Elstree WD6 ......169 C3
  Kings Langley WD4 ..139 A1
  Moor Park HA6 ...175 A4
  Radlett WD7 ......155 F4
Watford Sch of Music
  WD17 ............154 A1
Watford Sta WD18 ..166 F6
Watkin Mews EN3 ..163 A2
Watkins Cl HA6 ...174 F2
Watkins Rise EN6 ..159 B7
Watling Cl 1 HP2 ..124 E6
Watling Ct WD6 ...169 D3
Watling Knoll WD7 ..155 F6
Watling Mans WD7 ..156 B3
Watling St
  Park Street AL2 ...141 D6
  St Albans AL1 ...141 C8
Watling View AL1 ..141 C8
Watling View Sch AL1 ..141 D7
Watlington Rd CM17 ..118 D4
Watson Ave AL3 ...127 C4
Watson's Wlk AL1 ..127 E2
Watton at Stone Prim Sch
  SG14 ............70 D3
Watton at Stone Sta
  SG14 ............70 D3
Watton Ho SG14 ..70 F3
Watton Rd Knebworth SG3 ..69 A5
  Ware SG12 ........93 C2
  Watton at S SG3,SG14 ..70 D2
Watts Cl SG11 ....57 C2
Waulud Prim Sch LU3 ..44 E7
Waulud's Bank Dr LU3 ..44 E7
Wavell Cl EN8 ....148 E4
Wavell Ho AL1 ....128 A2
Waveney HP2 .....124 F8
Waveney Rd AL5 ..86 C3
Waverley Cl SG2 ..69 A8
Waverley Gdns HA6 ..175 A2
Waverley Lodge AL3 ..127 D5
Waverley Rd AL3 ..127 D5
Waxhouse Gate AL1 ..127 D3
Waxwell Cl HA5 ...175 D1
Waxwell La HA5 ...175 D1
Wayfarers Pk HP4 ..121 F4
Wayletts Dr CM23 ..77 B7
Waynes Ct 9 LU1 ..63 E7
Wayre St CM17 ...118 C4
Wayre The CM17 ..118 C4
Waysbrook SG6 ...23 B5
Wayside
  Chipperfield WD4 ..138 B1
  Potters Bar EN6 ..159 D6
  Shenley WD7 .....156 D6
Wayside Ave WD23 ..168 D3
Wayside Ct AL2 ...140 F1
Wayside The HP3 ..125 C2
Waysmeet SG6 ....23 B4
Waytemore Castle★
  CM23 ............77 A7
Waytemore Rd CM23 ..76 E6

Weald Fst Sch HA3 ....**176** F3
Weald La HA3 .......**176** D2
Weald Mid Sch HA3 ....**176** F3
Weald Rise HA3 .....**176** F2
Wealdwood Gdns HA5 .**176** B4
Weall Gn WD25 .......**154** B7
Weardale Ct EN5 ....**171** C4
Weatherby Rd LU4 .....**44** D2
Weaver St CM23 ......**76** C4
Weavers Orch SG15 ....**11** A4
Weavers Rd HP23 .....**99** E4
Weavers Way SG7 .....**24** A8
Webb Cl SG6 .........**23** C5
Webb Rise SG1 .......**50** F7
Webber Cl WD6 ......**169** D3
Webley Ct EN3 ......**163** A2
Wedgewood Cl HA6 ..**174** C4
Wedgewood Pk SG1 ....**37** C2
Wedgewood Rd SG4 ....**35** B7
Wedgewood Way SG1 ...**37** B2
Wedgwood Ct SG1 .....**37** C2
Wedgwood Gate SG1 ...**37** B2
Wedmore Rd SG4 ......**35** B7
Wedon Way SG7 .......**13** C4
Weedon Cl SG16 ......**10** C5
Weighton Rd HA3 ....**176** D2
Welbeck Cl WD6 .....**170** A6
Welbeck Rd **3** LU2 ...**63** E8
Welbeck Rise AL5 ...**107** D6
Welbury Ave LU3 .....**45** C7
Welch Pl HA5 .......**175** C2
Welclose St AL3 ....**127** C3
Welcote Dr HA6 ....**174** D4
Weldon Cl LU2 .......**46** E1
Welham Cl
  Borehamwood WD6 ..**170** A4
  Welham Green AL9 ..**144** C7
Welham Ct AL9 .....**144** C7
Welham Green Sta AL9 **144** D8
Welham Manor AL9 ..**144** C7
Welkin Gn HP2 .....**125** C4
Well App EN5 ......**171** C4
Well Croft HP1 .....**124** B4
Well End Rd WD6 ...**157** D1
Well Garth AL7 ....**110** E5
Well Gn SG14 .......**91** C4
Well La Harlow CM19 .**117** A1
  Mentmore LU7 .......**61** B8
  Northaw EN6 ........**145** E2
Well Rd Barnet EN5 .**171** C4
Well Row SG13 .....**132** F6
Wellands AL10 .....**130** A7
Wellbrook Mews HP23 **100** B4
Wellbury Terr HP2 ..**125** C3
Wellcroft LU7 .......**80** F5
Wellcroft Cl AL7 ...**111** A4
Wellcroft Rd AL7 ...**111** A4
Wellen Rise HP3 ....**138** E8
Wellers Gr EN7 ....**148** A3
Wellesley Ave HA6 ..**174** F5
Wellesley Cres EN6 .**158** C6
Wellfield Ave LU3 ...**44** C8
Wellfield Cl AL10 ..**130** A6
Wellfield Ct SG1 ....**37** B1
Wellfield Rd AL10 ..**130** A7
Wellgate Rd LU4 .....**44** D2
Wellhouse Cl LU1 ....**63** A7
Wellhouse La EN5 ..**171** D5
Wellingham Ave SG5 ..**21** D1
Wellington Ave HA5 .**175** F2
Wellington Cl WD17 .**175** F7
Wellington Cotts SG11 .**73** B7
Wellington Ct **3** LU1 ..**63** D6
Wellington Dr AL7 ..**111** C6
Wellington Ho **1** WD24 **167** C7
Wellington Pl
  Cheshunt EN10 ....**148** C8
  Kneesworth SG8 ......**2** B5
Wellington Rd
  London Colney AL2 ..**142** D5
  Pinner HA5 .........**175** F2
  St Albans AL1 ......**128** B2
  Stevenage SG1 ......**51** C5
  Watford WD17 ......**167** B7
Wellington St
  Hertford SG14 .....**113** B7
  Luton LU1 ..........**63** D7
Wells Cl
  Hammond Street EN7 .**147** C6
  Harpenden AL5 ......**85** E4
  St Albans AL3 ......**127** C4
Wells Yd **8** Ware SG12 ..**93** D1
  Watford WD17 ......**167** B6
Wellside Cl EN5 ....**171** C5
Wellstones WD18 ...**167** B5
Wellswood Cl HP2 ...**125** C4
Welsummer Way EN8 .**148** D3
Weltmore Rd LU3 .....**44** F6
Welwyn By Pass Rd AL6 .**89** C5
Welwyn Ct HP2 .....**124** F7
Welwyn Garden City Sta
  AL8 ...............**110** D6
Welwyn Hall Gdns AL6 .**89** C5
Welwyn North Sta AL6 .**89** F3
Welwyn Rd SG14 ....**112** F7
Wendover Cl
  Harpenden AL5 ......**86** D1
  St Albans AL4 .....**128** C8
Wendover Ct AL6 ....**89** C5
Wendover Dr AL6 ....**89** C5
Wendover Rd WD18 ..**166** E2
Wendover Way
  Bushey WD23 ......**168** C3
  Luton LU2 ..........**45** F3
Wengeo La SG12 .....**93** B2

Wenham Ct SG2 ......**52** B8
Wenlock CE Jun Sch LU2 **64** B8
Wenlock St .........**63** E8
Wensley Cl AL5 ....**107** D6
Wensleydale
  Hemel Hempstead HP2 .**124** F6
  Luton LU2 ..........**45** E1
Wensum Rd SG1 ......**36** F3
Wensum Way WD3 ...**165** D1
Wenta Bsns Ctr WD24 .**154** D2
Wentbridge Path WD6 .**157** A1
Wentworth Ave
  Borehamwood WD6 ..**169** F4
  Luton LU4 ..........**44** C6
Wentworth Cl
  Potters Bar EN6 ...**159** A8
  Watford WD17 .....**153** F1
Wentworth Cotts
  Dane End SG11 ......**53** F2
  Hoddesdon EN10 ...**134** E1
Wentworth Ct EN5 ..**171** E6
Wentworth Dr CM23 ..**76** D6
Wentworth Rd
  Barnet EN5 ........**171** D6
  Hertford SG13 ....**113** C3
Wenwell Cl HP22 .....**99** A3
Wesley Cl Arlesey SG15 .**11** A4
  Goff's Oak EN7 ....**147** C3
Wesley Ho **7** AL1 ...**127** D3
Wesley Rd AL3 ......**83** E5
Wessex Cl **7** EN5 ..**171** D5
Wessex Dr HA5 .....**175** E3
West Alley **3** SG5 ...**34** E7
West Ave Baldock SG7 ..**23** E8
  Chiswell Green AL2 .**141** B6
West Burrowfield AL7 **110** D4
West Chantry HA3 ..**176** B2
West Cl Barnet EN5 .**171** B4
  Hitchin SG4 ........**22** B1
  Hoddesdon EN11 ...**135** A8
  Stevenage SG1 ......**50** F5
West Comm
  Harpenden AL5 .....**107** B6
  Redbourn AL3 ......**106** A4
West Common Cl AL5 .**107** B5
West Common Gr AL5 .**107** B5
West Common Way
  AL5 ...............**107** A5
West Ct CM21 .......**97** E3
West Dene HP2 .....**104** A8
West Dr Arlesey SG15 ..**11** B4
  Stanmore HA3 .....**176** D4
  Watford WD25 .....**154** A4
West Drive Gdns HA3 .**176** D4
West End SG7 ........**4** C3
West End La Barnet EN5 **171** D5
  Essendon AL9 ......**131** C5
West End Rd EN7 ...**147** F8
West Gate CM20 ....**117** C1
West Herts Bsns Ctr
  WD6 ..............**170** B6
West Herts Coll (Dacorum
  Campus) HP1 ......**124** C4
West Herts Coll Cassio
  Campus WD17 .....**154** A1
West Herts Coll Leggatts
  Campus WD24 .....**154** A5
West Herts Coll Watford
  Campus WD17 .....**167** A6
West Hill SG5 .......**34** D7
West Hill Rd
  Hoddesdon EN11 ...**134** F8
  Luton LU1 ..........**63** E5
West Hyde La SL9 ..**172** A4
West La Great Offley SG5 .**33** C2
  Pirton SG5 .........**20** D5
West Lieth HP23 .....**99** F1
West Lodge Cotts LU2 .**46** D5
West Mead AL7 .....**111** B3
West Pas HP23 .....**100** A3
West Pl CM20 ......**118** A4
West Rd
  Berkhamsted HP4 ..**122** A5
  Bishop's Stortford CM23 ..**76** E6
  Harlow CM20 ......**118** A4
  Sawbridgeworth CM21 ..**97** C3
  Stansted Mountfitchet
    CM24 ...........**59** E6
West Reach SG2 .....**50** F2
West Riding
  Bricket Wood AL2 ..**140** F1
  Tewin AL6 ..........**90** D5
West Side EN10 ....**148** E6
West Sq CM20 ......**117** C1
West St Hertford SG13 **113** C5
  Lilley LU2 ..........**32** D1
  Ware SG12 ..........**93** D1
  Watford WD17 .....**167** B7
West Valley Rd HP3 .**138** D7
West View Hatfield AL10 **130** A7
West View Cl AL5 ....**86** D2
  Letchworth SG6 .....**22** E5
  Standon SG11 .......**73** A6
West View Ct WD6 ..**169** D3
West View Gdns WD6 **169** D3
West View Rd AL3 ..**127** D4
West Way Harpenden AL5 .**86** C2
  Luton LU4 ..........**44** C4
  Rickmansworth WD3 **165** B1
West Ways HA6 ....**175** A1
Westall AL5 ........**85** F4
Westall Mews SG13 .**113** C5
Westbourne Mews AL1 **127** D3
Westbourne Rd LU4 ..**45** B1
Westbrook Cl SG8 .....**5** B8
Westbrook SG4 ......**34** F5
Westbrook Hay Prep Sch
  HP1 ..............**137** D7
Westbury EN8 ......**148** D1

Westbury Cl SG5 ....**34** D8
Westbury Farm CM23 .**33** C3
Westbury Gdns LU2 ..**45** E3
Westbury Pl SG6 .....**22** E5
Westbury Prim Sch SG6 **22** E5
Westbury Rd
  Moor Park HA6 ....**174** E7
  Watford WD18 ....**167** B4
Westbush Cl EN11 ..**114** F1
Westcott AL7 ......**111** D7
Westcroft HP23 ....**100** A3
Westcroft Cl EN3 ..**162** C1
Westcroft Ct EN10 .**135** A4
Westell Cl SG7 ......**24** A8
Westerdale
  Hemel Hempstead HP2 .**124** E6
  Luton LU4 ..........**44** B5
Western Ave SG16 ...**10** B3
Western Cl SG6 .....**11** E1
Western House Hospl
  SG12 .............**93** E2
Western Rd
  Lower Nazeing EN9 .**135** E1
  Luton LU1 ..........**63** D6
  Tring HP23 .........**99** F3
Western Terr **1** EN11 **115** B1
Western Way SG6 ....**11** E1
Westfield
  Welham Green AL9 .**144** F8
  Welwyn Garden City AL7 **111** A7
Westfield Ave
  Harpenden AL5 ......**86** A3
  Watford WD24 .....**154** D1
Westfield Cl
  Bishop's Stortford CM23 ..**76** E8
  Cheshunt EN8 .....**162** F8
  Hitchin SG5 ........**34** D7
Westfield Com Prim Sch
  EN11 .............**134** F7
Westfield Com Tech Coll
  WD18 ............**166** F3
Westfield Ct AL4 ...**128** D6
Westfield Dr AL5 ....**86** B4
Westfield Fst Sch HP4 **121** F5
Westfield La SG5 ....**34** D7
Westfield Pk HA5 ..**175** F3
Westfield Pl AL5 ....**86** B4
Westfield Rd
  Berkhamsted HP4 ..**121** F5
  Bishop's Stortford CM23 ..**76** E8
  Harpenden AL5 ......**86** B4
  Hertford SG14 ....**113** C8
  Hoddesdon EN11 ...**134** F7
  Pitstone LU7 .......**80** C3
Westfield Wlk EN8 .**162** F8
Westfields AL3 ....**141** A8
Westgate SG1 .......**50** D5
Westgate Ct EN3 ..**162** D4
Westholm SG6 ......**22** F8
Westland Cl WD25 .**153** F5
Westland Dr AL9 ..**144** E4
Westland Rd
  Watford WD17 ....**167** B7
  Knebworth SG3 .....**69** A5
Westlea Ave WD25 .**154** E2
Westlea Cl EN10 ..**148** F8
Westlea Rd EN10 ..**148** F8
Westlecote Gdns LU2 .**45** D4
Westly Wood AL7 ..**111** A7
Westmeade Cl EN7 .**148** B2
Westmill La Hitchin SG5 .**21** C3
  Ickleford SG5 ......**21** C3
Westmill Lawns SG5 .**21** D1
Westmill Rd Hitchin SG5 **21** C1
  Thundridge SG12 ...**93** A3
Westminster Ct
  Cheshunt EN8 .....**162** F6
  St Albans AL1 .....**127** C1
Westminster Ho **6**
  WD24 ............**167** C7
Westmorland Ave LU3 .**44** F5
Weston Ave SG8 ......**7** C7
Weston Cl EN6 ....**158** F7
Weston Prim Sch SG4 ..**24** C1
Weston Rd SG1 ......**36** E1
Weston Way SG7 .....**23** E7
Westonia Ct EN3 ..**162** E3
Westray HP5 .......**125** C1
Westridge Cl HP1 ..**123** F3
Westron Gdns HP23 .**100** B4
Westview Rise HP2 .**124** D4
Westwick Cl HP2 ..**125** D2
Westwick Pl WD25 .**154** C5
Westwick Row HP2 .**125** E2
Westwood Ave SG4 ..**35** A6
Westwood Cl EN6 ..**145** A1
Wetherby Cl SG1 ....**51** C8
Wetherby Rd
  Borehamwood WD6 .**169** E8
  Enfield EN2 .......**161** C1
Wetherfield CM24 ...**59** D7
Wetherly Cl CM17 ..**118** F4
Wetherne Link LU4 ..**44** C5
Wexham Cl LU3 .....**44** B1
Weybourne Cl AL5 ...**86** D2
Weybourne Dr LU2 ..**45** C7
Weybrigge Cl AL3 ..**106** A5
Weymouth St HP3 ..**138** D7
Weyver Ct **3** AL1 ..**127** E4
Whaley Rd EN6 ....**159** C6
Wharf La
  Berkhamsted HP4 ..**121** C8
  Rickmansworth WD3 **165** E1
Wharf Pl CM23 ......**77** A6
Wharf Rd
  **12** Bishop's Stortford CM23 **76** F6
  Hemel Hempstead HP1 .**124** B1
  Hoddesdon EN10 ...**148** F8

Wharf Row HP22 .....**99** B4
Wharf Villas HP1 ...**124** B1
Wharfdale **7** LU4 ...**44** C5
Wharfedale HP2 ....**124** E6
Wheat Cl AL4 ......**128** A7
Wheat Croft CM23 ...**76** E4
Wheat Hill SG6 ......**22** F8
Wheatbarn AL7 ....**111** B7
Wheatcotes SG3 .....**69** C5
Wheatcroft EN7 ...**148** B3
Wheatcroft Prim Sch
  SG13 .............**114** A7
Wheatfield Hatfield AL10 **130** B6
  Hemel Hempstead HP2 .**124** D5
Wheatfield Ave AL5 .**107** A5
Wheatfield Cres SG8 ..**7** E6
Wheatfield Rd AL5 .**107** A4
Wheatfields CM17 ..**118** D6
Wheatfields Inf Sch
  AL4 ...............**128** B7
Wheatfields Jun Mix Sch
  AL4 ...............**128** B7
Wheathampstead Rd
  Harpenden AL5 .....**107** E8
  Wheathampstead AL5,AL4 **108** A8
Wheatlands SG12 ....**51** C7
Wheatley Cl
  Sawbridgeworth CM21 ..**97** C1
  Welwyn Garden City AL7 **111** A4
Wheatley Dr WD25 .**154** C5
Wheatley Rd AL7 ..**111** A4
Wheatleys AL4 ....**128** C5
Wheatlock Mead AL3 **106** A5
Wheatsheaf Dr SG12 .**93** B3
Wheatsheaf Rd SG12 ..**95** D1
Wheelers Cl EN9 ..**135** F1
Wheelers La HP3 ..**124** E1
Wheelright Cl WD23 **168** B3
Wheelwrights SG4 ...**66** C1
Wheelwrights Cl CM23 **76** C4
Whempstead La SG12 **71** B6
Whempstead Rd SG12 **71** B7
Whetstone Cl AL6 ...**89** E8
Whetstone Ct AL6 ...**89** E8
Whinbush Gr SG5 ...**34** E3
Whinbush Rd SG5 ...**34** F8
Whippendell Hill WD4 **138** C1
Whippendell Rd WD18 **166** F4
Whipperley Ct LU1 ..**63** A6
Whipperley Inf Sch LU1 **63** A6
Whipperley Ring LU1 .**63** A6
Whipperley Way LU1 ..**63** A6
Whipsnade Wild Animal Pk★
  LU6 ..............**81** E7
Whisper Mews LU4 ..**44** D4
Whisper Wood WD3 .**165** B6
Whisperwood Cl HA3 **176** E3
Whit Hern Ct EN8 ..**148** C1
Whitby Rd LU3 ......**45** C1
Whitchurch Cl LU2 ..**46** D2
White Beams AL2 ..**141** C3
White Bear CM24 ...**59** E8
White Craig Cl HA5 **176** A5
White Gate Gdns HA3 **176** F3
White Hart Cl SG9 ...**40** E8
White Hart Ct HP2 .**125** A2
White Hart Dr HP2 .**124** F2
White Hart Rd HP2 .**125** A2
White Hedge Dr AL3 **127** C5
White Hill
  Ashley Green HP3,HP5 .**136** C2
  Flamstead AL3 .....**105** B8
  Hemel Hempstead HP1 .**123** F2
  Rickmansworth WD3 **174** A4
  Walkern SG2 ........**38** C2
White Ho The **6** EN8 .**148** D3
White Horse La
  London Colney AL2 .**142** E5
  Welwyn AL6 .........**90** C7
White House Cl SG14 .**70** E3
White House The SG6 .**23** B5
White La SG4 .......**49** C7
White Lion St HP3 .**138** D7
White Orchards N20 .**171** F1
White Post Field CM21 .**97** D2
White Shack La WD3 **152** F2
White Stubbs La EN10,
  SG13 .............**133** C2
White Way The SG4 ..**51** C7
Whitebarns SG9 .....**43** A5
Whitebarns La SG9 ..**43** A6
Whitebeam Cl
  **4** Hammond Street EN7 **147** E5
  Shenley WD7 ......**156** F6
Whitebeams AL10 ..**130** A2
Whitebroom Rd HP1 .**123** E5
Whitechurch Gdns SG6 **23** C3
Whitecroft AL1 ....**142** B8
Whitecroft Rd LU2 ..**64** A8
Whitecrofts SG5 ....**11** F6
Whitefield Ave LU3 ..**44** C7
Whitefield Ho AL10 .**130** C7
Whitefield Inf Sch LU3 .**44** E8
Whitefield Jun Sch LU3 .**44** E8
Whitefields Rd EN8 .**148** C3
Whitefriars Ave HA3 **176** E1
Whitefriars Dr HA3 .**176** E1
Whitefriars Fst & Mid Sch
  HA3 ..............**176** E1
Whitefriars Teaching Sch
  HA3 ..............**176** D1
Whitefriars Trad Est
  HA3 ..............**176** D1
Whitegale Cl SG4 ....**35** A6
Whitegates Cl WD3 .**166** A5
Whitehall Cl EN11 ..**135** E1
Whitehall Coll CM23 .**58** E1
Whitehall Cotts SG12 **116** D8

Whitehall La CM23 ..**58** F1
Whitehall Rd HA3 ..**176** C2
Whitehands Cl EN11 **134** F6
Whitehart Cross HP3 **136** F3
Whitehaven Cl EN7 .**147** E3
Whitehicks SG6 .....**12** A1
Whitehill
  Berkhamsted HP4 ..**122** D5
  Welwyn AL6 .........**89** A3
Whitehill Ave LU1 ...**63** D5
Whitehill Cotts AL6 .**89** A3
Whitehill Cl HP4 ...**122** D5
Whitehill Jun Sch SG4 .**35** A5
Whitehill La LU7 .....**80** D3
Whitehill Rd SG4 ....**35** A6
Whitehills Cl SG4 ...**35** A6
Whitehorse St SG7 ..**23** F8
Whitehorse Vale LU3 .**31** A1
Whitehouse Ave WD6 **170** B5
Whitehouse Ct SG8 ..**7** D4
Whitehouse La WD5 .**140** C4
Whitehurst Ave SG5 ..**21** F1
Whitelands Ave WD3 **164** C5
Whiteleaf Rd HP3 ..**138** C8
Whiteley Cl SG12 ...**71** E7
Whiteley La SG9 ....**27** C8
Whitesmead Rd SG1 .**50** E7
Whitestone Wlk HP1 **124** A6
Whitethorn AL7 ....**111** B5
Whitethorn La SG6 ..**23** A4
Whitethorn Way LU1 .**63** A6
Whitewaites CM20 .**117** E1
Whiteway SG6 ......**23** C4
Whitewaybottom La LU2,
  SG4 ...............**66** A3
Whitewebbs La EN2 **161** F4
Whitewebbs Mus of
  Transport★ EN2 ...**161** B4
Whitewebbs Pk★ EN2 **161** D4
Whitewebbs Rd EN2 **161** C4
Whitewood Rd HP4 **122** A4
Whitfield Way WD3 .**164** F1
Whitings AL5 .......**86** D4
Whitings Hill Prim Sch
  EN5 ..............**171** C4
Whitings Rd EN5 ..**171** C4
Whitlars Dr WD4 ..**138** F3
Whitley Cl WD5 ...**154** A7
Whitley Ct EN11 ..**135** B8
Whitley Rd EN11 ..**135** B8
Whitmores Wood HP2 **125** B4
Whitney Dr SG1 .....**36** C3
Whittingham Cl LU2 .**46** F1
Whittingstall Rd EN11 **135** C8
Whittington La SG1 ..**50** E4
Whittington Way CM23 **76** F3
Whittle Cl
  Lower Stondon SG16 ..**10** B4
  Watford WD25 .....**153** F5
Whittlesea Cl HA3 .**176** C3
Whittlesea Path HA3 **176** C2
Whittlesea Rd HA3 .**176** C2
Whitwell Cl LU3 .....**45** B8
Whitwell Rd WD25 .**154** D4
Whitworth Cres EN3 **163** A2
Whitworth Jones Ave
  SG16 .............**10** C5
Whitworth Rd SG1 ..**37** B3
Whomerley Rd SG1 ..**50** E4
Whybrow Gdns HP4 .**122** E6
Whydale Rd SG8 .....**7** E5
Whytingham Rd HP23 **100** C4
Wick Ave AL4 .....**108** D8
Wick Hill LU6 .......**82** A4
Wick Rd HP23 .....**120** D8
Wick The Hertford SG14 ..**92** C1
  Kimpton SG4 .......**66** C1
Wicken Fields SG12 .**93** C3
Wickets End WD7 ..**156** E6
Wickets The LU2 ....**45** E4
Wickfield SG3 ......**69** A2
Wickford Cl SG3 ....**69** A2
Wickham Cl UB9 ...**173** D2
Wickham Rd HA3 ..**176** D1
Wickham Way SG11 .**55** E3
Wickhams Wharf SG12 ..**93** E1
Wicklands Rd SG12 .**116** D8
Wickmere Ct LU2 ...**45** C7
Wickstead Ave LU4 .**44** E4
Wickwood Ct AL1 ..**128** B5
Widbury Gdns SG12 .**93** F1
Widbury Hill SG12 ..**93** F1
Widbury Sch SG12 ...**94** A1
Widford Rd Hunsdon SG12 **95** D2
  Much Hadham SG10 ..**95** F7
  Welwyn Garden City AL7 **111** B6
Widford Sch SG12 ...**95** D4
Widford Terr HP2 ..**105** A1
Widgeon Way WD25 **154** E2
Widmore Dr HP2 ..**125** A5
Wieland Rd HA6 ...**175** A3
Wiggenhall Rd WD18 **167** C4
Wigginton Bottom
  HP23 .............**120** E8
Wiggles La HP23 .....**99** F7
Wight Ho WD18 ...**166** F4
Wigmore La LU2 .....**46** D2
Wigmore Park Sh Ctr
  LU2 ..............**46** E1
Wigmore Pl LU2 .....**46** E1
Wigmore Prim Sch LU2 .**46** E2
Wigmores N AL8 ..**110** D7
Wigmores S AL8 ..**110** D6
Wigram Way SG2 ...**51** B3
Wilbraham's Almshouses
  ........................**171** F7
Wilbury Cl SG6 .....**22** C7
Wilbury Hills Rd SG6 .**22** C7

Wilbury Jun Sch SG6 ....22 D6
Wilbury Lodge 2 EN5 .171 D5
Wilbury Rd SG6 .........22 E8
Wilbury Way SG4 .......22 A3
Wilcon Way WD25 ....154 D5
Wilcot Ave WD19 ......167 E2
Wilcot Cl WD19 ........167 E2
Wilcox Cl WD6 .........170 C8
Wild Cherry Dr LU1 .....63 D5
Wild Marsh Ct EN8 ....162 E2
Wildacres HA6 .........174 F7
Wilderness The 3 HP4 .122 C4
Wildhill rd AL9 ........131 B2
Wildman Ct SG13 ......114 A7
Wildoaks Cl HA6 .......174 F4
Wildwood HA6 .........174 D4
Wildwood Ave AL2 .....140 F1
Wildwood Cl WD3 .....164 F5
Wildwood La SG1 ......50 E3
Wilford Cl HA6 ........174 D3
Wilga Rd AL6 ..........89 B5
Wilkin's Green La AL4 .129 C4
Wilkins Gr AL8 ........110 D5
Wilkinsgreen Terr AL4 .129 B3
Wilkinson Cl EN7 .....147 C6
Willenhall Cl LU3 ......45 A7
Willetts Mews EN11 ...135 A7
William Austin Inf Sch
LU3 .................45 C4
William Austin Jun Sch
LU3 .................45 C4
William Covell Cl EN2 .160 F1
William Crook Ho HP1 .123 F3
William Ct HP3 ........138 D7
William Pl SG2 .........51 A3
William Ransom Prim Sch
SG4 .................35 B7
William St
18 Berkhamsted HP4 ..122 D4
Luton LU2 ............45 E1
Markyate AL3 ..........83 E5
Watford WD23 ........167 D6
William Sutton Ct LU2 .46 B5
Williams Way WD7 ....156 C4
Williamson St 1 LU1 ..63 E7
Williamson Way WD3 .165 A1
Willian Church Rd SG6 .23 A2
Willian Rd
Great Wymondley SG4 ..35 F7
Hitchin SG4,SG6 ......22 E1
Willian Way Baldock SG7 .23 E6
Letchworth SG6 .......23 A3
Willinghall Cl EN9 ....163 D7
Williton Rd LU2 .......46 C2
Willoughby Cl EN10 ..134 E2
Willoughby Ct AL2 ....142 D5
Willoughby Rd AL5 ....86 B4
Willoughby Way SG4 ..35 A6
Willow Cl
Bishop's Stortford CM23 ..76 E8
Great Hormead SG9 ....42 E8
Hammond Street EN7 .147 E5
Reed SG8 .............16 D5
Willow Cnr SG13 .....132 F5
Willow Cres AL1 ......128 C3
Willow Ct Harrow HA2 .176 C1
Harrow HA3 ..........176 F2
Luton LU3 ............44 E5
Willow Dene
Bushey WD23 ........168 E2
Pinner HA5 ...........175 D1
Willow Dr EN5 ........171 E5
Willow Edge WD4 .....139 A2
Willow End HA6 ......175 A4
Willow Gn WD6 ......170 D4
Willow La Hitchin SG5 ..34 D6
St Ippolyts SG4 ......35 B2
Watford WD18 ........167 A4
Willow Mead CM21 ....97 E2
Willow Path EN9 .....163 E5
Willow Tree Way SG5 ..21 F2
Willow Trees Cvn Site
SG16 ................10 A4
Willow View SG12 ....114 E8
Willow Way
Chiswell Green AL2 ...141 A4
Harpenden AL5 ........86 C4
Hatfield AL10 ........129 F2
Hemel Hempstead HP1 .124 B5
Luton LU3 ............44 E5
Potters Bar EN6 ......159 B6
Radlett WD7 .........155 E3
Willow Wlk AL6 .......89 C8
Willowdene EN8 ......148 E4
Willowfield Lower Sch
LU1 .................62 F4
Willowgate Trad Est LU3 .44 B8
Willows Cl HA5 .......175 C1
Willows La HP1 .......103 F1
Willows Link SG2 ......51 A1
Willows The
Buntingford SG9 ......40 D8
Hemel Hempstead HP2 .125 B5
Hitchin SG4 ...........35 A5
Rickmansworth WD3 ..173 A8
St Albans AL1 ........142 B7
Stevenage SG2 ........51 A1
Watford WD19 ........167 B2
Willowside AL2 .......142 E4
Willowside Way SG8 ....7 C8
Willowtree Lo HA6 ....174 F5
Willowtree Lodge 1
HA6 .................174 F5
Wilsden Ave LU1 .......63 D6
Wilshere Ave AL1 .....127 C1
Wilshere Cres SG4 .....35 C8

Wilshere Rd AL6 ........89 A5
Wilshere-Dacre Jun Sch
SG5 ..................34 E8
Wilsmere Dr HA3 .....176 E3
Wilson Cl
Bishop's Stortford CM23 ..76 F5
Stevenage SG1 ........36 D1
Wilsons La SG7 .........4 C4
Wilstone Dr AL4 ......128 C8
Wilton Cl CM23 ........77 B7
Wilton Cres SG13 ....113 C4
Wilton Ct WD17 ......167 C6
Wilton Rd SG5 .........21 E1
Wilton Way SG13 ....113 C4
Wiltshire Rd SG2 ......51 A4
Wimborne Cl CM21 ....97 D2
Wimborne Gr WD17 ..153 E2
Wimborne Rd LU1 .....63 C8
Wimple Rd LU4 ........44 A1
Winch Cl SG4 ..........88 F8
Winch St LU2 ..........45 F1
Winchdells HP3 ......139 A8
Winchester Cl
Bishop's Stortford CM23 ..76 D4
Stevenage SG1 ........37 B2
Winchester Ho AL3 ...127 C2
Winchester Rd HA6 ...174 F1
Winchester Way WD3 .166 B4
Winchfield LU1 ........62 E4
Winchfield Way WD3 .165 C2
Windermere Ave AL1 .128 B1
Windermere Cl
Chorleywood WD3 ....164 D1
Hemel Hempstead HP3 .125 C2
Stevenage SG1 ........37 D2
Windermere Cres LU3 ..44 F5
Windermere Ct 5
WD17 ...............167 A7
Windermere Prim Sch
AL1 .................128 B1
Windhill
Bishop's Stortford CM23 ..76 E7
Welwyn Garden City AL7 .111 A4
Windhill Old Rd CM23 ..76 E7
Winding Hill SG10 .....75 D4
Winding Shot HP1 ....124 A4
Winding Shott SG14 ...91 C4
Windmill Ave AL4 ....128 C5
Windmill Cl Barkway SG8 .17 C5
Pitstone LU7 ..........80 F5
Stansted Mountfitchet
CM24 ................59 D6
Waltham Abbey EN9 .163 E5
Windmill Cotts SG12 ..93 D6
Windmill Dr WD3 .....165 F3
Windmill Field SG12 .114 D8
Windmill Fields CM17 .118 F4
Windmill Hill
Buntingford SG9 .......40 F6
Chipperfield WD4 ....151 F7
Hitchin SG4 ...........34 F7
Windmill La Barnet EN5 .170 F3
Bushey WD23 ........168 E1
Cheshunt EN8 ........148 E1
Windmill Rd
Breachwood Green SG4 ..47 D2
Hemel Hempstead HP2 .124 F2
Luton LU1 ............63 F6
Markyate AL3,LU1 .....84 B6
Windmill St WD23 ...168 E1
Windmill Way
Much Hadham SG10 ...74 E1
Tring HP23 ...........99 F4
Windmills SG12 .......71 E8
Windmore Ave EN6 ..158 C8
Windmore Hall EN6 ..158 C8
Windridge Cl AL3 .....127 A1
Windrush Cl SG1 ......37 A3
Winds End Cl HP2 ....125 A5
Windsor Cl
Borehamwood WD6 ..170 A8
Bovingdon HP3 ......137 A3
Cheshunt EN7 ........148 A1
Hemel Hempstead HP3 .124 E2
Northwood HA6 ......175 A1
Stevenage SG2 ........69 B7
Welwyn AL6 ..........89 B3
Windsor Ct
Borehamwood WD6 ..170 C7
Bushey WD23 ........168 C2
Kings Langley WD4 ..139 B2
11 Luton LU1 ........63 D6
St Albans AL1 ........128 A2
Windsor Gdns CM23 ...76 C7
Windsor Rd Barnet EN5 .171 E3
Enfield EN3 ..........162 D4
Harrow HA3 ..........176 D2
Pitstone LU7 ..........80 D3
Royston SG8 ...........7 F6
Watford WD24 .......154 C1
Welwyn AL6 ..........89 B3
Windsor St LU1 ........63 D6
Windsor Way WD3 ...165 A1
Windsor Wlk 8 LU1 ...63 D6
Windsor Wood EN9 ..163 E6
Windward Cl EN3 ....162 D4
Windy Rise SG12 ......71 F7
Winford Dr EN10 ....134 F1
Wingate Cl LU4 .......44 F2
Wingate Gdns AL6 ....89 B5
Wingate Rd LU4 .......44 F2
Wingate Way AL1 ....128 A2
Wingrave CE Comb Sch
HP22 ................60 A3
Wingrave Rd Tring HP23 .100 B6
Wilstone HP23 ........79 D1
Winifred Cl HW7 .....170 D1
Winifred Rd HP3 .....138 D7

Winkfield Cl LU4 .......44 B1
Winnington Rd EN3 ..162 C2
Winsdon Ct 1 LU1 .....63 D6
Winslow Cl LU3 ........45 C4
Winslow Rd HP22 ......60 B3
Winston Churchill Way
EN8 .................162 D6
Winston Cl Harrow HA3 .176 E4
Hitchin SG5 ...........34 D7
Winston Ct HA3 ......176 B3
Winston Gdns HP4 ...121 F4
Winston Way EN6 ....159 A6
Winstre Rd WD6 .....170 A8
Winters La SG2 ........38 C1
Winterscroft Rd EN11 .134 F7
Winton App WD3 ....166 C4
Winton Cl Letchworth SG6 .23 D8
Luton LU2 ............45 D6
Winton Cres WD3 ....166 B4
Winton Dr Cheshunt EN8 .148 E2
Croxley Green WD3 ...166 C4
Winton Rd SG12 ......93 F1
Winton Terr AL1 .....127 C2
Wintons CM20 .......117 C2
Wisden Rd SG1 ........36 F1
Wisdom Dr SG13 .....113 E6
Wiseman Cl LU2 .......45 E7
Wisemans Gdns CM21 .97 C1
Wistaria Dr AL2 .....142 B5
Wistlea Cres AL4 .....129 B1
Wistow Rd LU3 ........45 A6
Witchford AL7 .......111 D6
Withy Cl LU4 ..........44 B4
Withy Pl AL2 .........141 C3
Witley Gn LU2 .........46 D2
Witney Cl HA5 .......175 F4
Witter Ave SG5 .......21 E4
Wiveton Cl LU2 .......45 D7
Woburn Ave CM23 ....76 C7
Woburn Cl Bushey WD23 168 C3
Stevenage SG2 ........69 C7
Woburn Ct LU4 .......44 D5
Wodecroft Rd LU3 .....45 A4
Wodson Park Sports & L Ctr
SG12 ................91 F5
Wolfsburg Ct 4 LU4 ...44 C5
Wolsey Ave EN7 .....147 F2
Wolsey Mans HA6 ...174 C7
Wolsey Rd
Hemel Hempstead HP2 .124 D2
Moor Park HA6 ......174 D7
Wolston Cl LU1 ........63 C7
Wolverley Ho SG7 ......4 D4
Wolves Mere SG3 .....69 A2
Wolvescroft SG3 ......69 A2
Wonnacott Pl EN3 ...162 D3
Wood Cl AL10 ........130 B5
Wood Comm AL10 ...130 B8
Wood Cres HP3 ......124 E1
Wood Dr SG2 ..........51 B2
Wood End AL2 .......141 C3
Wood End Cl HP2 ....125 C4
Wood End Hill AL5 ....85 D4
Wood End La AL3 ....104 E8
Wood End Rd AL5 .....85 D3
Wood End Sch AL5 ....85 D3
Wood Farm Rd HP2 ..124 E2
Wood Green Cl LU2 ...46 B5
Wood Green Rd LU2 ..46 C5
Wood Green Way EN8 .162 E1
Wood House La EN10 .134 A2
Wood La Birchanger CM23 .59 E2
Hemel Hempstead HP2 .124 D2
Meesden SG9 .........30 A6
Wood Lane End HP2 ..125 A3
Wood St Barnet EN5 ..171 D5
Luton LU1 ............63 F6
Wood Vale AL10 .....130 B5
Wood View Cuffley EN6 .146 E4
Hemel Hempstead HP1 .124 B5
Woodacre Dr AL6 .....90 A8
Woodbine Gr EN2 ....161 D1
Woodbridge Cl LU4 ...44 E4
Woodbrook Gdns EN9 .163 E6
Woodbury Hill LU2 ....45 E2
Woodcock Hill
Rickmansworth WD3 .173 E4
Sandridge AL4 .......108 C1
Woodcock Rd Luton LU3 .63 A7
Royston SG8 ...........7 E8
Stevenage SG2 ........51 D2
Woodcote Cl EN8 ....148 C1
Woodcote Ho 1 SG4 ..34 F7
Woodcroft HA5 ........34 E6
Woodcroft Rd SG12 .115 E4
Woodfall Ave EN5 ...171 F4
Woodfield Ave HA6 ..174 E6
Woodfield Cl CM24 ...59 E6
Woodfield Dr HP3 ...125 D1
Woodfield Gdns HP3 .125 D1
Woodfield La AL9 ....145 E8
Woodfield Rd
Radlett WD7 .........156 A3
Stevenage SG1 ........36 C1
Welwyn Garden City AL7 .110 F6
Woodfield Rise WD23 .168 D2
Woodfield Sch HP3 ..125 D1
Woodfield Terr
Harefield UB9 ........173 B1
Stansted Mountfitchet
CM24 ................59 E6
2 Watford WD18 ....167 C5

Woodford Cres HA5 ..175 B1
Woodford Rd WD17 ..167 C7
Woodforde Cl SG7 ......4 E4
Woodgate WD25 .....154 B6
Woodgate Ave EN6 ..160 B7
Woodgate Cres HA6 .175 A4
Woodgrange Ct EN11 .135 A5
Woodhall Ave HA5 ..175 B2
Woodhall Cl SG14 ...113 C8
Woodhall Ct AL7 ....110 E5
Woodhall Dr HA5 ....175 E2
Woodhall Gate HA5 .175 D2
Woodhall Gr
Hemel Hempstead HP2 .124 E4
Shenley WD7 ........156 F4
South Oxhey WD19 ..175 E6
Welwyn Garden City AL7 .110 C4
Woodhall Sch WD19 .175 E6
Woodham Way SG12 .115 C4
Woodhill Ho AL9 .....145 D8
Woodhouse Eaves HA6 .175 A5
Woodhurst SG6 .......22 F8
Woodhurst Ave WD25 .154 D4
Woodland Ave
Hemel Hempstead HP1 .124 B2
Luton LU2 ............45 B2
Woodland Cl
Hemel Hempstead HP1 .124 B2
Tring HP23 ...........99 F2
Woodland Ct AL3 ....127 F7
Woodland Dr
St Albans AL4 .......128 C4
Watford WD17 ......166 F8
Woodland La WD3 ...164 D6
Woodland Mount SG13 .113 F6
Woodland Pl
Chorleywood WD3 ...164 F5
Hemel Hempstead HP1 .124 B2
Woodland Rd
Hertford Heath SG13 .114 C3
Maple Cross WD3 ...172 D5
Woodland Rise
Studham LU6 .........82 B7
Welwyn Garden City AL8 .110 C8
Woodland Way
Baldock SG7 ..........23 F6
Bedmond WD5 .......139 F4
Goff's Oak EN7 ......147 B3
Stevenage SG2 ........51 A1
Welwyn AL6 ..........90 A7
Woodlands
Bishop's Stortford CM23 .77 C8
Brookmans Park AL9 .145 B4
Caddington LU1 .......62 E3
Chiswell Green AL2 ..141 C4
Harpenden AL5 ........85 E3
Radlett WD7 .........156 A5
Royston SG8 ...........7 F6
Woodlands Ave HP4 .122 D3
Woodlands Cl
Borehamwood WD6 ..170 B5
Hoddesdon EN11 .....135 A5
Woodlands Dr
Bedmond WD4 .......139 C3
Harrow HA7 .........176 F4
Hoddesdon EN11 .....135 A4
Woodlands Meade SG4 .37 B8
Woodlands Prim Sch
WD6 ................170 A8
Woodlands Rd
Enfield EN2 ..........161 D1
Hertford SG13 ......113 F6
Kings Langley HP3 ..139 A4
Thundridge SG12 .....93 D6
Watford WD23 .......167 E4
Woodlands Sec Sch LU3 .44 F7
Woodlea AL2 .........141 A6
Woodlea Gr HA6 .....174 C4
Woodley Rd SG12 .....93 F2
Woodleys CM20 .....118 A1
Woodman Rd 4 HP3 .124 E1
Woodmere LU3 ........31 A1
Woodmere Ave WD24 .154 E1
Woodmill Mews EN11 .135 A5
Woodpecker Cl
Bishop's Stortford CM23 .76 C6
Bushey WD23 ........168 C1
Harrow HA3 ..........176 F2
Hatfield AL10 ........129 F2
Woodridge Way HA6 .174 E4
Woodridings Ave HA5 .175 F2
Woodridings Cl HA5 .175 F3
Woods Ave AL10 .....130 B4
Woods Pl HP23 ......100 A3
Woods The Radlett WD7 .156 B5
South Oxhey WD19 ..175 A5
Woodshots Mdw WD18 .166 D4
Woodside
Bishop's Stortford CM23 .77 D8
Borehamwood WD6 ..169 F5
Cheshunt EN7 ........162 A8
Hertford Heath SG13 .114 C2
Watford WD24 .......154 A3
Woodside Farm & Wildfowl
Pk LU1 ...............84 A8
Woodside Gdns SG4 ...34 F7
Woodside Ho AL8 ....110 C2
Woodside Ind Pk SG6 ..23 D6
Woodside La AL9 ....131 A1
Woodside Prim Sch
EN7 .................147 B2
Woodside Rd
Abbots Langley WD25 .154 B8
Bricket Wood AL2 ...140 F2
Welwyn AL6 ..........89 F3
Woodside LU1 .........63 B3

Woodstock SG3 ........68 F3
Woodstock Cl SG13 ..114 B4
Woodstock Rd
Bushey WD23 ........168 F2
Hoddesdon EN10 ....134 E4
Woodstock Rd N AL1 .128 B4
Woodstock Rd S AL1 .128 B3
Woodvale AL6 ........162 C4
Woodville Court Mews
WD17 ...............167 A7
Woodville Cl WD17 ..167 A7
Woodville Pl SG14 ...113 B8
Woodward Gdns HA7 .176 F3
Woodwaye WD19 ....167 C2
Woodwicks WD3 .....172 D5
Woolenwick Inf Sch SG1 50 B6
Woolenwick Jun Sch
SG1 ..................50 B6
Woolgrove Ct SG4 .....22 B1
Woolgrove Rd SG4 ....22 B1
Woolgrove Sch SG6 ...23 D5
Woollam Cres AL3 ...127 C7
Woollams AL3 ........106 A4
Woollard St EN9 .....163 C5
Woolmans Cl WD6 ...134 F1
Woolmer Cl WD6 ....157 A1
Woolmer Dr HP2 ....125 C3
Woolmer's Park Mews
SG14 ................112 B1
Woolmerdine Ct WD23 .167 D6
Woolmers La SG14 ..112 B2
Woolners Way SG1 ....50 C6
Woolston Ave SG6 ....23 A4
Wootton Cl LU3 ......45 B7
Wootton Dr HP2 ....124 F8
Worboys Ct SG8 ........1 F5
Worcester Ct AL1 ....128 C4
Worcester Ho 12 WD6 .170 A7
Worcester Rd AL10 ..129 F6
Worcesters Ave EN1 .162 A1
Worcesters Prim Sch
EN1 .................161 F1
Wordsworth Cl SG8 ....2 D1
Wordsworth Gdns WD6 .170 A4
Wordsworth Rd
Harpenden AL5 ........86 A3
Luton LU4 ............44 A3
Works Rd SG6 .........23 C7
Worley Rd AL3 ......127 C4
Wormley Cl EN10 ....148 F7
Wormley Lodge Cl EN10 .148 E8
Wormley Prim Sch
EN10 ...............148 D8
Wormleybury EN10 .148 D8
Worsdell Way SG4 .....35 B7
Worsted La SG9 .......41 E6
Wortham Rd SG9 ......7 E4
Wortham Way SG2 ....51 B3
Wraglings The CM23 ..77 B5
Wratten Cl SG5 .......34 E6
Wratten Rd E SG5 ....34 E6
Wratten Rd W SG5 ...34 E6
Wrayfields SG5 .......12 B8
Wraysbury Cl LU4 ....44 D3
Wren Cl Kimpton SG4 ..66 B1
Luton LU2 ............46 C6
Stevenage SG2 ........51 B6
Wren Cres WD23 ....168 C1
Wren Wood AL7 .....111 B7
Wrenbrook Rd CM23 ..76 B3
Wrensfield HP1 ......124 B3
Wrestlers Cl AL10 ...130 C7
Wrexham Terr SG8 .....7 D7
Wright Cl AL4 .......108 E7
Wright's Bldgs WD17 .167 B7
Wrights Green La CM22 .98 D7
Wrights Mdw SG2 ....52 B8
Wrights Orch SG2 .....51 E2
Wrotham Pk EN5 ....158 F3
Wrotham Rd EN5 ....171 E7
Wroxham Ave SG2 ..124 D1
Wroxham Gdns
Crews Hill EN2 ......161 B4
Potters Bar EN6 .....158 D8
Wroxham Sch The EN6 .158 D8
Wroxham Way AL5 ....86 C3
Wulfrath Way SG12 ...93 C3
Wulstan Pk EN6 .....159 D7
Wulwards Cl LU1 ......63 B6
Wulwards Ct LU1 .....63 B6
Wyatt Cl Bushey WD23 .168 E2
Ickleford SG5 .........21 D4
Wyatt's Cl WD3 .....165 A6
Wyatt's Rd WD3 ....165 A6
Wyburn Ave EN5 ....171 F6
Wych Elm CM20 .....117 C1
Wych Elm La AL6,SG3 ..68 F2
Wych Elms AL2 ......141 B3
Wychdell SG2 .........69 C8
Wychford Dr CM21 ...97 C1
Wychwood Ave LU2 ...45 E3
Wychwood Way HA6 .174 F3
Wycklond Cl SG5 .....11 E6
Wycliffe Cl LU3 .......45 C6
Wycliffe Ct WD5 ....153 E7
Wycombe Pl AL4 ....128 B6
Wycombe Way Luton LU3 .45 C2
St Albans AL4 .......128 B6
Wyddial Gn AL7 .....111 B6
Wyddial Rd SG9 .......40 E8
Wye The HP2 ........125 A8
Wyedale AL2 .........142 F4
Wykeham Rise N20 ..171 E1
Wyken Cl LU3 ........45 A7
Wyldwood Cl CM17 .118 C6

**Wyllyotts Cl** EN6 ......**158** F7
**Wyllyotts La** EN6 ......**158** F7
**Wyllyotts Pl** EN6 ......**158** F7
**Wylo Dr** EN5 ..........**171** A3
**Wymondley Cl** SG4 .....**35** A7
Wymondley Jun Mix Inf Sch
SG4 ..................**35** E4
**Wymondley Rd**
Hitchin SG4 ...........**35** B6
Letchworth SG6 ........**23** A1
**Wynches Farm Dr** AL4 .**128** D3
**Wynchgate** HA3 ......**176** E3
**Wynchlands Cres** AL4 .**128** D3
**Wynd The** SG6 ........**22** F6
**Wyndham Rd** LU4 ......**44** C2
**Wyndhams End** AL7 ...**110** F2
**Wynlie Gdns** HA5 .....**175** B1
**Wynn Cl** SG7 ..........**13** A1

**Wyrley Dell** SG6 ........**23** A3
**Wysells Ct** SG6 ........**22** D7
**Wyton** AL7 ...........**111** D6
**Wyvern Cl** LU4 .........**44** E3

## Y

**Yardley** SG6 ..........**23** C4
**Yardley Ave** LU7 .......**80** D4
**Yardley Ct** 14 AL5 ......**86** B1
**Yarmouth Rd**
Stevenage SG1 .........**50** A7
Watford WD24 ........**154** C1
**Yarra Ho** 3 AL1 .......**127** E3
**Yately Cl** LU2 ..........**45** D7
**Ye Cnr** WD19 .........**167** E3
**Yearling Cl** SG12 ......**114** F7
**Yeatman Ho** WD24 ....**154** B3
**Yeats Cl** SG8 ............**2** D1
**Yeomanry Dr** SG7 ......**13** A1

**Yeomans Ave** AL5 .......**85** D3
**Yeomans Cl** CM23 .......**76** D6
**Yeomans Dr** SG2 ........**51** E2
**Yeomans Ride** HP2 ....**105** A1
**Yeovil Ct** LU2 ..........**46** B2
**Yeovil Rd** LU2 ..........**46** B2
**Yew Cl** EN7 ...........**147** E4
**Yew Gr** AL7 ...........**111** C5
**Yew Tree Cl** HP5 ......**136** A1
**Yew Tree Ct**
Elstree WD6 ..........**169** D3
Hemel Hempstead HP1 ..**124** A1
**Yew Tree Dr** HP3 ......**137** B3
**Yew Tree Pl** CM23 ......**76** F8
**Yew Wlk** EN11 .......**135** A5
**Yewlands**
Hoddesdon EN11 ......**135** A5
Sawbridgeworth CM21 ...**97** E1
**Yewlands Dr** EN11 .....**135** A5
**Yews Ave** EN1 ........**162** B3
**Yewstone Ct** WD18 ....**167** A6

**Yewtree Cl** LU7 .........**80** E5
**Yewtree End** AL2 ......**141** B4
**York Cl** WD4 ..........**139** A2
**York Cres** WD6 ........**170** D7
**York Ho**
18 Borehamwood WD6 ...**170** A7
St Albans AL3 ..........**127** C2
**York House Sch** WD3 ..**165** F7
**York Rd** Cheshunt EN8 ..**162** E6
Hitchin SG5 ............**34** E8
Northwood HA6 ........**175** A1
St Albans AL1 ..........**127** F4
Stevenage SG1 .........**36** F1
Watford WD18 ........**167** C4
**York St** LU2 ............**63** F8
**York Terr** EN2 ........**161** C1
**York Way**
Hemel Hempstead HP2 ..**124** E2
Royston SG8 ............**7** B8
Watford WD25 ........**154** E3
Welwyn AL6 ...........**89** C3

**Yorke Gate** WD17 .....**167** A7
Yorke Mead Prim Sch
WD3 ................**166** A4
**Yorke Rd** WD3 .........**166** A3
**Yorkes Mews** 16 SG12 ...**93** D1
**Youngfield Rd** HP1 ...**123** F4
**Youngs Mews** SG14 ...**113** C6
**Youngs Rise** AL8 ......**110** C6
**Youngsbury La** SG12 ...**93** E8
**Yule Cl** AL2 ...........**140** F1

## Z

**Zambesi Rd** CM23 ......**76** F5